Franz Daniel Pastorius
and
Transatlantic Culture

Franz Daniel Pastorius and Transatlantic Culture

German Beginnings,
Pennsylvania Conclusions

By John Weaver

© 2016, 2013 & 1985 by John Weaver. All rights reserved.

Published 2016 by John Weaver, 96047 Bamberg, Germany

ISBN 978-3-00-054901-4 (hardback)   978-3-00-055308-0 (paperback)

Publisher's Cataloging-in-Publication Data

Weaver, John.   1942 -
   Franz Daniel Pastorius and Transatlantic Culture: German Beginnings, Pennsylvania Conclusions / by John Weaver
   Bamberg, Germany
   John Weaver, 2016.
   346 p. Includes bibliographical references and an index. Includes English translations and German original texts.

   1. Pastorius, Franz Daniel, 1651-1719. 2. Pastorius, Francis Daniel, 1651-1719. 3. Poets, American--Colonial period, ca. 1600-1775--Biography. 4. Poetry, Modern--17th & 18th century. 5. Pietism--Germany--History--17th Century. 6. Child rearing--Germany--History--17th century. 7. Authoritarianism-Germany--History--17th century. 8. Fathers and sons--Germany. 9. Pastorius, Melchior Adam, 1624-1702. 10. Cultural critique.

Disconcerted by inequality in absolutist Europe, Franz Daniel Pastorius emigrated to William Penn's Quaker colony, and forged one of the most versatile careers in colonial America. This study traces his growth to maturity in Germany and delineates his bicultural perceptions and convictions as a jurist, classicist and radical social critic. His unique perspective provides a fresh critique of contemporaneous society, religion and politics.

Cover illustrations:

Franciszek Smuglewicz (1745-1807), The Battle of Chocim [Khotyn] in the Year 1673, c. 1800; oil on canvas; in the National Museum in Krakow, Poland. Origin: Laboratory stock provided by the National Museum in Krakow (image digitally enhanced). Used with permission.

German broadside view of Augsburg, Germany, with comets of 1680, 1682 (Halley), and 1683, and three horsemen of the Apocalypse. Adler Planetarium, Chicago. Used with permission. In "Science - Comets in Ancient Cultures" at http://solarsystem.nasa.gov/deepimpact/science/comets-cultures.cfm

Win[d]sheim by Matthäus Merian, *Topographia Franconiae*, Frankfurt, 1656, pp. 107-108. http://upload.wikimedia.org/wikipedia/commons/e/e7/De_Merian_Frankoniae_148.jpg

Edward Hicks (1780-1849), Penn's Treaty with the Indians, c. 1840/1844; oil on canvas (image digitally enhanced). Gift of Edgar William and Bernice Chrysler Garbisch. Courtesy National Gallery of Art, Washington. https://images.nga.gov/en/search/do_quick_search.html?q=%221980.62.11%22& qw=%22Open%20Access%20Available%22

Contents

	Preface	ix
	Acknowledgements	x
	Introduction	1
	PROLOGUE *Melchior Adam Pastorius and the Search for Salvation in Hapsburg Europe*	13
	CHAPTER ONE *New Beginnings in the Old World*	27
1.1	"To escape disaster in time and eternity": Leaving Germany in 1683	27
1.2	Scholarly Simplifications of Pastorius' Piety and Worldliness	30
1.3	Mixed Attitudes toward Germany	32
1.3.1	"The bond of a good conscience with God": An 'Unholy' Baptism Repudiated	32
1.3.2	The Self-Imposed "Exile" of a German "Alien"	34
1.4	An Idyllic and Ravaged Homeland: Franconia in the Age of Absolutism	37
1.4.1	The Cultural Environment	37
1.4.2	The Reformation and the Thirty Years' War	40
1.5	"To lead a godly life in a howling Wilderness": Embracing Lutheran Pietism, Relinquishing European Comforts	42
	CHAPTER TWO *Franconian Childhood*	47
2.1	The Early Years in Sommerhausen, 1651-59	48
2.1.1	Melchior Adam Pastorius' Beginning Law Career	48
2.1.2	Personal Recollections and the Family Record	49
2.1.3	Neighborly Proximity of Village Life	51
2.1.4	The Pastorius Family and the Sommerhausen Community	54
2.2	Moving to the Imperial City of Windsheim in 1659	56
2.3	Windsheim's Civic Life during the 1660s	57
2.3.1	Open-Air Markets and Sheltering Walls	57
2.3.2	Enjoying – and Limiting – Public Exuberance	60
2.3.3	Music and Fellowship at the Church of Saint Kilian	61
2.3.4	Political Gestures of Ostentation and Obeisance	64
2.3.5	A Highflying Toast to Common Endeavor	67
2.4	Treading the Path to Virtue at the Windsheim Gymnasium	68
2.4.1	Lutheran Pedagogy in the Imperial City	69
2.4.1.1	Luther's Humanist Ideals and Strict Discipline	70

2.4.1.2	Compulsions among Windsheim's Pious and Wanton Youth	71
2.4.1.3	Contention among the Teachers and Clergy	73
2.4.1.4	Codes of Education of 1595 and 1667	74
2.4.2	A Curriculum for the Mind and the Soul	77
2.4.2.1	The Classical Tradition of Contemporary Lutheranism (With Pennsylvania Adaptations)	77
2.4.2.2	Divining Lighthouse of Practical Philosophy: Rector Schumberg's Lessons in Ethics and Politics	81
2.5	Family Life and Upbringing	85
2.5.1	Dispersal of the Extended Family	85
2.5.2	Stepmothers within the Nuclear Family	86
2.5.3	Father and Son	89
2.5.3.1	The Warm Affection and Stylized Formalities of Franz Daniel's Correspondence	89
2.5.3.2	A Cultural Album of Childrearing from the "Beehive"	92
2.5.3.3	Establishing the Limits of Filial Obedience	99
2.6	Leaving Home with Friends in 1668	102

CHAPTER THREE
The University Years — 105

3.1	"In none of the objects of this worldly *theatrum* could I find any enduring delight": From the Foreword to *Beschreibung Pennsylvaniae*	105
3.2	Cultural Life in Academia	109
3.2.1	Student Career at Nürnberg, Strasbourg and Jena	109
3.2.2	Nürnberg's Student Milieu	110
3.2.2.1	University Offerings	110
3.2.2.2	Student Conduct	112
3.2.3	Assets and Costs of Cultural Attainment	114
3.3	Objects of Delight: Nürnberg's Cultural Influence, Germantown Applications	119
3.3.1	Art, Music and Drama in the Metropolis	120
3.3.2	Poetic Influences of City and Court	121
3.3.3	"The Preeminence of the Female Sex above ours": Gender and Sexuality in Pastorius' Scholarship and Poetry	123
3.3.3.1	Attitudes Toward Women and Sexuality	124
3.3.3.2	Husband and Wife	126
3.3.3.3	Flirtation and Sensuality in Pastorius' Poetry	128
3.3.3.4	A Prose 'Rhapsody' on Feminine Merits, and an Apian Poem on Sensual Rewards	134
3.3.4	Nürnberg Society in Pastorius' Personal Experience and Pennsylvania Commentary	138
3.3.4.1	A Brief Record of Illustrious Encounters	138
3.3.4.2	"A Syllogism represented to my view": Ambiguous Attitudes toward Government	139
3.3.4.3	"Laugh, lovely innocence, laugh!": A Pietist Mechanic Apostrophized	139
3.4	Scholarly Life among the Lutheran Aristotelians	141
3.4.1	"Physics and metaphysics and other superfluous *Argumentationibus*"	142

3.4.2	Pastorius and the Great Wagenseil	145
3.4.2.1	Gregarious Scholar Abroad: The Dynamics of Self-Interest	145
3.4.2.2	"Cheerful jestings for our learned friend": The Transatlantic Connection	147
3.4.3	Evading the Compulsions of Academia	148
3.4.3.1	Harlequin of Learnedness: Johann Leonard Schwäger	149
3.4.3.2	Strident Tones and Mute Voices	150
3.4.3.3	A Nürnberg Theologian's Flight to Strasbourg: Lucas Friedrich Reinhart	151
3.4.4	Pietist Influences at Strasbourg and a Special Windsheim Schoolmate: Johann Augustin Lietzheimer	153
3.4.5	Broadening Religious and Intellectual Views	156
3.5	The Life of the Law Student	161
3.5.1	Learning the *Corpus juris civilis*	161
3.5.2	The Liberal Impulses of Public Law	162
3.5.2.1	Daring Questions of Political Order	162
3.5.2.2	A Semblance of Moral Concern: Johann Heinrich Boeckler	163
3.5.3	Study at Jena	163
3.5.3.1	Natural Theology and a Philosophical Gadfly	163
3.5.3.2	Law Instructor Heinrich Linck	165
3.5.4	Interludes at Regensburg and Windsheim	165
3.5.4.1	Deadly Game of Reichstag Politics	166
3.5.4.2	The Headstrong Son	167
3.6	"Making an end of academical learning": The Doctorate in Civil and Canon Law	170
3.6.1	Practicing the Art of Disputation	170
3.6.2	The *Rigorosum* and *Disputatio Inauguralis*	171
3.7	"They keep on strutting about *a la mode*": Graduation Day without the Graduate	172

CHAPTER FOUR
Obeying the Father — 175

4.1	The Windsheim Insurrection of 1677-79	175
4.1.1	Franz Daniel's Personal and Collective Guilt	175
4.1.2	Political Developments in the Imperial City	178
4.1.2.1	Causes of Tension	178
4.1.2.2	Tumult of March and April, 1677	179
4.1.3	"Windsheim contra Windsheim": The People versus the Government	180
4.1.3.1	The Charges (and a Baptism of Note)	180
4.1.3.2	The Hearings (and Renewed Resistance)	182
4.1.3.3	The Verdict	184
4.1.4	Father and Son at a Moral Impasse	185
4.1.4.1	Conduct of Burgomaster Pastorius	185
4.1.4.2	The Learned Approach to the Insurrection	186
4.1.4.3	"Christ's Divine Light shall rise": Unresolved Moral Tensions in Franz Daniel's Correspondence with his Father	187
4.2	Godly Advice from a Good Friend: Pietist Johann Heinrich Horb in Windsheim	192

4.2.1	Clerical Conflicts and Church Reforms	192
4.2.2	An "Active Faith" Challenging Clerical Hypocrisy	194
4.2.3	Resolving the Tensions of 1677-79: The Mitigated Penitence of a Senate Loyal to Horb	196
4.2.4	Worldly Finesse and Pietist Commitment	198
4.3	Frankfurt Lawyer and European Traveler, 1679-83	200
4.3.1	Millennialist Premonitions and Political Realities	200
4.3.1.1	Legal Experience in Frankfurt and the Palatinate	200
4.3.1.2	Balance-of-Power Politics and the Palatine Devastation	202
4.3.2	The Saalhof Pietists	207
4.3.2.1	Muted Rebelliousness of Otherworldly Piety	207
4.3.2.2	A Theology of Universal Salvation: Johanna Eleonora von Merlau & Johann Wilhelm Petersen	211
4.4	The Transatlantic Message of *Beschreibung Pennsylvaniae*	215
4.4.1	A Scholarly Guide to the New World's Most Remote Colony	216
4.4.1.1	The Allure of America	216
4.4.1.2	Feudal Values and New Freedoms: The Founding of Pennsylvania	218
4.4.1.3	Incremental Levels of Reality: The Example of Pennsylvania's Abundance	219
4.4.2	The Modest Satisfactions of Pennsylvania	222
4.4.2.1	Personal Growth amid Societal Innovations	222
4.4.2.2	Provincial Politics and Economics	224
4.4.2.3	"A separate German province to avoid all oppression"	227
4.4.2.4	"Neither battle cries nor the sound of drums or muskets": Communal and Personal Contentments	229
4.4.3	The Native American: Personifying New World Potential	231
4.4.3.1	European Encroachment upon the Delaware Tribes	231
4.4.3.2	"Frank in spirit, unassuming": Anthropological Reporting	234
4.4.3.3	Bicultural Object Lessons and Cross-Cultural Interaction: Indian Virtue, Universalism, Anti-Chauvinism	236
4.4.3.4	"My unsavage savages": A Common Bond with the Delaware	240
4.5	The Rights of Blacks Asserted	242

Conclusion 244

Notes 251

Appendices
I. From "Genealogia Pastoriana" 297
II. Selections from Pastorius' German Texts 299

Bibliography 310

Index: "Alphabetical Hive" topics cited 324

Index 325

Preface
to the 2016 edition

This study provides a detailed introduction to Franz Daniel Pastorius in the context of his early life in Germany, delineating his bicultural perceptions and convictions as a jurist, classicist and radical social critic. It has been long in the making. I revised my Ph.D. dissertation on Pastorius (University of California, Davis, 1985) in the late 1980s, but did not manage to find a publisher for it. I eventually put the typescript aside, and continued my career as an English and American Studies lecturer at Bonn University. (I'd begun Pastorius research in 1976, but postponed the Ph.D. while adapting to an expatriate life and delving into German history.)

In 2010, after retiring from teaching, a query from a senior lecturer at Cambridge University reminded me of renewed interest in Pastorius. I retrieved the old typescript from my desk, examined it closely, and ultimately decided to digitize and publish it. I have added two paragraphs on recent Pastorius research, and critically and extensively re-edited the text. (Substantive changes and additions are indicated as updates in the notes.) I have not attempted to update the study as a whole. Brief commentary on Pastorius' millennialism, for example, still reflects the insecurities of the Cold War era rather than the increasing disintegration of world politics since 11 September 2001. This remains essentially a 1990 publication, delayed for two and a half decades.

I published this study in PDF format at http://www.pastorius.info in October, 2013, and registered it at the United States copyright office a month later. Production and editorial issues, and a few intervening projects, delayed book publication (with additional revisions and an index) until 2016. (Health issues and a move from Potsdam to Bamberg, Germany, also intervened.)

On a personal note, my own life has essentially inverted the transatlantic passage of Franz Daniel Pastorius. From a Pennsylvania-German family once called Weber, I moved to Germany in 1977 with my German-born wife and our two California children for a one-year exchange as a university lecturer. That led to further employment in Germany, but no equivalent offers back home. Needless to say, Germany in the modern world is far removed (politically, socially and, of course, economically) from the country Pastorius left in 1683, and it can provide as satisfactory a life as any other.

Bamberg, Germany
September, 2016

Acknowledgements

I gratefully acknowledge the assistance of the many individuals and institutions that have made this book possible, among them the librarians at the University of California, Davis, and Bonn University, and others who gave me access to documents, manuscripts and rare books: Prof. Harrison T. Meserole, the Historical Society of Pennsylvania, the Special Collections Staff of the University of Pennsylvania's Van Pelt Library, the Stadtarchiv and Delp Verlag in Bad Windsheim, Germany, and other institutions identified in the bibliography. Dr. Rolf Lenzen, a university Latin examiner (*Staatliches Prüfungsamt*) and assistant rector of Cardinal Frings Gymnasium in Bonn, assisted in translating the Latin texts cited here in English. Bonn University and the University of California, Davis, provided grants for travel and research. For several crucial years Prof. Hans-Martin Buchmann of Bonn enabled my teaching and Pastorius research to proceed harmoniously.

Numerous other colleagues offered criticism, new insights and suggestions for improvement, especially during several German-American history and literature conferences in the United States and Germany in 1983, as I was completing the first draft of my 1985 Ph.D. dissertation (a preliminary version of this study), and at a 1988 conference of the Society for German-American Studies in Millersville, Pennsylvania. Professors Brom Weber, James Woodress, and Clifford Bernd at Davis guided my dissertation research, and, among others, Professors Hartmut Lehmann, Rudolf Vierhaus, Johannes Wallmann, Hermann Wellenreuther and Alfred Wendehorst provided additional advice and encouragement in Germany. Above all, my wife Reinhild and our children Andrea and Stephan have sustained me, and this study of life and scholarship, with their continuing warmth and generosity.

Bonn - Bad Godesberg, Germany
June, 1990

Introduction

One day Diogenes went backwards; whereat, the people laughing: Are you not ashamed, saith he, to do that all your lifetime, which you deride? Nic. Culpeper, p. 450.

The World is a great and stately volume of natural things. [Wm. Penn,] Max[im] 3. And the characters thereof very legible to the children of wisdom. Idem, 11.
Living fish swim against the stream.

    -- Entries under the headings of "Absurdity," "Book" and "Custom" in Pastorius' "Alphabetical Hive" ("Beehive" manuscript)

Life is motion. Not an aimless ebb and flow but a purposeful moving forward, we presume, even when our navigation is most in doubt. As Franz Daniel Pastorius (1651-1719/20) moved through intricate currents, he measured his progress (and allayed the insecurities of passage) with a personal compass or sextant compounded of folk verities, traditional learning, and what can be called, quite simply, inner light. [1] He spent his youth in the German province of Franconia, attending a Gymnasium and German universities where he studied philosophy and classical and modern philology, and earned a doctorate in law. He then worked as a lawyer and law docent in Franconia and in Frankfurt am Main and the neighboring Palatinate cities, and took a grand tour of Switzerland, Holland, England and France before emigrating to America, where he began a multifaceted career almost immediately after landing in Quaker Philadelphia on 20 August 1683.

Pastorius energetically accepted the innovations and challenges of Pennsylvania, adding a generous portion of frontier pragmatism to his refinements as a classicist and jurist. He kept a farm, taught school and raised a family, and participated in the political and religious events that shaped the beginnings of Pennsylvania history. Thirteen families from Krefeld, Germany, most of them Quaker or Mennonite weavers, joined him in Philadelphia on 6 October 1683. Negotiating on-site with William Penn, Pastorius founded the village of Germantown with the Krefeld immigrants in a forest clearing near Philadelphia later that month, and helped it become a source of Delaware Valley trade and a way station for German families heading farther west as well as a new home for immigrants of various ethnic origins. He worked part-time as a scrivener and attorney or law clerk in Germantown, and held numerous public offices including town clerk, collector of rents, court recorder, town councilman, and bailiff, an office combining the duties of mayor and judge. Beyond Germantown, he was elected to the provincial legislature and appointed a judge in Philadelphia County. He was also an avid gardener and, his self-reliance offsetting scholarly aversions to manual labor, at least occasionally practiced crafts like masonry and weaving. And when the Philadelphia Quaker Meeting considered importing a printing press from England, Pastorius was the man who volunteered to operate it.

Through his many activities, Pastorius made himself at home in the diverse cultures of early Pennsylvania. Despite ethnic insecurities and tensions, he got on well with William Penn and other prominent English and Welsh Quakers in Philadelphia, and his personal statesmanship helped to keep Anglo-German relations on an even keel during the early years of Quaker government. At the same time, he kept in touch with friends in Germany, satisfying their curiosity about his frontier existence while challenging a number of their traditional attitudes. He wrote enthusiastic reports about Pennsylvania and served as business agent for a Frankfurt company that acquired around 25,000 acres of land in the colony, thus helping to get German immigration off to a solid start (although his plans to found a semi-autonomous German colony within Pennsylvania failed). Without denying cherished customs and values, he assimilated into Anglo-American society, a complex process imperfectly achieved, though facilitated by his cultural breadth and esteem.

His ethnicity tempered his approach to assimilation, and to the sensitive issues of minority rights in a multi-ethnic society. He criticized exploitation of the Native Americans, and contested ethnocentric views of tribal culture, especially in a few texts ignored or misinterpreted to the present day. When the property and inheritance rights of German and Dutch immigrants seemed jeopardized, he supported a naturalization law that gave them the full privileges of citizenship. When black slaves were brought to Pennsylvania from the Caribbean, he and three of his Germantown neighbors drafted the first recorded anti-slavery petition in America and fought, unsuccessfully, to establish equality under the law for blacks as well as whites. In a similar vein, he challenged religious conformity, and enjoyed deflating shibboleths and conventional ideas, arguing, for example, that females are, in "almost innumerable" ways, superior to males, an argument to some extent related to his flirtatiousness.

A feisty moralist and sensitive intellectual, he was a herald of the Enlightenment in America, encouraging open-mindedness and cultural diversity. He was pacifist, ecumenical and universalist, and, in various respects, anti-establishment. Despite his liberality, though, he retained traces of the pervasive parochialism or chauvinism of his age, once implicitly complaining, for example, that the women of his household did not have a properly sharpened scissors available when he needed one (see page 245 of this study). The darkest blemishes in the biographical record: As a schoolmaster, he once beat a recalcitrant pupil (page 100). As a scrivener, he composed a runaway slave notice commissioned by a slave-owning client (pages 243-44).

Pastorius rarely described his physical appearance, and he was part of a generation of Pennsylvania leaders who, wary of overt self-aggrandizement, did not generally have their portraits painted. He noted in a medical manuscript that he had

a Melancholy-Cholerick Complexion, and therefore [based on the "four humors" of contemporary psychology, could be described as] gentle, given to Sobriety, Solitary, Studious, doubtful, shame-faced, timorous, pensive, constant & true in action, of slow wit with obliviousness, &c [etc].
If any do him wrong,
He can't remember 't long. [2]

A "prating" schoolboy (the recalcitrant pupil just mentioned) once cited his nose, presumably because of its prominence, as indicating Pastorius "would prove an angry [school]master." [3] In his Poem 167 (composed around 1711), Pastorius admits he had become "almost too stout" from smoking tobacco – a fashion whose many followers in Virginia, Maryland and Pennsylvania he here compares, rather fancifully, with the daughters of Venus, "grow[n] gentler, tho' more plump" from the pipe-smoking habit. In terms of physical detail, there is little else to go on. This study thus traces his inner appearance, psychological or spiritual, with the help of his prolific Pennsylvania writings.

* * *

Pastorius' intellectual zeal matched his energy as a colonizer, in part reflecting the moral tensions of his learnedness and pragmatism. He read voraciously in Pennsylvania, assembling a personal library of more than 250 books in various languages, "undoubtedly the largest in the colony" during his lifetime, and also joining a provincial readers' circle: "I did read, pick and cull several hundred" predominantly English books "lent me by" Philadelphia and Germantown neighbors, he reported in 1718. [4] Amid this steady flow of knowledge, he absorbed English culture and kept abreast of new developments on the Continent. Copying compulsively, he filled numerous commonplace volumes from the borrowed books as well as those in his library, and wrote compositions of his own, in German, English and Latin, on a variety of practical, scientific and philosophical topics.

A number of his manuscripts illumine the politics, business practices and religious life of early Pennsylvania. His medical writings, compiled from over two dozen English, Latin, German and Dutch sources, seem to be the earliest and most eclectic in the British colonies. His law clerks' guide "is the oldest extant treatise on law written in British North America." When he needed textbooks for his pupils – in arithmetic, geometry, Latin and English – Pastorius compiled or wrote his own, and he had his English primer published (by the printer closest at hand, then 85 miles away in New York City). He recorded years of personal observation and scholarly research in a thick agricultural manuscript, describing both the challenges of domesticating nature and the pastoral satisfactions of Germantown fields, orchards and streams. [5]

Venturing beyond prose, Pastorius turned the exercise of versifying into a productive daily habit (Poem 483 notes) as poetic form and measure gratifyingly ordered the flow of his meditative and humorous thought. In an introduction to his collected poetry ("Beehive," p. 113), while noting that "some [Pennsylvanians] ... can't brook" poetry for moral or religious reasons, he denies any pretensions to the title of poet and ingeniously explains that his poems are little more than an arts-and-crafts experiment: "I made them ... only to try whether Versifying and Turning of the Spooling-wheel [at his son's loom] were things Compatible at the same time." His earliest English verse merely provided an enjoyable method of improving his English, a language he first learned in Pennsylvania (and used in his poetry along with Latin and German, and, infrequently, Dutch, French and Italian), but he was soon fascinated by his craft, and brash enough to challenge any critical reader of the manuscript volume of "my Contemplations" to prove he can do better (Poem 156):

> ... before he doth slight
> This, Pray! Let him grant m' a Sight
> Of his Rare Garden Meditations; ...

Pastorius knew he would not soon find anyone to take up the challenge, even if the manuscript collection includes flawed specimens of his craft, verses hurriedly penned and left for future polishing. In poems describing or commenting on political campaigns and neighborhood events, biblical themes, flirtation and domestic quarreling, the flowers, herbs and vegetables of his garden, philosophical disputes, the joys and limitations of poetry, and much, much more, he was steadily creating an impressive lyric effusiveness, a poetry of grace that celebrates the variety and complexity of nature and the mind as reflections of divine perfection. Expanding the Continental poetics of his youth, he consciously absorbed the English techniques of Francis Quarles, John Denham, Daniel Defoe and others ("Beehive," p. 139), and grew increasingly innovative. He wrote

> lyrics, epigrams, rhymed proverbs, hymns, dedicatory and prefatory verses, [elegies, anagrams, and verse paraphrases of Scripture] – poetry in an astonishing variety of forms, styles, and meters composed on an equally astonishing range of subjects. [6]

Especially from 1708 to 1719, in his poetic maturity, he frequently achieved a felicity of phrase and rhythm, the surprise and delight of thematic juxtapositions, fresh images and idioms, striking rhymes, experimental devices. Since the poet and his persona are largely identical, the poetry, too, offers new insights into the life he and others were leading in early Pennsylvania. These epigrams display a characteristic mix of learnedness and pragmatism, the creative tensions informing Pastorius' transatlantic life and culture:

> A Verse may stick, when tedious Sermons fly
> Beside the Mark, and unremembered die.

> Whoever Dutch and French and Latin speaks,
> May learn the English Tongue within Six Weeks.

> Zeal for the Good is good, with Love conjoin'd,
> Or else a Fire, void of Light, or blind.

> Know how to keep as well as gain your Chink
>   [coin, money (now archaic)].
> 'Tis strange but true: For want of Weight Men sink.

> Rather depend upon your Fingers' Ends
> Than fix your Expectations on your Friends.

> The Lust of Flesh and Eyes, the Pride of Life,
> Are three most noisome weeds, which rankly thrive
> In Rich men's well dung'd grounds; mine being poor,
> Thanks be to God, they are kept out of door.

> Transporting Joys, tormenting Fears,
> Reviving Smiles, succeeding Tears
> Are Cupid's various Train.

> Too late an Old Decrepit Fellow woos,
> Who cannot piss beyond his Boots or Shoes.
>
> One small Dram of good Life excels a Pound
> Of humane Learning, tho' the most profound.
>
> So live, as if Thou wert today to die:
> So learn, as if Thou could'st Death's Pow'r defy. [7]

Although little of his poetry was published, much of it was written for an audience, recited in small groups or on public occasions, or circulated in manuscript collections, creating delight, and sometimes consternation. Poem 329, for example, describes an altercation with an offended clergyman, its iambic pentameter effectively varied, and exploiting classical form and allusion to enhance the poet's (and poetry's) stature:

> Thou callst me Satyrist and yet thyself doest rage
> When on the Pulpit where None dare with Thee engage,
> The loudest Talker which was heard on any Stage.
> Thy Talent in the Tongue, mine in the Pen does lie:
> The Diff'rence is thy Words, as soon as born, die,
> I with Apelles paint ev'n to Eternity; Now, Stentor, cry. [8]

Embellishing his homespun fabric with exotic textures, Pastorius put a bit of finesse and élan into his arts-and-crafts experiment.

* * *

Despite the optimism of Pastorius' reformist impulses (a religious and secular mix of early Enlightenment ideas), his life and writings reveal the deep personal and intellectual insecurities of his formative years in a society experiencing rapid social and technological change as well as massive wartime destruction. Framed by the Thirty Years' War (1618-48) and the Palatine Devastation of 1688, these were years of apocalyptic angst and millennialist hope, an ambiguous intellectual climate in Germany that Pastorius reflected in his early reports and letters on Pennsylvania geography, government and culture, begun en route to America and published as *Umständige Geographische Beschreibung der zu allerletzt erfundenen Provintz Pen[n]sylvaniae*, 1700 (A Detailed Geographical Description of the Most Recently Discovered Province of Pennsylvania, subsequently cited as *Beschreibung Pennsylvaniae*). [9]

Political and spiritual decline on the Continent, he reported aboard ship for Pennsylvania and in later correspondence, had brought Europe to the verge of self-destruction. Like Lot escaping Sodom's annihilation or Aeneas fleeing the flames of Troy, Pastorius was driven from his homeland by fears he could no longer ignore – and he was drawn by hopes for a radically new beginning in Pennsylvania. He was part of a bold experiment tapping human potential ignored in previous Western societies. The experiment did not completely succeed, he later admitted, yet it succeeded more than it failed, and in ways not fully anticipated – nudging history closer to the era of modern democratic societies.

In his Pennsylvania scholarship, Pastorius countered the temptation to ignore the past while reshaping the future, a basic limitation of radically new beginnings. His zealous commitment to transmitting traditional learning – along with new ideas – reflects European cultural anxieties exacerbated in an American colony so far removed from its cultural and political sources, so tenuously bound to the past. His mammoth "Beehive" manuscript, begun in 1696 as a commonplace book of language and philosophy for the edification of his sons, grew to encyclopedic proportions as Pastorius emulated apian diligence for two and a half decades. [10] He jokingly describes it as an *"Alvearium Anglicanum Apiculae Germanopolitanae,"* thus identifying himself as the 'little Germantown bee' who gathered the 'nectar' of ancient, medieval and modern learning, filling the 'hive' with biblical piety, classical speculation and morality, scholastic syllogism, rationalist skepticism and neoclassical wit.

His simple explanation on the book's first page: "For as much as our Memory is not Capable to retain all remarkable Words, Phrases, Sciences, or Matters of Moment, which we do hear and read, It becomes every good Scholar to have a Common-Place-Book, & therein to Treasure up whatever Deserves his Notice, &c [etc]." He compiled from the writings of numerous English Quakers and lesser-known contemporaries such as the English millennialist Jane Ward Lead and the Pennsylvania almanac maker Daniel Leeds as well as authors like Virgil and Ovid, Saint Augustine and Thomas Aquinas, Cornelius Agrippa, Theophrastus Paracelcus and Jakob Boehme, and Francis Bacon, John Locke and the essayists Joseph Addison and Richard Steele – but he did not limit himself to the printed word.

His original purpose was, Pastorius writes, "to collect common proverbs, witty sentences, wise and godly sayings, [and] the like substantial marrow of other men's writing" in approximately one thousand alphabetically arranged "honeycombs" – sections or boxes created by drawing horizontal lines across each folio page, and filling them with the entries gleaned on subjects from absence and authority to zeal and zenith, thus yielding a typical page with commentary on cowards, "could" (i.e., the faint-hearted), crabs, the cradle, craftiness, "creature," credit, crime, criticism, crosses, the cross of Christ, and crowns. In the process of collecting, however, he became so impressed with "the copiousness of words, phrases & expressions in the English" that he eventually attempted to create both a selective commonplace encyclopedia – predominantly English but with citations in Latin, German and other languages as well – and a comprehensive English thesaurus in one alphabetical sequence: "I took as much pains & patience as to import into this alphabetical *alvearium* all & singular terms, idioms, manners of stile and speech used" in English.

As his alphabetical honeycombs filled up, he added a numerical sequence, both new headings and continuations of the old, that eventually contained more than 3000 supplementary sections averaging, conservatively estimated, two dozen entries each. Religious, political and scientific themes are treated along with mundane reality, be it courtship or cookery, falsehood or friendship, in a compendium of knowledge comparable in scope and breadth of opinion with many of the Renaissance and early Enlightenment encyclopedias which it emulates. [11] Pastorius distinguishes between his philosophical "honey," sentences and paragraphs quoted for their content, and the "wax" or "hive dross" of the individual words and phrases demonstrating the copiousness of English, yet he gathered "honey" and "dross" with equal determination, thus creating an unparalleled sourcebook on the English language as it was read and spoken in early Pennsylvania. [12] More than any of his other writings, furthermore, the thousands of entries in the "Alphabetical Hive" reveal his ongoing commitment to the delight and instruction of transmitted culture – the wisdom and wit of both the ancients and the moderns, the traditionalists and the innovators of Western civilization.

Yet this zealous scholarship became, in the context of his Pennsylvania life, little more than an exercise in futility, an attempt to sustain a level of cultural attainment made at least partially superfluous by the nature of the new society he was helping to create. Reflecting a basic shift in his values, the scholar's own sons never acquired the scholarly impulse that kept him at his encyclopedic compilations, or the social prominence deriving from his cultural attainments. Despite his personal influence on the culture of early Philadelphia, the Pastorius family name – along with knowledge of his weighty "Beehive" manuscript – lapsed nearly into obscurity.

* * *

The extent of Pastorius' contribution to colonial American culture has only gradually been gaining recognition. Even today, at least two of the minor hallmarks of Americana traceable to Pastorius are often attributed instead to Benjamin Franklin (1706-90): "A penny saved is a penny got" is listed under "Parsimony" in the "Alphabetical Hive," and Poem 116 offers both German and English versions of "Early to bed, early to rise, / Makes a man healthy, wealthy and wise." [13] Pastorius is best known in ethnic circles, where he has been acclaimed as "the father of German-American immigration" ever since Oswald Seidensticker discovered a cache of Pastorius documents in 1870. [14] Largely due to a paucity of reliable information about his life and works, there have been relatively few attempts to assess his achievement for a general audience.

His wide reading and scholarly attainment have led to comparisons with Cotton Mather (1663-1728), "the universal genius of New England," who owned around 3000 books and wrote 450 printed works. James Truslow Adams, for example, concluded that Pastorius "was, perhaps, the most learned man of his day in America – not forgetting Cotton Mather – and he was far in advance of the New England divine in the breadth of his education." Carl Bridenbaugh went a step further: "For sheer force of intellect coupled with sympathetic insight into human nature Pastorius, perhaps the most learned man who ever came to live in America, highly deserves attention." And Anthony Grafton recently provided a transatlantic context: "In the English-speaking world around 1700, Pastorius stands out as a [commonplace] compiler for his riotous polyglot learning and his manically associative habit of mind." Lawrence A. Cremin has identified Pastorius' shift from classical values to "a much more utilitarian view" of education in Pennsylvania, and Hans Fantel relates this insight to later political developments: "It was largely thanks to Pastorius and his group [of scholarly Pennsylvanians] that Philadelphia became America's first center of open intellectual inquiry." As Sydney E. Ahlstrom has concluded, "Pastorius was one of the most fascinating and profound figures in [early] Pennsylvania." [15]

Pastorius' literary reputation has attracted limited attention since 1872, when Oswald Seidensticker noted that "most of the poetry ... would bear being printed." In 1897 and 1898 Marion Dexter Learned published more than a hundred of Pastorius' poems in *Americana Germanica*, an ethnic journal that escaped the attention of most American literature scholars. "The range of Pastorius' literary activity," Learned insisted in his 1908 Pastorius biography, "has scarcely found a parallel in America from [his] time to the present day," but Learned turned to other matters without elucidating this claim, and without commenting on Pastorius' verse. In 1938 Carl Bridenbaugh concluded that Pastorius' "remarkable versatility made of him the leading poet of seventeenth century America" and one of the best in the colonial period as a whole (although in a general study of colonial society with no room for details on Pastorius). [16] Two Ph.D. dissertations began the task of evaluating the poetry, and in 1948 the *Literary History of the United States* encouraged further work, noting that Pastorius' "contribution to colonial literature deserves to be better known." [17]

Two decades later Harrison T. Meserole's anthology of colonial American poetry brought Pastorius to the attention of general readers for the first time. Meserole offered a sampling of Pastorius' English verse and evaluated his poetic achievement:

> [Pastorius'] wealth of garden and herbal imagery, his rollicking humor, his regularly gentle but occasionally sharp satire, and his experiments in rhythms, structures, and rebus effects establish him not only as the first poet of consequence in Pennsylvania but also as one of the most important poets of early America. [18]

In 1982, Christoph E. Schweitzer completed the first critical edition of any of Pastorius' manuscript works: *Deliciae Hortenses or Garden-Recreations and Voluptates Apianae*, a well-annotated text of two small multilingual volumes of verse (and occasionally prose) reflections on gardening and apiculture. [19] Appended to the text, a photographic reproduction of the manuscripts displays the poet's thoughtful and playful use of calligraphy, sketches and textual arrangement, and also reveals the difficulty of deciphering many of Pastorius' cramped lines, written when paper was scarce, a difficulty that has hampered the editing of other Pastorius texts. [20] Schweitzer has briefly analyzed the wit and dexterity of Pastorius' German verse, demonstrating that Pastorius "must be taken seriously as an author of German poetry, especially of epigrams." [21]

Since this study was first written, greater strides have been made, most notably the inclusion of Pastorius in *The New Oxford Book of Seventeenth Century Verse*, 1992, and in *American Poetry: The Seventeenth and Eighteenth Centuries*, 2007; a generous sampling of "The Beehive" in *The Multilingual Anthology of American Literature*, 2000; a high-resolution online version of "The Beehive" at the University of Pennsylvania, produced by 2009; and an impressive collection of Pastorius' manuscripts available online at the Historical Society of Pennsylvania as of 2012. [22]

* * *

Even aside from his scholarly zeal and poetic dexterity, Pastorius is of interest today for the sheer breadth of his experience, reflecting the historical context of his unusual personal growth. He absorbed the ideas of the early Enlightenment, helped to implement many of them in Pennsylvania, and contributed to what became an ongoing transatlantic debate of underlying cultural values. He knew the well delineated social order prescribed by aristocratic lords as well as a form of the 'mob rule' they feared, and it was the latter that became the accepted reality of Pennsylvania government in his lifetime. As a young lawyer in Franconia, he felt implicated in the injustices of a feudal system that oppressed the peasants on the land they worked for their overlords; as a land agent, bailiff and law clerk in Pennsylvania, he enabled former peasants to create farms of their own, altering their habits and attitudes in new terrain. In Germany and Pennsylvania, respectively, he experienced dogmatic state religion and relative freedom of conscience; the controls of political absolutism and the looseness of frontier settlement; a densely-populated and war-torn environment, and a sparsely-populated land that seemed large enough for all, and thus with the requisites of peace and prosperity. [23]

Reflecting these divergent influences, Pastorius combined common spiritual values with high culture, yet revealed typical predilections by praising the unspoiled integrity of the Delaware or Lenape Indians in Pennsylvania and deriding the arrogance of the learned. Although he had been part of a learned elite amid German cultural disparities that reinforced widespread belief in inherent inferiority and superiority, he challenged such convictions by teaching at Philadelphia and Germantown primary schools and offering Germantown evening classes for adults as well – all part of William Penn's plans (albeit not fully implemented) for a society in which free public education would bridge the gap between upper and lower classes and reduce the tensions and frustrations prevalent in highly stratified societies. [24] Even at the most personal level, Pastorius, entitled to learned esteem and privilege in Germany, broke well-established family tradition by enrolling his two Pennsylvania sons as apprentices in the trades of weaving and shoemaking, and encouraging them to live as ordinary citizens in Germantown.

As if to explain these sharp contrasts, he once quoted, among the 'honey' of his "Beehive" commonplaces, a seriocomic adage that had already gained currency among the independent souls who settled early Pennsylvania: "Many a learned head in Europe is ignorant of what our clowns know in America." [25] Steeped in European tradition yet promoting social innovation in Pennsylvania, Pastorius continually grappled with the "radical cultural question" that – both motive and result of a moral and material quest – was emerging in immigrant American society generally, challenging authority and tradition and not infrequently displaying contempt for elitist cultural attainment. [26]

He saw this quest as precarious, demanding dexterity and judgement, but he believed in its potential, and so did many who followed. A few decades after he moved to Pennsylvania, European liberals looked to the province as "a successful experiment in the life of reason, . . . an illustration of the belief that man could lead the good life without monarchy, feudalism, or religious uniformity." [27] And with Enlightenment ideals largely relegated to speculative philosophy in Europe, the Pennsylvania experiment attracted increasing numbers of Pastorius' compatriots. During the eighteenth century so many Germans poured into Pennsylvania, then being described despite immigrant hardships as "the best poor man's country in the world," that even level-headed Benjamin Franklin feared German would replace his native tongue in the province. Subsequent German immigration grew to such an extent that, by the 1980s, Americans claiming German descent constituted the largest ethnic group in the United States. [28]

The pragmatic idealism of ethnic Americans like Franz Daniel Pastorius adds significance to this historical phenomenon. Synthesizing biblical Christianity, traditional and Enlightenment learnedness, and the societal innovation of Pennsylvania, he evolved a liberal personal credo responsive to the desires for self-realization and social order that together sustain any vibrant culture. In an era of moral, political and economic uncertainty not unlike our own, as the opportunities and dangers of technological development were creating a modern mentality, he recognized that personal fulfillment involves both the intellect and the spirit, both individual assertions of will and an acceptance of universal interdependencies – a complex awareness that has not lost any of the relevance and urgency he gave it three centuries ago.

* * *

Despite his historical relevance and the intrinsic interest of his life and writings, Pastorius has not been examined comprehensively or coherently. Preliminary biographies by Oswald Seidensticker and Samuel Pennypacker near the end of the nineteenth century were supplemented, in 1908, by Marion Dexter Learned's *Life of Francis Daniel Pastorius*, more of a documentary catalogue than an interpretive biography. [29] None of the early biographers dealt with the evasions and misleading rhetoric of Pastorius' transatlantic writings, explored the humor and wisdom of his mature scholarship and poetry revealing the most intriguing aspects of his thought and personality, or resolved what were viewed as troubling inconsistencies in his conduct and character. Other articles about Pastorius up to the 1980s, many of them filiopietistic and derivative, added little significant detail. [30]

More recently, though, Pastorius has been generating renewed interest. Patrick M. Erben, Anthony Grafton and Brooke Palmieri have delved into "The Beehive," analyzing Pastorius' bookishness and his methods of collecting and compiling knowledge. Grafton traces the broad context of European learnedness that informs Pastorius, and Erben places him in the context of ethnic Pennsylvanians who sought to build community out of linguistic and religious diversity. Alfred L. Brophy examines Pastorius' legal activity in Pennsylvania, showing how he absorbed English legal procedures and supported Quaker efforts to simplify the law and make it accessible, and to enhance fairness and justice. Lyman W. Riley and Brophy, furthermore, have used Pastorius' "Beehive" citations to elucidate Quaker book culture in Pennsylvania, and Margo M. Lambert (among other things) traces his Pietist and Quaker influences through "Beehive" citations and some of the cited books. The growing interest in Pastorius can also be seen in numerous new reprints and online versions of his *Beschreibung Pennsylvaniae* and the early studies by Pennypacker, Learned and others. [31]

This study reconstructs the historical and cultural context of Pastorius' early life in Germany, and traces the contours of his biography. It is based on his Pennsylvania correspondence, autobiographical writing, poetry and scholarship as well as documentary evidence and historical evaluation from a great variety of German sources: government files, studies of folk culture and local history, religious and political monographs, baptismal and academic records, funeral sermons, biographies. (All translations not otherwise attributed are my own.) Throughout the book, epigraphs from Pastorius' writing and scholarship provide reflective commentary, and they also highlight many of his intriguing epigrams and poems. A prologue describes Pastorius' father Melchior Adam and his search for salvation in Hapsburg Europe. Chapter One examines contradictory approaches to Pastorius as a scholar-poet, social critic and pragmatic immigrant, and it introduces the Franconian and German culture of his youth, indicating historical reasons for his conversion to Lutheran Pietism in 1679 and his emigration in 1683.

Chapter Two describes Pastorius' childhood and youth, noting the vitality of his community and family life, and his disciplined growth from childhood spontaneity to an identity anticipating adult responsibilities as a Lutheran burgomaster's son in the free imperial city of Windsheim. The chapter identifies tensions involving authoritarianism and latent resistance to authority especially in Pastorius' Gymnasium schooling and in the complex relationship of father and son, and presents complementary views on upbringing from his Pennsylvania writings. Chapter Three traces his student career at Nürnberg and other German universities (1668-76), studying philosophy, language and law, observing a wartime Reichstag (or Imperial Diet) in Regensburg, and attaining a doctorate in civil and canon law. This academic milieu reveals learned compulsions related to the tensions of his upbringing. The chapter notes his courtly delights and cultural attainments as well as their social costs, and examines Pastorius' commentary, including commonplace entries and poetry on esthetic pleasures, and satire and criticism epitomized in Gospel references to rich Dives and the beggar Lazarus. A detailed description of his mature poetry of flirtation and sensuality augments his fervent social criticism.

Chapter Four presents Pastorius' adult experience of Europe and America, describing the start of his law career during two years of strife in Windsheim (1677-79), when his family and friends helped to suppress a popular insurrection against abuses of oligarchic rule. It examines the complicity and guilt that led him to reject the home and community he dearly loved, and to join the learned Lutheran Pietists of Frankfurt am Main, and it describes the baroque tensions he continued to encounter as he practiced law in Frankfurt and the Palatinate and toured Europe (1679-83). His predictions of a European Armageddon (1683-84), reflecting these tensions, are explained on several levels, including the destructive potential of the era of the Thirty Years' War and the 1688 Palatine Devastation. The chapter analyzes Pastorius' reports and letters from Pennsylvania, in which he piously urges humane reforms and pragmatically describes the economy, politics and society of the province, often focusing on the Lenni Lenape or Delaware tribe. It examines his opposition to black slavery and to the exploitation of Native Americans (and related criticism of European cultural imperialism in India) as well as his praise of material and ethical satisfactions in the New World. This context illumines his personal maturation in Pennsylvania, a diverse and evolving culture with secular influences of neoclassicism and the Enlightenment.

The study as a whole reflects Franconian and European culture through the prism of Pastorius' Pennsylvania writings. Overall, his unique perspective provides a fresh critique of contemporaneous society, religion and politics.

* * *

A 2013 postscript on my approach to Pastorius:
My own background seems relevant here. I grew up in a rural Protestant family. In 1953 (at the age of ten), I was among a dozen or more teens and pre-teens who had revival-meeting conversions and then joined the New Holland (Pennsylvania) Evangelical United Brethren Church. [32] In 1960, pursuing a love of language, I chose to study English literature. I left the church a few years later, and never returned. Yet even as a modern agnostic in graduate school, I was still drawn to religious themes in authors as varied as Philip Roth, Carson McCullers, James Joyce, Rainer Maria Rilke, William Blake and John Donne.

I encountered Pastorius in a University of California course on Colonial American literature, and later began a Ph.D. dissertation focusing on his poetry. The focus changed during German research as I uncovered his past in Sommerhausen and Windsheim. The critical skills acquired in graduate school helped me delve into seventeenth-century German history, but I got deeper into the project than intellectual curiosity alone would have justified. My rural Protestant upbringing may have drawn me into Pastorius' Franconian past. It certainly played a role in my research. Because of it, I was better able to explore his Lutheran roots and Pietist leanings, and to deal with his emotive, and often obscure, moral or religious discourse.

I gradually realized that, on the whole, Pastorius' Pietist message was genuine and legitimate. His rhetoric ultimately meshed with the social reality of his day. With this awareness, I was able to trace his growth to maturity in Franconia, and to refract his message through the historical record. I readily exploited modern German scholarship to fill in the details of his cultural biography.

Prologue

Melchior Adam Pastorius and the Search for Salvation in Hapsburg Europe

> Men can bear all things, except good days. When prosperity smileth on thee, stand then on thy watch. Philip, King of Macedon[ia], upon three sorts of good news arriving in one day, feared too much success might transport him immoderately; and therefore prayed for some small disappointments to season his prosperity . . . You cannot fare well but you must cry roast meat. The better [the] day, the better [the] deed. Better [to] be happy [i.e., fortunate] than wise. To own the water . . .By good Hap . . . He hath the wind with him. Leeward-tide . . . Our minds rise & fall with our fortunes . . . The folly of one man is the fortune of an other. Fr. Bacon. Worldly felicity, I know, makes the head giddy. Of the power of F[ortune] see Sen[eca]: L'Estr[ange] p. 206, 207. She throws her gifts among us, and we sweat and scuffle for them &c [etc]. p. 208 . . .Fortune throws out baits for us and sets traps . . . If they had anything in them that were Substantial, they would some time or other fill and quiet us, but they serve only to provoke our appetite . . . p. 209 . . . Prosperity like a fair gale upon a Strong Current carries man in a trice out of the very sight of peace and quiet. p. 566 . . . One beats the bush while an other catches the hare . . .
> Oh cruel fortune, stepdame to all joys,
> Plunging our hopes in troubled seas annoys. &c. Salmon, p. 362.
> -- "Fortune" ("Alphabetical Hive" commonplace entries)

The early life and travels of Melchior Adam Pastorius (1624-1702) presage the emigrant experience of his son Franz Daniel. Both father and son learned Christian values in their youth and rejected the unchristian excesses of the established church and state as young men, yet their youthful decisions were influenced by the radically different possibilities available to each. While Franz Daniel left his culture for a new beginning in Anglo-American society, Melchior Adam converted from Roman Catholicism to Lutheranism and remained within established European society. The father's conversion nevertheless involved a repudiation of the worldly values of the Catholic courts of the Hapsburg empire and a departure from the courtly environment of his youth, and these elements foreshadowed similar events in Franz Daniel's life.

Franz Daniel himself indicated the personal importance of his father's conversion. He wrote in "Genealogia Pastoriana" (Appendix I) that as a child he had "often heard" his father explain "why he forsook the Romish Religion," and in a 1699 letter (written with or on behalf of his sons Heinrich and Johann Samuel) he urged Melchior Adam to put the familiar story into writing for the benefit of his grandsons. [1] Franz Daniel had ulterior motives for this request. Although as a young man he had challenged his father's values and conduct, his filial affection for Melchior Adam seems to have increased as he lived in Pennsylvania, generating a desire to evaluate his father's defense of the Franconian existence Franz Daniel had rejected in 1679. Destined to life-long separation from his father, he longed for the eternal reunion his religious belief allowed him to anticipate – if only he could be convinced that Melchior Adam's life would end in spiritual salvation.

Melchior Adam, then 75 years old but by no means enfeebled, accepted the challenge of convincing his son, retelling the story of the "many strange fates and unfortunate circumstances" of his life that had left him "wholly amazed by the almighty hand of God, which has guided, nourished, protected and kept me in such miraculous ways." [2] The eighteen-page autobiography he sent his grandsons skillfully creates a portrait of resolute and harmonious living among the tensions of world and spirit in Hapsburg Europe. [3] In this retelling and in his earlier "Itinerarium et Vitae Curriculus" he proudly recalled his robust and active youth, the fulfillment of companionship, travel and adventure among scholars, monks, aristocrats and royalty. He dramatically portrayed the epiphanies of his travels, his mounting religious doubt and sharp existential fear, his search for redemption and his ultimate conversion, and the decisive departure from the Catholic court of Würzburg in 1649. These highlights revealed pure motives of Lutheran reform, an espousal of Christ's redeeming love, the common theme in the lives of father and son. But this was only the beginning of the story. Melchior Adam's account ignored the deeper tensions that would eventually influence the life of his eldest son.

Melchior Adam Pastorius was born in the eighth year of the Thirty Years' War, the son of Martin Pastorius (1576-1631), a Roman Catholic lawyer and judge employed in Protestant Erfurt by the archbishop-prince of Mainz, a Catholic Hapsburg elector. [4] The German family name, Schäfer or Hügelschäfer (variations of Shepherd), had been Latinized to Pastorius a few generations earlier, indicating social advancement from humble origins. In 1529, six years after Melchior Adam's birth, King Gustavus Adolphus of Sweden arranged a truce with Erfurt's city fathers and led his Protestant army into the city. As Melchior Adam recalled in 1699, this turn of events had dire consequences for his Catholic family:

> The [Swedish] King ... refused to extend the terms of the surrender to Roman Catholics, whose houses and cloisters were the only ones taken by the soldiers ... [who] then ... plundered them completely, and in most cases even pulled them down and demolished them utterly. ... My mother [Brigitta] escaped [from my father's house on Horsemarket Square] with only a little register of the family inheritance with the accounts of collection for various rents and monies due. We children, though, were driven forth by the soldiers with their naked swords, and we all saw how such manner of persuasion was

applied to cheat and misuse the Catholics of our city... My father Martinus Pastorius quickly prepared to journey to his prince at Mainz to report the destruction that had been endured. Along the route, however, he fell into the hands of the Swedish soldiers once more; they removed his clothing and, in his naked condition, beat him so severely that he died within a few weeks.... We children grew up under great difficulties with a widow who lived in distress and misery... My mother managed to support my studies even though we only had the bare essentials of food and clothing... When I [eventually] implored her to send me to the university, she... [managed to] borrow a ducat from my godfather, and gave it to me for my journey; I traveled several thousand land-miles around the world [i.e., in Europe] with that coin, yet never lived in want. [5]

Retelling this portion of his father's story in "Genealogia Pastoriana" around 1715, Franz Daniel revised its detail and underscored its symbolic import. He described his grandfather as "a man of a good Estate" and reported that Martin Pastorius'

several houses in [Erfurt] with all his goods were burnt in one night, and he himself in his Journey towards Mentz [Mainz], ... being oblig'd to lodge one Evening in a Village, where Swedish Souldiers did lie, hided himself in a Barn under some Straw, but was betrayed by his own Servant, and by the said Souldiers (searching & pricking after him with their naked Swords,) sore wounded in divers parts of his Body, so that not many days after he departed this Life.

Franz Daniel reported his grandfather's wealth and position more clearly than Melchior Adam did – "several houses" and "all his goods" supplement the one specified residence and impersonal account books – and he also mentioned the servant's betrayal that his father ignored in writing. A rich man's betrayal by his servant was one of the most unpleasant facts of life in upper-class Europe, evoking emotions like those that met disobedience and political upheaval generally. Citing this betrayal, Franz Daniel alluded indirectly to the wider theme of rebellion and upheaval that would later heighten personal emotions in the Franconian existence he shared with his father. In its implications, at least, his account admits that the social standing of his forebears contributed to the tensions of his Franconian life.

The son's report of the father's solitary ducat indicates the symbolic appeal of the coin anecdote:

When my Father at his Going to the University bade her [his mother] Farewel, she could give him but one Ducat (or two pieces of Eight) besides her good Blessing, neither did he ever get more (no, not a Farthing,) of all his patrimony, which made him the oft'ner remember the great Virtue or Efficacy of a Ducat given by a well wishing Mother.

In fact, Melchior Adam's material want or lack of it depended not on his ability to get by on a single ducat but rather on the general deprivation of war and the generosity of Hapsburg courts – as later details of the story vividly illustrate. Franz Daniel's added detail illumines the anecdote's symbolic meaning: Melchior Adam's Protestant conversion cut him and his progeny off from his Catholic family and heritage, and the nearly heroic resolve it demanded was, for Franz Daniel, the first step toward the ultimate independence of a new life in America. More immediately, the lack of a family inheritance increased Melchior Adam's incentive for material success and thus added to the tensions of world and spirit in Franz Daniel's youth. (In Seneca's terms, the baits thrown out by Fortune would provoke Melchior Adam's appetite, too.)

Within the household of his mother Brigitta Pastorius, Melchior Adam learned a warm Catholic piety, and concern for those whose poverty was not temporary. In a verse anagram recalling his departure from Erfurt in 1643, he recreated his mother's parting advice to him: Dear son, praise God from your heart always, love Him and be in spirit like a bride who jests lovingly, give freely to the needy poor, and thus will you know God's grace both here and hereafter. [6] His Catholic schooling taught ethical sensitivity and worldly finesse. He studied the classics at a Jesuit academy in Erfurt (graduating in 1643 with a diploma in poetry and rhetoric) and philosophy at the Catholic University of Würzburg in 1643-44, and he earned a doctorate of law at the University of Rome.

Pastorius got an unusually close view of the political and ecclesiastical workings of the Hapsburg Empire during his student years. His sponsor at Würzburg University, a Catholic baron, personally introduced him to Prince-Bishop Johann Philipp von Schönborn (1605-73), reigning at Würzburg's Marienberg Castle, the powerful territorial lord who would soon garner the additional titles of archbishop of Mainz and imperial elector, and Johann Philipp in turn recommended Melchior Adam to Cardinal Carolus Rosetti (b. 1610), en route to a papal election in 1644, and offered 19-year-old Pastorius a scholarship to study theology at the German Jesuit College in Rome. In the Eternal City, Pastorius was welcomed by his brother Johann Augustin Pastorius, a lawyer and historian who served the Prince-Bishop of Trier, Philipp Christoph von Sötern (1567-1652), as consul to the Papal See. Three months later he switched from theology to law. The strict religious regimen of the Jesuit College "was completely against my nature," he wrote later, "and I was not the least interested in a spiritual vocation." [7] He studied at the University of Rome, and gained first-hand legal experience in the Consulate of Trier run by his brother.

In 1646, touring the courts of Bavaria and Austria, he impressed some of his aristocratic hosts with his learning and tact. No less a personage than Emperor Ferdinand III (1608-57) rewarded Pastorius' courtly skills with a payment of 30 talers for his *Carmen Gratulatorum*, a flattering poem that, Pastorius reported, "I composed . . . , had printed, and presented [to the Emperor] . . . in the open court session" at Linz, Austria. [8] Back in Rome in 1647, he continued his legal studies and consular practicum, and won his doctorate in 1648. He briefly held his brother's post as Consul to Prince-Bishop Philipp Christoph of Trier – long enough, though, for him to negotiate with Vatican officials and to obtain "some bulls of dispensation for [Philipp Christoph] from the Pope." And when he returned to Germany later that year Philipp Christoph rewarded him with a cash payment for his success at the Vatican. [9] During these years of courtly apprenticeship, Pastorius mastered the political and ecclesiastical machinery regulating the affairs of Rome as well as the Holy Roman Empire, with its Hapsburg monarch and virtually autonomous princes and bishops.

As he immersed himself in courtly politics, Pastorius was also gaining the attitudes and skills that would make him a successful lawyer and politician in Protestant Franconia – attitudes and skills he later endeavored, more or less successfully, to pass on to his son Franz Daniel. His broad travels enhanced his ability to comprehend his surroundings. He was 18 when he toured central Germany before entering the university, observing courtly existence in Mainz, commercial bustle in Frankfurt am Main and village life in the provinces. Then, with Cardinal Rosetti, he witnessed lavish receptions at courts, manors and monasteries in southern Germany, Switzerland and Italy. Breaking away from the Cardinal's train in Italy, he sampled ordinary life in Cento, where the provincial Italians "were very amazed that the people in Germany speak differently than they, and that I couldn't speak their language." [10] One reason he left the German Jesuit College was to see more of Italy and the Italians, and to "learn the Roman [i.e., Italian] language, which would never have happened shut up in the College with other Germans." [11]

In Rome, he explored castles, monasteries, chapels and churches, admired the splendors of the Vatican halls, libraries and papal chambers, and enjoyed the city's fountains, statues, painting and music, all the while compiling a lengthy journal on the sights he saw. Traveling to and from Rome, Pastorius noted cultural landmarks and esthetic delights throughout the central and northern provinces of the Italian peninsula in locations like Venice, Trient, Florence and Mantua. Equally impressive sights awaited him on his tour of 1646-47 in cities such as Bavarian Passau and Munich and, across the Austrian border, in Salzburg, Innsbruck and Vienna. Finally, after ending his studies in Rome, he began another full year of broadening travel – north through Italy to Switzerland and Germany and then on to France. [12]

On his travels, Pastorius learned quickly from new circumstances, as his first Alpine adventure illustrates:

> I stared with amazement at the snow lying on the mountaintops despite the dog days of summer. I bet half a bucket [*eimer*] of wine [probably 30 liters] with a lieutenant [in Cardinal Rosetti's train] that I could walk there and fetch some snowballs within four hours. When I had already walked an hour and a half, I met a peasant, and asked him how far I still had to go to reach the snow. He told me it would take another three hours. I thought I had lost the contest, but then asked the peasant if he didn't know of any snow in that area. Whereupon he soon led me to a patch of snow, from which I packed four snowballs together, put them in my hat, and ran off toward [the starting point of] Schwaz, [Austria,] even managing to arrive a good quarter-hour ahead of my planned return, and thus winning the bet. [13]

For Pastorius, being "on the road" typically meant enjoying the hospitality of a court, manor or monastery for a week or two – and sometimes much longer – before traveling on to the next stopover. Since his traveling coincided with the traveling of others, he was involved in a crisscrossing network of social communication, meeting old friends and new, local inhabitants and foreigners from distant homelands.

"With the opportunity of dining at court day after day," Pastorius reported of a three-month stay at Würzburg's Marienberg Castle in 1649, "I was able to penetrate the full range of courtly existence." [14] He met the court steward, who ran the administrative affairs of the principality and introduced him to "the newly-invented arts of economics," ate his meals with squires and knights, watched musketeers and soldiers drilling in the courtyard, and got to know the learned itinerants – including a few alchemists – living off the largess of the court or awaiting permanent employment. Pastorius enjoyed the conviviality of the court, displaying his wit in learned discourse and youthful pranks:

> [While touring Würzburg] the castrati singers and the musicians from the Royal Court of Italy... invited me to their chambers for a drink and some good conversation... I invited them to my quarters in return, and they accepted but [at first] hesitated to specify a time because they didn't want me to go to any trouble and expense on their behalf. I promised them not to serve more than two pitchers of wine ... [and then instructed a friend to refill the pitchers

secretly]. Thus the good musicians got so drunk that their throats became raw and they could sing but poorly the following day. [15]

Even if Pastorius delighted in this life of courtly privilege, he could not long ignore the burdens it placed on society. Wherever he traveled, he saw examples of political and social excess that did not square with the Catholic teachings of his youth. This excess was shockingly obvious in Rome, at the very center of Catholic influence, during the papal tenure of Innocent X (r. 1644-55), whose top priorities included consolidating the political power of the Papal States in central Italy, ensconcing members of his family in Vatican offices and diverting papal wealth to the family coffers. The Pope reigned in an atmosphere of favoritism, opportunism, corruption and intrigue, reflecting the moral climate then prevailing generally in the Eternal City. [16] "In Rome," Pastorius wryly concluded, "the body has its heaven, the soul its hell, and the purse its purgatory." He composed a brief satirical travel-ogue to dissuade his contemporaries from witnessing the decadence of the city:

> *Peregrinationis Dissuasio*
> Tell me, what did you see in Rome?
> Among the rich, the mountain of pride and ruthlessness, and hearts full of the sins of avarice, licentiousness and sodomy. Among the poor, the valley of tears, of starvation and of disdain [i.e., disdainful treatment by the rich].
> Blessed are those who believe this without seeing it. [17]

Pastorius began to question the worldly manifestations of Catholicism while in Rome, and he later criticized the political power of the papacy and its role in establishing the Holy Roman Empire (even though he would himself hold imperial office):

> In redeeming us and establishing His Church, . . . the Lord Jesus did not intend to create a spiritual sovereignty and papal state to stand in opposition to all the well-established governments that had previously existed in every region and country, but spoke instead quite clearly: My kingdom is not of this world. [18]

He also grew dissatisfied with Catholic religious practices:

> In the city of Rome I had experienced enough of the abuses of the Roman Church, and in fact had become sick of them: the idolization of the pope, the saints, the relics, and the bones of the dead; the elevated status of the holy water, the Agnus Dei, the mass, the pilgrimages, the votive offerings in the cloisters, the rosary prayers, etc. [19]

Pastorius claimed that many of the Vatican's iron chests, allegedly filled with saintly paraphernalia, would prove to be empty if one managed to unlock them. In Mantua, where legend had it that Saint Francis' body had been miraculously preserved for centuries, he put the "miracle" to the test, and he ridiculed the Franciscan friars for sending him on a wild goose chase when he insisted on seeing the saint's remains. [20]

Exploiting popular superstition, Pastorius implied, the Church enhanced its wealth and power. After visiting the papal sacristy, he described the costliness of the Pope's ceremonial robes and jeweled accessories, and noted the "numerous chests filled with vain treasures which one pope or another had shipped to this spot in order to increase the wealth of his treasury." [21] He stopped at the House of Inquisition, and wrote that "all sorts of methods" ("auff aller-hand Weiße") were used there to force heretics to repent. [22] All in all, he felt disillusioned with Catholicism despite his Catholic predispositions:

I just couldn't get it through my head that the Church should not have a pope and a visible leader, or that it was possible to get to heaven without the pope. And because of these doubts I completely abstained from the practices of confession and Holy Communion for several years, and could hardly believe in anything. [23]

Pastorius thus ignored his conscience and played the role allotted to him as a friend and companion of Catholic priests, noblemen and scholars, and a participant in the political and ecclesiastical processes of the Holy Roman Empire. Nothing indicates the extent of his involvement more clearly than his willingness to obtain papal dispensations for Prince-Bishop Philipp Christoph of Trier, a man who personified the excesses of the age. [24]

Philipp Christoph, whose German principality bordered on present-day Belgium, Luxembourg and France, aggrandized his political power before and during the Thirty Years' War by enlarging his armies and constructing edifices of baroque grandeur throughout his territory – the castle and fort of Ehrenbreitstein, the fortification of Philippsburg and a sumptuous palace at Trier. And he repeatedly demanded tax increases to finance these ventures. When the Trier provincial assembly refused to grant a requested tax levy in 1627, charging that Philipp Christoph's pomp and greed were vainly sacrificing the blood and sweat of his subjects, the Prince-Bishop dissolved the assembly, tripled taxes on his own authority and threatened to use military force if the levies were not met. The city of Trier refused to collect the burdensome tax, so Philipp Christoph jailed every member of the city council until they were ready to pledge their obedience in writing – and he could justify this absolutism with some of the interpretations of princely rights then advanced by political theorists.

In subsequent maneuverings, Philipp Christoph flouted his allegiance to the Hapsburg Empire by aligning with France, the archfiend, in the midst of the Thirty Years' War, but this attempt to advance his influence backfired when he was captured and imprisoned by the imperial army. Thus, Melchior Adam's Vatican employer, out of prison and back in office by 1645, aggrandized his power and influence by blatantly ignoring both the Christian morality and the imperial policies that presumably entitled him to his position – and in this era his behavior was not an isolated instance of such misconduct.

Pastorius could not ignore his conscience for long, however – certainly not with the proddings that jolted him on his travels in war-torn Europe. Two brushes with death in Italy foreshadowed other harrowing experiences on his subsequent journey through France. On one occasion he barely managed to flee from "bandits and murderers" ("Banditen und Mörder") two miles outside of Rome, and when he stopped at a road-side inn late one night he was

> shown into a very dark chamber to sleep, where the body of a man who had been killed lay under the bed and gave off a repulsive stench, and on my arrival I had noticed a large, freshly-dug hole behind the inn, in which they tried to bury the dead man and me, but God graciously helped me, through the arrival of various traveling pilgrims, to get out of there, and in that very night I moved on toward Monte Frascon... [26]

Pastorius thus began to evaluate his personal conduct in the light of his mortality: "Laughing [at fate] was costly then, and my pondering keen and earnest: where would I, body and soul, have traveled if I had been killed with my sins upon me?" [27] As the dangers of the road honed his moral sensitivity, he slowly developed

Protestant leanings. Within a year of leaving Rome, his disillusionment with Catholicism resolved into worldly yet pious Lutheran convictions, his traveling came to an end in Protestant Franconia, and the stage was set for his mature life as the father of Franz Daniel Pastorius.

When Melchior Adam left Rome for good in September, 1648, peace was at hand – the Westphalian treaty ending the war was signed within a month – and he set off once more, this time with Dr. Bartholomeus Nagel, a Franconian physician, to meet old friends and seek new opportunities in Hapsburg Europe. Three months later, after crossing the Alps and laying over at Koblenz and Trier, the scenario abruptly changed when Pastorius and Nagel began a walking tour of France just as an insurrection broke out in the capital city. As Pastorius tells the story in his reports, the workings of weather and nature provided a fitting prelude to the war-time hysteria that, despite the Peace of Westphalia, they soon encountered on the road to Paris. [28]

After celebrating New Year's Eve in Châlon sur Marne, Pastorius and Nagel continued their journey on 3 January 1649, trudging along for hours through clammy weather and pea-soup fog, ultimately becoming disoriented. Barking dogs and crowing cocks signaled villages they could not see; loamy mud clung to their shoes, and they grew fatigued. As night descended, they failed to find a town where they could lodge, and were forced to camp out "under the open skies in our wet clothing and the bitter cold." [29] Fears of freezing to death or being attacked by wolves disturbed their sleep, and these fears presaged an awesome encounter in the dead of night:

> Then, from a great distance, we saw a light arise, which gradually rose higher in the sky as it came on, until it finally passed quite close to us, and circled around us, scintillating, far larger than a large horse, so that both of us trembled to the quick, and we began to cry aloud to God, and begged for deliverance; then it finally receded again, and at the very spot where it had first appeared, the light was extinguished once more, and it disappeared. God only knows what it was. [30]

Pastorius and Nagel barely managed to warm up and regain their composure the next day at Beaona – "we received very poor comfort, since one never finds heated rooms in such villages with their typical rural ways" [31] – and they were soon caught in heavy rains that had flooded the Marne by January 13, sweeping away the bridge at La Ferté and interrupting their progress toward Paris.

Before the flood receded, Pastorius and Nagel were up to their necks in a political deluge that moved as surely as the churning Marne. In Paris, a coalition of the aristocracy and parliament had revolted against the absolutist rule of Queen Anne of Austria (1601-66) and Cardinal Jules Mazarin (1602-61), and mobs of anti-royalists took to the streets. [32] Although the Queen and Mazarin had fled on January 6, both the royalists and the rebels were rallying their forces the day Pastorius and Nagel arrived in La Ferté. Several regiments were approaching the village on their march to Paris, and the villagers panicked, carting their furniture and valuables into the village church for safekeeping from marauders just as Pastorius and Nagel hiked through the churchyard. The villagers showed no mercy:

> They jumped on us furiously, accused us of being spies, took our swords and tried to cut our throats. I showed them my passport from the Prince of Trier, but they merely threw it in the mud, and so I very nearly had to relinquish my life, until a wealthy grain merchant came along and calmed the mob down,

gave us back our passports, then took us along to his fine house and wined and dined us on a young roast goat. [33]

Secreted across the Marne by boat before dawn the next day, Pastorius and Nagel appealed to a Catholic bishop in Meaux for shelter "until the marching regiments would have passed by" ("bis die marchirende Regimenter möchten vorbey sein"), but the bishop hustled them off to Paris in an overland carriage instead. They were placed under house arrest by the Paris Guard, and released as soon as their credentials were verified. The city's proverbial charm nevertheless proved evanescent:

> I rented a room from a Dr. Heilmann in the suburb of St. Germain, bought a good supply of victuals – peas, beans, lentils, cheese, butter, etc. – and didn't dare venture out of the house, since there was a great tumult in the city every day, and some people were stabbed to death while trying to buy bread, inasmuch as great price increases came about because Prince [Louis] Conde [(1621-86)] with his [royalist] troops had occupied all the roads out of the city, so that the 2000 wagons and carts of bread that usually entered the city every week could no longer arrive. That put an end to all normal business, and made things difficult for the general run of the populace, and furthermore no one would cash a foreigner's draft, and of course it was absolutely forbidden to leave the city, on pain of death. [34]

It was, in fact, a deadly encounter at the city gates that shocked Pastorius into probing the values he lived by. When the tensions of insurrection and siege became unbearable, he sought help in quitting Paris at the Embassy of Trier, where he was formally received by the ambassador, Baron Philipp Ludwig von Reiffenberg (d. 1686):

> This gentleman poured me a glass of wine and drank to my health, and he offered me every possible consolation, but that very afternoon he pretended to be taking a pleasant carriage ride to a garden outside the city, and he never came back to Paris. [35]

Pastorius soon befriended the Ambassador's faithful steward, who, disoriented by his superior's sudden desertion, agreed to escape the tumult of the city by moving in with Pastorius:

> When the steward had spent a number of days with me in hiding, he finally resolved to try to leave the city and get back to his lord the baron, against which I strongly advised, begging him to wait patiently just a few more days, telling him the tumult would soon be over; and since he was not willing to abide by my oft-repeated consolations and entreaties, I accompanied him as far as the city gates, and then went immediately atop the high wall. He had already passed the first and second sentries, but the third and final sentry (a mere lad of eleven or twelve years of age) shouted out, who was he, and where did he want to go, but since he went steadily onward without slackening his pace and repeatedly refused to answer, he was shot through and through and died instantly, was soon thereafter carried into the city by various soldiers, buried in a little hospital churchyard, *fine lux fine crux*, a man truly possessed of grand qualities, with a deep knowledge of jurisprudence and various languages. This tragic spectacle of my sleeping companion and the *recordatio* [recollection] of the dangerous happenings on the journey taught me to sit quietly in my little room of trial and endurance, to take the vanity of the world to heart, withal to search my own conscience, and to determine how it stands in relation to God, and in what manner my poor soul might be saved from eternal damnation. [36]

Elsewhere on his journey and throughout his life, death hovered close to Pastorius and touched his diurnal existence. [37] His father had been mortally wounded by Swedish soldiers. A brother, conscripted into the Hapsburg army, died in battle during the Thirty Years' War. A sister died in childbirth at Eltville on the Rhine shortly before Pastorius reached her home along his route from Rome to Paris. In subsequent years, funerals repeatedly followed weddings in Pastorius' own household – he was widowed in 1657, then in 1661 and again in 1674. When he married a twenty-year-old bride on his fiftieth birthday in September, 1674, he seemed to have overwhelmed the odds against him, for she lived beyond his own death in 1702. Nevertheless, he was caught in a losing game with high stakes: three of his eight children died at childbirth or within a year of birth. His second-oldest son, Pastorius' brightest hope for the future after Franz Daniel emigrated to America, died in 1687 at the age of twelve, and Pastorius poured out his grief in a rhymed epitaph and 38 stanzas of meditative verse. In retrospect, however, none of these deaths had a greater impact on Pastorius' life than the death of the baron's steward at the gates of Paris, for it was there that he most poignantly felt his complicity in the moral imperfections of Hapsburg Europe.

Leaving Paris in June, 1649, Pastorius pondered his future as he traveled on to Lyon and Nantua, then to Geneva and Basel in Switzerland and on through the German Black Forest to Tubingen, Stuttgart and Würzburg. Fully aware of his own mortality, he wanted to live morally and responsibly for the sake of his immortal soul, but he was too much a part of his culture to renounce the joys and privileges of his worldly existence. Trying to resolve this dilemma, he began exploring the meaning of Christianity with a few Protestant clergymen along his route, among them Johann Valentin Andreae (1586-1654) in Stuttgart, one of the liberal Lutherans whose writings would inspire Lutheran Pietists a few years later – a man in whom Pastorius sensed "the very spirit of God" ("Sanctus Spiritus ipse"). [38] Yet it was a mundane IOU that first drew Pastorius to the Protestant villages of rural Franconia, which seemed, on the surface, safely removed from the excesses of the Roman Catholic courts in Hapsburg Europe.

Financially pressed in Paris, Pastorius had badgered Dr. Bartholomeus Nagel to repay the money Pastorius had generously lent him during their journey from Rome. Just when he thought he was solvent once more, Pastorius discovered that Nagel had tricked him by freezing the funds another four weeks, critically intensifying his sense of destitution in a city where his own drafts were not negotiable. In a huff, Pastorius broke off their friendship, and vented his anger in a verse anagram wishing Nagel a poverty-stricken future. [39]

He kept Nagel's IOU and eventually, arriving in Franconia from Stuttgart, presented it to Nagel's stepfather Wilhelm Treuen, the village parson in Winterhausen, across the Main River from Sommerhausen thirteen kilometers south of Würzburg. The pennyless clergyman, paid in kind with Franconian wine instead of cash, needed time to sell off a supply of wine large enough to redeem the IOU. Meanwhile, Pastorius traveled on to Würzburg to pay his respects to Prince-Bishop Johann Philipp at Marienberg Castle, thanking him for the stipend that had supported Pastorius' studies in Rome and apologizing "most submissively" ("unterthänigst") for using it on the law instead of theology:

> His Grace the electoral Prince did not reveal the slightest indication of displeasure with me, but announced instead, with a cordial mien, that the clerical pro-

fession was not to everyone's liking. I should remain at the court, he would be wanting to speak to me again. [40]

While staying on at the court of Würzburg during the autumn of 1649, Pastorius returned to Winterhausen to prod Parson Treuen into liquidating his assets – and accepted instead a large barrel of the liquid that, transported back to Würzburg, enabled him to entertain guests like the Italian castrati singers on the eve of his conversion to Protestantism. "I had finally grown tired of courtly existence," Pastorius concluded by November, 1649 [41]:

> I frequently rode out to Winterhausen and Sommerhausen, and was always treated very politely by the residents there, so that I became more and more pleased with the locality and the conversations I had with the Protestant Christians who lived there, and I thus requested His most worthy Grace the electoral Prince [Johann Philipp] for his recommendation to the [Lutheran] Grafs of Limpurg, [lords of Sommerhausen and vicinity,] was granted the same, and was subsequently welcomed and made at home in the town in the most friendly manner.
> My first task [in Sommerhausen], however, was this: to read through the [Lutheran] Augsburg Confession, to examine the course of my life as I had lived it from one year to the next, and to be instructed in the value of always fastening one's eyes upon the Creator rather than the works of creation and of believing in the words of Christ more than human law and tradition, until I finally came to the realization that I had found the new man within and abandoned the nominal Christian without who relies on the worthiness of his own deeds, and I participated in Holy Communion for the first time in Sommerhausen on [Christmas Day,] 1649, standing next to his most honorable Graf and imperial Cupbearer, Georg Friedrich von Limpurg [1596-1651], and I also wrote up my profession of Christian faith in accordance with the Augsburg Confession, and dedicated it to his Grace the most esteemed Graf. [42]

Writing this narrative for his Pennsylvania son and grandsons in 1699, Melchior Adam carefully indicated both the worldly and spiritual motives behind his conversion to Protestantism half a century earlier. A one-sided approach would not have been very convincing. He had been a leading member of worldly society as a young lawyer in Sommerhausen, and when he moved his family to the free imperial city of Windsheim in 1659, he began one of the most energetic and illustrious careers in the history of this Franconian city. [43] In addition to running a prosperous law practice with some fifty nobles and affluent burghers as clients, he held 23 long-term offices in city government, including city advocate, supervisor of education, supervisor of the hospital, public works supervisor, housing inspector, water commissioner, district tax collector for the surrounding villages, fiscal overseer of various civic organizations, charities and altar funds as well as burgomaster for 26 years and, culminating his career from 1692 to 1698, lord mayor (or *Oberbürgermeister*) of the city. He compiled detailed ledgers, journals and governmental handbooks while diligently performing his civic duties, and he also wrote profusely in private life – manuscripts and printed works of local, regional and imperial history, travel description, autobiography, religious meditation, secular and religious poetry.

His civic and scholarly accomplishments won him influence and repute among the men of learning and station throughout Franconia, especially among the senators, or city magistrates, of Nürnberg and the representatives of the Provincial Assembly ("Fränckischer Kreis") and at the Protestant court of Brandenburg Bayreuth. (His conduct during the Windsheim insurrection of 1677-79 is described in

Chapter Four. His attempts to win influence at Bayreuth, described in Chapter Three, involved pandering to Margrave Christian Ernst (1644-1712), a Protestant prince whose ruthless ambition was similar to that of Philipp Christoph of Trier, the Catholic prince-bishop he had served decades earlier.)

Yet underlying this worldly success was a deep baroque uncertainty that, disguised as rock-steady paternal authority, touched the personality of young Franz Daniel Pastorius. Melchior Adam's civic career tested the hypothesis behind his religious conversion of 1649, often with discouraging results. Insisting that he could renounce Catholicism without giving up his privilege and station within German society, Pastorius had staked his very salvation upon the integrity of the Lutheran church and state – and initiated a running battle between his Christian ideals and conscience and the realities of pride and egotism in himself and in society.

The outward signs of this conflict became apparent only after Franz Daniel's emigration in 1683. When illness threatened his life in 1689 (two years after the death of his 12-year-old son Johann Samuel, and in the midst of attacks on the Hapsburg Empire by Turkey and France), Melchior Adam reported, he gave up his prosperous law practice and swore that from then on he would only represent needy clients like widows and orphans. [44] In these years, he increasingly challenged the upper-class attitudes of Windsheim. His history of Windsheim, published in 1692 (the same year he was named lord mayor), countered the governmental secrecy of the senate (or city council), even claiming on its title page that it would reveal the "true causes of such great decadence" in the city for the benefit of its "dear citizens." [45]

His conflict of conscience emerges poignantly in verse meditations on Christ's humility and the unchristian conduct of the rich and powerful. [46] In "Klage deß Welt Kindes über den Tod" ("Complaint of a Child of this World upon his Death"), for example, a civic leader regrets that he treated the poor unmercifully and obstructed justice during life. One of Pastorius' epigrams implicitly questions the existence – or regrets the necessity – of a privileged class: Where were the aristocrats when Adam hoed the earth and Eve spun her yarn? Unflinchingly introspective in a few poems, Pastorius admitted his own pursuit of honor and esteem, and confessed it had led him to love his titles and possessions and to disdain the members of the lower classes.

He moved beyond this conflict in his richest poetry, innocently celebrating worldly pleasures, which he could appreciate as a foretaste of heavenly fulfillment. Although he sometimes displayed self-centered attitudes in his religious expression, for example in the 1674 wedding poem quoted on page 168, he frequently wrote poems of maturity and depth, transcending the boundaries of temporal and spiritual, of life and death, even of human eroticism and divine love. Fat, round cabbages and turnips and full, ripe apples and grapes, for instance, image the "pregnant earth," always regenerating life ("Die Erd stets Schwanger ist ..."), just as the playful repartee of courting lovers builds to a statement of heavenly bliss ambiguously resonating between the physical and the spiritual. This perception of Immanence in diurnal life moved Pastorius to a spiritual lyricism of formal brilliance and sincerity, and – especially toward the end of his career – it also caused him to lash out vehemently at the excesses of his age.

All of Christendom is a barbarous wasteland, he wrote, and he claimed that the vices of cunning, insincerity, deceitfulness, greed and arrogance had become the predominant motives of his culture. Christians zealously studied the Bible and Luther's teachings at school and in church in the early days of the Reformation, he argued in the anagram "Pfui ein geplapp inn Sion" ("Phooey on the Babbling in Zion"), but today going through the motions has replaced genuine faith. He dwelt on Old Testament righteousness: the eyes of God flash through the darkness, he warned, and perceive all that does not conform to His law. And he described God's wrath toward the unrepentant with the dark imagery of the Book of Revelations. In a poem ostensibly about the biblical Jerusalem, but also reflecting Pastorius' growing impatience toward his own city of Windsheim, God describes his efforts to save the city like a hen protecting her chicks ("wie ein Henn ihr Kücklein decket") but then, angered by the city's debauchery and impenitence, predicts its ultimate destruction.

Pastorius' bitter and sarcastic "Absagung der weltlichen Gesellschaft" ("Rejection of Worldly Society") describes humanity as little children who selfishly and stubbornly follow cheap pleasures, rely on luck and malice to get ahead, and use friends one day and despise them the next. And Pastorius bids them all a curt yet painful farewell: Get away from me, society both high and low, leave me alone. Just keep on despising me, laugh or scorn as you will; I want to live in Christ's friendship and, yes, to be mocked by the world:

Drumb, Welt Kinder flihet hin,
Packt euch fortt aus meinem Sinn,
    Die Gesellschaft, gros und kleine,
    Heb dich fort, laß mich alleine.
Thut mich immerhin verachten,
    Lachet, oder spottet mein,
Ich will Christi Freundschafft achten,
    Der Welt auch verspottet sein.

The bitterness of these lines reflects Pastorius' experience in Windsheim. Latent rivalries came to a head in 1697 when Pastorius, then 73 years old, feuded with a Windsheim clergyman and – for lack of solidarity from his fellow senators (or city councilmen) – resigned from all public office, including his post as lord mayor, the city's highest honor. Irked by Pastorius' self-righteousness and breaches of decorum, the senators then tried and convicted him for tax evasions that ordinarily would have gone ignored within the chambers of government. Adding to his difficulties, his wife Dorothea Esther was exposed as the author of anonymous diatribes against upper-class neighbors. Pastorius was thus forced to leave his adopted city in public disgrace.

In the autobiography he sent to Pennsylvania, Pastorius ignored his fall from civic grace. He enumerated his 23 long-term public offices in Windsheim instead, and then simply reported that he had resigned from all of them and retired with his family to a modest garden home in Nürnberg: "I [now] devote my time to pious thoughts and meditation as if [I were living] in a religious hermitage." [47] Yet by 1699 the elder Pastorius had reached a turning point: He finally seemed convinced that his son Franz Daniel had found a way to avoid the conflicts of world and spirit in his European life. He announced his plans to emigrate to Pennsylvania, but was dissuaded by medical counsel that judged his health too fragile for the journey. He then gathered together Franz Daniel's Pennsylvania letters and reports for publication in Frankfurt, and added a two-page preface displaying his enthusiasm for America. [48]

Franz Daniel Pastorius could comprehend this belated enthusiasm with greater particularity than most, for he had all too keenly felt the tensions behind it. By teaching Christian morality to his son yet compromising his principles in his daily conduct, Melchior Adam had become personally involved in the events and emotions that convinced Franz Daniel to leave Germany in 1683.

CHAPTER ONE
New Beginnings in the Old World

1.1 *"To escape disaster in time and eternity":*
Leaving Germany in 1683

> Ever in pilgrimage, and yet never from home.
> -- "Pilgrimage"
>
> To quest as a spaniel.
> -- "Dog"
>
> [The Greek philosopher] Anaxagorus being asked, why he had no more love for his country than to leave it? Wrong me not, saith he, my greatest care is my country, pointing his finger towards heaven. Culpeper, p. 428 . . . Joseph [in Egypt, Gen. 39-50] found more kindness and friendship in a strange land than he had in his own country and among his own brethren. <u>Genes.</u>, p. 72.
> -- "Native Country"
>
> Cold winter's gone, the pleasant spring begun;
> Why fear we frost, and are so near the sun?
> -- Epigram 56

During the spring of 1683 Franz Daniel Pastorius, then a 31-year-old bachelor practicing law in Frankfurt am Main, reached a decision that altered the course of his life and added his name to the growing list of European emigrants seeking a new world. [1] It was not an easy decision. To make it, he had to give up the prospect of a comfortable law career, contemplate leaving family, friends and homeland, and accept the insecurities of an ocean voyage and a frontier existence. His plans had begun taking shape the preceding winter when, having returned from his European grand tour, he learned of a venture in international commerce and real estate that several Frankfurt merchants were embarking upon in the English colony of Pennsylvania, established by William Penn (1644-1718) in 1682. As Lutheran Pietists, the merchants embraced a religious movement with progressive social and political ideals that had taken root in Frankfurt a few years earlier and was increasingly attracting converts. Penn's "holy experiment" thus offered them both religious freedom and economic opportunity, and, as a bold departure from the status quo, appealed to visionary non-merchants as well. Some of the Pietists were already packing for the journey when Pastorius learned of their plans, while others, considering their financial and emotional ties to the homeland, said they would need about a year to prepare for emigration.

Pastorius, a friend of both merchants and visionaries, volunteered to spearhead the operation in Pennsylvania, but first attempted a partial reconciliation with his father, from whom he had been estranged since leaving home in 1679. He repeatedly wrote to Melchior Adam Pastorius in the province of Franconia, presenting his case for emigration, and requesting his father's "consent and approbation," including financial backing (Appendix I). Melchior Adam could not see any advantage to a reconciliation involving even greater separation, yet he was caught in a moral bind, and aware that opposing his son could be self-defeating. Eventually he reluctantly approved the emigration plans he must have considered foolhardy and spiteful, and, in an apparent display of love and contrition, forwarded a "Bill of Exchange of 250 rixdollars," the money Franz Daniel needed to arrange a 1000-acre purchase of Pennsylvania land as part of the Frankfurt venture.

Young Pastorius accepted the money, but decided against a final leave-taking from his family in southern Germany, instead shipping them a token of his disturbed affection, "a large Chest full of Books & other Rarities by me heretofore gathered" (Appendix I), thus ameliorating the logistical as well as the emotional strains of his removal to the New World. Packing books, clothing, and household and personal effects too numerous for the journey (and deciding which 'rarities' to leave behind), he could sympathize with the Pietists who needed more time to prepare for departure, and with those who admitted this new beginning was too radical for them. Yet he readied himself for departure, and bid farewell to Frankfurt friends, who gave him cash and practical gifts including a butter dish, a pocket watch, and a flintlock rifle betokening these friendships interrupted or terminated as well as the civilized comforts then being relinquished and frontier exigencies anticipated.

On 2 April 1683 Pastorius signed a contract as sole American agent for the Pietist merchants, collected starting capital, and set off down the Rhine toward Rotterdam and a tentative port call across the Channel in London. Along the way he recruited a party of nine German, Dutch and English employees for the Frankfurt enterprise, the workmen and maids who would build makeshift dwellings, clear the land and plant Indian corn to ensure the survival of the first immigrant families. He also met two groups of future emigrants, including some of the Mennonite or Quaker craftsmen at Krefeld, Germany, who, independent of the Frankfurt Pietists, would be departing for America with their families three months later. Despite the Krefelders' distrust of his upper-class Lutheranism, Pastorius managed to lay the groundwork for future cooperation in America. By working closely with Germans of various callings and confessions, he hoped to establish "a little Germany" – self-contained and essentially independent – within the larger colony of Pennsylvania.

After a two-week stopover in Rotterdam, home of Penn's Dutch affiliates, and a month of sailing preparations in London, where Pennsylvania agents sold him approximately 20,000 acres of land for private or communal estates and future resale to emigrating Germans, Pastorius and his party sailed from Gravesend to Deal aboard the "America" on June 6, the preliminary leg of their journey, and their ship was soon heading across the Atlantic. About a decade later, well established in Pennsylvania, he summarized this undertaking with a third-person report in an even-tempered style typifying much of his American writing:

> The entire German Company or society had commissioned the eager traveler *Franciscum Danielum Pastorium, J.U. licentiam* [licentiate of civil and canon law], as its authorized attorney. He set out from Frankfurt am Main and arrived in London, concluded a purchase, received a land deed with instructions for the surveyor, and, under God's escort, happily [or: successfully] sailed across the ocean. [2]

During a port-side layover at Deal on June 6, 1683, with a foretaste of the ocean voyage upon him, Pastorius had chosen a different style, also typical of his writing, as he tried to explain his departure in a letter to his father and friends in his former home town of Windsheim, Germany:

> After I had seen my fill of the regions and provinces of Europe and taken to heart the impending *motus belli* [passions of war] and the disturbing disruptions and transformations that war will bring to my fatherland, I allowed myself to be moved by the special urging of the Almighty to cross the ocean to Pennsylvania, living in the hope that this undertaking of mine will work out to the best for me and my dear brothers and sisters and, most of all, enhance the glory of God (which is my aim above all else), especially since the worldly impudence and sin of Europe are ever increasing from one day to the next, which is why the righteous judgement of God cannot be delayed for very much longer.
>
> In all of my doings I have truly taken these vanities and impertinences to heart and, in deep meditation, pondered where they will ultimately lead us, realizing that life and limb itself, worldly possessions, honor and sensual pleasures must all yield to death and corruption. But once an immortal soul is lost, it is lost forever. *Semel periisse aeternum est.* [Once to be lost is forever.]
>
> Thus, to escape disaster in time and eternity, I have all the more willingly set out upon this journey across the great ocean under God's holy guidance, and, along with nine individuals in my care, sailed from Deal in the company of various families of good standing on June 7, 1683, trusting that the Lord, who to this very hour has so richly blessed me and commanded his angels to watch over me, will govern my going out and coming in so that I will also be able to praise His holy name on the far side of the sea in unknown places.
>
> I thus commit my respected father and all my dear relatives to the protective hand of God, and as soon as He helps me across to Pennsylvania I will report about everything in a more detailed account. Should it be His holy will to claim me along the way, however, I am ready with all my heart, and I therefore bid my father the farewell befitting a child, again thanking him obediently for all the love and devotion he has so abundantly given me; may God repay him for this in time and eternity.
>
> One of the things I recall having seen on my grand tour was a tombstone with an epitaph which reads as follows:
>
> > Der ich bey frembder Grufft so manche Schrifft gelesen,
> > Und deren gute Zahl in dieses Buch gebracht,
> > Weiß nicht wo? wann? und wie? ich selbst werd verwesen,
> > Drum gib ich Welt-lust dir nun tausend gute Nacht.
> > [Since I, who have read many an inscription at foreign crypts,
> > And collected a goodly number of them in this book,

> Do not know where? when? or how? I myself will decay,
> I therefore bid thee, worldly desire, a thousand times good night.]
> If for this reason we do not see each other again beneath the heavens, then it will be *in* heaven, where we may accomplish God's will differently than here on earth, which I desire with all my soul; and I remain until death
>
> My respected father's
> most truly obedient son,
> F. D. P [3]

Pastorius thus reveals, in his earliest correspondence, the pragmatic determination and troubled idealism of his Pennsylvania enterprise.

1.2 Scholarly Simplifications of Pastorius' Piety and Worldliness

> The love of life, a sweet and sour desire,
> Is in man's breast an universal fire.
>
> -- Epigram 2330.9

> Twelve pennyworth of flesh with five shillings of cookery may happen to make a fashionable dish. [Wm.] Penn. They sin to their hability [ability; i.e., by overeating]. Cook . . . builds strange fabrics in pasta, towers and castles, which are offered to the assault of valiant teeth. The receipts [recipes] of cookery are swelled to a volume, but a good stomach excels them all. Max[im] 56 . . . General sauces, and sauces for every particular roasted or boiled creature. See <u>Closet</u>, p. 136.
>
> -- "Cookery"

> True God and true man . . . Christ was before [King] David was, for he was David's Lord, and David was before Christ, for Christ was the son of David, though David did not beget him. Christ had a father and mother, and yet he was without father and mother; he was the Son of Man, and yet no man's son. The son of God's desires and good pleasure, in whom he has heaped up the fullness of grace, and treasures of all perfection.
>
> -- "Christ" [4]

Although Pastorius' "Alphabetical Hive" entries on Christ and cookery indicate a healthy involvement in the life and thought of his day, they can also be equated with the contrast between his emotional letter of 1683 and the level-headed summary of his emigration written years later, and with similar contrasts throughout his life and writings. Pastorius enjoyed living fully in the physical world around him – whether that entailed traveling in Europe, launching an American business venture, growing turnips, muskmelons or forget-me-nots in his Germantown garden, drinking wine, smoking a clay pipe, savoring fresh Pennsylvania strawberries in West Indian rum, or encouraging female flirtation and male camaraderie. [5] Yet he also joined a religious movement that rejected a number of the worldly indulgences of his European contemporaries, and he freely used a rhetoric of piety to attack what he regarded as the moral inadequacies of European society. This rhetoric emerges repeatedly in his transatlantic correspondence with his father and friends in Germany, and it can easily mislead readers into forgetting that he lived a robust worldly existence even as he wrote his jeremiads and diatribes, especially since the grace and humor of his mature writing (most of it unpublished) has been largely ignored.

Because this pious rhetoric coincides with personal evasions, the transatlantic writings have remained virtually inaccessible even to historians, and they have inevitably been misinterpreted. In the letters to his father constituting the bulk of the published correspondence, Pastorius was too respectful to challenge paternal authority and the dominant values of German society in literal and readily-comprehended language, yet too headstrong to keep his controversial opinions to himself. Adopting a pious literary style, one of the most popular and respected in his day, he was able to combine the subtleties of indirect statement and veiled allusion with the persuasive force of colorful metaphor, emotive language, and biblical authority. And the deep convictions underlying this stylistic choice made it all the more convincing.

Pastorius communicated effectively with his father and the tradition-bound culture he had left behind, stimulating German-American immigration in the process, yet his use of a pious rhetoric has led to doubts and confusions about his character and the merits of his contribution to transatlantic culture. Gertrude S. Kimball, for example, revealed her inability to take Pastorius seriously by refusing to translate accurately his criticism of the scholastic Aristotelians cited on page 252 (note 9), and his biographer Marion D. Learned was clearly troubled by contradictions between Pastorius' apparent religiosity and his broad cultural accomplishments. Commenting on Pastorius' reiterated claim that God would soon destroy Europe, for instance, Learned refused to admit that Pastorius was swayed by Pietist millennialism during the 1680s:

> The impression of impending European disaster, so deeply engraved on Pastorius' mind, is not to be regarded as evidence that he entertained Chiliastic views of the approaching end of the world, but rather as a prophetic presentiment of the catastrophe which culminated in the French Revolution. [6]

Learned avoided basic aspects of Pastorius' robust personality and culture as well as his millennialist radicalism, and this scholarly evasiveness yielded a distorted image of Pastorius that has prevailed despite an occasional corrective touch such as that by Julius Goebel, who in 1904 sensed a "completely new aspect" ("ganz neue Seite") of Pastorius in the classical learning and rich humor of two uncollected letters, and hoped it would offset the prevalent image of a "somewhat humdrum and prosaic [German-American] hero despite all of his respectability and honesty." [7]

A few evaluations since then (cited on pages 7-8 and 10) reveal greater complexity, but until the 1980s Pastorius, for the most part, was caught in the time warp of turn-of-the-century research, which by ignoring or simplifying his beliefs produced a flat character whose piety has been overemphasized in most of the accounts of him up to the present. In his 1983 history of the Krefeld emigrants, for example, Ernst Köppen gives this grossly misleading picture of Pastorius on the book's very first page:

> His clothing was made of coarse fabric and tailored in the plainest fashion. He had a friendly greeting for everyone passing his way, but of course he never once raised his hat. [8]

Misreading the transatlantic writings, Köppen erroneously concluded that Pastorius must have looked and acted like a simple Quaker laborer or Mennonite peasant as he approached Krefeld on 11 April 1683, yet nothing is farther from the truth. [9] Tipping his hat, especially before his superiors, was one of the most basic and deep-seated forms of propriety Pastorius had learned as a Gymnasium pupil, and there is nothing in his personality or culture to suggest that he would have abandoned the habit before arriving in Quaker Pennsylvania, where his upper-class manner and dress, along with his learnedness and the land holdings of a genteel farmer, won him the confidence and respect of William Penn and other members of the Quaker elite, and among the average citizens marked him as a natural leader in their society. As this study points out, it was in fact his keen awareness of the requirements of social conformity that created problems for Pastorius in Germany; if he had been able to reject prevailing customs and live freely as a nonconformist within his own society – if he could have resisted the urge to tip his hat – he would not have had his particular reasons for leaving Europe in the first place.

Pastorius has thus been one of the least understood of colonial American writers even though he left voluminous and expressive testimony to his personality and values. Rather than bogging down in apparent contradictions of personality, this study accepts them as hallmarks of his complex humanity and moves on, assuming that analysis of his personal development will adequately explain them – especially if the analysis is comprehensive, refracting the documented historical and biographical evidence through the commentary of his multifaceted Pennsylvania writings.

1.3   Mixed Attitudes toward Germany
1.3.1   "The bond of a good conscience with God": An 'Unholy' Baptism Repudiated

> Felicity is near. But once begin
> A virtuous life, you'll find it all within.
>
> -- Epigram 103
>
> Hypocrites make clean the outside of the cup. Matt. 23:25 . . . The true Christian's sorrow [i.e., concern] is not water but purification of the heart by faith. I Pet. 3:21, Acts 15:9 . . . They lay hold of the shadow and figure instead of the substance, of the shell instead of the kernel. Shewen, p. 78.
>
> -- "Baptism"
>
> Original sin, a term not found in Scripture; nor grounded therein. The seed of sin is transmitted from Adam unto all men, but it is imputed to none, no, not to infants, until they actually join with it by sinning. Barclay, p. 41, 93. For Adam's eating [of the 'apple'], all the children's teeth must be set on edge, contrary to what God saith. Jer. 34:29, Ezek. 18:2 . . . We are not to look so much how sin came in, as how we may get it out. Geo. Keith, Reexam. . . . Original sin is a stirring evil, and never lies dormant. Boehm, Orig., p. 11 . . . The knowledge of our fall in Adam and of our recovery in Christ are the two great hinges whereon the whole structure of Christian religion moves . . . Ibid., p. 20. There is a real communication of Adam's corruption, and so there must be a real communication of Christ's righteousness. Ibid., p. 27.
>
> -- "Original Sin"

Approaching Pastorius through his writings, this study has thus far noted two puzzling contrasts. Radically different descriptions of his emigration reflect general stylistic contrasts in his prose and poetry, just as the robust living demonstrated in his poetry and scholarly jottings contrasts with the didactic morality of his transatlantic correspondence. A third basic contrast – differentiating his correspondence from his poetry and scholarship – will also be dealt with in this study, further indicating that cross-cultural analysis may resolve the apparent inconsistencies in Pastorius' character and conduct.

Privately collecting the wit and wisdom of others in his "Alphabetical Hive," Pastorius calmly and generously accepted opposing views, postponing final judgement on the nature of truth until all the evidence could be heard. Thus his entries on original sin include the somber undertones of Lutheran theology in the Pietist writings of Anton Wilhelm Boehme (1673-1722), a German chaplain at the English court of Queen Anne and King George I (where the final 'e' was dropped from his name), along with the enlightened spirituality of the English Quaker Robert Barclay (1648-90), a satirical or skeptical view from an unidentified source, and the pragmatic stance of Scotsman George Keith (1638-1716), a Quaker in Pennsylvania from 1685 to 1692 (and later an Anglican). An even broader range of opinion can be observed in many of his manuscript 'honeycombs' (such as the entries on atheism cited on page 157), and his poetry also explores a wide range of issues in a predominantly calm and patient manner, humorous, skeptical and compassionate. Commenting on German existence in his letters, however, he was typically uncalm and impatient toward the views of others, indicating that a verdict had already been reached.

Pastorius displays this impatience while greeting one of his Franconian godchildren in a letter of 30 March 1694, to his father Melchior Adam, then lord mayor of Windsheim. Since the passage refers to the very beginnings of life in the Franconian society of his day, it reflects on the traditions that both enriched and burdened young Pastorius' life in Germany, and begins to explain the ambiguous emotions accompanying his 1683 emigration. Pastorius, 42 years old and living with his 35-year-old wife Ennecke and their sons Johann Samuel, 4, and Heinrich, 2, wrote the passage in response to a letter he had received from a 23-year-old lawyer who would later become burgomaster of the free imperial city – an office Pastorius himself would have attained if he had followed the well-established traditions of the city that had been his home from 1659 to 1679:

> On Feb. 8 of this year 1694 I received a few lines from my godson Franz Jacob Mercklein, whom I had raised out of the font of holy baptism in my eighteenth year, before I myself had been baptized by the Holy Spirit or become a Christian. Please give him my friendly greetings, and earnestly exhort him to observe faithfully and zealously the covenant I then made with God on his behalf, and to resist the desire to break it, noting as well that I then renounced the devil, the world and the lusts of the flesh in his name; for this first promise is far, far more important than all other commitments, and true baptism is not the [ceremonial] cleansing of impurity from the flesh, but rather the bond of a good conscience with God, &c [etc]. [10]

For Franz Daniel Pastorius in 1694, a brief note from his namesake Franz Jakob Mercklein (1670-1742), who was only an eight-year-old child when they last saw each other in Windsheim, triggered emotions complicated by memories of his Franconian past and a present awareness, in his Pennsylvania life, of humane values he had not been able to apply while living with his upper-class family and friends in Germany. Emboldened by this juxtaposition, Pastorius employed a pietistic tone to offer blunt moral advice, and in the process he seemingly contradicted the facts of his own biography.

Despite his claim that he had not been spiritually baptized by the age of eighteen, both family and church records confirm that a Lutheran clergyman baptized

Franz Daniel at the Church of Saint Bartholomew in Sommerhausen on 27 September 1651, the day following his birth in this rural Franconian village. [11] The real water and the immanent Word of this rite, orthodox Lutherans maintained, cleansed the infant of the original sin and eternal guilt he had inherited from Adam, and conferred divine grace upon him, thus joining him with the dead and resurrected body of Christ and the visible community of His church in this world. [12] The baby was passively involved in the ritual, which also involved his father and the two godfathers who through their professed faith sponsored Franz Daniel before God, and through their social stature lent significance to the occasion. Doctor Melchior Adam Pastorius chose as godfathers for his first-born son a colleague who shared his vocation as a jurist and the young Graf who was his Sommerhausen lord, then noted their names and titles in his record of family history, and commemorated Franz Daniel's redemption through the blood of Christ in a Latin anagram verse of his own composition. [13]

Beginning with this baptism, Melchior Adam taught, and for a number of years his son diligently learned, the particular mix of worldly and spiritual values reiterated in so many aspects of Franz Daniel's upbringing in Sommerhausen and Windsheim. But Franz Daniel's letter of 30 March 1694 shows that he eventually asserted independent values precluding a role as an obedient son in his Franconian homeland. By denying the spirituality of his infant baptism, Pastorius challenged one of the most fundamental dogmas of his old community.

The German readers of *Beschreibung Pennsylvaniae*, after all (the published source of this letter), knew perfectly well that an ordained clergyman had admitted him into the Lutheran church by baptizing him in the name of the Father, and of the Son, and of the Holy Spirit: How else could he have later served as a baptismal sponsor? So they could not help inferring that Pastorius was denying the efficacy of church baptism and disparaging the Christianity of the established church. These readers knew that each inhabitant of the Lutheran state was baptized as a sign of acceptance into the community and, in practice, of subservience to it, and they generally accepted the orthodox Lutheran doctrine that any baptism performed by a minister of the state church was genuine and irrevocable, a holy sacrament ordained by God.

Writing from America, Pastorius was free to challenge this doctrine with a simple and far-reaching heresy: His church baptism had not been effused with the Holy Spirit, and he had not been a Christian in his Franconian youth. As corollaries to this, he elsewhere reports that he was brought to Christ by Lutheran Pietists in Frankfurt, and states that Franconian society, and Europe generally, ignored the real values of Christianity.

1.3.2 The Self-imposed 'Exile' of a German 'Alien'

> Only those noble souls are truly free,
> That can deny themselves their liberty.
>
> -- Epigram 2325.4

> If it be my duty to love my country, I must be kind also to my countrymen: If a veneration be due the whole, so is a piety also to the parts; we are all members of one body, &c. Seneca, p. 415. The place where I first drew the vital air. [The people] among whom I have received my natural breath. *Vincit amor patriae.* [He prevails over (or demonstrates) love of country.]

> Virgil. Nature has ingrafted in every creature an affection to the place whence it had its birth and beginning. <u>Genes.</u>, p. 71.
>
> -- "Native Country"
>
> A stranger, though never so long conversant amongst the English, carrieth evermore a watchword upon his tongue to descry him by.
>
> -- "Language"

In his reports and letters, Pastorius asserts his right as an individual to reject the standards of the community, yet this was a right not commonly recognized in his day. Fully aware of European constraints on the individual, he felt impelled to give up his membership in the community before freely asserting his individual rights. His rejection of communal standards thus involved a history of painful separation – deep emotions that can hardly be fathomed today. Although the Franconian community of his day demanded conformity of its members, it also offered them a sense of belonging rooted in the ritual and symbolism of communal life – deep and lasting bonds forged in vital daily contact, celebrated in boisterous festivities, and consecrated through sacramental observances of baptism and Holy Communion and the burial of the dead. Those who chose to remain in this closely-knit community could certainly understand why Pastorius inevitably employed a highly-charged emotional tone to express the morality that had forced him to break, at least physically, his bonds with the past.

Because of this sense of belonging, Pastorius for some time considered returning to Germany from Pennsylvania, "this then uncouth land," where he was "an Alien" in self-imposed "Exile" among Anglo-Americans, conversing with Quaker leaders in Latin or French until he became "a Stammerer of the English Tongue" (Poem 359, written 1714). Such thoughts led readily enough to biblical and classical consolations. All Christians are sojourners, pilgrims and travelers on earth, he writes (quoting the Psalms and Saint Paul's letter to the Hebrews) in his commonplace entries on banishment in the "Alphabetical Hive," which also describe a number of involuntary exiles. He read about a young idealist who "abjure[d] the realm as a man extermined from his native country" in the satirical dialogues of Johann Valentin Andreae's *Menippus*, 1618. Citing the popular English writings of Nicholas Culpeper (1616-54), he notes that Aristides the Just, banished from Athens in 482 B.C., "prayed to God that the affairs of his country would go so well as never to need his return." "The very founder of the Roman Empire was an exile," he writes, quoting or paraphrasing a reference to Virgil's Aeneas from an unidentified source.

"All the transportations of people," and thus all colonists, involve (or are involved in) a sort of "public banishment," Pastorius read in and interpolated from Lucius Seneca's *Morals* (English translation by Roger L'Estrange, 1679), and he quotes at length from the Roman Seneca, banished to Corsica from 41 to 49 A.D. "Thousands" have faced the "sad condition" of being "barred the freedom of [their] own country," Seneca wrote, and Pastorius notes the higher freedom Seneca attributed to exile:

> We have, however, this comfort, that we carry our virtues along with us . . . What signifies the being banished from one spot of ground to another, to a man that has his mind free and his thoughts above? . . . Wherever we go, we have the heavens over our heads, and no further from us than they were before – and so long as we can entertain our eyes and thoughts with those glories, what matter is it what ground we tread upon? (Pp. 330-33.)

Despite such consolations, Pastorius occasionally regretted the lack of cultural continuity in his immigrant existence, especially as his sons Johann Samuel and Heinrich – increasingly addressed, even within the Pastorius household, as John Samuel and Henry – were growing up in Anglo-American society, with little awareness of their German past. In the letter he wrote to Melchior Adam with or on behalf of his sons in 1699 (mentioned on page 14), the two boys expressed their love and concern for the 74-year-old grandfather they had never met, and gave their reasons for wanting to know more about Melchior Adam's life and their family history:

> so that, in case any of us should ever come on over to Germany, if God wills, we would be able to inquire about our relations, and we would also appreciate it if you would greet our dear cousins for us, and persuade them to write us letters frequently, which would please us very much both now and after the death of our father, since we will not lack the assistance of other pious people [who can read and write German] to continue the correspondence. [14]

John Samuel and Henry never went to Germany. This 1699 letter, with Melchior Adam's response, is the last of the extant family correspondence, and there is no evidence that it continued beyond 1702, when Pastorius was informed that his father had died. It may have been the finality of this separation – and his great distance from the friends with whom he infrequently corresponded in his later years – that deepened his longing for native roots, most clearly expressed in Poem 427, written in 1716 after he had read a book (recommended by his learned Anglo-American neighbor Christopher Witt) that seemed to predict Sweden and Turkey would soon subjugate continental Europe. Reflecting an inversion of his fears as a young emigrant, 64-year-old Pastorius was newly intrigued by "The Prophecies of Some, which Europe now alarms [sic], / Predicting Fire and Sword, and whatsoever harms." Even though he had stopped worrying about God's punishment of Europe approximately three decades earlier, and had also stated his belief that hopes for peace in Europe were largely utopian (Poem 414), here he was willing to see the Swedes and the Turks as agents of a renewal that would allow European emigrants or expatriates to return to the place that still seemed home:

> And after they have done, what they had in Command,
> True Worship and true Peace will flourish in that land,
> Whith'r many then shall be Returning out of hand.

Here and elsewhere in his writings, Pastorius reflects at least a few of the difficulties and disappointments of immigrant acculturation, a sense of nostalgia or uprootedness not wholly allayed by Pennsylvania satisfactions. He especially missed the learned camaraderie of upper-class Europe; a few learned Pennsylvanians, he notes in Poem 359, provided "the chiefest Charms, which forc'd me to abide" in the Pennsylvania "wilderness land." And while he praises the colony's political and religious freedom, he criticizes usury and religious strife as well as black slavery and the exploitation of Native Americans. "Alphabetical Hive" entries (in the epigraph below) also reveal his appreciation for the "blunt honesty" of the Germans which, at least in its idealized form, contrasted with the daily compromises of a multi-ethnic and relatively democratic society like Pennsylvania. Reflecting bicultural maturity and an awareness of societal imperfections in Poem 396 (composed in 1715), he writes America as "Amo(a)rica," or "a Countrey bitter-sweet," thus evoking immigrant disappointment or bitterness ("amar") as well as love ("amor"). In this country "the Lord ... gave us our desires," he concludes here (commemorating the 32nd anniversary of his arrival in Pennsylvania), but with this qualification (which evokes spiritual as well as physical "safety"):

> I know some thought that Pennsylvania's scheme
> Predicted better, and would of Utopia dream,
> That Extramundane place (by Thomas Morus found,
> Now with old Groenland lost,) where all are safe and sound;
> Yet is it parcel of the old and Cursed Ground. Genesis 3:17.

Such reflections indicate the cultural breadth of a man who was both colonist and expatriate, a man who never fully broke his ties to the homeland he had once rejected.

1.4 An Idyllic and Ravaged Homeland: Franconia in the Age of Absolutism
1.4.1 The Cultural Environment

> [Time] suddenly posts by,
> E'en in an Instant, and the Twinkling of an Eye.
> 'Tis nothing but a Now, a Now that can not last;
> Pronounce it with all Haste, and with all Haste it's past.
> A Weaver's Shuttle is not half so Swift or Fleet,
> This momentary Jot has rather Wings than Feet:
> It vanishes like Smoke, like Dust before the Wind,
> And leaves, as sounding Brass, an Echoing Voice behind.
>
> -- Poem 396 (reflecting, in 1715, on the passage of time, since his German youth, "in two parts of this Globe.")

> Firmamentum Declarat Gloriam Omni Potentis. Psalms 19:1.
> The Firmament Declares God's glorious Power,
> From under which Distills his Blessing's Plenteous Shower.
>
> -- "Symbola Onomastica" (described on page 92), no. 525

> The Frenchmen say that the German's heart and mouth is one thing. . . . They [Germans] love sincerity more than any other nation. . . . It is a maxim among the French, that 'tis impossible for a Dutchman [i.e., a German] to be a wit. <u>Ath. Oracle</u>, p. 478 . . . The German ambassadors [from Germanic tribes, according to medieval legend,] being asked by Alexander the Great what it was they feared most in the world, they replied, their only fear was that the sky might fall; at which haughty answer, he, without shewing the least resentment, only told them they were a proud generation, and so dismissed them without honour. Creech, p. 11. With true men of German tongues and hearts, always agree; for their proper virtue is, that their promise does not miss. [The preceding sentence bracketed by Pastorius, presumably for emphasis.] . . . The blunt, honest humour of the Germans. <u>Spectator</u>.
>
> -- "Germany"

The environment of his youth had encouraged Pastorius to value tradition and homeland deeply. His own father described, in local, provincial and imperial histories, the ubiquitous cultural traditions that had been evolving since the seventh-century Christianization of Germanic tribes like those whose valor or arrogance is noted under Germany in the "Alphabetical Hive." The regional landscape was rich and varied, with a natural integrity that, given human institutions of sufficient caliber, would have satisfied the soul. [15]

Sommerhausen, Pastorius' home for his first seven years, was a small agricultural town on the Main River – its official designation as a "Marktflecken" placed it somewhere between 'village' and 'town' in size and importance – with several dozen merchants' and peasants' houses, two churches, a Renaissance town hall almost too grand for a town of modest size, an even more stately castle, and, beyond the town walls, undulating hillsides profuse with vineyards established by the Romans centuries earlier. The free imperial city of Windsheim, nestled in the valley of the Aisch River between the forested mountains of Frankenhöhe and Steigerwald, was Pastorius' second boyhood home. It had a heterogeneous mix of peasants, guild craftsmen and merchants, and was governed by twenty-five enterprising 'senators' or city councilmen rather than by a single nobleman and his family, as was the case in Sommerhausen. Windsheim was a small imperial city, with 3000 to 3600 residents, but its medieval walls, towers and church steeples, symbolizing civic and commercial importance, dominated the landscape for miles around.

Throughout the region encompassing Windsheim and Sommerhausen, man's impress upon the environment was, in many respects, cause for repose and joy and self-congratulation. Gothic spires and castle towers dotted the countryside and gave it an uplifting perspective. Fields and orchards tamed nature and focused it upon the villages whose dwellings clustered along rivers and streams and on the crests of gentle hills. Taverns and churches provided conviviality and communal purpose, and half-timbered houses fused wood and earth into harmony, a balance of raw nature and domestic perfection. Yet such accomplishments of civilization were a mixed blessing for Pastorius' contemporaries in the seventeenth century.

Sommerhausen and Windsheim are both located in Franconia, now a part of Bavaria, where the Danube flows eastward to the Black Sea in Rumania and the Main flows westward into the Rhine at Mainz and on to the North Sea in Holland. In Pastorius' day the region was a crossroads of Europe, predominantly rural in character, yet with metropolitan centers that brought the conflicting currents of European life to the province. Würzburg, thirteen kilometers north of Sommerhausen, was a bishopric and center of ecclesiastical power, while Nürnberg, sixty kilometers west of Windsheim, was a free city and center of commercial influence. With its marked bourgeois character, Nürnberg went Protestant early in the Reformation, whereas the ecclesiastical influence of its bishop-prince kept most of the Würzburg territory firmly committed to Catholicism. The polarities of Nürnberg and Würzburg could be noted throughout Franconia, a loose federation of small territories within the Hapsburg Empire, in districts like Protestant Bayreuth and Ansbach, residential seats of the margraves of Brandenburg, and the Catholic bishopric of Bamberg. This polarity shaped Pastorius' awareness of religion and politics, and he eventually rejected the religious and political extremes it had generated in Germany, yet the cultural environment of Franconia gave him the vital heritage that later distinguished him from his Anglo-American neighbors in Pennsylvania.

The distinctive features of Würzburg and Nürnberg were clearly visible to travelers in the sixteenth and seventeenth centuries. [16] "The city of Nürnberg is without any doubt one of the most magnificent and distinguished cities of Germany," Frenchman Jacques Esprinchard reported in 1597. "It is known in the entire world for the important commerce that is carried on here, and for the fine craftsmanship of the work that is produced here in the most varied mechanical trades." The Englishman William Smith noted in 1594 that the city's industry and thrift were matched by its civility and cleanliness. "Through the politik & wyse government [of the 'senators'] the [common] people are kept in quyetnes, dew aw, & obaysance," he wrote. And for a man who knew London, the "faire & brode" streets of Nürnberg were a marvel to behold:

> For they have no doung hilles in all their streets, but in certayne odd by corners. Neither is it the custome there to make water in the streets... Yea so precyse are they, in the sweet keeping of their cittie: that... swyne [must be kept] without the cittie.

Travelers were equally awed by Würzburg, but for different reasons. The Dutch Jesuit scholar Daniel Papebroch enjoyed the beautiful contrasts of hill and dale approaching Würzburg along the Main River in the autumn of 1660. He described the ripe scents of heavy-laden orchards and vineyards, and he also noted a political aspect of the area's geographical highs and lows: "Here on this side down in the valley is Würzburg, and over on the other side [of the river], up on a high hill, is the very attractive [Marienberg] Castle... with the magnificent gardens of the prince-bishop." Like other esteemed visitors, Papebroch was invited to ride up to Marienberg Castle in a stately carriage, approaching the prince-bishop's estate over a bridge that, the scholar noted, could be cut off from the city in case of attack from below. The city itself, Sebastian Münster had reported in 1567, contained

> many magnificent temples, cloisters, sumptuous residences and villas that are owned not only by officials of the Church but also by the [free] citizens... The citizens are largely in the courtly employment of the prince-bishop, but the common people work in the vineyards [owned by the Church], the grapes of which grow to excess in this area, and are thus made into wine and transported by ship and wagon to the surrounding lands.

The cultural differences between Nürnberg and Würzburg were especially clear to the well-traveled Frenchman Balthasar de Monconys when he toured Franconia in 1663. In Nürnberg he found city life centered upon the broad market square, flanked by a grand Lutheran church and the city hall he considered more beautiful than Amsterdam's. Everywhere in the city, he was astonished by the many merchants and their wares – intricate mechanical toys and clocks, artistic productions, guns of advanced design, technical inventions of all kinds. Most of the city's churches, he noted in passing, were not worth seeing. Describing Würzburg, though, de Monconys did not even mention the merchants or the life of the streets, but lavished praise on the churches and cloisters, including a mass at the Augustinian monastery with "the most beautiful music, both in vocal quality and composition, that I have ever heard in my life." He nevertheless devoted most of his reporting to the marvels of Marienberg Castle on the hill overlooking Würzburg – elaborate bastions fortified with rows of cannon, a magnificent outer court, impressive fountains supplied with water pumped up from the Main, sumptuous reception halls, and an immense wine cellar with intricately-carved vats containing a vast assortment of wines, including a 123-year-old variety of superb clarity that de Monconys was graciously allowed to sample. Franconia was a province of grand accomplishments, one jewel in the intricate mosaic of the Hapsburg Empire.

1.4.2 The Reformation and the Thirty Years War

> Democritus still laughs, Heraclitus sheds tears
> At the great Folly which in these our Days aPpears.
>
> -- "Symbola Onomastica," no. 600

> That great body of so many princes and circles [district governments] is slow in motion. A body so differently composed as the German Empire. Temple. Since the reign of Rudolf I [1273-91], above 200 principalities and states are fallen off from the Empire. Mamut, v. 7, p. 130 . . . That mighty Empire was at last catonized, rent in pieces, and dwindled into that narrow dominion which it now possesses under the tutelage of the House of Austria. Idem, p. 299.
>
> -- "Germany"

> [Where the state punishes religious nonconformity] men must offer up their understandings to their fears, and dissemble conviction to be safe . . . Penn . . . Christ once whipped out the profaners of his Father's temple, but he never whipped any in. Idem.
>
> -- "Persecution"

Technological development and social awareness were generating new ideals and insecurities throughout Europe, and especially in Hapsburg Germany, where a proliferation of interest groups and principalities had frequently threatened the stability of a well-organized imperial government. [17] The civilized landscape of rural Franconia and the cultural achievement of its cities and courts owed their existence to institutions inaugurated during the medieval Carolingian empire – a feudal system that gave the lords and bishops virtual autonomy over their subjects. (It continued with little fundamental change until the nineteenth century.) Even as Renaissance humanism and Martin Luther's German translation of the Bible were encouraging independent convictions, both Catholic and Protestant princes were demanding political and religious conformity, and using increasingly sophisticated military force to combat their opponents, win new territory, and secure their rights and privileges.

Although Luther's dramatic defiance of the Pope and the Emperor early in the sixteenth century had threatened the power of the consolidated church and state in Germany, and inspired the Peasants' Revolt of 1525, Luther condemned the excesses of this rebellion and supported established authority with his theory of the "two kingdoms." True Christians experience the Kingdom of God, a realm of love and peace; but, Luther argued, they live in the Kingdom of the World, where the might of the sword holds sway, and while on earth they must obey worldly power, the guarantor of social order and a tool of God's unfathomed purpose. Protestant sectists, Lutheran humanists and mystics helped to create a nonconformist tradition in Germany – and were decried as religious heretics or political anarchists – but the orthodox Lutheran church generally heeded the will of its worldly lords while demanding conformity to its religious dogma and practice. Unrighteous Christians, Luther maintained, "will be compelled by the civil authorities to be pious and righteous before the world." [18]

Political unrest was checked, but tensions did not abate. Germany's contending princes formed Protestant and Catholic alliances at home and abroad as the seventeenth century began. As in the Calvinist Palatinate, whose repeated destruction helps to explain Pastorius' millennialism, even liberal political and economic measures could have dire consequences. Economic gains in one principality, also increasing matériel, heightened the insecurities of rival princes, and complicated the regional and continental balance of power all the more. To avoid the dissension and instability of continued rivalry, Catholics and Protestants each attempted to gain political control throughout the German provinces, and – aided by foreign allies – became involved in the Thirty Years' War (1618-48), a war of attrition that caused unprecedented death and destruction.

In regions like Franconia, population fell to about one-half its pre-war level. The economy collapsed. Foreign trade ceased, productivity in manufacturing and handcrafts decreased drastically (although opportunists grew rich on war profiteering), agriculture nearly came to a standstill: farming villages were decimated, the cattle were slaughtered, fields lay fallow and overrun with weeds. In the imperial city of Windsheim, Melchior Adam Pastorius later reported, occupying soldiers insulted, harassed, extorted and robbed the citizenry. At times school, church and other civic functions ceased. Malnutrition and lack of sanitation created plague epidemics: "The dead . . . lay everywhere in the streets, and every day they were carted off across the fields to an open pit where they were all buried together." Unbearable tax levies and "contributions" demanded by the emperor and numerous military commanders, furthermore, compounded the economic woes accumulating in Windsheim during these thirty years. [19]

The Peace of Westphalia ended the war in 1648, just three years before the birth of Franz Daniel Pastorius, but Germany managed only a partial recovery during the second half of the seventeenth century. [20] The weakened economy aggravated the gap between rich and poor as Franz Daniel grew to adulthood in Windsheim, generating social and political tensions that complicated the youth's existence as the eldest son of Burgomaster Pastorius. Local tensions reflected the general political climate. French influence on the Westphalian treaty had limited the power of the Hapsburg Emperor and increased the autonomy of the German territorial princes, thus debilitating Germany as a nation. As the German states vied for ascendency and vacillated between the Hapsburgs and the French, political instability as well as economic weakness threatened social order, and reinforced a rigidity and conformity that was especially pronounced in Germany:

> Social distinctions were jealously heeded, privileges and "distance" (aloofness of the socially superior) were emphasized, a tight system of social controls in cities and villages [demanded conformity]. . . . Servility and real or feigned humility toward one's "superiors" . . . were deeply ingrained in the thought and behavior of the populace . . . The conduct of lawyers, clergymen and other men of learning was governed by a sense of exclusivity and station. [21]

These personal and cultural constraints gave the age a peculiar and pervasive tension, reflecting the intricate interworkings of culture and politics, and the sense of involvement or complicity each individual felt in a society that was becoming increasingly complex and impersonal. Particularly in Germany, where territorial lords were soon aping the manners of Versailles, this age of European absolutism was characterized by the rise of France under Louis XIV (r. 1643-1715), an obsessive ruler who systematically exploited his own populace and destroyed enemy territory to enhance the splendor and might of his empire, cynically manipulating national allegiances with payoffs to statesmen and princes, and generating the domestic unrest that would culminate in the French Revolution of 1789.

In his transatlantic correspondence, Pastorius criticized the multifaceted decadence he perceived in these developments, and in Poem 411 he also ridiculed "Louis le Grand, Venereal King of France," for fornicating with innumerable "Paramours": "As Boars do grunt, so lustful Sows will brim." [22] His poem comments on the French King's sexual exploits as reported in *The Secret Amours of Marquise de Maintenon* [23] and, implicitly, on the moral tensions of the age. Royal paramours, Pastorius knew, were not the only individuals to enjoy ambiguous courtly favors while indulging a lord's desire for conquest.

Pastorius' animalistic image of all restraints abandoned coexists with rigidity and conformity in this age, and this tension suggests a variety of compulsions he had observed especially among the learned leaders of his society. Like royal paramours, the learned might be enticed into roles of dubious satisfaction, and denied control over their lives, just as their world, subjected to the machinations of European politics and warfare, was moving ever closer to some vaguely perceived brink, beyond which it would lose all semblance of rationality and order. Compelled to affirm an orderly existence, statesmen and scholars redoubled their efforts to define and control – efforts that, in Pastorius' early experience, at times verged on the hysterical.

1.5 "To lead a godly life in a howling Wilderness": Embracing Lutheran Pietism, Relinquishing European Comforts

> These times, the foulest undoubtedly and the most execrable of all others since the very apostasy of the angels. [Translator's] Preface, Seneca . . . The corruption of the present times is the general complaint of all times, &c. One while whoring is in fashion, another while gluttony: today excells in apparel, tomorrow comes up the humor of scoffing; and after that perchance a vein of drinking, &c. Seneca, p. 543 . . .
> But if one truth may slip my harmless pen,
> Times would be better, had we but better men.
>
> -- "Complaint of Times"
>
> Wahn und Gewohnheit, zwei Tyrannen,
> Fast alle Menschen übermannen.
> [Delusion and custom, two tyrants, / Overwhelm almost everyone.]
>
> -- Poem 50
>
> As by degrees ill customs have been taken
> So by degrees the worst may be forsaken.
>
> -- Epigram 2311.5
>
> Custom, a mighty tyrant . . . Christ called himself truth, not custom . . . That which is bred in the bone will not out of the flesh . . . Custom and opinion oft times take so deep a root that judgement has no free power to act. Phillips, Preface . . . Custom must give place to verity. Augustine. There is no hope of remedy where that which sometime were vices be turned into manners. Seneca.
>
> -- "Custom"

Even though his upbringing interpreted the Lutheran Reformation as a return to the redemptive faith of early Christianity, Pastorius came to believe that the history of Germany following the Reformation denied the regenerative impulse symbolized in Christ's resurrection and heralded anew by Martin Luther. Pastorius became one of many who longed for a change of heart in his fellow man – for a rebirth of the spirit radical enough to get society back to the basics of freedom and dignity expressed in Christ's message of universal love. He and others turned to Lutheran Pietism, a movement that developed in the context of German culture after the Thirty Years' War, when religious sensibility also encouraged George Fox, William Penn and Robert Barclay to spread their Quaker message on preaching tours of Germany. European artists and poets reflected the tensions of the age in the style of the baroque – bold expression, rich imagery, striking metaphor, bombast, contradiction, paradox. Existentially, a growing number of Germans found in Pietism a special type of baroque expressiveness – a bold message of millennial hope – that helped them resolve the disparities between human aspiration and everyday reality.

Philipp Jakob Spener (1635-1705), superintendent of Frankfurt's Lutheran churches, published his *Pia Desideria* in 1675, arguing that a religion of the heart should replace the dogmatic scholastic orthodoxy of contemporary Lutheran theology. Moderate and radical forms of Pietism soon emerged:

> The Pietists [sought] to replace outward observances with an inner spirit of union with God ... They thought of the Second Advent not as a vague doctrine of theology, but as a warm and active inspiration of their daily lives. At any moment now Christ would reappear on earth; he would still the strife of faiths and end the reign of force and war; he would establish a purely "spiritual church," without organization, without ritual, without priests, but practicing with joy a generous Christianity of the heart. [24]

Measuring the conduct of both rich and poor by Christ's Golden Rule (Luke 6, 31), many of the Pietists challenged the lopsided social structure of the age; civic and clerical authorities, fearing the movement's populist appeal, often suppressed it as dangerously unorthodox or anarchic. [25] Yet Philipp Jakob Spener was personally serene and doctrinally irenic. In his teens he had avidly read the writings of the English Puritans Lewis Bayly (d. 1631) and Richard Baxter (1615-91), the German mystic and reformer Johann Arndt (1555-1621), and the Dutch political scholars Justice Lipsius (1547-1606) and Hugo Grotius (1583-1645). At Lutheran and Calvinist universities in Strasbourg and Basel he studied the breadth of the humanities – language, philosophy, history and theology – and later earned the friendship and respect of intellectuals throughout Germany and Europe, men and women like the political theorist Veit Ludwig von Seckendorf (1626-92), the French Quietist theologian Jean de Labadie (1610-74), the Danish Princess Anne Sophia (1647-1717, wife of the Elector of Saxony), and the philosopher-statesman Gottfried Wilhelm von Leibniz (1646-1716).

With the breadth and fervor of men like Spener, Pietism gave liberal impetus to the Enlightenment and eventually influenced the German Idealism of Johann Gottfried Herder (1744-1803) and Johann Wolfgang von Goethe (1749-1832) as well as the Methodist tenets of John Wesley (1703-91). Some of the Pietists, as dogmatic as their orthodox Lutheran antagonists, endlessly debated old theological arguments, and a later generation of deists and rationalists dismissed them as irrelevant, but in Pastorius' day theological debate was lively, sophisticated, and potent. Spener and other Pietists attacked what they saw as reactionary illiberality in the church and state of Protestant Germany. Although the fervor and liberality of Pietism reformed Lutheranism in the long run, especially in colonial America, the Pietists remained a small minority group for most of the seventeenth century.

Spener's efforts to inspire Christian understanding did not significantly moderate social or political excesses in his lifetime.

At the age of 27 in 1679 Franz Daniel Pastorius, a scholar of classical and modern literature and doctor of canon and civil law, joined the Pietist dissenters by moving from Windsheim to Frankfurt and meeting Spener, "that brave patriarch of the Pietists," as Pastorius called him (Appendix I of this study), whose living faith won Pastorius' conversion. Pastorius admired the irenic attitudes of Spener, who sought to reach all nominal Christians in Protestant Germany – each member of Lutheran society – by generating religious renewal especially among the political and clerical leaders in the hierarchy of church and state. In Frankfurt, too, Pastorius was increasingly attracted to the radical views of the "Saalhof" Pietists, Spener's separatist friends who condemned the hierarchy of the church, rejected the possibility of a genuine Christian faith encompassing all members of the community, and formed a tight circle of true believers among themselves. It was a small group of well-to-do merchants and mystics among the Saalhof Pietists who began to make plans for a community of Pennsylvania Pietists in 1682 and sent Pastorius off to the New World the following year.

By taking the radical views of the Saalhof Pietists seriously, a man of Pastorius' great learning and social standing inevitably shocked and disappointed the majority of his peers in a metropolis like Frankfurt. An unlikely candidate for Pietist zeal, Pastorius nevertheless proved to be the one member of the Saalhof group to demonstrate the courage of his convictions by actually leaving Germany. As the originators of the emigration plan backed out one by one – but continued to invest in Pennsylvania trade and real estate – Pastorius was left to found Germantown with a group of simple craftsmen from Krefeld whose fear of religious persecution, like that of the English Pilgrims before them, was one of the factors that led them to leave their homeland. [26]

Pastorius' religious convictions were similar to those of the Krefelders, but he did not have to face persecution as long as he lived as an upper-class Lutheran in Protestant Germany. Knowing that most of his Pietist friends in Frankfurt were motivated by personal choice rather than driven by necessity, he urged them to come to America for conscience' sake but cautioned those who could not give up, at least temporarily, "the accustomed comforts of Germany such as stone dwellings and rarity of food and drink" to stay at home in their affluent Frankfurt surroundings. [27] Although his friend Philipp Jakob Spener wished Pastorius well in Pennsylvania, the clergyman shared the sedentary attitudes that separated the original Frankfurt Pietists from their American harbinger. As long as his territorial lord tolerated his preaching, Spener refused to consider leaving his homeland:

> I must leave those who seek a refuge there [in Pennsylvania] to their own cogitations; I could not advise anyone to flee before the Lord drives us out [of Germany].... My purpose has always been to stay where the Lord has placed us as long as He allows ... [28]

None of the leaders of the Frankfurt Pietists ever came to Pennsylvania, Pastorius reported in 1698, "because they fear the barren wastes, the isolation and boredom [of the colony], all of which I have in the meantime become thoroughly accustomed to, thank God, and so I'll remain accustomed to it until my dying day." [29]

In time Pietists, Mennonites, Schwenckfelders and other sectists (as well as Calvinists, orthodox Lutherans, and Roman Catholics) would head off for Pennsylvania in droves, but German immigration did not gain any real momentum until well into the eighteenth century, and even then it was predominantly the poor and the oppressed who left Germany to try their luck in America. With his learning and station in Germany, Pastorius would have been an extraordinary emigrant at any point in history, but in 1683 he was the only one of his kind. None of his upper-class peers were ready to sacrifice a life of European comforts and privileges "to lead a quiet, godly and honest life in a howling wilderness," as Pastorius wryly described his undertaking around 1715 (Appendix I), and few of them were prepared to admit any moral grounds for sacrifices of this kind in Europe or America. By contrast Pastorius was aware that the needs of the underprivileged should place limits on the rights of the privileged, and he was ahead of his time in this recognition. Such an awareness was evolving but slowly in Western civilization – and it would everywhere coexist with desires for inordinate wealth or power ignoring the needs of the many – but it would nevertheless gain impetus as more and more Europeans followed Pastorius to America or, within Europe, allowed their view of mankind to be shaped by the higher ideals of this emerging transatlantic culture.

What led Pastorius to take his radical stand in 1683? The historical events of the Thirty Years' War and postwar reconstruction affected the entire populace but did not produce any large-scale exodus from Germany in the seventeenth century, so these events alone do not explain Pastorius' isolated decision to leave the country. Numerous Germans, furthermore, shared some or all of his dissatisfactions with their society yet did not remove themselves from it as he did. Some of his contemporaries criticized the church hierarchy, noted the inordinate power of the rich, decried the insidious decline of morality, desired pervasive spiritual rebirth or social reform, or feared the destruction of war and longed for enduring peace – yet in 1683 they were not prepared to risk their very existence in an ocean crossing or face the uncertainties of life in the New World, then considered a distant and awesome realm known predominantly to the buccaneer and the savage. Beyond the culture shared by all of his contemporaries and the critical attitudes expressed by some of his fellows, Pastorius had compelling personal reasons for emigrating that can be ascertained in his particular experience of society – in the attitudes and emotions that were developing within him as he grew to maturity in Germany.

Chapter Two
Franconian Childhood

> We laugh at [children's] foolish sports, but their game is our ernest; their drums, rattles and hobbyhorses but the emblems of men's business . . . Our childhood we rattle away in toys and fooleries. His very babyish days declared of what stock and lineage he were . . . Valour exerts itself even in the cradle (Emblem 1), and then art draws its draughts as on blank canvas (Emblem 2), fortifying and adorning the body with honourable exercises (Emblem 3), and the mind with liberal sciences and polite learning (Emblems 4, 6). Saavedre.
>
>   -- "Childhood"
>
> Experience best is gained without much cost:
> Read men and books; then practice what thou know'st.
>
>   -- Epigram 88

Pastorius grew up in two picturesque Franconian towns, among a robust populace that lived in neighborly proximity, with a lively cultural heritage reflecting ancient pagan traditions as well as the mores of medieval Catholicism and the Reformation. Numerous institutions constructively channeled the boundless energy of this vital culture, generating personal tensions in the process, especially among the sons of its leaders, who were exposed to elitist values and to strict morality in their homes and in the upper-class schools known as Gymnasiums. This chapter uses biographical and historical detail to delineate the spontaneity of Franz Daniel's childhood and his disciplined growth toward an identity largely defined by his society and family. Pastorius' Pennsylvania commentary, furthermore, provides adult reflections on the child's experience, though from a distance in time, geography and mentality. This distance will itself be used reflectively, so that the child and the man emerge in motifs and images refracted through each other, disclosing notable similarities and differences.

2.1 The Early Years in Sommerhausen, 1651-59
2.1.1 Melchior Adam Pastorius' Beginning Law Career

> Lo, here's a trade surpasseth all the rest,
> No change annoys the lawyer's interest:
> His tongue buys land, builds houses without toil;
> The pen's his plow, the parchment is his soil.
> Him storms disturb not, militia bands:
> The tree roots best that in the weather stands. Leeds, 1706.
>
> -- "Lawyer"
>
> Young fellows almost ravish old widows into matrimony, if they have any appurtenances worth angling for. Ath. Oracle, p. 305.
>
> -- "To Court or to Woo"

When Melchior Adam Pastorius had persuaded Johann Philipp von Schönborn, the Catholic archbishop-prince of Würzburg and Mainz, to accept his conversion to Lutheranism and recommend him to the Protestant lord of Sommerhausen in late November, 1649, Melchior Adam called upon Graf Georg Friedrich at the Sommerhausen castle and presented the elaborately-sealed document that, when opened, attested to "the special character of our dear and very learned Melchior Adam Pastorius" and urged Georg Friedrich to offer Pastorius, "in accordance with his [excellent] qualities, accommodation and advancement to the fullest extent." [1]

Georg Friedrich naturally respected the wishes of his liege lord Johann Philipp, and Melchior Adam soon joined the small staff of learned men who ran the Graf's legal and administrative affairs, the courtly element in rural Sommerhausen. He quickly made himself at home among the influential citizens of Sommerhausen. He had already met Magdalena Frischmann (1607-57), the widow of Bailiff (`Schultheiß') Johann Johms, until his death in 1648 Georg Friedrich's chief administrator and judge. On 22 January 1650, less than two months after moving to the town, Pastorius married the widow Johms, 17 years his senior, apparently his reason for moving to Sommerhausen in the first place, since the marriage solidified his position and enhanced his career, as could be noted in the ritual of the wedding day, particularly the festive banquet presided over by Graf Georg Friedrich, who honored the bride and groom with a toast from the silver chalice normally reserved for coronations of the emperors of the Holy Roman Empire – a family heirloom signifying the Graf's ceremonial role as cupbearer to the emperor.

Pastorius worked energetically for Georg Friedrich and his son Franz, who assumed the titles of graf and cupbearer at the age of 14 when his father died in October, 1651, just nine days after young Franz served as godfather to his newly-born namesake Franz Daniel Pastorius. Establishing a private law practice in Sommerhausen as well, Melchior Adam accumulated the cash needed to build a costly half-timbered house in the lean post-war years, and, paying little heed to the envy of less fortunate neighbors, had it adorned with a datestone bearing the Pastorius coat of arms and an inscription in Latin affirming the young lawyer's acumen [2]:

> Melchior Adam Pastorius built this dwelling from its foundations up with his own money for the use of himself and his family. In the year of our Lord 1655.

Such inscriptions were common on the houses of the well-to-do in Germany. Typically, though, they displayed humility, piety or humor, often beseeching God's blessing. Melchior Adam's blunt wording reflects the extremes of the post-war era as well as his own goal-oriented personality.

Sommerhausen thus provided an auspicious beginning to Melchior Adam's career, offering natural and civilized satisfactions in a well-regulated feudal existence, as the elder Pastorius indicates in a description of the town appended to his history of Franconia:

> Sommerhausen – a beautiful 'Flecken' [town or village] across from Winterhausen on the Main belonging to the von Limpurg Grafs, hereditary imperial cupbearers, who in turn hold it as a fiefdom from the bishops of Würzburg. There is a baronial residence [the Graf's castle] and a beautiful church within the town, also a winery and the office of the bailiff, healthy springs, and marvelous vineyards as well as richly-bearing orchards. [3]

Melchior Adam's journals and poetry indicate that he and his family enjoyed a convivial existence in Sommerhausen and throughout Franz Daniel's Franconian life. He describes "the most friendly manner" of Sommerhausen residents (page 23 of this study), and poetically celebrates the pleasures of festive eating and drinking while rejoicing in the bounty of God the provider.

2.1.2 Personal Recollections and the Family Record

> His soul is yet a white paper unscribbled with observations of the world, wherewith at length it becomes a blarr'd notebook [i.e., copiously or overwhelmingly filled (cf. "blare," *OED*)]. He is the Christian's example, and the old man's relapse; his parents little story, wherein they read those days of their life that they cannot remember; and see what innocence they have outlived ... A hopeful offspring. Sweet babes, the pledges (product) of chaste, connubial love. Children and fools live merry lives. Children will do, like children.
> -- "Child"

Franz Daniel Pastorius describes essential details of his early years in Sommerhausen in "Genealogia Pastoriana" (Appendix I), and in a German-language biographical sketch entitled (in Latin) "Res Propriae." [4] His mother's marriage to Bailiff Johms, he writes, had given her "four children, whereof two died when I was but very young, but her Daughter Margaret[a] & her Son Ladowick [Johann Ludwig] Johms I knew, and loved as my own self." Although he does not describe Margareta and Johann Ludwig or his childhood friends, a list of six "important weddings" ("principale Hochzeiten") he attended in Germany (in "Res Propriae") reveals that at least two of these relationships endured beyond the Sommerhausen years. He took part in the wedding of "my brother Johann Ludwig Johms" in 1663, when he was nearly twelve years old, and at the age of 23 he led 22-year-old Magdalena Eichen to the alter when she married in 1675. Magdalena was his mother's godchild, and she had been "my dear playmate" ("mein liebe Gespielin") in Sommerhausen.

Describing his departure from Sommerhausen as a boy of seven in 1659, Pastorius notes that young Graf Franz "clothed me in red Scarlet, giving me also a little Sword, a hat with three plumes of Feathers & a pair of white boots, &c. [etc.], making a fool of me, even in my earliest years." Graf Franz had made his mark in the Hapsburg Empire in 1653, when he was 16 and Franz Daniel was still a toddler, by insisting on his hereditary right to bear the imperial chalice at the coronation of Ferdinand IV (r. 1653-54) despite efforts to keep him out of the ceremony, and when Pastorius was four the Graf left home to study at Nürnberg University and travel in France and Italy, returning on furloughs to attend to the affairs of his territory – and to 'make a fool' of his young godson. [5] Pastorius' ambiguous wording suggests the aristocrat's warm affection for the child and the child's naive delight in the lavish gifts (or pride in being so honored) as well as the adult's social awareness that would eventually complicate even such innocent enjoyments as a child's being indulged by a generous aristocrat.

Supplementing these few details, the most direct evidence of a healthy and robust childhood in Sommerhausen, Pastorius describes his earliest life in Poem 396 (written in 1715), an anniversary commemoration of his arrival in Philadelphia on a ship filled with immigrants including the family of Thomas Lloyd (1640-94), a Welsh Quaker physician and deputy governor of Pennsylvania. An obviously fictional account that nevertheless suggests the warmth and sustenance Pastorius knew as a small child, the poem describes gestation in the womb, childbirth, and nursing: the pleasures of being kissed, "dandled" and suckled as they were presumably experienced not only by the poet but also by his former shipmates and contemporary readers, the three adult daughters of Thomas Lloyd (then married to prominent Philadelphians). The segment on nursing immediately follows birth:

> But presently we wept, quite overwhelm'd with fears,
> Forecasting that we came into a vale of tears.
> How be 't they kiss'd, they buss'd, and dandled us so long,
> Till with their cogging and melodious midwife's song,
> They dunn'd our juicy ears, and in our nurse's lap,
> Outwearied by these tunes, we took a gentle nap;
> Anon awakening, they laid us to the breast,
> The which of all the sports (me thinks) has been the best; . . .

The baby's first cry presages "fears . . . [in] a vale of tears" that are not wholly allayed by all the singing, kissing, dandling and breast-feeding of an anonymous nurse. Along with childhood joys in a relatively secure upper-class home, Pastorius knew deprivation and disruption in a post-war era whose insecurities were reflected in his mother's troubled life and early death. Magdalena Pastorius had lost two husbands during the Thirty Years' War, and five of her eight children died young. Franz Daniel was the only child of her third marriage. Aged 44 when he was born, she died little more than six years later. In an anagram verse upon her death, Melchior Adam gives a first-person narrative of her life, here in unrhymed translation:

> I floundered in distress from childhood on,
> I feared the inundating tides of war and plundering:
> I had to flee my father's hearth and home,
> And then lost all my husband had acquired;
> A widow, I looked back on what could never be retrieved.
>> Such lessons of the Cross taught me to scorn the world,
>> To view its vanity from sources deep within.
>> I said: O save me, God, from all this pain some day;
>> O Jesus, with all my love to thee I cling. [6]

Franz Daniel summarized his mother's biography in "Genealogia Pastoriana" (birth, marriages, children) and then sought to crystalize the meaning she had for him. He describes her funeral, the ultimate focus of his memories of her, and recaptures a domestic image of her helping Sommerhausen neighbors. Unwilling to revive the emotions of a parental relationship "lost too early," or to dwell on his distance from it, he ends the paragraph inconclusively:

> My s[ai]d father testif[ied] his sincere & constant affection towards her in a printed Funeral Comment upon the words of Holy David, Psal. 73: v. 25 & 26, which were in a manner her *Symbolum*, Motto or Device, and found according to Martin Luther's Dutch [i.e., German] translation verbatim thus: "When I have but Thee, I care not for Heaven and Earth, And though my body & Soul do pine away, yet art Thou, O God, always the Comfort of my heart & my Portion." She was a Woman fearing the Lord, and ready to help the poor and the Sick as much as in her lied, having for that end a small Apothecary-shop in her own house, being herself pretty skilful in Physick [i.e., medicine], &c. I shall say no more of her, whom I lost too early, but 6 years and 6 months old.

The death of Magdalena Pastorius in March, 1657, initiated a series of transitions and disruptions recorded in Melchior Adam's family journals. In February, 1658, Melchior Adam married Eva Margareta Gelchsheimer, daughter of Doctor Johann Gelchsheimer, 54, city advocate and senator (or city councilman) of Windsheim. Franz Daniel's first baby sister, born in December, 1658, lived only four months. Her death in April, 1659, was followed a month later by the death of Johann Gelchsheimer, and the family moved to Windsheim about three months thereafter. The move separated Franz Daniel from Margareta and Johann Ludwig Johms, who must have had other family ties in Sommerhausen and were adults (or nearly so) at the time; the notice of Johann Ludwig's wedding is the only record of continuing contact with his Sommerhausen relatives. A second sister was born in June, 1660, but died after nine days, and a year later Franz Daniel's stepmother died following the delivery of a third child, stillborn, by Caesarean section. Absorbed in Windsheim politics and his law practice, Melchior Adam, in 1662, married a 56-year-old widow who served as housekeeper and raised 10-year-old Franz Daniel until the boy left home for the university six years later.

Repeatedly experiencing death at close hand, Franz Daniel remained an only child in a post-war society that stressed repopulation and fostered large families. The disruptions of his early life also emphasized his dependence upon Melchior Adam Pastorius, creating an unusually strong – and demanding – bond between father and son.

2.1.3 Neighborly Proximity of Village Life

> Put with thy labour mirth sometimes in ure [use, practice],
> That thou the better may'st thy work endure.
>
> -- Epigram 2326.5
>
> To find in joy what we lost in sorrow. Good to be merry and wise. . . . Clear up your brow. Makes a man as merry as a cricket . . In truth, you live like fiddlers. You live merry lives on it.
>
> -- "Joy"
>
> Drinking to people . . . [is] a provocation to drink more than doth people good. Wm. Penn . . . To ply one with Cups. Drinking-Clubs & other Conventicles of that nature. "Here's to you!" i.e. "Prosit!" . . . This your wine mirth is but the smothering, if not the drowning, of a deeper grief; like the lustick fit in some countries of such as are going to execution. . . . New jovial drinking, vide in Ac. Compl. p. 111 . . . I'll pledge that loving health with all my heart, From any thing that's good I never part. Id. p. 91 . . .

> Sound the trumpets, boys, sound,
> And let each man stand his ground,
> Till this glass is handed round . . .
>
> Examine your cup,
> To drink it all up,
> And leave not a drop.
>
> -- "Drinking of Healths"

Local history gives Pastorius' early biography focus and meaning. It was in Sommerhausen that he first experienced the deep and lasting bonds of Franconian community, and also began to sense a rift in communal accord. The village history shows that its residents were robust and spontaneous men and women and children; the circumstances of the Pastorius family show why many of these hearty individuals nevertheless treated the son of Melchior Adam Pastorius with deference or restraint.

Sommerhausen, like many other villages and towns in Lower Franconia (the Main Valley region surrounding Würzburg), had reacted to centuries of regional confrontation by concentrating its existence within a compact but protected living space. [7] Its walls, gates and towers – many of them since fallen – encircled houses and shops that still crowd up against each other along narrow streets and alleys, and its residents had learned to get along with each other under circumstances that non-villagers today might consider too close for comfort:

> Like members of a single household, the village community had to work hand in hand for the good of all . . . to keep differing temperaments from colliding with each other under the exhausting labor requirements of daily life. [8]

Time-worn rituals and customs assured social order and enhanced "good neighborliness" ("gute Nachbarschaft") among residents. [9] Ceremonial observances accompanied legal and business transactions, births, weddings and deaths, and the numerous public events and holidays recurring year after year. Public ceremonies centered around the village square and the adjoining town hall – a Renaissance arcade with pointed arches graced its massive stone walls and towers from without, and intricately carved wood paneling and beams (along with the Graf's coat of arms) its interior. These ceremonies generally involved festive eating and drinking, the keynote of communal life. The town council frequently concluded its meetings with a banquet, held an annual oxhead feast for the Graf's officials, and dispensed wine (particularly for the Graf's officials) from its capacious *Ratskellar*, or communal wine cellar, on numerous similar occasions, such as the outdoor pageants and plays of traveling artists. Festivities like *Kirchweih* (meaning church dedication) and a boundary procession involved the entire community.

Symbolizing territorial rights and responsibilities, the procession around the village boundaries retained traces of pre-Roman tribal cultism, initiated schoolboys into civic life, and gave the villagers a grand occasion for celebration despite the strict hierarchy of its ritualistic march:

> At the front marched the keeper of the meadows [who maintained the boundary markers] with the schoolboys, two tambourine players, four musicians, and the four [honorary] jurymen, [who deciphered the slate or ceramic hieroglyphs buried under the boundary markers and judged boundary disputes,] bearing [green] switches that were decorated with silk ribbons; next followed the Graf's official representative, the bailiff, the town secretary and other officials, two members of the town council in gown and sword, the rifle company with its pennants and its commanding officer; and [then came] the militia [including all adult males of sound body] which was led by two tambourine players, three musicians, the captain of the militia, the militiamen with their

town flag, their superior and inferior officers, one tambourine player and two pipers, and finally a corporal with the company of the young men of the village. [10]

As festivities continued the following day, all the males were given Ratskellar wine – a full measure (about one liter) for youths and adults, and half a measure for the young boys – and a small loaf of bread in token of their disparate unity with the chief celebrants:

> The participants in the festive meal that filled two banquet tables at the town hall included the Graf's officials, the village clergyman, the bailiff, the town secretary, [and] the officers of the rifle company and the militia ...

Despite its medieval religious origins (recognized in a morning church service), the autumn *Kirchweih* was raucously celebrated in all Lower Franconian villages:

> Gambling tables and market booths were set up, cooks and vintners prepared their meals and served their wines on the village square, and visitors from neighboring villages poured in from all directions. Dance music resounded from the official dance [for the village elite] and from the dance floors where the innkeepers had organized the public dancing [for the common folk]. Groups of revelers sat drinking around the tables that had been set up on the village streets or in the pubs ... The shouting and jubilation of the dancers and drinkers filled the air, and quarrels flared up now and then [typically when the youths of one village defended their honor against their rivals from another] ... The events of the day warmed the sensual appetites as well as the fighting spirits. It is a matter of record that many a mortal owed their existence to the intoxication of the dancing and drinking at the *Kirchweih* festival. Many a young maiden, no matter how virtuous she might have been to this hour of destiny, met her undoing on the walk back home that night or even while catching a breath of fresh air in the courtyard of an inn after the excitement of the dancing. [11]

Children enjoyed the carnival atmosphere of *Kirchweih* as well as the spontaneity of large family gatherings, with uncles and aunts and cousins arriving from the countryside, and in many villages they were given special attention as well. They were rewarded with a meal for performing in the morning church service, for example, or, in at least one local town, invited from neighboring villages and treated to food and drink at the town's expense. [12] Sommerhausen asserted local pride with an unusually diverse *Kirchweih* program. Along with the drinking, feasting, gambling and dancing, it also offered a parade that included militia "corporals, drummers and officers" (who received *Ratskellar* wine for their participation), a marksmanship contest with a fully-grown sheep as first prize, and an autumn variant of a Maypole festival, during which village youths accompanied by pipers carried a tall birch from the communal forest to the village square, raised the tree, and danced around it. [13]

Kirchweih exuberance typified neighborly conviviality:

> The enjoyment of robust pleasures found its expression not only in eating and drinking together at the various festivals of public and private life. It also shaped – and spiced – everyday existence. [14]

The villagers celebrated life insistently, undaunted by its burdens. And because they celebrated, they were able to endure their generous share of toil and trouble. Throughout the year they "grabbed every available opportunity" for dancing or playing games – cards, dice, nine-pins, contests of strength – and for many of them a visit to the neighborhood pub habitually ended the work day. Wine was the usual drink. It loosened the tongue, and neighbors told each other what they thought, sometimes so bluntly that tempers rose or fisticuffs ensued. Yet the habit of gathering convivially kept them together through thick and thin, and carried them on to death itself. [15]

Although festivities like baptism and marriage were predominantly family affairs in Lower Franconian villages, the end of life concerned the community as a whole. When anyone died in Sommerhausen, churchbells tolled and townspeople broke their daily routine. Friends and neighbors attended a funeral service at the Church of Saint Bartholomew and took part in the procession to the cemetery outside the town walls, singing hymns of death and resurrection as they went. At the grave the parson commemorated the completion of life's cycle; two choirboys chanted, "We beseech Thee, O Lord, let Thy servant now depart in peace;" and the church choir responded, "For mine eyes have seen Thy salvation, O Lord." [16] And when the ceremony concluded, Lower Franconians paid their respects to the dead by celebrating life in the manner they knew best:

> Right after the funeral, [the] neighbors ... gathered together in the local pub or in the house of the deceased for a funeral drink. On such occasions they would not be satisfied with the wine contributed by the family, but instead provided – naturally to honor the deceased – additional drink for all the guests ... [which in some instances led to] drunkenness and undignified behavior. [17]

2.1.4 The Pastorius Family and the Sommerhausen Community

> To walk an alderman's pace. Honours change manners. It must be a strong brain that bears heady wine.
>
> -- "Grandeur"
>
> The Princes of this World and their Grandees,
> Like sturdy Oaks, and lofty Cedar Trees,
> Are oft'ner hurt by Thunderbolts and Wind
> Than dwarfish Shrubs, or Plants of lesser Kind;
> Who therefore would Exalt himself at all?
> Not I, keep me my Lord, keep me but small,
> And that I never may into Temptation fall.
>
> -- Poem 306 (entire)

Touched by the vitality of Sommerhausen, Franz Daniel Pastorius lived more or less in harmony with his community during his early years, not yet aware that his family's rank and privilege might disrupt "the bond of a good conscience with God." Melchior Adam's joy in conviviality, displayed in his biography and poetry, was well suited to Sommerhausen's neighborliness, and Franz Daniel's appreciation of life was enhanced by his father's willingness to indulge in the social pleasures of eating and drinking, of 'communing' with his neighbors. Within the Pastorius family, Franconian warmth and spontaneity generated the deep attachments common in traditional societies – in this context Franz Daniel's claim that he loved his brother Johann Ludwig and sister Margareta "as my own self" does not seem exaggerated – and the family had countless opportunities to share these feelings festively, in the company of Magdalena's children, other relatives, or even in-laws by previous marriage, with the families of friends like Franz Daniel's second godfather Daniel Gering or Magdalena's godchild Magdalena Eichen, or with other members of the Graf's official staff and their families. In moments of loss, too, especially at the death of his mother, young Pastorius surely felt the warm support of rituals observed in neighborly proximity.

In the jubilation of a *Kirchweih* festival, of course, Franz Daniel could also enjoy the privilege of special treatment among "the lord's officials [and] the bailiff . . . [who] sat in the midst of the hubbub and consumed their *Kirchweih* banquet at the expense of the community." [18] It was, in the long run, this privileged status that complicated his life in Franconia. Franz Daniel would have to learn to curb the love and spontaneity of early childhood in a manner prescribed by social convention and political necessity, erecting barriers between himself and his fellow Franconians that, he eventually believed, negated the "first promise" of Christian baptism. The role of his family in Sommerhausen indicates the pattern he was expected to follow.

Even if Melchior Adam had not deliberately emphasized his social position and authority – standing beside Graf Georg Friedrich for his first Holy Communion in the town, marrying the former bailiff's widow, choosing young Graf Franz as Franz Daniel's godfather, building a fine house with its proud and insensitive datestone – his job as legal administrator, or assistant to the bailiff of Sommerhausen, would have been enough to keep him and Franz Daniel living in the shadow of the ruling family, whose relationship with the citizenry was clearly regulated by law and tradition. [19]

Although the Graf and his heirs had full authority over the town, everyday government was shared by the Graf's appointed officials and civic leaders – a burgomaster and six town councilmen – who represented the citizens. Court procedures at two levels demonstrate the distribution of power. The appointed officials and civic leaders together presided over the lower court ("gemeindliche Gericht"), which handled petty civil and criminal cases with relative informality. The high court, on the other hand, adjudicated serious crimes and formally delineated the hierarchy of the community in sessions all adult males were required to attend thrice yearly whether or not there were any cases on the docket.

In a public reading of the town's charter and laws, the citizens were informed of their duties toward their lord as well as their rights to security and justice ("Schutz und Schirm"), and in the main solemnity of the assembly, the burgomaster and councilmen deferentially passed the ceremonial staff of the court to the bailiff, who then presided over the court in the name of the Graf and administered the oath of citizenship to the young men who had reached their majority. As these new citizens pledged their allegiance to the Graf, each member of the assembled community was reminded that his existence rested upon dutiful obedience to his lord and the appointed officials of Sommerhausen.

Doctor Melchior Adam Pastorius, like the bailiff of Sommerhausen, represented the Graf's interests and resolved disputes among neighbors with magisterial probity, thus working in "a sphere of tension":

> The villagers had occasion enough in their private lives to rub up against the old inherited privileges of their lord, a festering wound that chafed and burned. The fear of being exploited kept them vigilant, and their suspicions were easily aroused. Thus, having to represent the interests of the lord in the village was not a very desirable assignment – a fact the bailiff in particular had to confront time and again ... His function created a quite obvious gap between himself and the rest of the villagers. [20]

This gap marked the existence of the Pastorius family in Sommerhausen and, with minor formal variations, played an important role later in Windsheim as well. Although its effect on Franz Daniel in Sommerhausen cannot be directly ascertained, his growing awareness of it eventually kept him from affirming the traditions of his family and homeland in the form they had assumed in seventeenth-century Germany.

2.2 Moving to the Imperial City of Windsheim in 1659

> East or west, at home is best. Travel east, or travel west, a man's own house is still the best. Home is home, though never so homely. Every bird praiseth its own nest. A tired horse seeth a foul stable rather than a fair way. His land is the dunghill, and he the cock that crows over it. To one bewailing himself that he should not die in his own country, Diogenes said, be of comfort, for the way to heaven is alike in every place. Culpeper, p. 450.
>
> -- "Home"

The death of his step-grandfather Johann Gelchsheimer in Windsheim dramatically ended Franz Daniel's early childhood in Sommerhausen, for it opened a key post in Windsheim's government and drew the Pastorius family to the imperial city. When seven-year-old Franz Daniel accompanied his father and stepmother to Windsheim in July, 1659, probably in a horse-drawn coach provided by the Windsheim senate, he traveled some forty kilometers through a varied terrain of riverbank, field, forest and hillside – stimulatingly new but not radically different from the Lower Franconian landscape he was leaving behind. [21]

Heading south along the Main, the family must have crossed the river by ferry at its southernmost point in Ochsenfurt and then struck a southeastward course away from the river, along the Ansbach road toward Windsheim. As Franz Daniel and his parents then traversed the hills of the Steigerwald forest near Uffenheim, about a dozen kilometers from their destination, they left the Main Valley and Würzburg's sphere of influence, and entered Middle Franconia, where the imperial city of Nürnberg provided the focus for trade, government and culture, and middle-sized Ansbach, residential seat of the Margrave of Brandenburg, competed with Nürnberg for influence in the countryside and the smaller population centers of the region, including the subsidiary imperial cities of Dinkelsbühl, Rothenburg ob der Tauber, Weißenburg and Windsheim.

As the Pastorius family descended the Steigerwald hills into the Aisch River valley, they could see Windsheim's picturesque stone walls and towers and church steeples in the distance, and they could sense the elation of homecoming and anticipate a bright future. Eva Margareta was returning to girlhood friends and relatives after a year and a half of married life in Sommerhausen. Melchior Adam had already gained the friendship and respect of the city's most powerful men, and they were well prepared for his arrival. The Windsheim senate would grant him citizenship within a matter of days, elect him to its twelve-man outer chamber a month later, and appoint him, on November 16 of that year, to the inner chamber of the senate, whose thirteen members, many of them practicing attorneys, actually ran the city government. [22] The joyful anticipation of this journey surely touched Franz Daniel Pastorius along the Ansbach road, a boy who could view the distant towers and walls of Windsheim as if in a benign fairy tale, where such symbols of strength and order reassure and sustain rather than threaten or oppress those who behold them.

Windsheim would be Franz Daniel's home for the next two decades, and under normal circumstances it would have been his home for the rest of his life. Nine years of growth in the city gave him a sense of belonging and taught him the communal values that repeatedly urged him back to Windsheim once he had ventured off to the University of Nürnberg as a lad of sixteen in 1668. Even as an accomplished young man of the world eight years later – an alumnus of Nürnberg, Strasbourg and Jena, fluent in Latin, French and Italian, and with a doctorate in law – Pastorius dutifully returned to Windsheim to take on adult responsibilities among family and friends in the environment he knew best. Everything in his experience of the city had taught him to remain loyal to it, and he would not lightly break the communal bonds nurtured amid the vitality and order of his youth.

To define the elements that sustained and burdened young Pastorius, this chapter places his upbringing and education in the context of Windsheim's civic life during the 1660s, which offered the expressiveness of public celebration and church fellowship along with governmental restraints on popular vitality and a mood of insecurity and submissiveness reflecting the influence of European politics and warfare. The various strains of vitality and order in Windsheim's daily life were also reflected in Franz Daniel's education, which emphasized orderliness over spontaneity, and thus fostered the complex loyalty that made his ultimate departure from the imperial city an event of emotional or even traumatic intensity.

2.3 Windsheim's Civic Life during the 1660s
2.3.1 Open-Air Markets and Sheltering Walls

> They [husbandmen] seem to have the punishment of Nebuchadnezzar [Daniel 4, 32-33], for their conversation is among beasts, and their talons none of the shortest; only they eat no grass because they love not salads. Their hands guide the plough, and the plough their thoughts; they sweat as much at their dinner as at their labour.
>
> -- "Husbandry"
>
> Let the tailor keep to his shop board, and the shoemaker to his last . . . Some Christ called from the plow, some from their dray-nets.
>
> -- "Calling"
>
> Everyman's nose will not make a shoeing horn . . . None is born a master [craftsman]. A man is never the less an artist [i.e. craftsman] for not having his tools about him, or a musician because he wants his fiddle. Seneca, p. 91 . . . Dull working tools,
> One's courage cools. Tusser, p. 51.
>
> -- "Instrument"
>
> High fortunes are the way to high minds . . . The chief (choicest) men of the city. A grandee . . . The proud zamzummins of the earth. The false and dazzling splendours of greatness.
>
> -- "Grandeur"

Seventeenth-century Windsheim combined rural and citified vitality in a cultural life influenced by peasants, guild craftsmen, and merchants. [23] The peasants, though few in number by Pastorius' day, had inhabited the city for centuries. Sheep-herding and cattle-raising still went on in Windsheim, and commercial activity centered on the agricultural needs of the surrounding countryside – even if the learned of Windsheim might view such simplicity with condescension. Recording a few English comments on the uncouth peasantry in his "Alphabetical Hive" entries on husbandry – most of which describe agrarian virtues and satisfactions – Pastorius reflects a bias of his youth that can be seen, though faintly, in his own writing. Poem 386, for example, criticizes an uncultivated cultivator of the soil in moralistic terms:

> Hans tills his ground; his mind lies fallow:
> That he plows deep, and this but shallow.
> The first bears wheat, the other weeds;
> To wit, bad words and evil deeds.

A remnant of his upbringing, this bias is modified throughout Pastorius' writings, for example in Poem 340 (where "Doctors" identifies the learned in various professions):

> A man us'd to the Spade, or such like Instrument,
> Oft to the Purpose speaks Things very congruent;
> But Doctors frequently do miss, and cannot hit
> The nail upon the head: Are talking more than 't's fit.
> ...
> By the Tiller of the ground,
> Strong of limbs and Reason sound,
> Seasonable words abound.

Of course the child was not encouraged to develop this sort of appreciation in Windsheim, even if folk vitality (and, presumably, congruent speech) abounded. The city's trade guilds multiplied during the sixteenth and seventeenth centuries, indicating the growing diversity of its economy, which included weavers, dyers, lace-makers, stocking-knitters, furriers, comb-makers, gunsmiths, cutlers, pewter-founders, harness makers, potters, carpenters, beer-brewers, bakers and butchers. Master guildsmen operated their own shops, employing journeymen and training apprentices, and sold their wares directly to the townspeople, but they ranked below the merchant class in Windsheim society.

The astute, smartly-dressed merchants and government leaders gave the city its cultural tone. A few of them mixed in Nürnberg society and frequented its stock market, an exclusive association of leading businessmen with a courier service to cities like Vienna, Antwerp, Lyon, Strasbourg and Hamburg. Nürnberg's senate, controlled by wealthy merchants and aristocrats, also set the tone for city government in Windsheim. Although the economy of Nürnberg and other free cities was weakened by the Thirty Years' War and the mercantilist policies of the post-war era, a few prominent Windsheim families continued to build respectable fortunes and make a name for themselves well beyond the city limits.

Yet for all the sophistication of the merchant class, Windsheim's daily commerce was conducted with country simplicity in open-air markets where housewives, peasants and craftsmen shouted greetings, aired gripes, bantered and argued, traded shop talk and gossip, and dickered over prices in the spirited give-and-take and colorful metaphor of Middle Franconian life and speech. The names of various streets and market squares – among them Holzmarkt, Kornmarkt, Metzgergasse, Weinmarkt and Marktplatz – identify the locations where products such as lumber, grain, meat, wine and farm produce were bought and sold in this informal manner. And there were the small shops located in Shopkeepers' Alley (Krämergasse), too. Selling meant giving of one's personality – the master guildsman knew how much

care and discipline went into each of his wares – and the buyer received his fellow townsman's product with appreciation or, when occasion demanded, openly criticized the product and its producer, just as (in Poem 328) Pastorius criticizes, along with derelict physicians and clergymen, the craftsmen who "make things not strong nor plain," and (in Epigram 670) he also notes:
> What needless works are done by these most needful tools
> Call'd needles, pins and awls when in the hands of fools.

The social overtones of buying and selling were most evident during the "seven big fairs" held annually in Windsheim. These events, glorified market days that attracted buyers from the surrounding villages, had transformed medieval religious holidays such as Walpurgis and given them a festive air reminiscent of Sommerhausen's *Kirchweih* celebration. Well before the 1660s, the city's commercial bustle had become the warp in the fabric of civic interaction.

Although the towns of Middle Franconia did not all fit the tight pattern that characterized their Lower Franconian counterparts – some had broad streets and generous dimensions – the city of Windsheim was a large-scale model of Sommerhausen with narrow, winding streets and compact houses built up against each other within its protective walls. [24] Expanded with new walls and towers during the fifteenth century, the growing city kept its medieval atmosphere of seclusion, shelter and intimacy, characteristics that impressed Franz Daniel as a child and occupied him years later when he tried to communicate his experience in the New World to his friends in the Old.

After laying out Germantown with the straight and wide streets of new commercial towns like Philadelphia, Pastorius wrote that it was like Rome because "no walls protect our village other than those Romulus once drew around his new city with a plow," and although he noted that God protected the villagers from attack in peaceful Pennsylvania, his boyhood feelings still convinced him that unwalled Germantown was somehow incomplete. At least half of Germantown "is fortified," he once argued ingeniously, "with pleasant springs that form a natural wall around it," and in a letter to a boyhood friend he described "walk[ing] out through the town gates" to explore the countryside – even though no such gates existed in Germantown. [25]

Despite such differences, the robust give-and-take of Windsheim's daily commerce reveals continuities with Pastorius' life in Pennsylvania, where he reported on his commercial activities on behalf of the Frankfurt Pietist merchants, and versified about Philadelphia and Germantown housewives who traveled six miles through the forest to sell each other tulips and turnips (Poem 168) and Germantown families who took their produce to market in Philadelphia (Epigram 862):
> The husband, coming from Philad$^{\underline{a}}$ Market, says to his Wife:
> How hard a Task, my Honey,
> To get a little Money!

Pastorius (whose Poem 154 suggests he owned a dog himself) immortalized a joke about a local tavernkeeper's dog in Poem 378, thus indicating his familiarity with the tavern, a place of everyday conviviality in both Windsheim and Germantown:
> A taverner at Germantown having a dog, called Onepound might truly say:
> Besides what I by mine Inn-keeping win,
> One Pound I'm sure to me comes daily in.

2.3.2 Enjoying – and Limiting – Public Exuberance

> The best theatre of natures, where they are not played, but truly acted. Some friends come hither to quarrel, others who are quarreling to be made friends . . . The common consumption of the afternoon, and maker away of rainy days. The busy man's recreation, and the idle man's business. The stranger's welcome, and the citizen's courtesy . . . Some in one night of the week spend there what they have gathered all the days of the same at home, to the prejudice of their poor wives and children. Upon the Lord's Day they quench and drown there all the good lessons they have heard at church.
>
> -- "Inn & Innkeeper"

> Constraint in all things makes the pleasure less;
> Sweet is the love that comes with willingness.
>
> -- Epigram 59

In terms of its public celebrations, at least, Windsheim outdid Sommerhausen, an agricultural town with a limited budget that had to be content with a few major celebrations each year. Like the other Middle Franconian cities inspired by Nürnberg, Windsheim sought to achieve festive surfeit on the cosmopolitan scale, although with more decorum than its boisterous populace would muster. Notations in city ledgers and account books show that its

> calendar of annual festivities . . . included Carnival, Lent, Easter, Whitsunday, Corpus Christi, Saint Martin's Day, Christmas and New Year's Day. These holidays were celebrated, at the very least, with senate banquets at the city hall. Carnival was characterized by pageants and dances organized by the craftsmen's guilds. New Year's Day was also commemorated in an especially festive manner. Of course the city's big political events – especially the [annual] elections of the senators and the [four rotating] burgomasters – were given [festive] prominence as well. Musicians and diplomats representing foreign sovereigns [including other Franconian cities and territories] arrived throughout the year and enjoyed the city's generous hospitality. [26]

Young Pastorius experienced both abandon and limits in Windsheim's civic life. The exuberance of the festivities involving the youth of Middle Franconia has been reconstructed from the court records and government mandates of villages and cities alike:

> Swarms of peasant youths or [predominantly lower-class] city boys raucously hurried along the dusty streets from every direction, all of them heading toward . . . an inn that was already teeming with commotion, where beer and wine flowed with abandon, where laughing and cursing filled the air and a host of musicians were warming up for the dance . . . It is not difficult to imagine that these hoards of youth did not return home quietly, that they raised a ruckus drumming and piping back in their home towns even if it was the middle of the night, that the streets suddenly rang with "wild and bawdy shouting, rejoicing and singing" [to quote a sixteenth century ordinance]. [27]

Franz Daniel would have witnessed such boisterousness, but not have been allowed to participate in it, one aspect of the gap between the social classes affecting his early life. As the son of a Windsheim senator committed to moral reform, he was at least indirectly drawn into a conflict over standards of behavior involving the citizenry and their upper-class leaders (more evidence of which appears in his Gymnasium schooling). Franconian governments repeatedly tried to limit the spontaneity and enthusiasm of popular celebrations, typically involving young and old alike. [28]

In 1653 and 1659 (and again in 1711), for example, the Nürnberg senate unsuccessfully attempted to keep the city's children and adults from celebrating the summer solstice with a pagan bonfire and excessive "eating and drinking, dancing and jumping as well as all other related superstitious practices and unchristian improprieties which evoke God's wrath and teach the young to conduct themselves reproachably, and which in manifold instances have caused vexation and annoyance." [29] Similar attitudes prevailed in Windsheim after the Thirty Years' War. A 1650 senate proclamation "Against the Abuses that Have Taken Hold in the City", particularly those involving baptisms, weddings and funerals, documents the vitality of the citizens in Pastorius' day, and the senate's efforts to restrain them. [30]

The senate limited wedding feasting and dancing to two days' duration, prohibited drinking more than one glass of wine before the morning wedding ceremony, prescribed restrained violin music for the serenade to the church – with senate approval required for trumpets or cornets – and warned guests to return home after the evening celebrations without playing music or shouting boisterously. It also authorized the officiating pastor to refuse to marry any couples who delayed arriving at the church until "long after the sermon had begun or even after it was concluded." In related measures, it prohibited "unrestrained drunkenness," gambling, loud celebrating in the streets, and "all manner of pomp and arrogance preeminently among the womenfolk."

In 1667, when Franz Daniel was fifteen, the senate expanded its provisions for civic order with a comprehensive ten-page "Policey Ordtnung," and pledged itself to curbing the unruly behavior of the city's teenage boys. [31] The young and old of Windsheim thus continued to live exuberantly during the 1660s, such evidence indicates, giving Franz Daniel much of the vitality that would be displayed in his active Pennsylvania life, even if he would live by essentially genteel values, with Aristotle's golden mean moderating his social pleasures. He nevertheless argues, in Epigram 59 (in the epigraph above), for pleasure over constraint.

2.3.3 *Music and Fellowship at the Church of Saint Kilian*

> Singing in the spirit and power of God, with a melodious sound. Fox, Journal, p. 277 . . . He that in Christ would still rejoice, / Must sing his praise with heart and voice. Whenever our hearts are warmed with a sense of divine love, our tongues will sing aloud of God's goodness. Ps. 40:10, 89:1. Piggott, Sermon, p. 19.
> -- "Singing"

> Our modern Christians have cleverly dropped the harsher doctrines of taking up the cross [of self-denial, Matt. 16,24] . . . and have modelled religion so fashionable that it may be liked of by the profanest worldling that can be. Boehm, Lud., p. 36.
> -- "Articles of Faith"

> The nearer the church, the farther from God . . . The church is the house of God, the pillar and ground of truth. I Tim. 3:15.
> -- "Church"

In contrast to the raucousness of popular celebration, religious and civic observances demonstrated official Windsheim's respect for high culture and grand formality, influences Pastorius absorbed in childhood yet partially rejected in Pennsylvania (just as Windsheim's struggling citizenry generally resented the costs of culture). The focus of religious festivity was the Church of Saint Kilian, a Romanesque edifice with eight flying buttresses located next to the city hall in the center of Windsheim. An obvious symbol of the civic pride and religious conformity that would later cause problems for Franz Daniel, it was lovingly described by Melchior Adam Pastorius in his history of Windsheim.

The elder Pastorius detailed the exquisite sculpture, paintings, carvings, altars and grand organ as well as the large chiming clock in a cupola of the steeple, an impressive array of cultural artifacts commissioned by the senate and paid for with tax expenditures over the years. [32] His description of the large and lavishly-carved pulpit reflects esthetic and religious sensitivity as well as acceptance of strict theology, and, apparently, of clerical pride as well:

> The pulpit . . . was constructed in 1600 A.D. by Georg Brenck, citizen and sculptor, in this manner: The laws of Moses with their two tablets stand at the very bottom, and on this base six angels with extended wings support the pulpit as well as the atlantes. Encircling the pulpit are figures of Christ the Saviour, the four evangelists, Saint John the Baptist and several prophets. These words appear along the upper cornice: According to the Law and the Testament: If you do not follow them you will not see the Dawn [of Judgement]. On the inside of the uppermost section, the story of the outpouring of the Holy Spirit is portrayed with this inscription: And He appeared unto each of them, and they were filled with the Holy Ghost. Encircling the outside of this upper section are the twelve apostles and twelve angels who stand watch for the Christian Church and serve the holy trinity, which is portrayed at the very top. On the door of the pulpit is the fall of Adam and Eve and a likeness of Christ separating the sheep from the goats, and along its outer edges are the seven works of charity. Above the door [Windsheim's] clergymen of that era are portrayed, and at the very top the dead and resurrected Lord Jesus, and next to Him two angels with trumpets proclaiming the final judgement.

Franz Daniel may well have been thinking of Saint Kilian's grandeur – and the pride of its upper-class parishioners and clergymen – when he reported that the citizens of Germantown built a simple wooden church in 1686:

> We ... did not give consideration to the externals of a grand stone edifice, but instead hoped that the temple of God (which we believers are ourselves) would be established, and that we may all be holy and undefiled. The Lutheran preachers ... [should be] servants of Christ rather than servants of the flesh, and dedicated to the *theologiae internae* instead of reciting the letter of the Law. [34]

Criticizing the Old Testament legalism of orthodox Lutherans and evoking, at least implicitly, the radical mysticism of Valetin Weigel (1533-88) and Jakob Boehme (1575-1624), who compared the cold "stone church" of Lutheranism to the inner warmth of Christ's temple, Pastorius presumably alludes to the frustration of children compelled to obey strict rules as well as that of adult conformity to the state church. [35] Yet as a child he also experienced religious satisfactions, above all through music at Saint Kilian's, which provided "an impressively diverse program ... of instrumental and choral music dedicated to the greater glory of God ('*ad maiorem gloriam Dei*')" – psalms, hymns, cantatas, motets and oratorios by local and international composers sung by the choir (or the congregation and choir) and performed on church instruments including violins, bass viols, cornets, trumpets and drums in addition to the deeply resonant organ. [36]

The influence of Saint Kilian's can be seen in Pastorius' American poetry, whose lyricism, rhythm and form derive in part from folk and church music. Celebrating the anticipated joys of heavenly song in the English Poem 212, for example, he reverts to his native German to conclude with an allusion to the sonorous and uplifting Lutheran liturgical hymn, "Heilig ist unser Gott," the canticum or doxology that, in an English equivalent, begins, "Holy, holy, holy, Lord God Almighty":

> Men and angels in one Quire
> Then together will conspire,
> And singing the Canticum   Rev. 4:8
> To Him that sitteth on the Throne
> Say day and night
> With great delight:
> Triumph and Glory be forever!
> To God, from whom we never sever,
> Heilig ist unser Gott,
> Der Herre Zebaoth.   Cant. 2

The melody and incantation of church hymns and prayers gave Franz Daniel a sense of devotional participation with his fellow Windsheimers as a child, and it was at this level of communication – this blending of esthetics, religious belief and human feeling – that he was once more able to express, by the 1690s, the love he still felt for some of his Windsheim friends. "A few lines" received from his godson Franz Jakob Mercklein in 1694, for instance, led him to reflect on his youth in Windsheim (*Beschreibung Pennsylvaniae*, pp. 67-68). After exhorting his godchild to respect the "first promise" of Christian baptism in a letter to Melchior Adam (see page 33), he recalls Franz Jakob's father and uncles, a few older friends and his cousin Lukas Klein. "Are [they] still alive?" he asks. ("Leb[en sie] ... noch?") He then warmly greets these friends and relatives, hoping that he and they will all grow in the "active and ardent love" ("thätiger brünstiger Liebe") of Christ and thus meet again in heaven to "thank Him with eternal hallelujahs and sing 'Holy, Holy, Holy'" ("ihme mit ewigen Alleluja dancken / und das Heilig / Heilig / Heilig singen").

Pastorius' love of high church music was intellectual as well as esthetic or emotive, in part because he and other Windsheim pupils were taught musical theory and practice by the church cantor. The city also boasted its own church hymnal, edited by Cantor Georg Österreicher (1580-1622), who, in addition to teaching music and directing the church choir and musicians, was long remembered for staging productions of religious dramas in German and Latin, at least one of which managed to include each of Windsheim's citizens (the adult males) in the supporting cast. [37]

The cantor's multiple job functions eventually provided a model for other employees in the cultural sector. In a budget ploy first conceived in 1641, the senate even managed to combine the arts with defense outlays by hiring three full-time 'Stadtmusikanten' who doubled as keepers of the watchtower atop the Church of Saint Kilian. When the musicians were not busy performing at religious and civic observances of every variety, they rotated shifts as sentinels in the tower, where they were required "to signal their vigilance from all four sides every fifteen minutes." [38] As compensation they were given a cozy little 'room with a view' that, as described by Melchior Adam Pastorius, seems to have been one of the most romantic spots in picturesque Windsheim:

Outside of the church to the right of the chancel, an eight-sided church tower was built in 1439 A.D. To climb the tower, with its trim crenelated roof, one walks up a [narrow] stone staircase that spirals like a snail, and in the first room are the bells, and in the one above it the living quarters of the watchmen or musicians, from [the windows of] which one can view the entire horizon. At the very top of the tower hangs the chiming clock, which the watchman chimes by tugging [the rope]. [39]

2.3.4 Political Gestures of Ostentation and Obeisance

In time of peace	Who gains the most
Wealth does increase,	May cease to boast
By war the same is diminished:	When all accounts are finished.

-- "Peace"

Hospitality is good, if the poorer sort are the subjects of our bounty; else too mere a superfluity. Max[im] 46. Generally men invite such as can invite them again. <u>Miscellanea</u>, p. 120. To the poor they assign the coarsest fare. Ibid. . . . Fresh fish & strangers stink in three days. To keep a good table . . . To tarry all night.

-- "Hospitality"

The horse pisseth most where it is wet [i.e., public expenditures are lavished on the rich and powerful].

-- "Liberality"

Hunger eats through stone walls. No gold so red, but it must out for bread . . . Hungry dogs will eat dirty puddings. Hard [soup] bones for sweet beans. If thou rise from table with an appetite, thou art sure never to sit down without one. Max[im] 59.

-- "Hunger"

The vigilant 'Stadtmusikanten' proved indispensable during the 1660s, a decade of political uncertainty when the city repeatedly tested its alliances in diplomatic gatherings marked by pomp and ceremony. [40] When Windsheim envoys negotiated a commercial and political treaty with its most powerful neighboring sovereigns in 1663, the senate invited the signatories – the Graf von Castell, Graf Christian von Hohenlohe, and Christian Ernst and Georg Albrecht, margraves of Brandenburg at Bayreuth and Ansbach respectively – to a ratification ceremony in Windsheim on October 21. The Brandenburg margraves mobilized their diplomatic staffs and their spouses for the event, arriving at the city gates with a train of sixty horse, and a seven-gun salute marked their processional entry into Windsheim.

The following year, when senators frequently consulted over defensive measures to counter a Turkish invasion of Hungary, numerous high-ranking guests arrived: the Prince of Paderborn, the Bishop of Strasbourg, the Graf of Hanau, Graf Königsmarck of Sweden, Bishop Christoph Bernhard of Münster, and Archbishop-Elector Carl Caspar of Trier. Each of these sovereigns displayed his grandeur and importance in the size and ostentation of his train – which in the case of Elector Carl Caspar numbered 160 horse, decisively trumping the local Brandenburg margraves – and Windsheim, to the extent its coffers permitted, responded in kind by generously wining and dining its guests and lavishing ceremony upon them.

During these lean years, when some of Windsheim's residents knew hunger like that described in Pastorius' "Alphabetical Hive" entries, the senate was more concerned with imperial politics than local poverty, and could justify its liberality toward wealthy dignitaries as part of concerted efforts to balance European power. [41] Ever since Archbishop-Elector Johann Philipp of Mainz and Würzburg, Melchior Adam's host at Marienberg Castle in 1649, began forming a Rhineland Alliance of neutral German princes in 1654, Franconians had felt the tension of potential clashes between the Hapsburg dynasty and the emerging French empire of Louis XIV. During the 1650s the Spanish and Austrian Hapsburgs seemed more of a threat than France. Louis XIV was, in 1654, a lad of 16 vaguely dreaming of empire, but Philip IV (1605-65), the Hapsburg King of Sicily, Naples and Spain, was battling to restore Spain's waning glory in Italy and Holland, and he urged his Austrian cousin, Emperor Ferdinand III, to join the effort to regain Hapsburg hegemony in Europe. Prince Johann Philipp worried that Ferdinand III would march Hapsburg forces through Franconia to Holland, involving it and the Rhineland in another crippling war, so to put some muscle behind his peace initiative he encouraged France to join his Rhineland Alliance. Before long, however, France seemed all too eager to "defend" central Germany, and the Franconian lords and imperial cities eventually realized they needed the emperor to protect them from their "protector."

France had not yet begun displaying its might when Ferdinand III died in 1657, but the tension-filled interregnum following his death shifted the European balance of power in its favor. As the German princes prepared to elect a new emperor, they refused to consider the Hapsburg candidate a foregone conclusion, ignoring tradition that had held through centuries. Only after Johann Philipp and Friedrich Wilhelm (1620-88), the "Great Elector" of Brandenburg Prussia, won a Hapsburg guarantee that Austria would not aid Spain on its Dutch and Italian battlefields did the electoral princes choose Leopold I (1640-1705), the 18-year-old King of Austria and Bohemia, as emperor of the Holy Roman Empire.

In February, 1659, Windsheimers felt the awesome presence of Hapsburg power when the Emperor Elect paid the imperial city a two-day visit en route to his coronation in Frankfurt am Main. [42] Young Leopold personified the force that, in its resolution or caprice, could bring peace and prosperity or war and destruction to Windsheim, and the citizens indulged their ambiguous emotions in celebration and homage. Guildsmen set to work constructing two provisional kitchens on the market square days before the new emperor arrived. Their exertions were well advised. When Leopold entered the city on February 16, he was accompanied by his Uncle Leopold Wilhelm (1614-62), the Archduke of Austria, and a court retinue that required two thousand horses and a hundred wagons for transportation and matériel support.

The city fed the court retainers and feasted the royal party, and, Melchior Adam Pastorius later reported, when Leopold and his entourage departed the following day

> the entire senate walked beside the [royal] coaches with their heads bared, and 25 of the noblest citizens followed on horseback behind the coaches until the royal party reached the boundary markers of the city at [the village of] Wibelsheim, where all those present lined up in a row [beside the passing royal train] and bid farewell to the potentates, bowing abjectly before them. [43]

Windsheim observed Leopold's coronation with "a celebration of thanksgiving and joy" ("Dank und Freudenfest") on July 25. The Emperor later ratified the city's royal privileges and sent his imperial commissioner to receive the oath of homage and obedience from Windsheim's citizens and senators, who assembled in front of the city hall for the ceremony on 13 January 1660.

In the political developments of the 1660s, the Emperor put Windsheim's loyalty to the test with repeated demands for military assistance. The citizens of Windsheim and its villages were required to house and feed imperial troops in 1662, 1664 and 1669, and to raise defense funds exceeding 3000 gulden in 1663 and 1664. Leopold I had meddled in Hungarian national politics – attempting to curb Turkish interests in the area despite Hungarian distrust of the Emperor's motives – and Fazil Ahmed Pasha (1635-76), Grand Vizier of the Ottoman Empire, responded in 1663 by invading Hungary with 120,000 Turkish soldiers. Although the Hungarians were out-manned, they refused to accept Hapsburg reinforcements and lost a decisive battle at Neuhäusel in September, opening the way for a Turkish advance toward Austria's borders. [44]

The Turkish threat caused alarm throughout the empire:

> The [Windsheim] senate forbade all festivities and amusements, and proclaimed October 1 [1663] a day of penitence and prayer. The fear of the Turks was so great, even in Franconia, that the senators saw repairing the city's defensive walls as a necessity and many people from the surrounding area secured their valuables within the city. [45]

Windsheim citizens practiced military drills, and the senate held its frequent consultations with high-ranking guests. [46] The Reichstag (Imperial Diet) at Regensburg approved mobilization, and Leopold I's forces routed the enemy the following year, just as it reached the Austro-Hungarian frontier. To build this army, Franconian sovereigns and imperial cities were required to raise two regiments, or nearly 2500 soldiers, and Windsheim's contingent – peasants conscripted from its outlying villages – marched off to the Turkish war on 26 April 1664. [47] Melchior Adam Pastorius described their fate in his history of Windsheim:

> 1664. On July 22 the bloody battle of Saint Gotthard in Hungary took place along the Raab River. Colonel Bleittner, Lieutenant-Colonel Buttlar, Guard Commander Beck and most of the soldiers of the [Franconian] regiment were mowed down by the sabered Turks. The city of Windsheim had recruited every fifth man from all of its [village] subjects, more than 90 head, and the only ones to come back were two corporals and eight privates. [They were] discharged with gratitude on December 5, and each of them received, along with his discharge papers, three and one-half talers. [48]

Although Windsheimers fought for the Emperor in Hungary again in 1669 and the city was threatened by war with France in subsequent years, the Peace of Vasvar with the Turks in 1665 lasted until 1683, the year Franz Daniel Pastorius finally had enough of European warmongering. The Turks laid siege to Vienna itself in July of that year, and (in Poem 359) Pastorius reported that his ship to America once escaped a pursuing vessel believed to be manned by "the Cruel, Enslaving Turks." Yet neither the Turks nor the French were the enemy he identified when he reflected upon the cycle of history that had characterized his 31 years of life in Europe. In one of his earliest English poems, enti-

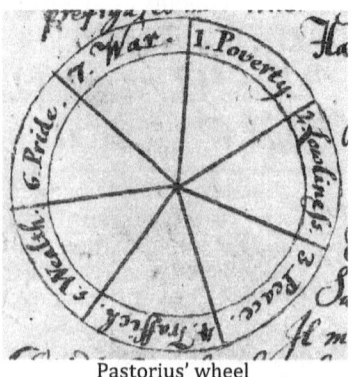

Pastorius' wheel ("Beehive," I, 141)

tled "The Revolution or Changeable Course and Recourse of this present World" (Poem 12), he illustrates the cycle with a seven-spoked wheel and a verse commentary including these lines [49]:

> War begets Poverty, Poverty Peace,
> Then people will traffick [i.e., trade], & Riches increase,
> Riches produceth Pride; Pride is War's ground,
> War begets Poverty, So we go round.

2.3.5 A Highflying Toast to Common Endeavor

> He stands taller on his own bottom, than others on the advantaged ground of fortune.
> -- "Grandeur"

> A churchbell gently tolling; bells ringing in peal solemnly, as at a funeral; merry round ringing as at weddings. Beaumont, p. 187.
> -- "Bell"

> Conquerors through all vicissitudes. [To] outmaster . . . To bear the bell away . . . To give one a foil. To get above. He got the better of it at every exercise . . . Victory suddenly appears like the sun after a long overcasting of clouds and mists. Hill. To overcome this storm of adversity.
> -- "Victory"

No matter how the wheel of history with its vicissitudes of war and peace, of pride and poverty, might have affected Windsheim during the 1660s (the city's peasant soldiers submitting to combat and death for the Empire, and its esteemed senators to rituals of obeisance before the Emperor), Franz Daniel's fellow townspeople refused to consider themselves mere cogs in a wheel as they robustly lived together within their walled city. When lightning struck and burned the church tower of Saint Kilian's in 1666, for example, the citizens reacted with heroic determination, and before long, with the tower crowned to perfection once more, a nimble artisan celebrated this civic triumph with lordly aplomb, illustrating the Franconian customs that ameliorated life's burdens.

Melchior Adam Pastorius reports these events simply, but with appreciation for the endeavor of his townspeople and the manifold talents of the artisan:

> The little tower at the very top, which houses the chiming clock, . . . remained in flames for almost two hours. The fire-fighters could not reach that height from the outside with any of their devices, and on the inside [the tower] was so constricted that one individual could barely stand on the ladder. The citizens gathered all the milk from [the city dairy at] the hospital and elsewhere, carried it [in fire buckets] across the lengthy church building, and handed one fire bucket after the other up to Thomas Wagner, who stood at the top next to the fire, until with God's help it was finally extinguished.
>
> The city subsequently commissioned the carpenters' guild to build a new clock tower from good oak lumber in the pattern of the original, and hired the slater from Kitzingen [in Lower Franconia] to roof it with crenelated [copper] metal. This master, after completing the last stage of his work on Wednesday the 23rd of May, climbed to the pinnacle [of the tower roof], and there he put on a new pair of stockings and shoes, drank a full measure of wine [about one liter] from a pewter vessel in three long pulls, and tossed the empty vessel down [to the appreciative crowd] in front of the new edifice. [50]

When the citizens of Windsheim gathered at the city hall and swore allegiance to Leopold I in January, 1660, eight-year-old Franz Daniel Pastorius, at home in the imperial city for about half a year, was in his first year of school at the Windsheim Gymnasium. When fear of the Turks led the senate to proclaim a day of penitence and prayer in October, 1663, young Pastorius had just celebrated his twelfth birthday; he entered his teens before Windsheim's decimated contingent of soldiers returned from Hungary the following year. When the slater from Kitzingen put a new copper roof on the steeple of Saint Kilian's in May, 1666, Franz Daniel was a fourteen-year-old scholar mastering intermediate lessons at the Gymnasium, and the glistening spire would only have begun to tarnish when he headed off to Nürnberg University with three of his classmates two years later. As a boy involved in the daily life of Windsheim during the 1660s, Franz Daniel was able to absorb impressions and attitudes from all that transpired around him – from the toil and celebration of peasants and craftsmen, the give-and-take of open-air markets, the order and pageantry of political ceremony and diplomatic consultation, the fervor of church sermons and the grace of devotional motets.

As Pastorius indicates in his references to protective city walls and gates and to hymns joyfully sung, much of this daily life provided sustenance and fulfillment for the child, enabling him to develop the vitality of spirit so often displayed in the warmth and humor of his Pennsylvania poetry and prose. Despite threats of war and acts of obeisance, the civic life of Windsheim in the 1660s generally exhibits an attractive combination of vitality and order, a public surface where ingrained habits and long-established rituals constructively channeled the energies of an exuberant populace.

Of course this smooth surface was not all that Pastorius experienced in Windsheim, for if it had been he would never have felt compelled to leave the city, or to appeal to his former townspeople with the emotional piety repeatedly displayed in his transatlantic writings. To identify the deep structure of his Windsheim experience, this study probes Franz Daniel's upbringing and education, levels of personal and cultural existence revealing, beneath the seemingly benign order of public ritual, tensions and frustrations that resulted from the process of ingraining the habits demanded by the peculiar orderliness of the age.

2.4 *Treading the Path to Virtue at the Windsheim Gymnasium*

> The learning instilled into my early years. Hill.
> -- "Doctrine"
>
> Youth is like the first cogitations, not so wise as the second. Bacon.
> -- "Youth"
>
> As more and more our understanding clears,
> So more and more our ignorance appears.
>
> Easier and sooner learning's lost than gained
> If by fresh applications not maintain'd.
> -- Epigrams 5, 2315.2

Young Pastorius' moral and intellectual growth in Windsheim was most directly influenced by his formal education at the Lutheran Gymnasium, also known as the Latin School, and by the upbringing he experienced in the Pastorius home, two spheres that overlapped. His father Melchior Adam not only wrote poetry and prose revealing a firm commitment to strict Lutheran education; beginning in 1663 he also served as one of the two supervisors of education ('Scholarchen') on the Windsheim senate responsible for the conduct of the Gymnasium. Franz Daniel's formal education will be defined with the aid of historical detail placing the policies and conduct of the Windsheim Gymnasium in the context of Lutheran educational traditions. Since his upbringing and family life centered upon the relationship of father and son, which was strongly influenced by the concepts of filial obedience and paternal authority prevalent in his culture, an analysis of these aspects will conclude this description of his Windsheim youth.

Obedience and authority were recurring themes in his upbringing, schooling and young adult experience, and this study increasingly focuses upon them. Pastorius, who became one of Pennsylvania's first educators, absorbed Lutheran humanist learning at the Windsheim Gymnasium, and he affirms much of this morality and learning in his Pennsylvania writings. Yet he eventually rejected the elitist goals of the Gymnasium. This pillar of the Lutheran church and state insisted on strict obedience to an establishment that, Pastorius believed, denied in practice the Christian values it advanced in theory. (His American commentary on Gymnasium education is one aspect of his general criticism of European learnedness explored in Chapter Three.)

2.4.1 Lutheran Pedagogy in the Imperial City

> A calling every way cumbersome, and full of toil ... Scholars must have a willing mind, an attentive ear, and a ready hand.
> -- "Schoole"
>
> A man without Learning (as Cato doth say)
> May justly be called an Image of Clay.
>
> What things by studious care a boy does find
> In curious arts, lodge longest in the mind.
> -- Epigrams 19, 2335.4

Melchior Adam Pastorius provides, in his history of Windsheim, an introduction to the Gymnasium indicating the city's emphasis on diligent learning and religious training:

> The [three-story] Latin schoolhouse, a short distance from the main church and the city hall, was constructed by order of the honorable Senate in the year of our Lord 1573 at a spot so situated that not much of the din made by the guild workers can be heard ... On the first floor, the youngest boys are taught to comprehend the alphabet and to read and write German, and are also induced to pray and to memorize the short [Lutheran] catechism ... There are three [intermediate] classes on the second floor ... On the top floor, the rector lectures the grown youths, and sharpens their wits so that they will be capable of journeying to a university and taking up advanced studies. All of the *praeceptores* [teachers] are retained by the honorable Senate, and given free room and board and a minimal salary. In return, they are required to sign a declaration that they will instruct the youths in the fear of the Lord and in the liberal arts with all necessary diligence, demonstrate exemplary conduct in their personal lives, and obey the orders of the Senate. [51]

2.4.1.1 Luther's Humanist Ideals and Strict Discipline

> Those who at school well throve in grammar's eight parts,
> Now think themselves above all masters of arts [i.e. craftsmen].
>
> -- Epigram 615
>
> Hebrew and Greek a pair of spectacles to the learned priests ... In the beginning (before Babel) was the Word [of God, John 1,1], the saints' original; since the beginning was Babel, and tongues, the priests' original ... The natural man perceives not the things of God, though he hath Hebrew, Greek and Latin. E.M. Mod., p. 4.
>
> -- "Original Tongues"
>
> Arts and sciences [ought to] be taught in the mother tongue, so that young gentlemen may attend them without so much trouble and cracking their brains so many years about learning the languages. Reynell, p. 76.
>
> -- "Learning"

Informing Melchior Adam's text – and the realities of Windsheim education – was an unbroken history of Lutheran educational endeavor beginning with Martin Luther himself, who had signaled his battle against the Powers of Darkness by hurling his inkwell at the Devil while hiding out from the Emperor and the Pope in 1521. [52] Language, Luther knew, was the key to salvation in the course of history as in the life of each individual. God in His wisdom had caused the diaspora of the Greeks and the rise of the Roman Empire so that the seed of the Gospel, in the Greek and Latin texts of the Bible, would fall on fallow ground and bear fruit through the ages. In the era of print, studying the Greek, Latin and Hebrew languages could give each Christian direct access to the transmitted Word of God; yet as the Reformation began Satan was cunningly and secretly pursuing his work of spiritual destruction, effecting a decline in liberal education of unprecedented magnitude.

Luther, German translator of the Bible par excellence, scorned those critics who disparaged the liberal arts and argued that the Gospel in German was all that anyone needed. They were "German fools" who wanted "us Germans to remain brutes and raving animals forever." Why should we vainly consume foreign luxuries that impoverish and ruin the nation, Luther challenged the philistines, yet reject the foreign languages and liberal arts that enrich and embellish the human spirit?

Seeking an ally in his battle against ignorance, Luther published *An Appeal to the Magistrates of all the Cities of Germany for the Establishment and Maintenance of Christian Schools* in 1524. He saw the leaders of the free cities as the last resort for a spiritual and cultural rebirth in Germany. The peasants and workers were mired in ignorance and poverty, he noted, and the princes and lords intoxicated with frivolous pleasures and worldly pursuits. He particularly appealed to the material interests of these civic leaders:

> A city attains its best and richest prosperity, welfare and strength by having many refined, educated, reasonable, honorable, well-bred citizens ... Even if the soul did not exist ... and schools and languages were not needed for the sake of God and the Scriptures, there would still be more than enough reason for establishing the very best schools for both boys and girls in every location: in order to maintain the forms of temporal society, the world would still need men and women of refinement and skill, so that the men could govern the state and its people with facility and the women could proficiently take charge of the household, children and servants. Naturally enough, it is the little boys

who have to become men of this sort, and the little girls who must develop into this kind of woman. [53]

Responding to Luther's appeal, the Nürnberg senate established one of the first Protestant Gymnasiums under the guidance of Luther's colleague Philipp Melanchthon (1497-1560), who developed a curriculum that served as a model for Windsheim and other cities. [54] The Gymnasium in Windsheim combined worldly and religious instruction as Luther envisioned, but it never provided the "very best" for the "many." With about 150 pupils in the 1660s, it remained small and elitist. For those who could not attend – lower-class youths, and (despite Luther's appeal) girls of all classes – the city's one-room German school provided only the most rudimentary education, and only for those whose parents would pay the teacher of this "private" school. [55] Franz Daniel Pastorius and his schoolmates might nevertheless have considered admission to the "public" Gymnasium a mixed blessing, since the Lutheran process of making "men of this sort" out of these "little boys" tended to create a vicious cycle of bad conduct and punishment, generally reassuring Windsheim's educators that Luther's view of childhood was all too true.

With his stark awareness of original sin, Luther rejected the claim of Desiderius Erasmus (1466?-1536) of Rotterdam that gentle and imaginative teaching could engender a godlike being in innocent children. [56] The childlike innocence praised by Christ as the key to heaven (Matt. 18, 3 and 19, 14) is not innocence per se, Luther countered, but rather the redeemed innocence gained through baptism in Christ. Children are evil by nature – inherently disobedient to parents, teachers and God – and can be saved only by exercising authority over them, by demanding discipline and obedience from them, by breaking the child's will. "By beating your child with a stick," he advised parents, "you will save its soul from Hell." Luther was callous and unyielding in his attitudes toward human development, but his personal warmth and redemptive vision helped to assuage the psychic wounds of childhood. Even young children felt God's grace and presence in the vibrant hymns and devotional prose that flowed from his pen.

2.4.1.2 Compulsions among Windsheim's Pious and Wanton Youth

By sad experience this is known to some,
Who hate instruction to destruction come.

-- Epigram 34

A discreet and cool hand may direct the blow right, and hit the mark, when men of fury rather ease their passion than mend their youth; especially if the correction exceed the fault, for that hardens. Penn.

-- "Punishment"

Some I pardoned for their youth; others for their age; I spare one man for his dignity, another for his humility; and when I find no other matter to work upon, I spare myself, says the merciful prince, examining his own conscience. Seneca, p. 435.

-- "Pardon"

In the life of the most profligate wretch, we may read our own character; for there is no sin in his life, but what is in our nature. Boehm, p. 26.

-- "Original Sin"

Luther's approach to childrearing reflected the disciplinary attitudes of his age, attitudes that prevailed virtually unchanged in Windsheim until well after the 1660s. In the preamble to the Code of Education of 1595 (retained until 1667), the senate classified children as basically good or evil, and ordered its teachers to act accordingly:

> All pupils should emulate... the pious pupils who demonstrate all due obedience of their own accord because they love honor and virtue; we therefore earnestly order and command the preceptors [teachers], each and every one, to impel the bad and ill-bred pupils to dutiful obedience with appropriate punishment, and in particular to make use of the rod in greater earnest than has been the case up to the present. We propose, on the other hand, to demonstrate our greatest good will and encouragement to both the preceptors and the pious pupils. [57]

In 1667, a year before Pastorius graduated from the Gymnasium, the senators omitted the reference to corporal punishment, perhaps because beating pupils had not improved behavior. Updating the 1595 Code of Education, the senate declared its goal was

> to promote the usefulness and piety, the eternal and temporal welfare of the dear youths who will be growing up in the future and, on the other hand, to do everything within our power to terminate all of their abuses against good conduct and prevent the laziness, wantonness and obstinacy that have taken hold, as well as the unchristian and dishonorable conduct that, in the world's present state of decline, has so unfortunately been gaining the upper hand in this city to an alarming extent. [58]

The educational codes of 1595 and 1667 both demanded strict obedience from the school boys of Windsheim, and sought to instill piety and virtue through a regimen of church attendance, Bible-reading, prayer, and catechism instruction. Many boys submitted, and strove to attain godly righteousness, rejecting some of their natural impulses as sinful aberrations. Others rebelled, reveling in prankish behavior or, in extreme cases, plunging into an abyss of despair and self-destruction. Three students who boarded at the Gymnasium, accused of sodomy and brought to trial in 1656, confessed to a life of depravity contemporaries found almost beyond belief. [59] One of the three, Hans Dötsch, admitted to signing a pact with the Devil in his own blood, selling body and soul in return for "learnedness and the talent of being able to win the favors of the female sex." He said he had placed the pact under a stone in the chapel but, torn by guilt and fear a few days later, retrieved it and ripped it to shreds before the Devil claimed it.

The sins of these pariahs cried to heaven for castigation by fire, a Windsheim chronicler wrote, adding that the court showed leniency because the offenders were minors (though without mentioning their ages, apparently in the early teens). Dötsch and his friend Hans Fleck were flogged in prison and released for a final weekend with their parents before being banished from the city for ten and two years respectively, and Dötsch was also made to stand bareheaded in front of Saint Kilian's holding a scourge for several hours before being marched to the city gates. In a separate trial a few days later, Sebastian Summa was found guilty of having corrupted his two schoolmates, apparently by involving them in unspecified homosexual conduct. Young Summa was then sentenced to be beheaded by sword. Following an appeal for leniency, tentatively advanced by parents and neighbors, the boy was first placed in the pillory, and then repeatedly flogged as he was led through the streets to the city gates and banished from Windsheim for life.

Melchior Adam Pastorius chronicles a century of crime and punishment in his 1692 history of Windsheim – adulterers, fornicators and murderers beheaded by sword or bound and thrown into the Aisch River to drown, thieves hung at the gallows, a war-time spy drawn and quartered, witches burned at the stake in the witch hunt of 1596-97 – but he does not describe the crimes of Sebastian Summa and his friends or their sentencing and punishment. [60] A concentrated image of the personal and societal compulsions and severe discipline that complicated and frustrated behavior in Windsheim, this dramatic event occurred within memory of many of his townspeople, and it could not be recalled without raising complex and destructive emotions – private and familial anguish and shame as well as deep resentment of judicial and governmental authority that festered below the surface of the city's public life.

Franz Daniel was spared the trauma of these and similar punishments. He did not arrive in Windsheim until three years after the sodomy trials, and no public floggings or executions are recorded for the years when he was living in the city. All the same, these trials show the extent to which sexual conduct and gender identity were circumscribed in this era. (In "Some Onomastical Considerations," no. 762, Pastorius himself refers to homosexual conduct as "filthy wickedness... preposterous Venery... this unnatural Sin of Buggery." [60a]) Furthermore, Hans Dötsch's willingness to sell his soul for learned attainments and sensual satisfactions reveals similarities with the learned compulsions Pastorius encountered at the Gymnasium and universities that fostered his own willingness to attain erudition at considerable personal cost. This compulsiveness was pervasive, and traces of it can be noted in Pastorius along with the humor, generosity and philosophical depth of his maturity, a vital and resilient personality displaying the beneficial influences of his Pennsylvania life, and the emotive sustenance of his Franconian childhood, which provided warm and loving approval as well as strict discipline.

2.4.1.3 *Contention among the Teachers and Clergy*

> Many teachers need to be taught.
> -- "Doctor"
>
> Dissembling cats take the flesh out of the pot ... A waterman, looking one way and rowing another.
> -- "Simulation"
>
> An ounce of mother wit is worth a pound of clergy. Antid., p. 31.
> -- "Learning"
>
> Be bold, but cautious; follow wisdom's voice:
> Integrity is all, the rest a noise.
> -- Epigram 33

Windsheim's teachers and clergymen, employees of the city, dutifully instilled piety and virtue in their pupils, yet were not always able to practice what they preached – thus adding to the tensions of Pastorius' youth. [61] The job of teaching was difficult and demoralizing, and it commanded a low salary and little esteem. Clergymen were grudgingly respected as educated men but poorly paid, and school teachers were usually the younger or less-qualified theologians who hoped to work their way a bit farther up the social and economic ladder with a promotion into the ranks of the clergy. School and church finances were in a shambles after the Thirty

Years' War, and teachers and clergymen bitterly complained that they lived as paupers, often forced to wait months on end for their miserly wages.

Jealousies over rank and salary festered. Clergyman Johannes Model (1610-75), whose son was a school chum of Pastorius', precipitated a row when he won a promotion to the city's best-paid clerical post during salary negotiations in 1662, with Chaplain Johannes Petermann (1630-79) accusing him of "grabbing up everything for himself alone," and resentments flared up again four years later. Petermann and Model then greedily argued over percentages of the take when a sick parishioner gave the clergy a gift in return for prayers offered. The incident turned into a free-for-all of insults and name-calling among four of the city's six or seven clergymen. When two of the parsons began beating each other, colleagues were forced to restrain them physically. Taking to the courts, the disputants filed charges and counter-charges, one of which refuted eighteen "lies" in an opponent's brief. To restore order, the senate had to threaten the clergymen with dismissal.

Similar infighting occurred at the Gymnasium, too. In 1664 Rector Johann Wolfgang Gilg (1625-97) challenged Chaplain Petermann for offering a course in logic to advanced students whom Gilg believed should have been getting their logic from him. The two learned men castigated each other repeatedly until the senate was forced to intervene. The disturbance was apparently not an isolated instance. In the 1667 education code, the senate instructed its teachers "to comport themselves peaceably and reasonably [not only in public but] also among each other, without antipathies, quarreling or hatred," and to develop "a truly Christian and amiable manner toward their colleagues," evidence of disturbing everyday tensions. [62]

Theological disputes also demanded senate action, including a categorical prohibition of "all malicious improprieties from the pulpit" in 1662. Two clergymen had waged pulpit warfare over the precise nature of Christ's incarnation in 1658 – so indefatigably, in fact, that the senate called a special session to hear both arguments. Senator Johann Gelchsheimer, Franz Daniel's step-grandfather, ingeniously resolved the issue by observing that

> he thought each of these disputants is simply using different words to say the same thing. This struck both of the clergymen as an innovation of unprecedented nature. They stopped short, and after they had reflected a few moments, the matter seemed to them exactly as Gelchsheimer had said. [63]

2.4.1.4 Codes of Education of 1595 and 1667

> Childhood is over-fond, youth mad and vain,
> Manhood is vindictive, old age but pain.
> -- Epigram 63
>
> An old cat plays with no ball. Boys will have toys . . . Children do things in jest, old men in earnest, so that the works of old men are nothing in the world but the progress and improvement of children's errors. Seneca, p. 224.
> -- "Childhood"

No matter how pupils, teachers and clergy actually behaved, the city's standards were clearly defined by the educational codes of 1595 and 1667. [64] In a barrage of prohibitions, restrictions, threats and insinuations, the city fathers spelled out a program for reforming human conduct by properly training the youth of Windsheim. They wrote concretely and colorfully, and their dictates tell a lot about the education Franz Daniel and his schoolmates received. Since the document of 1667 amends that of 1595, comparing the two yields a reliable picture of the principles and reality of Gymnasium life during the 1660s. In reaffirming the principles of 1595, the 1667 senate held on to the educational traditions of Lutheran humanism. By amending and expanding the code, it showed how educational practices in Windsheim fell short of Luther's goals and the senate's own expectations.

The code adopted in 1595 consists of three sections, with eight articles on religious instruction and thirteen on general deportment that were reissued essentially unchanged in 1667, and nine paragraphs on scholarly habits shortened and simplified when the 1667 senate added reformist goals to the regulations.

The first eight articles instruct each child to conduct himself as follows: to fear and love God, to praise and thank Him at all times, and to obey Him patiently through trial and tribulation; to heartily thank God for His goodness with a prayer at daybreak and to begin classes joyfully, arriving punctually for morning prayers; to avoid profanity and blasphemy; on Sundays and holidays, to enter the school with his copy of Luther's Book of Hymns and Psalms at the first bell, to proceed to the church two by two, orderly and properly, with head bared and without dragging his feet "like a lazy and sluggish snake," and to take his assigned place quietly and politely; if he is one of the young pupils excused from the sermon because of the cold in winter, to leave the church without disturbing the preaching by shouting and running about; to pay close attention to the sermon and to take notes or comprehend it well enough to answer when questioned about its central argument, to avoid gossip and idle talk during the sermon, and to avoid being found taking a walk, playing outside or "engaging in any other improper behavior" while church services are being held; to leave the church in procession with his class, and if his class is singing the recessional hymn, to take his place with the group in front of the pulpit without having to be reminded, and to sing in unison slowly and understandably; when singing or praying as a class during Holy Communion or for the collection, to sing or say his part as soon as his turn comes, to kneel and pray meditatively, and to avoid setting a bad example by leaning on the pews or standing in an unruly manner.

Thirteen articles on proper conduct generally, section two of the code, admonish each pupil to behave in this manner: to conduct himself honorably and morally at all times, to love and obey parents and preceptors as God commands and especially to respect teachers regardless of rank by deferentially carrying out all of their commands at school and elsewhere; to avoid mocking or making fun of teachers or spitefully spreading untrue complaints about them; to show reverence and respect for members of the senate and "other persons of eminence" as well as their virtuous wives by removing his cap when passing such persons on the street and genuflecting when addressing them; to wear honorable and conservative clothing suitable to his station, to avoid wearing roguish or faddish clothing or the clothing of rascals and peasant youths, and to abstain from carrying weapons like daggers and hunting knives; to comport himself commendably in public, always closing his gown, combing his hair and washing his hands properly before leaving his quarters, and without shouting or running about or otherwise behaving improperly; to abstain from drinking alcoholic beverages in any pub or inn, and from attending weddings and dances uninvited or without his teacher's permission; for health's sake to avoid bathing, fishing or, in winter, ice-skating or sledding in, on or near rivers, ponds and streams; to play only honorable and proper games (ball, foot-racing, "knight's race," etc.), exercising Ciceronian restraint (i.e., by dispensing with scholarly chores before playing); to avoid buying and selling among his fellow pupils without the consent of the teacher; to behave, in short, so honorably and virtuously that the general public "notices there is a difference between an idiot or guild apprentice and a Gymnasium pupil," especially avoiding "frivolous, scandalous, godless, indecent and vulgar talk and gossip" as well as brawls and unseemly arguments, appealing to his teacher for justice rather than fighting back if insulted or unjustly treated by malicious individuals (i.e., lower-class boys who would dare to challenge a Gymnasium youth).

A third section of the code, on scholarly habits, prohibits disturbing the lessons by eating, whispering, gossiping, behaving eccentrically or running back and forth on the benches; regulates attendance keeping and punishment for absence and tardiness; describes the scholars' "tools" – books, paper, quill and ink – and their use, consisting primarily of copying maxims, commonplaces, "artistic and beautiful expressions and phrases" and other content taught or dictated by the teacher; prescribes punishment for inattentive or careless pupils doodling, drawing, or besmirching books or paper; defines the standards for memorizing and reciting assigned texts, emphasizing clear and precise enunciation of grammatically significant final syllables in Latin; stipulates that Latin be used instead of German at school and when talking to learned persons; urges attending to music lessons to increase the joy and vitality of school routines; requires that homework be done carefully and thoroughly, and without assisting or copying from others; and defines the standards for grammatical analysis and written composition in German, Latin and Greek.

Reviewing these regulations in October, 1667, the senate modified style and tone by omitting a few robust phrases, and some specific references to disapproved conduct like "disturbing the preaching by shouting and running about," shortened to "disturbing the preaching." In the first two sections, excisions were kept to a minimum. The reference to "lazy and sluggish snakes" disappeared, for example, but the cruelly disparaging "idiots or guild apprentices" remained. The section on scholarly habits, though, was compressed to nearly half its original length, dispensing with repetitive phrases and unnecessary detail as well as some fine Renaissance prose describing the attainment of language skills in terms of their elements and ideals, much as a pragmatic painter might explain the use of brushes, oils and canvas yet evoke a deeper sense of his art – evocative detail sacrificed, in the lengthy revised code, to make way for the senate's new code preamble (quoted on page 72) and fifteen new articles outlining a rigorous program of educational reform. The senators had grown dissatisfied with Windsheim's educational performance since the Thirty Years' War, and they were moved to action by inside reports detailing scholarly and moral laxity among Gymnasium teachers and pupils. [65]

The reports were presented by the city's two supervisors of education, Senator Melchior Adam Pastorius and his superior, Burgomaster Johann Georg Stellwag (1621-91). As the city's education experts, Pastorius and Stellwag offered many of the suggestions for change, and as the junior supervisor, Pastorius was probably responsible for drafting the code revisions. A third contributor to the reform program was Tobias Schumberg (1627-1713), hired as the new rector four months earlier, and, under the revised code, given greater authority over school personnel and curriculum than his predecessors. The timing of Schumberg's appointment was not coincidental. Johann Gilg had dutifully served as rector since 1655 and, promoted to assistant parson at the city hospital, was finally winning release from the educational treadmill.

Fervently reasserting the goals of Lutheran humanism, the code revisions of 1667 nevertheless include pedagogical theory somewhat more enlightened than in the past. Teachers are advised to emulate adult society in the classroom by appointing class leaders, equitably distributing honorary positions, and encouraging reasonable social order, thus eliminating "torment and servile fear" among pupils. An article approving competitive academic games (long popular in Franconia) notes that youthful competition "sometimes achieves more than the teacher does with reprimands, threats and punishment." All in all, however, the new code reemphasizes negative incentives, strict discipline and moral indoctrination.

Advanced pupils who speak German instead of Latin in class, it warns, "may expect severe punishment." "All malevolent and negligent conduct" accompanying religious observances would be "prohibit[ed] with painstaking energy and heavy punishment." "Diligent" catechism instruction was introduced for young pupils on Sunday mornings, and the older boys were required to attend Sunday afternoon classes to analyze the morning's sermon and "read diligently" in the Old and New Testaments. Hymns, prayers and meditation would precede classes each weekday morning and afternoon, and teachers were to be present and "in a proper meditative mood." Each preceptor was to admonish his pupils to godly and moral conduct "conscientiously and zealously," to teach "with all the diligence and intellect at his command," and to constantly control the unruliness of his pupils in school, at church and in religious processions. "Observe all of your underlings," the 1667 code instructs, "at all times keeping them within view."

Even the enlightened pedagogy reveals unenlightened ulterior motives. Classroom leaders were instructed to "secretly inform their preceptor" of any negligence or mischief observed among their classmates. Competitive games had booby prizes "such as a crown of straw or a painted wooden donkey" as well as "awards and tokens of excellence" including a crown or scepter, and the classroom dunce was forced to wear the straw crown or strap the donkey around his neck. Such reward and punishment, the revised code notes, incites pupils to "the appropriate diligence and zeal, and intimidates against indifference or neglect." The Windsheim Gymnasium had fallen into "noticeable decline and ruin," the senate proclaimed, and strong measures were needed to recapture its lost splendor "for the glory of God and the welfare of the state." Martin Luther's battle had not yet been won in Windsheim. And with societal tensions as high as ever, efforts at reform were assuming proportions that today might be seen as verging on the hysterical.

2.4.2 A Curriculum for the Mind and the Soul
2.4.2.1 The Classical Tradition of Contemporary Lutheranism (With Pennsylvania Adaptations)

> He has some snatch of a scholar, and yet uses Latin very hardly, and lest it should accuse him, cuts it off in the midst [rather than openly display embarrassing deficiencies of case and tense] . . . Shreds of Latin and superannuated pedantry. Ser. Apology, p. 142. Papists' trusty Latin hides

so many of their cheats from the eyes of the common people. Julian, p. 154. Of the natural love to Latin, vide Spectator, no. 221.

-- "Latin"

The breaking a rule of grammar is more noticed than any error in life and conversation.

-- "Grammar"

Many [memories] are like sieves taken out of the water: all runs out . . . He reads it so long till he gets it without book . . . The lesson a scholar hath learned by heart and that in the book are still one and the same lesson.

-- "Memory"

Labour does strengthen and refine our brains;
But those who take no pains, shall have no gains.

-- Epigram 2321.2

Vainly seeking to crop the lavish blossom of youth down to a tight pistil of Lutheran virtue, the Windsheim senate also demonstrated that its Gymnasium pupils were true sons of Franconia, little human beings whose vitality and exuberance flowed unchecked regardless of time or place. It's prohibitions responded to actual conduct. The boys of Windsheim, they imply, knew riotous hours of play in field, forest and stream, and resisted the uninspired lines and boxes of school experience. Ranged in rows of benches or desks, meticulously penning columns of letters and numbers within the neat margins of their copybooks, they naturally conspired with their classmates to break the routine and enliven the atmosphere. At the same time, however, convinced that education was more or less synonymous with compulsion, they quickly responded to the gruff proddings of their harassed teachers – and absorbed a demanding curriculum.

In Windsheim, a city with limited resources and a competitive spirit, the future of most upper-class families depended upon the academic achievement of their sons. Although rank and privilege may have encouraged special treatment in a few instances, the boys generally accepted, freely or grudgingly, the duties as well as the prerogatives of their social position, and at the Gymnasium – where classes grew smaller as the boys advanced – learning energetically was a boy's primary duty. Ambiguously encouraging and checking learned arrogance, the Lutheran Gymnasium instilled academic values of elitist perfectionism – values that constantly reminded the boys of their own imperfection – as well as religious values with an egalitarian strain. The boys learned the cleverness and wit that separated them from the "idiots or guild apprentices" of Windsheim, and they also learned to value – or at least to intone – biblical phrases about brotherly love and the grace of God for all mankind. This curricular blend left indelible traces upon the character of Franz Daniel Pastorius, and affected his conduct in Germany and America.

Young Pastorius learned to read and write German and to do arithmetic in the first-floor classroom, and was then promoted to the intermediate grades where he began his Latin schooling. [66] Since Windsheim and other cities had long since abandoned the trilingual education advanced by Luther and Melanchthon, Pastorius received little if any Greek instruction in Windsheim. He began learning Latin by reading, repeating, memorizing and analyzing short phrases. Even the early stages demanded intellectual discipline. Pastorius and his classmates were judged on their ability to recall vocabulary items, sort out syntax, assign case and number, identify tense and mood. Like many of his contemporaries, Pastorius probably beamed with pride when encouraged for a correct response and cringed with shame and self-doubt when he erred. Negative incentives may have overwhelmed the slow learners, but the clever boys gradually found strategies to win the "carrot" and avoid the "stick."

The discipline of Latin remained the mainstay of Pastorius' Windsheim education. Grammatical analysis expanded as the phrases increased in length and complexity. Pastorius memorized the precepts of grammar, and learned to interpret the Latin phrases as examples of the precepts. He copied verse and prose models from Classical and Renaissance Latin authors into his exercise books, and imitated them in his writing practice which, completing the cycle, demonstrated the precepts of grammar anew. He was also trained to speak and debate from models of Latin eloquence, for his education emphasized both literacy and rhetorical skill. The process was tiresomely pedantic, but productive after its fashion. All advanced pupils learned to speak with an awareness of grace and decorum and to write prose and poetry more or less like the models they read from the classics, and they all absorbed a classical European heritage in the process. The content of Latin – in proverbs, aphorisms, epigrams, verse stanzas, Bible readings and, in advanced lessons, treatises on history and philosophy – was as important as its form.

Although the learnedness of Pastorius' university and Pennsylvania years reveals a broader classicism, the Latin texts selected for Gymnasium lessons emphasized biblical values and avoided or reinterpreted the pagan elements of Greek and Roman culture. The myths of Ovid's *Metamorphoses*, Lutheran humanists maintained, were rich symbols of God's Grace and Wrath, vivid testimony that He rewards the just and punishes the wicked. The Lutheran humanism Pastorius learned in Windsheim taught him to appreciate the classics for the eloquence they contained and the Christian morality they displayed. Latin texts were taught along with music and the Lutheran catechism, and for much the same reason. Bible verses, instrumental music and song, and the classics all mirrored the fullness of God's creation. They were examples of His grand precepts. Imitating their grace and truth, Godly pupils demonstrated the order and certainty of the Grammar of Life.

For pupils like Pastorius, delight in language and a search for universal truth merged with and then supplanted the external compulsions of the Gymnasium, yielding a personal sense of grace and order, and the deep satisfaction of classical attainments shared with other learned men, attainments that also served as a badge of social distinction. Pastorius frequently demonstrated this satisfaction in Pennsylvania; he circulated collections of poetry and of emblems and their predominantly Latin mottoes, gave William Penn a learned compendium entitled "A Few Onomastical Considerations" (described on page 252, n. 10), and wrote a fellow graduate of the Windsheim Gymnasium at least one Latin letter rich in classical allusions and resonances of word and phrase that can only be fully appreciated by other classical scholars. [67]

Adapting old-fashioned learned exhibitionism to his Pennsylvania surroundings, he composed numerous Latin emblematical mottoes for his flowers, herbs and vegetables, and displayed them in his Germantown garden (Poem 241 indicates), but he complains that many of his visitors were unprepared for Latin mottoes or learned repartee: "But with our young Gentry the Latin being scarce / Ask 'em a Question: they may term it a Farce." Thus in numerous instances his garden adornments (or "Emblematical Merriments," as he calls them) were more likely to cause frustration or embarrassment than the amusement or delight that would otherwise have fostered learned camaraderie among the gardener-poet and his callers.

Yet his classical learnedness repeatedly drew respect and admiration particularly among the Quaker elite of Philadelphia. When William Penn visited the temporary home Pastorius had built shortly after arriving in Philadelphia, for example, Penn read the inscription above the door and burst out laughing (*Beschreibung Pa.*, p. 23). It read: "Parva domus sed amica bonis, procul este prophani" or "It's a little house but welcoming to good people: profane men, keep your distance." Penn, who rarely laughed, got the allusion to Virgil's *Aeneid* and could appreciate the incongruity of this line of graceful Latin verse on a crudely-built, squat cottage (its entrance half above ground and half below) with windows made of oil-soaked paper for lack of glass. (It was a line Pastorius had copied from a house in Paris on his grand tour a year or so earlier.) In the *Aeneid* (Book 6), the Cumaean Sibyl tells Aeneas how to descend to the Underworld and then cries "procul, o procul este prophani" ("profane men, keep your distance") as priests make sacrifices to the chthonic gods. [68]

Aeneas' descent to the Underworld was a witty allusion well suited to Pastorius' cave-like cottage, and it might also have seemed analogous to the arduous tasks of settling the wilderness Pastorius and Penn confronted together in 1683. Penn and numerous fellow Pennsylvanians (among them Thomas Lloyd, Griffith Owen, Samuel Preston, Richard Hill, Christopher Witt and James Logan) clearly appreciated Pastorius' humanist learning and wit.

All the same, Pastorius admitted that Latin was difficult to learn, and that the learned often flaunted their knowledge of it, but he encouraged his son Johann Samuel to learn "at least a little Latin" along with other academic skills in order to enjoy modest success as an independent tradesman (Poem 55). (He encouraged his younger son Heinrich to learn French, giving him a grammar of French written in English.) [69] In Poem 364, penned into the Latin-English dictionary he bought in London to learn English, he describes "learn[ing] to comprehend our Canting Scholars' Rattle" (i.e., Latin speech) as sailing through an "Ocean of Words ... / Through twice four Parts of Speech, and many Cases" to arrive at "old Latium" or "the Land of Labour." He frequently versified in Latin (ironically deprecated, in "A Few Onomastical Considerations," as his "Latin poetical jingling and tingling"), and recalled Latin phrases and proverbs to suit virtually any context, but he reflected an Anglo-American trend toward monolingualism – and increased literacy – in his preference for English books (which became the source and subject of his "Alphabetical Hive") even when he had ready access to Latin originals.

Although he owned and consulted the collected writings of Seneca in the Latin *Opera*, for example, he read, with relish and deep appreciation, the English translation of Seneca's *Morals* by Roger L'Estrange. He compiled extensively from this translation, and, in Poem 80, praises the rhetorical accomplishments of the essayist Sir William Temple, the unnamed author of *The Turkish Spy* (apparently Giovanni Paolo Marana) and L'Estrange, three skilled writers who "Our English tongue thus amplify, / That great and small may learn thereby." Literacy is an unadulterated "Delight in Books" as well as "the Art of true Levelling," he notes in Poem 35: "Delight in books, for books do bring / Poor men to learn most every thing," and such knowledge provides the only real weapon

> to fling
> On waspish men (who taking wing
> Surround us) that they cannot Sting.

Similar considerations led him to translate passages from Dutch and Latin texts for English compilation in the "Beehive" (among them the item on banishment from Johann Valentin Andreae's Latin *Menippus* quoted, in Pastorius' translation, on page 35). His poetry and scholarship thus reveal an essentially democratic impetus.

2.4.2.2 Divining Lighthouse of Practical Philosophy: Rector Schumberg's Lessons in Ethics and Politics

> Beauty, like peach trees, her bloss'ms soon casts,
> But virtue's golden fruit for evermore lasts.
> -- Epigram 40

> This world is his [a philosopher's] book, his study, his university. He cloisters not his meditations in the narrow darkness of a room . . . Aristotle, the oracle of philosophy to these very times. Culpeper, p. 451. To steer by the compass of right reason, not by the winds of deluding *sophisius* [sophistry]. Every true Christian is a philosopher (a lover of wisdom), and yet abhorring that philosophy and vain deceit after the tradition of men and rudiments of this world . . . Keith, <u>Reexam.</u>, p. 41.
> -- "Philosophy"

> Houses of clay, the houses of our minds, the most curious structure of the world; a living, walking tabernacle. Max[ims].
> -- "Body"

> Beyond the golden mean strive not to go;
> His wants are boundless, whose desires are so.
> -- Epigram 36

Shying away from the compulsions of his youth, Pastorius never fully or accurately described his Gymnasium education, but he did include one sentence on the subject when he wrote his brief autobiography in "Genealogia Pastoriana" "above 30 years" after leaving Germany – between 1714 and his death at the age of 68 in December, 1719, or January, 1720:

> In Win[d]sheim I had a good Schooling, & mostly twenty or more young Earls, Baronets & Noblemens Children for Schoolfellows, there being then an excellent Rector of the Gymnasium by name Tobias Schumberg, a Hungarian by birth, who could speak almost no [high] Dutch [i.e., German], so that it was not allowed, to use any other language but Latin, &c.

Here Pastorius provides an enigmatic "&c." (or "et cetera") to substitute for all he leaves unsaid, and thus evades and misinterprets his youthful experience. He distances himself from his schoolmates by ascribing them to the nobility although most of them were, like himself, the sons of influential but untitled burghers (merchants, lawyers and clergymen). He also implies that Rector Schumberg ran the school during the nine years he attended even though Schumberg first arrived in Windsheim a year before he graduated. In effect, Pastorius ignores his first eight years of Gymnasium education while describing his "good schooling" under this "excellent Rector," thus accentuating the concluding year of his Windsheim education, when he was refining his scholarly habits and clarifying his values under an educator who was then considered liberal, and whose moral outlook influenced the ethical choices that led Pastorius to turn his back on Windsheim a decade later as a young attorney. In Poem 396 (quoted on page 88), he indicates that he learned more "bad" than "good" from the teachers of his earlier years.

Pastorius' recollections to the contrary, Schumberg spoke German well enough but insisted his pupils use Latin in the classroom, affirming Windsheim policy and the "direct method" of foreign-language teaching advocated by the educational reformers Wolfgang Ratke (1571-1635) and Johannes Amos Comenius (1592-1671), the latter of whom was the author of four volumes later owned by Pastorius. [70] The son of expatriate Germans living in Hungary, Schumberg had studied philosophy and law at German universities and won a reputation for his liberal and pious views before he was hired to run the Windsheim Gymnasium, predominantly at the instigation of Melchior Adam Pastorius. Schumberg's progressive friends included Johann Michael Dilherr (1604-69), Nürnberg's school and church superintendent, whose church reform movement contributed to the birth of Lutheran Pietism around 1675, and the jurist Veit Ludwig von Seckendorf, whose writings – including *Teutscher Fürstenstaat*, 1656 (The German Princely State) – confirmed the absolutist rights of the prince but argued that each lord had an obligation to serve the welfare of the community rather than his own private or dynastic ambitions. A pragmatic scholar, Schumberg won a seat on the Windsheim senate after six years at the Gymnasium, enabling him to resign as rector a year later; he also held office as supervisor of education and, late in life, burgomaster of Windsheim.

His teaching and writing reveal a love of learning, and strict authoritarianism compensating for basic insecurities, a combination typical of the age. He held Latin rhetoric contests in the classroom, and invited the public to Latin debates and comedies performed by his advanced pupils – "heathen comedies," some narrow-minded citizens claimed, that were corrupting the morality of Windsheim's youth. His authoritarianism, apparent in his Latin textbook *Pharus divina philosophiae practicae*, 1663 (Divining Lighthouse of Practical Philosophy), seems to have contributed, within his own family, to compulsions that could only be held in check as long as Schumberg himself was exercising familial authority. When he died in 1713, his son Johann Samuel, then an esteemed Windsheim senator, became involved in "a spectacular affair" with the wife of a Windsheim citizen that ended in the senator's disgrace and ultimate defeat far from home in Schaffhausen, Switzerland, and Vienna.

Schumberg ordered the second edition of his Latin textbook on practical philosophy when he moved to Windsheim in 1667, evidence that he used this advanced text for the instruction Pastorius received from him in 1667-68. A typical Lutheran humanist textbook, the 260-page volume consists of 49 chapters on ethics, economics and government, each including basic definitions, illustrative aphorisms and a list of guiding questions and answers along with *exempla* from history and readings from the Bible and from a broad range of classical Latin and Greek authors (all in Latin). [71] Seeking the golden mean of Christian virtue between perilous extremes of defective and excessive temperament in the individual and society, Schumberg applies scholastic logic and the teachings of Aristotle to the moral choices of everyday existence but avoids the abstruse Aristotelian sophistries later ridiculed by Pastorius, who also praises Aristotelian moderation in poetry like his early Epigram 36 (quoted above) and the opening couplet of Poem 81, attached to the weaver's loom he bought his son John Samuel in 1707:

My shuttle through the middle flies,
Let all men shun extremities.

Schumberg fosters youthful idealism, encouraging virtuous friendships in language echoed in the "Alphabetical Hive," and provides ethical advice similar to that espoused by Pastorius in Pennsylvania. Analyzing the economic activities of the extended family in simple and complex societies, for example, he praises agrarian virtues, opposes the acquisition of wealth, and warns against earning one's living at the expense of others. Nevertheless, the tedious and repetitive pedantry of this textbook demands the exaggerated diligence typical of Gymnasium and university training in the seventeenth century. Schumberg accepts the Scriptures and the classics as venerable authorities, and expects dedication to them. As the book's emblematic frontispiece indicates, the "Lighthouse" of practical philosophy illumines the "Arduous Path to Virtue" ("Ardua Virtutis Via"), and diligent pupils followed this narrow and lonely path toward its distant goal – an ephemeral castle high on a coastal hill in this view of sea and shore – rather than enjoying the worldly pleasures of their less dedicated peers, a number of whom can be seen feasting and lazing about on an expansive and inviting lawn or meadow in the foreground of the emblem.

Despite the certitudes of faith and knowledge, Schumberg, in his analysis of government, reveals deep uncertainties that could only be assuaged with irrational appeals to authority. He presents a double vision of hope and despair, the prospect of virtuous monarchies, aristocracies and democracies generating peace and prosperity for all, or – transformed into tyrannies, oligarchies and ochlocracies – inducing general strife and destruction. The power of government, Schumberg indicates, is awesome, its balance precarious, its mechanisms complicated. In a chapter "On the Composition of Society," he presents a list of 23 basic definitions (longer than any other), but then metaphorically confesses (quoting Psalms 127, 1b) that scrutinizing or running governments transcends human limits: "Except the Lord keep the city, the watchman waketh in vain."

Contrasts between political reality and Schumberg's ideals help to explain this intellectual impotence. In these basic definitions he states that the people form a government through honorable association, that government provides for the common welfare, and that the affairs of state are decided with the consent of the majority, but he elsewhere ignores these principles and accepts radical compromises demanded by the age, such as this endorsement of 'the lesser evil' in a chapter on governmental administration: "The political conditions in a state with a bad emperor and good counselors are more tolerable than in a state with a good emperor and bad counselors." Despite this bleak reality – or indeed because of it – Schumberg encourages his pupils with instruction on the virtues of good leaders, including piety, authority, compassion and prudence, and describes well-educated leaders as mediating between the prince and the populace, in principle governing fairly. Aware that the principle is often violated, he cites Isaiah 10, 1-3, presumably as a warning to his pupils, future leaders of church and state:

> Woe to those who decree iniquitous decrees, and ... turn aside the needy from justice ... What will you do on the day of punishment ... ? To whom will you flee for help, and where will you leave your wealth?

Increasingly, though, he alludes to potential or imminent disorder that can be averted only by unqualified submission and obedience. In a chapter "On Subjection or Homage" he defines obedience as that which keeps the state from "degenerating into confusion," and he twice warns the citizens to show their political superiors "obedience, love, honor and reverence, and of course to pay their taxes" – prerequisites, he writes, for public order. In a chapter "On the Causes of Corruption and Overthrow of the State" he identifies "secondary causes" in the behavior of the populace and of governmental leaders. Magistrates or senators contribute to the state's downfall by administering the law unjustly, by bickering among themselves, by acting out of ambition and avarice, or by abdicating office inopportunely. Secondary causes involving violations of public discipline include laxity in religious worship, idolatry, blasphemy, perjury, "confusion" of the sexual appetites, arrogance and extravagance, and oppressive poverty. Ultimately, though, Schumberg attributes the primary causes of political "annihilation" to "God's wrath and justice" and to "malignant aspects and influences of the constellations." "Religion is the basis and foundation of the state," he intones here. "Comets, eclipses and earthquakes portend future mutations in the empire."

Young Franz Daniel Pastorius thus encountered in his Windsheim schooling some of the insecurities of the age contributing to his own sense of unease or hysteria as he set off for America over a decade later. He also derived some of his moral fervor and awareness of governmental complexity from Schumberg's lessons in ethics and politics even though he later recognized that any system obliging the populace to obey its leaders under all circumstances places no effective limits on government or the abuse of governmental authority, a logical flaw of Schumberg's textbook arguments. Reflecting Quaker influence (especially that of the "peace testimony"), Pastorius categorically denies Schumberg's authoritarianism in Pennsylvania writings like "The matter of Taxes & Contributions briefly Examined," which supports nonviolent resistance to government, including refusing to pay taxes levied for purposes in "Violation of our Conscience" even if such refusal could lead to expropriation of personal property – an attitude indicating the relative liberality of Pennsylvania government (he anticipates expropriation rather than imprisonment) and presaging the civil disobedience of individuals like Henry David Thoreau.

Nevertheless, Pastorius twice expressed his appreciation for the guidance and training Schumberg gave him as a youth, and presumably for moral support during the family and community crisis of 1676-79. He dedicated a 244-page compendium of ecclesiastical history to Schumberg when he had it published in 1690, and in 1693 he sent his former schoolmaster a scholarly Latin poem entitled "De Mundi Vanitate" (Of the Vanities of the World), noting that Death claims all men, both the ancients and the moderns, including proudly courageous soldiers, the learned who seek the favor of their mighty lords, and the princes who live off the sweat of their subjects – and that Christ offers eternal joy to the repentant. [73] Through the poem's dexterity of rhyme, meter and word-play and its classical allusion, Pastorius pays tribute to the traditions Schumberg espoused, but he also distances himself from these traditions with his deep irony and his deep religious feeling, which convey in this rich and lively poem a genuine sense of renunciation toward the social order – the orderliness that was affirmed at the Windsheim Gymnasium, but which Pastorius eventually held responsible for unchristian excesses among the elite of Europe.

2.5 Family Life and Upbringing
2.5.1 Dispersal of the Extended Family

> If [as head of the household] thou wouldst be happy and easy in thy family, above all things observe discipline. Max[im] 50. That all in it may know their duty; and there be a time and place for every thing. Idem 51. Suppress tales in the general; but where a matter requires notice, encourage the complaint, and right the aggrieved. Idem 183. Wishers and woulders are no good householders.
>
> -- "OEconomy"

"The father is the foremost member of the family, governing family matters as a monarch" does the state, Tobias Schumberg writes in *Pharus divina philosophiae practicae*, reflecting the values that prevailed in the Pastorius home. [75] While Gymnasium experience and daily life in Windsheim each played a key role in forming Franz Daniel's adult character, the unusual circumstances of his family life were just as basic. This was the factor that, in subsequent years, exacerbated the difficulties young Pastorius had in applying the widely-held concepts of filial obedience towards paternal authority.

Franz Daniel was the one youth in Schumberg's third-floor Gymnasium classroom in 1667-68 who came from a family that did not fit the predominant pattern of family structure in Windsheim society. Most upper-class families had closely-knit ties and long-standing traditions. Sons, fathers and grandfathers affirmed the continuity of the family, and they helped it acquire the wealth and position that was passed from one generation to the next. The extended family was, as Schumberg indicates in the economic lessons of *Pharus divina philosophiae practicae*, the basic unit of social, economic and political life, and its very size and heterogeneity provided a degree of egalitarianism to offset the authority of the fathers who governed its affairs.

A typical son in Windsheim, as in traditional families everywhere, could turn any number of potential family rivalries to his advantage if he felt pressured by his own father – be it those involving the grandmother and aunts who watched over personal conduct, buffered sharp emotions and consoled hurt pride, the uncles who anxiously counseled with each other and consented to every decision affecting their common weal, or the grandfather who exercised authority over the father. As the only son in an isolated nuclear family, and with three stepmothers instead of a mother, Franz Daniel Pastorius lacked the familial buffer zone that usually modulated the relations of father and son. Observing typical elitist contradictions in his father's personal conduct, Franz Daniel increasingly felt this lack as he grew to maturity.

Pastorius reveals his awareness of familial isolation in "Genealogia Pastoriana" (Appendix I), the document containing, along with autobiographical recollections, descriptions of his father, mother, grandfather and other family members. As a Protestant convert, Melchior Adam was the black sheep of his Roman Catholic family, and Franz Daniel was thus alienated from the four uncles and two aunts – his father's brothers and sisters – who would have normally helped create his sense of family identity. Franz Daniel was never able to attend any Pastorius family gatherings, and two isolated encounters with his relatives only served to emphasize the gulf between his life and theirs. He met his uncle Johann Augustin, the influential

Hapsburg official who had supervised Melchior Adam's legal training years earlier in Rome,

> before I was seven Years of age, he then sojourning for a few weeks at Sommerhausen, where (as a very Zealous Papist, together with a Couple of fi[e]ry Jesuits), he laboured hard to bring my Father back to the Roman Church; but seeing his endeavours fruitless, my s[ai]d Uncle dis[in]herited his own Brother & me too; not withstanding he himself was never married, & had gotten a deal of Wealth by his Lawyership both at the Court of Rome, & that of the Elector of Mentz [Mainz], as also a fast [vast] Estate in Hungary, the Emperour having given him the Title of a Baron, by the Name of Augustin von Hirthenfels.

On his way to study law at Jena University sixteen years later, Franz Daniel had his only other encounter with any of his father's relatives when he briefly visited his Aunt Rebecca, a Catholic nun living in a cloister at Erfurt, his father's native city. He barely got to speak to his aunt, a meek woman of few words, for the visit took place in the company of "an ancient Canonicus" employed at the Erfurt cathedral who all the while held "many pretty Discourses" with young Pastorius, during one of which the canon described "this harmless Nun (pointing to my sd Aunt)" as one of those who receive but little of "the Sundry Gifts which God bestows upon his Creatures." Indulging in a theological joke, Pastorius notes, "And really, She look'd to be extreme Innocent, & if not meriting Heaven through her self-conceited Good Works, I thought, it would be pity she should deserve Hell." Even if he was essentially sympathetic toward his aunt, young Franz Daniel considered her good works "self-conceited" because he accepted Luther's emphasis on grace over works, and a similar Protestant bias is also evident in his brief mention of his Uncle "Caspar, who became a Popish Priest, & so a Voluntary Eunuch, &c."

At home in a Lutheran community, young Pastorius could not easily comprehend the lives or values of the relatives who lived in the environment of Catholic monasteries, churches and courts, and he was thus disinherited not only from baronial estates and fortunes but also from the security and identity a family tradition would have given him. With no paternal cousins, aunts, uncles and grandparents around, he found his identity to an unusual extent through his father, the constant factor in his upbringing. Even the influence of his stepmothers contributed to the tensions that eventually developed between father and son.

2.5.2 Stepmothers within the Nuclear Family

> He that begets thee owns thee, and has a natural right over thee. Max[im] 159. Next to God thy parents, next to them the magistrate. Idem 160. Rebellion in children was therefore made death by God's law [Exod. 21:15]; and the next sin to idolatry, which is renouncing of God, the great parent of all. Idem 162. Obedience to parents is not only our duty but our interest; we receive our life from them, and prolong it by obeying them [Exod. 20,12]: for obedience is the first commandment with promise [i.e., that of long life]. Idem 163.
>
> -- "Parents"

Although Franz Daniel writes approvingly of his mother and his second stepmother in "Genealogia Pastoriana," he does not characterize his first stepmother, whom he refers to merely as Melchior Adam's "Second Wife Eve Margaret, the youngest daughter of Johannes Gelchsheimer J[uris] U[triusque] D[octor (i.e, doctor of civil and canon law)] & Counsellor of the Imperial City of Win[d]sheim in Franck-

enland [or Franconia] afores[ai]d." In his only other reference to her, he lists the vital statistics of births and deaths in the family, ending with this cool recollection:
> Anno 1661. the 28th of May she his sd wife being great with young & not able to bring forth, a dead male-child was cut or ripped out of her belly, & the next ensuing 11th of June she also died herself.

Melchior Adam, equally restrained in a third-person journal entry, indicates that he began his relationship with Eva Margareta as a marriage of convenience giving him access to governmental position in Windsheim:
> Since he was not willing . . . to stay on indefinitely with his son Francisco Daniele in Sommerhausen, he married Eva Marageta, maiden daughter of the right honorable and very learned gentleman Johann Gelchsheimer, doctor of the laws and the duly-appointed counsel of the Holy Roman Imperial City of Windsheim, on Feb. 9, 1658. [76]

With his flexible German syntax, Melchior Adam places the name and titles of his father-in-law in front of "married Eva Margareta, maiden daughter," emphasizing the family connection rather than the personal relationship. Further notations record births and deaths, and report that he won his father-in-law's seat on the Windsheim senate, but he does not comment on Eva Margareta's personality or character. Commemorating her death in a Latin verse anagram, "Passa Amara Ergo Initetur," he notes that Christ's cross imaged and resolved her worldly sorrows.

With their reticence about Eva Margareta, both father and son might well have been indicating that she was less than an ideal mother and wife, in which case Melchior Adam's subsequent comment that he enjoyed "a peaceful marriage" with his third wife would stand in contrast to his marital experience with the youngest daughter of one of Windsheim's most influential citizens. The elder Pastorius decided, at any rate, to ignore youth and station as criteria in selecting the woman who reared his son during most of their family life in Windsheim.

The deaths of Eva Margareta and her infant children "practically intimidated him from marrying again," Melchior Adam writes, yet it would have been "rather difficult" to raise Franz Daniel on his own. (The demands of his multifaceted career, in fact, would have made it virtually impossible.) So he resolved to
> seek a mature matron and hard-working housekeeper with the help of whom he would be able to give his son a proper upbringing. On 21 January 1662, he therefore married the very virtuous and honorable Barbara Greulich, née Heider, a [56-year-old] widow from Hüttenheim [a village 22 kilometers from Windsheim], and lived with her in a peaceful marriage for 12 years and 8 weeks, but without any heirs. She died in God's peace 26 March anno 1674. She was a pious matron, well read in the Holy Scriptures, to whose memory the following rhymes are dedicated: [In four stanzas, the persona of the deceased matron notes that pain and anxiety precede a longing for true repentance and criticizes the haughtiness and hypocrisy of nominal Christians.] [77]

Franz Daniel reports, in "Genealogia Pastoriana," that Melchior Adam
> took his Third Wife Barbara . . . who of her former Husband had one Daughter & three Sons, viz. Michael, Erasmus and Johannes, who at my Departure out of Germany had every one of 'em their Wives & Children living at Hüttenheim, a matter of three Dutch miles from Win[d]sheim. She was a noble, kind & very loving Mother in Law [sic] to me, dying the 26th of March in the year 1674 and never bore any Child to my sd Father.

Marrying a matronly housekeeper from a village beyond Windsheim just two and a half years after moving to the city, Melchior Adam ignored the custom of intermarrying within upper-class Windsheim society and signaled his distrust of its predominant values at the very time he was energetically establishing himself as one of its most competent and respected leaders. [78] Although Melchior Adam emphasizes Barbara Greulich's moral virtue and housewifely industry, Franz Daniel recalls what really mattered to him as a boy of ten growing up in Windsheim – her children, who became his relatives, too, and her warm maternal love for him, a double fulfillment of his deep Franconian desire for close relationships. The prominence he gives to her children in this brief entry and his continuing awareness of them years after her death supports this interpretation, even if the children were adults in Hüttenheim when their mother married his father. (He seems to have stayed in touch with them even after moving to Frankfurt in 1679.)

Her warmth and fortitude, furthermore, presumably informed their lives just as her personality reflected the mores of rural Hüttenheim, a small Franconian village that offered a simple and rugged existence governed more by the rhythms of nature than by the social conventions of a city like Windsheim. Since neither Franz Daniel nor Melchior Adam reports the name or profession of Barbara Greulich's father or former husband – despite Melchior Adam's eagerness to state ranks and titles – her village background apparently reflected relatively modest social station and antecedents (though consonant with the literacy of a Bible reader). Influenced by this stepmother and her rural environment, young Pastorius could learn to appreciate biblical decency and simplicity as elements of daily experience and not merely as doctrinal abstractions in learned Lutheran sermons. Pastorius emphasizes this distinction by describing the corrective influence his home life had on the unchristian "wit" of Gymnasium schoolmasters – a description immediately following that of childbirth and suckling in the commemorative verse addressed to the daughters of Deputy Governor Thomas Lloyd (Poem 396):

> For, when we grew some years, discerning sad from glad,
> They sent us to the school, where we learn'd good and bad:
> More of the last than first – Had not our parents' skill
> Surpass'd our masters' wit, how ill, alas! how ill
> Would things still be with us? Had God withheld his Light,
> We were as blind as moles; but thanks to Him! our sight
> Increased with our age: Wherefore I humbly bless
> The Fountain of this gift, the Sun of Righteousness . . .

Even as a child in Germany, Pastorius claims in retrospect, he was blessed with God's "Light," saved from blindness, given "sight". ("Christ's divine light" is a reiterated theme of his Pennsylvania theology.) Barbara Greulich obviously played a key role in his formative years, which helps to explain his reaction to her death years later (described in Chapter 3).

As Melchior Adam indicates in his journal entry, marrying Barbara Greulich was his attempt to influence Franz Daniel's upbringing among an elite whose pride and selfishness he repeatedly criticizes in his poetry and meditative writings. By giving Franz Daniel an identity that transcended upper-class Windsheim values, he could hope to raise a son who would combine moral sensitivity and intellectual prowess, a responsible elitist who would perpetuate the family's worldly existence and assure its spiritual salvation. Barbara Greulich certainly met his expectations of her, giving his son moral and emotional sustenance. But at some point in their marriage – he was 37 when they wed and 49 when she died at the age of 68 – he seems to have realized that his sense of paternal duty was denying him some of the nuptial joys and fulfillments he might otherwise have known. As the years of all too peaceful domesticity accumulated, what must have been the painful disappointments of his marriage to young Eva Margareta receded in memory even as he began to enjoy the advantages of his widening social perspectives.

During these years Melchior Adam rose in stature as he gained ever more local authority, including the office of burgomaster in 1670, and began representing Windsheim in diplomatic gatherings throughout Franconia, making influential friendships, and socializing in the courtly and upper-class circles of Bayreuth and Nürnberg, where he also met a number of spirited and charming young ladies, at least one of whom was susceptible to his worldly finesse. Within weeks of his matronly wife's death in 1674, the elder Pastorius began courting 20-year-old Dorothea Esther Volckmann of Bayreuth, whose family included several of Franconia's most esteemed men of learning and station. He soon began a robust family life with her as his fourth wife, fathering four healthy children, yet the circumstances of his courtship and marriage underscored the unresolved tensions between worldly and spiritual values in Melchior Adam's life – tensions that, by that time, had become glaringly obvious to his son Franz Daniel.

2.5.3   Father and Son

2.5.3.1   The Warm Affection and Stylized Formalities of Franz Daniel's Correspondence

> A child, when the smart of the rod is past, smiles on his beater . . . Children increase the cares of life, but they mitigate the remembrance of death. Like sire, like son. A chip of[f] the old block. An ill bird, a worse egg. If thou wouldst be obeyed being a father, being a son be obedient. Max[im] 158.   Make not thy father's heart to bleed,
> Thy children will revenge the deed. . . .
> Children one of God's chief blessings. <u>Closet</u>, p. 175.
>
> -- "Child"

Unaware of these tensions in his earliest experience, Franz Daniel loved and was loved with all the warmth and spontaneity befitting his vital Franconian environment. It was in fact the depth of his love and respect for Melchior Adam that colored his growing awareness of tension and made his inevitable reactions – youthful rebellion and, ultimately, lifelong separation – so painful. "I bid my father the farewell befitting a child," 31-year-old Pastorius wrote aboard ship for Pennsylvania in 1683, "again thanking him obediently for all the love and devotion he has so abundantly given me," and he stated his childish affection for Melchior Adam with increasing fervor over the years. [79]

"Let us ... embrace each other in hearty affection as one in Christ, which neither the physical distance between us nor the danger of pirates at sea [who might have intercepted and destroyed Pastorius' letter] nor any other circumstances can prevent," he wrote in 1691, explaining that as a 40-year-old father he could better appreciate "all the love, devotion and good deeds [my father] demonstrated toward me" as a child, and more completely understand the proverb, *"amorem descendere potius quam ascendere,"* or "love descends [from parent to child] more than it ascends," and he labeled his father's expressed desire to do more for him in the future "a more than profuse affect of his paternal love." He felt "incomparable joy" to learn that his father and family were in good health in June, 1693, and, he reported in May, 1697, "I could not read" a newly-arrived letter "without shedding joyful tears of love." In March of the same year he wrote: "I can barely express the joy I felt to learn that my father is in good health ... since I had gradually lost all hope of seeing his worthy person in this world or receiving a few more syllables from the hand generously opened to me so often in the past."

Because of the unreliability of sea passage during a time of war in 1695, Franz Daniel "could not hope to receive many more letters from [my father's] worthy hand," but nevertheless "I childishly beg for more." Given the related meanings of the German word for 'beg' ['anhalten (um)'] – 'press,' 'hold on (to),' 'ask for (one's hand in marriage)' – and the context of the father's hand, this sentence suggests the image of a little child coyly begging his or her father ("Please, Daddy, please ..."), holding the father's hand in supplication until the favor is granted. Closing a letter in 1698, Franz Daniel evokes a spontaneous child's warm affection for a loving father: "I greet my father a thousand times through the air and kiss him with a child's hearty kisses."

Ignoring biographical evidence to the contrary, Franz Daniel portrays his father as a man of unadulterated virtue in "Genealogia Pastoriana," and thus indicates the great respect he still felt in his final years – or, more accurately, had by then regained – for the man who had seemed almost larger than life during his childhood. Franz Daniel's reluctance to acknowledge the poetic accomplishment of Melchior Adam merely demonstrates that this was the one area in which the son, a rival poet, could still feel threatened by the father's stature years after Melchior Adam's death:

> My dear and well-beloved Father ... was of a Settled & Composed Countenance, ... free from pride and affectation, courteous and affable to the poorest sort of men, cheerful sweet and pleasant in his discourses, not willing to give any offence to the very least in the company; a man of singular learning and divers languages, speaking Latin, Italian & French as perfect as his own Mother-tongue, given a little to Poetry, quick in Apprehension, sound in Judgment, slow to be provoked: a lover of pure Religion & Mystical Theologie, hating priestcraft & formalities; In his Lucubrations & Candle-light-Writings almost indefatigable, and as good a Lawyer as any needs to be, and never theless not Covetous, &c. but of a Spotless Reputation ...

His great respect for Melchior Adam begins to explain the discrepancy between the substance of the filial love Franz Daniel expressed and the style of expression he used in his letters to his father, or perhaps, more fundamentally, the ambiguity of this love itself. His epistolary outpourings of childish love and joy correspond to the reciprocated love Franz Daniel must have known as a young child with his father – innocently and unabashedly embracing, kissing and holding hands – just as the artificial formality of many passages in these letters reveals the influence of the conventions that transformed spontaneous filial love into obedience toward paternal authority and thus distanced sons from their fathers.

Bidding his father "the farewell befitting a child" ("kindgebührlichen Abschied") and "thanking him obediently" ("gehorsamer Dancksagung") aboard ship in 1683, Pastorius reveals this contrast between style and content or the ambiguity of his adult love. And he frequently addresses his father with similar formal expressions, sending him "the greetings fully expected of a child" ("kindschuldigster Gruß"), expressing his "genuine contestation that my soul is full of love, esteem and obligation toward you" ("wahrhafftiger Contestation, daß Meine Seele voll Lieb, Ehrerbietung und Diesntwilligkeit gegen Euch [ist]"), or beginning a letter with this cool formality: "At the present occasion, along with the rendering of my cordial love and respect, I cannot avoid briefly reporting on the good health of myself and my family ..." ("Bey gegenwärtiger Gelegenheit habe, nebst Abstattung meiner cordialen Lieb und Respects, nicht vorbey gekonnt meinen und der Meinigen guten Zustand kürtzlichen zu berichten ...") [80]

Franz Daniel repeatedly refers to Melchior Adam with phrases like "his honored person" ("dessen geehrte Person") or "his worthy hand" ("dessen werthen Hand"), and consistently uses the indirect form of address, "der Herr Vater," a formal substitute for direct address translated simply as "my father" in this study even though it combines the meaning of 'sir' and 'father' and could be translated as "my respected father," a level of formality rarely used within the family in English. In nearly two decades of recorded correspondence, he never directly addresses his father with the informal second-person singular pronoun 'du' ('dir'/'dich') or as Papa, Vati or Vater, the customary forms of informal and formal paternal address in German, but instead uses the stylized formality of "der Herr Vater" at all times.

Equally stilted in his salutations and complimentary closings, Pastorius uses formulas such as "My most beloved Father" ("Liebwerthester Herr Vater") and "My respected father's most truly obedient son" ("Des Herrn Vaters Treugehorsamster Sohn"). He closes a 1684 letter that, despite its polite formality, reads like a sermon against the sins of upper-class Europe – including those of Melchior Adam and his wife Dorothea Esther – with the reassuring phrase, "Des Herrn Vaters und Frau Mutter auch in America treugehorsamer Sohn," which translates, somewhat awkwardly, as "From my respected father and mother's son, [who remains] truly obedient even in America." Although he expresses himself formally throughout his correspondence, the degree of formality gradually decreased as he won distance from the complex emotions that had prompted his separation from Melchior Adam – just as the examples of warm affection quoted here were all written during the 1690s, more than a decade after he left Windsheim.

One exception proves, and elucidates, the rule of formality in Pastorius' correspondence. Writing his 1699 letter on behalf of six- and eight-year-old Heinrich and Johann Samuel (the last letter published in *Beschreibung Pennsylvaniae*), he decided that his Pennsylvania sons were entitled to use the informal pronoun 'du' ('you') when they informed Melchior Adam "we wish ... you were here" and "we would appreciate it if you would greet our dear cousins for us." This letter also contains ten instances of other informal or intimate second-person pronouns and adjectives (dich, dir, and dein as well as the plural euch), giving the entire letter the refreshingly direct and personal quality (elsewhere lacking in the correspondence) that can only be achieved with the everyday, down-to-earth simplicity of 'you' – and the especially informal or intimate German 'du,' differentiated as it is from the formal 'Sie.' After twenty years of separation (sixteen in Pennsylvania), Pastorius was finally able to abandon the strict formalities of his upbringing – not for himself, of course, but for the two boys who were growing up in the more relaxed and open society of early Pennsylvania.

How can Pastorius' stylized formality be reconciled with his genuine expression of filial love? The contrast reflects both his culture and his personality, the accumulated effects of childrearing as it was practiced in the upper-class homes of seventeenth century Germany and the particular experience of father and son during

Franz Daniel's formative years. Sensing the importance of these influences while studying and traveling in Europe, Pastorius began to record his culture's attitudes toward children, childrearing and the roles of fathers and sons in a literary album that reflects his own upbringing and illustrates the complexities of filial decision-making so crucial to his experience. His relationship with Melchior Adam – and his attitudes toward tradition and authority – can be defined with the help of this album and the biographical context of his youth and early adulthood in Windsheim.

2.5.3.2 A Cultural Album of Childrearing from the "Beehive"

> Aeneas carrying his Father upon his Shoulders: Digna Ciconia Laude. [Praised be the stork.]
> A Scholar on the back of winged Pegasus: Sic itur ad Astra. [This is the way to get to the stars (or to immortality).]
> -- "Emblematical Recreations"
> Father into thy hands I commenD my sPirit.
> -- "Symbola Onomastica," no.135 [from Luke 23,46]

Along with countless entries on topics such as childhood, discipline, fathers, love, obedience and sonship in his "Alphabetical Hive," the encyclopedic commonplace book of his American readings, Pastorius reveals his special interest in childrearing in the emblems and mottoes of "Emblematical Recreations" and the original and paraphrased sentences of "Symbola Onomastica," two compilations he bound together with the "Alphabetical Hive" in the huge manuscript known today as the "Beehive." In "Emblematical Recreations," Pastorius catalogued hundreds of emblems and mottoes from the art and architecture he observed on his European travels and from the emblem books he read in Europe and America, quoting emblem titles and mottoes verbatim and describing the untitled emblematic pictures with his own brief prose entries. (The actual images are not reproduced.) He also composed hundreds of "Symbola Onomastica" (onomastic "tokens" or "symbols"), brief prose and occasionally verse reflections, variously humorous or meditative, each of which contains the capitalized letters FDP, separated but in sequence (and sometimes repeated as a double or triple onomastic), thus identifying Pastorius' "onomastic" relationship to the idea it expresses. (The initials "stand in for" his name; creating the sentences with the initials properly placed was an intellectual pastime of his, a bit like doing acrostic or crossword puzzles.) [81]

Pastorius' album of childhood, gathered together from these sources, reflects the general experience of children as well as the cultural significance of childrearing in his age. The entries alluding to Virgil's *Aeneid* and Luke 23,46 (in the epigraph here) indicate the range of Pastorius' heritage and the depth and complexity of his own response to the meaning of the father-and-son relationship, just as the emblem of a scholar borne to the heavens or immortality upon the fabulous winged horse Pegasus, the darling of the Muses, shows the learned idealism – not wholly distinct from learned compulsion – that was expected to motivate aspiring sons in Pastorius' day.

The Aeneas emblem illustrates the episode described in the *Aeneid*, 2, 700-30. Fleeing Troy, Aeneas with his family and their ancestral gods carries his father Anchises to safety as he undertakes his epic task of founding Roman civilization. The motto "Digna Ciconia Laude" ("praised be the stork") refers to the stork as symbol of the obedient child in Roman mythology and as the bringer of babies in German folklore, commenting seriocomically on the role reversals implicit in Virgil's story: the heroic son must "bear" the burden of the father and "deliver" the tradition of the fathers into the world anew, thus assuring cultural continuity from one generation to the next. [82] In Sentence 135 from "Symbola Onomastica," Pastorius imbeds his initials into the dying words of Christ, the son of God, hanging on the cross at Calvary – the epitome of filial obedience and sacrifice – and thus indicates the motive force of Christian obedience in his personal life. These and other mythic images of filial sacrifice taught the child Franz Daniel to obey the Heavenly Father, which in terms of Christian precepts also meant obeying Melchior Adam Pastorius, and gave him a sense of idealism and self-sacrifice that was as spontaneous as his love for Melchior Adam and as universal as his understanding of God. Complementing the historical evidence of this study, Pastorius' emblems help to show how the process of cultural attainment could pervert idealism of this sort into the compulsions of an authoritarian upbringing.

Although a great variety of secular and biblical emblems define the context of childhood, it is the secular emblems that best describe or illumine the child's daily experience and growth. They demonstrate that the innocent child needs protection and guidance, that parental love involves both giving and controlling. Thus the child, in theory passive, receives protection and accepts guidance. His unbridled impulses are destructive, and he learns to control them by sacrificing natural desires and striving toward a future fulfillment he cannot yet perceive. He need not see, for his parental guide is blessed with vision, and he, in trust, may follow blindly. These are the lessons of childhood portrayed time and again in Pastorius' emblem catalogue.

The innocence of childhood embodies adult potential. A child with his drums, rattles and hobby-horses symbolizes the time of youth, tenderness, frailty: "A teneris." A child blowing soap bubbles is a "badge" of boyhood innocence. ("Bulla facit bullas.") Yet just as the husbandman sows, the seed "will yield fruit in its own time." ("Fructum dabit in ternpore suo.") An eaglet still too young to fly proclaims its futurity – "Ad sidera nascor," or "I grow toward the heavens" – and a lion's cub embodies an innocence it will soon lose: "Animus tener Se corpore prodit," or "The tender spirit forsakes the body." Children are pictured with mottoes announcing that strength of character matures with the body ("Vis animi cum corpore crescet"), that prudence or discretion cannot be expected before the child grows hair on his chin. ("Nec ante pilos prudentia rerum.") The smallness of the child is a matter of perspective, and childhood can be understood ("Parva videtur") in the image of "a great Ship afar off."

Parental security protects the child, and parental authority guides its potential. A dove feeding her young symbolizes the concern of the parent for its child. ("Hoc cura parentis.") A young halcyon in its nest proclaims, "I grow in (or spring forth from) loving peace" ("Nascor pacis amans"), illustrating the Greek myth in which Zeus stilled the sea winds for fourteen halcyon days while the birds were hatching in their nests at the water's edge. A mother, singing, rocks her child's cradle: "She brings peace to the restless." ("Parit irrequieta quietem.") "An old Man setting a young Tree" shows concern for the young. He is "creating a shady spot for his grandsons." ("Factura nepotibus umbrum.")

Security alone does not foster potential. Thus the parent is like the gardener who trims and bends the tree "from earliest youth on" ("a teneris") or prunes the superfluous branches from his vines. The enlightened branches know he does not act out of dislike or hate. ("Non tamen odit.") "We are sacrificed," they explain, "so that we may promulgate." ("Caduntur ut edant.") An artificially "suppressed" palm tree symbolizes growth in civilization, and its meanings are various: "Reshaped, I flourish anew. Bearing this burden, I grow green. Henceforth [I am] the cream of the crop. Glory through severity. Virtue thrives under a burden. You [i.e., the gardener] suppress, you do not destroy." ("Curvata resurgo. Sub mole viresco. Hinc robur. Ex duris gloria. Crescit sub pondere virtus. Premis, non perimis.") Imaging the aspirations of father and son, a valorous eagle holds his eaglet toward the sun. The lessons are manifold: "With my guidance. Getting used to [difficult tasks] from early youth on is productive. [The father is] the bearer [of tradition, of the son] (or giver of laws) under this heaven. When this [sun or son] shines (or becomes illustrious), I will be lifted up (or released or comforted). Thus does he imbibe of the celestial heights." ("Me duce. A teneris assuescere prodest. Hoc sidere lator. Illo splendente levabor. Ut caelestem combibat auram.")

To attain the eagle's grandeur or the palm tree's perfection, a child must control his natural impulses. Boys fighting each other behave "stupidly" ("Commutant stolide"); like some other boys observed throwing stones, their destructive impulses harm themselves and others. ("Ludere dum tentant, laeduntur.") They stand in contrast to the well-behaved sons portrayed with this verse motto: "Frome [sic] Knaben Gottes Gaben. /Glücklich sind, die solche haben." ("Pious boys are God's blessing; happy are those [parents] who have such.") An undisciplined child is like an unbridled horse, and a creature of this sort may be seen "throwing himself headlong down from the Brow of a Hill," inspiring the emblem writer to sophist irony: "Libertas Libertate perit," or "Liberty destroys liberty."

Keeping harmful impulses in check may require prodding. A bridle is pictured with the explanation, "It governs and improves." A rod or switch explains its raison d'etre, and concludes with a word of caution: "I punish those I love. This pain will benefit you in the future. Frequent beating generates considerable outcry (or noise)." ("Quos diligo castigo. Dolor hic tibi proderit olim. Multo fit clamor ab ictu.") A mother "whipping" her child explains, "I punish [because] he is not restrained." ("Castigo, ne castigatur.") A child who refuses to put his fingers into the flame of a burning candle has learned the hard lessons of restraint: "That which harms is instructive. Experience produces caution. This won't happen the same way twice." ("Quae nocent decent. Facit experientia cautum. Nec bis contingit eadem.") In "An hot Iron upon an Anvil" the flame and the hammer are implied as agents, metaphorically, in the painful process of shaping behavior and character. The iron, reluctantly accepting the heat and the pressure, cries: "À poco, à poco!" or "Just a little, just a little!"

Along with restraint, the aspiring child learns endurance, a virtue he will need to attain the adult goals provided for him. A child "swimming against the Stream in a tempestuous Sea" illustrates this virtue: "The spirit perseveres in spite of all." ("Animus tamen idem.") And the depiction of "some books in a funnel over a schoolboy's head" demonstrates its application: "Knowledge may flow (or pour) into the brain." ("Influat in cerebrum.") Amid the "flood" of knowledge, keeping one's neck above water does not come easy. "A child swimming upon bladders and bulrushes" bears the motto "Sublevat Ingenium," indicating that his life preserver is his own character, temperament or genius. The child swimming without bladders or bulrushes, on the other hand, demonstrates success. He is "sine cortice": "without a life preserver" and, in the Latin idiom, "on his own." For most pupils, however, the "sea" of knowledge seems, at least in the early stages, overwhelming. "A ship loaden [sic] with schoolboys" is captioned: "We are sailing for Latium [i.e., studying Latin], Our port [of debarkation] is in the unknown. In this sea we are hoping for (or looking forward to) the seashore." ("Tendimus in Latium. Portus in ignoto. Speramus in aequore litus.")

As the child becomes a schoolboy and then a university scholar, he accepts discipline and perseverance as mainstays of his existence. A verse inscription from a school portal or wall notes: "Arbeit, Zwang und Lehren / Bringt Kinder oft zu Ehren." ("Toil, compulsion and instruction often lead children to honors.") Holding a gong and a metal rod, a pupil indicates that many were governed by negative incentives rather than internalized values: "Force is needed to produce its tones. It slacks off (or does nothing) when the beating (or flogging) stops." ("Durch den Zwang komt der Klang. Sine verbere cessat.") A scholar holding a book and an oil lamp symbolizes the virtues of effort and alertness ("labor et vigilantia"). Another, bent over his lessons, anticipates the light at the end of the tunnel: "Erudition is acquired through practice (or familiarity). Some day recalling this activity will bring pleasure." ("Doctrina acquiritur usu. Olim meminisse juvabit.") To these two mottoes Pastorius adds, in the English of his American years: "My Book & Heart shall never part." "Emblematical Recreations" also includes a personalized emblem and motto showing him at one of his favorite Pennsylvania pastimes: "FDP and a good Book before him: Habet hic sua guadia pauper." ("In this he finds his own meager pleasures.")

Thus, confirming the evidence of his poetry and scholarship generally, these secular emblems indicate that Pastorius was one of the Gymnasium pupils who successfully completed a painful process of growth, internalizing intellectual values despite the rigors of scholarship, and discovering the rewards of liberating knowledge such as those implied in several dozen emblems of "Profane Histories and Fables" that pay tribute to classical philosophers, poets and kings, heroes and heroines, gods and goddesses. The Titan "Atlas bearing the heavens," enigmatic "Janus with two faces," lovely "Venus and her son [Cupid or Aeneas] warming their hands and feet at a fire," the bold voyager "Ulysses passing the Sirens," the beautiful "Adonis slain by a Boar," Zeus' accomplished daughter "Pallas [Athena], or Minerva, figuring forth or representing Wisdom, Knowledge, Arts and Wit," foolish King "Midas with a pair of Asses' ears," the fearless "Hercules Squeezing a Serpent in his Cradle," pragmatic "Alexander [the Great] cutting Gordius' Knot asunder" – these and similar emblems reflecting Pastorius' broad reading were part of the cultivated Pennsylvania life that culminated his German upbringing and fostered a relaxation of its compulsions.

Both biblical and secular emblems indicate the blend of idealism and compulsion involved in maturation. Biblical and classical stories are rich in narrative detail and mythic complexity, yet subject to simplistic interpretation. The heroic endeavor of a Ulysses or a Hercules might help a youth through his tedious academic labors, just as the obedience of Isaac might suggest filial compliance at all costs. Numerous biblical emblems in "Emblematical Recreations" reveal deeply-ingrained attitudes toward authority that complicated Pastorius' Franconian upbringing. They include didactic emblems illustrating filial virtues and vices along with dramatic cameos alluding to the emotions that bound Old Testament fathers and sons.

"Eli and his wicked Sons," an emblem depicting the story in 1 Samuel 2 and 3, illustrates the father's responsibility for the conduct of his sons during their childhood and beyond. God tells young Samuel in a dream, "I will judge [Eli's] house for ever for the iniquity [of his adult sons] which he knoweth; because his sons made themselves vile, and he restrained them not." "The Child Samuel ministering in the Tabernacle" alludes to 1 Samuel 1-3, which notes that Samuel's dutiful obedience to God and family wins him the gift of prophecy, and "Saul seeking his Father's Asses" (1 Samuel 9, 10) reveals a similar lesson. After proving his obedience by persisting in a search that takes him far from home and marks him as God's annointed, Saul, despite his inauspicious origins, is crowned King of Israel. "Esau selling his Birthright for a red Pottage" (Genesis 25, 19-34) depicts filial ingratitude. When Esau is faint with hunger and close to starvation, his brother Jacob refuses him a meal of lentil beans until he has agreed to relinquish his rights as the first-born son. Esau reasons, "Behold, I am at the point to die: and what profit shall this birthright do me?" but the author of Genesis comments unsympathetically, "thus Esau despised his birthright." By contrast Jacob's unbrotherly opportunism, reflecting the morality of Genesis, draws no editorial comment.

"Ham the Son of Noah a Scoffer" (Genesis 9, 18-27) points up the imprecise and precarious nature of filial duty. Ham happens to be in his father's tent while Noah imbibes to excess and thus sees "the nakedness of his father" that accompanies Noah's drunkenness. He then reports the father's indiscretion to his elder brothers Shem and Japheth. Mature and well-trained sons, they dexterously manage to enter Noah's tent walking side-by-side and backwards while carrying one garment between them, and because "their faces [are] backward" they are able to cover Noah with the garment without actually seeing his disgraceful state. When he sobers up, Noah curses Ham and his descendents and prophesies that God will bless Shem and Japheth with progeny. Although Pastorius' source calls Ham a "scoffer," Genesis nowhere indicates that Ham acted unkindly. His real offense as a son was in not turning his back to the impropriety of the father. Depending on the context of paternal conduct, the emblem indicates, a son's mere passivity may prove disrespectful.

In a brief and sprightly "epic" of agricultural history (Poem 220), Pastorius recalls that, following the biblical flood, "Just Noah obtained that Grace / (Renewing the world,) to Continue Man's Race," but he describes Noah's drunkenness humorously, and he then moves on to agricultural episodes involving Lot and Abraham without commenting on Ham – two indications that he came to believe paternal conduct has an impact on paternal authority and filial obedience:

> And altho' Jehova had Cursed the Ground,
> By reason of Evils, that in it abound,
> Yet Noah, soon after the Deluge, to get
> Some Comfort in Troubles, a Vineyard did set.
> He dress'd it, no question, like Adam his Field,
> Which therefore but sorry sow'r Clusters could yield,
> And hereof poor Noah, redoubling a Dram,
> Was fuddled, his Nakedness seen by Ham.

Compiling emblems depicting the lives of Jacob and his son Joseph, David and Absolom, and Abraham and Isaac, Pastorius reveals his awareness of some of the most dramatic father-and-son stories in the Judeo-Christian tradition, familiar tales of tragedy and fulfillment that added to his childhood understanding of filial obedience. He refers to the story of Joseph told in Genesis 37-50 with four emblems ranging from "Joseph sold by his Brethern into Egypt" to "Joseph making himself known to his Brethern." Jealous of Joseph because their father Isaac loves him deeply as the child of his old age, the other sons secretly sell Joseph into captivity in Egypt. Following long years of separation, Joseph meets his brothers and forgives them after revealing himself to them with these words: "I am Joseph; doth my father yet live?" Joseph is reunited with his father in a denoument that accepts the brothers' evil conduct as a part of God's plan: The family is saved from starvation because of Joseph's connections in fertile Egypt, and his captivity becomes their release.

The emblem "Absolom hanging on an Oak" is an image of filial perversity with undying paternal love as its reverse (2 Samuel 13-18). After King David forgives his best-loved son Absolom for previous wrongs, the son, heir to the throne, grows impatient for power and foments sedition against his father. When David and his army are forced to desert the capital, Absolom desecrates the house of David by going "in unto his father's concubines in the sight of all Israel." On the eve of battle Absolom listens approvingly to a plan to kill his father and save the army. "Behold," David laments, "my son, which came forth of my bowels, seeketh my life." In battle, however, justice prevails:

> And Absolom rode upon a mule, and the mule went under the thick boughs of a great oak, and his head caught hold of the oak, and he was taken up between the heaven and the earth; and the mule that was under him went away.

Soldiers kill Absolom as he hangs, yet David mourns inconsolably: "Would God I had died for thee, O Absolom, my son, my son!" As it was read in family circles and dramatically explicated from the pulpit, this story provided a cathartic cleansing of latent or actual sins against the father and an affirmation of the purity of paternal love.

Pastorius records three emblems of the story of Isaac and Abraham – one described as "Isaac carrying the Wood, wherewith he himself was to be made a burnt Offering" – thus indicating his interest in a myth with multiple levels of filial and paternal love and obedience (Genesis 22, 1-18). God tests Abraham by ordering him to sacrifice, on a distant mountain, "thy son, thine only son Isaac, whom thou lovest." Abraham's love for Isaac is indeed great, for God granted Abraham and his barren wife Sarah this son in their old age, yet Abraham dutifully takes Isaac and journeys forth, on the third day preparing a sacrificial altar at the appointed place. As he binds his innocent son on the altar and raises the knife for the kill, God speaks to Abraham and reveals "behind him a ram caught in a thicket by his horns." Isaac is thus spared, "for now I know that thou fearest God, seeing thou hast not withheld thy son, thine only son from me."

The myth reveals two levels of authority and two levels of obedience. The father obeys divine authority, which is omnipotent and omniscient, and the son obeys the father. The father sees the natural consequences of the actions of father and son, and bears the burden of this knowledge. Carrying the firewood as he is told, Isaac asks his father, "but where is the lamb for a burnt offering?" He receives a placating answer, and remains the archetypal son, innocent and obedient. The story may have a happy ending, but its message is oppressively authoritarian. Pastorius recognized this as he copied the motto accompanying the emblem entitled "Isaac upon the Altar for a burnt Offering." It reads, "Voluisse Sat Est": "Willingness has reached its limit." In a garden meditation on the bleeding heart (Poem 238), Pastorius writes that the myth of Isaac and Abraham "much ... inflamed" his soul, and, citing Hebrews 11,17 (By faith Abraham ... offered up Isaac ...), he expresses its meaning as a paradox of religious faith. Despite his own "bleeding heart," Abraham "Most faithfully God's voice obeys, / His only child not slaying slays."

The "monogrammed" sentences of "Symbola Onomastica" reveal the ambiguous interconnections Pastorius sensed in human and divine authority – along with traditional attitudes such as "Foolish Children are Disobedient to their Parents" (Sentence 183) and "Fathers by InDulgence Press their Children unto Idleness" (Sentence 574) and humane advice like "Ye Fathers Do not Provoke your Children to Wrath" (Sentence 240, paraphrasing Ephesians 6,4). Sentence 650 encourages submissive obedience, presumably toward divine authority: "IF thou woulDst have a RecomPense, Continue in Obedience." Pastorius shows an attitude of humility, probably toward the Heavenly Father, in Sentence 667: "Father Dearest Pardon me, wherein I offended thee." With a reference to Colossians 1, 13 and John 3, 16 in Sentence 761, he gives another interpretation of Christ's sacrifice, with overtones of secular meaning: "Filius Dilectionis Paterna," or "The Son is the one beloved of (or chosen or esteemed by) the Father." In Sentence 194, paraphrasing Matthew 5, 48, Pastorius draws a parallel between divine and human virtue, noting the perfection of God or the "father" and the imperfection of mankind or the "child": "Our Father, which is in Heaven, being perfect, his Dear Children here on Earth should likewise endeavour for Perfection."

These sentences skim the surface of Pastorius' complex thought and deep emotions regarding the Heavenly Father, which he lyrically expressed with a piety deriving in part from the childish love upon which obedience was predicated. In Poem 242, for example, the low, overarching branches of an olive tree image the protection of the Lord, "Hugging us as in his lap;" the forget-me-not (Poem 236, in German) reminds Pastorius of God's undying love, of "your fatherly heart" which, like a human father above his small child (re-imaging the flower on its stem a few inches from the earth), bends down to embrace the persona with a love that "forgets me not, no never," a love that is constant and true yet "every morning new":

> Doch ich weiß, dein Vater Hertz
> Neigt in Lieb sich niederwarts,
> Ist in Treu auff mich gericht,
> Und vergisst mein nimmer nicht.
> > Deine Lieb und Treu
> > Ist alle Morgen neu.

Thus both childish spontaneity and childhood training, both religious feeling and doctrine, predisposed Pastorius to accept authority, and his writings generally indicate that he considered parental as well as political authority as deriving from and reflecting the authority of God. Duty to God and family were, from this perspective, one and the same – a theoretical approach that clashed with Franconian social reality as he eventually perceived it.

2.5.3.3   Establishing the Limits of Filial Obedience

> Let my experienced advice and fatherly instruction sink deep into thy heart. Culpeper, p. 519.
>
> -- "Admonishing"
>
> 'Tis obedience to disobey parents, etc., wherein we cannot obey them unless we disobey God. If we be disobedient, we are abominable. Tit. 1:16, Job 10:15. Those that are disobedient, rebelling and gainsayers, forfeit the benefit of Christ's obedience unto his Father. Eph. 5:6, Col. 3:6 ... Subjects and children dishonour their superiors and parents in complying with their unrighteous commands. Culpeper, p. 158. Those resist and quench the Spirit, who rebel against its motions, reproofs, and instructions in them. Idem, p. 372.
>
> -- "Disobedience"
>
> [Patience is] the art of bearing troubles without much troubling of ourselves.
>
> -- "Patience"
>
> Quietly learn all crosses to endure,
> Repining does more misery procure.
>
> -- Epigram 2327.6

The calm rationality of a few "Alphabetical Hive" entries on virtuous disobedience (by independent-minded Englishmen like Nicholas Culpeper, the scholar and physician whom the staid College of Physicians accused of disseminating attitudes "of rebellion and atheism" in 1649 [83]) does not fit the context of Pastorius' youth, which encouraged him to play the role of the heroic son, bearing the burden of tradition and assuring cultural continuity – and living with learned compulsion. As familial tensions gradually disturbed his sense of filial love and fostered a reluctant rebelliousness, obedience and authority became imbued with a complexity and emotionality that influenced his conduct as a learned son in Germany as well as his acculturation in Pennsylvania.

In Pennsylvania, Pastorius inevitably displayed some of the authoritarian traits so pervasively asserted in his childhood, like many of his contemporaries continuing habits that had generated emotional scars in his own youth, even if Pennsylvania innovations gradually encouraged him to break a number of these habits. In his 1698 school primer, for example (in a chapter entitled "General and Particular Duties of True Christians"), he summarizes biblical views on childrearing that include corporal punishment – views moderated, during the 1710s, in spirited references to Christian freedom (including a citation from Saint Paul on page 141).

> Parents ... bring and train up their Children in the way they should go (Prov. 22:6), in the nurture and admonition of the Lord, not provoking them to Wrath (Ephes. 6:4) nor Anger, lest they be discouraged (Col. 3:21), love them, by chastening them betimes (Prov. 13:24), not withholding Correction from them, but beating them with the Rod (chap. 23:13, Heb. 12:9), instruct them in the Truth (Isa. 38:19, Deut. 6:6, Joel 1:3), and give them good gifts (Mat. 7:11) ... Children honour and reverence their Father and Mother (Heb. 12:9), are subject unto them (Luke 2:51), obey them (Eph. 6:1) in all things (Col. 3:20), do not mock, despise, nor curse them, but honour and assist them when old and poor (Mat. 15:5, Gen. 45:9, 10, 11). [84]

When he cofounded and began teaching at a Philadelphia Friends' School early in 1698, Pastorius emphasized old-fashioned diligence and obedience as he taught

English and Latin to girls and boys who included future provincial leaders. He praised two girls of timid but "good disposition" in April, 1698, noting that "the very shadow of the rod will do more with them than the spur with others." Two months later an antagonistic thirteen-year-old English youth, Israel Pemberton, charged that Pastorius (whom he described as "a German one" and nicknamed "D. P. Sowerness") beat him about the head and arms severely enough to produce bleeding and swelling, and "the tokens of his correction" were "still to be seen" five weeks thereafter. [85] Even Pastorius' six- and eight-year-old sons alluded to their reluctant obedience in attending school (and thus to the beginnings of compulsiveness) in the letter to their grandfather of March, 1699, composed by their father:

> Oh, if only you were here, and lived in our house in Germantown, which has a nice orchard, and is unoccupied for the time being, since we are living in Philadelphia, and have to go to school a full eight hours each day, except for the last day of the week [Saturday], when we are allowed to stay home in the afternoon. [86]

This muted complaint suggests the adjustments Pastorius was making from classical learnedness to frontier pragmatism, in part encouraged by the sensitive and loving attitudes he commonly displayed toward children (thus reflecting his view of divine love in the poems cited on page 98). An exchange between father and child (Poem 243), for example, shows a world view fostering gentleness:

> The child's question:
> Who made these things so excellent and fair
> Which we in gardens see, smell, taste, feel, hear?
> The father's answer:
> God made 'em all, and gave to us the same
> To magnify his great and pow'rful name.
> What God made is good,
> He still the best raiment gives, and food;
> In him I rest.

The attitudes of his fellow Pennsylvanians helped Pastorius resolve tensions between gentleness and authoritarianism similar to those felt by many European schoolmasters. Beating young Israel Pemberton in 1698 violated Quaker principles of childrearing (despite William Penn's authoritarian maxims in the "Alphabetical Hive"), a violation Quakers immediately challenged. Pemberton's father withdrew the boy from the Philadelphia Friends' School; the headmaster (Pastorius' fellow teacher) wrote the father an apology commenting on "thy great resentment of" Pastorius, and asked Pastorius to write an apology of his own, an embarrassing situation cautioning him to respect the standards of his new community.

Pastorius continued to absorb the new values around him, moderating his traditionalism in the process. He soon adjusted to the moderate levels of scholarly attainment generally considered appropriate for Pennsylvania living, and eventually encouraged his own sons to live as self-sufficient craftsmen in Germantown, just as he himself accepted the role of village schoolteacher beginning in 1700 (moving his family back to Germantown after two years in Philadelphia, also reflecting accommodation to village life). He also developed an abiding interest in innovative pedagogy demonstrated in numerous "Alphabetical Hive" entries and in a number of the pedagogical books in his library. His transatlantic writings (described in Chapters Three and Four) indicate his awareness that compromises were needed to avoid the insecurity and arrogance generated along with erudition in upper-class Europe. He became convinced that learned Europeans – and Americans who emulated them – were generally unprepared for everyday reality, and thus inordinately dependent on their social inferiors for their daily needs, which partially explains why many of them resorted to assertiveness and arrogance rather than face the personal insecurities resulting from this dependence, one of the fundamental sources of learned compulsion.

Pastorius was, it seems, groping his way to new awareness, not necessarily without faltering in the process. A man capable of beating one of his pupils would not always have shown patience toward his own children, especially as he attempted to instill virtue and learning in them. Although the record is not clear on this point, it seems likely that he only gradually consented to having his sons become modest tradesmen, perhaps the result of frustrations encountered while attempting to educate them in an environment that did not fully support the compulsive learning of his youth. In fact, the Pennsylvania Quakers encouraged or required apprenticeships in the trades (see page 225). Even late in life, at any rate, Pastorius still showed enthusiasm for learnedness, encouraging youths like Lloyd Zachary to scholarly attainment.

He thus demonstrated some sense of continuity with his Windsheim childhood, which had been marked not only by pervasive authority, but also by family tensions that can be reasonably well defined even though he refused to comment on them, and in time acted as if they had never existed. His society had demanded a dutiful submissiveness that, even in the best of circumstances, would have frustrated a growing child's natural desire for increasing autonomy, and the circumstances of his upbringing were less than ideal in several respects. Along with the disadvantages of living as an only child in a more or less isolated nuclear family, Franz Daniel increasingly noted sharp qualifications to the very advantages of his existence – especially the great stature of Melchior Adam and the privileges of his upper-class existence.

Even in Franz Daniel's earliest years, Melchior Adam's "almost indefatigable" energies as a lawyer and scholar were, if not downright inhibiting, as awesome as they were inspiring to a child who could not even form the letters and words that flowed from the endless pages of his father's "Lucubrations & Candle-light Writings." Yet these energies served not only as a model but also as a prod for the son of the man who helped implement Windsheim's educational reforms of 1667 and wrote fervent poems about dedicating oneself to learning the Bible and Luther's teachings at school and in church. Along with his religious fervor and intellectual vigor, furthermore, Melchior Adam displayed a feistiness and disputatiousness that belies his son's description of him as consistently "settled and composed... courteous and affable." This can be seen in various details from his biography including his petulance toward a penniless friend in Paris and his disputes with other Windsheim leaders, and in numerous spirited and even cantankerous passages in his poetry, and it would become especially obvious in his official conduct during the popular dissension that preceded Franz Daniel's departure for Frankfurt in 1679. An energetic perfectionist who displayed impatience toward normal human failings, Melchior Adam was certainly a demanding father for young Franz Daniel Pastorius.

Trained to accept his father's authority in whatever guise it might assume, and craving paternal love, Franz Daniel did his best to meet the demands placed upon him as a youth in Windsheim even when these demands seemed excessive. Although the first evidence of his unwillingness or inability to meet his father's demands does not emerge until he was well along in his university career, a 1697 Pennsylvania letter reveals the frustration a teenager might experience as a Gymnasium pupil and the only son in Melchior Adam's home. Inspired by Pastorius' departure from Windsheim eighteen years earlier, 14-year-old Augustin Adam Pastorius (a half-brother Pastorius never met) became so obsessed with the idea of leaving home and emigrating to Pennsylvania that he managed to communicate his desire secretly in a letter sent on to Pastorius, presumably with the aid of a sympathetic adult in Windsheim. Writing to Melchior Adam in May, 1697, Franz Daniel responded with the formality demanded by his well-trained sense of filial loyalty:

> I was very pleased to learn that my dearly-beloved brother Augustin Adam has been thinking about coming over to me, convinced as I am that we would live harmoniously with each other in brotherly love, and constantly show true, heartfelt and unadulterated affection for each other. No matter how happy I would be to have him here with me, however, I must in all friendliness request and implore that he by no means leave home without the knowledge and consent of his parents, who deserve his respect, and I hereby inform him that under such circumstances he would not receive any welcome from me whatsoever. [87]

Like Isaac upon Abraham's sacrificial altar, young Franz Daniel Pastorius would learn that the willingness to obey can be pushed to the limit and beyond, but demarcating that limit would involve disappointing his father's expectations of him, and burden him with guilt in the process. Siding with his father in 1697 (even at the risk of cruelly affronting his desperate half-brother) was one of the ways he atoned for the breach of filial virtue that, in terms of traditional values, characterized his 1679 departure from Windsheim and his emigration to Pennsylvania four years later.

2.6 Leaving Home with Friends in 1668

> Libertas Amicitiae Zenith. True FrienDshiP is altogether Free, and Drags no Piece of slavish Flattery, Dissimulation & Partiality after her.
>
> -- "Beehive," p. 221 (an unnumbered triple onomastic)
>
> Friendship built on opinion first looks fair;
> But soon is but a castle in the air.
>
> -- Epigram 2316.2
>
> Friendship multiplieth joys, and divideth grief. Bacon. No greater wilderness, than to be without true friends. Idem. A true friend will never dissemble. One God, no more: but friends good store. Virtuous persons are always friends, sayeth [the Greek philosopher] Antisthenes. Friendship is an union of spirits, a marriage of hearts, and the bond thereof virtue. Max[im] 101 . . . Friends are true twins in soul . . . A friend in need, a friend indeed. Adversity tries friends . . . Choose a friend as thou dost a wife, til death separate you. Max[im] 109. Yet be not a friend beyond the altar [of God]; but let virtue bound thy friendship; else it is not friendship but an evil confederacy. Idem 110. Make not friends in haste, nor hastily part with them. Solon. Culpeper, p. 419.
>
> -- "Friendship"

On 31 July 1668, 16-year-old Franz Daniel Pastorius left Windsheim for Nürnberg University in the company of three fellow graduates of the local Gymnasium,

Georg Leonhart Model (1650-1713), Johannes Mathias Stellwag (b. 1650) and Johannes Joachim Mercklein (1650-1714) – boys who had been his upper-class friends for nearly a decade of neighborly proximity within the walled city. [88] For Franz Daniel and his young friends, a university career was about to culminate the Franconian upbringing that would lead two of these youths to follow in the footsteps of their fathers, attaining the rank of clergyman or senator and thus assuming a place of authority in Windsheim's well-ordered civic existence.

After studying philosophy with Franz Daniel at Nürnberg, Georg Leonhart Model, the son of Windsheim's highest-ranking and best-paid clergyman, went on to Wittenberg University, developing orthodox Lutheran erudition and rhetorical skills in seminars and disputations on homiletics, metaphysics, pneumatology and various theological doctrines. [89] A diligent student, Model even devised a special alarm clock with a rope attached to his feet that yanked him back to scholarly consciousness well before less energetic students began to stir. He ranked fifth among Wittenberg's twenty philosophy students graduating as "Magister" (master) in 1672. Following an extended tour of Magdeburg, Hamburg, Helmstedt and Leipzig, Model returned to Windsheim in 1674, and was appointed assistant rector of the Gymnasium in recognition of his "exemplary learnedness." Serving as rector from 1682 to 1689, Model "hardly managed to endure the arduous and incessant tasks" of inculcating piety and knowledge into another generation of Windsheim's youth, but his dedication won him the clergyman's post he held from then on in Windsheim. A stalwart upper-class Lutheran, Model displayed authoritarian attitudes by insisting on religious conformity in belief and conduct:

> In the midst of vanity his character was but slightly vain ... If he saw any who erred in religion, he could not rest until he had brought them back to the true path ... If he saw godless Children of the World, who were drowning in untold sin and vice, he pursued them until he had snatched them from the jaws of the Devil once more. [90]

Franz Daniel's friends Johannes Mathias Stellwag and Johannes Joachim Mercklein, like young Pastorius the sons of Windsheim senators and burgomasters, studied philosophy and law to prepare themselves for government careers in Windsheim. [91] Stellwag's father was Burgomaster Johann Georg Stellwag, appointed Lord Mayor in 1671, whose high-handed approach to government helped to generate popular dissension during the 1670s. Young Mercklein's civic attainment, like that of many of the sons of Windsheim's first families, reflected similar attainments in his family over generations. When he returned to Windsheim after finishing his law studies in 1674, he married into another upper-class Windsheim family, began a private law practice and was chosen for a seat on the Windsheim senate. He was appointed to the powerful inner chamber of the senate in 1691, and in 1698 named burgomaster and supervisor of education, offices he held until his death sixteen years later. The Mercklein family was so well established in Windsheim that from 1650 to 1750 ten of its members were able to hold – usually for a decade or more – the office of burgomaster, one of whom wrote, as a young attorney in 1694, the letter to his godfather Franz Daniel Pastorius eliciting Franz Daniel's fervent exhortation to honor the "first promise" of Christian baptism above "all other commitments" to family and class in Windsheim.

As family and friends bid them farewell on their day of departure in 1668, Franz Daniel and his fellow graduates could anticipate a productive future and appreciate the camaraderie and good will generated, on such occasions, within the Franconian bonds of family and community. The youths might have been overwhelmed by their previous duties as Gymnasium pupils, but now, with these tasks behind them, they could feel a sense of accomplishment and enjoy the admiration and respect many Windsheimers felt for their young scholars. The boys might yet have trepidations about the duties and freedoms awaiting them at universities known for strict academic discipline and lax student conduct, but they also knew that the sons of Windsheim's best families had bravely and willingly met such challenges in the past, and would continue to do so now and in the future.

In the hour of departure, surely enjoying the warm acceptance of those they loved, these Windsheim youths had every reason for confidence and good cheer. Surrounded by friends and relatives who would have naturally chatted and joked and offered words of advice and encouragement, fervently hugging and kissing them and unceasingly waving good-bye, the boys might well perceive that the discipline of their young lives was part of a benign orderliness extending from birth to death, joining their lives with the lives of past and future generations and (as long as this orderliness could be affirmed) encompassing all members of society and creation, from high to low, in what could well be imaged as a great chain of being. It was this sense of order – though commingled with the compulsions of their upbringing, and the commitments to family and class generating much of this compulsiveness – that carried the boys through their lives of privilege and responsibility in the imperial city of Windsheim. Like most of their peers in Windsheim and all of Franconia, and indeed throughout Europe, they were merely living the lives society expected of them.

CHAPTER THREE
The University Years

3.1 *"In none of the objects of this worldly* theatrum *could I find any enduring delight":*
From the Foreword to Beschreibung Pennsylvaniae

> The World's a dang'rous Sea,
> Man may wrack ev'ry way;
> Woe! Woe! therefore to him,
> That has not learned to Swim.
> -- Poem 350

> The world's fawning is worse than its frowning . . . A full delight in earthly things argues a neglect of heavenly. Many lose an eternal kingdom for the gain of toys and vanities.
> -- "Love of the World"

Franz Daniel Pastorius, through no fault of his own, was not able to affirm the benign orderliness of society as he pursued the life of a German law student and then accepted adult responsibilities in Windsheim eight years after first leaving the city with his youthful friends. This inability ultimately cheated him of a number of European fulfillments, separating him from the friends of his youth, from his family and his community, and denying him the sense of identity with this family and community that, through all of his experience, had come to mean more to him than life itself – more, at any rate, than a life bereft of community could ever mean to a man of his temperament. His student and professional experience in Germany, Pastorius came to believe, revealed deep truths demanding a personal rejection of his community – yet rejecting the community left a void that could only be filled with the slowly accumulating balm of time.

Although he often made veiled allusions to his rejection of the Franconian community, he only once attempted a sustained description of the course of events that led him to emigrate to Pennsylvania in 1683. Largely a critique of his university years and European grand tour, this description readily serves as prelude to a detailed evaluation of the personal and cultural experience that brought young

Pastorius ever closer to open confrontation with the dominant values of his society. He composed the text, a personal credo or confession, as the foreword to his *Beschreibung Pennsylvaniae* [1]:

> As everyone in my family well knows, I have been directing my course along the path of this world toward a joyous Eternity ever since my little legs could carry me, or at least since outgrowing the shoes of childhood, and in all my doings I have tried to learn how I might recognize the benign will of God, fear his great omnipotence, and love, praise and honor his unfathomable goodness and mercy. It was my good fortune to study law, along with other general disciplines of the liberal arts, and I successfully completed my law degree. I also became sufficiently familiar with the Italian and French languages, and thereafter made a so-called grand tour through various countries among good society. No matter where I traveled, however, I took great pains to learn one thing above all else: Where and among which people and nations might one possibly find and apprehend a true devotion, love, knowledge and fear of God? At universities and academies I found men of learning in numbers practically without end – but such sorts of intellect, such religions and sects, such contrived thought and pointed *Quaestiones* [examination]; in short, this vain worldly wisdom produced such a surfeit of pomposity and garrulity as that which led the Apostle [Paul in 1 Corinthians 8,1] to write: "*Scientia inflat*" [knowledge puffeth up].
>
> Nor can I write with a clear conscience that I ever saw, in any parts of the Netherlands or France, a professor who, with all of his heart and soul, with the heart of a lad and the soul of a disciple, earnestly taught the pure love of Jesus and a knowledge of the holy trinity.
>
> Nominal Christians are certainly not in short supply. They go around mouthing their religion, puffed up with conceited worldly wit and coveting the lusts of the flesh, the lusts of the eye and a haughty nature (the trifolium of the devil). But those who sought to attain bliss in fear and trembling, lived without deceit and, with all of their powers of spirit, penetrated to the center of their being, to God the supreme good – such Christians were *rara avis in terris* [rare birds on the earth].
>
> Finally, at the University of Cambridge [in England] and in the city of Ghent [in Flanders, or present-day Belgium], I did manage to find some devoted men who, secretly retired from the world, had resigned themselves wholly to God, and having discovered my earnest searching, they taught me many good lessons and greatly fortified me in my resolution; they also gave me a helping hand in various ways, and thus at the royal court of Ghent I was shown the birth chamber of the illustrious Emperor Charles V (which is only four ells long and four ells wide) with the recollection that one of his godfathers gave this new-born prince a richly-bound Bible with the inscription "Scrutamini scripturas" in gold lettering, and the prince then read this Bible diligently, and therein learned that he would have to die in the merits of Jesus Christ alone.
>
> While on my grand tour, furthermore, at Orleans, Paris, Avignon, Marseille, Lyon and Geneva, I saw thousands of young people from Germany, most of them aristocrats, whose occupation away from home consists solely of pursuing the vanities of dress, speech, foreign customs and ceremonies, and whose learning involves spending incredible sums on horseback-riding and -jumping, on dancing, fencing, dashing lances and waving banners. In such fashion they use up great portions of their German patrimony on worldly frivolities that profit no one, but they do not give even a single moment's reflection to the love of God or to the wisdom, so pleasing to Him, of following Christ's example. In fact, anyone who wants to discuss the writings and *soliloquis cum Deo* [meditations] of Saint Augustine, [Johann] Tauler, [Johann] Arndt and other men of Godly learning has to face being ridiculed as a Pietist, sectarian and heretic;

and none of the men who have drowned in Aristotelian worldly wisdom can be convinced of anything anymore, and they will not let the spirit of God taughten them [i.e., their presumably water-logged flaccidity], either.

For their sakes I sat down for a little *retirade* [retreat] in my *cabinet* [room] after my tour was over, and recalled to memory everything that this worldly *theatrum* had presented to my eyes, and in none of its objects could I find any enduring delight; I despaired, furthermore, that any place could be found in my Fatherland [i.e., Franconia] or in all of Germany where, now or in future, a person could lay down the old habits of mere *Operis operati* [going through the motions] and take up the pure love of God with all of his heart and all of his soul and all of his strength, and likewise love his neighbor as himself.

I thus considered whether it might not be better for me to expound, for the benefit of the newly-discovered American tribes in Pennsylvania, the knowledge given me by the grace of the highest Giver and Father of Light, and thus enable them to participate in the true knowledge of the holy trinity and genuine Christianity.

Since the province and region of Pennsylvania is situated on the farthest frontiers of America, however, it will be necessary to precede [my description of this province] with a brief consideration of the divisions of the globe and *in specie* of America as a whole, the fourth continent of the world...

In this foreword to his German readers, Pastorius vividly describes what he perceived as the moral essence of his student years from 1668 to 1676 and his grand tour of 1680-82 (pointedly omitting any reference to his Windsheim life of 1676-79). His indictment of arrogance, disputatiousness, vanity, hypocrisy and godlessness among students, professors and young aristocrats is convincingly sincere, and his stylized portrait of personal ennui provides a plausible motivation for his emigration in 1683. The worldly "*theatrum*" of European capitals, courts and universities could not offer enduring pleasure, and as Pastorius turns his back on these decadent players and settings the reader may well experience a cathartic mix of pleasure and pain. The somber tones of the drama are tragic, but its denouement suggests a resolution not unlike that of high comedy.

With his reference to Native American tribes, Pastorius implicitly shifts his focus from damnation to redemption, from ineluctable loss to anticipated fulfillment among a different sort of humanity, and his intended readers could readily supply the elements of romance that linked their mundane reality with the novel milieu of Pennsylvania. As Pastorius turns to his discourse on the continents of the world culminating with "the farthest frontiers of America," these readers vicariously experience the rolling waves and outstretched sails that took him on his quest, just as the wisdom attained through the trial and endurance of the quest is revealed to them in the New World experience recorded in the book's succeeding 122 pages.

This foreword contains autobiographical simplifications and evasions that will be clarified in this study. For his prospective readers, however, it presented a familiar reality in terms they readily understood. Many of them were convinced that most learned men were arrogant and disputatious. Average taxpayers shared Pastorius' scorn for squandered German patrimonies, well aware that squires, lords and princes financed their sons' lives of luxury from the public or semi-public coffers, and many of them sensed the social injustice of this waste. Protestants readily appreciated the story of Hapsburg Emperor Charles V (1500-58), affirming Luther's emphasis on grace over works. Although Pastorius' Ghent hosts could recall Charles as the potentate who had quelled rebellions in Ghent and other Catholic cities of the Spanish Netherlands, revoking imperial privileges and contributing to economic decline [2], historically conscious Protestants recognized him as the emperor who had tried and failed to nip the Reformation in the bud, and such readers could enjoy the wry ironic humor of this Catholic sovereign reading in his ornate Latin Bible the simple truths they read in Luther's German translation.

Some of Pastorius' readers undoubtedly got the message encoded in his reference to a professor in the Netherlands or France. A possible allusion to the radical French theologian Jean de Labadie and his Dutch Labadist followers, it served to clarify Pastorius' theological allegiances or to deny reports that placed him in radical company – sensitive issues demanding subtle exposition. Pastorius cryptically alluded to Quakerism and radical mysticism with references to meditative trembling, the "Father of Light" and the divine center of one's being, indirectly mentioned German Pietism, and focused most clearly on English and Flemish groups safely removed from the turbulence of German religion and politics.

The closing reference to the Native Americans, while evasive and misleading, suggests a spellbinding reality beyond the experience of Pastorius' readers. Although he went to Pennsylvania as the personal friend and business agent of Frankfurt Pietists and never lived as a missionary or preacher, Pastorius had good reasons for referring to the Indian tribes at this crucial point. He had become convinced of their integrity, and this was a basic insight of his book, so he needed them thematically. And since their presence shifted the focus from Europe to America, they abruptly resolved the personal narrative as it verged on intimate revelation.

Pastorius was not willing to describe the euphoric emigration plans he had made with his Pietist friends in 1683, since these friends reneged on their plans and thus disappointed and embarrassed him. Nor was he willing to describe his most personal reasons for emigration, involving the moral and psychological tensions of his beginning law career in Franconia and the Windsheim insurrection of 1677-79. Nevertheless unable to ignore these compelling motivations, he bared his soul in his own fashion, proclaiming the despair he felt in realizing he could not find a satisfying moral life anywhere in Franconia or Germany – a confession made especially poignant for his father (his most important reader) since its description of meditative seclusion echoes Melchior Adam's oft-repeated description of similar private meditations inspiring the father's Protestant conversion in 1649. Carrying personal revelation any farther would have violated the canons of good taste and brought into focus the most painful details of his early adult life – details that, despite Pastorius' reticence, can be approached through the context of his years as student, lawyer and traveler in Europe.

This chapter describes the student experience of a man who combined outspoken academic criticism with extraordinary cultural achievement, paying particular attention to the city and university of Nürnberg, where Pastorius was most at home. Nürnberg typifies the cultural and academic advantages and shortcomings of Europe as Pastorius knew them, just as Pastorius himself typifies the well motivated student of his day, delighting in high cultural attainment yet aware of moral deficiencies in the cultural establishment that would soon be demanding his full participation. Since Pastorius was free to express this awareness in his Pennsylvania commentary, his experience delineates, with unusual clarity, the complex web of academic, cultural, political and religious influences that went into the making of the man of learning in the age of the baroque, when the learned generally behaved with steadfast determination yet not infrequently experienced grave spiritual uncertainties. The chapter exploits Pastorius' prose, poetry and commonplace jottings to define these cultural themes.

3.2 Cultural Life in Academia
3.2.1 Student Career at Nürnberg, Strasbourg and Jena

> Plodding students would fain change the dull lead of their brain into finer metal ... [I was so] mightily addicted to reading and study (such employments of the brain) that I abridged myself of my sleep and rest. Tryon, Mem., p. 18 ... A spendthrift scholar, to get money of his father, wrote to him that he was dead, and entreated him to send ten pounds to defray his funeral charges. Ac. Compl., p.16.
> – "Student"
>
> Wander far, and gather nothing but empty notions, husks indeed. Penn. Young gentlemen are sent thither, because there are the best fencing and dancing schools. Schools of wrangling . . . Superficial scholars return as wise, as they came thither . . . Signal places for idleness, looseness, prodigality, &c. Truth.
> – "University"

In July, 1668, Pastorius began his student career by enrolling in the faculty of philosophy at Lutheran Nürnberg University, studying the liberal arts there for two years. [3] He visited Windsheim in July, 1670, serving as godfather at the baptism of Franz Jakob Mercklein, and in August he moved on to Strasbourg University in Alsace for two years of politics, law and French. Strasbourg ("Straßburg" in German) on the Rhine was a German free city when Pastorius lived there; it first fell to the French in 1681. Despite its Lutheran affiliation, the city boasted a diverse cosmopolitan culture reflecting its commercial ties with Catholic France just west of the Rhine and the Calvinist influence of the Swiss cantons to the south. During a summer trip to Calvinist Basel University in 1672, Pastorius explored French and Swiss territory beyond Germany and Lutheranism.

He returned to Strasbourg in August, but political tensions between the Hapsburgs and France under Louis XIV were making life difficult there. [4] The city tried and executed Georg Obrecht, a doctor of the laws and one of its own senators, for circulating reports that its government had made a deal with France. Law Professor Johann Heinrich Boeckler (1611-72), who taught liberal politics yet peddled his influence for favors both in Vienna and at the French court, died as tensions mounted in September. French troops violated Strasbourg's sovereignty in November, burning the Rhine bridge and cutting the main Hapsburg route to Holland, where France had begun its Dutch War (1672-79).

Pastorius left the turmoil of Strasbourg in November, and spent the winter at home in Windsheim. His father was then beginning his third year as burgomaster; this was the last time he would see his stepmother Barbara. He returned to Nürnberg University for the spring of 1673, but, "not liking the place for some reasons" (among them, apparently, the arrogance of its law professors), he journeyed on to Jena University in the province of Thuringia, a liberal Lutheran university, where he continued his legal studies under Dr. Heinrich Linck (1642-96) and studied Italian during 1673 and 1674. He toured Erfurt on his way to Jena, and "Naumburg, Gotha and other Towns of that Countrey" while in Thuringia.

Well advanced in law by August, 1674, Pastorius traveled to the "Reichstag" (imperial diet) at Regensburg in northern Bavaria, where he observed politics in the making for eight months as war broke out with France and Sweden in Alsace, in Prussia and in the Rhineland. Reluctant to finish his law degree, he returned to Windsheim for half a year in April, 1675. In his absence his stepmother had died in March, 1674, and his father had married for the fourth time in September of that year – a ceremony Franz Daniel had pointedly refused to attend. Meanwhile Dr. Linck, Pastorius' favorite law instructor at Jena, had won a professorship at Nürnberg University, and Pastorius dutifully joined him there for a final year of law study beginning in September, 1675. Culminating his student career, Pastorius received a doctorate in civil and canon law following his inaugural disputation at Nürnberg in November, 1676.

3.2.2 Nürnberg's Student Milieu
3.2.2.1 University Offerings

> The exemplary works of others mind,
> Till thy brave genius can no equals find.
>
> -- Epigram 2330.2
>
> The study of wisdom or knowledge in things rational, natural and moral ... Philosophy is a quiet study, and even the worst have an esteem for it; the world can never be so wicked, but the very name of a philosopher shall still continue venerable and sacred. Seneca, p. 293 ... Philosophy teaches us ... to hit the white [bull's-eye] at any distance. P. 156 ... To dispute with Socrates, to doubt with Carneades, to set up my rest with Epicurus, to master my appetites with the Stoics, and to renounce the world with the Cynic, is better than all impertinent niceties and cavils. P. 505 ... It becomes the gravity of philosophers, first to be sure of matter of fact, and then to search after the reason of the thing. <u>Ath. Oracle</u>, p. 478.
>
> -- "Philosophy"

Pastorius' student milieu is exemplified by Nürnberg University, also known as Altdorf University because it was located, 18 kilometers from central Nürnberg, in the village of Altdorf – part of the large territory governed in the seventeenth century by the city then known as the Republic of Nürnberg. [5] The city's original Lutheran Gymnasium, founded by Philipp Melanchthon in 1526, was expanded and reorganized as a "school for nobles and patricians [i.e., wealthy members of the upper class]" ("schola nobilis et patricia") and built anew in the idyllic environs of Altdorf in the 1570s. The school's "collegium," still standing today despite the university's demise in 1809, consists of three four-story stone buildings in the Renaissance style – the central college with its high bell tower, long arcade and arched portals and windows, and two large wings built at right angles to the main edifice. Joined on the fourth side by a long stone wall with a high arched gate, they surrounded a spacious open courtyard embellished with a decorative and functional copper fountain from the guild shops of Nürnberg. Pallas Athena, the helmeted goddess of wisdom, presided over it, and three cast-iron dolphins spewed forth fresh water piped through the town from a nearby mountain spring. Nürnberg's city fathers had endowed a physical plant "worthy of the largest and most famous university" ("der berühmtesten und größten Universität würdig").

The school received imperial charters as an academy (1578) and then as a university (1622), and expanded its facilities throughout the seventeenth century. The library, established in 1598, was repeatedly enlarged through endowments and bequests. A botanical garden, begun in 1626 and expanded three decades later, was the largest in Germany, rivaling Leyden's for its physical beauty and the variety of its medicinal herbs, many of which are catalogued in Pastorius' Pennsylvania manuscripts. A "theater of anatomy," opened in 1650, included skeletons, large-scale pictures and special anatomical equipment. An astronomy observatory was built in 1657. The growing interest in chemistry, already evident in Pastorius' day, led the university to equip a chemistry laboratory in 1685. Altdorf also attracted several printers to meet its need for a wide range of publications – poetry, academic catalogues, graduation programs, university mandates, scholarly disputations.

The faculties of philosophy, law, theology and medicine, each with three to five professors, provided the meat of the curriculum. The professors of philosophy, the broadest field, taught year-long courses in dialectics or logic, metaphysics, ethics, politics, oratory or eloquence, poetics, history, physics and mathematics, and private instructors and tutors supplemented these essentials with "non-academic" offerings in fencing, dancing, music, art and the modern languages. Choral and instrumental music was taught by a professor of music and the university cantor, and students could borrow musical instruments to stage their own concerts and festivities. The resident artist doubled as the art instructor. The language instructors were native speakers, usually from France and Italy. Unlike most universities, Nürnberg did not offer riding instruction until 1721, but students could make use of the city's riding stables in central Nürnberg.

Along with the formality of lecture halls and classrooms, spacious grounds beyond the "collegium" offered opportunities for quiet reflection and animated conversation. "Manifold and attractive promenades" ("mannichfaltigen und reizenden Spaziergänge") and pathways with names like Via Philosophica, Via Scipionis and Poets' Grove ("das Poetenwäldgen") led through the botanical garden, along the gardens and town walls of Altdorf, and to adjacent fields and nearby hillsides. Reflecting moments of personal rumination and camaraderie while strolling at Altdorf, Pastorius recorded cultural landmarks of the campus, including an anonymous poem, inscribed at the entrance to the orchard of the botanical garden, describing the ephemeral beauty of the rose and the narcissus as images of human transience. [6] Numerous "Alphabetical Hive" entries indicate the philosophical idealism that was generated, among contemplative students, in such surroundings.

Nürnberg, a medium-sized German university, had 111 new students when Pastorius enrolled in 1668, and a student body that can be estimated at three to four hundred, a select group of future leaders of varied background. It commonly drew students from Bohemia, Poland, Austria and Hungary as well as most regions of Germany and, less frequently, from Egypt, Greece, Transylvania, Denmark, Sweden, France, England, Scotland and Ireland. Its alumni included some of the big names of seventeenth century Germany, among them the poets Friedrich von Logau (1604-55) and Georg Philipp Harsdörffer (1607-55), philosopher-statesman Gottfried Wilhelm von Leibniz, and General Albrecht von Wallenstein (1583-1634), the chief strategist of the Thirty Years' War.

Altdorf professors were equally renowned. [7] The oft-published theologian Lucas Friedrich Reinhart (1623-88), Pastorius' teacher and friend, has earned a place in modern scholarship for introducing the concept of dogmatics into the study of theology. The mathematician and astronomer Abdias Trew (1597-1669) won the praise of Gottfried Wilhelm von Leibniz, the inventor of the calculus, for his textbooks incorporating the scientific views of Nicolaus Copernicus (1473-1543) and Galileo Galilei (1564-1642) at a time when many similar textbooks were still based on the Ptolemaic universe and outdated mathematics. When Trew died during Pastorius' first year at Altdorf, his post was filled by Johann Christoph Sturm (1635-1704), whose advances in mathematical thought and experimental science won him honorary membership in the Royal Society of London.

Pastorius' professors included several polymaths (or polyhistors) – men whose training and research cut a broad swath across various disciplines. Johann Conrad Dürr (1625-77) was appointed professor of ethics in 1654 and won a second professorship for poetics the following year; promoted to professor of theology in 1657, he relinquished the poetry chair but continued to publish works on philology and history as well as theology and philosophy. Johann Christoph Wagenseil (1633-1705) held the chairs of history, oriental languages (i.e., Hebrew and Arabic), public law and canon law, translated the entire Hebrew Talmud into German, assembled an anthropological compendium on world cultures and compiled a six-volume encyclopedia on oratory, poetics, geography, history, philosophy, the Latin language and law. Although his life typifies the learned vanity Pastorius ridiculed in America and Wagenseil's historical writings have long been criticized for their inaccuracies, his studies of "Meistersang" and Yiddish were genuine contributions to Europe's growing corpus of scholarly knowledge.

3.2.2.2 Student Conduct

> A handsome hostess... is the lode stone that attracts men of iron... Her lips are your welcome, which is put into the reckoning, too, and sometimes the dearest parcel in it. Here the purse is emptied of money, the head of reason, the heart of all former grace...
> A vintner's boy holds the candle and the door,
> Lets out the drunkard, and lets in the whore.
>
> -- "Inn & Innkeeper"
>
> By following whores, and cards and dice,
> We're pox'd and beggar'd in a trice.
>
> Keep at a distance from the sons of vice,
> Once known, endanger not your soul's health twice.
>
> -- Epigrams 45, 2320.4
>
> One fool makes many... Be good company of bad fellows. Keep such company as thou need'st not blush at. Shun the society of inbred envy and pride... It is merry when knaves meet... Bad and base company, like Delilah, binds us, blinds us, undoes us.
>
> -- "Company"
>
> Fool, giggle on, and waste thy wanton breath,
> Thy morning laughter breeds an evening death. Quarles.
>
> -- "Laughter"

Pastorius alludes to student conduct at Altdorf in "Genealogia Pastoriana," stating that he was "initiated among Students (which they call Deponiren,) giving to those Novices with abundance of impertinent Ceremonies the Salt of Wisdom, *Sal*

Sapientiae, &c." German universities repeatedly attempted to curb the excesses of "pennalism," the unwritten code that required all new students to submit to initiation ceremonies upon their arrival and hazing activities throughout their first year, thus demonstrating their inferiority and subservience to upperclassmen. Professor Dürr had battled pennalism during his term as rector in 1660-61, but Pastorius indicates it was flourishing once more by 1668. [8] The university sought to check rowdiness generally, and maintained three jail cells for student offenders, whose ranks included such famous men as Albrecht von Wallenstein, who caused "a lot of trouble and difficulty" ("viel Unruhe und Ärgernis") in 1599, and Friedrich von Logau, punished for dueling and damaging a churchyard wall in 1627. Punishment in the dungeon beneath the bell tower was reserved for severe offenses, but confinement in the two cells up in the tower was considered "not detrimental to the health [of the students] but very humane and mild" ("der Gesundheit nicht schädlich, sondern sehr menschenfreundlich und gelind"), and it was thus imposed "merely as a disciplinary measure" ("bei bloßen Disciplinstrafen"). [9]

As young aristocrats, Wallenstein and Logau were more prone to uncivil behavior than students of non-aristocratic rank. Nürnberg showed its respect for aristocratic privilege by reserving luxurious rooms and suites for students from fourteen of the aristocratic families of Franconia and, like all universities, it did not require young noblemen to take their studies seriously. As heirs to estates, they generally did not complete any degree program because they would be hiring graduates to handle the details of government and administration for them. [10] When Pastorius took inventory of his manuscript collection late in his Pennsylvania life, he recalled the young aristocrat from Hamburg who had once been his roommate, and revealed a resentment that was not untypical of student feelings toward the nobility. Pastorius had energetically filled two copy books with scholarly sentences on unspecified themes and then lent them to this fellow law student as a personal favor. Decades later he noted, "My Altdorf roommate Wilhelm von Düten never returned my two phrase books to me" ("Mein zu Altdorf gewesener Stubengesell Wilhelm von Düten J. U. Lic. enthielt mir 2 geschriebene Phrasesbüchlein"). [11]

Although many students, at Altdorf and elsewhere, resented aristocratic privilege, they generally aped the behavior of the aristocrats all the same. In fact, the tendency to display luxury and pomp in dress and manner waxed as the seventeenth century wore on. The typical student at Strasbourg, for example, portrayed by a contemporary artist in 1628, wore a cavalier's outfit with feathered hat and a sword, yet this attire is unpretentious in comparison with the rich elegance of embroidered, ruffled and frilled velvets and satins – shirts, waistcoats and gowns – fashioned for Strasbourg students at the end of the century. Pastorius' generation only briefly resisted wearing ostentatious wigs as a badge of social superiority, a fashion that increasingly obliged even the young to sacrifice their natural good looks for the artificiality introduced by Louis XIII of France (r. 1610-43) to hide his premature baldness. [12] When a bewigged trend-setter appeared at Altdorf in 1671, his fellow students ripped the wig from his head and tore it to shreds, but the fashion had become so widespread by 1692 that a wig maker then decided to set up shop in the village. Students wore gowns and swords at Altdorf, too, but luxurious red velvet gowns apparently did not become the fashion until after Pastorius' day. [13]

Despite the refinements of dress, student conduct was often unrefined, reflecting the social tensions that generated ennui and cynicism among upper-class youth. Pastorius' Pennsylvania writings indicate that he witnessed scenes of dissipation similar to those portrayed by an anonymous Jena artist during the 1620s and the Strasbourg artist Jakob van der Heyden (1573-1645). [14] The Jena painting, an aquarelle, shows a hung-over student seated, on an especially bleak morning, at his bedroom desk amid the scattered remnants of his self-indulgent life. Games and playing cards, drinking glasses and tankards, a lute, sword and stiletto strew the floor, and two blackboards on the wall tally his great debts to gamblers, pub-keepers and bar-maids and his bills for good meals and fine apparel. An old girl-friend, unexpected company, has just arrived, and she reveals his true state of bankruptcy as she accusingly holds up his newly-born illegitimate child instead of offering the cash he vainly awaits.

In Poem 424 (a prose reflection included among his poetry), Pastorius blends literal and metaphorical interpretations of an insignia allegedly identifying Cambridge University, and shows dismay for the typical excesses displayed in the Jena painting. He describes the insignia as " a woman with large naked breasts, three flowers on her head, holding in her right hand a cup, and in her left the sun, with this motto: Hinc Lucem et Pocula Sacra" ("This is a place of light, or elucidation, and sacred drink"). In his own Latin response, though, he notes with "anguish" that the universities have generated "nothing but thirst and indebtedness": "Proh dolor! Expectant hinc lucem et pocula sacra, hactenus unde nihil ni sitis et fenebrae." Adding Gospel references, he indicates that most students "walk in darkness" (1 John 1, 6) and ironically comments (John 4, 13): "Everyone who drinks of this water will thirst again."

In his university experience, the drinking cup was profane, and all too literal. One in ten drank himself to death while pursuing hedonistic excesses, Pastorius claimed in a letter he sent his father in 1699. University living could lead the best of youths astray. Even the well-trained son of a Melchior Adam Pastorius, he admitted with deep emotion, might backslide in this worldly environment. In a fervent epistle to Pietist friends, he briefly confessed to losing his religious faith as a student, and reported that he overcame "the godlessness of the universities [that was] deeply rooted in me." [15] Along with student excesses, Pastorius also encountered a wholesome, everyday sociability at German universities and on his later travels, evidence of which appears in his biographical notations on the men and women who provided him room and board over the years, including the armorer Abraham Klinger at Altdorf, a bookseller and a "Frau Lucretia" in Strasbourg, a printer by the name of Bauhoffer at Jena, a widow and an innkeeper at Regensburg, and "an old & merry-hearted Gentleman call'd Junker [i.e., Squire] Fichard" in Frankfurt.

3.2.3 Assets and Costs of Cultural Attainment

> Studies perfect nature, and are perfected by experience. Bacon. Bought wit is best. How few, alas, are learned, either in the macrocosm, or their microcosm. Petry. True beatitude consists not in understanding, but in living understandingly; neither is it great learning, but good will that joins men to God . . . To study such commendable arts as arithmetic, geometry, navigation, husbandry, handicraft, medicine, histories. Culpeper, p. 304. A hard lesson to learn to forget his learning . . . Learning, that honey of all humanity! . . . None are so learned that

they need not learn ... Learning of the schools lies chiefly in the abuse
of words, and such learning of ill consequence. Locke.
-- "Learning"

Knowledge that puffs up the possessor's mind,
Is evermore of a pernicious kind.
-- Epigram 2320.3

There are impertinent studies as well as impertinent men. Seneca, p. 504. There is more of trick and artifice in it than solidity; and yet there is matter of diversion, too: enough perhaps to pass away a winter's evening, and keep a man waking that's heavy-headed. P. 44.
-- "Pedantry"

The rich man's table, Luke 16:
    Of days thus spent,
    We must repent.
-- "Emblematical Recreations"
(On Lazarus and Dives)

During eight years of philosophy, rhetoric, modern languages, politics and law at his three German universities, Pastorius experienced typical intellectual delights and compulsions while pursuing a student career of unusual breadth and intensity. He absorbed a rich and varied culture in the daily life of his university towns, during his Switzerland trip, and on cultural excursions to cities like Bayreuth in Franconia, Erfurt, Naumburg and Gotha in Thuringia, and Sélestat and Colmar in the French province of Alsace. He was already developing the avid interests in art, architecture, popular graffiti and learned inscription that later led him to compile a lengthy manuscript journal of his grand tour containing hundreds or even thousands of detailed entries on the cultural artifacts he observed in dozens of cities – paintings, stained-glass windows, altars, fountains, statues, city halls, guild halls, private dwellings, cathedrals, palaces, stock exchanges. [16] His penchant for scholarly notation was firmly established during his youth. "I collected when yet a Lad and Scholar," Pastorius reported in 1698 (but without mentioning the title of this manuscript collection), "a good store of all sorts of [proverbs and] the like sharp and witty Apothegms ... under [a] Thousand Heads" [17] – an indication that his "Alphabetical Hive" in the "Beehive" manuscript, a similar but much larger collection, continued the intellectual habits formed at German universities.

Although students generally traveled from one university to another during the "wandering years" ("Wanderjahre") of late youth and frequently concluded their education with a grand tour of foreign countries – thus preparing themselves for lives of responsibility and satisfaction in their local communities – young Pastorius displayed unusual dedication to cultural pursuits in his prolific manuscript jottings on art and architecture, in his immense collection of proverbs and apothegms, and in his formal and informal study of language and literature, areas not directly related to his supposed interest in the law. In the notations of "Res Propriae," his brief autobiography in German, he indicated that he repeatedly hired private instructors for individual and small-group language lessons, applying to French and Italian the skills he had developed in Latin, the language of instruction in all of his academic courses.

He made impressive progress in Italian at Jena University. Supplementing his law studies on 1 August 1673, he began taking Italian lessons from Dr. Carlo Gaffa, a Roman scholar educated by the Dominicans, and by April 18 of the following year he had gained enough facility to deliver his own translation of a formal legal disputation he had first presented three months earlier in a seminar conducted by Instructor Heinrich Linck. Among his Pennsylvania dictionaries and grammar books – English, German, French, Italian, Spanish, Flemish or Belgian, Latin and Greek – Pastorius kept an annotated manuscript of Caffa's Italian grammar, a reminder of his linguistic accomplishment. Not yet satisfied with his proficiency in French after two years of the language with three or four instructors at Strasbourg, he again hired a French tutor for six more months during his stay at Regensburg in 1674-75.

Apparently in poetics courses and informal readings and discussions, Pastorius also learned the baroque tastes in literature popularized in Germany by academic poets like Martin Opitz (1597-1639) and Paul Fleming (1609-40), who had introduced a rich variety of forms and themes from vernacular Italian, French and Dutch models and insisted that German was, like the other vernacular tongues, as suitable as Latin for formal poetic expression. Interest in modern literature flourished in Pastorius' day, especially in university towns, where scholars and poets debated the nature of language and the rules of versification and read their own poetry in the festive gatherings of language or poetry societies ("Sprachgesellschaften"). [18]

Pastorius indicated the importance of these new developments in his "Beehive" manuscript (p. 321), noting that the folksy compositions of Hans Sachs (1494-1576), Nürnberg's most popular "Meistersinger" poet, "were as valuable in that age as those of Opitz and Fleming in ours." Pastorius' delight in the modern, fostered in Germany, continued to flourish in America. His commonplace jottings and literary commentary show his appreciation for periodicals like *The Freeholder*, *The Medley* and *The Spectator* (all published in the 1710s) and popular poets, novelists and playwrights like Henry Peacham (1576-1643), Francis Quarles (1592-1644), Edmund Waller (1606-87), Sir John Denham (1615-69), Sir Roger L'Estrange (1616-1704), Abraham Cowley (1618-67), John Wilson (1627-96), Sir William Temple (1628-99) and Daniel Defoe (1660-1731). [19] Although his enthusiasm or intensity was above average, Pastorius' youthful interests in art, literature and language were typical for the age of Louis XIV, when German students were eagerly absorbing the latest attitudes and mannerisms of the French court. [20]

Pastorius endeavored, as a student, to stay abreast of the times. Two days before signing up for Italian lessons at Jena University, for example, "Res Propriae" indicates, he began taking lessons in fencing from the university's fencing master – a man customarily addressed as "Monsieur Ebart" – apparently anticipating his own participation in the upper-class "vanities" of "dashing lances and waving banners" criticized in *Beschreibung Pennsylvaniae*. In like manner, on his grand tour of 1680-82, later condemned for the aristocratic excesses it revealed, Pastorius did not behave antisocially or dourly while accompanying the "noble young Spark called Johannes Bonaventura von Bodeck in his travels through Holland, England, France, Switzerland, &c," as he described the grand tour decades later in "Genealogia Pastoriana." [21] "We did ... happily perform our s[ai]d Voyage," he comments here, and he lists "feasting, dancing, &c" as hallmarks of the tour.

He also recalled delights of a personal nature in these two "monogrammed" sentences from "Symbola Onomastica" (no. 214): "Fashions Differ in the various Provinces of the world. French Damosels are Pleasant." He once wrote that he had met attractive females throughout his youthful travels, with the "fair Women & Girls" of Nürnberg "foreprized" above all others (see page 135). Even in 1683, when the "worldly *theatrum*" had lost its allure, Pastorius still considered it necessary to pack his formal clothing, wigs, and other upper-class paraphernalia as he set off for Pennsylvania (page 262, n. 9), indicating that he was not willing or able, at any point in his European existence, to dissociate himself from the norms of his society, or at least from outward conformity to the behavior and appearance his society expected of him.

These habits were deep-seated because they had been so thoroughly acquired. At considerable expense to his family, Pastorius indulged his tastes for learning and culture far more than students with limited resources were able to do. Future Windsheim clergymen like his friend Georg Model, for example, received four-year scholarships from the city in return for a pledge to enter public service, and their families usually could not afford to support a life of leisure away from home beyond this restricted period, just as the less fortunate students without scholarships were often forced to quit the university after one or two years. Well-to-do merchants and attorneys, however, freely supported their sons' extensive educations in the knowledge that titles like "doctor of the laws" (J. U. D.) would eventually pay big dividends in superior learning, reputation and status for the few who persevered.

Although Pastorius stated he had wasted time and money on useless scholastic learning, he also acknowledged the "great sums" ("große Summen") Melchior Adam had repeatedly sent him during his university years – a total of 949 talers, conservatively estimated as around $100,000 in today's money, an extraordinary amount in an age when the majority lived in or near poverty – and he gratefully concluded that his father had done more for him "than I will ever be able to repay" ("als ich . . . [n]immer fähig sein werde zu vergelten"). [22] The costs of cultural attainment generated guilt as well as gratitude, which in part accounts for the compulsive scholarliness of Pastorius' era. Transferring more than a hundred sundial inscriptions from his 600-page travel journal to his "Tantum Quantum" collection of learned inscriptions, Pastorius recognized he had been overly zealous as a note-taking student and traveler. "There are more of this sort in my 'Itinerario,'" he writes at the end of the list, "but it is not worth the time and the paper to copy them here." [23]

In the title-page introduction to "Emblematical Recreations," the collection of emblems and mottoes he presented to friends in Pennsylvania, he humorously describes the eagerly wandering eyes with which he observed cultural artifacts, and he gives this humor a serious context by citing Luke 16, 19 and thus referring to the story of the beggar Lazarus and the impenitent rich man Dives (Luke 16, 19-31). In effect, he satirizes the curiosity and compulsiveness that motivated his overly energetic observation of and compilation from cultural landmarks:

> Whereas [pictorial] Examples everywhere prevail above Precepts, I . . . shall [here] Collect, or rather Recollect as many [emblems and mottoes], as are not worn out of my Memory, Being once a Traveller in the World, mine eyes wandered about, hither & thither, up & down, over & under, especially gazing on the painted Walls & Tombs of Great Men, falsely so esteemed, Luke 16:19, and besides the following Emblems did observe several other Literal [i.e., literary] Plays and Ingenious Sports [including "Hieroglyphiks, or Egyptian Characters," "Rebus, or European Hieroglyphiks," epitaphs, inscriptions, "Posies," symbols and anagrams] . . . But I must not enlarge beyond mine own Intention, & tell you of other fine Poetical Knacks, as Ecchos, Achrostiches, Serpentine Verses, Recurrents, Numerals, &c., which I saw not only in Print, but even upon Columns & Tables of Marble.

Despite the moral ambiguity perceived in the artistic displays of great men, the emphasis here is on cultural satisfactions. His catalog of verse forms reflects the intellectual playfulness that made them popular, and Pastorius also conveys a thoughtful playfulness in his brief accompanying treatise on emblems. Tracing the meaning of "emblem" to the Greek phrase for "inserting or putting in," he shows his delight in esthetic complexity: "Whatsoever is laid in, embroidered, checkered or engraved of many pieces of divers Colours, may properly be called an Emblem." He explains that "Emblems are Speaking Pictures," and thus have both "a Body, viz. a fair representation" and a "Soul," which "give[s] life to the body" and, in some instances, "points at the mystical or hidden Sense" of the picture, so that creating emblems "require[s] as well an artificious Hand of either a Painter or Engraver, as likewise a quibbling Brain of a Word-measuring Poet." A good emblematic caption, he notes, is "a short but witty Motto or Word, answerable to the Picture, not too obscure, nor too plain. Best of all an Hemistich of some different language." Pastorius thus communicated some of his literary and artistic enthusiasms to fellow Pennsylvanians whom he considered literate enough to read and enjoy hundreds of Latin mottoes, yet capable of increasing their learned delights through the lessons he gladly provided.

The Gospel reference to Lazarus and Dives suggests the emotional issues of art and society that frustrated Pastorius' enjoyments in Germany, and contributed to the compulsiveness that typically accompanied the intellectual attainment of the learned. Pastorius was seeking truth as well as delight as he compiled proverbs, mottoes and poems from marble tablets and columns and other cultural artifacts, yet, in terms of authentic human values, much of this culture was insincere and ultimately pernicious – this, at any rate, is the conclusion suggested by the biblical citation in Pastorius' text. In the Gospel, Christ says that Dives "was clothed in purple and fine linen, and fared sumptuously every day," while the beggar Lazarus "was laid at his gate, full of sores, and desiring to be fed with the crumbs which fell from the rich man's table." Dives later suffers "torments" in hell, and learns "there is a great gulf fixed" between the impenitent and the virtuous in afterlife, reflecting a similar gap between the rich and the poor on earth. "In a coarse Frieze [coat or cloak] there is less Danger than in Purple and Scarlet," Pastorius writes in "Symbola Onomastica" (no. 211), commenting on the implications of this biblical story.

Following a relaxation of moral tensions in Pennsylvania, Pastorius would joke, in his full maturity, that "Our Painters and Poets are re-so-lute men" having more in common with the beggar Lazarus than with "poor Dives," but he was not prepared to advance such light-hearted arguments during his final years in Germany. [24] Even while enjoying the richness of cultural attainment, he was moving ever closer to the realization that the delights presented to his eyes by "this worldly *theatrum*" could not endure because (as he indicated in the foreword to *Beschreibung Pennsylvaniae*) they conflicted with his humane desire for Christian charity or neighborly love. His delight faded, at least temporarily, with the knowledge that he was enjoying high culture at the expense of his fellow citizens – and at the cost of his own moral and intellectual integrity. In his earliest American poetry, written before he resolved the moral tensions accompanying his emigration, Pastorius uses a simple opposition to express the urgency of this awareness (Poem 25):

> I loved luxury and gold and honour once,
> But loving now the LORD,
> I hate them for the nonce.

The contrast between his love of luxury and his love for God – or, more precisely, the manner in or extent to which he experienced a fading of cultural delights – is at the very heart of his bicultural experience, drawing together aspects of his character and conduct that have previously been misinterpreted. It is hardly surprising that Pastorius should have displayed mixed attitudes or evasiveness toward this crucial area of his personal development since, in the baroque era, the social costs of cultural attainment frequently evoked deeply emotional reactions from the most learned of men. Pastorius' emotions, furthermore, were increasingly complicated by the demands of obedience and authority that pervaded his experience at the university and in society generally, ultimately convincing him to sacrifice some of the satisfactions of his vital culture.

3.3   Objects of Delight:
Nürnberg's Cultural Influence, Germantown Applications

> Of artificial music neither precept nor example in the New Testament. Barclay, p. 473 . . . Jubal and his jolly jovial lads are wholly upon their merry pins [i.e., those of stringed instruments], timbrel, harp and organs (Gen. 4:21, Job 21:12) whilst Noah is building his ark. The ravishing strains of a sweet-tuned voice married to the warbles of the artful instrument. With songs an house can not be well ordered, was Diogenes' saying to one that bragged of his skill in music. Titillation of the ear. It is a kind of disparagement to be a cunning fiddler. There are hallelujahs sung in heaven . . . The superlative sweetness of the music. Mamut. After a skillful musician has put a viol in tune, some blundering hand new-turns the pegs, and spoils its harmony. Idem. Solacing his ear with several strains of music, harp, bagpipes, cymbal and taboret; lute, opharion, viol, sack-butt, cornet and organs . . . Music an intellectual as well as a sensible pleasure. Ath. Oracle, p. 439
> . . .   Music alone without women and wine
>   Does relish but dully though never so fine.
>
>   -- "Music"

Just as Altdorf offered the charms of gardens, promenades and Renaissance architecture along with the high ideals of post-Renaissance learning yet also revealed student excesses and academic demands typifying baroque tensions in the age of absolutism, seventeenth-century Nürnberg society effused grace and urbanity despite the tensions that could be felt beneath its convivial surface – a social charm that was most effusive in the learned idealism of youthful friends, in the flirtation of young lovers, and in the cultivated pleasures of art, music and poetry enjoyed especially by the young.

Despite the moral emphasis of his transatlantic correspondence, Pastorius obviously enjoyed the esthetic and the sensual that, as suggested by some of his "Alphabetical Hive" entries on music, together characterized the most delightful aspects of courtly and upper-class society. This enjoyment can be demonstrated, first of all, in the culture of Nürnberg, the city Pastorius knew best as a student, and, secondly, in his flirtatious and sexually allusive poetry, which owes some of its inspiration to Nürnberg. Taken together, Nürnberg culture and the Pennsylvania poetry also help to elucidate the distinction Pastorius made between fading and enduring delights.

120 | Franz Daniel Pastorius

This cross-cultural perspective reveals a number of pleasures that still flourished – or flourished anew – in Pennsylvania.

3.3.1 Art, Music and Drama in the Metropolis

> A fine woman who sings well is a trap doubly baited. Ath. Oracle, p. 272. Most songsters neither know when to begin nor make an end. Idem... The newest opera airs. Spectator... Of the theatrical manner of singing the Psalms, vide Spectator, No. 205. Children in the Wood, a ballad; wherein to be commended. Idem, vol. 2, p. 16. Mirth and music; or a collection of the newest and choicest songs sung at either playhouse or court, containing love songs, merry catches, and jovial healths, vide in Ac. Compl., p. 96 &c.
> – "Singing"

Although decentralized Germany did not have a capital matching the splendor of London or Paris until Prussian might drew the arts to Berlin in the nineteenth century, the cultural achievement of Nürnberg during the Renaissance and the seventeenth century was not surpassed by that of any other German city. [25] The grandeur of the city hall and church on its central plaza, the versatility of its craftsmen and merchants, the vitality of its folk festivals – these manifestations (briefly described on pages 38-39 and 61) only begin to characterize the Republic of Nürnberg as young Pastorius was developing cultural interests like those indicated in his "Alphabetical Hive" entries on the music of playhouse and court. These entries, from his readings two or three decades after emigrating, also reveal the personal growth that allowed him to move from at least partial rejection of upper-class culture to enjoyment of moderate cultural satisfactions essentially in consonance with the well-being of society as a whole.

Nürnberg's international colony of artists competed with local guild painters and carried on the traditions established in the city by Albrecht Dürer (1471-1528) and numerous immigrant Dutch masters of the Renaissance. Joachim von Sandrat (1606-88) and his nephew Jakob (1630-1708) founded the first German academy of art in 1661, achieving new standards in art publishing, engraving and portraiture. Nürnberg's musicians, composers, instrument makers and music publishers all contributed to the manifold forms of worldly and religious music that enriched baroque life. The Nürnberg composers Leonhard Lechner (1553-1606) and Hans Leo Haßler (1564-1612) had brought late Renaissance German song to its height of complexity and beauty, and later accomplishments of the Nürnberg School, combining strict formal complexity with the lyric simplicity of folk music, were exemplified in composer Johann Pachelbel (1653-1706), a fellow student of Pastorius' at Altdorf in 1669, whose sophisticated technique ranks him as one of the most important predecessors of Johann Sebastian Bach (1685-1750). [26]

As Pastorius enrolled at Nürnberg in 1668, the city was opening its stately new House of Opera and Comedy with a year-round theater season, augmenting the summer performances of an older open-air theater. Director Michael Treu (d. 1708) began producing plays like Shakespeare's *King Lear*, Christopher Marlowe's *Faust* and works by Jean Baptiste Moliére (1622-73), and a ballet staged that year featured a cast of 67 dancing children. It was a fascinating theater program. The poet Sigmund von Birken (1626-81) listed 36 comedies and pastoral entertainments that were performed in the old and new theaters from 1667 to 1669, two of which he attended twice and only one of which he did not get to see. Birken regretted the omission, for the comedy had been warmly recommended by friends.

3.3.2 Poetic Influences of City and Court

> Far from court, far from fear . . . What affronts must we endure to be admitted, and how much greater when we are in? Seneca, p. 228. Courts are only the schools of avarice and ambition. P. 559. . . . Courtiers are like those locusts in the Revelations, having men's faces but a lion's teeth. Saavedra. Of the servitude of great courtiers, vide <u>Spectator</u>, no. 193.
>
> -- "Court"
>
> An Narren und Poeten ist nie kein Mangel gewest.
> [There has never been any lack of poets and fools.]
>
> -- German proverb ironically concluding Poem 492, an English tribute to 53 poets from Homer to Shakespeare and Milton.
>
> Flatterers and Detractors are spiders in kings' Palaces. Prov. 30:28. [By imagining a large spider population not mentioned in Proverbs, Pastorius explains the presence of "small, but . . . exceedingly wise" lizards "in kings' palaces," and anticipates the wholesome feasting that would achieve ecological balance.]

Rich Folks Debauch and jump [i.e., dance],	Four and five good cups of Rhenish [wine]
And waste their goods with Pomp.	Does dull Poets' veins replenish.
First Deserve, and then Pretend:	If in Favour with the Lord,
On men's Favour not DePend.	I with Dukes and Princes bor'd.

> -- "Symbola Onomastica,"
> nos. 186, 520, 521, 528, 529

Poetry had a natural affinity with art, music and drama in Nürnberg. [27] Sigmund von Birken was president of the Worthy Order of Shepherds and Blossoms (Löblicher Hirten- und Blumen-Orden) on the Pegnitz, a society of predominantly local poets whose principles had been formulated by fellow poet Georg Philipp Harsdörffer and the clergyman-poet Johann Klaj (1616-56) in idyllic retreats along the Pegnitz River just outside of Nürnberg. Like Opitz and Flemming, Harsdörffer admired Italian and French verse and championed the German vernacular as a poetic medium. He also taught that music and art provided keys to poetic language, popularizing emblematic verse and experiments with onomatopoeia and melodic forms among the Pegnitz Shepherds.

The Nürnberg poets saw their art as both sensual and social. Harsdörffer combined literature – poetry, stories and plays framed by a rambling and intermittent novel – and intellectual parlor games in his nine-volume *Gesprechspiele*, 1641-49 (Conversational Recreations). Occasional verse flourished, and the poets collaborated with musicians and set designers to stage grand theatrical productions. When the Thirty Years' War ended in 1649, Klaj and Birken attained celebrity by producing an overwhelming combination of oratory, poetry, allegorical drama and song for an imperial banquet celebrating the conclusion of peace negotiations in Nürnberg, and Birken continued his career with "Singspiele" (musical plays or operas), ballets and other productions for the performing arts.

Along with worldly verse in these manifold forms, the Nürnberg poets – stimulated by Church Superintendent Johann Michael Dilherr, the friend of Windsheim's Rector Tobias Schumberg – produced religious verse of warm piety. Harsdörffer translated books by the English religious writers Joseph Hall (1574-1656) and William Ames (1576-1633), other editions of which were part of Pastorius' Pennsylvania library, and a small group of Protestant Austrian exiles in Nürnberg and Regensburg directly influenced Pastorius' writing. [28] The group included Catharina von Greiffenberg (1633-94), "the greatest female lyricist of seventeenth century German literature," [29] and Wolfgang Helmhard von Hohberg (1612-88), whose *Georgica Curiosa, Oder Adelisches Land- und Feldleben*, 1692 (Lordly [or Aristocratic] Life of the Country and Fields) is repeatedly cited in Pastorius' poetry and agricultural writing, revealing his enthusiasm for the life of rural virtue espoused by the Austrian exiles.

Given this array of secular and religious impulses in the poetry of Nürnberg, it is not surprising that Franz Daniel Pastorius would develop broad literary tastes there, especially favoring occasional and emblematic verse (even if Strasbourg and Frankfurt might further encourage these predilections), or that he would later produce sophisticated verse with a great variety of forms, styles and themes. No matter how indebted he might have been to Nürnberg, however, he would become dissatisfied with the illusions that sustained the Pegnitz Shepherds, who evoked pastoral scenes and ideals but accepted European social reality readily enough.

Harsdörffer and Birken wrote paeans to the emperor in Vienna and won aristocratic titles in return. Klaj accepted an appointment as clergyman at Kitzingen in rural Franconia, a truly pastoral locale, but town residents soon described the learned shepherd as "an arrogant and pompous man" who neglected his parishioners and "was only concerned with earning a large salary." [30] A number of the Pegnitz Shepherds wrote little if any poetry worthy of the name. Some of them joined to advance a career or gain social prominence, and others were asked to join because of their wealth or station. In this atmosphere, genuine literary expression easily degenerated into trite and dull mimicry. All too often, the Nürnberg poets displayed the limits of their social conventions in highly conventionalized poetic expression.

Even Sigmund von Birken, with his aristocratic title, his fame as a poet and his influence as president of the Pegnitz Shepherds, engaged in flattery and servility as he sought literary contracts among the city functionaries and prominent citizens of Nürnberg, the aristocrats of Franconia, and the officials at the Hapsburg court in Vienna. [31] Austrian and Franconian court officials repeatedly nagged at him and insulted his integrity, demanding textual revisions that conformed to the glorified image of emperor or prince. Caught between his ideals and the realities of his existence as a poet, Birken increasingly sought release in alcoholic intoxication. He aged prematurely, and grew so obese from compulsive eating and drinking that he could no longer climb the stairs unassisted. He clung to his pious Lutheran faith despite these tribulations, and decried the vanities of this world – particularly the flattery and duplicity of courtly existence – until, at age 55 (two years before Pastorius sailed for America), he found respite in death.

Young Pastorius would indirectly confront Birken's courtly travails as his own father gained influence at the court of Margrave Christian Ernst of Bayreuth, an absolutist prince who bankrupted his territory with military campaigns abroad and exorbitant luxury at home, yet was lavishly praised in the writings of both Birken and the elder Pastorius, two learned men of religious fervor and humane ideals who felt obliged to sacrifice personal integrity for courtly favor. [32] Having come so close to what he perceived as learned perniciousness, Pastorius would have abundant reason for praising the pristine delights and cultured satisfactions of early Pennsylvania, or, conversely, for criticizing or satirizing the compromises of courtly life – as in "Symbola Onomastica" items quoted above. Even reflecting on his garden catnip (Poem 174, in German), he satirizes a chameleon-like panderer whose hypocrisy and back-biting, the poem indicates, epitomize courtly behavior. The Pennsylvania setting, such reflection suggests, permitted a few essential modifications of tone and character in his life and poetry, reinforcing the anti-courtly attitudes that coexisted with his robust worldliness.

3.3.3 "The Preeminence of the Female Sex above ours": Gender and Sexuality in Pastorius' Scholarship and Poetry

> Many kiss the child for the nurse's sake . . . To kiss a yard higher. The common salutation of women [e.g., kissing] to be abhorred; if a piece of civility, it is not a calmly sight . . . To buss. She clasped him about the neck. A colling. To embrace. To hose. To hug . . . To smack a kiss. To twine about . . . Alain Chartier, secretary to King Louis XI of France, by whose Queen the Lady Anne of Britain he was so admired for his poetry, that one day she finding him asleep on a table's end, said in the hearing of many, we may not of princely courtesy pass by, and not honour with a kiss the mouth from whence so many sweet ditties and golden poems have issued. Phillips. Of kisses between different sexes, <u>Ath. Oracle</u>, p. 111. Kissing is a luscious diet. Id.
>
>   And shall I boldly seize a kiss,
>   The prelude to a greater bliss?
>
>   -- "Kiss"
>
> Dick swears that Nell is neat and handy,
> And kisses sweet as sugar candy.
>
>   -- "Brave Woman"

Pastorius may have criticized courtly servitude and duplicity, but he did not categorically reject the cultural delights of his youth. This is especially obvious in his flirtatious poetry, with its mellowed but essentially youthful spontaneity, and its blending of the sensual and the esthetic, as well as in "Alphabetical Hive" entries like the anecdote of Lady Anne of Britain boldly kissing her French troubadour, with a refined sensuality complementing the bawdiness of "to kiss a yard higher," presumably from a joke then circulating in Germantown and Philadelphia. The lively sensuality of Pastorius' poetry (part of a conviviality also expressed in a number of poems celebrating male camaraderie) demonstrates that his condemnation of social excess did not encompass the range of human pleasures so often presumed to be rejected by men and women (be they Puritans, Quakers or Pietists) with well-defined standards of morality. A rich sampling of colonial American sensual expression, this poetry (most of it written in 1708-19) shows Pastorius in a predominant mood of his full maturity, as he relaxed and enjoyed – and contributed to – the culture of early eighteenth-century Philadelphia, principally Anglo-American, increasingly secular and neoclassical, and already developing the cosmopolitan traits that would make it one of the British colonies' liveliest and most important cities. The poetry will be described here in the context of the gender issues presented in Pastorius' commonplace scholarship.

3.3.3.1 Attitudes Toward Women and Sexuality

> There is much to be said in praise of women, and not a little in their disparagement. Mamut. They are the gates of life and death, the very avenues to heaven or hell, according as they are used. Ibid., vol. 7, p. 64. 'Tis neither safe to vex 'em in the least, or humour 'em too much. Ibid. Your windings and turnings are intricate as those of serpents; Daedalus himself were he now alive, though once the glory of labyrinth makers, yet would be puzzled to trace your sex in all your secret, wild, unknown meanders. Ibid. . . . Of a more than feminine wit and fancy . . . Women in fact have managed affairs as well [as men], even when placed upon thrones. Ath. Oracle, p. 444.
>
> Now to describe a woman to the life,
> Whether virgin, maid or married wife . . .
> She is a tender thing, refined and pure,
> And cannot harsh, rough handling well endure;
> For like a Venice glass she breaks asunder
> When boistrous men will strive to keep her under. Leeds, 1712.
>
> -- "Woman"
>
> Beauty never tempted men
> To lasciviousness, but when
> Careless idleness has brought
> Wicked longings into thought.
>
> -- Epigram 40

Although both Nürnberg and Philadelphia reveal cosmopolitan traits fostering poetic sensuality, Pastorius also encountered mores and attitudes discouraging unrestrained flirtation and generous appreciation for the opposite sex. His morality, enlightened and biblical, retained some of the emphasis on good and evil stressed in his often compulsive upbringing, the sexual aspects of which inform his early Epigram 40 on beauty and lasciviousness as well as "Symbola Onomastica," no. 231, a rendering of Proverbs 22, 14, suggesting a linkage between sexual adventure and damnation: "Kiss not the mouth of a Strange Woman, For it is a Deep Pit." Despite this tendency, Pastorius rarely criticizes sexual conduct, and then only if it violates his humane standards of decency.

In "Symbola Onomastica" he censures apparently biblical "arrant Whores" (no. 216) and, probably reflecting scenes witnessed as a young man, concludes (no. 526): "Of all things the French have, the most Detestable are their Pocks [i.e., syphilis], a long repentance Following a short Delight or Pleasure." He sums up French prostitution in Poem 262: "proffer'd service stinks." His sharp ridicule of "venereal" Louis XIV's sexual exploits has already been mentioned. Outraged by the innocent suffering of rape victims, he ignores, in Poem 259, the liberal punishment evoked in his commentary on the Native Americans and numerous "Alphabetical Hive" entries:

> To force a Woman, once was Death,
> No Ruffians suffered were to breathe,
> But now deflow'ring whom they will,
> Says Rosamund, We must be still. Jer. 23:10.

Although Pastorius repeatedly criticizes immoral conduct, these are the only poems of sexual criticism in his collected verse. Even in his "Alphabet of Sinful Men and Women" (Poem 440) demonstrating "That Learning's first Degree / Depends on the A, B, C" and describing 28 individuals (mostly biblical, four female) who committed sins ranging from disdain and deceit to murder, he cites only two for sexual offenses – Reuben for "defil[ing] his Father's own Couch" and Tamar for "play[ing] the Whore" – and reports that Adam and Eve "in Eden did fall" without accusing or moralizing, just as his only other verse about them (Poem 14) is a witty German play on words defining human earthiness. [33] His morality usually has a nonsexual focus, indicating a liberality that gained ascendance over his early compulsions, and he moved ever closer to an awareness that inflexible sexual codes are based in part on unhealthy inhibitions artificially keeping the sexes isolated from each other. Such an awareness, although not commonly accepted in his day, is reflected in a few "Alphabetical Hive" entries such as the bluntly humorous observation (from "The Privy Parts") that "a man's prick may cause a prick of conscience" and (from "Womanish") "to be amorous of women is a sign of good nature."

Augmenting and intensifying sexual inhibitions, the superiority and standoffishness of learned men created sexual barriers of the sort Pastorius undermined with his appreciative flirtation (even if he remained sexist in his understanding of family roles). Most of the "Alphabetical Hive" entries on "Woman," "Woman's Wit," "Womanish" and "Woman's Imperiousness" display supercilious criticism, sardonic wit or outright ridicule – and thus lack the appreciative irony of Mamut, the "Turkish Spy" quoted in the epigraph here. (In real life, the 'spy' was apparently Giovanni Paolo Marana (1642-1693), a witty Italian). Pastorius' scholarly peers infrequently and ambiguously mention the "gentle wit" and "soft rhetoric" of the female, faint praise at best, but repeatedly criticize women as deceitful, crafty, wily, "hurtful things," purveyors of "glittering promises" soon broken – evidence of male authority subverted, and egos deflated, by attractive but intractable females.

"He is not in his wits that puts any trust in women," a simple rendering of the theme, also receives rhetorical embellishment: "Many are their wiles, and guile goes forward upon the earth." A man swayed by the female is categorized as womanish, effeminate, uxorious, unmanly, unmanned; or ridiculed as "henpeckt," a meacock (meaning someone effeminate or cowardly), a "smell-smock." Pastorius' peers do not show any sympathy for "imperious" women, either. "Socrates said he kept his froward wife Xanthippe to exercise his patience," one of them notes, and Francis Quarles (one of Pastorius' favorite emblem writers) observes:

> I know not which live most unnatural lives,
> Obeying husbands or commanding wives.

Judgmental and punitive attitudes indicate deep-seated sexual tension. Equestrian and feminine virtues are judged comparatively in a popular proverb: "It is a good (horse) woman that never (stumbles) grumbles." "Though no wickedness be above that of a woman," one superior male intones, "yet has she less brain in her head than a man." With one notable exception epitomizing the hearty appreciation of marital partners for each other ("A good woman is best pleased with her own good man"), the entries under "Wife" exhort women to virtue and obedience or patronizingly praise wifely virtue, just as those under "Woman's Beating" reveal learned men accepting or condoning repressive conduct meant to prevent or overwhelm female intractability. "The wickedness of the beating husband is often a whetstone to the wife's devotion and prayer," one source ingeniously argues, and another reduces this to its ultimate simplification: "The worse he is the better she grows." Such devious male logic accepts dehumanized roles of dominance and submission: "The more they are beaten the better they be."

The only challenge to punitive attitudes is from Daniel Leeds' 1712 Pennsylvania almanac (in the epigraph above), a sympathetic voice protesting in light verse against "harsh, rough handling," its image of shattering Venetian crystal poignantly capturing the despair of women pushed to the breaking point in male-dominated society. This is one of very few liberal entries in "Woman," others of which show that Pastorius read about "female excellency" in an unclearly-identified source, and (in Edward Phillips' *Theatrum Poetarium*) about the Italian Lucrezia Marinella (1571-1653), who "wrote a poem of the divinity and preeminence of women," apparently a reference to *La nobiltà et l'eccellenza delle donne, co' difetti et mancamenti de gli uomini (The Nobility and Excellence of Women and the Defects and Vices of Men)*, 1601, cogently refuting misogynist treatises. [33a] Pastorius also collected generous appraisals of women under the heading of "Brave Woman," both sexist judgements of female beauty and charm, and attitudes more conducive to gender understanding. A few liberal opinions from "Woman" and "Brave Woman" are quoted on pages 134-35.

3.3.3.2 Husband and Wife

Modesty is her ornament, and a moving rhetoric in itself. <u>Closet</u>, p. 204 . . . Modesty the chief adornment of the female sex, <u>Spectator</u>, no. 6.

-- "Modesty"

One man is hankering after his neighbour's wife, another is in pain about his own. Senaca, p. 597. The foot on the cradle and the hand on the distaff [for spinning flax or wool] is the sign of a good housewife. The more women look to their glasses [of beer or wine], the less they look to their houses. Women among Christians take more care to show themselves than to hide themselves. Mamut, vol 1, p. 5. Some women can conceal nothing but what they do not know. Ibid. A man that would have a wife not talkative, should marry a mute as Turks do. Ibid. p. 16 . . . Women will be wasps if angered. Leeds, 1709. Women will be quiet when well pleased. Ibid . . . Women are fitter to conceive children than to conceal secrets. Leeds, 1713. If it were not for women, hell would be but thinly peopled.

-- "Woman"

Bad is the fate, sad is the life,
Of him that has a scolding wife.

-- Epigram 46

Illiberal comments about women in Leeds' almanacs and Marana's *Turkish Spy (Mamut the Arabian)* indicate the tentativeness of contemporary male generosity toward female partners or antagonists, a trait shared to some extent by Pastorius. In comments of a general nature, at least, his male chauvinism is of the mildest sort. "Young Maidens fain would Husbands have, / And then of them do Children crave," he notes in Epigram 677 (citing Genesis 30, 1), and endorses feminine modesty in references to the story of demure and spirited Rebecca divinely chosen as the bride of Isaac (Genesis 24, in "Symbola Onomastica," nos. 207, 208). His male bias is more pronounced in a few comments on wives based to some extent on his own marital experience. [34] Nettles teach "how bad Wives / Are Vexations to Men's Lives," he writes in Poem 233 (warning against superficially equating the natural and the spiritual yet drawing a few lessons from nature), and his "Alphabet of Sinful Men and Women" includes Delilah for betraying "her Husband" Samson and "long-tongued" Xanthippe for vexing Socrates. He does not deal with cuckoldry in his collected poetry, but gives it passing notice in Epigram 77:

> Debauched Wives and Back Doors in a House
> Soon make a Man as naked as a Louse.

He was so impressed with a widower's witty arguments against marrying a second time (in the "Secret History" of Madame de Maintenon, 1690, also his source for the sexual exploits of Louis XIV) that he paraphrased them in a series of twelve epigrams including these (nos. 1, 2, 8, 11):

> The Husband's the Pilot, the Wife is the Ocean,
> He's always in Danger, she always in Motion.

> A Man that in Wedlock twice hazards his Body,
> Twice ventures a Drowning, a pitiful Noddy.

> If you're unactive, there's nothing but Scorning,
> Night's Failures are sore reproached next Morning.

> Flood, Fire and Female begin with the same letter,
> And for 'em we are not a Farthing the better.

The domestic frustration of Epigram 46 on a "scolding wife" (in the epigraph above) reappears in Poem 102 (in Latin, German and English), which plays on the meanings of mellis and fellis (honey and bile or gall), the herbal name amara-dulcis (bittersweet) and the ambiguous phrase je länger, je lieber (here meaning she will improve with age, or the more I/you know her, the more I/you like her). It unsympathetically describes "a woman" ("ein Weib") whose courtship allurements are utterly transformed by marital existence:

> This sweet and kind Creature
> Of honey-like Nature,
> Soon makes herself all
> As bitter as Gall.

Those who do not know the wife merely laugh at the husband or his perception of her, Pastorius notes in German, and claim she will improve with age (or that she evokes the adage, "the more I know her, the more I like her"). He later turned this poem into a graceful German lyric (Poem 190) that pithily contrasts amara-dulcis (its first word) and je länger, je lieber (its final line), here specifying that "ein Weib" ("a woman") is actually "mein Weib" ("my wife"), but attenuating the sharp mood of Poem 102 by omitting the Latin and English references to honey and gall. [35] Poem 351, with a persona not in the first person (though presumably voicing ideas similar to Pastorius'), mixes fatalism and light satire in its comments on marriage and divorce. A husband called Tom says he would prefer three-month marriages to the social or religious mores that keep him in a bad marriage, but does not refute his wife's claim that "Death's hand alone can write our General Release, / And change our daily Broils with Everlasting Peace."

This sharp conjugal tension is moderated elsewhere in Pastorius' poetry (see pages 133-34) and, it seems, in much of his life as well. His poetry reflects numerous domestic satisfactions such as the high adventure of the poet, his wife Anne and their 16-year-old son John Samuel guiding a swarm of bees to a new hive in the orchard of "our Country-farm" (Poem 77, composed in 1706, and dedicated to Anne). Having commented on "bittersweet" aspects of marriage, he later wrote religious meditations also employing the 'amara-dulcis' and 'je länger, je lieber' motifs (Poems 234, 235), indicating an awareness that marriage and life entail burdens that can only be appreciated with experience, that a mix of bitter and sweet is more realistic, and presumably more satisfying, than unmitigated sweetness.

His mature poetry embodies a complex psychology accepting tension in conjugal relationships, and it also reveals a generous appreciation of females that raises the battle of the sexes above the level of petty disagreement. As he interacted with his wife and other women, learning from personal experience in Pennsylvania's new society and from his broad reading (and epitomizing this blend of knowledge in his poetry), he joked and versified sexually, growing increasingly unrestrained in his sexual references (though not entirely freed of his inhibitions), and ultimately so "amorous of women" that he acknowledged feminine "preeminence" in a small but significant treatise refuting a number of the biases of male supremacy.

3.3.3.3 *Flirtation and Sensuality in Pastorius' Poetry*

> The love of women is natural to our sex; and there is no man who at one time or other has not felt the warmths of this amorous passion. Mamut. The greatest men in the world have been subject to this passion of love, see Ibid. vol. 8, p. 190. United in the chaste endearments of reciprocal love. Closet. Tho' love is the supreme matter, yet it ought to be attended with prudence, or else it will waste itself and totter in its sphere. Ibid. p. 223. Lovers fall out and in again . . . A woman's man described, with his necessary qualifications, Spectator, no. 156 & 158 . . . He that fears womankind, can't be counted mankind. Newb.
>
>   -- "Love of Woman"
>
> A maid that laughs is half taken.
>
>   -- "Laughter"
>
> Variety is most taking . . . Variety has, to say truth, a strange charm in it. Ath. Oracle.
>
>   -- "Variety"

Variously coy and explicit in his verse, Pastorius repeatedly alludes to sexual themes suggested by the organic growth of his garden, in the German and Latin Poem 144 described as a varied neighborhood where "all get used to living together" ("alle sich Zusamm gewöhnen") even though some "neighbors" have to be kept apart and, typifying equally strange human couplings, "a rose fragrant, beautiful and tender" frequently "mates" with a stinging nettle:

> Die Nachbarschaft ist mancher Art,
> Ein Ros, wohlriechend, schön und zart
> Sich oftmals mit Brenn Nessel paart.

Pastorius wastes not a word on the rough, masculine stinging nettle but, ambiguously invoking female or flower, waxes learnedly lyrical over the luscious rose, or "Rosa, the delight of the gods":

> Rosa, Honor Decusque Florum,
> Rosa, Cura Amorque Veneris,
> Rosa, Coelitum Voluptas.

Similarly, in a garden revealing literal as well as figurative neighbors, Pastorius (in Poem 141) is particularly intrigued by the variety of his female callers, some of them "Gentle women" who "delight chiefly in those Flowers, / That are as beautiful as they themselves," while others search out "sweet Smells" with their "Grocers-Noses" or debate the medicinal effects of the garden herbs – and immediately get some teasing advice from the gardener-poet about the effectiveness of "Ladies-Smocks," a flowering cress (also known as the cuckoo flower, and thus evoking cuckoldry as well as undergarments) whose name alone, if spoken with a knowing look or tone of voice, might elicit a modest blush or sprightly laughter. (The meaning of "smock" as "undergarment" has since become archaic.)

Stretching the similarity between herbal names and girls' names in Poem 169, he suggests the process of selecting from a variety of females – "I love" and "prefer Angelicam and Barberry" (herbs with names sounding like Angelica and Barbara) to "Sweet Maudlin and Sweet Margery /am " (combining marjoram and Margery) – just as he elsewhere suggests cosmopolitan variety, in part reflecting on his youth and early travels. In his version of a popular German lyric on kissing and making love, "Darf man dich Corinna küss?" (Would you let me kiss you, Corinna?), a too-hesitant lover learns that his girl means yes when she says no. Its graceful poetry implies a healthy antidote to sexual repression in a light-hearted context far removed from modern considerations of consent. [36] Poem 261 describes a pert "French Damosel" who tells "an English Gentleman: / I am the fairest Flower in all the Town," but learns that he "to Demoiselles prefer[s] an English Wench." In the following poem Pastorius himself confesses, "The British Marigolds are pretty things, me thinks," but then goes on to indicate he is referring to the flowers – or is it (yes, it is!) the females and the flowers.

He observes "Many Women, many Minds / All of quite Contrary kinds" as Philadelphia ladies "buy Tulips" and Germantown villagers "sell Turnips" (Poem 168), and then he wryly identifies a common denominator in the flirtation or lovemaking of the maidens and wives from the village and the town:

> How be't the most, when in their mood,
> Love William sweet and Henry good:
> And then are playing Hide and Seek,
> Call'd Apodidrascind [or apodidraskinda] in Greek.

In Poem 167 he describes "Girls and their Wooers" smoking tobacco, and notes that "Both Sexes are enamoured of what I call a Weed [i.e., tobacco] / They take it for mere Fashions Sake, and also when 'tis need" (i.e., medicinally), thus suggesting that smoking was an American pastime where gender equality prevailed.

Descriptions of newlywed sex and a striptease artist reveal warmhearted humor and witty satire. In Poem 260 a new husband's "achings" are cured when his bride takes artichokes, or "heartichokes," as an aphrodisiac, with subtle wordplay (hard and heart merge into hart) suggesting physical and emotional aspects of love consummated as well as the male deer, agile and fleet, and traditionally imaging erotic sensation:

> The same way soon restored them,
> And [she] cry'd I am entangled,
> Very hart beset
> In the Wedlock's Net.

Poem 337, identifying the outer petals of a pea blossom with a lady's gown (and the young green pod with her petticoat), teasingly compares the pea to a stripping lady. The personification is especially effective – and humorous – since "rounceval" identifies several varieties of the garden pea with its tiny, delicate blossom as well as a woman "of large build and boisterous or loose manners" (*OED*, 8, 820):

> When Madam Rounceval, now being piping-hot,
> Puts off her purple Gown, Young Folks despise her not;
> She looks the lovelier in her green Petticoat.

Pastorius also treats virgins and widows humorously. He coyly defines virginity in Poem 278:

> White lilies yield the sweetest Smell
> When Virgin like they stand;
> I mean, when (understand me well)
> Untouch'd by human hand.

In a German carpe diem parody (Poem 165), a pure, white snowdrop (the flower 'leucojum bulbosum'), personified as a virgin, bitterly complains that she is languishing because "nobody has taken me in marriage." ("... Ach und Wehe, / Niemand nimmet mich zur Ehe"). In contrast, Poem 279 objectively describes maidens who, beguiled and disarmed by compliments and "shining talents" ("güldner Gaben glantz"), lose the purity they might otherwise have kept. The herb melancholy cures despair, he writes in Poem 288, and "Makes men like merry Crickets, / Or newly married Widows." When "pirate" bees robbed his hive in 1708, leaving him as a honeyless "widow," he notes in the German Poem 128, grief "penetrated through my belly to the heart" ("Drung mir durchs Wammes bis ans Hertz"), and he did not relinquish his "old sorrows" for a new "marriage" (replenishing his hive) until the following year: a young widow mourns loudly, he reflects, and doesn't even want to think about another husband until she's buried the first.

Using humor and satire, Pastorius in these poems deals with sexual themes frequently considered inappropriate for public expression, an awareness that explains why he omitted most of his lively sexual verse from the manuscripts he circulated in Pennsylvania, and some of the sexual allusions from the poems he did include. The sensual poem most obviously intended for recitation in mixed company (Poem 253) combines delight and instruction of the most traditional variety. Deliberately confusing botanical and feminine traits, Pastorius here notes, "My well-shaped Flowers by Age do wear away, / Red Cheeks grow pale, and yellow hairs wax gray," and he lightheartedly addresses his readers or listeners:

> Mind this, You Beauties of our Time,
> And thank the Poet of his Rime,
> Who also, gallant Dames, tells you beside,
> No Vice offends the Lord so much as Pride,
>   The Frailty of his Flowers
>   An Emblem is of yours.

Pastorius dexterously employs his literary skills to get beneath the public surface of sexual attitudes, ambiguously expressing the feelings of attraction or desire that could not be openly stated. Poem 191, for example, can be taken either as romantic parody, ironic botanical realism, or a proclamation of his love for the addressee:

> Why did thou send me Violets my Dear?
> To make me burn more violent, I fear:
> With these thy Cordial Flowers too vehement thou art
> To set on Fire and to violate my heart.
> Some from an other hand did Cool my Sore,
> But thine (tho' very fresh) inflame it more and more.

> My head-ache, thirst, hot Ague, Pleurisie,
> Are not remov'd; they are Increas'd thereby.

The poem was probably a response to flowers sent to his sick bed, and it was probably addressed to a good friend. But the tension between the two quatrains (the second is either a contradiction or a culmination of the first) suggests a deeper ambiguity as well – genuine feelings of attraction, a "fever" that is metaphorical, an irony doubly ironic.

Some of his poetic tête-à-têtes were not quite this ambiguous. In a 1718 letter he sent "Jane Fenn, my lovely Poetess," 66-year-old Pastorius cites the example of accomplished females from "famous Sappho" of Lesbos to Anne Bradstreet (misspelled Broadstreet), "the Tenth [female British muse], sprung up in New England," to encourage this young and inexperienced Pennsylvania poetess, who might "most of thy Sex surpass" if, he gently advises, she would master the basics of scansion demonstrated in the verse of his letter to her (Poem 474). [37] While his attraction for young Jane Fenn might have been predominantly intellectual, Pastorius, in Poem 339, playfully employs sensual imagery and botanical metaphor to evoke sexual attraction. The poet or his persona describes "Thy two Lips, Dulcimouth, / Bright red and fine," while addressing a beloved, Dorcas (the Latin-English hybrid "Dulcimouth" describes her delightful mouth), who is admiring "this Tulip-Bed of mine," with its "Ninety nine Chosen Flowers." As he tentatively invites her into his bed (with the other ninety-nine), he indicates that this enchanting woman is not just one among a hundred, but his flower of flowers – and Pastorius calls attention to his double entendre with a technical footnote (in Latin and with biblical citations, complexity that might have moved "Dorcas" to seek further elucidation from the poet himself):

> If, dear Dorcas, thou wert free,[*]
> Amongst them to set thy Shoe,
> Thou soon wouldst the Hundredst be,
> And of all the Fairest too.

---

[*] Shoe for Foot. Metonymice, Continens sumitur pro re Contenta [Metonymy, a main feature is selected instead of (but as if comprising) the thing itself]; vide Deut. 28:5, I Cor. 10:21 & 11:26. [Pastorius' note.]

Pastorius repeatedly uses verbal devices including two lips / tulips (evoking visual and tactile satisfactions of enduring appeal) and the horticultural and physical or sexual connotations of "bed" along with sensual and organic imagery, colors, and color contrasts to suggest the vitality of sexual desire, a vitality variously mature and innocent. He describes the spontaneous delight of a youthful kiss in a German riddle and its English paraphrase (Poem 278). How can you change white lilies into red roses? Unexpectedly kiss your Polyxena, and she will laugh blushingly (the word "erröthen," German for 'blush,' actually contains the red ['rot'] of the girl's cheeks within it):

> Q. Wie wilstu weise Lilien
>   Zu rothen Rosen machen?
> A. Küss unversehens dein Polyxen,
>   Sie wird erröthet lachen.
>   White lilies presently
>   One may Metamorphose

>By kissing Margery (Dorothy, &c.)
>Into a Damask-Rose.

He repeats the tulips / two lips device in Poem 202, with a comic realism deriving from fanciful reflections on red and yellow tulips, round and stout figures in their separate beds (one old and the other young), and on popular attitudes toward garden design and/or hybridization:

>Now't was stout Hans that said
>To Belly Bell the Maid, viz.
>My Two-Lips stale and pale,
>Your Two-Lips neat and red,
>Let, dear Belly Bell,
>Be Joyned in one Bed.
>But She, displeas'd hereby,
>Did suddenly reply, viz.
>Hans, Mine you say, are red,
>And yours do look like yellow,
>Therefore each by themselves!
>Dream not of *this* Bed-fellow.

Poems 163 (mostly in English but also with German, Latin and French lines) and 164 (in German and English) reveal a complex approach to sensuality combining linguistic and imagistic devices, humor, indirection, and a willingness to push introspection beyond the limits imposed by social convention. Poem 163 argues for hearty gustatory and olfactory satisfactions instead of merely visual pleasures as Pastorius addresses "Du liebe Jungfer" (You, dear virgin), an inexperienced young woman who gazes too appreciatively at the rich display of "unwont Colors" in her bed of tulips, flowers without odor. The poem asserts the merits of a vegetable meal over this floral view, an ordinary garden theme, but with phallic or sexual possibilities suggested when the poet announces "my Sparagus" (or asparagus "shoots") as his choice of vegetable and then blusters on:

>But I forever am so blunt,
>That what things happen will may hap,
>No words nor Swords move me to Swap
>A hundred Sperage Shoots of mine
>For thousand smelless Flowers of thine,
>Which never hungry Men could eat.
>This good Stalk with and without Meat
>Can make for me a Stately Meal;
>(I only wish I had a deal).

Despite the Freudian potential of these lines, the poem seems so lighthearted and, at the level of explicit discourse, so non-erotic that even "This good Stalk with and without meat" would not necessarily evoke sexual connotations were it not for a concluding joke about tulips and two lips (in the sequence of the collected poetry the first use of this device), and a variation of it in the following poem. But is Pastorius joking? At times in this poem he seems moody or even petulant, and, apparently, he grudgingly admits a physical attraction for this "dear virgin" that he considers "injurious" [37a]. The tone of the next poem is lighter even though it breaks a taboo by playfully comparing the herb cowslip with girls' lips and laps (Poem 164 entire):

Cowslips never hurted none;
But let Girls' L $_i^a$ ps alone:
Thereby Many were undone.
Therefore, Fare well my Cowslips Sweet,
Fare well, til we again do meet.
Schwartze Augen, rothe Lippen,
Zwei bekannte Schiffbruchs-klippen.
[Black eyes and red lips,
Two well-known shoals of shipwreck.]

These two poems frankly probe the limits of a mature man's enjoyment of youthful beauty and reveal the mind (and libido) of a man who is apparently considering whether to resist or to yield to physical attraction felt for a particular female. Note that "girl" for Pastorius can mean any single young woman; he uses "Innuptas" in Poem 163, refers to "Girls and their Wooers" in Poem 167 (cited on page 129), and, mentioning Nürnberg's "fair Women & Girls" (page 116), distinguishes married women from unmarried. Pastorius included a shortened and simplified version of Poem 163 in his circulated "Deliciae Hortenses" manuscript (deleting the most obvious sexual imagery and dropping the identity of "you" as a young virgin), and he omitted Poem 164 entirely, indicating his sensitivity to conventional attitudes toward sexuality. His own willingness to probe the conventions, even to broach taboo themes, reveals a maturity benefitting from insights unavailable to those who repressed or sublimated feelings not approved by society. These insights can be seen in his prose reflections on feminine merits generally, and in a few mature poems deriving from his domestic experience.

The literary evidence suggests that flirting with other women and writing sensuous poetry strengthened rather than undermined Pastorius' relationship with his wife Anne. Exploiting the phallic connotations of the trumpet rose while evoking the domestic satisfactions described in numerous poems, he humorously compares his staid marital existence with a bachelor's presumed lack of sexual restraint (Poem 275, in German, Latin and English):

The Trumpet-Rose
Thrives best with those
Who live a Batch'lors life,
But mine soon rots
In Beds or Pots,
Because I have a Wife;
Yet I, O strange!
Would not exchange
My Consort as she is,
Chaste, clean and pure,
(No Strumpet, sure)
For all their Trumperies. [38]

In Poem 337 (part of a learned exchange with James Logan of Philadelphia), "A Scolding Fit of Botanical Bynames between Husband and Wife, the Honey-Moon being over" follows "Some herbal Epithets, which a couple of young overfond Paramours foolishly bestowed one upon another." Pastorius thus transmutes the thin honey-and-gall frustrations of earlier domestic poems into hearty and humorous art. In these extended "dialogues," the young lovers call each other sonorous and suggestive names like (addressed to the female) honeysuckle, lambs tongue, hay-maid, vine of Virginia and "Allheal, pure Ladies-smock," and (to the male) cull-me-to-you, sugar pea, muskmelon, spikenard, "One-blade and Sauce-alone." The wife begins her scolding with the energetic outburst, "Thou Hore hound, Butterbur, Cockshead and Cuckowpint, / Satyrion, Dragon wort, Bistort, Puff, Calamint," and the husband responds in kind. Poem 299 (entire) provides a mature appreciation of a temperamental or "scolding wife," apparently a tribute to Anne, whose robust personality he had earlier criticized:

> If thou wouldst Rose's Scent mend,
> And make more excellent,
> Than thou formerly hadst them,
> Plant but Garlick to their Stem;
> Likewise, if a Friend of thine
> Should to Goodness so incline,
> As to lead a Virtuous Life,
> Let him take a Scolding Wife:
> Thus Nature works, you see,
> Sometimes by Antipathy.

The view of the Pastorius' marriage is, unfortunately, entirely one-sided. Despite the vast documentation of his life and writings, Anne's voice and attitudes are nowhere recorded.

3.3.3.4 A Prose 'Rhapsody' on Feminine Merits, And an Apian Poem on Sensual Rewards

> A spider gathereth poison where a bee would find honey. A bee chuseth rather to go to the flowers in the field, and there to lade their thighs securely and with leasure; but a wasp comes to the apothecaries shop and falls into the honey and is drowned. . . . The bee that wanders, and slips from every flower, disposes what she has gathered into her cells. Seneca, p. 471 . . . The cattle afford us plenty of milk, and the bees are no niggards of their honey. Mamut . . . Are there no chastisements amongst them? Every hive is a pattern of a well-governed commonwealth; all doing their duty with cheerfulness, all uniting their powers for the promoting of one interest, which is the ready way to prosper and flourish.
>
> -- "Bee"
>
> Women not to be considered merely objects of sight. <u>Spectator</u>, no. 33 . . . That sex which is the fairest part of the visible creation, Ibid. The dearer part of mankind. Ibid.
>
> -- "Woman"
>
> One more fair than ever Apelles drew. Chaste as Diana, yet as kind as Venus. Mamut. Of a sweet disposition (flexible and merciful). . . . A young lady who is one of the wonders of the age for [her] piety, wit, beauty, birth and fortune. <u>Ath. Oracle</u>, p. 266. The fair sex, instructed with wit, and armed with beauty. Ibid. . . . Those women that are many times the free'st in conversation are the most virtuous in reality . . . You are the object of the world's wide eye, your bounteous mind and matchless piety and reason. Peacham . . . I think the universities would do well to consider whether they should not fill their rhetoric chairs with She Professors. <u>Spectator</u>, no. 247. Female orators branch out many a long extemporary dissertation upon the edging of a petticoat. Ibid. . . . Of a beautiful and virtuous woman, two perfections gloriously united in one person. Ibid., no. 302. A lady of a free and disengaged behaviour, ever in good humour. Ibid.

> Of all wives that were since Adam,
> You're the best, my dear madam.
>
> -- "Brave Woman"

Supplementing his poetry, Pastorius expresses appreciation for the female sex in an informal treatise he wrote in 1719, part of an intellectual game or exercise involving him as mentor and two teenage correspondents from nearby Philadelphia. [39] Citing biblical and Quaker arguments for sexual equality in spiritual matters, he goes beyond Quaker liberality as he presents physiological, psychological and philological evidence convincing him that females are generally – or in many particulars – superior to "the stronger sex." This essay also provides a far more sustained and comprehensive liberality than any of the remarks recorded in his "Alphabetical Hive" entries on women.

He observes with verve and humor that lively "Wives & Maidens" often have "Dull-pated Husbands and he-Companions." Having noted that in Hebrew Eve, meaning "Mother of all living," is "a more excellent Name" than Adam, "signify[ing] only red Earth," he ironically criticizes English translators for rendering the Hebrew *ish* and *ishshah* as man and "WO-man, as if she were the sole Cause of all the WO and misery abounding among mankind." Confusing enculturation and biology, he explains the "tragical Stories" of Penelope, Lucretia and Philomena with his only mention of a female deficiency (nevertheless seen as a virtue, and related to the patience of young women waiting to be courted): "Women being naturally of a colder temperament, are Consequently more Chaste than Men."

Feminine "Handsomeness, Luster and Beauty," Pastorius notes, is "not the least" of the "almost innumerable Prerogatives they have in their outward Bodies above us." He mentions the "fine Skin" and "Delicateness of rare Complexion in a Woman's Body," depicts Adam's "first Sight of this fair Sex (le bien Gens, saith the French man);" describes Eve as "this noblest piece of the divine Creation, of so pleasant a Feature & Countenance;" mentions a painter who – striving to capture the hue or texture of female flesh – chose "five of the most well-favoured Virgins to unite, as it were, all their Elegancies into one;" and describes women's breasts as a physical "Ornament" and as the "mammary Paps or Sucking Bottles [Nature] gave them . . . for the nutritious Use of their little Babes, therewith to comfort them as with Clusters of the Vine." Here he also recalls the attractive females he met on his youthful travels, with those of Nürnberg "foreprized" above all others. In his unabashedly sexual praise of women, a natural response to the divine spark sustaining male-female attractions throughout history, he liberally asserts female preeminence over males. In one biblical reference, though, he seems to imply an unwillingness to relinquish a male conception of conjugal priorities:

> The Lord formed (or as the Hebrew text imparts) builded [sic] [the first female] in Paradise itself, as the last & best of his Handiworks, the most Illustrious of all Sublunary Beings. *In Fine Corona*. [In ending the creation, crowning it.] Prov. 12:4. ["A good wife is the crown of her husband . . ."]

Yet his most basic insight is also his widest-ranging: Greater flexibility, compassion and good-naturedness among women, he concludes, derive from "a secret and hidden Source of Nature deserving our solid Inquiry and profound Consideration."

In this appreciative treatise and in the flirtation of his garden poetry, with its repeated identification of females and flowers, Pastorius displays a basic aspect of his broadly inclusive poetic vision, a celebration of God's bounty and grace that ranges freely through a continuum of the physical and the spiritual. It is this approach that allows him to combine lighthearted flirtation with advice against pride in Poem 253 (quoted on page 130), to describe the "Divine Poems" of the Bible (books like the Psalms and the Song of Solomon) and biblical poetesses (among them Mary, "the blessed Virgin, Mother of our Lord and Saviour") in his 1718 letter to the young poetess Jane Fenn, and to criticize the impurity of biblical commentaries in Poem 278 – the same poem that describes real lilies standing "Virgin like" and the unexpected kisses that transform metaphorical lilies to blushing roses. [40] And in Poem 163, where he apparently wrestles with feelings of attraction for a young woman, he concludes with references to 1 John 2,27 and 1 Peter 3,13 ("And who is he that will harm you, if ye be followers of that which is good").

A poem of 28 stanzas in "Voluptates Apianae" (*Deliciae Hortenses*, pp. 79-85, composed during the 1710s) most clearly demonstrates his belief that sensual imagery aptly embellishes moral instruction. In this poem about his Pennsylvania bees, Pastorius sums up apian common sense (stanza 28):

> This I take notice of,
> That they do mostly scoff
> At things esteemed by the great,
> And gather more (I see)
> From Peach and Cherry tree,
> From Fennel, Turnips and Buck wheat,
> Than from the blooms of Pome-granate.

And he contrasts his industrious and self-sufficient bees, the skilled builders of apian "private houses" and a "Royal Palace," with affluent humans who "eat the bread of Idleness" (stanza 12):

> But you, not half so able,
> Can hardly make a Stable,
> Unless one Mason you do call,
> Besides two Carpenters,
> And three strong Labourers;
> To speak the Truth here, as I shall,
> You are poor Sluggards, These do all.

Yet enhancing this didactic theme is a playful sexual motif of male/apian attraction, restraint, and energy in the midst of female/botanical plenitude, with bees and flowers corresponding to the men and women who tease each other and are teased by the poem. Pastorius establishes the correspondence, in stanzas 16-20, as "Overseers bid" the bees to "search what's hid" in forests and fields, "to rove / Through Gardens such as women love" for "Liquors" including "The Sap of Apricocks / Of Thyme and Ladies-Smocks" and "Balm / For those who swoon and qualm." The bees are "too too Chaste" for "wanton" and "leach'rous" tulips and other flowers lacking "Smell and Taste," the overseers advise, but once aroused by the truly sensual they can barely be restrained (stanza 18):

> But do ye never pluck
> No Blossom; Only suck
> The Bosom of Dames-Violet,
> And if ye can, then hose [kiss]
> Sweet Marjoram or Rose;
> And finally tug hard to get
> The Juice of Mint and Alkanet.

Early in the poem, Pastorius personifies the bees as models of civic and religious virtue, obeying their "King" and kneeling for their prayers, virtues he links to their diligence. In an ironic culmination, though, he describes the rewards of diligence as rewards attained in unrestrained rambling among the enticing flowers (stanzas 21-26):

> And seeing Buds must soon decay,
> To most they but a visit pay.
>
> One prick of time with Nep,
> And then they change their step
> And wander to Dandelion,
> To Daisies, Sassafras,
> Whorts and Five-leaved grass,
> Moreover to Satyrion,
> To Basil and Rose Campion.
>
> . . .
>
> How comely they engross
> Their Honey, Wax and Dross;
> And lade their Thighs, ev'n whilst they Swarve [climb or swerve],
> Lest in a Cook's Shop they should starve.

Despite the bold implications of apian rewards thus perceived, Pastorius does not explicitly address human sexuality in this suggestive poem. He confesses, in its penultimate stanza, that he has not penetrated the secrets of the hive "nor those of Hell," a vestige of early compulsions evoked by his awareness or acceptance of sexual taboos, and the poem concludes with the bees safely scoffing "At things esteemed by the great," and gathering their nectar among the everyday turnips and buckwheat of the Pennsylvania fields. Thus Pastorius would seem to consider, and then back away from, an espousal of unrestrained sexuality, evidence of a reflective mentality probing the mores of his society, and encouraging others to do likewise. This graceful poem is the final entry in the "Voluptates Apianae" manuscript circulated among friends in Pennsylvania, and thus early evidence of the appreciation for neoclassical charm then developing in Philadelphia culture.

The playful ambiguity of Pastorius' sensual poetry seems its most striking characteristic – the teasing (or even titillation) that takes him to the verge of the socially acceptable or beyond, testing his own moral limits (and those of his contemporaries) while constructing a rich poetic world related to the real world as he envisioned it. This is a world where one may live fully, in lively sociability, at ease with oneself and one's fellows, in harmony with God and nature yet relishing the variety and contrariety of species, personalities and sexes. His poetry embodies a European understanding of social grace and divine grace enhanced in an American setting, where it attained a natural vitality and maturity transcending some of the conformist limitations of baroque culture in absolutist Europe.

3.3.4 Nürnberg Society in Pastorius' Personal Experience and Pennsylvania Commentary

3.3.4.1 A Brief Record of Illustrious Encounters

> A Scepter or Baton of Command: Unius ad natum. [For the one born (or naturally suited) to it.] A Scepter, upon a Cushion: Imperiosa quies. Claudiori. [Magisterial rest. Very defective. I.e., nonvigilant magistrates govern poorly.] A Scepter, with an Eye at the Top: Et regit, & regitur. [He (or it) governs, and is also (i.e. divinely) governed.] A Caltrap, with 3 sharp spikes: ... Principes non irritandi. [Leaders are not to be provoked.] Prov. 25:15. ["With patience a ruler may be persuaded, and a soft tongue will break a bone."] ... The Sword of a Magistrate: non est contemnere tutum. [It is not prudent (or safe) to disregard (or defy) this.]
>
> -- "Emblematical Recreations"

Just as Pastorius' Pennsylvania poetry illustrates the social delights of this early German-American, his Nürnberg experience elucidates the baroque tensions he keenly felt as a young man, particularly in this Franconian city, where he was known as the eldest son of an influential burgomaster with numerous important connections and, from 1674 on, the stepson of a young lady from one of Nürnberg's leading families. Although he did not record his daily comings and goings, Pastorius apparently had an active social life among the men as well as the "fair Women & Girls" of the city. He noted in "Res Propriae" that "various friends" ("verschiedene Freunde") in Nürnberg gave him cash gifts totaling seventeen talers when he left for Strasbourg in 1670, and when Altdorf dissatisfied him upon his return in 1673, "Genealogia Pastoriana" indicates, he spent about a week visiting friends in Nürnberg as the first stopover on his way to Jena. Again in August 1674, he stopped over in Nürnberg on his trip from Jena to Regensburg.

Highlighting a few especially illustrious encounters, Pastorius noted that he began his trip to Jena on 2 July 1673 by traveling into Nürnberg with Burgomaster Bühler, and that, a week before his graduation in 1676, he was formally received by Magnus Fetzer (d. 1692), vice chancellor of the university and a high official of the city. Both of these men were lawyers and politicians, acquainted personally or by reputation with Melchior Adam, and they had every reason to show courtesy and approbation toward young Pastorius.

In Regensburg from 1 October 1674 to 16 April 1675, Pastorius records in "Res Propriae," "I went to the family of the Nürnberg ambassador for both meals and lodging, where the ambassador and his wife treated me very kindly." In "Genealogia Pastoriana" he specifies that his Regensburg host was "Dr. Völcker, Embassadour of Nürnberg and the rest of the Imperial Cities of Frankenland," i.e., Franconia. The reference is to Christoph Karl Wölcker (1632-80), a Nürnberg diplomat's son who had enough political influence to win a private audience with Cardinal Mazarin and the young Louis XIV at court in Paris when he was only 22. Wölcker was customarily given Nürnberg's "most distinguished and important diplomatic assignments" ("vornehmsten und wichtigsten Gesandtschaften") after achieving the high rank of "consulent" to the city court in 1662. [41]

Moving into the Franconian embassy for six of his eight months in Regensburg, Pastorius took full advantage of his connections in Nürnberg society, albeit at a time of particular need (described on pages 168-69). For the first two months of his Regensburg stay, he had used private funds to pay for his room at an inn called "Im

Grünen Krantz" (At the Green Wreath) and for the meals he took in a dining hall for staff secretaries. Thereafter, however, he lived at the expense of Franconian taxpayers as one of the privileged guests of the ambassador – a high public official who by training and accustomed usage brooked no opposition to his authority and whose prerogatives naturally included a flexible budget.

3.3.4.2 "A Syllogism represented to my view": Ambiguous Attitudes toward Government

> In all disputations use proper media, or arguments to prove your tenets by; never draw spiritual conclusions from natural premises. I Cor. 2:13 . . . Puffed up in their sophistical way of contending: for or against . . . Fallacious way of reasoning: a cock hath two legs; you all have two legs, therefore you are all cocks. Fox. Nature itself makes every man a logician. This tailor is a good honest fellow; ergo a good tailor. *Nego consequentiam*, every honest man is not fit to make a doublet. Naked reason the best logic.
>
> -- "Logic"

Even though Pastorius could still indulge in the prerogatives of his upper-class life in 1674, he was already developing the ambiguity toward this society displayed in his American writings. Entries in his "Emblematical Recreations" (cited on page 138) warn against provoking or defying leaders, and advise stoicism or extreme patience. (How long does it take a "soft tongue" to "break a bone"?) Yet he concludes the introduction to this collection of emblems (after describing the manifold forms of European culture presented to his "wandering eyes") by referring to

> a Syllogism, I remember was represented to my view in a Glass-Window of the Senate-House of Nürnberg, viz.
> Incuria est Vituperanda,
> Consul Nürnberg est in Curia,
> Ergo Consul Nürnberg est Vituperandus.

Punning on "curia" (senate house) and "incuria" (carelessness, neglect or negligence), it offers nonsense logic with ambiguous shades of serious meaning: Carelessness ("incuria") is to be censured or reproached; the high magistrate of Nürnberg is in the "curia" (senate house) or "in curia"; thus, the high magistrate is to be censured or reproached.

The meaning of the syllogism is elusive: Does it satirize weak logic? Criticize governmental leaders? Or even the arbitrariness of the law? Equally puzzling: Why did Pastorius give it prominence as the final observation in this introduction, which comments on falsely esteemed great men and refers to Dives and Lazarus? Although he recorded it here without comment, some of the meaning it had for him can be gleaned from two of his Pennsylvania poems involving Nürnberg experience.

3.3.4.3 "Laugh, lovely innocence, laugh!": A Pietist Mechanic Apostrophized

> When one that's Eloquent does bawl,
> Then Congregate both great and small;
> But if Truth-speaking Preachers come,
> Both great and small will stay at home.
>
> -- Poem 469

> We ought to have a special care to express our mind and meaning most plainly . . . Fit words are better than fine.
>
> -- "Eloquence"
>
> The Lord is angering the wise and learned by pouring out his Spirit upon illiterate tradesmen not bred up at schools and universities. Barclay, p. 885.
>
> -- "Calling"
>
> Ignorance in the laity increases according to the clergy's power in any place. <u>Chr. Rights</u>, p. 229. Laity are obliged to renounce their teachers if erroneous. P. 242.
>
> -- "Lay People"
>
> If reason and Scripture will not prevail, imprisonment, etc. are not like to do it.
>
> -- "Persuasion"

The Nürnberg city fathers of the Renaissance may have displayed a spirit of aloof generosity in allowing their window artists to poke fun at governmental authority or popular attitudes toward government, but the city's mood was not always so free. Commenting on a book called *Wunder- und Gnaden-volle Führung Gottes*, 1704 (God's Marvelous and Blessed Guidance), Pastorius criticized constricting authority in Nürnberg years after he had left Franconia. The author of the book was Johann Georg Rosenbach (1678-1747), a simple mechanic who wrote so poorly that an Altdorf student had to rewrite the text for him before it went to press. [42] Rosenbach, a prodigal son whose father had wished him to the gallows for his disobedient and riotous living, described his religious conversion and the Pietist "conventicles," or religious meetings, he held on his travels through Franconia and other parts of Germany – combating what an "Alphabetical Hive" source terms "ignorance in the laity," and being subjected to persuasion by imprisonment in both Protestant and Catholic territories.

When Rosenbach found a following among students at Altdorf in September, 1703, Theology Professor Christoph Sonntag obtained a decree from the Nürnberg senate ordering Rosenbach to leave the city and its territory. The decree claimed the Pietist mechanic was "one of those idiots devoted to fanatic opinions and conceited visions who could easily lead youthful students astray and give the University a bad reputation." [43] Two opposing professors rushed to Rosenbach's defense, writing character references that were filed with the city and appended to the book Pastorius read. Theology Professor Johann Michael Long, a young adherent of Pietism, argued that truly Christian laymen were needed to interpret the word of God because "the artificial and intellectual knowledge of pedants has been gaining ground at the expense of the spirit and vigor" of the Lutheran faith. Georg Paul Rötenbeck, professor of logic and politics, claimed Rosenbach was being persecuted

> by the worldly-minded [members of the clergy], some of them Pharisees and pedantic theologians who destroy the spiritual vineyard as cunning and rabid scholastic foxes, and others of them godless priests of Baal and libertine gluttons who root up [the vineyard] as raving sows. [44]

Although the references did not sway Nürnberg's senators, Rosenbach ignored the decree and, his book dramatically reports, was jailed for twelve days.

Despite the arrogant tone of Rosenbach's writing and his presumptuous claims – that his understanding of God's will placed him above man's law, for example, or that his enemies were, quoting Matthew 15, 13, plants that would be rooted up –

Pastorius understood Rosenbach's motivations, and applauds his conduct in a German poem he penned on the flyleaf of the book (Poem 419). "Laugh, lovely innocence, laugh!" he heartily apostrophizes, "for your dear Rosenbach is converting many souls." And he vividly describes the indignant cries of the ordained preachers, the satanic revenge that did not quench Rosenbach's spirit, the vain efforts to conceal God's truth by banishing the mechanic preacher.

Summing up the meaning of Rosenbach's story in Poem 428, Pastorius takes as his text 2 Corinthians 3, 12 ("Seeing then that we have such hope, we use great plainness of speech") and affirms Saint Paul's evocation of the liberty that comes to the hearts and minds of men when the Spirit of the Lord lifts the veil of tradition from the books of Moses and reveals the true glory of God (2 Corinthians 3, 12-18). By accepting persecution, the poem concludes, Rosenbach furthered the cause of Christ. [45] Reacting to the environment of his youth in these American poems (written around 1715, and typifying the piety that coexists with enlightened liberality in his mature poetry), Pastorius reveals a bold strain of nonconformity that was beginning to germinate during his years of personal experience in Nürnberg. Rosenbach's challenge to established society touched deep emotions, indicating the grave difficulties Pastorius had had conforming to this society as a young adult – to its politics, religion and education. His praise of the Pietist mechanic's innocence and truth is thus related to his ridicule of the scholastic Aristotelians he endured at Nürnberg University.

3.4 Scholarly Life among the Lutheran Aristotelians

> Christendom . . . has Apostatiz'd from Faith, and from the Form of words
> Sound, Good and Scriptural . . .
> Instead hereof a heap of Crabbed Terms remains,
> By Councils, Popes, Divines (Oh! Interfering Brains)
> Hatch'd, patch'd and Idoliz'd, Set up for Sacred Creeds,
> On which their Offspring now, as dainty Victuals, feeds.
>
> -- Poem 83
>
> Luther calls [universities] . . . the stews [bordellos] of Anti-Christ . . . The outward form of gross popery has been taken away from our universities, but the brains, heart, bowels, bones, marrow, sinews and blood thereof is the self-same as heretofore. Dell, p. 88 . . . The truest design of academical learning are evasions, equivocations, and dark fetches to secure themselves from the very dint of Scripture and reason. Ser. Apology, p. 121.
>
> -- "University"

Although Pastorius later rejected the scholastic learning that "drowned" many of his peers, he was himself, as it were, immersed in Aristotelian "waters" (or feeding on "dainty victuals") from 1668 to 1676. Despite Luther's conviction that Christian faith could not be explored in Aristotelian terms, Lutheran universities under Melanchthon's influence grew increasingly committed to the scholastic heritage embodied in lengthy Aristotelian texts and detailed commentaries on the corpus – logic, rhetoric, poetics, the practical sciences of ethics and politics, and the theoretical sciences of metaphysics and physics as well as, peripherally, astronomy, biology and psychology. The consummate methodology of Aristotelian philosophy equipped young theologians to fight the battle of Christ, the orthodox Lutheran spokesman Johann Gerhard (1582-1637) argued in 1620, and he noted that the opponents of Protestantism were already well fortified with the logical prowess of scholastic Aristotelianism.

Gerhard's rather cumbersome battle-ax had been forged by medieval schoolmen in endless debates that never resolved the contradictions between Aristotle and Christianity, and it seemed little more than a dull bludgeon to independent minds of the seventeenth century. "How could I convince those Aristotelians?" Galileo complained after the Inquisition convicted him of heresy in 1633. "With their minds full of vain propositions, they show themselves unable to follow even the simplest and easiest of demonstrations." The definitions and proofs of the Aristotelians, claimed Lutherans like Johann Valentin Andreae (whom Pastorius read and quoted, and his father had visited in 1649), completely missed the point of Christian love. Other critics derided these scholastics as blind and arrogant fools, disciples of the devil, the whores of Babylon. Attacked on various fronts, the seventeenth-century Aristotelians entrenched themselves in the ivory towers of the universities, steeled with the scholastic formalities that denied modern science and impeded personal faith. [46]

3.4.1 "Physics and metaphysics and other superfluous Argumentationibus"

Sophisters, to evade the truth, raise distinctions; *materialiter, formaliter*, strict and late (poor threadbare terms) then are tossed up and down like tennis balls. The craft whereby they and their families are maintained in pride and idleness. Their divinity becomes demonity. Vide Polemica [in Johann Valentin] Andreae, . . . [and] Agrippa, Ch. 97. . . . Scholastic divinity is for the most part entangled in useless questions invented chiefly by Lombard, Scotus, and other patriarchs of pedantry, says Sieur [Samuel] Pufendorf. Chr. Rights, p. 225 . . . Metaphysic and school divinity filled with uninstructive propositions. Locke.

-- "Theologia scholastica"

Sound Doctrine I approve
As much as men behoove;
Yet talking is but foul,
And meerly idle Noise,
If I to Wisdom's Voice
Not hearken in my Soul . . .

What foolishness to quarrel
About an empty Barrel?
When we can have the taste
Of holy Kingdom's Wine;
When we can richly dine
With Christ, as at a feast.

-- Poem 38

Especially during his first two years at Nürnberg, Pastorius diligently learned the Aristotelian corpus and honed the scholarly habits that held for a lifetime, but he gradually became convinced that his learned professors could not satisfy his worldly or spiritual needs. Taught to respect and emulate authority, he did his best to cope with an academic routine that many students considered rigorous, dull and even demeaning. Although progressive educators like Strasbourg's Mattheus Bernegger (1582-1640) condemned the procedure as inhumane, most professors read their pedantic lessons from prepared Latin texts in boring monotones, and students were generally obliged to copy each precious word. Many of the professors delighted in devising refined terminology and proving exceptionally subtle theories; they published erudite disputations demolishing counter-arguments and insulting those who advanced them, and not infrequently treated average students with condescension or scorn while reserving their praise for a few especially zealous or emulative young scholars. [47]

Preceding his comments about student drinking in 1699, Pastorius criticized the "inhumanity" of European universities, where the professors "waste their precious time with nothing but useless questions and *indagationibus*" (investigations), and he ridiculed those who "go searching through the Greek declensions for the ablative case, but why they are trying fo find it, they don't even know themselves." (Latin has an ablative case, but Greek does not). He thus implied it was the frustrations of academia that drove many German students to drink. [48] He had indicated some of his own frustrations with scholastic impracticalities in a 1697 letter to his father (again implying an interest in converting the Native Americans):

> I myself would gladly pay many hundreds of imperial talers right now if I would have spent my precious time on the arts of engineering or printing instead of learning the physics and metaphysics of [Johannes] Sperling and other superfluous *Argumentationibus* and *Arguitionibus* [argumentations and subtleties]. These practical arts would certainly prove more useful and delightful for me and my fellow Christians than such physics, metaphysics and all the Aristotelian *Elenchi and Sylochismi* [pearls and syllogisms], which are not any help in bringing Indians and non-Christians to God or even in earning a slice of bread. [49]

Johannes Sperling (1603-58) never wrote a metaphysics textbook, but Pastorius cannot be blamed for failing to distinguish his Aristotelian physics from the metaphysics of his student years. Sperling, educated in theology as well as medicine, remained firmly committed to the scholastic principle that physics was speculative rather than experimental, and his *Institutiones physicae*, 1646, the authorized physics textbook at most German universities in Pastorius' day, made a last-ditch effort to salvage Aristotelian physics from the inroads of the empiricism of Francis Bacon (1561-1626) and the rationalism of Rene Descartes (1596-1650). Sensing the mood of his age, Sperling begins with a rhetorical flourish in praise of the book of nature with its three pages of earth, water and the heavens, warning against blindly following Aristotle, and in "Book V" he even contradicts the master with a learned disputation in favor of atomism, yet the work as a whole follows the pattern familiar through centuries, tracing Aristotelian causes, forms and "materia," and eventually defining the universal soul itself. Sperling's heavenly bodies remained perfect and immutable, protected from earthly scrutiny by the adept use of syllogistic thought, and the Aristotelian universe still seemed more or less intact. [50]

Pastorius apparently got his fill of Sperling's physics in lectures held at Altdorf by Johann Sturm, later honored by the Royal Society, whose own *Physicae electiva sive hypothetica* was not published until 1697. Sturm mastered the theoretical advances of Descartes and Isaac Newton (1642-1727) and pioneered experimental physics in Germany, yet he was well versed in Aristotelian tradition. The scholastics, Sturm wrote in 1697, had fought for Aristotle's concepts to the point of desperation. Rather than battle with or against them in his weighty textbook, Sturm advanced ingenious interpretations that strained to harmonize the ancients and the moderns, all the while publishing mathematically precise experimental studies that helped physics develop beyond these feeble compromises. [51] Given this context, Pastorius in Pennsylvania naturally criticized Aristotelian physics and metaphysics as he developed scientific interests, in part by stocking his library with various books on geography, hydrography, cosmography, astronomy and physics, and compiling five manuscripts of his own on arithmetic and geometry.

While Aristotelian physics imperfectly described the real world, the *Metaphysics* as Pastorius learned it failed to reflect his spiritual awareness. Aristotle's text, a miscellany from teaching notes and lectures lacking unity and consistency, rejected Plato's ideal categories, attempted to differentiate appearance and reality, or matter and form, and postulated a hierarchy of being, which was set in motion by the Unmoved Mover and analyzed by theology, the highest and most desirable of the sciences. Out of this complexity Lutheran theologians constructed an inflexible system of orthodox exegesis and dogma only loosely related to the original text. The *Metaphysics* was taught from lengthy commentaries that displayed the petty disputes of the theologians but lacked the full context of Aristotle's thought, essential portions of which were no longer read by the commentators themselves. Instead of confronting Aristotle's texts, students were obliged to memorize meaningless lists and tables of terminology and definitions. [52]

The only professor of metaphysics at Nürnberg was Johann Paul Felwinger (1606-81), and it was from him that Pastorius must have gotten his metaphysics. Felwinger published his mammoth commentary *Collegium metaphysicum ex Aristotele* in installments from 1638 to 1666, and he paid tribute to Altdorf's long and turbulent metaphysical tradition by editing the unpublished works of his predecessors. Ernst Soner had written his erudite *In libros XII metaphysicos Aristotelis commentarius* at the beginning of the century, but it was so tainted with Socinianism, a unitarian doctrine long considered heretical, that Felwinger could not get it published until 1657. Although Felwinger had changed the spelling of his name (substituting a "w" for the "b" of Felbinger) to obscure his connections with a Socinianist family, he was by no means faint-hearted. In the course of his 45-year career at Nürnberg, he published more than 110 works, most of them long-winded scholastic disputations on minor points of doctrine. The year Pastorius arrived at Nürnberg, for example, Felwinger released *A Disputation on Evil*, *A Tractate upon Magistracy*, *A Disputation on Distinctions relating To Procreation*, and *Discreet Indiscretions* and *Segregating the Segregated*, both of the latter attacking the "Photinian" doctrines of Daniel Zwicker and the Transylvanian Valentin Baumgart. [53]

Although scholastic hair-splitting and nit-picking left young Pastorius cold, he nevertheless learned from the Lutheran Aristotelians, and carried this knowledge with him to Pennsylvania. To cite the most obvious example, Pastorius attended the ethics lectures of Johann Conrad Dürr based on Dürr's *Compendium Theologiae Moralis*, 1662, the first comprehensive ethics textbook for Lutheran theologians. Dürr took his ethical knowledge from Saint Augustine, Saint Ambrose and other early church fathers, from medieval scholastics like Lombard and Vivres, and from the reformers Luther, Melanchthon and Johann Arndt. The "Alphabetical Hive" reflects this range of traditional and reformist Christian viewpoints along with its great variety of contemporary opinion. Pastorius did not pay tribute to Dürr, however, who published many disputatious writings, and had been publicly chastised, at the beginning of his career, by one of his former professors for arrogantly pursuing "Scotist subtleties" – a reference to John Duns Scotus (1265/66-1308), the medieval scholastic known as Doctor Subtlety. [54]

3.4.2 Pastorius and the Great Wagenseil

> Folly is set in great Dignity, truly wise men in low Places.
> -- "Symbola Onomastica," no. 178

> Contend not with a man of great pow'r;
> By sea and land strong beasts the weak devour.
> -- Epigram 53

> Sometimes a well-managed silence is the best eloquence. Ath. Oracle, p. 268.
> --"Eloquence"

Pastorius may not have felt deep respect for many of his professors, but of course he would have kept his feelings to himself. In the age of absolutism, students customarily displayed obeisance toward their superiors. Even years later in Pennsylvania, his transatlantic connection with Professor Johann Christoph Wagenseil indicates, he had enough social finesse to maintain a more or less civil disposition toward one of the most opportunistic men of learning he had ever met.

3.4.2.1 Gregarious Scholar Abroad: The Dynamics of Self-Interest

> Greatness except with goodness qualified
> Is but at best eye-dazzling peacock's pride.
>
> Envious men at best their own tormentors are,
> Whilst those who're envied still the better fare.
> -- Epigrams 111, 87

> Bacon calleth a man's self the arch flatterer, with whom all the petty flatterers have intelligence.
> -- "Self"

> They cannot lay an egg but must cackle.
> -- "Self-Praise"

> Every man for himself, and God for us all . . . Every man has a good opinion of his own opinion . . . His charity begins at home, and ends there, too.
> -- "Self-Love"

The year before Pastorius began studying at Nürnberg, Wagenseil, then 33 years old, was appointed professor of history and public law after completing a six-year grand tour as tutor to Graf Ferdinand Ernst von Traun. [55] "We will want to use every available opportunity in France and Italy to work hard at winning invitations," he had instructed the young Graf, "since that's the way you get to be known among the very cleverest people, and return home with greater refinement as well." The well-educated son of a widely-traveled Nürnberg merchant, Wagenseil proved adept at winning friends and influencing people wherever he went. In Florence he quickly became the close friend of a ranking orientalist and thus deepened his knowledge of Hebrew and picked up the rudiments of Arabic and Persian. He won honorary membership to learned societies in Turin and Padua. Among uncatalogued objects in a Turin museum, he spotted a bronze Egyptian "Isis tablet" considered missing since 1630, and happily touted his discovery.

Arriving in Paris at the beginning of 1665, Wagenseil sought out none other than poet and scholar Jean Chapelain (1595-1674), the co-founder of the Académie Francaise who dictated classic tastes in French literature and controlled the purse strings of court patronage for the artists and scholars whose works furthered the glory of Louis XIV. In a dedication to the Sun King prefacing his translation of one of the books of the Talmud, a project encouraged by Chapelain, Wagenseil claimed he was moved to call on Chapelain after having seen the sovereign of the world's largest empire in public – so awed was he by this divine form, whose radiance nearly blinded him. Wagenseil flattered Chapelain in person, lavishing praise upon his French national epic, which remained unfinished because of the poor reception its first twelve cantos had received in 1656 – this poem, Wagenseil told Chapelain (undoubtedly without batting an eye), was poetry such as France had never known before and would never know again!

Wagenseil became an immediate success at the French court, mixing with a wide assortment of famous and learned men, and his role in French affairs brought handsome rewards. He translated the prospectus of the newly-established French East India Company for German circulation and sought mercantile contacts for the French when he traveled on to Spain and Morocco later that year. His letters from Spain reported political details that may have helped the French decide when to invade the Spanish Netherlands, or present-day Belgium, in the first aggressive step toward realizing Louis' plans for a "universal monarchy" (the War of Devolution, 1667-68). In return, Wagenseil was placed on the roster of "donees" who received generous cash "gifts" for their support of France, and on his way back to Paris at year's end he was able to pick up his doctorate of the laws during a brief stop-over at the University of Orleans – one of several French and Italian institutions criticized for making deals or even selling the doctoral degree for a set price.

Back in Nürnberg, Wagenseil played the cosmopolitan to the hilt. He was one of the first Altdorf professors to don a wig and, initiating a custom observed in Spain, he insisted that his wife follow several paces behind as he strolled along the town's graceful promenades. He filled his home with curiosities collected on his journeys, and kept up a steady flow of correspondence with the scholars and politicians he had met everywhere on his travels. Politically flexible, he later visited Emperor Leopold I in Vienna, and promptly won an imperial commission to produce a liberal arts textbook especially designed for the royal household: *On the Education of a Young Prince Who Loathes All Learning, Yet May Nevertheless Become Learned and Refined*, 1705. With his great reputation, Wagenseil was idolized in Nürnberg. The Senate elected him to its outer chamber the year Pastorius began his studies, and various professors tried to emulate his quick success. Johann Paul Felwinger made several attempts to elicit French generosity with fawning dedications and learned treatises – when his piece "On War" was curtly rejected he undauntedly cranked out another "On Peace" – but in letters to Wagenseil Chapelain expressed his great irritation toward men of small reputation like Felwinger who thought unsolicited treatises would get them on the "donees" list: "Of course everyone may seek his personal advantage, but he should do so tactfully."

3.4.2.2 "Cheerful jestings for our learned friend": The Transatlantic Connection

> Blessed conjunction, happy band,
> Wisdom and virtue hand in hand.
> Knowledge and practice
>
> Think humbly of thyself. No commendation
> Can mount thee then above thy proper station.
>
> -- Epigrams 32, 2330.5
>
> A small motion of the passions causes a smile, a little greater causes laughing outright, a little more than that causes such a hearty laughter that is accompanied with tears, the next degree above that causes weeping, the next above that such a confusion of the spirits that we can neither cry nor laugh. <u>Ath. Oracle</u>, p. 426.
>
> -- "Laughter"

In theory Pastorius would have had good reason for studying under Wagenseil, a professor of public law and history, but when he was ready for public law he headed off to Strasbourg, and later stated with a touch of pride that he had studied this discipline under Strasbourg's renowned Professor Boeckler. The name of Wagenseil, by contrast, does not appear in Pastorius' biographical jottings. When Pastorius first returned to Altdorf in 1673, he was looking for a professor of law with whom he could work intensively in advanced seminars and disputations leading to the doctorate. Pastorius decided that Wagenseil and his colleagues did not meet his expectations, and thus set off for Jena without delay. Although he undoubtedly attended some of Wagenseil's lectures as a beginning student, Pastorius (for whatever reasons) apparently avoided him in subsequent years – at least until he took his oral exams in 1676, administered by all four of Nürnberg's law professors, including Wagenseil. In the long run, however, Wagenseil's scholarly interests coincided with Pastorius' practical experience, and these men of divergent views had one final, if oblique, confrontation – part of the philosophical give-and-take that transpired, with growing frequency, across the Atlantic Ocean.

Wagenseil appears to have learned, in 1688, that a former Nürnberg student had emigrated to America and was living a pioneering life among the Native Americans, which must have suggested yet another opportunity to enhance his knowledge and reputation as a connoisseur of world cultures. He knew Pastorius, at least remotely, as the young classicist and jurist who had attained doctoral honors twelve years earlier, yet the current information on Pastorius placed him in the company of Pietists and Quakers, radicals and mystics beyond the ken of a learned professor who based his contacts on the dynamics of self-interest. Unsure of himself when it came to Pastorius, Wagenseil apparently turned to his former student Georg Leonhart Model, then the Gymnasium rector in the imperial city of Windsheim, a predictable member of society who could be relied upon to reach his unpredictable friend. [56]

Any news from home was good news, and Pastorius was not offended to learn that the great Wagenseil wanted to know more about his Pennsylvania existence. In his response to the letter he received from Model, Pastorius defers Wagenseil's request while considering Model's predicament. Model, failing in health and spirit in his final year as rector, apparently complained about his care-worn existence, but Pastorius shows little sympathy as he gets to the heart of the matter, criticizing

Gymnasium education and offering suggestions for reform. [57] His old frustrations thus vented, Pastorius beckons Model to America by referring him to his world map at home in Windsheim and guiding him on a journey by fingertip across the ocean to Philadelphia, where the former school chums enjoy a leisurely walk along the Delaware River and a fireside chat in Pastorius' modest Germantown home. Humor and satire complement the factual detail that fills this fictional form. Having lured his friend away from European constraints, Pastorius demonstrates his American perspectives by deflating Wagenseil's pomposity with a few deft strokes of his pen:

> Now we can head out through the town gates, and in just a little while we'll be among the Indians. But first of all let's finish off this glass [of wine] so that we'll be fortified for the outing. And you, my cook, may roast this rabbit over the fire in the meantime, and when we return we'll spice it with cheerful jestings for our learned friend here. So we're all set now, Modelius. Let's go! To keep from ambling along in silence, though, let's talk about the Nile or, waters just as obscure, the origin of our Indians. There are people who believe they are descended from the Jews, and of course evidence can be found to support this theory. The language of the Indians living farther from us, however, would indicate that they originally came from Wales. When they would have crossed the Atlantic Ocean and which means of water transport they might possibly have employed – these matters can be better explained by your Altdorf polymath [Wagenseil]. Since I myself have not found anything about this in any of the books I have read, I cannot even start a learned dispute over the issue. I would prefer to ask for your patience in listening to the answer I would now like to attempt, as in a foreword, to the question put by your Virgil: What race of human beings is this? [58]

Pastorius' three-page answer to this question (described in Chapter Four) summarizes his first-hand knowledge of the Pennsylvania Indians, and it concludes with a final jest at the expense of Rector Model: "If you can determine the origin of the Indians with the help of these 'elements' ... then you must be a good philologian." Earlier in the letter, having concluded his criticism of Gymnasium education, Pastorius briefly considers whether to oblige Wagenseil with a full description of Pennsylvania. The playwright Publius Syrus writes that politely refusing a request is half as good as fulfilling it, he notes as he refers Model to information on Pennsylvania already published in Holland and Germany, and then limits his brief treatise to the Delaware Indians. Pastorius also notes in passing that Model has every right to ask him for a description of Pennsylvania, especially since "you show consideration for the earnest demands of your great Wagenseil." The tone of Pastorius' response shows his qualified consideration for European learnedness. His irony or satire here distances him from its pretentiousness just as his knowledge helped to satisfy its craving for substance.

3.4.3 Evading the Compulsions of Academia

> A learned man may perhaps give a better account of the history; but a saint of the mystery; the first may have more science, the other conscience. Rich in literal [i.e., bookish] knowledge, poor in spirit.
> -- "Learning"
>
> That magisterial sourness, which sticks so close to most pedagogues. <u>Ath. Oracle</u>, p. 442.
> -- "Pedantry"

> As by diff'rent Fruits wise Orchard-keepers see,
> And say, This is a good, but That an evil Tree;
> So on the sameself foot impartially I judge
> Of men of all degrees, without Respect or Grudge;
> . . .
> Great Scholars, fit to speak the Hebrew and the Greek,
> Being thereby puffed up, praise Hectors, slight the Meek,
> Can never Wisdom find, wherever they may seek.
>
> -- Poem 328

As a student in Germany, Pastorius could not satirize the pretensions and absurdities of academia, or even focus on a need for such satire if he were to keep his integrity as a student. Yet he was both sincere and sensitive, and probably hesitant to display obeisance. How best to survive the exigencies of a student career? He seems to have carefully observed the character of his mentors, and chosen accordingly.

All of his teachers had exerted great effort to acquire their knowledge and reputation, and these efforts had various effects upon their humanity. Especially arrogant or unprincipled professors might well have dispensed a knowledge so vain and superficial that learning it was, as Pastorius claims, a waste of time; and even those who offered a fascinating wealth of knowledge had, in many instances, constrained their potential warmth and decency in the struggle to attain it. Although Pastorius also met a few professors who had not unduly sacrificed for knowledge or position, two of whom receive special mention in his biographical notations, they were not the ones who established the general tone of academia as he experienced it in the 1670s.

3.4.3.1 Harlequin of Learnedness: Johann Leonhard Schwäger

> Inkhorn terms. A downright scholar. Men laugh at him [i.e., scholars generally] by tradition. He [a particular scholar] has not put on the quaint garb of the age; his scrape is homely, and his nod worse . . . The dunghill pedants, beggarly tatterdemalions, these contemplative idiots . . . An intelligible [i.e., intelligent] ass.
>
> -- "Pedantry"
>
> Pride and ambition lend men spreading wings
> To act the most ridiculous of things.
>
> -- Epigram 2326.7

As Pastorius struggled to acquire knowledge while holding on to his own truer humanity, he encountered one professor at Altdorf who was paying too dearly for the wisdom he attained. The pitiful condition of this learned man underscores the psychological tensions that generated arrogance in academia, and increasingly dampened Pastorius' enthusiasm for his studies. [59]

Johann Leonhard Schwäger (1628-1708) had shown unusual discipline as a youth at Nürnberg's Saint Lawrence School, supplementing his full-time studies with private lessons in astronomy and Hebrew, and then at Altdorf from 1644 to 1650. A phenomenal student, he managed to deliver his first learned disputation, in logic, just two years after entering the university, and he was soon learning theology and mastering the Hebrew, Chaldaic and Syrian languages. Hoping to qualify for an academic career as he worked toward his degree, he energetically prepared disputations and perorations at the extraordinary rate of almost one per week. After receiving his master's degree with honors in 1650, Schwäger joined the staff of the ambassador of Sweden and traveled internationally until, at Utrecht, Holland, in 1655, he contracted an "illness" beyond the comprehension of his doctors – an emotional or mental disorder that gradually deprived him of his speech, his memory, and his senses.

Back in Nürnberg under the care of friends, Schwäger recovered within a year. His great learning was rewarded with the Altdorf chairs of oratory and poetics in 1657, and he served with distinction as dean of the faculty of philosophy in 1659 and 1663, but his earlier disturbance reappeared and slowly drove him "totally insane" ("gänzlicher Wahnsinn"). His biographer, a Nürnberg professor, blamed his condition on domestic problems following his marriage to a professor's daughter in 1659, and Schwäger himself thought it must have been a long-term side-effect of a love potion he had taken in 1653. At Altdorf Schwäger became the fool of academia:

> All manner of improper, vexatious and ridiculous language, gestures and behavior could be observed [in his lectures and] even [in sermons] from the pulpit. He once preached a sermon with the words "Printed by the University Press of Baltasar Scherf" from the title page of a catechism as his text. The sermon dealt with the benefits of printing, and although it was not necessarily unlearned or totally unsuited to devotional needs, it nevertheless could not be delivered without drawing the ridicule of the congregation... For many years he wandered about the town dressed in a long Greek robe and carrying a walking staff, and with a hideous beard that grew longer and longer; he collected all the paper he found on the streets and carried it home, and generally acted very childish and foolish. [60]

Schwäger's disorientation was obvious during Pastorius' years at Nürnberg. From 1659 to 1662 Schwäger had displayed scholarly pride and thoroughness by writing course descriptions for the annual university catalogue of twelve, fifteen and seventeen lines – easily matching all but a few loquacious eighteen and twenty-line entries – but thereafter his descriptions rapidly sank well below the catalogue average of eight to nine lines. From 1665 to 1675 they averaged a mere two lines, dropping in 1672 to a feeble spurt of five words ("In Locis Communibus Philippi perget," or "General Topics from [Saint Paul's epistle to the] Philippians Continued") – abnormal brevity reflecting Schwäger's mental state.

3.4.3.2 Strident Tones and Mute Voices

> Quarrelsome natures meet their unkind kind,
> And commonly what such men seek, they find.
>
> A truly wise man knows, he nought does know,
> The fool says he knows all, but thinks but so.
>
> -- Epigrams 2327.5, 2311.7
>
> Nothing more certain than uncertainty in all human things.
>
> -- "Certainty"
>
> Self-confident men are the first that recoil and turn their backs ... A man's own strength is his exceeding weakness, and his own confidence great folly.
>
> -- "Self-confident"

> Smatterers are the most confident; but deep, solid men modest, always ready to acknowledge the greatest part of what they know is but the least of what they are ignorant of. Tryon, Mem.
> -- "Pedantry"

The conditions most likely to have turned Johann Leonhard Schwäger into a mockery of learnedness also generated learned compulsions in many of his peers. In an era that demanded absolute truths, the learned were plagued with uncertainties, insecurities and even self-doubts. Philosophy was the handmaiden of theology, and theology and law were charged with defining and implementing the values that governed society. These values, increasingly polarized during the sixteenth century, defied coherent definition in the age of absolutism. Serious scholars might restlessly and hectically consume one book after the other – not uncommonly studying ten, twelve or even fifteen hours a day, and rationing their sleep and social life – but they seldom resolved their search for truth, perhaps because they could not dispel the incongruities in society at large. [61] Overwhelmed by the demands placed upon them, many of the professors covered their insecurities with strident tones that, in the mass, produced an unpleasant cacophony. Some of them, sensitive to harmony, refused to join the yelping chorus. Few managed to stay calm and collected.

Georg Matthias König (1616-99) was the steady rock in Altdorf's stormy sea. He taught Greek, history and poetry for 51 years, and lived to the age of 84, and he also kept an even-tempered approach to knowledge. "Although our König wrote a lot [principally for his learned lectures], he published very little, and it is especially remarkable that he never published a single disputation." [62] Christoph Molitor (1627-74), professor of eloquence and oriental languages, was strong in body but otherwise unsuited to the disputatious life. "He was praised for his energy, honesty and modesty; the latter virtue was in fact compounded by a strain of timidity, at least to the extent that it was almost impossible to get him to release his writings for publication." [63] Another of the reluctant combatants of academia gained some prominence in Pastorius' student career, reflecting the humane attitudes that encouraged Pastorius to disdain disputatiousness even as he was learning the academic skills of disputation.

3.4.3.3 A Nürnberg Theologian's Flight to Strasbourg: Lucas Friedrich Reinhart

> Brabble not with him, whom quarrelsome you know;
> The greatest strife from few words may grow.
> -- Epigram 39
>
> Laugh not, when you do see me Run and others Beat;
> Fools ([John] Denham says) will fight, but prudent men retreat.
> -- Poem 377
>
> Socrates being told that one railed on him, said, Let him beat me too, so I be absent I care not . . . Do not flame at every vain tongue's puff.
> -- "Pardon"
>
> [Universalists] cannot drive into their fancy the circumscription of truth to our corner. You may sooner pick all religions out of them than one . . . To make one shoe serve for all feet . . . Where there is not a [theological] unity, we may exercise charity and forebearance . . . Barclay, p. 27. Universal love

begins to enlarge some souls dammed up all along by the narrow precincts of private interest and party. Franck, <u>Orph.</u>, pt. 2, p. 50. Some generous spirits are more zealous to propagate the interest of the church universal than their own hereditary form and usual way of worship. Id. p. 51.

-- "Universalists"

Lucas Friedrich Reinhart, who gave modern theology the concept of dogmatics, wrote with "moderation and extreme circumspection" ("Bescheidenheit und äusserste Behutsamkeit"), and his many publications revealed

> the discretion, modesty and love that could be seen in all of his actions. He preferred being alone to mingling in society, and as a theologian he was an irenic in the best and truest sense ... Reinhart was ... a Calixtian with all of his heart, but he had enough intelligence and discretion to keep his private opinions out of his lectures and sermons ... It was in fact an exaggerated sense of shyness and timidity rather than simple modesty that kept him from expressing, even in private, his opinion about any theological disagreement whatsoever. For precisely this reason, even though he was a professor for 39 years, he hardly ever wrote a disputation, so concerned was he to keep from getting mixed up in controversies. [64]

As a friend and student of Lutheran theologian Georg Calixt (1586-1656), the "syncretist" leader who sought to unite Catholics, Lutherans and Calvinists in one ecumenical community, Reinhart could not avoid controversy no matter how he tried to keep his opinions to himself. [65] After earning a master's in theology at Altdorf, Reinhart was urged, by Nürnberg's liberal Johann Michael Dilherr, to study under Calixt at Helmstedt University in 1644, and when Calixt headed off to the Colloquy of Thorn in Poland the following year, the Nürnberg Senate commissioned 22-year-old Reinhart to join Calixt and send the city weekly dispatches. The conference of Catholic, Lutheran and Calvinist Reformed theologians, convened by Polish King Vladislav IV four years before the Peace of Westphalia, had great potential for all of Europe. Billed as the *"colloquium caritativum"* ("colloquy of love"), it briefly offered hopes of political and religious detente, but the disputatious theologians fell upon each other's throats over mere formalities, and it ended in futility three months later, derided as the *"colloquium irritativum."* The orthodox Lutherans had started off with a dispute over Calixt himself, one of very few Lutherans willing to make meaningful compromises. They refused to grant him voting or debating rights as a member of their faction, and he watched helplessly from the sidelines, joining the Calvinists as an unofficial observer.

Disillusioned by the failure of Thorn, Reinhart had good reason to tread softly at Nürnberg, where he was appointed professor of theology in 1649. [66] He was particularly worried about his colleague Johann Weinmann (1599-1672), who had a reputation as an extremely disputatious orthodox Lutheran theologian. "Obstinate and quarrelsome" ("hartnäckig und zänkisch"), Weinmann frequently started "unmannerly and vehement disputes" ("unanständige Heftigkeiten") and liberally spiced his declamations with language that was "too harsh and blunt" ("zu hart und plumb"). It was, furthermore, precisely the issue of Calixtian "syncretism" that heated orthodox tempers most effectively. The issue produced such a furor at Altdorf that, in 1668, the Nürnberg Senate passed a decree forbidding all further syncretist discussion in the lecture hall, from the pulpit and in printed disputations. Weinmann was certainly irked that Reinhart, a syncretist par excellence, never let himself open for attack, so he eventually took the offensive by filing an order to prohibit the use of Reinhart's 1667 catechism text in the city schools. Reinhart, backed by Johann Michael Dilherr, filed suit and won. His book prevailed.

Pastorius encountered Reinhart at Nürnberg in the midst of the syncretist uproar and this legal dispute, and, "Res Propriae" indicates, developed a relationship with him considerably warmer than the average relationship of student and professor. According to Pastorius' jottings, Reinhart left Altdorf for Strasbourg around the time Pastorius left in 1670. Pastorius enrolled in Reinhart's year-long course in ethics and politics at Strasbourg on October 3, and by August of the following year Pastorius and Reinhart, along with Pastorius' Windsheim friend Johannes Joachim Mercklein, flouted academic protocol by taking private French lessons together at the university. Pastorius' report on Reinhart's sabbatical leave in 1670 and 1671, omitted from the professor's Nürnberg biography, is altogether consistent with Reinhart's character. Shaken by Weinmann's attack and the level of controversy at Altdorf, the sensitive theologian could find respite at a university more congenial to his temperament. Yet when Weinmann died in August, 1672, amid the acrimony that had alienated most of his colleagues, it was Reinhart (back at Altdorf once again) who agreed to preach the funeral sermon, honoring the memory of his antagonist with an unalloyed Christian charity uncommon at his Lutheran university. [67]

3.4.4   Pietist Influences at Strasbourg and a Special Windsheim Schoolmate: Johann Augustin Lietzheimer

> Man's business is virtue, not words. Seneca, p. 471. Wisdom delights in openness and simplicity; in the forming of our lives, rather than in the niceties of the schools, which at best do but bring us pleasure without profit. Ibid.
>
> -- "Pedantry"
>
> The doctrine of Christ is likened to honey and the honeycomb, to wine and milk (Ps. 19:11, 119:103, Isa. 55:1, I Pet. 2:2) because sweet, comfortable and wholesome. Ainsworth, [add] Cant. 5:1.
>
> -- "Doctrine"
>
> Virtue, though clad in rags, may challenge more
> Than Vice, adorn'd with silk, in midst of store.
>
> Disdain not such as are with virtues crown'd,
> They are, or shall, or ought to be renown'd.
>
> -- Epigrams 2314.1, 2334.3
>
> Live well, and you will not die ill.
>
> -- "Piety"

Reinhart's liberal Lutheranism shared basic tendencies with the Lutheran Pietism then coming into existence, especially at Strasbourg University, whose students and staff, during Pastorius' tenure, included the two men who would become Windsheim's foremost Pietist clergymen. The academic climate had not changed since the days of Johann Conrad Dannhauer (1606-66), an aggressive and disputatious orthodox Lutheran who nevertheless impressed some of the Pietists with his deep faith and openness to religious reform. [68] Philipp Jakob Spener got much of his theology from Dannhauer, just one aspect of the broad education in theology, language and history he acquired at Strasbourg from 1651 to 1659. Before accepting a call to direct the churches of Frankfurt in 1666, Spener preached and taught at Strasbourg, attracting many students with his combination of worldly knowledge and religious fervor. Johann Heinrich Horb (1645-95), later a Pietist clergyman in Windsheim described by Pastorius as "a good friend of mine," studied under Dannhauer and Spener, and then returned from a grand tour of England, Holland and France to lecture at Strasbourg in 1670 and 1671. [69]

Pastorius arrived in Strasbourg in September, 1670, with his Windsheim friend Johannes Mathias Stellwag, joining their friend Mercklein, who had been there since July of that year. A fourth Windsheim graduate, Johann Augustin Lietzheimer (1653-84), two years younger than Pastorius, began his university studies at Strasbourg in May, 1671, remaining there until transferring to Jena University in October, 1672, a month before Pastorius' departure for Jena. Pastorius naturally associated with all of his former schoolmates at Strasbourg – traveling to Basel with Mercklein and Lietzheimer in July, 1672 – and he joined Stellwag and Lietzheimer again at Jena. Yet it was more than schoolboy camaraderie that attracted him to Lietzheimer, a sensitive youth whose brief career as a Pietist clergyman in Windsheim influenced Pastorius' American writings.

Lietzheimer's biography, which accompanies a funeral sermon by his friend Johann Heinrich Horb published the year after Pastorius left Germany for Pennsylvania, exemplifies a number of Pastorius' own dissatisfactions with his culture and indicates, at a personal level, some of the factors that led Pastorius to espouse Pietism and reject the dogmatic authoritarianism of the Lutheran church and state. [70]

Taught to read and write by his father, the parson of one of Windsheim's outlying villages, young Lietzheimer never adapted to the upper-class culture of Windsheim, even after attending its Gymnasium from the age of ten and studying philosophy, philology and theology at German universities on one of Windsheim's four-year scholarships. His Gymnasium experience convinced him that the institutions of the Lutheran church had become a worldly Babel fit for God's destruction, he once told Clergyman Horb, and although he studied diligently he could never bring himself to face the academic hurdles leading to a university degree. He was so intimidated by his professors, Lietzheimer himself wrote, that "[I] hardly ever managed to open [my] mouth" in the classroom. He learned more than the lifeless theology of the scholastics, Horb reported, because "God inspired him to read, diligently and on his own, the Holy Scriptures and our dear Luther's books, and he thus obtained an unsophisticated yet wonderful understanding of God and His holy will."

Serving as one of Windsheim's village parsons from 1675 to 1680, Lietzheimer soon rejected the biblical authoritarianism he had learned at the university, and preached a message of grace and forgiveness. Enforcing obedience to God's law produced hypocrites, he proclaimed, but God's love brought a joyful awareness of human redemption. Lietzheimer sought to improve the conduct of his villagers with quiet advice and a good example rather than censorious attitudes or threats of damnation. Giving the peasant children religious instruction, he explained his own tenets of faith in simple, childlike language, and he did not destroy his pupils' innocent delight in Christian learning by forcing them to memorize lengthy catechism responses. Lietzheimer's preaching lacked the sophisticated formality characteristic of university graduates but, Horb maintained, his sermons touched the hearts of his listeners. Lietzheimer accepted his life as a simple village parson on a meager salary without "grumbling or complaining" ("klagen oder murren") yet sensed some degree of social injustice in the lot of the poor villagers, himself included. "There were times," Horb reported (alluding to the familiar story of Lazarus and Dives), "when he only wished he might have had the drops of wine or the substantial crumbs that fall from the tables of the rich or, often enough, are even wasted without serving anyone's needs."

In the dedication to his *Sabbaths-Bedancken*, 1675 (Sabbath Ponderings, a collection of Sunday meditations), Lietzheimer vacillated between submission and rebellion, meekly praising the presumed virtues of his influential Windsheim patrons yet vigorously or even insultingly attacking the abuses of wealth, learnedness and power familiar to the "honor-seeking reader" ("Ehrsüchtiger Leser") of his book. Especially after moving to Windsheim as Horb's assistant at the Church of Saint Kilian in 1680, Lietzheimer was unable to reconcile his conscience with his role in society. He complained that his life as a clergyman was making a hypocrite of him, and that some of his official duties endangered his immortal soul. He contemplated resigning from the clergy to live a Christian life. In 1683 he deliberately courted death, testing his faith by caring for Franconian soldiers who, back from another European war, were suffering and dying from scarlet fever. His faith had been too weak, he said on his deathbed. He had become sick only after following well-meant advice to take a prophylactic dose of the medicine he carried to his patients. Faint and enfevered, sometimes delirious, he suffered pangs of conscience and doubted his salvation. The maid who kept the parsonage assured him God knew he had been a good clergyman. He smiled, and marveled that a poor house-maid had become his holy priest.

Lietzheimer died peacefully a few days later, smiling with inner joy, assured of God's mercy and forgiveness. Any man in this age who can feast and carouse and live in splendor – anyone who gains a position of eminence and honor or inherits a grand estate – is deemed blissful by the world, Reverend Horb told those gathered for the funeral in Saint Kilian's. But Lietzheimer knew that honor and riches end with death, that the sins man commits to attain them burden his life and follow him to God's final judgement. It was this awareness, Horb explained, that had led Lietzheimer to preach many variations on a single theme during his last year in Windsheim. Taste the bliss of Christ's love in this Age of Grace, he had repeatedly urged his parishioners. A single drop of its balm refreshes your soul so richly that you will never again be satisfied with the bland diet of worldly possessions, honors and desires.

Although Pastorius left Windsheim before Lietzheimer preached at the Church of Saint Kilian, he read Lietzheimer's published sermons and meditations in Pennsylvania, lyrically expressed Lietzheimer's theme that living decently is more important than being labeled Christian or heathen (Poem 344), reported in a Pennsylvania letter that he "always" thought of Lietzheimer when he reflected on the natural piety of the Native Americans, and bound his friend's publications with the popular writings of August Hermann Francke (1663-1727), the theologian and educational reformer who led a second generation of Lutheran Pietists at Halle, Germany. Pastorius repeatedly referred to the moral issues raised by Lietzheimer's life and preaching, perhaps most vividly in the multilingual verse of Poem 85, which criticizes, in English, the oppression of the poor in capitalist rather than feudalist terms, but then switches to German to offer an especially sharp summary comment before concluding with about a dozen Latin, Dutch, German and English proverbs or commonplaces on the satisfactions of a modest life (omitted here, and in the short version of the poem in *Deliciae Hortenses*):

> The usurer lives in the city!
> And he who is opprest
> Must pay him interest,
> Eat in his thatched cottage
> A peas or barley pottage,
> And carry from his field
> What good things that doth yield
> To usurers in the city,
> Alas! What great a pity.
> Der Reiche frisst den Armen,
> Dess woll sich Gott erbarmen.
> [The rich devour the poor,
> For which may God have mercy.]

3.4.5   Broadening Religious and Intellectual Views

> Christianity consisteth chiefly in the renewing of the heart, by virtue of the operation of God's light and grace. True Christians are the children of God, of the day, and light . . . Christianity is not only an outward profession, but the very power of God (Rom. 1:16), whereby He renews . . . His own image and likeness in man, . . . setting it again in [its] former brightness and perfection.
>
> -- "Christianity"

> It is a base coin that needs imposition to make it current; true metal passeth for its own intrinsic value. Penn, <u>Address</u> . . . The will is no longer will if not free, nor conscience to be reputed conscience where it is compelled. Idem.
>
> -- "Liberty of Conscience"

> In Kirchen, Mosqueen, Pagoden, Synagogen,
> Wird vieles gepredigt, so erdicht und gelogen,
> Nechst Christen und Turcken, Heyden und Juden betrogen.
> [Much is preached, so falsified and fabricated,
> In churches, mosques, pagodas, synagogues,
> Deceiving (or: cheating, defrauding) Christians and Turks
> (i.e., Muslims) along with heathens and Jews.]
>
> -- Poem 460 (entire)

> Easy it is to write; but to write well
> Is very hard, much harder to excell.
>
> -- Epigram 2315.1

Pastorius' American interest in Lietzheimer's writings reflects the years they spent together at Strasbourg (1671-72) and Jena (1673-74) as well as their shared experience of political tribulation in Windsheim (1676-79). At Strasbourg their moral and religious growth included a trip they took to Roman Catholic monasteries in Alsace and to Calvinist Basel University in Switzerland. The syncretism of Nürnberg's Professor Reinhart encouraged their broadening travel. At one stopover on this trip, Pastorius made such a conciliatory impression that, he reported in "Genealogia Pastoriana," "I . . . was . . . strangely attack'd by the prior of [a] monastery, to stay & read over the Books of St. Augustine & these *Patres* that might convince me" to become a Catholic. The feisty prior had obviously mistaken Pastorius' openness to differing religious views as a sign of his willingness to convert, unaware that Pastorius and a growing number of young Protestants were pursuing religious truth without restricting themselves to orthodox Lutheran dogma. Young Pastorius had listened carefully to the prior's clever arguments in favor of Catholicism, and he was impressed enough to be able to give a sprightly paraphrase of them two decades later. [71]

The company of men like Lietzheimer and Reinhart and their liberal thought form part of the general pattern of moral and intellectual growth that can be traced from Pastorius' Windsheim schooling to his life with Frankfurt Pietists and then with Pennsylvania Quakers. As he matured, he found more and more friends of moral sensitivity and religious conviction who rejected narrow-minded creeds and self-righteous attitudes. Many individuals of this character hoped that increasing liberality and secularity would allow each individual to live honestly, conforming to personal values that gave life meaning and dignity. Thus the relevance of his entries by William Penn under "Liberty of Conscience" in the "Alphabetical Hive" (quoted above).

He may well have believed there was one true way to salvation, but Pastorius was too universalist or ecumenical to insist that any particular church, denomination or religion monopolized this truth. At times he seems radical or extreme, apparently probing even his own Christian convictions. He went so far as to challenge orthodoxy of whatever stripe – as in the German Poem 460 (quoted above) with its enlightened cynicism or irony – and he also recorded for posterity the most varied points of view available to him.

His entries in the "Alphabetical Hive" on atheism, for example, include criticism of Benedictus Spinoza and Thomas Hobbes, and of various attitudes generally considered atheistic, along with surprisingly detailed accounts of a number of these attitudes. Religion is "a mere state trick," one of them states, and entries like the following expand upon this thesis with Aristotelian, Epicurean and other theories rejecting physical creationism or spiritual immortality:

> [Atheists] say that the formidable notions of conscience, heaven, hell, futurity and the immortality of the soul are but politic inventions of priests and cunning magistrates to enrich themselves and keep the vulgar in awe, who are naturally superstitious and fearful; that the soul is material and mortal, and that it will dissolve with the body.

One of Pastorius' sources argues that "a fortuitous concourse of atoms stretched forth the heavens, and laid the foundations of the earth," and another description, based on Epicurean atomism, reveals a playfully speculative mind probing fundamental aspects of existence and morality:

> Some atheists say . . . the world made itself by mere chance, by a casual conjunction of atoms or small particles, as they were eternally dancing about in an infinite ultramundan[e] space, and so by their perpetual motion (caused by their internal vigour or gravity) danced themselves into all visible beings. They say that . . . nothing is above man, and so he is his own law . . . [with] no distinction of good and evil. . . . They believe that both their joy and sorrow terminates with this life.

Recording these nonconformist views (a relaxation of the compulsions of his youth), Pastorius displayed the open-minded curiosity motivating his Pennsylvania intellectual pursuits, which also included quoting extensively from the writings of

Francis Bacon, compiling an eight-page extract from Robert Boyle's *Medicinal Experiments* (1692) for his "Medicus Dilectus" manuscript, and reading John Locke's *An Essay Concerning Humane Understanding* (edition of 1710) and commenting on it in Poem 421, a brief and sprightly explication of the Platonic doctrine of ideas, or "Plato's Cabinet... by Locke unlock'd at last." These were continuations of the curiosity and moral concern Pastorius developed as a university student, perhaps most characteristically by reading a wide assortment of books by predominantly Lutheran reformers and mystics. Reflecting broad religious views first encountered in Germany, the works of men like Thomas a Kempis, Jakob Boehme, Heinrich Cornelius Agrippa, Peter Ramus, Erasmus of Rotterdam, Johann Tauler, Johann Arndt and Johann Valentin Andreae later lined his bookshelves in Germantown.

Pastorius typically appreciated religious scholars of linguistic subtlety and psychological depth, and impatiently rejected religionists "unable to indite" or unwilling "to lop" their verbosity, faults compounded by a narrow-minded refusal to listen to opposing views, "the Top of foolish Wickedness" (Poems 394, 395). He ridiculed the uncritical personal insights of a German commentary on the Book of Revelations (Poem 458), and criticized the credulity with which Joseph Glanvill reported incidents of witchcraft in *Sadducismus Triumphatus*, 1681 edition (Poem 437): "He that would not into Temptation fall, / Believes in part; but never Credits all." This healthy skepticism may reflect an awareness of the Salem witch trials of 1692, influenced to some extent by Cotton Mather's acceptance of Glanvill's reports on witchcraft. [71a]

Pastorius was so committed to good writing that he even risked offending acquaintances like Lydia Norton, a Quaker then visiting in Pennsylvania (probably a Caribbean missionary or colonist's wife), whom he instructed by letter after copying 44 pages of her Barbados journal, a frustrating mix of the essential and the superfluous that he graced (tempering his criticism) with Poem 485 praising her religious sincerity. "Thou seest ... that I deal plainly, being by Birth a [frank] Franconian, and measurably by Regeneration a Free-man of the Lord," he explains in the letter, his attempt at humor barely disguising his irritation over "the frequent Repetitions" of irrelevant detail that "almost wearied" him:

> Journals that contain only remarkable Passages (in mine Eyes) are the best, seeing we can the sooner peruse 'em, and the things therein related will stick the more firmly in our Memory. I do not hint this to thee, as if I was any way displeased with Thine, but Simply because now a days most Readers loathe Superfluities in all Sorts of Writings, and much more those to whose Task it falls to Copy or transcribe them. [72]

Although Pastorius appreciated the subjective aspect of religious experience, and used an emotional piety particularly in contexts where his upbringing did not permit explicit statement, he nevertheless endorsed clear communication in both science and religion, which he saw as complimentary approaches to universal truth.

Pastorius' liberal theology, developing but not fully developed in his student years, also explains why he left Europe as a Lutheran Pietist and later played an active role in the Quaker Meetings of Germantown and Philadelphia. Appalled by doctrinal disputes and confessional prejudice, however, he repeatedly avoided questions from Germany about the denomination of his Germantown church – and obscured the issue of his confessional allegiance in the process.

He was especially guarded in letters to his father. Even when Melchior Adam, contemplating emigration in 1698, asked for specific details on the types of church services held in Pennsylvania, Franz Daniel avoided the issue, pleading instead for the religious freedom that would encourage true spiritual growth rather than hypocritical conformity to a state church, arguing that all true Christians are of one spirit with the Lord but that the established churches are deficient in their awareness of unity with Christ, noting the beneficial reform efforts of Roman Catholic Quietists like Miguel de Molinos (1640-96) and the Lutheran Pietists, and reporting that all sects were allowed freedom of Sunday worship in Pennsylvania – but avoiding any mention of the Quakers or Society of Friends. [73]

Aware that learned Germans generally considered Quakerism disturbingly radical, he endorsed, in most of his transatlantic correspondence, a familiar Christian piety rather than the exotic doctrine of the Inner Light. He revealed Quaker influence by describing God as "the Father of Light" and the Holy Spirit as "His divine light" ("Foreword" and p. 29 of *Beschreibung Pennsylvaniae*), and further indicated his religious liberality in the "Foreword" by identifying as sources of inspiration the learned Christians of Catholic Ghent and Protestant Cambridge, the latter well known for the Cambridge Platonist movement, which combined religious fervor and enlightened moral and scientific attitudes precursing eighteenth-century deism in a manner complementing Pastorius' own blending of fervor and pragmatism. [74]

Nevertheless, Pastorius reacted decisively to a published German report that claimed the "vain and foolish" ("Eitelkeit und Thorheit") Quaker church leaders in Pennsylvania denied basic Christian beliefs, above all Christ's "righteousness, blood and death" ("Gerechtigkeit / Blut und Todt"). These were "malicious lies" ("boßhafftig[e] Lügen"), he wrote in a 15-page letter to Pietist friends, spread against "loyal witnesses and servants of Jesus Christ, most of whose books I have read, and for more than 13 years I have frequently listened to their spoken explanations and sermons." He recalled that many of the Lutheran clergy of his youth – "those strutting cocks that are allowed to crow the loudest from their own dung-heap (the pulpit)" – had repeatedly castigated "Quakers and enthusiasts" even though they either had no idea of what they were talking about, or far worse, they knew better, but ignored their conscience and preached hypocritically because they were "unwilling to walk the narrow way of the cross of Christ" in their own lives.

Pastorius regretted that so few Germans had firsthand knowledge of the Quakers even though "they are so well known in England and here in America through their countless publications, their lives of Christlike virtue and their patient suffering." And he defined the Christian principles of the Quakers in terms familiar to his German readers in a lengthy passage displaying the fervor and precision of a learned Pietist sermon (yet with a Quaker emphasis on God's 'Light'):

> They profess steadfastly and unanimously that Christ Jesus is the eternal only-begotten son of God created by his Heavenly Father for our salvation and righteousness . . . and that we follow in his footsteps, in his Light, Power and Strength (I Peter 2:21), that is, we walk even as he walked (I John 2:6) . . . and their teachers . . . preach with one accord that the blood of the immaculate Lamb of God sacrificed from the beginning of time purifies from all sin, sanctifies and justifies eternally before God all those who believe in the Light and walk in it in childlike obedience . . . [75]

This spirited defense of the Quakers is one aspect of Pastorius' universalism or ecumenicalism, which also includes praising the natural piety of the Delaware Indians and defending Malabar 'heathens' against Protestant proselytizing (see page 238). Pastorius actively participated in Quaker religious services and avidly read and copied commonplaces from dozens or even hundreds of Quaker publications, thus revealing a clear religious preference. [76] Nevertheless, his mature beliefs, liberal and open yet firmly Christian, seem not to have been restricted by Quaker doctrine or any other orthodoxy. He lived, essentially, by his own 'inner light' – a light that also left room for wide-ranging secular thought as well as the strains of Lutheran Pietist theology that never faded away.

Pastorius thus reveals an unusually broad theological or intellectual range – evolving strikingly from his earliest collected poetry, written predominantly in German and Latin during his early adult years, when European moral tensions weighed upon him. Here he combines reflections on time and eternity with pietist moralizing and fundamentalist preaching on sin, death and hell. "Look at this circle, the image of eternity" ("Schau diesem Circkel an, das Bild der Ewigkeit"), he advises in Poem 15, and urges readers to fight valiantly against "devil, world and flesh" ("Teuffel, Welt und Fleisch") to win the rewards the Lord will provide "in eternal heavenly bliss" ("in Ew'ger Himmelsfreud"). He composes a poetic warning to be placed next to his clock (Poem 13):

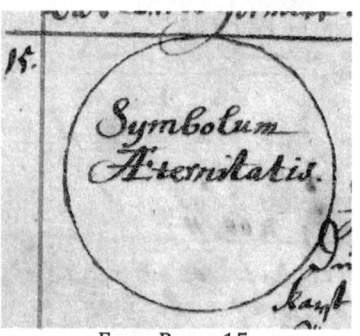

From Poem 15: "Symbolum AEternitatis"

> Windgeschwind vergeht die Zeit,
> Mensch! Mach dich zum Tod bereit,
> Und Denck an die Ewigkeit.
> [Time passes with the speed of the wind,
> Mortal! Get ready for your death,
> And think about Eternity.]

Poems 18 and 19 describe loving the cross of Christ "with all your heart" ("von hertzen liebt"): "Dying... is easy for those who have arduously striven to live by the ✝." ("Leicht [fällt das Sterben]... dem der schwerlich in der ✝ Schul hat gestrebt.") In Poems 20 and 21 he praises unity in Christ, ("UNIO CHRISTI"), "the salvation of every Christian" ("aller Christen heil"): " I fear you [Christ] as a faithful peasant [does his lord], / Since your divine nature deserves as much" ("Dich fürcht ich als ein treuer Knecht, / Dann das ist deiner Gottheit recht"). "Oh, Fear of God,... you are truly the beginning of wisdom," he writes in Poem 26 ("O Gottes-Furcht, du... magst mit recht der Weissheit Anfang heissen"). You protect us from evil, and help us to avoid sin and disgrace. (Love supplants fear, he eventually argued, for example in the epigraph on page 211.) Sometime later, now in English, sprightly verse enlivens the dry theology of Poem 62 (entire). Here he employs a lighter, almost playful, tone undercutting the bleak message – an indication that he is beginning to overcome his obsession with sin, death and the hereafter:

> Many go to hell,
> For not doing well,   Matt. 24: 42, Luke 12: 47
> More go to the Devil,
> That are doing evil.   1. Cor. 6: 9, Matt. 7: 23
> But few go to Heaven,   Matt. 7: 14
> The rest resist the Leaven,
> Which would work in these noddies
> Their Spirits, Souls & Bodies.

These verses display the pious Lutheran beginnings of Pastorius' social and theological world, which expanded dramatically in the course of a redeeming Pennsylvania life.

3.5 The Life of the Law Student
3.5.1 Learning the Corpus juris civilis

> The philosopher Anacharsis compared the laws to cobwebs that caught poor flies but let the hornets and wasps escape.
>
> -- "Spider"
>
> The studies of physic [i.e., medicine] and of the law are now exceedingly corrupt . . . We think lawyers to be wise, but they know us to be fools. Leeds, 1710 . . . It is with justice as with sick men; in time past, when we had fewer doctors (as well of law as of physick), we had more right and more health. Quevedo. In the days of old one single book of laws was enough for the best ordered government in the world; but now, institutes, digests, pandects, codes, reports, cases, judgements, glosses (idem) [apparently indicating the end of this direct quotation from Quevedo, followed by paraphrase] embroil us in endless suits and confusion. Lawyers and solicitors are but so many smoke merchants, sellers of wind, and troublers of the public peace. Idem. What a train of mischief does not one wretched pettifogger draw after him? Idem.
>
> -- "Lawyer"

Despite the moral stimulation of Strasbourg, Pastorius' main reason for being there was to prepare for a law career, pursuing a discipline that satisfied neither his predilection for literature and philosophy nor his moral idealism. (Negative attitudes on lawyers like those in the "Alphabetical Hive" were not uncommon in his student days.) As consolation, Pastorius was gaining a detailed awareness of the systematic complexity of his society, and also discovering humane principles that suggested the possibility of social reform. The discipline encompassed civil, canon, feudal, trial, criminal, public and natural law yet placed greatest emphasis on the *Corpus juris civilis* compiled during the reign of Justinian I (527-565) – the Justinian code of civil law inherited from ancient Rome. [77]

A codification of immense length and complexity, it was absorbed piecemeal in year-long lecture courses and seminars exploring its main components or selected portions thereof: the Institutes, the official textbook of Roman law in four books; the Pandects or Digests, a compilation from about 2000 legal writings by 40 classical Roman jurists; the Codex itself, a compilation of Roman imperial law in twelve books; and the Novelle, amendments and individual laws added during Justinian's reign. These venerable texts contained the intricate blueprint of political structure within the Hapsburg empire, where even the relations of lords and peasants were spelled out in contracts written in terms of the Roman civil code.

Pastorius recorded various stages marking his progress toward full accomplishment in this system. He enrolled in Professor Ulrici's "collegium" in the Institutes in September, 1670, and began another course in the Institutes taught by Professor Obrecht in January of the following year. Building upon this foundation at Jena in 1673-74, he studied the Pandects in Instructor Linck's "Collegium in Scotani Exerc. Juris," a course using a textbook by Bernardus Schotanus (1598-1652). He also took two intermediate courses from Instructor Tillemann for the two months preceding his journey to Regensburg, and at Nürnberg in 1675-76 his advanced studies under

Linck were based on textbooks and commentaries by Amadeus Eckolt (1623-68) and Wilhelm Ludwell (1589-1663). These courses showed some traces of innovative organization and presentation, yet for the most part they used the same cumbersome scholastic methods that had made Pastorius' study of philosophy such a heavy and unrewarding task. Future lawyers, too, Pastorius learned, were expected to swim in deep Aristotelian waters.

3.5.2 The Liberal Impulses of Public Law
3.5.2.1 Daring Questions of Political Order

Ahab covets Naboth's land,
And bids the Owner sell;
Deny'd is sad and sorry, and
Solac'd by Jezebel,   I Kings 21.
[She has the "elders and nobles"
execute Naboth on false charges,
and Ahab takes the coveted land.]
This is the manner of the Kings,
As well now, as of old,
To take away their Subjects' things
Like Samuel foretold.

Not only those upon the Throne,
But upon Bench and Stools
[i.e., officials like judges and
professors ("stool" = Ger."Stuhl")]
Do make (and so have always done)
Of their Inferiors Fools:
But will the Lord God suffer it
For ever to be so?
And this their Cruelty permit?
The holy Writ says, No.
Isa. 10, 51:3, Ezek. 31, Dan. 4, Joel 2, Micah
7, Zeph. 3, Luke 1:52, Sap. 6:8, Eccl. 10:8

-- Poem 214 (entire)

Privileged individuals of wealth and influence may turn the complexity of the law to their advantage, but the very existence of laws implies the possibility of fairness and justice. Along with its view of pervasive corruption, Poem 214 suggests the truism that, for any society, systemic injustice is ultimately self-defeating. This awareness may well have inspired the growth of public law in Germany, a subject Pastorius studied under Strasbourg's Professor Boeckler in 1671-72.

Focusing on aspects of Roman and feudal law, public law became established during the seventeenth century as a special field combining history and politics with the technicalities of law. [78] Along with the related field of natural law, it was the forerunner of political science – the discipline that dared to raise questions about the philosophical principles behind social organization. It was a lively field of study, since it could tackle the sensitive political issues involving the rights of peasants, burghers, gentry, lords and bishops, imperial cities and the emperor himself.

The rights of the peasants generally remained too sensitive for public discussion, but defining and limiting the power of the emperor began the historical process that gradually led to a concern for individual rights. It was Pastorius' interest in public law that prompted him to visit the Regensburg Reichstag in 1674-75, and while at Jena this interest also drew him to the court of Duke Ernst the Pious (1601-75) at Gotha, whose liberal government served as the model for Veit Ludwig von Seckendorf's *Teutscher Fürstenstaat* (German Princely State), 1655. Visiting Gotha as an advanced law student on 13 May 1674, "Res Propriae" notes, Pastorius was granted an interview with one of Seckendorf's successors as *"cancelarius,"* or chief administrator of the court.

3.5.2.2 A Semblance of Moral Concern: Johann Heinrich Boeckler

> Zeal is the strength of love, which breeds delight
> To do those actions that are just and right.
> -- Epigram 2331.1

> This famous nursery of letters. Those seminaries which publicly instill into the minds of their pupils destructive notions . . . are the well-springs of sedition, and nurseries of faction for times to come. Vide <u>Medley</u>, no. 14.
> -- "University"

Johann Heinrich Boeckler's students had included Seckendorf and other young liberals, among them Gottfried Wilhelm von Leibniz and Philipp Jakob Spener. [79] Boeckler, a polymath renowned for his broad learning in history, language and law, took a critical attitude toward the power of the emperor, insisted that moral principles be applied to state actions, popularized the liberal views of the Dutch jurist Hugo Grotius, the "father" of international law, and supported the work of Hermann Conring (1606-81) to establish the historical relevance of the German legal traditions long suppressed by the empire's emphasis on Roman law.

Although Pastorius stated he "was taught some certain principles by the renowned Dr. Böckler at Strassburg," he nevertheless had reason enough to include Boeckler in his blanket condemnation of learned arrogance in Europe. Despite his liberal theory, Boeckler courted power and influence with the finesse of the connoisseur. Garnering titles, honors and monetary awards in addition to academic posts, he was court historian to Queen Christine (1626-89) of Sweden, counselor to Archbishop Johann Philipp of Mainz and Würzburg, and "imperial retainer" ("Comes palatinus Caesareus") to Emperor Ferdinand III, and he also gained a permanent position on the "donee's list" of Louis XIV long before Nürnberg's Wagenseil earned the same dubious distinction. The strains caused by his contradictory allegiances apparently took their toll during the explosive autumn of 1672. Caught between the battle lines of his Hapsburg and French masters, Boeckler died of unspecified natural causes while conducting his 1672-73 course on public law, and Pastorius then had to look elsewhere for legal instruction with a semblance of moral concern.

3.5.3   Study at Jena
3.5.3.1   Natural Theology and a Philosophical Gadfly

> . . . Sift out everything. I'll have a taste of ev'ry thing that's good; / Of ev'ry thing that God ordain'd for food. How can you tell except you try? . . . To try with a touch-stone. More ways to the wood than one. Error only looseth upon Trial. Penn, <u>Address</u> . . . Truth never lost ground by Enquiry, because she is most of all reasonable. Max[im], 2^d 164. Thus we learn its intrinsic worth. Id. 163 . . . None should borrow other's eyes, when he can see with his own. Saavedre. . . . Men must inquire into Religion, but in many places they are hindered from inquiring. Locke. Whet your wits upon it, & they will be the sharper. Culpeper. . . . Socrates held that a life without examination, was no life. Assay, I pray!
> -- "Try all things"

> Examples are brave imitation's law;
> Precepts may lead us but good patterns draw.
> -- Epigram 93

> Tho' Philosophers may know,
> In what manner Turnips grow;
> Yet still there is a difference:
> Some from Books upon their Shelves,
> Others having seen 't themselves,
> Speak by their own Experience.
> These (not those) do rightly know,
> In what manner Turnips grow.
>
> -- Poem 247 (entire)

Dissatisfied with Nürnberg's law faculty in 1673, Pastorius did not have to think twice about where he would continue his legal training. By 1665 Jena had gained a reputation for innovations in teaching method and content of the sort that would eventually replace scholasticism in Germany. [80] This academic climate provided impulses similar to those that later urged him to "see with his own" eyes, to "Try all things" – the pragmatic values (then admittedly still bookish) that would germinate along with the turnips of his Pennsylvania garden or fields. At Jena, Georg Adam Struve (1619-92) applied empirical methods to the study of law and legal texts. Johann Musäus (1613-81) introduced a moderate "natural theology" based on reason, and his student Johann Wilhelm Baier (1647-95), named professor of theology in 1674, fought the orthodox Lutherans on behalf of the Calixtians. Baier's liberality eventually placed him in the Pietist camp, and when the Pietists won an intellectual foothold with the founding of Halle University in 1694, he became the first rector of the new university.

Most of Jena's philosophy professors were dedicated scholastics, but one innovative genius inspired advances in philosophy, law and pedagogy. The mathematician Erhart Weigel (1625-99) saw mathematical principles behind all of nature, and declared nature and technology as the true objects of learning. In 1667 he opened his peculiar private home for the study of the earth and the heavens replete with technical instruments and gadgets like the hydraulic pumps that conveyed water and wine from the cellar and an elevator for his visitors. Weigel, whose concept of mathematics included harmony in society, broke a scholastic taboo by holding some of his lectures in German instead of Latin, and in 1684 he opened an experimental elementary school where children were playfully taught language and practical skills with no dull drills or anxiety-inducing punishment, an experiment Pastorius read about in America after it had been continued at Pietist Halle University.

Extending mathematics to politics, Weigel taught the enlightened theories of Hugo Grotius and Thomas Hobbes (1588-1679), and his pupil Samuel Pufendorf (1632-94) – cited in an anti-scholastic "Alphabetical Hive" entry in the epigraph on page 142 – successfully systematized and secularized natural law and its premises of rational social order. Weigel was, in short, Jena's gadfly. He repeatedly challenged the authority traditionally exercised by church and state officials in the Lutheran provinces and cities of Germany, and students flocked to his lectures despite protests that he was spreading "great confusion" ("große Confusion") among them.

3.5.3.2 Law Instructor Heinrich Linck

> Be reserved, but not sour; grave, not formal; bold, not rash; humble, not servile; patient, not insensible; constant, not obstinate; cheerful, not light; rather sweet than familiar; familiar than intimate; and intimate to the very few, and upon very good grounds. Max[im] 114.
>
> -- "Rules"
>
> Be good to all men, to the best be best;
> Court peace, with no contentious man contest.
> Greatness with goodness make a man complete,
> But few there are, that are both good and great.
>
> -- Epigrams 2312.4, 2317.6

Weigel's influence to some extent ameliorated Pastorius' subsequent study of law. More or less content with the scholarly energy and humanity combined in law instructor Heinrich Linck, one of Weigel's former students, Pastorius could not bring himself to study under any other teacher. He attended Linck's classes faithfully until Linck left Jena to become professor of the Institutes at Nürnberg in the spring of 1674. Presumably dissatisfied with the lectures of the Jena law professors, he opted on June 1 for two courses by instructor Tillemann, but Tillemann could not hold his interest for long. By July 31 he was on his way to the Regensburg imperial diet, well aware that the excitement of European politics would break the dull routine of his formal studies, and when he finally returned to Nürnberg University in September of the following year, it was to conclude his degree program under the tutorage of Linck, then at Altdorf.

Linck's sober realism differed from the idealism of Weigel, who was only one of the young attorney's former professors. [81] While still a student at Jena, Linck had served one of his professors as private amanuensis; he married another professor's widow when he won his doctorate in 1668, and soon gained a reputation for "industriousness and worldly dexterity" ("Fleis und Geschicklichkeit in der Welt"). During his Nürnberg career he won various honors and positions in academia and government, published a comprehensive commentary on canon law as well as 79 learned disputations, and "through his legal consultation, briefs and decisions was able to influence the political world at large." Linck nevertheless managed to combine human decency with his energy and finesse. He "was in point of fact naturally endowed as a university teacher, since he had, along with his great learnedness, a serious demeanor tempered by a friendly disposition, and all the students were thus attracted to him." Moderate to liberal in his legal opinions, Linck was influenced by Weigel, Hermann Conring and the new trends of natural law. His historical scholarship on canon law was still highly regarded by scholars of legal history at the turn of the century (around 1900).

3.5.4 Interludes at Regensburg and Windsheim

> The world's peace is soon at an end. Barclay, p. 711 . . . Peace is the greatest treasure man e'er knew, / A thousand triumphs to it seem but few. Sil. Ital. . . . Our peace with God is the foundation both of our peace with ourselves and with our fellow creatures also. Ludolf, p. 114.
>
> -- "Peace"

166 | Franz Daniel Pastorius

> Grasp not for fame, for transient is earth's glory,
> And fades away within one age's story.
>
> Where all is govern'd by noble blood,
> Nor wit, nor virtue does no good.
>
> -- Epigrams 2317.1, 2335.8

The fourteen-month interval between the end of Pastorius' studies at Jena and the start of his final year at Nürnberg was marked by political turmoil in Europe and personal difficulties within the Pastorius family, two interrelated crises. Pastorius' growing dissatisfaction with his university education did not diminish as he observed the events of the Reichstag at Regensburg – where statesmen pursued sensual pleasures and ego satisfactions while their soldiers were fighting and dying on the battlefield. What he learned at Regensburg must have convinced him that his legal training was not likely to lead to a Christian career in Franconia, and this conviction added to the domestic tensions that erupted when Melchior Adam married, for the fourth time, less than two months after Franz Daniel traveled to the imperial diet.

3.5.4.1 Deadly Game of Reichstag Politics

> Fullers, Dyers, Perriwigmakers,
> Farriers, Drapers and Pie bakers,
> Are the men most excellent
> In our civil government.
>
> -- "Symbola Onomastica," no.651

> There is not upon the face of the earth a bolder or more indefatigable nation than the Germans . . . yet broken through their temerity even by the most effeminate of men. Seneca, p. 369 . . . Drunkenness is said to be the original sin of Germany, from whence it spread itself into other countries. Mamut, vol. 7, p. 131. They can bear the debauch well – always maintain a regiment of whores in their camp. Ibid. Their generals take more pride in their feathers, than in their military arms. Idem.
>
> -- "Germany"

> If ever the wit of man went beyond itself, it was in the invention of these engines of war . . . Guns, powder, bullets, shot, swords, drums I may properly call mischievous tools, devilish instruments . . . Nitre from earth, and brimstone fetched from Hell. Denham.
>
> -- "Gun"

> Death's mottos have it all, his scythe mows down
> The rich and poor, the emperour and clown.
>
> -- Epigram 72

In the political developments of 1674, a further increasing of tensions between France and Hapsburg Europe, Emperor Leopold I convinced most of the German princes, often fighting among themselves, to join him in a campaign to push the French out of Holland, which France had invaded in 1672, and win back territory occupied by the French since 1660. [82] Even the independent Elector Friedrich Wilhelm of Brandenburg Prussia joined Leopold's alliance with Spain and the Netherlands in July, just before Pastorius decided to view further developments at first hand, and while Pastorius was at the Reichstag, the Empire declared war on France, effecting political realignments and adjustments from Poland to England. The

French marched their troops from the Spanish Netherlands to battle the Germans at Trier and along the Rhine in Alsace and the Rhineland. The Swedes invaded Prussia, giving Friedrich Wilhelm an excuse to attack Pomerania, and Denmark and the Netherlands eagerly joined the fray against Sweden. To the east, meanwhile, the Polish-Ottoman War of 1672-76 further exacerbated European insecurity. The Battle of Khotyn in 1673 (portrayed on the book cover) is often seen as a prelude to the Turkish siege of Vienna a decade later as Pastorius was sailing to Pennsylvania.

Viewing these developments from Regensburg, Pastorius saw the heart-rending combination of foibles and vices that constituted the deadly game of European power politics. The jealousies of his professors hardly vied with those of the lords and princes and their ambassadors at the Reichstag. Endless hassles over protocol impeded the diet's real tasks, and those in power, augmenting burdensome military expenditures, squandered large sums on pomp and ceremony to display their grand importance. Regensburg artists, sacrificing esthetics to accent the values of the Reichstag in their paintings and engravings of official proceedings, placed large sequential numbers above the heads of all Reichstag deputies as keys to a list of names and titles that also indicated the rank each held in the *Stände* (estates) of bishops, princes and free cities. Portraying Archbishop of Mainz Johann Philipp's glorious entry into Regensburg in 1663, an artist created a perspective of the entire procession at the top of his copper plate and, in seven close-up rows beneath the perspective, detailed the horsemen, carriages and personages in each of 34 processional elements, keyed of course to a printed "Order of the Procession" with names and titles that filled the bottom half of his ceremonial prints.

Seeking relief from the tedium of protocol or from their awareness of the human costs of war, many ambassadors and functionaries drank and partied excessively. The Restoration playwright Sir George Etherege (1636-92), whose reputation as a rake had drawn censure in England, complained during his tenure as King James II's envoy that Regensburg's unrestrained hedonism far exceeded his capacities:

> To this day the Germans make good the Observation that Tacitus made of their Ancestors; I mean, that their Affairs (let them be never so serious and pressing) never put a stop to good Eating and Drinking, and that they debate their weightiest Negotiations over their Cups ... They are such unmerciful Plyers of the Bottle, so wholy given up to what our Sots call Good-fellowship, that 'tis as great a Constraint upon my Nature to sit out a Night's Entertainment with them, as it would be to hear half a score long-winded Presbyterian Divines Cant successively one after another. [83]

3.5.4.2 *The Headstrong Son*

> The constant hunter catcheth the deer. By labour men get fire out of a stone. It's best to woo where a man can see the smoke. He that will lay out [i.e., spend] but little seldom buyeth good flesh. That which is gotten with trouble is possessed with love ... Faint heart never won fair lady. Lovers live by love as larks live by leeks ... If one will not, another will ... A castle often battered, is either taken, or surrendered. I have plied this charming woman with visits, loved her even to idolatry. Mamut ... Ladies should not be in such haste to yield at the first appearance of a foe, to hang out the white flag before the cannon be drawn down. <u>Ath. Oracle</u>, p. 302.
>
> -- "Courting"

> Beg help of known friends in any grief,
> No doctor like to them can give relief.
>
> Before you undertake, consider well,
> And then resolve; next in dispatch excell.
>
> -- Epigrams 38, 2312.5

In his personal life, Pastorius, who had been accustomed to a humble and matronly stepmother for half of his life, was apparently shocked to learn that his father was planning to marry a twenty-year-old from the courtly circles of Bayreuth and Nürnberg. His father's haste, furthermore, dishonored the memory of his stepmother, who had died less than six months before Melchior Adam's new wedding date. Melchior Adam, imperfectly aware of Franz Daniel's sensitivities, relied too heavily on his expectation of filial obedience as he elaborated an insensitive justification of his marriage, using the poetic skills that had already proved effective in courting his young fiancée. "Vocatio Melchioris Adami Pastory ad Quartas Nuptias, Educato iam Filio Francisco," a German poem of eight quatrains, is the wedding invitation meant to educate and summon his son from Regensburg to the wedding (the Latin title indicates) as well as the entertaining and instructive text he read, on 22 September 1674, to the learned guests partaking of the nuptial festivities in Nürnberg, a relatively easy journey of 95 kilometers from the Reichstag.

This wedding, the poem proclaims, demonstrates anew God's marvelous ways to man. Humor and personal conviction go hand in hand as the elder Pastorius argues that the grand events of European history were part of a divine scheme leading him to Dorothea Esther Volckmann, the daughter of a deceased doctor of the laws who had held an influential post as counselor to Margrave Christian Ernst of Bayreuth. If the Dutch had not been riding the crest of fortune with such pride, the French would not have attacked out of envy and the Emperor would not have come to their defense. The French would have stayed on their side of the Rhine, the residents of the court of Bayreuth would not have sought refuge within the walls of Nürnberg, and Pastorius would not have been attending emergency sessions of the Franconian Assembly and visiting the Nürnberg friends who were sheltering "this child, . . . my dear bride." These nuptials were ordained by God himself, Pastorius declares. But in three concluding stanzas, thanking friend and foe for their part in God's plan, he reveals egocentric attitudes undermining the charm and humor of the poem. The three stanzas, here in free verse translation:

> Thanks be to you, almighty God, thanks be to all of you, my friends.
> Thanks (of a special kind) to you, the enemies of Germany,
> For having brought fear and flight to Esther's heart.
> And now I wish you would be slaughtered by the German sword.
>
> I have that which God through you has sent me,
> My intention has been achieved to the fullest satisfaction of my desires.
> The Lord will soon reward you, however, according to the deserts of tyranny,
> With misery, death, ridicule, fear and mockery.
>
> May God bless us, however, with His merciful peace,
> His goodness keep us from all that might cause harm.
> May He so fully unite and bind these two hearts,
> That we may enjoy constant bliss both here and hereafter. [84]

Reading and pondering his father's sentiments at Regensburg, 22-year-old Franz Daniel had obvious reasons for the moral repulsion and embarrassment that, through his conspicuous absence from the Nürnberg wedding, forced him into the role of a self-willed and disobedient son. [85] As he studied law and read mystic authors, young Pastorius was sharpening his social awareness and redefining Christian love in terms of his everyday experience, which increasingly impinged upon the experience of Melchior Adam. Visiting Windsheim on his student furlough of 1672-73, for example, after four years of affluent university living, he could not help noticing anew the plight of the ordinary citizens in an era of war and wartime taxation, a citizenry later described by his own father as overtaxed, "immersed in misery, danger, cares and sorrows, and penury, even agonizing" under the burdens that could only be relieved by a return to peacetime prosperity or "the release of the soul from these mortal bodies" in death. [86] Young Pastorius could also perceive, during the 1670s and especially in this 1674 wedding invitation, the compromises his father was making as a leading citizen of Franconia, compromises indicating Melchior Adam's willingness to take personal gain at the expense of others.

Having married his third wife out of Christian duty and pursued the most varied and demanding government tasks with what appeared to be selfless energy and dedication, the elder Pastorius, at the age of 50, flouted the respect for the dead traditionally expressed in year-long mourning and embarked upon his May-and-December courtship with poetry describing his beloved in the trite phrases of romantic schoolboys – "You are my heart's adornment... Oh, you, life of my life," he proclaims, stating that life with Dorothea Esther would be "Like the sunshine following rain" [87] – and this courtship won him, along with his virgin bride, connections at the court of Bayreuth that he would later use to personal advantage. Since connections of this sort were not secured by marriage alone, Melchior Adam, in his wedding poem, also espouses the cold-hearted bellicosity of Margrave Christian Ernst, and thus endorses the political circumstances that contributed to widespread poverty and disparities of wealth and station. Franz Daniel Pastorius, in the midst of wartime wrangling at Regensburg, could not appreciate the superficial humor of his father's wedding poem. The contrast of one man's wedded bliss with the slaughter of thousands was too crass for him to swallow.

Franz Daniel stayed on at Regensburg another seven months, moving into the embassy of Nürnberg and Franconia within a week of his father's wedding. Melchior Adam apparently cut off his son's allowance at this point, which must have been one of the reasons Franz Daniel expressed his appreciation for the "very kind" treatment he received from Ambassador Wölcker and his wife. As mature members of Nürnberg society, the Wölckers undoubtedly consoled young Pastorius and patiently explained Melchior Adam's motives to him, helping him recover the sense of filial obedience he had temporarily lost. On 16 April 1675 Franz Daniel atoned for this lapse by riding the postal coach the 125 kilometers to Bayreuth, the residential city of Margrave Christian Ernst, known in Germany for its splendor long before the operas of Richard Wagner gave it an international reputation. In this city Dorothea Esther's older sister Anna Maria was marrying Georg Roth, a learned official at Christian Ernst's court, and young Pastorius was finally prepared to meet his new stepmother. He joined his parents at the wedding, participated in the festivities that followed, and rode home to Windsheim in a private coach with Dorothea Esther and Melchior Adam.

Pastorius lived at home another five months, deliberately avoiding the formal study of law for more than a year. On July 6 he led his childhood playmate Magdalena Eichen down the aisle at her wedding in the village of Segnitz, affirming communal ties in rural Franconia. At some point during this stay in Windsheim, possibly as a result of discussions with his father about Christian values and his place in society, he became convinced that it was his duty to finish his law degree and assume the responsibilities and prerogatives awaiting him as Melchior Adam's son. Five months together in his father's home produced at least a semblance of family solidarity. He saw his stepmother Dorothea Esther, two or three years younger than he was, assume her role as wife and future mother, and became aware that Melchior Adam's family had a promising future. Three months pregnant when he met her, Dorothea Esther gave birth to her first child in October, 1675.

3.6 "Making an end of academical learning": The Doctorate in Civil and Canon Law
3.6.1 Practicing the Art of Disputation

> Boldness and readiness of speech with the most (though not with the most judicious) bears away the bell. Phocion [of Athens, c. 402-318 B.C.] compared an orator to a cypress tree, fair and great, but fruitless. Culpeper, p. 384. Rhetoricians (p. 385) will speak well, not do well (p. 447).
>
> -- "Eloquence"

> Such is the subtilty of sophistical reasonings, that men may almost distinguish themselves into and out of any opinion; and some people who are masters of the art of nice arguing often lose both themselves and their religion in the labyrinths of words.
>
> -- "Theologia scholastica"

By the time Dorothea Esther's son Johannes Samuel was born, Pastorius had returned to Nürnberg, where, he notes in "Genealogia Pastoriana," "I at last made an end of my academical learning." He had taken up lodgings in Altdorf on September 27, receiving his meals in the home of Professor Linck. He studied more legal theory, and refined the rhetorical skills he had first practiced in Latin and Italian legal disputations at Jena a year and a half earlier. On November 10 he began a *disputatorium* training him for future rhetorical performances, and on May 31 of the following year, ready for the first big hurdle, he entered one of the two enclosed and elevated rostrums at the front of the Welserischen Auditorium, the university's grandest hall, used for large lectures, official ceremonies and banquets, and for formal disputations. Professor Linck occupied the other rostrum. The two of them were the opponents in a two-hour private disputation preparing Pastorius for his forthcoming doctoral disputation.

Writing in 1794, Professor Georg Andreas Will described the Nürnberg tradition that Pastorius got to know so well:

> If the useful practice of disputing has ever had a home anywhere, then it can verily be said that from time immemorial this home has existed above all at Altdorf. We have public and private disputations at this university. For the public disputations, the rector and the dean of the faculty appear in their official habits, and all the professors are required to attend. Public disputations are held either as practice disputations presided over by one of the professors ... or by private instructors who are qualifying for academic inauguration or simply want the practice, or finally for the attainment of the highest academic honor [i.e., the doctorate] ... The private disputations represent a develop-

ment unique to this university. Although they are distinguished from public disputations, they are nevertheless held in an auditorium and are open to faculty and students, but the professors are not especially required to attend ... This worthy institution, established in our early history and renewed in 1627, is one of the reasons such an extremely large number of disputations have been held at Altdorf, among them those of [twenty-four of the most disputatious professors in Nürnberg's history, including Dürr, Felwinger, Linck, Sturm, Wagenseil, Weinmann and, from a later generation, Christoph Sonntag, the anti-Pietist who hounded Johann Georg Rosenbach out of Nürnberg, and Georg Paul Rötenbeck, who in turn lambasted Sonntag] ... As a matter of fact, all four of the faculties have held private disputations every week since time out of memory. [88]

3.6.2 *The* Rigorosum *and* Disputatio Inauguralis

Flesh, World and Devil are three
against Poor F. D. P.
Father, Son anD sPirit
assist him above merit.

It's better to be mute,
Than Foolishly DisPute
Of things not understood:
Strive rather to be good.

-- "Symbola Onomastica," nos. 707, 708

Pastorius thus disputed with one of the grand masters of the art, and he disputed to his mentor's complete satisfaction. His performance on May 31 was the first in a series of formalities assuring his full qualification for Nürnberg's highest academic degree. [89] He concluded his study of law in subsequent months, and on October 26 he was invited to a formal interview with all the professors of law – Linck, Wagenseil, Georg Reichard Hammer, and the dean of law, Johann Anton Geiger, who was authorized to award certificates of recommendation (*lieris systaticus*) for advancement to the examinations for the degree of doctor of civil and canon law (*Juris utriusque Doctor*).

Pastorius was awarded such a certificate, and he took it with him when he called on Chancellor Magnus Fetzer in central Nürnberg on November 2. As chancellor, Fetzer was empowered, by the four city officials who made up the university's board of trustees, to run the university in accordance with the city's mandates and guidelines for education and the charter granted by the emperor. He personally authorized each degree candidate to participate in the oral exams and to hold the inaugural disputation and, along with the dean, censored the disputation texts "to make sure that nothing prejudicial to the constitution and laws of the German empire and the city of Nürnberg found its way into them." [90] Fetzer was satisfied with Pastorius' credentials and character, and on November 7 and 8 Pastorius was grilled by the law professors during the two days of final examinations known as the *Rigorosum*, which tested his general knowledge of the law and his ability to interpret specific passages from both the civil and canon law texts of the Justinian Code.

In a three-hour inaugural disputation on 23 November 1676, Pastorius defended, before some of his fellow students and the entire faculty of the university assembled in the Welserischen Auditorium, the forty theses and twelve corollaries printed in his 25-page text entitled *Disputatio Inauguralis De Rasura Documentorum* (Inaugural Disputation on Deleting [or obscuring legal] Documentation). [91] Although many of his contemporaries paid their professors to produce their disputation texts for them, Pastorius wrote anagrams into his twelve corollaries giving them his personal signature. In handwritten notations on his Pennsylvania copy of the disputation, Pastorius showed that the first letter of the first word of each corollary formed a series of four acrostics in this order: MAP for Melchior Adam Pastorius, DEV for Dorthea Esther Volckmann, FDP for Franz Daniel Pastorius, and JSP for Johannes Samuel Pastorius, the half brother who was one year old when Franz Daniel published his disputation. In addition to these family acrostics, Pastorius dedicated his printed disputation "To my God, native land, father, supporters and friends" ("Deo, Patriae, Genitori, Fautoribus & Amicis"), two indications he was asserting a solidarity with his family and community that he could barely hope to realize as matters stood at the moment.

As his twelve personalized corollaries indicate, Pastorius was assigned doctoral research on a miscellaneous assortment of legal topics, some of which merely demonstrated that even bagatelles could take on legal significance if they affected the interests of an influential burgher or lord. Despite the more or less arbitrary nature of his legal assignments, they nevertheless reveal two basic areas of tension, personal and social, that had been bothering him at least since the beginning of his Regensburg stay two years earlier. Although Pastorius was convinced that much of his education was unproductive and even unchristian, he obediently researched and disputed according to the desires of his professors – denying a contradiction between Aristotle and Christianity, asserting that women could not legally object to unwanted sexual advances, that overlords could present a case for legally robbing their vassals, that men of learning could refuse to accept the unlearned as neighbors. [92]

Although these establishment views differed from his personal convictions, Pastorius nevertheless found a way to register a protest against authority even as he defended his disputation and signaled a willingness to accept his place in Franconian society. He managed to arrange his twelve personalized corollaries so that the very first one, beginning with "M" for Melchior, quietly but defiantly proclaimed the resentment he felt toward his authoritarian society, symbolized for him in the single act that most clearly represented the uncharitable – and thus unchristian – conduct of his own father. In English paraphrase, the corollary states: "A husband is not legally bound to mourn his wife, but he creates a scandal by becoming engaged to marry upon her death."

3.7 "*They keep on strutting about* a la mode": Graduation Day without the Graduate

If ev'ry man or reasonable Creature,
Would only use what's requisite by Nature,
Then all might feed on Wheaten Flow'r most fine,
Drink Beer and ale, Yea nothing else than Wine;
But, O Great But! the richest and the greatest
Amongst Mankind do prove the Degeneratest,
Misspend and waste their Liquor and their Food:
What's left for us? Scarce any thing that's good.

-- Poem 369 (entire)

If Pastorius had been a typical graduate of Nürnberg University, he would have returned to Altdorf for the graduation ceremonies that accompanied the festival of Saint Peter and Saint Paul on 29 June 1677, but by that date he had witnessed political confrontation in Windsheim and found cogent reasons for refusing to participate in the orderly ceremonies that bestowed legitimacy upon the learned men who practiced his profession in Franconia. [93] If the spring of 1677 had not already shattered his hopes for familial and communal solidarity, he would have joined the procession of students and professors and representatives of the Nürnberg Senate who marched from the Lutheran church adjoining the village square of Altdorf to the campus at the edge of town – through the sweeping arch of the main gate, across the spacious lawn of the central courtyard, past the bronze fountain of Pallas Athena, and on to the main portal of the Renaissance "collegium" – and within the Welserischen Auditorium he would have stood opposite Dean Johann Anton Geiger to swear an oath to perpetuate the honor and dignity of the law and to be invested with the doctoral robe and hat, signifying an authority and esteem equal to that of the nobility itself, and finally he would have joined in the eloquent speech-making and festive eating and drinking that marked the conclusion of the graduation ceremonies each year at Nürnberg University.

Since doctoral investment followed the inaugural disputation but was always "repeated and confirmed" at the annual festivities in June, not participating in these ceremonies was as much an affront to authority as not attending Melchior Adam's wedding in 1674. [94] What can be taken as an explanation of Pastorius' absence from the Altdorf formalities is contained in a letter of 1699 advising his father not to have his younger half-brother study law, an argument further elucidated by Franz Daniel's Windsheim experience during 1676-79:

> I only regret that anyone who, like my dear brother Johann Samuel, has learned piety and the fear of the Lord from his dear parents and *Praeceptore domestico* [tutor] at home, may then lose this piety again while at the university, and experience so much *dediscinda* [matters better forgotten] at extreme danger to his mortal soul, and I would much rather advise him, with hearty brotherly love, to learn a decent and readily-comprehensible trade in which he could serve God and his fellow man; although the crafts are despised and held in low esteem among you, they are nevertheless far more in keeping with God's laws and the teachings of the Apostles than all the strange conceits of the scholastics; since most of the highly learned are grandly foolish and *scientia mundana inflat* [worldly knowledge puffeth up], high arrogant souls of this sort expect to live in pomp and finery after finishing the university, and thus they need great sums of money, which they try to obtain at the cost of their neighbors *per fas et nefas* [by means both legal and illegal], just so their wives and children can keep on strutting about *a la mode* no matter what. [95]

Perceiving that European learnedness contributed to the political and social tensions of Europe, Pastorius criticized both Aristotelian scholasticism, an academic tradition that gradually gave way to the learning of a more enlightened and scientific age, and the cultural biases of the learned that did not disappear with the passing of scholastic learning. The commentary of his American correspondence was both a diagnosis of the contemporary ills of European society and a prognosis for a healthier society in America, where individual rights might be newly defined, and (for a number of generations, at any rate) the special rights and privileges of cultural elites diminished.

Chapter Four
Obeying the Father

4.1   The Windsheim Insurrection of 1677-79
4.1.1   Franz Daniel's Personal and Collective Guilt

> Count that day spent in vain, whose setting sun
> Views from thy hands no worthy action done.
>
> Conscience abus'd is the worst of furies,
> And will condemn more than a thousand juries.
>
> Plead never for a thing, the which is evil,
> Or else you are attornies for the Devil.
>
> -- Epigrams 49, 51, 609

> [Conscience] is the throne of God, and free from the power of all men. Barclay . . . It is called the heart. Eccl. 7:22. I John 3:20. Man's inseparable companion at all times and in all places. God's notary or recorder, writing down all particulars of our whole life, good or ill, with an indelible character, which nothing can raze out but Christ's blood. [Sin is written] With a pen of iron, with the point of diamond. Jer. 17:1 . . . Conscience, according to a common saying, is a thousand witnesses. Good conscience, as David's harp, drives away the evil spirit.
>
> -- "Conscience"

As a learned doctor of the laws in 1676, 25-year-old Pastorius could have had his pick of career opportunities at almost any of the courts of Protestant Germany, yet he chose to return home to Windsheim, where his opportunities were severely limited. He was expected to follow in his father's footsteps, marrying into the upper class and attaining governmental power and social influence, and his community was not prepared for any deviations from these expectations. Pastorius assumed the roles of country lawyer and burgomaster's son but did not fully meet the community's expectations of him. He postponed marriage indefinitely, essentially an affront to upper-class families and their daughters of marriageable age. Thus, unlike other sons of Windsheim senators returning home with a law degree (including his friend Johannes Joachim Mercklein), Pastorius was not appointed to the outer chamber of the senate. He tried to fit in, but apparently could not. Moral qualms stood in the way.

Despite his best efforts, Pastorius could not deny his own inner feelings. The Lutheran faith that had nurtured him and the pious and mystic influences that supplemented his learning at the university assumed growing importance as he confronted the choices of daily life in Windsheim. He had been repelled, in the lecture hall, by the lifeless doctrines of the Aristotelian theologians, and he could not separate religious belief from everyday conduct. If the teachings he had absorbed all his life meant anything at all, then they amounted to a living religious faith that informed one's entire being and flowed richly into the community through individual conduct. Denying this potential richness, Pastorius well knew, led unfailingly to guilt. He was acutely aware that his religion demanded obedience to the authority of the Heavenly Father, and he had been taught that disobedience would be punished. Where punishment was delayed, guilt accumulated, and produced fears of eternal damnation in the hereafter or even of immanent destruction in this world. "Conscience abus'd is the worst of furies," he would later conclude (quoted above).

Try as he might, Pastorius could not obey the Father in his daily conduct – either as attorney or as burgomaster's son. He felt tainted with sin as he provided legal services to his clients, the landed gentry who, with their feudal rights as landlords, judges and tax-collectors over the peasants, owned the estates and controlled the hamlets of middle Franconia. [1] Although the German peasants had attempted to overthrow the feudal system in the Peasants' War of 1525, their lords overwhelmingly defeated them and forced them to accept repressive measures that generally kept them politically impotent and, especially after the Thirty Years' War, poverty-stricken as well. Thus Pastorius' legal duties involved the gentry's contractual demands for substantial portions of the peasants' goods, services and cash – demands that accentuated the gap between the power and affluence of the few and the impotence and destitution of many of the peasants.

Diligently performing these tasks, Pastorius had accumulated "an abundance" ("einen Überfluss") of legal forms by 1678, he writes in his Pennsylvania "Collection of the Young Country Clerk's Solemn Forms" (Poem 74), but "since I did not want to save them" ("Weil ich Jene nicht wolt spahren") he was collecting similar forms again in Germantown years later. This evasive statement, combined with specific mention of the year 1678, suggests young Pastorius was so appalled by his duties, and by Windsheim politics, that he destroyed his legal forms in an emotional gesture of resignation.

His father later reported in a family journal that Franz Daniel's letters convinced his half brother Augustin Adam not to study law "because he [Franz Daniel] really does consider such a course of study a *Lusus de alieno corio* [a game at another's expense]... creat[ing] hate between brothers," and Melchior Adam reflected Franz Daniel's attitudes with an emblem and epigram attached to this report. The emblem portrays a jurist, the victim of his own talents, as a man with a lobster in his right hand ("Si laxes, erepit") and a serpent in the left ("Si stringas, erumpit"): If he relaxes his grip, the lobster will claw him, but too much pressure will cause the serpent to vent its venom. The epigram, in German, describes the opportunism of the country lawyer who interprets the law according to his clients' needs, and is rewarded in kind:

> He is right in any saddle,
> And drapes his cloak according to the wind.
> If he can't get a steer he'll settle for a cow. [2]

Franz Daniel indicates in "Genealogia Pastoriana" that he did not develop the moral insensitivity demanded of his profession in Windsheim:

> Here I practiced above two years & an half, keeping mine own horse, marching from one nobleman's house in the province unto the other, (auff der Wurst herumb [i.e., riding a live sausage], as they [are] use[d] to speak[ing],) and in short making nothing but work for repentance.

As if to atone for these sins, Pastorius repeatedly copied, from his English readings, moral and satirical descriptions under the heading of "Lawyer" in the "Alphabetical Hive," eventually assembling one of the lengthiest listings in the hive, a scathing cumulative judgement that helped to assuage the psychic wounds of early adulthood. Some of his poems and epigrams likewise criticize lawyers, in Poem 328 described as men who "perversely Plead" against orphans, widows and their own friends, evoking the prophet Micah's condemnation of governments in which all the officials are corrupt (Mic. 7,4): "The best of them is as a briar: The most upright is sharper than a thorn hedge." In contrast, reflecting positive attitudes toward the law, the many legal forms he collected in Pennsylvania illustrate his extensive legal activity helping to build a new society with a reformed legal system.

For a young lawyer with qualms about his profession, upper-class Windsheim would have presented difficulties even under normal circumstances. (Franz Daniel was virtually enmeshed in the legal profession: His father and various friends and some of their fathers and uncles were lawyers, too.) In fact, the circumstances in Windsheim were far from normal during these years. With his return to the imperial city on 29 November 1676, he had to face rising political tensions that led to open confrontation during the spring of 1677 and remained unresolved until after his final departure in 1679. Even more than his personal guilt as an attorney, it was the unspeakable horrors of insurrection and his collective guilt as a member of Windsheim's ruling class that robbed him of inner peace, and convinced him that a life of Christian love was not possible in his homeland, where economic conditions and militaristic policies kept many of the average citizens in oppressive poverty.

Despite the emphasis his society placed on civil obedience, young Pastorius realized that the citizens of Windsheim were justified in many of their claims against the government even though his own father was instrumental in suppressing the popular uprising. Thus the demands of filial duty and family solidarity obliged him to condone attitudes and conduct he must have found unconscionable. In the heat of civil confrontation, furthermore, he keenly felt the pressures the government exerted upon the Lutheran clergy, and realized that the state church was not able to affirm the Christian values he espoused. If he were to live honestly, he would be forced to reject both church and state – and to break his ties with his family and community. Obeying the Father, he painfully realized, meant turning his back on his own father, and this was the bitterest lesson he would learn in all of his filial experience.

4.1.2 Political Developments in the Imperial City
4.1.2.1 Causes of Tension

> How soon can God a pleasant calm transform
> Into a hurricane or dreadful storm!
>
> -- Epigram 126

> When men are grown high, God hath no better way with them than to brew them a cup of wormwood.
>
> -- "Adversity"

> We cannot submit unto the unjust things commanded by governments any other way than through a patient suffering under it . . . I am altogether under the jurisdiction of my friends, where their commands do not interfere with conscience. Obedience the mother of common prosperity; viz. when, as Solon said, the citizens are obedient to the magistrates, and the magistrates to the laws.
>
> -- "Obedience"

Windsheim's government, never fully recovered from the economic decline of the Thirty Years' War, was burdened by the demands of renewed warfare – and complicated by the attitudes of those who governed. [3] "This city is administered almost aristocratically by a lord mayor and 24 senators," Melchior Adam Pastorius admitted in his history of Windsheim, [4] and in fact it was the twelve members of the senate's inner chamber (including four burgomasters serving by rotation) who, with the lord mayor ("Oberbürgermeister"), ran the government on a daily basis, held most if not all of the important city offices, and exercised a voting majority on those rare occasions when the outer chamber might hesitate to approve their decisions. The senators usually held office for life – annual "elections" within the senate generally confirmed each member's status for another year – and when a senator died his successor was elected by the incumbents rather than by the citizenry. Intermarriage and nepotism, practiced for generations, had concentrated power in the hands of a few affluent merchants and well-educated lawyers. These were the men who headed the elite families of Windsheim and held obvious credentials as city administrators, yet there was arrogance in their administration and, aside from religious belief, little effective control over their self-interest.

Although the popular frustrations generated by this government were normally held in check, amid the economic difficulties of the 1670s they attained the force of unbearable insult, and dissension among government leaders – especially between Burgomaster Pastorius and Lord Mayor Johann Georg Stellwag – did not ameliorate the impending crisis. With civic pride demanding physical renewal and expansion, the empire direly needing new martial revenues, and old debts still left over from the Thirty Years' War, the senators saw themselves forced to run the city on a deficit, piling up even more long-term debts, and to levy crippling taxes on the populace. Their fiscal policies and aristocratic bearing gave the impression that they were driving the citizenry to the poorhouse while going easy on their personal estates. A 1677 government document indicates that 395 out of a total of about 530 households lived in "total poverty" ("ganz verarmt") or at a bare subsistence level, and some of the senators were in fact collecting interest payments on capital loaned to the city, one of the methods of enhancing their fortunes in difficult times, yet it was the repeated presence of imperial troops in Windsheim from 1673 onward that led to open resistence.

4.1.2.2 Tumult of March and April, 1677

> We are not against magistracy, but for it (it being God's ordinance), and are only against that in magistrates, which doth pollute and defile the place of magistracy. Fox, Sal. You that sit at the stern, whether of little barques or greater ships, whether counties or countries, you should not (like the heads of Israel) abhor justice and pervert equity for the love of money. By nature it is ordained that the better command the worse. The magistrate is bound to act according to the law, and not to set up his will in the stead thereof.
> -- "Magistrate"

> Only to see proves of small consequence;
> But to foresee shews wisdom's excellence.
> -- Epigram 2325.1

Tempers had been rising during the winter of 1676-77, when the citizens were required to open their homes to a regiment of soldiers, providing room and board at their personal inconvenience and expense, while the senators exempted themselves from this demeaning civic duty. [5] As the regiment prepared to leave in March, its commander demanded a "contribution" of 6000 talers to secure its subsistence en route to Holland, and on March 25 the senate complied by issuing a decree that set the citizenry in an uproar. It announced a doubling of the annual taxes to meet the demand, and it gave the citizens a mere eight days to raise the needed funds. The next day a committee of angry citizens appeared at the city hall with a petition of supplication and a list of grievances, demanding to inspect the fiscal records, but the senate refused to open the city's account books and would not consider alternate sources of revenue. Numerous citizens met in pubs to air their complaints on March 30 and 31, and four days later about 70 of them vowed to present their case before Emperor Leopold I in Vienna.

When a group of citizens again marched to the city hall on April 6, the senate reluctantly agreed to let a few individuals inspect the fiscal records, but then it reconsidered and, witnesses reported, attempted to jail one of the citizens' spokesmen instead. Three days later the citizens hired a lawyer from out of town and started drawing up a comprehensive "*gravamina*," or formal protest petition, that eventually listed 62 specific infringements of their freedoms, many of which represented repeated offenses. The senators countered by beginning to interrogate the citizens and, the next day, forbidding all public assembly, but on April 12 they permitted the citizens to read the first draft of their protest petition in the senate chambers. Since the senate refused to acknowledge the grievances, one hundred citizens met their attorney on April 20 to consider further legal steps, and the senate responded with an insulting order to cease and desist.

For nearly a month the citizens had been trying to impress their leaders with the injustice of governmental demands, yet the government remained adamant. The citizens grew belligerent in turn – individuals who did not join the rebellion were reportedly warned they would not be safe beyond the city gates – and increasingly afraid of heavy-handed repercussions. When two regiments of imperial troops approached Windsheim on April 21, the populace refused to believe a senate proclamation that the city would not be occupied. Organized as a militia and ready

180 | Franz Daniel Pastorius

to begin armed conflict, the citizens manned defensive positions along the city walls and, on April 25 and 26, forbade military passage. Resistance had now become open insurrection, and Burgomaster Pastorius and another senator visited Nürnberg to consult with its senate – possibly to request military assistance. A day or two later, apparently informed of this consultation, citizens guarding the city gates refused to let Burgomaster Pastorius leave the city, even though his task this time was the routine spring-time distribution of meadowlands.

4.1.3 "Windsheim contra Windsheim": The People versus the Government
4.1.3.1 The Charges (and a Baptism of Note)

> Zealously serve thy Maker, keep thy station,
> Truth, faith, hope, love: Thy coin and reputation.
>
> -- Epigram 2331.3

> They that make laws must keep them, sayeth Xenophanes. Culpeper, p. 381. [King] Archidamus being asked, who was master of Lacedaemonia [Sparta]? The laws, sayeth he, and after them the magistrates. P. 382. The law of God is perfect, and written in the heart. Fox. There is no law to be compared with love. Between just laws and righteous men no antipathy.
>
> -- "Law"

> Clouds of disdain are commonly raised by the wind of ostentation . . . 'Tis the froth only that gets to the top of the water . . . I am not scared with your big words.
>
> -- "Boasting"

Although these explosive tensions gradually diminished, the citizens remained convinced that their demands were justified, and – after collecting a set fee from each household to cover their expenses despite a senate order prohibiting such illegal "taxation" – they actually dispatched a party of three to Vienna, where the deputation presented its *gravamina* at the court of Leopold I before the end of May, thus initiating the case that was labeled "Windsheim contra [versus] Windsheim" in government files. The petition reveals numerous complaints against the fiscal policies of the city government and the privileges of the senators, which included using the city's day laborers and its horses in their private undertakings, unofficially exempting themselves from property taxes even though some of them owned several luxurious houses, and allegedly squandering tax money on costly official journeys. The citizens further argued that excessive nepotism hindered the proper functioning of government, and bolstered this argument by claiming that Gymnasium and university scholarships intended for the poor were awarded to senators' sons, who then wasted their years at the university in riotous living only to be handed a senate post upon their return to Windsheim, "where, to the appreciation of their elders, they soon can be seen exercising their domination over the poor, suffering citizenry, and engage in forbidden carnal pleasures, seduce the wives of virtuous citizens and rape their daughters, despite which they are tolerated in the senate." [6]

Deep class resentments marked the tone of these complaints, and may have led to some exaggeration. Despite the plural forms of the latter charge, for example, it cited only one case of a citizen whose wife and daughter were allegedly seduced or raped with impunity by a young senator. But the overwhelming array of specific charges could not be ignored, especially since a number of them were leveled at Lord Mayor Johann Georg Stellwag, appointed to the city's highest office by his fellow senators and confirmed as Windsheim's imperial representative by Leopold I in 1671. The citizens charged that Stellwag had privately sold church ornamentation, removed a beautiful altar from the church, and accepted a bribe from an apothecary who gained monopoly powers in return, that he repeatedly authorized funeral sermons only after receiving cash "gifts" from the relatives of the deceased, granted illegal tax benefits to favored citizens, interfered in civil court cases normally adjudicated by the acting burgomaster if Stellwag had a grudge against the complainant or a special interest in the outcome, insulted citizens in the public chambers of the senate, and beat them in the streets.

Government remained unstable as the citizens awaited the appointment of an imperial commission to inquire into the validity of their grievances. When Margrave Christian Ernst of Bayreuth opportunistically attempted to intervene on behalf of the citizens, the senators jealously reasserted their sovereignty within the free city. Burgomaster Georg Andreas Dienst accused the Windsheim clergy of unwarranted permissiveness; instead of keeping the citizens in check, he complained, they encouraged sedition by claiming it was only "dissension." The critical process of appointing an investigatory commission extended on through the summer as the citizenry and senate filed petitions and counter-petitions on behalf of various parties sympathetic to their cause. Citizens refused to obey a senate decree forbidding marksmanship contests and dancing during the autumn "Kirchweih" festivities, and ignored summonses to appear in court for the offense. When two companies of soldiers arrived for the winter of 1677-78, the citizens assembled publicly once more, and after convening another of many special sessions, the senate issued a warning to comply with its procedures for quartering the military.

How Franz Daniel coped with these tensions is, for the most part, not recorded. He does note, in "Res Propriae," that on 6 August 1677 he served as the godfather at the baptism of the son of Michael Schmidt, a Windsheim saltpeter gatherer ("Salpetersieder"), and the baby was given the name Franz Daniel. At this point Pastorius was treading a thin line between loyalty and disloyalty to family and class. The saltpeterman was a lowly laborer whose job it was to go from village to village digging up nitrous soil soaked in urine and excrement from stables, outhouses and other such locations, and then to boil down his extractions in a large vat to win saltpeter, or the nitrates used in making gunpowder. [6a] Saltpeter gatherers were endured as a public nuisance or treated as pariahs since they were authorized to intrude wherever nitrous soil could be found, inside barns and underneath houses or even inside them. Legal disputes ensued, which would explain how Pastorius first encountered Schmidt. Still, it is hard to imagine that two men of such disparate standing would have gotten to know each other. And even harder to imagine that a common workman like Schmidt would have dared to ask young Doctor Pastorius to be his son's godfather.

Pastorius does not comment on his "Res Propriae" notation. All that can be said is this: The learned country lawyer standing beside this itinerant laborer at a Lutheran baptismal font with Schmidt's wife and baby presented a poignant image of neighborly love or Christian charity, essentially the inverse of the parable of Lazarus and Dives. Young Pastorius might have seen his decision to stand with the Schmidt family as penitence or atonement for the sins of his family and class.

Windsheim society was more likely to have seen it as foolhardy behavior, or even as betrayal. Yet Pastorius would later insist that Christ's Golden Rule can prevail in society, even giving it title-page status in his copy of Pennsylvania's "Great Law" (in the epigraph below). "There is no law to be compared with love," one of his commonplace jottings affirms (quoted above).

4.1.3.2 The Hearings (and Renewed Resistance)

> If men split twice on the same rocks and shelves,
> Let them blame none, but rather thank themselves.
>
> -- Epigram 2319.5

> Do as you would be done unto! The obeying these seven words is more than the reading, hearing, and professing seven times seven thousand words. It is indeed a golden rule, a royal law, the standard of equity according to which we must converse with all men.
>
> -- "Rules"

> ***Leges Pennsilvanianae,***
> h.e. The Great Law of the Province of Pennsylvania.
> Gal. 5:14. All the law is fulfilled in one word, in this: Thou shalt love thy neighbour as thy self. add. Rom. 13:8.
> Matth. 7:12. All things, whatsoever ye would, that men should do to you, do ye even so to them, for this is the law and the prophets. add Cap. 22 v. 35 etc.
> *Salus Populi Suprema Lex isto.*
> [The welfare of the people is the highest law.]
> Francis Daniel Pastorius his Book.
> 1690
>
> -- Manuscript title page

> If we did reason right   To do to Others as
> And perfect Logick chop,   We would be done by them.
> Endeav'ring day and night   This was Christ's doctrine and,
> To get to Wisdom's Top,   If fully understood,
> We should in stead of glass   Is the Eternal Band
> Meet with the precious Gem,   Of Peace, the noblest Good.
>
> -- Poem 331, to James Logan of Philadelphia

The commissioners finally arrived on 16 November 1677 and were welcomed with opening ceremonies conducted by Lord Mayor Stellwag. Their formal hearings, punctuated by lengthy recesses, lasted eight months. In December the citizens declared the commission biased, and in Vienna on 31 January 1678, their representatives requested that it be reconstituted and that Stellwag be removed from office at least until the hearings ended. The senate countered with a demand that the citizens' attorney be debarred, presumably because representing the citizens was seditious. The Vienna officials asked Stellwag to refrain from attending Senate sessions dealing with his personal conduct but refused to appoint a new commission. On March 25 an imperial decree, anticipating that citizens might sense defeat and evade punishment, prohibited moving away from Windsheim. To clarify a charge that the citizens' attorney was not their legitimate representative, the commission conducted a poll of the citizens in May, revealing that – despite the likelihood of repercussions – 69.2 percent still supported the protest, 20 percent then favored the government, and 5.5 percent considered themselves "neutral." (Those not available for questioning accounted for the remaining 5.3 percent.)

At lengthy hearings during June and early July, 1678, more than a year after the uprising, the commission investigated city finances, heard evidence relating to the complaint petition, examined the charges against Lord Mayor Stellwag, and identified the instigators of the insurrection in a special "inquisition" ("*inquisitio in authores seditionis*"). Several incidents during June revealed new complaints and renewed tensions: The bailiffs of various villages in the city's jurisdiction appeared with protests against the senate; three individuals were fined for wrangling with other citizens; a number of inhabitants held public diatribes against the senate, two of whom were imprisoned for 24 hours by the commission; and a second attorney representing the citizens, after refusing to appear to be sworn in, was placed under arrest but managed to escape from the arresting officials. After concluding the hearings on July 12, the commission reached three findings, announced before the senate, that completely ignored the central issues: 1) Senators should be punished if they discuss confidential issues outside the senate chambers. 2) Senators may not seek to influence other senate members while a vote is in progress. 3) Lord Mayor Stellwag and Burgomaster Pastorius must end their public discord.

Disturbed by the commission's imminent departure six days later, the citizens tried to turn the commissioners' attention to essentials with a new petition requesting a complete account of city finances and a list of the creditors who earned interest from the city, and threatening that the citizenry would leave Windsheim if Stellwag was not removed from office. The following day the commission announced that its Windsheim investigation was concluded, and prepared to leave the city. Responding to the new petition, it revealed that the city's debts amounted to 40,000 florins, but it refused to name the creditors without the specific authorization of the Emperor. It dismissed the request for fiscal documentation, arguing that the process would be costly and would not benefit the citizenry. Referring to the threat to leave Windsheim, it warned that subjects should never presume to instruct their Emperor, and added that imperial rescripts protected the lord mayor in the conduct of his office. It admonished the citizens to reconciliation and warned them to stop holding "conventicles" or assemblies. Before leaving town, it admonished the clergy to be sure that their sermons contained proper information in the future.

While Windsheim was awaiting the official results of the hearings for another full year – two imperial decrees of 31 May 1679 were not announced until that August – the insurrection broke out anew with a repetition of the very same issues, but this time the city government, benefitting from past experience, nipped it in the bud with firm and decisive action. Again soldiers were quartered in the city for the winter, and extraordinary expenses led the senate to demand one and one-half times the normal taxes. Again the citizens refused to pay, and on 2 February 1679, their representatives presented their case in the senate chambers. The senate immediately appealed to Vienna. An imperial decree of March 10 ordered the citizens to pay the tax or face the displeasure of his imperial majesty, and an imperial rescript ordered the Windsheim commission to imprison and punish the leaders of the protest.

Tensions remained high. When Clergyman Johannes Petermann died on April 27, his chambers were sealed, apparently to allow an official search of his papers, since he had helped the citizens prepare their documents for the commission. On

May 1 citizens demanded that the twelve-man outer chamber of the senate meet to discuss pressing issues, and a meeting was convened six days later, but the twelve-man inner chamber, with Lord Mayor Stellwag and Burgomaster Pastorius, refused to let the citizens present their arguments, aimed at a "categorical resolution" of the political tensions. Clergyman Johann Philipp Groß kept an appointment with the citizens' attorney in a neighboring village in July, and he apparently spoke publicly in favor of the citizens. On July 16, the senate suspended him from office for creating a scandal and placed him under house arrest pending the final session of the imperial commission.

In May of 1678, Franz Daniel Pastorius served as godfather when his friend Johannes Joachim Mercklein's infant son was baptized. This seems to have been the last time he would attempt to affirm communal bonds in Franconia. It was sometime during 1678 that he apparently destroyed all of the legal forms he had been collecting as a country lawyer, privately indicating his resolve to end his Franconian law career. Indecisive and agonizing, he delayed leaving Windsheim for good until April, 1679, as Vienna was aiding the senate in its efforts to restrain the citizens and punish their leaders.

4.1.3.3   The Verdict

> That Sov'raign, that but pricks, Waspishly does sting
> His loyal Subjects, is a Tyrant, not a King:
> He, when the City burns, with Nero falls to Sing.
> And those who Taxes take, and at their pleasure Spend,
> Should (like my Roses I) the Innocent defend,
> Else certainly they will be Taxed at the End. Isa. 10:1,2.
>
> -- Poem 328, alluding to brambles and roses

The commissioners returned to Windsheim on 10 August 1679, and two days later convened the senators and citizens for a reading of the two decrees signed by Leopold I. In the first decree, the Emperor reprimanded the citizenry for revolting against their legitimate government and disobediently submitting their grievances to him, forbade public assembly and rebellion, demanded that the citizens show respect and obedience toward their government officials, and displayed his mercy by punishing only the ringleaders of the insurrection. Six of them were sentenced to eight days in the tower on bread and water, and the three chief offenders were banished from the city, a punishment that was later reduced to fourteen days on bread and water. In the second decree, Leopold I dismissed the charges against Lord Mayor Stellwag and exhorted the citizens to be dutifully respectful of Windsheim's highest official, yet commanded Stellwag to deal justly with the citizens in the future, thus tacitly admitting the Lord Mayor's past offenses. In a related decision, the Emperor prohibited the citizens' attorney from representing his Windsheim clients any longer, leaving the citizens with no legal recourse.

After the decrees were read, the citizens and senators ritually demonstrated their obeisance by kneeling and renewing their oath of allegiance to Leopold I. In a private session with senate members the following day, the commission presented suggestions for administrative reforms, and on August 19 a citizens' committee accepted a limited reform program that included minor revisions of the tax law but did not address the basic faults of government. In one instance, the senate all too willingly responded to civic protest. Some of the citizens had complained that

Jewish craftsmen or merchants tolerated in the city were gaining too much of Windsheim's mercantile income, and demanded a revocation of selling privileges. The Senate reacted by proclaiming that all the Jews of Windsheim – whose presence was reflected in the street name "Judengasse," or "Jews' Alley" – would be required to leave the city.

The political structure of Windsheim was not affected by these modifications. The Senate retained its rights and privileges, and the citizens were forced to live with the frustrations that continued to complicate civic life in the decades following Franz Daniel Pastorius' departure. [7] The leading families of the imperial city pursued the goals of baroque and rococo culture and absolutist government: The city built a magnificent lord mayor's residence (1705) and other imposing public buildings in "the style of the Brandenburg margraves" ("Markgrafenstil"), a style emulated in new private mansions as well. It toppled the half-timbered medieval and Renaissance city hall and constructed, from 1713 to 1717, a palatial baroque edifice of Italian design in its stead. It commissioned new religious paintings, altars and an organ for the Church of Saint Kilian and new statues and fountains, and landscaped a formal garden with promenades and a tree-lined avenue to give it the proper courtly perspective.

Windsheim's citizens continued to bear the burdens of heavy taxation and governmental arrogance, generally but not continuously in submissive obedience. Following widespread protest in 1731, the senate ceremoniously burned anonymous petitions accusing it of injustices after its aggressive investigation failed to identify the authors of the petitions. In the protests of 1749-50, the citizenry, in a 42-point petition, again formally accused the senate of abusing its authority. Although the Emperor censured the citizens and threatened to restore order forcibly, this time the verdict of an imperial commission confirmed the charges of senatorial nepotism and other irregularities instead of imprisoning the protestors – indications that the European establishment, influenced by Enlightenment views on the rational use of authority, was beginning to develop a political awareness not unlike that displayed seven decades earlier by Franz Daniel Pastorius.

4.1.4 Father and Son at a Moral Impasse
4.1.4.1 Conduct of Burgomaster Pastorius

> If we must not disobey God to obey [our parents], at least we must let them see that there is nothing else in our refusal. Max[im] 165 . . . Blessed, yea thrice blessed, are those children whose parents (like Jacob) walked in His integrity. Prov. 20:7. <u>Genes.</u>, p. 103.
>
> -- "Parents"
>
> Wrath is blind . . . A man may do that in his passion, which exceedeth all compassion.
>
> -- "Anger"

The family circumstances affecting young Pastorius during the insurrection of 1677-79 can be inferred from the documentary evidence of his father's attitudes and conduct. Although Melchior Adam objected to governmental excess in principle, he was by no means willing to let the common citizens challenge his authority as burgomaster. Aside from Lord Mayor Stellwag, in fact, Burgomaster Pastorius was the only ranking official personally criticized in the citizens' *gravamina*:

> The honorable citizenry ... finds itself extremely aggrieved by Burgomaster Pastorius because, during the recently-endured heavy occupation, he readily threatened some citizens with severe punishment in the prison and the tower, accused others of being rebels, and in an exceedingly abusive manner showed a third group the way to the city gates, declaring they should be banished, and he subsequently made the same accusations against [three other citizens], and more than once was heard proclaiming in public that yet another citizen should be whipped and driven beyond the city gates and banished from the city at the earliest opportunity. [8]

Melchior Adam's feuding with Lord Mayor Stellwag, also documented in the *gravamina*, may have had its origins in his moral condemnation of Stellwag's abuses of power, but in 1677 the citizens made no moral distinctions and impartially criticized both leaders:

> It also appears very grievous to the honorable citizenry that Lord Mayor Stellwag and Burgomaster Pastorius are completely unable to get along with each other, as the latter openly proclaims that he cannot continue to govern and exist alongside Mr. Stellwag but would rather consider leaving the city for this reason, which [dispute] not only noticeably inhibits the healing process of justice and curtails the rights of the oppressed citizens but also severely endangers the city government itself. [9]

The imperial commission concluded, in its findings of July, 1678, that the "constant quarreling" ("ständige Streitigkeiten") between Lord Mayor Stellwag and Burgomaster Pastorius constituted a "defect" ("*Defectus*") in the city government; it ordered the two to reconcile their differences publicly by shaking hands and forgiving each other, and declared that renewing the feud would be punishable by a fine of fifty talers. [10] The commission thus indicated that government officials, regardless of their private scruples, could be forced to accept the limitations of the status quo if they wished to retain their place in society – yet another reason why Franz Daniel Pastorius felt obliged to leave Franconia and Germany.

4.1.4.2 The Learned Approach to the Insurrection

You first-rate men and topping-ones,	That oft a tall Tree falls,
On Princely Chairs and Royal Thrones,	When down-bent Bushes stand;
For ought set not at nought	That Kings are us'd as Thralls,
This Poetaster Thought,	When Slaves and knaves command.
	Ezek. 31 and Dan. 4.

-- Poem 304

Events like the Windsheim insurrection of 1677-79 defied the widely-held premises of social organization in seventeenth-century Germany, where, in theory, loyal citizens invariably obeyed their virtuous leaders, and disobedient individuals were social outcasts. The mere suggestion that citizens might have legitimate complaints against government threatened the hierarchy itself, and – in the most prevalent arguments of the learned – such suggestions had to be denied. Given this interpretation of reality, popular rebellion becomes by logical necessity a figment of the imagination, and the learned of Franconia long treated the Windsheim uprising accordingly. Although Melchior Adam published histories of Windsheim and Franconia, he never mentioned the insurrection of 1677-79 in his writings, and other historians with access to the government files likewise treated it as a non-event.

When Johann Heinrich Zedler (1706-63), a counselor to the King of Prussia, produced the 57th folio volume of his universal encyclopedia in 1748, one of his contributors described the history and culture of Windsheim in 41 lengthy columns but refused to report various civil disturbances from the Peasants' Revolt onward:

> The conflicts [in and around Windsheim are] ... matters that do not amount to anything of significance ... Windsheim's chief concern has been, as with the other imperial cities, to maintain constant ties with his imperial majesty and the empire, and within the city itself to remain intent upon the aims of peace, calm and unity ... in order to insure that it may enjoy a flourishing state at all times. [11]

Christian Wilhelm Schirmer, whose comprehensive and generally reliable history of Windsheim was published in 1848 (a year of revolution in Germany), limited his description of the 1677-79 insurrection to one sentence: "Since the citizens believed they could no longer bear the burdens [of housing and feeding imperial soldiers during the winter of 1677], they indulged in insubordination, and even registered a complaint in Vienna." [12]

Even in the twentieth century, the insurrection has been ignored or played down, resulting in historical inaccuracies that are only now being corrected. [13] Details of the uprising did not become generally available until Werner Korndörfer's archival research in Windsheim and Vienna was published in 1971. In the context of Franz Daniel Pastorius' upbringing and adult experience in Europe, these long-ignored details now reveal one of the most basic factors ultimately leading to his emigration and to the moral tone of his transatlantic writings. His emphasis on modest living and neighborly love (or the Golden Rule) was a keenly-felt response to upper-class excesses particularly in Windsheim.

4.1.4.3 "Christ's Divine Light shall rise": Unresolved Moral Tensions in Franz Daniel's Correspondence with his Father

> Fraud veil'd with friendship makes the greatest foe;
> Think most men rogues, but yet tell no man so.
> -- Epigram 99

> At [Babel's] dreadful Fall Christ's Divine Light shall rise,
> And make all Emperours, all Kings and Princes Wise,
> Nay, Wiser than once the Wisest, (Solomon);
> Pray! loyal Subjects pray, that this be hasten'd on
> By God; For human hands and Brains are too too weak,
> Her Bulwarks, Trenches, Walls and Bastions so to break
> Down to the ground, that they there in their Rubbish lie,
> An Ensign of His Wrath, to all Eternity.
> -- Poem 341, to James Logan, inspired by Saavedre's political emblems

The social and political conditions in Frankfurt am Main, Germany, Pastorius' home beginning in April 1679, and in Europe generally, as he experienced them during his grand tour from June 1680 to November 1682 did not relieve the personal tensions he had felt in Windsheim from 1676 to 1679. Since inequities of wealth and power could be seen anywhere, not just in a city like Windsheim where rebellion made them acutely noticeable, Pastorius, as a privileged doctor of the laws, felt complicity in an establishment he considered unchristian, and his personal guilt, projected upon the European establishment as a whole, created fears of divine retribution that were reinforced by Christian millennialism and the actual and potential destruction of European warfare and balance-of-power politics. These emotions were further heightened by his awareness that avoiding such complicity involved giving up his friends and relatives and the many satisfactions of his upper-class existence in Franconia and Germany.

This explains his 1683 farewell letter from Deal, England, announcing his desire "to escape disaster in time and eternity" by fleeing "the worldly impudence and sin of Europe," and it helps to account for the morality and satire that continued to invigorate his poetry and prose after his personal fears had waned. This sharp moral awareness informs Poem 341 (in the epigraph here), with its yearning for governmental wisdom and for the destruction of the instruments or monuments of belligerent empire, and it also lies behind his sympathy for his Pietist friend Johann Augustin Lietzheimer and for the somber rebelliousness of the Pietist mechanic Johann Georg Rosenbach as well as his criticism of rich and aristocratic young Germans throughout Europe who wasted "their German patrimony on worldly frivolities that profit no one" and of the "high arrogant souls" who used legal and illegal means "to live in pomp and finery after finishing the university."

Although he left Windsheim because he could not directly oppose the authority of his father – or the tradition-bound authority of the imperial city – Pastorius, through long soul-searching and separation, achieved a tone of independent authority in his Pennsylvania correspondence, persistently expressing basic truths even when they contradicted the values most revered by many of his peers. In the early 1680s, at least, he was not immune to the emotionality or isolation of the seer or prophet, especially since his most important opponent in this contest of values was his father, the man he had most respected and emulated during his early life. His isolation is particularly apparent in a letter to his parents dated 7 March 1684. Dramatically describing the apocalyptic fears that had preceded his emigration and still preoccupied him nine months later, Pastorius admitted the loss he felt separated from his home and family even as he preached a moral regeneration inspired by the innovative potential of Pennsylvania:

> I surely wish that I could have you and my dear brothers and sisters here with me, well knowing that neither you nor they would regret having made a change of this kind. For even though I may have been robbed of your physical presence, I nevertheless am always present with you in childly love, and I see the judgement of woeful wrath and heavy punishment that, in the inevitable course of divine justice upon Europe, will be poured out over this abominable Babylon to the point of total destruction. If you want to escape the calamity awaiting Germany, dear parents, then do not become accomplices in its sin, but note well: depart from it!
>
> I am not talking about a [purely] physical departure, which in itself would have little benefit, but rather a spiritual leave-taking that can only be achieved if you refuse to subject yourselves to the Babylonian vanities and disordered human laws and precepts that have the upper hand on your side [of the Atlantic], and refuse to recognize as master any but Jesus Christ the son of almighty God, who sent Him to us so that He might be the way and the truth and life everlasting for us.
>
> If your conviction is such that you indeed wish to remain in your Fatherland (inasmuch as you do not feel inwardly moved by God to leave the same), then live as Lot did in Sodom, remaining undefiled by the arrogance, affluence and wantonness that there prevailed.

Since, however, I have ascertained upon valid grounds that the rain of fire and brimstone of divine wrath will soon descend upon the Gomorrah of Germany, it is my earnest wish that you may be spared from it in both body and soul. In this as in all matters, determine what God's benign will is so that you may accomplish the same, for whoever does this will not perish with the horde of the Godless but has the promise of eternity &c.

... I assure [my dear brothers and sisters] that I would, for their sakes, gladly make the dangerous and difficult journey [across the Atlantic] one more time, if it should be God's holy will, in order to bring them here &c. [14]

The disturbed relationship of father and son was one of the basic tensions reflected in this letter. Young Pastorius was obviously frustrated as the civil impasse of 1679 went unresolved even after his departure from Windsheim, yet he remained convinced of his father's misconduct – two factors contributing to his assertive tone, which further distanced father and son. Melchior Adam eventually learned to accept Franz Daniel's American independence, but his sense of propriety and his expectations of filial loyalty were deeply offended by this 1684 letter. He later printed a shortened and inoffensive form of it in *Beschreibung Pennsylvaniae*, and he apparently refused to reply to this letter for seven years, a time lapse reflected in the published letters.

Because of this breach in their relationship, Franz Daniel did not report his Germantown marriage to Ennecke Klostermanns in 1688 or the births of their sons in 1690 and 1692 until June, 1693. Melchior Adam had written again by 1691, following the bereavement of a twelve-year-old son's death in 1687 and the wide-spread destruction of German wars with France and Turkey (as well as Franz Daniel's 1688 report to Georg Leonhart Model). He then expressed his desire to do more for his eldest son in the future, Franz Daniel's paraphrase of what apparently involved an offer to publish one or more of his Pennsylvania reports. The letters in *Beschreibung Pennsylvaniae* resume with the son's response to this letter, dated 10 October 1691, in which Franz Daniel declares his love and concern for Melchior Adam, and explains that God was punishing "European impenitence through the Turks and the French" ("die Europäische Unbußfertigkeit durch Turcken und Frantzosen"). Presumably as a guide to avoiding impenitence, he includes eleven biblical citations in the letter – injunctions to govern justly and follow Christ's Golden Rule – and reports that these precepts guide the government of Germantown.

When he congratulated Melchior Adam for becoming lord mayor in June, 1693, Franz Daniel indulged in word play – designating Melchior Adam the "Superior Judge" ("Ober-Richter"), one of the lord mayor's titles, and God the "Most Superior Judge" ("Aller-Obriste-Richter") – as he lectured on the holy responsibility of worldly office:

I am congratulating [my father] because he has now received greater opportunity and capability to serve the poor city of Windsheim advantageously ... May we constantly bear in mind that the Most Superior Judge of the living and the dead confers such governmental power upon us for the sake of the common good rather than for our personal advantage, and that, on the great Day of Final Judgment, He will expect much of those who were given much. [15]

Melchior Adam apparently accepted Franz Daniel's justification for this admonition – that "compassionate love" ("erbarmende Liebe") moved one Christian to use "all occasions to encourage another to Godliness. Oh, to true Godliness!" ("bey allen Vorfallenheiten einer den andern zur Heiligkeit auffzumuntern. Ach zur wahren Heiligkeit!"). In his reply, at any rate, he assured his son that God was the only source of his inner peace. This assurance "delighted" Franz Daniel in March, 1694, but did not prove fully convincing, as Franz Daniel indicated on 30 May 1698, in his contradictory response to the news that Melchior Adam had resigned his Windsheim offices and moved away from the imperial city, and had virtually decided to emigrate to Pennsylvania:

> I am very happy to hear that my father has reached the decision to live here himself and serve God. Oh, what a blessed foretaste of all that awaits us in the fullness of Eternity after we have laid down the tents of the flesh.
> Oh, blessed guidance of the Holy Spirit! For what else could it be, what else could possibly be mentioned other than the sacred grace of God, which led my father (after growing old and grey in the service of many offices in Windsheim), so that the Lord God finally made him so innocent in his heart and soul that he could recognize the incorrigible nature of humanity [or: of the people in Windsheim] and for this reason departed from Babel. May the Heavenly Father of all light keep this endowment of the Holy Spirit within my father's heart until his final release and leap into Eternity. [16]

Along with the satisfaction of knowing his father had followed his own lead in leaving the corruption of Windsheim society, this letter reveals, Franz Daniel still had second thoughts about Melchior Adam's conduct. (As noted in the Prologue, his father had in fact been disgraced and virtually banished from Windsheim.) Melchior Adam, familiar with courtly flattery, wanted to know whether he should write "a few complimentary lines" ("einige Compliment-Zeilen") to William Penn, proprietor of the colony he was planning to inhabit. But Franz Daniel replied that Penn was "a good Christian, and has thus wholly renounced the vain worldly formality of compliments" ("ein guter Christ, und folglich von der Welt eitelen Complimenten gantz abgekehret"). Penn, he added, would nevertheless respond to "sound and true words" ("gesunde und wahre Worte") addressed to him. [17]

In the same letter, Franz Daniel also used his father's physical well-being as an excuse for delivering another moral admonition:

> That our merciful God so graciously preserved my father and dear relatives from the most recent attack of the French army gives me great cause to praise His never-ending Goodness, and fervently to implore this mild and fatherly Goodness to continue to keep you from all harm, and most especially to encourage, ever more and more, a wholesome fear and obedience of the Lord, so that we will loathe offending Him and instead want to accomplish His holy will with a joyful heart. [18]

Given the nature of the culture Melchior Adam and Franz Daniel had shared, these moral proddings can be seen as evidence of the deep personal feelings that bound father and son – and kept them competing spiritually – through years of separation. In concluding his lengthy letter of 30 May 1698, Franz Daniel could recognize his father's paternal love and affirm his own filial love with an allusion to the tensions that had driven them apart in 1679. Preparing to leave Windsheim on April 24, as Vienna and the Windsheim Senate were jointly suppressing the tax revolt of that winter, Franz Daniel had gathered together in the family garden with Melchior Adam, Dorothea Esther, three-year-old Johann Samuel and one-year-old Anna Katharina – he would never meet his half-sister Margareta Barbara and half-brother Augustin Adam, born in 1680 and 1682 respectively – for a small ceremony that typified the ritual of Franconian existence yet anticipated an untypical career.

Twenty-seven-year-old Pastorius knelt to the earth and planted a young tree in the garden soil, and he undoubtedly spoke a few learned words about the unity of spirit it would demonstrate no matter what distances might separate them. Although this tree-planting ceremony marked the finality of Franz Daniel's departure – he carefully avoided Windsheim even when he traveled widely in Germany and Europe on his grand tour of 1680-82 – Melchior Adam nevertheless found solace in the tree's growth over the years. By 1698, however, he wrote to Franz Daniel, he had become aware that the tree was withering and dying, and this had given him bad dreams that seemed to portend sickness or death for his eldest son. Yes, Franz Daniel responded, he and his wife and youngest son had been very sick,

> but, praise God, we have been restored to full health once more. Matters of this sort [bad dreams and ill health] are nevertheless reminders of our mortality. All things must come to an end, and this letter is one of them, so in closing I greet my father a thousand times through the air, and kiss him with a child's hearty kisses, perhaps for the last time, and may God's salutary hand protect and guide you with us, and us with you, and I remain
> My father's truly obedient son,
> F. D. P. [19]

Although Franz Daniel was able to conclude his 1698 letter with a touch of grace and humor and warm affection, he never managed to hide the bitter disappointment and moral outrage he had felt toward his father and friends in Windsheim during 1677-79 – toward the fathers who ran the government and the sons who passively and obediently accepted the decisions of their fathers and gradually assumed roles of authority themselves. For the citizens of Windsheim, the trauma of rebellion and punishment slowly healed in the routines of work, celebration and worship that sustained Franconian life, but for young Pastorius departure abruptly halted the round of daily activity in Windsheim, leaving, in a kind of suspended animation, an enduring image of public upheaval and immoral repression, and emotional scars that would never feel the healing touch of human intercourse with those who had shared the same traumatic experience. And no matter how often he alluded to it in his transatlantic correspondence, Pastorius could assimilate the Windsheim experience imperfectly at best.

Real assimilation could only have come through concrete discussion of specific behavior – the acts of his father and friends that he perceived as betraying his personal trust and his Christian faith, and his own acts that must have betrayed his family and class and added to his sense of guilt. Yet this specific behavior would remain unmentionable all his life. For in his extant writings (which seem definitive in this respect) he never could bring himself to break the taboo observed by his father and the learned of Franconia with a direct reference to the insurrection of 1677-79. Because of this taboo, Pastorius continued to employ an emotional rhetoric of piety in most of his allusions to the events preceding his departure from Windsheim.

Yet the moral force of his pious rhetoric and satirical verse was both a symptom and a cure – or rather one part of a variegated remedy consisting of his dedicated scholarship and writing as well as the everyday pursuits of his active Pennsylvania life. The rich conviviality and humor of his poetry demonstrate the effectiveness of this cure, and so does the philosophical tone of an oblique reference to his Windsheim experience made for English readers years later. Arguing for equitable taxation in "The Matter of Taxes & Contributions briefly Examined," he wrote, "Where the thickest Joices [i.e., those with the greatest juices, or "the emoluments or profits of a profession or office" (OED, 5, 624)] bear the least [tax] burden ... others will grow unwilling and rebell." Thus the Windsheim insurrection left at least one fairly direct imprint in Pastorius' American writings. But when he actually mentioned his Windsheim departure in "Genealogia Pastoriana" some thirty-five years afterwards, he did so with the briefest of all his entries, evading the crucial experience itself: "Anno 1679. the 24th of April I went (by persuasion of Dr. Horb, a godly man & good friend of mine,) to Franckfort upon the Meyn, where I still plaid the lawyer... "

4.2 Godly Advice from a Good Friend: Pietist Johann Heinrich Horb in Windsheim
4.2.1 Clerical Conflicts and Church Reforms

> God makes our adversity our university . . . Be by a heroic courage above those troubles, which thou canst not be without.
> -- "Adversity"
>
> Run virtue, run the race thou hast begun,
> 'Tis shame and death to thee, to be outrun.
> --Epigram 2328.1

Few men in Windsheim could better understand Pastorius' frustrations in the city than newcomer Johann Heinrich Horb – just as Horb's brief Windsheim career indicates why young Pastorius confided in Horb and took the advice of this "godly man" to move to Frankfurt in April 1679. [20] Charged with "heterodoxy" (or a lack of orthodoxy) by a fellow clergyman while initiating Pietist reforms as a Lutheran pastor and church inspector in Trarbach on the Mosel, Horb was suspended from office in February 1678 by the Count Palatine Christian von Birkenfeld, his territorial lord, and later advised to seek new employment elsewhere. He thus learned that Christian renewal could only be accomplished with the support of the civil authorities, a lesson that guided his conduct in Windsheim following his arrival for job interviews on 12 November 1678 – four months after the imperial commission concluded its Windsheim hearings and less than three months before the citizenry again resisted governmental authority in February 1679.

Horb had been recommended for the post of clergyman and church superintendent by Church Superintendent Johann Ludwig Hartmann of neighboring Rothenburg on the Tauber, a friend of Horb's brother-in-law, the Pietist Philipp Jakob Spener. Horb was greeted in Windsheim by an official welcoming committee consisting of Lord Mayor Stellwag, Senator Tobias Schumberg (Pastorius' former teacher serving on the Senate since 1673), and Burgomaster Georg Andreas Dienst (who had criticized the Windsheim clergy for treating the insurrection as mere "dissension"). Two days later, after demonstrating his preaching ability, Horb was hired by the senate, and in January 1679, when he moved to Windsheim with his wife and four children, he began tackling the nearly impossible task of restoring order among Windsheim's clergy.

The two clergymen serving at Saint Kilian's, Georg Erhard Neubert (1630-88) and Johann Philipp Groß, the latter of whom would be placed under house arrest for "scandalous" conduct supporting the citizenry in July 1679, stated their opposition to Horb even before his appointment – their reasons are not recorded – and their continued criticism of the new superintendent was countered with a senate order to desist. When Horb was invested in mid January 1679, the Windsheim clergymen refused to relinquish the first church pew, designated for the superintendent, until the senate ordered their compliance. Horb's public neutrality during the renewed opposition to the government in February and March did not improve his chances for acceptance among his fellow clergymen. After Reverend Groß had begun attacking Horb from the pulpit at some point during the spring, Lord Mayor Stellwag, in his role as church supervisor, delivered a report to the senate on June 23 noting the "bad intentions" ("Üble Intentionen") shown Horb by Neubert and Groß, "but most especially by Mr. Groß" ("absonderlich aber Herr Groß"), and two days later the senate resolved that Groß was to be "admonished" ("gemahnet") and instructed not to preach "for some time" ("einige Zeit lang") – a sanction preceding Groß's house arrest by three weeks.

Thus Pietist Horb had become, more or less unwillingly, a religious leader whose authority symbolized the unpopular yet all-powerful government of Windsheim, and the senate, grateful to have a superintendent who did not obstruct its policies, wholeheartedly supported Horb during his tenure in Windsheim. With the theological assistance of Rothenburg's Superintendent Hartmann, the senate cleared Horb of charges that he espoused unorthodox religious principles in a resolution of 30 July 1679, the day Hartmann also managed to end Reverend Groß's feud with Horb by obtaining an apology from Groß. The senate filled a clerical and a Gymnasium vacancy with Horb's appointees in 1679 and 1680. It also established a church consistory and named four senators to serve on this supervisory body, but Horb and his first appointee, the Frankfurt Pietist Johann Adolf Rhein (1646-1709), were the only clergymen appointed to the consistory. These moves did not appease the local clergymen and teachers. When Gymnasium teacher Michael Eckard (1647-1729) interrupted a sermon of Horb's in September 1680 by shouting out, "Horb, you are lying! Your teachings are perfidious!" ("Horb, du lügst! Deine Lehre ist falsch!"), the senate had Eckard arrested and imprisoned, and demanded a public retraction and apology before reinstating him at the Gymnasium.

In August 1681 it ordered Burgomaster Augustin Keget (1639-1712), vehemently opposed to Horb's religious reforms, to cease his malicious and unsuccessful campaign to gather evidence demonstrating that Horb's two appointees had not displayed unblemished character during their student years at various universities. Although it imprisoned and accepted the resignation of Gymnasium Rector Daniel Caspar Jakobi, Horb's second appointee, for allegedly homosexual conduct in January 1682, it reasserted its loyalty to Horb in April 1683 by reprimanding Burgomaster Keget and fining him 200 ducats for attempting to revive long-discredited rumors about Horb's Trarbach past. When, in May 1684, Horb was offered a prestigious post in Düsseldorf, a much larger city, a senate delegation including Lord Mayor Stellwag, Burgomaster Pastorius and Tobias Schumberg begged him to stay in Windsheim, and in February 1685, when Horb accepted a post in Hamburg, Germany's largest port and a member of the influential Hanseatic League, the senate expressed its sorrow that Windsheim was losing "our loyal, diligent, conscientious and exemplary pastor and preacher" ("unseren treuen, eifrigen, sorgfältigen und exemplarischen Seelsorger und Prediger").

Despite his loyalty to Windsheim and its senators, Horb also remained loyal to his Christian principles. Under his influence Windsheim acquired new church and preaching regulations ("Kirchenordnung" and "Predigtordnung," both 1679) and a penitential regulation ("Bußordnung," 1681); selling was prohibited while church services were being held, and non-religious celebrations and fairs were rescheduled from Sundays to other days of the week; drinking alcoholic beverages was forbidden at the Gymnasium, and despite opposition particularly from Burgomaster Keget, "sinful" ("sündliche") or excessive drinking was prohibited within the senate.

Horb furthered the most characteristic goals of Lutheran Pietism by holding devotional meetings ("Erbauungsstunden") and emphasizing the religious instruction of the young. He published a commentary (*Grundlicher Wortverstand*, 1683) on Martin Luther's *Small Catechism* under the sponsorship of the senate, a book that was later used by August Hermann Francke at a Pietist orphans' school in Halle, and he personally conducted a children's church service, for which the church bells were rung, by senate proclamation, at twelve noon each Sunday. At Horb's recommendation, children and adults were allowed to say their confession before the Windsheim clergyman of their choice rather than by arbitrary assignment, and the penitents were no longer required to pay their confessor a "confessional penny" ("Beichtpfennig"). Horb's sermon of penitence on the comet of 1680 was published in Frankfurt, adding to the popular literature on the moral significance of supernatural and astronomical phenomena. Entitled *Gottes gnädige Heimsuchung der Reichsstadt Windsheim* (God's Visitation of Grace upon the Imperial City of Windsheim), the sermon had as its text Exodus 20, 20: "And Moses said unto the people, Fear not: for God is come to prove you, and that his fear may be before your faces, that ye sin not." [21]

4.2.2 An "Active Faith" Challenging Clerical Hypocrisy

> Most Fraudfully those teachers Deal, who steal, and Preach men should not steal, Rom. 2:21, who eat the lambs out of the Flock, and love to Domineer, and to have the Preeminence.
>
> | | Lawyers | | Dissentions |
> |---|---|---|---|
> | Foh! that | Divines | so called should Feed upon the | Disbelief |
> | | Physicians | | Diseases |
> | | | Farms and estates. | |
> | of the People in and about their | | Doctrines and traditions. | |
> | | | bodily Parts or members. | |
>
>   -- "Symbola Onomastica," nos. 204, 244
>   (double and triple onomastics)
>
> Thomas Tusser's <u>Belief</u>, p. 147, begins thus:
> This is my steadfast creed, my faith and all my trust,
> That there forever is a God most mild and just,
> Who all and everything made wonderfully well,
> And power has of life, of heaven, death, and hell. &c.
>
>   --"Articles of Faith"

Although Horb's spiritual fervor distinguished him from many of the orthodox Lutherans of his day, his reformist impulse nevertheless had its roots in orthodox traditions. As church inspector in Trarbach he had renewed strict censorship regulations, and insisted on his right to fine his parishioners for their religious offenses even though the civil authorities increasingly opposed ecclesiastical punishment in this era. (Horb later explained that he stopped using punishment when he realized it created conformist hypocrites rather than loving Christians.) [22] His suspension in Trarbach can be traced in part to his espousal of anti-Catholic doctrines in a region that had both Lutheran and Catholic lords and to the youthful pride or arrogance that led him to proclaim, prematurely, in a letter to his lord the Count Palatine:

> Your Excellency will undoubtedly have heard, with utmost satisfaction, that our *Pia desideria* [book of Pietist reform] has already made a splendid *progressus* through all of Germany... The whole world recognizes what we have written to be the pure Truth. [23]

Along with these early excesses, indicating some of the dangers inherent in any program of reform zealously pursued, Horb increasingly demonstrated the loving spirituality that characterized the noblest of the Pietists throughout the movement's history. Many of his parishioners, in Trarbach, Windsheim and in Hamburg, were impressed with the sincerity of his vocation – with his genuine concern for their spiritual needs. Their loyalty and admiration was one of the reasons Horb generated animosity or jealousy among ungenerous colleagues – especially among the cynics who saw the clerical profession as a means to leading an easy life or flaunting their academic or social superiority. Insisting, in his contribution to *Pia desideria*, that Lutheran clergymen should live by Christian values, Horb drew the ire of sophisticated theologians like Georg Konrad Dilfeld, who argued that attaining academic skills was the essential prerequisite for the ministry and added that theology can be learned by

> a diligent theology student without any special dispensation from the Holy Spirit... yes, even if he should happen to be a Godless student, as surely has often been the case, and is living a life of sinful abandon in opposition to his conscience.... Daily experience shows us that many of the most corrupt students, by applying their fine ingenuity and diligence, have excelled over others in theology [and thus become skillful theologians]. [24]

Disparaging Horb with ironic sophistry, Dilfeld revealed the degree of learned arrogance and hypocrisy among the Lutheran clergy during the age of absolutism – attitudes that angered Franz Daniel Pastorius and help to explain why he remained zealously committed to the ideals of German Pietism in Quaker Pennsylvania. He satirized hypocritical clergymen – in these "sharp" and "chattering" lines from Poem 475 – as sharp-tongued, chattering monkeys who castigate and punish others while "grabbing up everything" for themselves, and advised his readers not to have anything to do with them:

> Mit kläffenden Pfaffen,
> Die and're bestraffen,
> Und gleichwie die Affen
> Durch spitz-Wort und Waffen
> Gern all nach sich raffen,
> Hab nichts nicht zu schaffen.

Writing to his father shortly after reading a report from "a reliable friend in Frankfurt" in 1694, Pastorius approvingly noted that "the indifferent Lutheran preachers... were being somewhat assailed and shaken by the Pietists," and warned that trying to silence the Pietists was "like resisting Divine counsel and dictating over the conscience of man" – and thus an assault upon God and his crucified Son. Those who were attempting to persecute the Lutheran Pietists – and the Quietist reformers within the Roman Catholic church – "will sooner or later realize whose body they have pierced. *Verbum Domini manet in aeternum* [The Word of the Lord endures forever]. God's Word and the Truth cannot be suppressed." [25] When his father wanted to know, in 1698, whether the American Indians were civilized, Pastorius replied that he considered them "reasonable, and capable of comprehending good teachings and customs, ... and they have in fact shown themselves to be much more eager for divine knowledge than many of those among you who expound the words of Christ from the pulpit but deny [Christ's teachings] through their ungodly living." [26] By satirizing hypocritical clergymen and contrasting them with "reasonable" Native Americans, and by implying that orthodox Lutherans, metaphorically, were thrusting their swords into the wounds of Christ, Pastorius revealed the indignation he felt for the clergymen who took advantage of the political and social inequities of the age rather than assert the Christian principles that would have helped alleviate social tensions. In contrast, "the Pietists [were] urging others toward an active faith," Pastorius wrote, and this distinction contributed to his warm feelings for Windsheim's Superintendent Horb. [27]

4.2.3 Resolving the Tensions of 1677-79: The Mitigated Penitence of a Senate Loyal to Horb

> Rash anger is a short phrensy, *brevis insania*. Seneca ... The end of passion, the beginning of repentance.
>
> -- "Anger"
>
> Know thyself [from the Greek] ... is an old divine saying come down from heaven. Everyone knoweth where the shoe wrings him. Where everyone searcheth himself, no man is lost.
>
> -- "Self-Knowledge"
>
> As things require, be either stern or kind;
> For wise men without blame oft change their mind.
>
> Experience tells us, If we will amend,
> Living here well, shall make a happy end.
>
> -- Epigrams 8, 2332.2

As he gained influence in Windsheim, Horb demonstrated a delicate balance of political finesse and Christian idealism. Given the timing of his arrival and the necessities of his office, he was inevitably a focus of discontent, yet as he made shrewd compromises and preached his Christian message he helped the citizenry and the government to resolve the tensions of 1677-79, and gradually won the trust or allayed the suspicions of a number of his opponents. The very fact that the Windsheim senate sought out a pious religious leader in 1678 – by obtaining its recommendation from Rothenburg's Superintendent Hartmann, who, invited by the senate, had preached a fervent Pentecost, or Whitsunday, sermon in Windsheim earlier that year and was known as a religious reformer – suggests that the majority of the senators were then acutely aware that the state of governmental affairs was, as Senator Tobias Schumberg had earlier taught his Gymnasium pupils, too intricate to be left entirely in human hands. (It was apparently for similar reasons that young Senator Johannes Joachim Mercklein chose Hartmann and his friend Franz Daniel Pastorius as godfathers when his infant son was baptized in May, 1678.) A leader like Burgomaster Pastorius or Lord Mayor Stellwag inevitably faced conflicting emotions as the citizenry exposed the base motivations of some of his deeds, underscoring the disparities between his professed religious faith and his daily conduct and, by resisting his authority, driving him to highly emotional reactions that, at least in private meditation, surely caused him to recognize and ponder the sinful nature of his immortal soul.

Since history not infrequently reveals a stubborn persistence in following established social norms as well as susceptibility to guilt and expiation and spiritual renewal, it is not an overwhelming paradox that the Windsheim senate continued to run the affairs of the city with a firm hand yet showed a remarkable willingness to institute religious reforms during Johann Heinrich Horb's tenure in the city, or that Lord Mayor Stellwag, as leader of this senate, became one of Horb's most loyal defenders, spearheading the move to penalize Burgomaster Keget for his dogged anti-Pietist tactics with such devotion that the senate felt moved, in April, 1683, to arrange a formal reconciliation between Keget and Stellwag reminiscent of the formalities thrust upon Burgomaster Pastorius and Stellwag five years earlier.

On the eve of Horb's departure for Hamburg Stellwag again bitterly attacked Keget, this time for not having done everything possible to convince Horb to remain in Windsheim, since Keget had meanwhile revised his tactics or his opinion of Horb enough to have drafted, a few weeks earlier, the senate's official letter asking Horb to continue as Windsheim's church superintendent. Melchior Adam Pastorius' Windsheim biographer has noted that Melchior Adam dramatically increased his productivity of religious verse during these years, and attributed the increase to Melchior Adam's fondness for Horb, [28] although the emotional effects of the insurrection and Franz Daniel's departure – and the latter's repeated censure of his father's conduct, whether actually stated or merely implied – were at least as important as Horb's influence. In the aftermath of insurrection, Windsheim was obviously ready for a church leader whose convictions were more than skin deep.

Within the senate, this readiness by no means implied dependence or passivity. The tough, worldly-minded men who ran the government repeatedly weighed and evaluated Horb's programs, conduct and character, and the conduct and character of his appointees, and reached independent conclusions. When they found themselves willing to believe reports that Rector Jakobi had made homosexual advances toward some of the boys at the Gymnasium, they ignored Horb's and Jakobi's repeated protestations of innocence and even refused to accept Horb's formal written plea on behalf of Jakobi, so that after five days in jail Jakobi was forced to resign or face the prospect of extended imprisonment pending legal proceedings the Senate indicated it would deliberately complicate by filing a request for the legal or theological opinion of an "impartial" panel of university consultants. When the Senate learned, in February, 1682, that Reverend Rhein was being considered for a position elsewhere and concluded that Rhein's departure could benefit Windsheim, it sent a delegation to tell Rhein that he might want to accept the new position because it would advance his career, and that members of his congregation had been complaining for some time about the inordinate length of his sermons, and in many instances were even avoiding the Sunday morning service for this reason.

Not so with their Superintendent Horb. At the first indication that he might consider leaving them, the Senate convened and excitedly considered strategies to satisfy him, on two occasions sending delegations to persuade him and, in December, 1684, even consenting to Horb's request that they submit their proposal in writing – only to discover in the urgency and excitement of the next senate session that no agreement could be reached on the precise wording and stylistic revisions of their draft proposal, and thus as a final resort accepting, with a few revisions, cool-headed Burgomaster Keget's draft submitted late in the evening.

Why did the senators try so hard to keep Horb in Windsheim? Obviously not because they trusted him as an administrator with the ability to select reliable church and school personnel, for when his first two appointees left Windsheim the senate decided to return to the established procedure of hiring and promoting Windsheim's own young theologians and tactfully rejected Horb's subsequent candidates from Pietist circles elsewhere in Germany. Horb's impartiality during the popular resistance of 1679 – easily interpreted as governmental loyalty in troubled times – does not alone explain the senate's reliance upon him five years later, especially since Windsheim's populace had long since returned to the well-ordered rounds of daily existence, and by January 1684 (following the death of Johann Augustin Lietzheimer), even the clergymen were working together so amicably that Lord Mayor Stellwag could report there was "a good sense of harmony" ("eine gute Harmonie") among them.

Any adequate explanation of the senate's continued devotion to Horb has to recognize the importance Horb's Christian message and example had for the senators in 1684. They sensed in Horb rare qualities that not only inspired their citizens to accept virtuous ideals of Christian obedience but also kept the senators aware, during these post-insurrection years, that they should themselves attempt to live by Christian principles. Horb's message and example, as long as it was heard and felt, conveyed humanitarian values that helped to reduce the ever-present tensions of daily life in Windsheim, and it was not until after his departure that Windsheim returned to non-reformist Lutheranism and the senate gradually distanced itself from the lessons of 1677-79.

4.2.4 Worldly Finesse and Pietist Commitment

> [A lawyer] commonly chooses the worst [cause], because that brings the best fee: true to none but himself, and false to all parties, to serve his own turn ... A dapper lawyer, with a tongue steeped in oil, able to make the best of a bad cause; for he had all the shifts and starting holes in the law at his fingers' ends. Quevedo ...
> Here sweet-lipped fraud, with her divided face,
> Must act [goddess of justice] Astrea's part, must take Astrea's place. Quarles.... [Lawyers]
> Take money of the rich, and hang the poor,
> And lash the strumpet, they debauched before. [Defoe,] Trueborn.
> See, how he rides the circuit with the judge,
> To law and lewdness a devoted drudge. Idem.
>
> -- "Lawyers"

It was Horb's combination of Christian morality and worldly awareness that gradually won him the respect of the Windsheim senate – and, in 1679, the confidence of Franz Daniel Pastorius. Describing, in his contribution to *Pia desideria*, the sinfulness of the courts of law in Germany, for example, Horb referred to procedure and terminology more specifically – and displayed greater practical insight – than might have been expected of a moralizing clergyman. Along with criticizing those who accepted bribes and allowed respect for person or station to influence their legal decisions, Horb objected to the attorneys who complicated their legal briefs with obscure and imprecise language or delayed court proceedings through their negligent unpreparedness or with deliberate ploys to increase their fees as well as the judges who did not take the time and effort to read the charges carefully or to understand the issues and facts of the case – all of these acts or omissions were, in Pietist terms, grievous sins against God and His divine order. [29] In a similar vein, while criticizing scholastic learnedness in his Windsheim funeral sermon and biography for clergyman Johann Augustin Lietzheimer (January 1684), Horb praised both philology and modern mathematics, the latter of which rewarded the time and effort spent attaining it with "something consummate and certain" ("etwas vollkommen und gewiß").

Lietzheimer's funeral sermon also demonstrates the warmth and trust Horb had for his close friends, and this humane quality pervades the letters he wrote fellow Pietists as he was ending his Windsheim career with the decision to accept the post of supervising clergyman at the Church of Saint Nicholas in Hamburg, where orthodox Lutheran clergymen would wage an anti-Pietist campaign that led to Horb's expulsion from office in 1693. Despite deep misgivings, Horb promised his friend and brother-in-law Philipp Jakob Spener, in a letter of 20 December 1684, that he would accept a call to Hamburg if it came. Spener recognized the importance of cities like Hamburg in his efforts to revitalize German Protestantism, and through his influence among progressive city leaders he had managed to get Clergyman Johann Winckler (1642-1705) appointed in Hamburg earlier in 1684. Winckler in turn recommended Horb for the next Hamburg vacancy, and the Hamburg church consistory unanimously chose Horb despite the concerted efforts of anti-Pietist clergymen to impugn Horb's orthodoxy – revealing prejudices against him, Horb wrote Spener, "of such severe consequence that I cannot think of them without sighing" in trepidation. [30]

"When I consider . . . what is in store for me," he wrote his good friend Winckler in early January, 1685, "and in contrast how peacefully I could [live and] die here [in Windsheim], it is easy enough to imagine what sort of thoughts begin to occur to me." Submitting his acceptance with another letter to Winckler on January 20, Horb wrote:

> Oh Lord Jesus, how difficult it has been for me to reach the decision to move to Hamburg. I have had to struggle with this day and night to the extent that I no longer knew whether I still had my faith and human reason, since I could not help thinking it highly dangerous to leave a peaceful community in my deteriorated physical condition and weak resolve [following recent sickness], a community where my studies are not overtaxing and I have overcome most of the difficulties, in order to move to a location where there are so many cares and dangers, so much human erudition, and so many difficult tasks awaiting me.

In these letters Horb indicated that it was his deep friendship for Spener and Winckler, and his trust in their shared goals, that led him to accept the uncertainties of Hamburg. A more generalized sense of love and trust was revealed in his farewell sermon in Windsheim, which attracted friends from Nürnberg to hear him preach for the last time, and in the departure of Horb and his family from Windsheim, during which there was "such an outcry and lamentation among the young and the old, the eminent and the common people, and so many who wept and followed after us." [31]

As Franz Daniel Pastorius was developing his friendship with Horb during the winter and early spring of 1679 (or deepening a friendship that might have begun during his student days in Strasbourg), he discovered a personality much like that revealed in this profile of Horb's Windsheim career – a man of warmth and intensity, convinced that a living Christian faith could improve his society, yet cautious in his actions and perhaps even fearful of the challenges then facing him in Windsheim. The two men were, in these respects, kindred souls. And Horb was able to offer Pastorius an enticing alternative to the frustrations he was then facing in the imperial city. As Horb described his Pietist friends in Frankfurt and their ideals – probably together with Johann Augustin Lietzheimer, Horb's first and best friend among the Windsheim clergy – Franz Daniel had good reason to compare the sense of community awaiting him there with the alienation he felt among his family and most of his friends in Windsheim, and he also knew the metropolis would provide him a livelihood as long as he remained in the legal profession. Pastorius could hope to make his way in the world even while getting to know other individuals who were contemplating the possibility – or even the establishment – of a social order that would not violate the moral foundations of pristine Christianity.

4.3 Frankfurt Lawyer and European Traveler, 1679-83
4.3.1 Millennialist Premonitions and Political Realities
4.3.1.1 Legal Experience in Frankfurt and the Palatinate

> All former monarchies, great empires, mighty pow'rs,
> Devour'd by hungry time, had their allotted hours.
>
> Vice triumphs over grace, virtue like grass
> Is trampled on: the world's at a rare pass.
>
> Christ, the Lamb of God, innocent and dumb,   Isa. 53:7
> Lion-like once more will to Judgment come.   Rev. 4:5
>
>   -- Epigrams 26, 2334.1, 60

"Even if the whole world opposed us, our own parents included, we will nevertheless want to remain true to that which is our real Father," Philipp Jakob Spener wrote in a letter of 1689 that also mentions Franz Daniel Pastorius and the Pennsylvania Quakers. The awareness that an earthly father might comprehend the words of the Gospel but not their deeper significance, especially when this leads to separation and the loss of "all paternal love," is "surely one of the most oppressive sorrows that any soul may have to experience." [32]

With the friendship and support of Spener and the Saalhof Pietists, young Pastorius coped with "oppressive sorrows," including parental separation and the guilt he felt as a lawyer, that were intensified by the political insecurities of 1679-83, when France was aggressively expanding into the Rhine territories while oppressive Hapsburg policies were leading to revolt in Hungary and the subsequent siege of Vienna by the Turks in 1683, military events in a spiral of destruction offering some justification for Pastorius' claim that God would soon destroy Europe. At the same time, however, his contact with religious diversity and modern commerce in Frankfurt and on excursions to the Calvinist Palatinate were providing some of the insights that would convince him to join William Penn's "holy experiment" in Pennsylvania and escape the escalating violence then centered upon Europe.

Despite personal misgivings, Pastorius "still plaid the Lawyer & kept *Collegia privata Juris* [i.e., taught law courses as a private docent, or instructor] to some young *Patriciis* of" the city, sons or close relatives of ruling city aristocrats, known as the Frankfurt patricians. He was thus sponsored, in effect, by the city's elite not only in Frankfurt but also on his grand tour of Europe, undertaken as "Conductor & Guide" to Johann Bonaventura von Bodeck, a young aristocrat from a family of rich patrician bankers. (Spener had recommended him to Bodeck's family.) Setting off on 26 June 1680, Pastorius traveled the first stretch of this tour (from Frankfurt to Mainz) with the city officials he identified as "Juncker Günterod" and "Juncker Lerssner," and the wives of Günderode and Lersner (to use the official spellings of these names). ("Junker" designates a nobleman or squire.) A typical patrician outing, it reflected the exclusivity that had long prevailed in Frankfurt government. Young Bodeck, Pastorius notes in this "Res Propriae" entry, was a relative or "in-law" of both Günderode and Lersner. Intermarriage and nepotism were as *de rigueur* among the Frankfurt patricians as they were in a small imperial city like Windsheim. [33]

With its unusual concentration of merchants, bankers and oligarchs, Frankfurt offered Pastorius job security but little peace of mind. Its senate resolutely opposed guild attempts to gain a role in city government, which led to violent uprisings in 1355, 1525 and 1614, and, beginning in 1705, to a 27-year legal battle for a modicum of political representation ("Frankfurt contra Frankfurt"). Protestant Frankfurt nevertheless avoided the economic stagnation that plagued many German cities, in part by accommodating an influx of Jewish and Calvinist Dutch and Walloon guildsmen and merchants, although popular and ecclesiastical intolerance limited the success of this accommodation. Family or business ties to Holland among the Frankfurt Pietists (like those of the Krefeld emigrants and Pennsylvania Quakers) would encourage Pastorius' interest in enlightened Dutch ideas engendered by the political and religious diversity of the Netherlands, whose Stadtholder, William of Orange (1650-1702), would be proclaimed king of Britain and Ireland following the Glorious Revolution of 1688. As the traditional site of imperial elections and coronations, the Frankfurt cathedral remained by treaty a Catholic enclave, reflecting the city's strategic importance – and precarious position – within the empire. A huge ring of fortification around the city, constructed during and after the Thirty Years' War, offered some degree of security until it was demolished during the Napoleonic Wars in 1804-09.

As he traveled south to the Palatinate, a territory devastated by the Thirty Years' War and threatened by French expansion, Pastorius encountered burgeoning commerce and religious diversity along with reminders of wartime destruction and forebodings of wars to come. While practicing law in Frankfurt, he writes in "Genealogia Pastoriana," he had "good Opportunity to see Worms, Mannheim, Speyer & other places of the [Palatine] Neighbourhood." He went to Mannheim, "Res Propriae" notes, on behalf of "Samuel the Jew," providing (and being "abundantly paid" for) unspecified legal services at the court of the Elector Palatine Karl Ludwig (1617-80) in September 1679 and March and April 1680. Planning his emigration in 1683, he would return to the Mannheim area to visit a small Quaker community at Kriegsheim, future Germantown immigrants.

In March 1680 he traveled to Speyer with a "Dr. Fuchsen," presumably a senior attorney with a case to present before the Imperial High Court there, the only apparent reason for the journey of about one hundred kilometers from Frankfurt. Indulging in word play on "Spira" (Latin for Speyer) in Pennsylvania, Pastorius once wryly noted of the Imperial High Court: "in qua plurimae lites spirant, sed non exspirant,"or "here many lawsuits breathe, but never breathe their last" (i.e., they are prolonged interminably). [34] Such dark jurisprudential humor, vaguely reminiscent of Charles Dickens' *Bleak House*, is at least indirectly related to Pastorius' apocalyptic views of the 1680s. His business trips to Palatine cities provided abundant inspiration for reflection on the interplay of European politics and divine justice.

4.3.1.2 Balance-of-Power Politics and the Palatine Devastation

> It passes for a mark of greatness to burn cities, & lay whole kingdoms waste ... But it is not the spoils of war & bloody trophies that make a prince glorious, but the divine power of preserving unity & peace &c. Seneca. L'Estrange, p. 426. All the bonds of humane society cancell'd &c. p. 545 ... What a madness is it to pursue mischiefs; to fall foul upon those we do not know; to be angry without a cause, and worse than beasts to kill what we have no quarrel to? p. 581. When war begins, hell opens.
>
> -- "War"
>
> Blazing star. A terrible, fearful sight. *Lux tristior umbris*. [A very dismal and ghostly light.] Mankind in vain did never gaze, / When comets in the heavens blaze. Great comets always denunciate great calamities ... Many affront God really for fear of affronting Him [i.e., guiltily fearing comets affronts God]; He is no daily labourer, but in an eternal rest and sabbatism, &c. Mamut, vol. 8, p. 275. [The comet] hath no stable place among the stars, and instead of a healing virtue, it sends forth nothing but vapours of a malignant nature. Boehm, <u>Epiph.</u>, p. 22.
>
> -- "Comets"

Lacking a modern economic base, the old cathedral cities of Speyer and Worms had been reduced to small-town obscurity by the Thirty Years' War despite their central role in medieval and Reformation history, and, exacerbating this decline, Speyer would soon lose even the Imperial High Court, moved to Vienna in 1688. Modern Mannheim, however, managed to image both the transience and the persistence of civilization, proudly or poignantly rising and falling and rising again in little more than half a century, with further cyclic repetitions occurring after Pastorius' departure for Pennsylvania. [35]

In 1606, before the Thirty Years' War, the Elector Palatine Friedrich IV (1574-1610) established Mannheim as a center of commerce and a Calvinist bulwark at the confluence of the Neckar and Rhine rivers just twenty kilometers from his Heidelberg court. Sixteen years later, then a town of some 1200 inhabitants, Mannheim was bombarded and captured by Hapsburg forces even though its defenses included the "impregnable" citadel of Friedrichsburg and massive city walls with eight newly designed bastions. Further wartime devastation, including fire and plague, reduced Mannheim to an uninhabited wasteland of pillaged and burned-out buildings. After the war, though, the liberality and determination of Elector Karl Ludwig, back from exile in Holland and England, helped Mannheim attain all-too-enviable wealth and influence. He rebuilt the city and its citadel during the 1650s, and brought relative prosperity to the Palatinate, in part by offering religious freedom and economic opportunity to immigrants – predominantly Calvinists but also Lutherans, Mennonites and Jews – from Switzerland, France, Walloon Belgium, Holland and Portugal. The population swelled to around 12,000 by 1688, profit-making industries flourished, especially in wine, tobacco and textiles, and experimentation led to advances such as cheaply-brewed beer, and potatoes for nourishment during the long winters.

With his first wife residing at Heidelberg Castle, Karl Ludwig built a palace of French design within the citadel of Friedrichsburg, where Italian musicians and artists and the comedies of Molière and Shakespeare entertained the Elector and his second wife, derided as a paramour by those who contested his self-proclaimed divorce. He avoided exorbitant lavishness, and supported the education of his populace, but proudly envisioned Mannheim as a second Rome and, having established a territorial army, aggressively defended or expanded his influence, which led to a brief war with Lorraine in 1668. He became a master of the popular art of appeasing Louis XIV, not only accepting the French "subsidies" that assured the neutrality of many German princes but also, in 1671, marrying his daughter Liselotte to the French king's brother – and, among the Calvinists, pretending ignorance of her Catholic conversion.

Despite this alliance, the Palatinate had become a target of French expansion by the time Pastorius visited Karl Ludwig's Mannheim court in 1679-80. [36] Following attacks on the Palatinate in the mid-1670s – part of the Dutch War concluded in 1679, when Leopold I ceded the German free city of Freiburg to France – Louis XIV embarked upon the "reunions" of 1679-84, an audacious scheme of bribing or coercing Rhineland princes into recognizing his sovereignty over German territory that had presumably been "separated" from French principalities in the course of centuries. Alsace was "annexed" in 1680, Strasbourg and portions of the Palatinate and Trier provinces in 1681, shortly after Karl Ludwig's death. By 1685, preparing for war, Louis XIV claimed the entire Palatinate as an "inheritance" through his sister-in-law Liselotte, the Palatine princess, silenced and scorned at the French court when the devastating battles began.

Patriotic outrage swelled among the German populace during Pastorius' Frankfurt years, especially when Strasbourg was taken without a battle. The Reichstag created a standing army, and then negotiated unsuccessfully with France at Frankfurt in 1681-82 (while Pastorius was touring Europe), but numerous princes had decided their own interests were best served by appeasing the mighty French indefinitely.

Autocratic Hapsburg rule, meanwhile, was creating violent unrest to the east. In 1680 peasants throughout Bohemia, armed with scythes and pitchforks, were dispersed or captured by the army and hanged, beheaded, quartered or impaled. In Hungary, rejecting military occupation and enforced recatholicization, aristocrats and nationalists had organized a Protestant crusade against Leopold I in 1678. The Hungarian rebels later sought Turkish assistance, an opportunity the Grand Vizier, by 1682, had turned into the last great campaign to subject Christendom to Muslim conquest. In March 1683 (with Pastorius back in Frankfurt, and deciding to leave Germany), the Turkish legions began heading north from Adrianople, convincing Poland and most of the German princes to join Leopold I and Pope Innocent XI in a counteroffensive against the Turks, although even then Louis XIV refused to aid the Hapsburgs. When the Turks began their siege of Vienna in July, Pastorius was halfway across the ocean, and he had safely arrived in Philadelphia weeks before they were routed in an awesome September battle that claimed some 15,000 lives, two-thirds of which, reflecting superior Western strategy and technology, were Turkish. As the dead were carted from the battlefield, Pastorius was already going about the rewarding tasks of building a new – and essentially pacifist – colony in America.

Before gaining the option of emigration – and for a good while thereafter – Pastorius was subjected to intense psychological pressures that, in varying degrees, were also felt by many men of learning and conscience who found themselves forced into unacceptable compromises by their careers in church, state and commerce. These widespread personal, religious and political tensions, in a period described as the Age of Angst, helped create a genre of popular literature and art that Pastorius could draw upon as he reported on his emigration and criticized European society. [37] The theme of God's retribution on an unrepentant humanity was illustrated in Windsheim textbook references to comets and earthquakes, in Johann Heinrich Horb's 1680 penitential sermon, and in countless other references to imminent or future violence or calamity, many of which involved interpreting heavenly portents in the context of anticipated political events, above all war or rebellion. Related millennial beliefs, based on biblical prophecies that Christ would come again and reign a thousand years, found adherents in the established churches and among the general populace as well as in radical religious groups like the Saalhof Pietists of Frankfurt.

A series of comets accompanying the political excitation of Pastorius' final years in Europe – those of 1675, 1677 and 1680 were followed by Halley's Comet in 1682 (though first identified as such in 1705) – generated exceptional interest in celestial events, a combination of awe or fear and, increasingly, scientific curiosity. In Germany these four comets, often described as fiery rods of divine punishment, elicited several dozen published sermons, poems and artistic depictions. One illustration (on the cover of this book) shows a contemporary view of Augsburg with three comets and three horsemen of the Apocalypse within a clock face that has Roman numerals made of weapons and bones, thus focusing on war and death. Meteors and planets were also mistaken for or exaggerated as portentous comets. Even a local lightning storm could be described, in the dramatic prose and poetry of a Nürnberg broadside, as a warning to "the Turks as well as the Christians," especially since an accompanying illustration placed a huge but fictive comet in the midst of the storm.

The emotionality of these predictions of punitive destruction often reflected more political realism than otherworldly mysticism. The massive destruction of the Thirty Years' War could still be seen in the landscape of Germany, and was felt in the consciousness of many Germans. At the same time, men like Pastorius – who observed dozens of young German aristocrats complacently practicing the martial arts and enjoying life at French courts despite the open confrontation of France and Hapsburg Germany – knew that political cynicism and military technology were together capable of producing calamity on a scale similar to or even greater than that of the Thirty Years' War. In fact, history would soon provide partial confirmation of Pastorius' 1683 and 1684 predictions, as Pastorius himself noted in later correspondence. There is a captivating portentousness in these predictions, a fascination deriving less from their religious emotion than from the political and psychological depth that seems to have motivated them. Pastorius could again reflect on this blend of religious and political insight as he recalled his visits to the Palatine cities of Worms, Speyer and Mannheim in the "Genealogia Pastoriana" jottings of around 1715.

Balance-of-power politics virtually demanded new conquests, and escalating destruction. [38] Hapsburg victories against the Turks added Hungary to the empire and opened the possibility of further conquests in the Balkans, greatly enhancing Leopold's influence among the German princes, which also swelled his military ranks, and threatened France's European predominance. Louis XIV, countering these developments in 1688, forced Leopold to fight on two fronts by having French forces invade the Palatinate and other Rhine territories as the Turkish War continued to the east. Then the French advanced on into Swabia and Franconia, spreading destruction and terror in the west and south of Germany. At the outset, France had expected token opposition in a short war, but even reluctant princes felt obliged to join a decisive counterattack that, under normal circumstances, would have meant a rapid and embarrassing French retreat.

Slowing its retreat and simultaneously denying the enemy potential matériel, Louis XIV ordered his army to employ the most systematic destruction then conceivable, violating all previous conventions of war. Palatine towns, villages, fields and orchards were devastated, as were castles all along the Rhine and Mosel rivers. Worms, Speyer and other cities were burned to the ground, and in the Speyer cathedral crypt, the graves of medieval emperors were desecrated and destroyed.

Louis XIV and his war minister together consulted over the fate of Mannheim, the pride of the Palatinate, and decided it was to be "so completely destroyed," the minister wrote, "that not a single stone remains standing upon another." Two days after ordering its evacuation, an occupation army began plundering and demolishing. Then torches and mines were laid and ignited according to a coolly executed plan that might have been meant to symbolize civilization's transience or ultimate futility. As the homes of 12,000 Mannheimers caught fire singly and (with sudden incendiary bursts) in clusters, a wall of flame raged through the city toward the castle and fortress of the Elector Palatine and, in pyrotechnic culmination, engulfed and consumed this monument of regal might and splendor – simultaneously marking the end of Karl Ludwig's experiment in religious tolerance and benevolent despotism, and the ascendancy of a new line of absolutist princes.

Ignoring orders to resettle in Catholic Alsace, many of the Mannheim refugees fled to neighboring Lutheran provinces, to Calvinist Brandenburg, or to England and ultimately to America. Although Mannheim would flourish again, and again be destroyed and subsequently reconstructed in the Napoleonic Wars and World War II, the Palatinate was ruined for decades to come. Despite the appeasement or complicity that had encouraged the French to miscalculate their position – even Leopold I had accepted French "subsidies" – this massive and fortuitous destruction created deep-seated resentments that would lead to renewed aggression and counter-aggression, part of the cycle of violence repeated throughout European history, increasing in geographical scope and destructive potential to such an extent that Pastorius' 1684 prediction of total European destruction now finds an altered context in global fears of cataclysmic regional unrest or nuclear Armageddon, a reinterpretation of the Revelations 16 text Pastorius paraphrased as God's "woeful wrath ... poured out over" Europe.

Although a number of German poets, historians and propagandists up to World War II would see in the Palatine devastation a moral inspiring vigilance and commitment to the Fatherland, the lesson most directly related to Pastorius' German experience is reflected in the reaction of Princess Liselotte, the daughter of Elector

Karl Ludwig, whose name was repeatedly invoked as her brother-in-law Louis XIV attacked and destroyed his "inheritance" and her Palatine homeland. Writing to relatives in Germany, Liselotte described her feelings of complicity in this destruction, and her overwhelming depression, expressed in an impotent and belated resistance that could not relieve Palatine distress:

> What causes me the most pain is that my name was used to drive the poor people [of the Palatinate] to such dire extremity, and when I cry out in protest, they [French court officials] accuse me of ingratitude and ridicule me. But even if they were to take my life for it, I simply cannot keep from weeping and complaining ... Oh, I have such an aversion for everything that was demolished in this manner, that every night, as soon as I have begun to fall asleep, I get the impression I am at Heidelberg or Mannheim and I see all the devastation, and then I am wide awake again, and I cannot get back to sleep for at least two hours; then I invariably think about how everything was when I was there, and the condition it is in now, and then I think about the condition I am in, and I just cannot keep from sobbing out loud any longer. [39]

Princess Liselotte's sense of depression in 1689 was not very different from the desperation Franz Daniel Pastorius experienced in introspective moments as a Frankfurt lawyer and European traveler in 1679-83. "Here in this province," he writes in his October 1691 letter to his father, "we have listened with compassion to reports of that barbarous French conduct which involved destroying or even murderously burning down such beautiful cities, churches and emperors' graves." These reports convinced him that no bulwark of stone or masonry can protect Germans or Americans from enemy attack, "that we should rely solely upon the protective hand of God ... instead of physical force and mighty fortresses," a sentiment reiterated in poems opposing war and empire. [40] It is in this letter that he describes the French and the Turks as instruments of God's punishment of "European impenitence," and lists Christian principles of government contrasting with "the Babylonian vanities and disordered human laws and precepts" he saw, in 1684, as the object or source of the divine punishment he was then anticipating.

Both Pastorius and Princess Liselotte were, in short, responding to the human suffering which they perceived around them, and which they also perceived as resulting in part from their own involvement in the social fabric of the era, and the political deeds that were its weft – the sum total of the conformist or callous attitudes of all of those who merely played the roles thrust upon them by their society. Like the more generalized compulsions of men and women of learning or station, to some extent the result of resisting a similar awareness, Liselotte's morose sleeplessness and Franz Daniel's millennialist piety reveal individuals confronting an awareness that there can be no abiding satisfaction in a life of callous behavior, or of passive conformity to values perceived (no matter how obscurely) as ungenerous or inhumane – an awareness so basic that it became, in essence, the leitmotif of all of Pastorius' transatlantic correspondence.

In Pennsylvania, Pastorius retained an interest in natural cataclysm or divine intervention in nature, most clearly evidenced in a 1692 report on a Jamaican earthquake that spared a Philadelphia friend visiting the island but turned some wealthy European colonists into corporeal emblems of the punishments of hell. [41] He kept a copy of Johann Heinrich Horb's penitential sermon on the comet of 1680 on his Germantown bookshelf, and compiled related entries on topics like chiliasm and comets in his "Alphabetical Hive." The entries on chiliasm include a prediction in Daniel Leeds' 1703 Pennsylvania almanac that "the Sabbath of the world will enter about the year of the world 5740," but most of these entries favor a spiritual interpretation of the Second Coming, or criticize what one source calls "the sottish notions of some carnal millenarians and false enthusiasts." Pastorius reflects ambiguity in this citation from G. W. Innoe: "To question some men's notion of a fleshly coming of Christ, personally to reign on earth, is not to oppose the prophesy of his reign a thousand years, Rev. 20."

During his Pennsylvania years, Pastorius seems to have transmuted his early fear of divine retribution against Europe into a yearning for Godly purification of human institutions. The Swedes and the Turks might serve as God's agents in cleansing or redeeming Europe, and thus entice expatriates to return to their homeland (Poem 427, cited on page 36). Humans are "too, too weak" to break Babylonia's bulwarks and bastions "Down to the ground," so we should "Pray! . . . that this be hastened on / By God" to enable "Christ's Divine Light" to rise from the rubble of the "dreadful Fall." In this manner Poem 341 (in the epigraph on page 187) employs lyrical grace to deliver a potent millennialist message opposing 'unwise' rulers, militarism and empire.

4.3.2 The Saalhof Pietists
4.3.2.1 Muted Rebelliousness of Otherworldly Piety

> The disbeliever of the principles of a fellowship excludes himself therefrom. Barclay . . . If we communicate with bad bishops, we are accessory to their guilt . . . Paul . . . forbids conjunction [with idolaters]. 2 Cor. 6. Communion with God and good men, oh, blessed fellowship! Communion with the saints in the Light.
>
> -- "Communion"
>
> Better alone than with bad company. He that lieth with dogs gets fleas . . . One rotten apple in the basket spoileth also the sound fruit. Among wolves, men learn to howl . . . Lot was the world's miracle, who kept himself fresh in Sodom's salt water.
>
> -- "Company"
>
> Good God, most full of Grace, whose Mercy has no End,
> Receiving Sinners still, which do repent and mend;
> Grant that I so my knees may penitentially bend,
> As never thee, O Lord, hence forward to Offend.
>
> -- Poem 111 (entire)
>
> Christ found us maimed on the ground,
> With wine and oil does heal the wound.
>
> -- Epigram 59a

Where personal and societal values diverge – and insincerity or cynicism infects ordinary intercourse – sensitive or spontaneous individuals will seek each other out, and develop especially meaningful relationships. Pastorius' description of the Frankfurt Pietists in "Genealogia Pastoriana" reveals the warmth and trust he found among "those Christian friends who frequently assembled together in a house, called the Saalhof," the men and women whose "ancient familiarity" cheered him upon his return from his grand tour in November 1682, and provided much-needed relief from all of the "feasting, dancing, &c." that by then seemed more wearying than enjoyable. The Pietists' emigration plans "begat such a desire in my soul to continue in their society, and with them to lead a quiet, godly & honest life in a howling wilderness" that Pastorius was soon "prepar[ing] myself for this farthermost Journey, that I as yet ever had done or dreamed of." The Saalhof Pietists, something of a spiritual underground, had established the international connections required for the Pennsylvania venture several years before Pastorius joined them, especially in their travels and correspondence with Dutch Labadists or Quietists and English and Dutch Quakers.

Inspired by the fervor of the Frankfurt Pietists during a preaching tour of what he described as "desolate" and "dark" Germany, William Penn had written an epistle *To the churches of Jesus throughout the world* from Frankfurt in June 1677. [42] "There is a breathing, hungering, seeking people, solitarily scattered up and down this great land of Germany," Penn reported, and he sensed that "the full time is come," that "the day of the breaking-up of the nations about you, and of the sounding of the gospel trumpet unto the inhabitants of the earth, is just at the door." National origin had become irrelevant, for God "hath made us a people" – one supranational community imbued with the Light that generates "the riches of life," and striving to become "perfectly disentangled from the cares of this world," yet resisting worldly authority like the martyrs of early Christianity. If we are all "zealous and valiant for truth on earth," Penn argued, then "the liberty of all may stand in the cross [of Christ], which alone preserveth." A "young virgin" and "a widow, both of noble birth" – references to Johanna Eleonora von Merlau (1644-1724) and Maria Juliana Baur von Eyseneck (1641-84) – noted that Penn's message helped to relieve the "fearful spirit" inhibiting some Frankfurt believers, and Merlau urged one of Penn's audiences to "'lift up your voices without fear; for,' said she, 'It will never be well with us till persecution come, and some of us be lodged in the stadthouse;' that is, the prison." This mood of fervent seeking – of inner conviction combating fearfulness – had not diminished by the time Pastorius joined the Frankfurt Pietists less than two years later.

"Genealogia Pastoriana" lists Merlau and Baur von Eyseneck as well as Clergyman Philipp Jakob Spener and four Pietist laymen among the friends Pastorius frequently met at the Frankfurt Saalhof, a medieval estate house or castle and the residence of Merlau and Baur von Eyseneck. [43] Spener visited the Saalhof as a good friend of the leading Saalhof Pietists but, pressed to defend his orthodoxy, publicly rejected their separatist beliefs in 1684. Jakob van de Walle (fl. 1661-86), one of William Penn's hosts in 1677, was a Calvinist merchant and porcelain manufacturer with family and business connections in Holland. Signing up for 2500 acres of Pennsylvania land in 1683, he became one of the principle stockholders in the German Company around the same time he and his son Jakob began a lucrative business importing and processing English wool. He greeted Pastorius as "My heartily beloved Friend & Dear Brother" in a business letter of 1686. Maximillian von Lersner, head of one of Frankfurt's most prominent patrician families, became known as "Maximillian the Pious" for his participation, beginning in 1670, in a small society of learned men who wished to discuss spiritual matters without being ridiculed behind their backs or having to face the embarrassed silence such topics elicited in worldly society. Lersner and a few others later joined the Saalhof Pietists when their assemblies (named the "*Collegium pietatis*" under the influence of Spener, the group's spiritual leader) grew into large public meetings with no opportunity for conversation and meditation among close friends.

Maria Juliana Baur von Eyseneck, who in 1678 became the subject of a church inquiry because of her mystic and separatist beliefs, stated that God helped her "recognize, and avoid, the deceit" that motivates worldly society even "in the best of its undertakings." She was also one of several Pietists, Pastorius reported in "Res Propriae", who had "already packed" ("allschon zusamm gepackt") for Pennsylvania in 1683, and thus influenced his decision to leave Germany, just as her death in April 1684, may help to explain why the Saalhof Pietists did not emigrate. Reading the German funeral sermon published following her death, he was moved by its account of her selfless living and her own admonitions to reject prevailing social values and live honestly and simply in neighborly love, advice written (in a ten-page letter accompanying the sermon) to her three aristocratic children: "Do not say that your social rank demands that you do what Christ has forbidden ... Woe to you eternally, if you seek honors and riches opposed to the meekness of Christ." Pastorius penned a commemorative German verse on his copy of the funeral sermon (Poem 345) expressing his belief that Baur von Eyseneck had inherited the Heavenly Kingdom and his hope that he might stand next to her before Jesus in Eternity.

Doctor Johann Jakob Schütz (1640-90), a rich and influential Frankfurt lawyer, was illumined and consoled as he read the mystic writings of Johann Tauler after having concluded that orthodox Lutheran teachings could not allay his growing doubts about his salvation and even about the truth of the Christian religion itself. Thereafter a separatist who criticized the disputatiousness of the Lutheran theologians and claimed the clergy made a business of salvation, Schütz refused to defile his faith in church-administered Holy Communion, and was ultimately denied a Christian burial for this and other heresies. His radical millennialism was a mainstay of his friendship with Merlau and with Anna Maria van Schuurmann (1607-78), known as "the wonder of her epoch" for her learned accomplishments in art, poetry and music, all of which she renounced when she converted, at the age of sixty, to the French and Dutch Pietism of Jean de Labadie, also known as Quietism or Labadism. Convinced that the legal profession was sinful, Schütz helped establish the *Collegium pietatis* and increasingly devoted his time to religious meditation. In the foreword to his *Compendium Juris*, 1677, a popular law textbook, he urged a return to "the true laws of our most holy Saviour" based on "pure love" and criticized "the inexperience, negligence and malice of the judges, lawyers and litigants, whose outrageous behavior is creating nothing but disorder." Schütz, with a 4000-acre land purchase, became the largest shareholder in the German Company, and helped develop the plans for a Pietist colony in Pennsylvania.

In 1675 Schütz employed the notary Christian Fenda (1651-1746), who through contact with Schütz and Spener soon regretted his former life of "drinking, whoring and carousing." When Fenda told Schütz he still felt oppressed by sin despite his lengthy and detailed confession before a Lutheran pastor, Schütz compellingly urged Fenda to cast his old sins into the depths of the sea and go in salvation, and Fenda was overcome with delirious exultation. The learned Fenda subsequently married a laundress as an act of enduring humility – but in the course of his long life nevertheless acquired wealth and influence – and he was subjected to a church "inquisition," or investigation, of his unorthodox religious practices, which, thanks to his legal expertise and connections, ended inconclusively.

When Pastorius first taught and practiced law in Frankfurt, he lodged at the home of Dr. Schütz and dined with Christian Fenda at the Saalhof "for a while," but then, for unspecified reasons, temporarily lodged with a "Captain Daniel Repage" until he arranged for both meals and lodging with the "old & merry-hearted gentleman call'd Juncker Fichard," perhaps preferring 'merry-heartedness' to the learned intensity of Schütz and Fenda. He nevertheless corresponded with Schütz in Pennsylvania, formally addressing the attorney as "my most worthy bosom friend" ("mein werthester Hertzens-freund"), and he kept a copy of Schütz' *Compendium Juris* on his Germantown bookshelf throughout his life. Showing his appreciation for Schütz' Labadist interests in "Some Onomastical Considerations," he praises Jean de Labadie's Christian communism and describes Anna Maria van Schuurmann as "a Hollandish lady" who "made very good verses both in Latin, Greek and Hebrew," and, modestly or jokingly, he also labeled the box containing his thick scholarly manuscripts with one of her mottos (Poem 34): "Aus einem kleinen brünnlein trincket man sich auch satt," or "You can drink your fill even from a small fountain." [44] When Schütz and other Pietists, among them Johann Heinrich Horb's friend Johann Winckler, then preaching near Frankfurt, were challenged for holding private "conventicles" or assemblies in their homes, and thus fostering religious opinions not authorized by the state church, Pastorius sided with the Pietists. Winckler personally gave Pastorius a copy of the commentary he had written in defense of private assemblies, which Pastorius kept in Pennsylvania and commemorated, late in life, in Poem 453.

Pastorius recaptured the mood of fervent unity he had felt among the Saalhof Pietists in a 1684 report to the members of the German Company (*Sichere Nachricht*, pp. 7-8), seeking to express "with this eagle's feather the love I have for you ... My heart is joined to your [hearts] through the bond of love." He hoped they might all "grow together" like trees planted by the water that bear fruit in due time – "Fruit of penitence, fruit of peace, fruit of righteousness!" – and he unabashedly preached piety to the pious by noting that the gardener uproots and casts into the fire those "useless trees" that do not bear fruit even though diligently nurtured year after year. Pastorius learned an otherworldly piety of muted rebelliousness among the Saalhof Pietists, who generally stressed proper personal conduct and doctrine, especially within their select group, and thus avoided both the cynicism or guilt of complicity with the establishment and the despair or defeatism that necessarily followed open confrontation with governmental authority. He dwells upon Christian duty and obedience in a number of his poems, sometimes in pietistic meditation reflecting the psychic or spiritual uncertainties shared by many German intellectuals and mystics in the age of absolutism. His early religious verse emphasizes sin and death (see page 160), and in Epigram 857 he notes:

> Christ Jesus never laught, but often wept,
> And prayed all the Night, when Others slept;
> That we should follow Him likewise in this,
> There in our gloomy Days great Reason is.

Yet even in this somberness, Pastorius espouses active commitment rather than passive unconcern (here, Christ's prayerful coming to terms with destiny in Gethsemane versus the sleep of his disciples), indicating the basic optimism that could dispel the mood of "our gloomy Days" and reestablish the exuberance that predominates in his Pennsylvania life and poetry.

4.3.2.2 A Theology of Universal Salvation: Johanna Eleonora von Merlau and Johann Wilhelm Petersen

> Beauty's Dame Nature's pride, a skin-deep grace;
> But virtue makes the soul outshine the face.
>
> -- Epigram 2312.2
>
> Christ outlawed the law, and turned the curse into a blessing [i.e., by preaching the Beatitudes instead of Thou shalt nots]. By the law of the spirit of life we overcome the law of sin and death. Rom. 8:2. The Spirit leadeth through the law from under the law to Grace. Shewen, p. 46. Christ bringing in everlasting righteousness. Dan. 9:24. The law is fulfilled. I Tim. 1:9. [I.e., a Christian lives by the "charity of a good heart" and ignores the "vain jangling" of commandments (1 Tim. 1, 5-10).]
>
> -- "Law"
>
> Every moment a jubilee. As a few drops in regard of that bottomless sea of God's enjoyment. With unspeakable joy, ravishment of heart, and exultation of spirit. Mirth, music and delight. Merriment and gladness. None so glad, as those of an upright heart and good conscience; they sing, skip, and shout for joy. Psalms 97:11, 32:11 & 132:16, Prov. 29:6, II Cor. 1:12. An overflowing exuberance of holy jollity. There is nothing that men desire more than to live merrily, and many stumble at religion, under the idle conceit that it is the way to mar all their mirth. The Devil and his lying agents make people believe that religion renders a man lumpish and melancholy.
>
> -- "Joy"
>
> Fear must Depart out of the ♥, when PerFect love Does therein take its Place.
>
> -- "Symbola Onomastica," no. 678

Although Pastorius expresses attitudes similar to those of Attorney Schütz, especially toward the law profession and in his millennialist letters of the early 1680s, he does not record admiration for Schütz as he does for Maria Juliana Baur von Eyseneck and Johanna Eleonora von Merlau. "I have been most Intimately Acquainted" with Johanna Eleonora "these 40 years past," he writes in 1719, reporting that he received an unspecified number of letters from her and Johann Wilhelm Petersen (1649- 1727), whom she married in 1680, since arriving in Pennsylvania. He describes her as "of noble Extraction and more [i.e., even] nobler spirit," praises the "very notable things" she wrote during the 1690s "upon the *Apocalypsis* or Revelation of St. John," and notes that she is, like Petersen, "a true Pietist in deed." Pastorius thus singles out the freest spirit among the Saalhof Pietists as the member of the group he most admired, and indicates the continuing influence the Petersens' evolving liberal theology had on his own moral and religious attitudes as they developed in Pennsylvania. The following description of the Petersens highlights biographical detail (essential aspects of which have been ignored in previous biographies) that further illustrates the societal tensions and learned compulsions Pastorius rejected, and criticized in his writings. [45]

Unlike most of the learned men Pastorius met among the Pietists and elsewhere in Europe, feminist Merlau generally kept her distance from paternal authority, and held on to much of the childhood spontaneity – and purity of spirit – so often lost in the process of passing cultural traditions from father to son. She concludes her lively autobiography by noting that Hebraic sacred writings designate the Holy

Spirit "by the female gender as a fertile mother and brooding dove," and a contemporary critic in turn describes her style as "much more mature and, so to speak, masculine" than her husband's – converse indications that her life itself challenged the preconceptions and conventions of her society. Inevitably disturbing conservative dispositions, Merlau was the only Saalhof Pietist constrained by official decree. When a Hessian lord complained, in 1678, that the Pietists were disseminating "suspicious" religious books, the Frankfurt senate concluded Merlau was the cause of their difficulties and ordered her to leave the city. Her good friend Schütz used his influence to obtain a two-month extension, enough time for the excitement to die down, and the city did not insist upon the expulsion thereafter.

Merlau experienced an unusual polarity of maternal and paternal character. As young children she and her two sisters lived with their mother on a rural estate near Frankfurt. Merlau vividly recalled her mother's warmth and protection – holding her hand, for instance, as soldiers in combat passed threateningly close to them in a forest or field during the Thirty Years' War. Her father Georg Adolf von Merlau, the steward at a neighboring Hessian court with little time or inclination for his family, does not get any prominence in the autobiography until after the mother's death, when Merlau was about eleven.

Georg Adolf made his daughter responsible for the household when she refused to be humiliated and intimidated by two successive housekeepers. On periodic visits to the family estate, he personally tyrannized her, repeatedly berating and punishing her for the slightest offense, and he ultimately "demanded everything . . . of me." Although Merlau kept her natural ebullience and her "maidenly chastity," she "felt nothing but disgust for anything that was unchaste," even refusing to play house – "games like getting married or baptizing a child" – with other children because she was "so ashamed," and she shuddered with "servile fear . . . whenever I so much as heard a voice like the voice of my father." Young Merlau meditated on Christ's pure love, and sensed that oppressive paternal authority was a temporary condition: "As soon as [my father] had left [the estate] again, I was happy and in a good mood, I would sing and jump and was very joyful in spirit."

Moving away from Georg Adolf, Merlau lived at court from the age of twelve – for the most part in the care of a duchess who loved her dearly – until she moved in with the 34-year-old widow Baur von Eyseneck in 1675, when she was thirty. She stayed single despite her maidenly allure and her youthful enthusiasm for "dancing . . . lovely clothing and similar vanities." "The joyful spirit that was within me" attracted friends and admirers of both sexes, but potential suitors were quickly dissuaded: She remained engaged to an aristocrat she had not wanted in the first place, a young officer who, stationed far from her court, for years alternately wooed other fiancees and wrote letters assuring her of his steadfast intentions.

"God had let this happen to protect me from other aristocratic marriages," she later argued. By the time the engagement was terminated, she had lost "all interest in getting married" – and concluded that courtly living violated Christian love. Even though there were a few young noblemen of refined character, she explained, aristocratic society as such was so corrupt – especially in its prejudices against the commoners and in the drinking and dueling she considered most pronounced among the aristocrats – that she feared for the souls of her future offspring:

> [I] thus turned my thoughts from marriage completely, as if there wasn't a single man living in the world anymore who concerned me in this respect,

since I wouldn't be allowed, I thought, to marry into another class because my father was very impressed with his old family.

Merlau was attracted to men whose sensitivity and intelligence matched her own. When Philipp Jakob Spener, "through the special providence of God," sat next to her while traveling down the Main by riverboat in 1672, they were soon "talking together without stopping," so that time seemed to stand still and it "was as if he could see into my heart," perceiving the restless dissatisfaction with courtly superficialities that urged her to follow an inner vision of beatific Love. But she could not develop any enthusiasm for the men of learning and station who tried to win her hand. "Not a single thought in favor of marriage would take place within me" when a high-ranking but non-aristocratic church official proposed to her around 1674, so Merlau decided to place the matter in God's hands – by turning the proposal over to her father, who opposed a non-aristocratic marriage on principle. Despite an unexpected setback, providence prevailed:

> My father submitted the matter to the lord of my court, and my lord sent his permission to the clerical official, but I appealed to the will of my father and would not give my yes or no, but instead insisted that my father's yes should be my yes and his no my no.

She used the same approach six years later when she received a proposal from Johann Wilhelm Petersen, church superintendent in the bishopric of Lübeck, and again felt absolutely no urge to marry, remaining in the interim "as calm as if this didn't concern me." But this time her aging and impatient father feared opposing the marriage would be against God's will and argued, "Everyone knows she wouldn't marry beneath her station for frivolous reasons." 36-year-old Merlau accepted this decision as a sign of God's approval, and applied as much energy and intelligence to her marital existence as she had to preserving her independence.

Petersen had begun his career as a dedicated scholar and disputatious professor of philosophy at the orthodox Lutheran University of Gießen in 1673, but during a stay in Frankfurt two years later he participated in Philipp Jakob Spener's *Collegium pietatis*, got involved in discussions of mystic millennialism with Johann Jakob Schütz, and met the woman he would marry five years later. Unaware that Merlau was variously angered and depressed by theologians who "damn each other because of their opinions rather than trying to support each other in the true imitation of Christ," Petersen proudly submitted a copy of one of his anti-Calvinist disputations for her perusal and comment, and was "deeply moved" by her response: He "was honoring the god Petersen" with "such erudite superficialities," putting on airs as the scholars were wont to do instead of trying to attain "the divine simplicity of heavenly things."

Writing down these and other new spiritual insights in a scholarly notebook, Petersen set about mending his ways. He gradually moderated but did not quell his disputatiousness. Two Jesuit canons tried to have him arrested for libeling or lampooning Roman Catholicism after he delivered a Latin verse oration attacking the celibacy of the priesthood at a wedding feast in 1676. Spener once admitted that Petersen's spirited defense of Pietism did his cause more harm than good. Forced to resign from clerical office for his unorthodox views in 1692, Petersen voluminously expounded and defended his increasingly esoteric theology, immersed himself in mystic scholarship, and produced an impressive corpus of Latin poetry and hymns and German free-verse meditations or psalms. Throughout these years he was gaining spiritual proximity to his wife, who between 1688 and 1698 published three books of prayer and meditation revealing a progression from stylized or escapist expressions of mystic love, probably written during her courtly years, to a rich piety harmonizing soulful inwardness with outer-directed love, in part reflecting her maturity as a wife and mother.

Just as Petersen had rejected Calvinist predestination in his earliest disputations, Merlau as a child had been unwilling to believe that a loving God would damn all non-Christians to hell ("yes, even the poor children of the heathens, who never had the chance to know God, supposedly remain in such never-ending torment"), and by 1695 this spiritual sensitivity had evolved into a complex theology of universal salvation influenced by the mystic Philadelphianism of Jane Ward Lead (1623-1704) and the intuitions of Merlau's dreams, and supported with humane and methodical biblical exegesis. The Petersens jointly concluded that all souls, following Christ's imminent reign on earth for a thousand years, would return to the state of innocence prevailing before the Fall from Grace, and that Satan would then regain his status among the heavenly angels. God is love essential, they argued, and evil is rooted in time rather than eternity. Christ had died for all the creatures of God's creation, regardless of race, creed or calling, and even the Devil could not be excluded.

The Petersens have been ridiculed for their naiveté – especially for befriending and supporting, in 1691, 19-year-old Rosamunde Juliane von Asseburg, convinced by her mystic visions that Christ had personally chosen her as His bride-to-be – but reflective critics have noted the generosity and charity of their theology, a liberating challenge to the orthodox Lutheran emphasis on hell and damnation that influenced later church history. Gotthold Ephraim Lessing (1729-81), critical theorist of the German Enlightenment, distinguished between the insincere and self-serving Pietism of Christoph Martin Wieland's *Empfindungen eines Christen* (Sentiments of a Christian, 1756) and the genuine religious feeling of Petersen's free-verse psalms (*Stimmen aus Zion*, 1696-1701), inspired poetry "rich in vigorous ideas and grand conceptions" yet with the "noble simplicity" of biblical language. Johann Gottfried Herder, the critic and historian who taught Goethe to consider poetry "an endowment . . . of the people" rather than the "private inheritance of a few well-bred gentlemen," wrote that Petersen combined clear-sighted intelligence with a gentle heart, and Herder blamed the psychological pressures of constant antagonism for Petersen's preoccupation with millennialist hopes for the future, a preoccupation he believed would not have developed under other circumstances. Petersen and those sharing his reasonable principles and "hopeful religious enthusiasm," Herder concluded, were nevertheless instrumental in attaining lasting improvement in German society.

Herder's thesis about the cause of Petersen's preoccupation finds a converse of sorts in the biography of Franz Daniel Pastorius, whose American experience served essentially as a filter separating fanciful hopes from sound principles. Pastorius became less concerned with millennialism as the Petersens were getting more involved in it, but they nevertheless remained kindred spirits. When Pastorius writes, in the foreword to *Beschreibung Pennsylvaniae*, that Europe in his day had few Christians who "penetrated to the center of their being, to God the supreme good," he reveals a sense of personal divinity expressed in a similar fashion in Merlau's meditations of the 1690s, an unorthodox religious point of view deriving in part from the mystic pantheism of Jakob Boehme. In 1707 Petersen wrote that

Christ was the redeeming natural Light in every human being, even in heathens and Turks (i.e. Muslims) who had never heard of Him – a stance related to the universalist theology Pastorius had voiced, in similar language, more than a decade earlier in his descriptions of the Native Americans (page 238). "Christ's Divine Light shall rise," quoted from Poem 341 (page 187), encapsulates a recurring motif of Pastorius' thought, which seems to combine Pietist redemption, Quaker "Light" and early Enlightenment ideals into one, thus similar to, and in advance of, the Petersens.

The correspondence between Pastorius and the Petersens, which was not available for this study, would presumably account for these and other similarities involving points of view developed after Pastorius left the Saalhof Pietists in 1683. This correspondence may also account for the Petersens' renewed interest in Quakerism around 1695, more or less coinciding with Pastorius' 1696 letter defending Quakerism to the German Pietists, most likely sent to the Petersens. Expressing this interest, Petersen praised similarities between Pietism and Quakerism – and appalled the moderate Pietists who, reflecting political sensitivities in Germany, denied any relationship whatsoever between their faith and Quaker radicalism. In short, Pastorius' ongoing relationship with the Petersens underscores the common ground he continued to share with German Pietists while living in Pennsylvania. Pastorius himself, in his transatlantic writings, indicates a number of the differences emerging after 1683.

4.4 The Transatlantic Message of Beschreibung Pennsylvaniae

> This World, some say, is (found By Navigation) round, To wit just as a Churn;
> For what way Goodmen turn, They must be laughing Stocks, And meet with Shocks and Knocks.
>
> -- Poem 375

"Our German Company and Brotherhood" of Pietists was founded, Pastorius writes in a 1698 letter, "not especially for the sake of temporal gain but to a much greater extent to give its members and other honest countrymen a Pella [Palestinian city of Christian refuge in A.D. 67] or place of refuge when a just God would pour out the vessels of His wrath upon a sinful Europe." [46] His transatlantic correspondence clarifies the nature of this undertaking, and explains the shifts in grammatical tense and personal mood that transpired between his emotional statements of 1683-84 and this brief restatement of an apocalyptic vision modified by Pennsylvania experience.

God's wrath "will be poured out over this abominable Babylon," he wrote in June 1684. As this "will" evolved into the "would" of his 1698 recapitulation Pastorius was working at the arduous tasks of building a revitalized European society on the Pennsylvania frontier and, in the process, absorbing new values from his Native American and Anglo-American neighbors. In his reports and letters about his new home and his activities in it, Pastorius not only provides moral insight for sedentary Europeans and practical advice for anyone with the fortitude to start their life anew in America. He also reflects his personal growth in this environment. A summary of the message he communicated to his German homeland rounds out this study of Pastorius and the traditions of his early life, revealing his awareness of continuities and discontinuities between his native culture and that evolving in colonial Pennsylvania. [47]

To indicate both Pastorius' bicultural awareness and his personal growth in Pennsylvania, the following summary highlights the form and content of *Beschreibung Pennsylvaniae* and places this publication in the context of his transatlantic writing as a whole, noting contrasts between the earliest texts and those written after Pastorius became acclimated to the New World.

The extant transatlantic writings include his letter to his parents of June 1684 (*Copia, eines ... Brieffes*); a June 1684 report to the German Society or Company, also known as the Frankfurt Land Company, published as *Sichere Nachricht auß America* (Reliable Information from America), a seven-page brochure that includes portions of a report written in March 1684 and edited into the later text; the 1688 letter to Georg Leonhart Model and a letter of 20 June 1692 to Melchior Adam Pastorius published in the *Monatlichen Unterredungen* periodical issues of April 1691 and February 1693, respectively; and *Beschreibung Pennsylvaniae*, which includes twelve letters to Melchior Adam, excerpts from the two reports to the German Company combined in *Sichere Nachricht* and from a 1685 letter to Johann Jakob Schütz, and a condensed translation, probably by Melchior Adam Pastorius, of the Latin letter to Model, all of which are appended to a 47-page report on Pennsylvania life and culture with a foreword, introduction and seventeen chapters whose titles include "Of the Discovery of Pennsylvania," "Of the Fertility of this Land," "Of the Opportunities for Sailing to this Province," and "The Manner in Which William Penn Intends to Inhabit This Empty Province, Which He Received as a Gift; Terms of Sale." An earlier version of this report, entitled *Kurtze Beschreibung von der allerneulichst erfundenen Americanischen Landschafft Pensylvanien* (A Short Description of the Most Recently Discovered American Province of Pennsylvania), was published in 1690 or 1691. Responding to critical feedback from Germany, Pastorius revised, reorganized and expanded the report during the early and mid 1690s, thus giving it the form here described. [48]

4.4.1 A Scholarly Guide to the New World's Most Remote Colony
4.4.1.1 The Allure of America

> Few can resist the tempting shine of gold,
> From pole to pole men are by that controll'd.
>
>   -- Epigram 96
>
> I love the World, if you take out the L,
> This crooked letter is the way to Hell:
> Hell, at the Tail whereof You that behold,
> Without which we read God, and with it Gold.
> Gold is some people's God; but mine the Lord,
> In Him I only trust, and in His Word,
> His Word His pow'rful World . . .
>
>   -- Poem 358
>
> Oh! Time and Death make always haste,
> To Kill, Consume and Spend,
> Stones, Pebbles, Steel and Iron waste,
> And bring all to an End.
> Here ev'ry thing Wax is,
> Come Ovid, and explain it,
> Mors etiam Saxis,

> Marmoribusque venit.
> [Destruction (or death) comes even to rocks and marble.]
>> -- Poem 430, "On an old Tortoise Shell (resembling a man's Skull or Brainpan), hang'd up in my Garden"

After admitting, in the foreword to *Beschreibung Pennsylvaniae*, that he could not find moral satisfaction anywhere in Franconia or Germany, Pastorius reminds his German readers of their limited horizons with a lesson on global geography concluding the forward (pp. vii-x). Reflecting his practical experience and scholarly knowledge, he writes with refreshing and assuring authority. "I divide the globe into four continents," he begins, and explains that Europe, the first continent, is "the smallest of them all but, because of its arts and Christian religion, the best known." The world beyond Europe remains for the most part, in this brief treatise, remote and obscure. Africa, Pastorius reports on the strength of his sources, "is a very hot, unfertile and partially uninhabited land full of poisonous animals." Even less is known about some portions of the globe: "To this day no one has dared to venture" onto the island of Tierra del Fuego, "the great unknown land to the south ... which ... is aglow at night, as if the entire region were in raging flames." America, though divided into two subcontinents and described in greater detail in the "Introduction" (pp. 1-5), is treated here as one colossal entity:

> The fourth continent is America, or the so-called New World ... It ... is the largest portion of the globe, in fact almost as large as the entire Old World combined, Europe, Asia and Africa. And this is the land in which gold, silver, precious stones, sugar, spices and various rarities are to be found in superfluity, of which the fleets of silver arriving from thence each year offer us clear testimony. (P. ix.)

In his introduction Pastorius guides his readers on a scholarly journey of quest and discovery and colonization, enumerating the colonial powers – Spain, France, Holland and England – and describing their American territories and cities, and rivers like the Amazon and Plata in South America, "upon which the wealth of America is transported to sea and thus forth to Spain." Yet (like his sources) he depicts the early voyages of discovery in terms of Renaissance ideals, and fails to mention the death and destruction that accompanied colonization and conquest.

Describing Christopher Columbus (1451?-1506), for example, he cites the learnedness, sailing experience and entrepreneurial determination that enabled this explorer to hypothesize, by careful study of prevailing winds, the existence of a distant continent and to find the financial backing for the equipment, crew and ships needed "to explore this foreign land and sail beyond the Pillars of Hercules" – the African and European land areas separated by the Straits of Gibraltar that, according to modern scholarship, had once marked "the limits of enterprise for the seafaring peoples of the Mediterranean world" and were named after the Greco-Roman hero or god whose hardiness, valor and adventurousness are characterized in the labors of Hercules. [49]

Naive wonder still veils America at this point in Pastorius' narration. Columbus and his successor Amerigo Vespucci (1451?-1512) meet naked natives, discover "the Island of the Cannibals" and an island laden with riches, encounter "a fire-belching mountain" (otherwise known as a volcano) and a marvelous fountain whose waters cause the unsuspecting to die of laughter unless they get an antidote from another fountain to stop their laughing fit.

4.4.1.2 Feudal Values and New Freedoms: The Founding of Pennsylvania

> Let him that built high now creep low to shelter,
> When potentates must tumble, helter skelter.
>
> -- "Out of Sir John Denham's <u>Directions to a Painter</u>," "Beehive," p. 70

> The Govern[ou]r, Council & Assembly: These laws we hatch / For them that watch. *Vigilantibus Jura Scripta sunt.* [Written laws are for the watchful.] Not to help fools, but to prevent knaves.
>
> -- "Emblematical Recreations"

> Governments owe their being to consent, not conquest. <u>Chr. Rights</u>, p. 9. Government necessarily supposes a right of judging and determining all matters within its sphere. Id., p. 400. Alterations in government are by consent of the parties concerned. Id., p. 9 . . . Good governours ought to be apprehensive [i.e., aware] of the notion of two independent powers. P. 258. Self-preservation the original [cause] of appointing governments. P. 10 . . . Subjects are not born for the king, but the king for the subjects. Saavedre, p. 145 . . . The chief ends of government are the preservation of people's lives, the security of their fortunes, and the determination of justice between man and man. <u>Freeholder</u>.
>
> -- "Government"

> People should have a share in the making of their own laws, and likewise in the judicatory power to apply those laws made. <u>Engl. Pref. Int.</u>, pp. 14 & 17.
>
> -- "Law"

"Even though many colonies and plantations [ranging from Brazil and Peru to Virginia and New England] . . . were successively established from the days of Christopher Columbus and Amerigo Vespucci onward," Pastorius reports in Chapter One, "yet another was added to them when in 1665 . . . a vast new land was discovered lying far beyond the other provinces here described." Pastorius explains how this remote territory became the province of Pennsylvania with the makings of a self-contained German colony – not in terms of Pietist or Quaker religious beliefs but in the context of aristocratic birthrights, monarchist ideals, and new economic opportunities for the common man. The regicide of Charles I at the conclusion of the English Civil War in 1649 precedes the virtual martyrdom of Sir William Penn (1621-70) in the loyalist cause, and Charles II, once restored to the Crown, deeds Pennsylvania to Sir William's only son in a gesture of friendship and gratitude.

Pastorius' lively and pointed narrative admittedly sacrifices historical validity in a few basic details. Sir William (called "Lord Penn" in the German text) actually attained the rank of admiral and was awarded estates in Ireland under Oliver Cromwell's anti-royalist Protectorate, and he died peacefully in Essex, England, after the Restoration. [50] Yet it underscores the sharp contrasts between the debilitating chaos of the Civil War and the wholesome undertaking of William Penn the younger, who appears here as a benefactor of the people and esteemed member of the establishment and not as a proponent of radical Quaker theology or politics:

> . . . a tragedy of the most horrible nature, such as had never before been imagined, occurred to King Charles I when he was pursued by his own subjects, captured, and even beheaded with an axe. His son Charles II hastily assembled an army to avenge his father's death and defend his kingdom, and

engaged his forces but was defeated on the battlefield, and was pursued by enemies seeking to kill him, which would most certainly have been his fate had it not been for his General, Lord Penn, who disguised him and took him across to France by ship; as a result of this deed, all of Lord Penn's estates, castles and villages were burnt down, and he himself was driven into exile, where he then died before Charles II was restored to the royal throne.

With the King once more in possession of scepter and crown, William Penn (the only son of Lord Penn) appeared as a guest at court, was received by Charles II in a very friendly manner, and was presented with [the proprietary rights to] this newly-discovered land in recompense for the loyal service rendered by his father...

This William Penn issued general and public tidings in the city of London that he would be inclined to establish various colonies and cities in this land, and for anyone who might perchance take pleasure and delight in sailing with him to the colony, Penn announced his willingness to sell each acre of land for no more than a single English crown ("Kopstück"). Thus many people signed up for a particular parcel of land in his book of title, and very many families journeyed with him into the province, where he founded the city of Philadelphia for himself and his people. In particular, however, a German Company joined into association, and bargained for the purchase of many thousand acres of land so that it could establish a German colony there. The province as a whole, however, was named Pennsylvania (Penn's wilderness), since it was completely overgrown with forests and wilderness. (Pp. 6-7.)

As if to validate this account of the founding of Pennsylvania, Pastorius concludes Chapter One with a five-page German translation of the 1681 royal charter declaring the King's "special trust in the wisdom and justice of the aforementioned William Penn" and granting Penn and his descendants proprietary rights to the colony in perpetuity – subject to an annual fealty payment of two beaver pelts, a small token of the feudal order, still dominant in Germany, that was being fundamentally modified, in seventeenth-century England and especially in colonial Pennsylvania, by a great number of independent-minded thinkers and causes (among them rationalists, Cambridge Platonists and Levellers, Presbyterians, Puritans and Quakers, and the followers of Francis Bacon, Thomas Hobbes and James Harrington), and by related historical developments generating the Commonwealth and Interregnum of 1649-60 and the Glorious Revolution of 1688. [51] Although Pastorius simplifies English history to place himself and Penn on the side of old-fashioned feudal values in this introductory narrative, successive chapters reveal many of the freedoms he enjoyed under England's limited monarchy in a colony far removed from its central government.

4.4.1.3 *Incremental Levels of Reality: The Example of Pennsylvania's Abundance*

> Whoever sleeps when he should sow,
> May likewise sleep when he would mow.
>
> Love spurs on labour, and this gains by use
> Experience, and these three rare works produce.
>
> Quickly on quick-expiring moments seize;
> Be labour's friend, a foe to sloath and ease.
>
> -- Epigrams 660, 2321.1, 2327.2

> [Thomas] Tusser makes Husbandry say:
> So many as love me, and use me aright,
> With treasure and pleasure I richly acquite . . . From p. 121:
> Good husbandry weepeth, where huswifery sleepeth . . .
> Good husbands and huswives look always about,
> Not careless within doors, nor lazy without.
> -- "Husbandry"
>
> An idle person is the devil's pillow. No sheep runs into the mouth of a sleeping wolf . . . A plow that worketh, glisteneth: but rest makes it rusty . . Ah, I have consumed my life in laboriously doing nothing. Culpeper, p. 557 . . . I keep a-talking here, as if I had nothing else to do . . . They [the idle] think . . . they should be rocked asleep, and jogged to heaven unawares in a dream. Heywood, p. 67.
> -- "Idleness"

Although these seventeen chapters seem repetitive because they describe particular events and basic themes more than once – the founding of Philadelphia or the functioning of the German Company, for example – Pastorius actually develops these themes incrementally, expanding his preliminary descriptions, to some extent simplified or idealized, with realistic detail in subsequent reiterations. He gradually initiates his German readers into American experience, charting unfamiliar ground in tentative forays that do not overwhelm the novitiates. William Penn, introduced in a royal setting, soon reappears as the author of democratic doctrines, and in Chapter Twelve Pastorius finally identifies the proprietor as a Quaker who "nevertheless does not force anyone to accept a particular religion, but instead allows religious freedom to those of every nation" living in Pennsylvania.

Penn's call for colonists in Chapter One may have the air of a leisurely picnic outing, but it is later augmented with exact details about the costs and conditions of purchasing land and booking passage, just as Pastorius' description of his own ocean voyage, delayed to the penultimate chapter, warns emigrants to avoid certain ships entirely, criticizes the meager portions and awful taste of shipboard food – pea soup, salted fish, and meat so dried out it is "almost hard" – and advises all passengers to bring additional food with them or to bargain with the shipping agents "concerning the quality as well as the quantity of the food" and to refuse to pay full fare in advance as a means of forcing the captain to honor this commitment, all of which reveals that leisurely outings and romantic quests had little in common with real transatlantic travel.

In Chapter Nine Pastorius likewise disenchants readers dazzled by the spurious attractions of American gold, silver and precious stones with criticism reflecting his distaste for the excessive luxury of the wealthy:

> We do not have any precious stones in this region, nor do we have any desire for them, and we cannot confer any great praise upon those who first dug gold and gemstones up out of the dark and secret regions of the earth, for even though these gems are rare objects of God's creation and in themselves good, they have through misuse been shockingly defiled and, as unwilling subjects, forced into the service of vanity. (P. 25.)

Rather than offering illusory wealth, colonial beginnings demanded personal sacrifice. Do not come to Pennsylvania if you fear the "hardships and dangers of the wearisome journey" or are not prepared to live "in poor housing and on a modest diet" at least until "we have been able to improve the housing and commerce of the province," Pastorius advises in the version of *Sichere Nachricht* appended to *Be-*

schreibung Pennsylvaniae, and he indicates the extent of material wants the colony could not supply in 1684:
> Anyone who has made the earnest resolution to cross the ocean . . . should bring with him butter, cheese, sugar, wine, brandy, a great variety of farm and garden seeds, cast-iron pots, kettles, a gun for hunting game, &c. (P. 42.)

Concerned both with establishing a complex society and regaining some degree of pristine simplicity, Pastorius describes the bounty of nature as a blessing and as a challenge for European settlers. The natural satisfactions of Pennsylvania were almost overwhelming. As William Penn and his flotilla of twenty ships approached Pennsylvania in October 1682, Pastorius reports in Chapter Six, they could inhale "while yet rather far from land . . . a fragrance in the air as delightful as that from a freshly blossoming garden." He describes the Pennsylvania environment in Chapter Five, especially noting "various beautiful new stars . . . that were until now unknown to the European astrologers;" the Delaware River, two English miles wide at Philadelphia, he exaggerates, and "so magnificent that there is nothing comparable to it in all of Europe;" and natural delights to calm the soul and satisfy the palate:
> The fresh streams and springs are practically beyond number. The shady thickets and bushes are everywhere filled to overflowing with birds whose rare colors and varied song splendidly magnify the glory of their Creator. There is also a superabundance of wild goose, duck, turkey, partridge, dove, snipe, and similar game. (P. 20.)

Chapter Nine summarizes the qualities that made Pennsylvania especially fertile for agriculture and trade, including its commerce with the Caribbean Islands, the availability of fish, game and furs provided by the Native Americans, and the natural advantages of its geographical location:
> Since this province has the latitude of Montpellier [on the Mediterranean in France] and Naples [in Italy] but is blessed with far more rivers and springs than either of those areas, it goes almost without saying that a land such as this is easily capable of yielding many noble fruits of the soil. The air is light and pleasant, the summer longer and warmer than in Germany, and as a result we obtain plentiful and varied harvests in this area, and our work in the fields is justly rewarded. (P. 24.)

Since this glorious abundance could also be a hindrance to civilization, Pastorius warns, in his final chapter, that Pennsylvania is not a biblical paradise:
> My newly-established locality of Germantown is already flourishing with 64 households. Now in order to provide for these inhabitants as well as for others arriving here, the fields have to be cleared and farms have to be established. No matter where one turns, however, the story is the same: *Itur in antiquam sylvam* [you are walking in the ancient forests], and everything is overgrown with timber, so that I often wished I had had several dozen strong Tirolese who could have toppled the thick oak trees for us, but bit by bit we have had to clear the land ourselves, and in the process it has struck me that we descendants of Adam in this province are also subject to the dictates with which God punished Adam's disobedience, namely that he should eat his bread in the sweat of his face [Genesis 3, 19], for here the saying is: *Hic opus, hic labor est* [there is no achievement without labor], and it will not suffice to arrive here with money but without the willingness to work . . . (Pp. 38-39.)

In 1684 Pastorius criticized the "bad farmers" in the colony (mostly Swedish and Dutch immigrants in a few small settlements established earlier in the seventeenth century), "some of whom have neither barns nor stables, let their grain lie out under the open sky unthreshed year after year and their steers, horses, cows, pigs &c. run loose in the thickets summer and winter, and thus obtain little advantage from them." (*Sichere Nachricht*, pp. 2-3.) "Be labour's friend," he advises in his epigrams (page 219). The emphasis Pastorius gives to hard work and efficient techniques, the latter in his agricultural writings, indicates the beginning of a trend that, during the eighteenth century, won Pennsylvania Germans a reputation for clearing heavily-forested but fertile land and establishing prosperous farms, a significant contribution to America's agrarian traditions. [52]

4.4.2 The Modest Satisfactions of Pennsylvania
4.4.2.1 Personal Growth amid Societal Innovations

> Whatever in my garden grows,
> God's Goodness, Might and Wisdom shows;
> This threefold Attribute I see
> In ev'ry Herb, Flow'r, Shrub and Tree;
> Each Tree, Shrub, Herb, Flower cries,
> He's bounteous, powerful and wise.
> -- Poem 207

> Godliness is profitable for all things; it makes for the quiet of our minds, the health of our bodies, the increase of our estates, and procures us much credit and esteem, much love and good will among our neighbours. Chr. Monitor, p. 18.
> -- "Piety"

Ultimately resolving his earlier images of abundance by endorsing a robust form of the Protestant work ethic, Pastorius uses the same organizing device that allows him to present Pennsylvania in a reassuringly feudal context before describing the innovations of its society, politics and economy. Romantic images of America and the societal innovation of Pennsylvania complicated Pastorius' own first experience of the colony, and taught him to proceed cautiously as he interpreted Pennsylvania existence for his fellow Germans. Coming from a relatively homogeneous culture, Pastorius was surprised to find himself among a truly heterogeneous group of emigrants as he sailed for Pennsylvania in 1683, and he reacted typically, a few months later, by joking to his Pietist friends that his ship was a Noah's ark containing some "unclean animals" – his implicit designation for those who practiced 'unreasonable' religions. (His tally of Quakers on board, by the way, was obviously fudged.)

> There was a medical doctor with his wife and eight children, a French captain, a Dutch baker, an apothecary, glassblower, mason, blacksmith, cartwright, joiner, cooper, hatter, cobbler, tailor, gardener, farmers, seamstresses, &c., all together more than 80 people in addition to the crew of the ship. They were differentiated not only by their ages (which ranged from our oldest woman, aged 60, to the youngest child who was only twelve weeks old) and their trades, but also by such a variety of religions and attitudes that I could compare the ship that brought them hither, not inappropriately, with Noah's ark, since there were no fewer unclean animals than clean (reasonable) to be found on board. My company included individuals who sided with the Roman Catholics, the Lutherans, the Calvinists, the Baptists and the Anglicans, and only one Quaker. (*Sichere Nachricht*, p. 2.)

On top of the culture shock experienced aboard ship, Pastorius met his first Native Americans even before setting foot on Pennsylvania soil (he reports in *Sich-*

ere Nachricht) in an episode that reveals his eagerness to encounter the exotic or bravely face the unknown (as well as his awareness that Native Americans might be befriended or placated with alcohol):

> The first [so-called savages] I laid my eyes upon were the two who rowed their canoe up to our ship near Upland [Chester, Pennsylvania]. I offered them a brandy, and they wanted to pay me half a crown for it, but when I declined their money they shook hands with me and said, "Thank you, brother!"

Soon Native American curiosity turned the tables on Pastorius, and he must have then realized that people like himself were the exotic element in his new environment. Despite the absorbing tasks of colonization, he found the time and mustered the resolve to cope with the unrestrained neighborliness that challenged his European sense of decorum and hierarchy:

> [One of the chiefs] paid me a visit at my house on 3 October [1683] and on 12 December another king and queen [chief and his squaw] did the same. Many of the ordinary Indians very frequently overwhelm me with similar visits, but nevertheless I almost always demonstrate my love for them with a slice of bread and a glass of beer, and this awakens in them a love for me in return ... (P. 4.)

Early encounters with native and immigrant Americans demanded adaptation, and fostered personal growth, enhancing the liberal views subtly proclaimed in *Beschreibung Pennsylvaniae*. Pastorius' accounts of Native Americans are among the most open-minded and mature of the seventeenth century. [53] The tolerance he developed for differing religious views, displayed in his manuscript writings and, somewhat cautiously, in letters to his father, can also be noted in Chapter Thirteen of *Beschreibung Pennsylvaniae* ("Of the Religions in This Province"), objectively reporting on the four main faiths or denominations then established: The Native Americans, lacking "any written articles of faith, ... through their native language inform their children *per traditionem* of that which they have heard and learned from their parents;" the Dutch and English are predominantly Calvinists; the Quakers have become established in Philadelphia with William Penn; the Swedes and Germans are Lutherans.

Pastorius simplifies this description by playing down the importance of the Quakers and by implying that the Germans then in Germantown were Lutheran rather than predominantly Quaker or Mennonite, details omitted to avoid alarming conservative readers in Germany. The only comments indicating a religious bias are his report that the colony's Lutheran preacher was "very much given to drink, and still practically blind to the Inner Man" of Christian renewal (the word 'still' suggests Pastorius was working on the parson's 'blindness') and the disparaging remark about Lutheran clergymen that followed his report on the simple wooden church erected in Germantown in 1686, the denomination of which (Quaker or possibly Mennonite and Quaker) goes unmentioned. Although his 1684 joke about Noah's ark may imply a degree of intolerance toward some religions, the only religious bias of *Beschreibung Pennsylvaniae*, written after Pastorius had accepted the diversity of Pennsylvania, served his ongoing campaign against the bigotry of German Protestantism. His liberality is epitomized in the universalism espoused in his reports on Native Americans (see page 238).

Pastorius' commentary on Pennsylvania living shows that tolerance could be expected to increase in a diversified society with new opportunities for economic and political accomplishment. As he managed the affairs of the German Company in Philadelphia and Germantown and worked at colonizing Pennsylvania, Pastorius found spiritual satisfactions of a practical sort yet had little time available for meditation, a combination that moderated the religious intensity he had known among the Frankfurt Pietists. In the 1684 letter urging his parents "to escape the calamity awaiting Germany" (*Copia, eines ... Brieffes*), he describes the spiritual satisfactions of his worldly pursuits:

> Along with Germantown, W. Penn has assigned us a tract of land of 12,000 acres, which he named New Franconia, and, the Lord willing, I hope to make arrangements for the founding of numerous other towns in this region in the near future. In addition to this tract, we will be able to obtain another 20,000 acres of adjoining territory if a fairly large number of Germans immigrate (which I expect to happen), and thus establish a little Germany! with our own rights and privileges as well, and under our Governor, who loves integrity and justice, live a peaceful and quiet life in all blessed decency, Amen!
>
> Consider now, dear parents, whether these activities will bear more fruit in the service of God and my fellow man than would be the case if I were to help create disputes among brothers *via Juris* [practicing law] like other *rabulae forenses* [ranting lawyers] and unconscionable and scandalous attorneys who clean out the purses of their clients. In my present calling I at least find a more merciful God and an undisturbed conscience, and I value these two things incomparably higher than all the treasures of Egypt.

It seems that most of the Frankfurt Pietists have become immersed in worldly affairs, Pastorius observes in his 1685 letter to fellow Pietist Johann Jakob Schütz, and have lost their good intentions "to serve God and His justice with a tranquil heart here in Pennsylvania." He understood their lack of resolve:

> I myself, here in this province, am no longer able to do anything but direct my thoughts toward Philadelphia [when I am in Germantown], and then to Germantown again [when in Philadelphia], even though I would most prefer having them fixed forever upon the Holy Jerusalem, the future City of the Lord, which exists eternally and should be sought in good earnest by me and all who love God. But of course the many duties of supervision entrusted to me [by the German Company], among other tasks, must also be performed with as much diligence and devotion as possible. (*Beschreibung Pa.*, p. 48.)

Although his poetry and some of the letters to his father show that Pastorius also reflected maturely on religious themes, sixteen of the seventeen chapters of *Beschreibung Pennsylvaniae* are devoted almost exclusively to the temporal existence of immigrants and Native Americans, focusing particularly on the Anglo- and German-American activities that (for most of the colony's ethnic groups) were creating new material opportunities and improving the prospects for human dignity – and thus, for individuals like Franz Daniel Pastorius, infusing mundane existence with some of the grace and purity of God's ineffable spirit.

4.4.2.2 Provincial Politics and Economics

> A true Christian will not put forth his hand against the person, life, liberty, or estate of others because of their conscientious errors and religious practices . . . Shewen. A land where the sweat of the brow is not made the forfeit of the conscience. Penn . . . To be deprived of liberty of conscience is a slavery in the midst of the greatest liberty. gr Case, p. 11.
>
> -- "Liberty of Conscience"

> Freedom of conscience the most Desirable Privilege Freely enjoy'D in Pennsilvania.
>
> -- "Symbola Onomastica," no. 238
>
> When fortune smiles, of pride beware,
> And though it frown, do not despair.
>
> -- Epigram 2335.10

Pastorius marvels at the rapid growth of the colony even as he describes the political freedom and economic opportunity that made such growth possible. A brief political primer, Chapters Four and Seven summarize Pennsylvania's first constitution and the basic laws passed under William Penn. As Pastorius describes it, the constitution provided annual elections by secret ballot to keep public officials responsible to the people, a taxation policy requiring the consent of two-thirds of the legislature for each tax measure, a legal system eliminating the need for attorneys, freedom of conscience with no enforced church attendance, and strict morality among the citizenry and in business dealings. The basic laws, Pastorius reports, allowed all "nations" within Pennsylvania to establish their own schools and churches; declared Sunday as a day of worship; set up guidelines for establishing village communities – instead of isolated farms – to facilitate education, public worship and neighborly cooperation; regulated judicial appointments and guaranteed public court sessions; proposed the stocks as punishment for crimes like cheating, swearing, and quarreling among neighbors (a measure that, court records reveal, was not employed in Germantown [54]); set wage levels for craftsmen; and required that every twelve-year-old be apprenticed in "a trade or other honest undertaking."

While this list of rights and responsibilities combines conservative and innovative measures, Pastorius emphasizes the innovations in a 1698 summary of the essentials of Pennsylvania government: The "entire citizenry" annually elects a provincial legislature that "enacts necessary laws and ..., along with the governor, provides for the common weal." All court cases are heard by a jury of twelve neighbors, who decide on the facts, and the judges are all appointed from those who have served as elected members of the legislature. "And all judicial matters take place *in publica Curia* [in open court sessions], where every individual great and small may enter and listen to the proceedings" (pp. 82-83). Pastorius summarizes briefly and without commentary, aware that Germany was not yet ready for any grand proclamations of American political freedoms, yet he does not resist clearly stating the principle of "no taxation without representation" – essentially the same principle that, long before the American Revolution, had generated tensions among his fellow citizens in Windsheim:

> As far as taxation and tribute among the subjects of this province is concerned, the same considerations apply here as in the English nation, where neither the king himself nor his representatives, prefects or governors are permitted to impose military assessments or taxes of any sort, unless the subjects themselves have previously resolved and passed a particular approval [of the tax measure], and according to the Constitution [of Pennsylvania] no tax may be continued longer than a single year [without legislative renewal]. (Pp. 83-84.)

Despite its brevity, Pastorius' commentary on the English freedoms enjoyed in Pennsylvania marks one of the earliest stages in transferring the liberal ideology of limited monarchy – established with the Glorious Revolution of 1688 – from

England to the Continent, in this instance via an American colony. The process of transferal culminated in 1748 when Charles-Louis de Montesquieu (1689-1755), the French Enlightenment jurist, published his analysis of English constitutional rights in *De l'Esprit des Lois* (Of the Spirit of the Laws). [55]

The colony's reasonable laws and natural bounty, if combined with a willingness to work, enhanced the potential for material as well as spiritual well-being – this is the theme implied throughout the seventeen chapters of *Beschreibung Pennsylvaniae*. Anyone who manages to finance the journey but cannot afford to get established, Pastorius announces in Chapter Two, will be given fifty acres of land in return for a minimal quitrent – and it will be his to keep "just as if he had purchased the land in perpetuity for himself and his heirs." Servants who complete their term of service and children who come of age likewise receive a land grant of fifty acres and the full liberties of citizenship. For readers appalled by the prospect of servants suddenly becoming propertied men, Pastorius calmly explains that this measure was designed "to encourage [servants] to greater diligence and obedience."

Since land grants seemed to presuppose an agrarian society, Pastorius corrects this impression by describing, especially in Chapter Eight, new Pennsylvania towns and cities ("angehende Städte") and new opportunities for craftsmen, commerce and industry. Philadelphia is situated on two navigable rivers, and "the water is deep enough to enable the big ships to sail right up to the riverbank about a stone's throw from the city." An English company had founded the town of Frankford (like Germantown, part of present-day Philadelphia), erected company warehouses, and established "several mills, a glass factory and a brick kiln." The province also included the growing towns of Newcastle with a good harbor, and Upland with its predominantly Swedish population. The German Company had a chain of agents and merchants stretching from Philadelphia to London and across the Channel to Rotterdam, then up the Rhine to Frankfurt on the Main, with links along the way at Wesel and Duisburg in Germany (Chapter Fourteen). The company dealt in "wool and linen cloth as well as goods of every conceivable nature" (Chapter Seventeen).

In the 1684 letter to his parents (*Copia, eines ... Brieffes*), Pastorius mentions a hardworking Franconian relative or neighbor (whose name was deleted from the published text), apparently a craftsman or peasant, and notes that the man and his wife

> would be very useful in this country, and the country in turn would be very beneficial for them; in a few years, through the honest work of their hands, they could expect God's rich blessing to an extent they would not even dare to imagine in your area.

A similar conviction informs *Beschreibung Pennsylvaniae*, as Chapter Ten admirably illustrates. Entitled "Of the Growth of This Province," it evokes modest satisfactions amid economic self sufficiency:

> Although this distant region of the earth consisted of nothing but wilderness, and did not begin to serve the needs of Christian society until very recently, it is all the more astonishing to see how rapidly the colony has ascended under God's blessing, and how it is visibly growing from day to day. Even if, at the very beginning, we had to pay rather dearly of our own money to have food supplies brought over from [New] Jersey, for example, we at present are nevertheless able – may God be praised – to serve neighboring communities [with Pennsylvania's productivity].

We have most of the craftsmen needed to meet our needs, a tolerable wage has been established, and the most essential mills and brick kilns are now in operation.

We trade our surpluses of grain and cattle for brandy, sirup, sugar and salt from Barbados [in the Caribbean], although we ship our rare furs back to England.

Aside from this, we are devoting our energies to expanding textile weaving and vineyards for wine production in order to keep our money in the province, and for this reason we have already established annual trade fairs, not for the sake of profit or grievous usury but rather to enable any of those among us to purchase whatever another has produced beyond his own needs, so that individuals do not have to sail over to the neighboring islands, carrying their money with them. (Pp. 26-27.)

4.4.2.3 *"A separate German province to avoid all oppression"*

Land is the foundation, and regular labour is the great raiser of riches to a nation. Beller . . . To increase our manufactures and not our corn, puts more people to table, but no sufficient food upon it. Idem, p. 2 . . . The Delphic oracle declared Aglaus [the poorest Arcadian] the happiest of men, because he was busied in nothing but manuring and cultivating a little farm, never molesting himself with vain cares or passions, nor increasing the miseries of human life by tampering with foreign and unnecessary pleasures, which though full of blandishments, and sweet in the front, yet carry a sting in their tail, embittering all our joys. Mamut, vol. 8, p. 171.

-- "Husbandry"

I'll get me home. Hankering after home. Home bred . . . To settle. A settlement. They seated themselves [i.e., settled] about Germantown . . . Dry bread at home is better than roast meat abroad . . . Kings delight to dwell in goodly pleasant places. Ainsworth, ad. Cant. 6:4 . . . Dwell not where superfluous expenses surmount the revenues, nor where ill men are made more of than good ones, nor where the rulers for the most part are liars, sayeth Plato.

-- "Home"

Unlike the Philadelphia Quaker grandees who established a trade empire during his lifetime, Pastorius concentrated on modest satisfactions for the individual rather than the intricacies of commerce, and it was this goal that motivated his efforts to establish a colony for Germans within Pennsylvania. In *Sichere Nachricht* (pp. 5-6) he describes the shrewd bargaining of 1683-84 that, along with his warm friendship for William Penn, enabled him to win a number of important concessions for the German Company, in part because its members were "the forerunners of all the Germans" – ideal locations for warehouses and merchant dwellings in Philadelphia, one huge tract of land instead of various smaller plots, the separate town of Germantown to be settled jointly by the thirteen families from Krefeld and the Frankfurt Pietists then making plans for emigration, and the possibility of territorial expansion. The reason for these efforts was, Pastorius reports in Chapter Eight of *Beschreibung Pennsylvaniae*, "so that we Germans may receive a separate little province, and be more assured of our ability to avoid all oppression." Penn was agreeable, he explains: "Just the day before yesterday the Governor told me that he was very pleased by the diligence of the Germans as colonists, and that he preferred them to the English, and was willing to extend certain privileges [i.e., of limited self-government] to them."

Although Germantown became a way station for Germans settling farther west, Pastorius never established an independent colony on the territory of the German Company, in part because the well-to-do leaders of the Saalhof Pietists in Frankfurt were able to enjoy increased religious tolerance without emigrating to Pennsylvania. Apparently because the government did not wish to lose revenues generated by the Pietist community, Frankfurt officials took a more liberal attitude toward a few radical Pietists after the emigration plans were devised than they had before, and Pietists "entirely resolved" to emigrate in 1683 ("Genealogia Pastoriana") soon decided they could live according to their principles without giving up the comforts of home – the first indication that the "Pella or place of refuge" established by Franz Daniel Pastorius was creating new possibilities in Germany as well as in America. [56]

Nevertheless, Pastorius' claim that the German Company was more concerned with helping Germans leave Europe than with making a profit may reflect a personal bias rather than the aims of the stockholders. Pastorius, wholly absorbed in colonizing, serving in government and numerous other tasks and pleasures including farming and gardening, repeatedly asked the German Company to relieve him of his business duties once its members had decided not to emigrate. In the long run the company did not flourish under his supervision, although this might have reflected German rather than American disinterest, and it appointed new Pennsylvania agents in 1700, following reorganization in Germany. [57]

Pastorius briefly lived in Philadelphia – in 1683-84 and while teaching school there in 1698-99 – and had many friends in the city, but *Beschreibung Pennsylvaniae* indicates that his colonial hopes and daily life centered upon the village of Germantown, the potential city of "Germanopolis" that would have become the center of a thriving German territory if immigration had swelled immediately as Pastorius anticipated instead of several decades later. With this future city in mind, Pastorius described its modest yet auspicious beginnings – and his own role as founder and first citizen – in Chapter Eight, "Of the Incipient Cities in This Province":

> On October 24, 1683, I Franciscus Daniel Pastorius, with the consent of our Governor, laid out another new town, named Germantown or Germanopolis, two hours by footpath from Philadelphia in an area that has a good topsoil, black and fertile, many fresh and healthy springs, and lots of oak, walnut and chestnut trees as well as good pasture for the cattle. In the beginning there were only twelve families with forty-one individuals, most of them German craftsmen and weavers, since I realized that one would not be able to do without linen.
>
> I made the main street of this town sixty feet wide and the intersecting streets forty feet, and the *spatium* or plot of ground for every house and garden is a full three acres, although the plot for my residence is twice as large.

Pastorius thus highlights the town's invigorating natural surroundings, supporting a mixed economy of agriculture and small trades, with wide streets to facilitate commerce and large gardens to give Germantown craftsmen greater self-sufficiency. Describing his own double-sized lot, and reporting in 1684 that he was profitably farming "a good portion" of the 600 acres of land he then owned (p. 40), Pastorius reveals some of the privileges he enjoyed in the 1680s – and reflects class attitudes modified by Pennsylvania experience over the years. [58] His own awareness of the need for linen, furthermore, misrepresents the historical facts: The Krefelders had arranged their land purchase and immigration through Penn and his agents, not through Pastorius.

He reports a declining rate of growth following early expansion in Germantown. In his 1688 letter to Georg Leonhart Model, he describes early growth and accomplishment in a terrain of forest and partially-overgrown clearings, the latter indicating previous civilization by the Delaware Indians:

> Although we began with just thirteen households in 1683, the number has grown to fifty within a scant five years. Houses, stables and barns are now standing where a dense, wild forest then prevailed. Fields, orchards and gardens have been created from a wilderness of briars and undergrowth.

In a 1691 letter (pp. 50-51) he writes that William Penn had issued a town charter and appointed him the town's first mayor and justice of the peace. (He was later elected to the office of bailiff.) He adds that the official seal of the town council – a trifolium with a grape vine, flax plant and weaver's spool and the motto "Vinum, Linum & Textrinum" – symbolized Germantown's wine and flax production and the weaving and other trades then in operation or being established, although he bitterly notes, in 1716, that Germantown's soil had proved unsuitable for viniculture. [59] Even though Germantown had welcomed fewer immigrants than expected recently, he reports in 1692 (*Monatlichen Unterredungen*, Feb. 1693), immigration and propagation together would nevertheless enable the community to establish one or more subsidiary villages soon, "for just as hardly anyone has died, our children have been growing like olive trees on the banks of a stream." He describes the town's government, rural economy and modest growth in a 1698 letter:

> This town has its own court, its own mayor and town council, including the needed government officials, and well-established town laws, council rules and town seal. The inhabitants of this town are predominantly craftsmen such as textile, fustian and linen weavers, tailors, cobblers, mechanics and carpenters, all of whom, nevertheless, are also involved in farming and raising cattle. The locality could sustain twice as many inhabitants as are actually living here at the present time. (P. 83.)

4.4.2.4 "Neither battle cries nor the sound of drums or muskets": Communal and Personal Contentments

> Here in my Garden I enjoy
> What Want can't pinch, Fullness cloy.
> . . .
> God forbid! that I may not
> An over huge Plantation pog;
> For, the largest Tract or Spot
> Would but be uneasiest Clog.
> We spring, we bud, we blossom and we blast,
> Before we Count our days; they flee so fast.
>
> -- Poem 320, reflecting on Quarles' emblems

> I never had more land,   Than when I had the least:
> Enough, and that at hand   Does make a Stately Feast.
> Of these two lines the first Is best, because I dream'd it;
> The next (a Proverb) worst,   By reason that I maim'd it.

> Let Kings and Princes keep the Wide World's Ball,
> I would not change my Garden with them all.
>
> -- Poem 298 (entire)

Despite the disappointment of Germantown's slow development, Pastorius never tired of expressing the modest satisfactions of civilized life close to nature on the Pennsylvania frontier. Even though a Philadelphia prison was being built "so that those who are not willing to live in a Philadelphian manner [i.e., in brotherly love] may be disciplined," he writes in his *Sichere Nachricht* of 1684 (pp. 3-4), "there is no shortage of pious, God-fearing people either, and I can affirm in all truth that in Europe I never saw anything to compare with the [lost and found] notices that are posted in our Philadelphia" indicating the basic honesty of the great majority. "We have been living in peace and security for a long time now," he reports from Germantown eight years later (*Monatlichen Unterredungen*, Feb. 1693), "so much so that I have never yet locked my front door for the night." He writes (1692 and 1693) that some of those who "claim to know the closest and straightest way to heaven" were creating religious strife in the colony (a complaint repeated in 1697) and that "our Indians from this province" had advanced toward Canada to defend against attack by Indians allied with the French, yet these disturbances only emphasized the abiding sense of peace in Pennsylvania life:

> Throughout the ten years I have been here, God in His fundamental benevolence has so graciously sheltered this province under the wings of His mercy that neither hostile battle cries nor the sound of drums or muskets has ever disturbed our daily labor or nocturnal rest. We did not even have to pay a single cent for military or other *contributionen* [special taxes] during these many years, until about five weeks ago... [when] we consented to restituting the travel expenses [of New York's Governor Benjamin Fletcher, temporarily overseeing Pennsylvania government]. (1693, pp. 54-55.)

Civil peace and material satisfaction reflected the modest goals of Pennsylvania existence and "God's generosity and providence" in "richly" meeting "all our needs," Pastorius notes (1695, p. 69). A 1691 passage (p. 52) provides a moral and religious context: "To the extent that we live peacefully and contentedly, without a desire for ephemeral wealth, and have only food and apparel in this pilgrimage of ours, we are all the more able to keep our eyes directed ahead toward the heavenly Jerusalem, our true native land." He knew that not all Pennsylvanians enjoyed contentedness of this sort, which accounts for the hypothetical form of his statement. Or perhaps he was referring to desires of his own, more or less related to the inability to resolve worldly and spiritual aims he had confessed to Johann Jakob Schütz in 1685. By 1694, though, he was able to report a resolution of such feelings:

> My dear family and I continue to enjoy the health and happiness I reported in my last letter, in a quiet and peaceful manner among ourselves, and although I am still fully occupied with the supervision of the justice system in Germantown as well as in Philadelphia, such external functions do not by any means keep me from the inner feelings of a gentle and humble private life in Christ Jesus, so much so that even in the midst of these tasks I can truly say: *revertere anima mea in requiem tuam* [my soul reverts to Your peace (or relaxation or recreation)]. (Pp. 64-65.)

The genuinely pious tone of this and other letters to his father emphasizes the spiritual aspect of what Pastorius increasingly perceived as a unity of world and spirit. The decade preceding this letter had of course been an active one for Pastorius. He had married and twice become a father, managed the affairs of the German Company and Germantown, worked at farming and gardening, served as legislator and judge, and pursued countless other scholarly and practical tasks involving religious as well as secular or scientific interests. Thus his perceived ability to combine religious feeling and worldly activity indicates a basic change of attitude during the decade, a release from the compelling sense that all meditation excluded the outer world, a mature acceptance of worldly endeavor as integral to his Christian calling. A decade of Pennsylvania acculturation, this letter suggests, significantly reduced the tensions of world and spirit Pastorius had known during his final years in absolutist Europe.

4.4.3 The Native American: Personifying New World Potential

> An Indian of Pennsylvania in his Match-Coat: *Modicum Natura requiret.*
> [Nature (or the world) requires (or seeks) moderation.]
>
> -- "Emblematical Recreations"
>
> Contentment is a spring whose pleasant streams still hold
> In summer's scorching heat and winter's freezing cold.
>
> -- Epigram 52

As described in *Beschreibung Pennsylvaniae*, the material and spiritual satisfactions of the province went hand in hand, illustrating Pastorius' conviction that society, with an enlightened government and sufficient economic opportunity, could move beyond the imperfections of European institutions and approach a realization of the humane ideals embodied in the most fundamental teachings of Christianity. His reports on the Delaware or Lenni Lenape underscore this conviction. Anthropological detail broadened one's horizons, revealing that human behavior is not limited to one's own conventions. Pastorius became convinced that Native American life reflected a natural integrity and dignity that had been lost – or was being ignored – in Europe's complex society, and he could hope that his transatlantic message would infuse outworn modes of thought with a new innocence and sensitivity.

In these reports, he asserts a universalist conviction that Native Americans (and all mankind) are imbued with divinity and, one poem indicates, he even allowed Delaware theology to moderate his Christian ideology (just as he elsewhere opposes missionary ethnocentrism). In short, his reports suggest, contact with America was opening up new possibilities for Western civilization, and might even help to give the human spirit a much-needed rejuvenation.

4.4.3.1 European Encroachment upon the Delaware Tribes

> Quakers are both Pilgrims and Usufructuaries in this World . . .
> God of this World Proprietary is;
> It's Use and Profit have those Friends of His,
> Who once this Foot-stool shall as Sons Inherit
> By a free Legacy, and not by Merit.
>
> -- Poem 476
>
> Let Heroic Poets Tote of War and warlike Men,
> My Reed (shrill Oaten-Straw!) does welcome William Penn,
> A man of Love and Peace, abominating Strife . . .

> [During Penn's first stay (1682-84) in Philadelphia,
> then a frontier settlement,]
> There in thy Company I with my soul's delight
> At Intervals might sit till mid-time of the night.
> [By the time of Penn's second stay (1699-1701)]
> ... the country [was] full of Folks,
> The City stately built, some houses 's tall as Oaks,
> The Markets stall'd with Beef, whereof we nothing Knew,
> When (as aforesaid) Huts and Wig-wams were so few.
>
>   -- Poem 372,   to Wm. Penn [upon his planned third visit,
>   cancelled after the poem was written]

Pastorius praises the European transformation of Pennsylvania – and (in Poem 476, above) might imply theological justification of it as well – even though he seems to have realized the European presence was itself the most formidable challenge to Native American culture. [60] William Penn's Indian policies were enlightened and fair – indeed the most liberal anywhere in seventeenth-century America – yet from the beginning they were subject to compromise, and Pastorius noted violations that fit the shameful pattern of Native American abuse repeatedly demonstrated in colonial history. He also knew that, in the context of the Western technological superiority he praised in the discoveries of a Vespucci or Columbus but condemned when it took the form of militaristic destructiveness, the spiritual strengths of Indian culture involved strategic weaknesses when cultural interaction degenerated into confrontation.

This awareness accounts for some defensiveness in his description of European encroachments upon the Delaware, especially in these two respects: 1) Although he admitted the societal complexity of the Delaware, he also depicted them as nomads inhabiting seemingly endless forests. In fact, a mixed economy (hunting, fishing and farming or gardening) and the practice of relocating their villages as the land was depleted (estimated at 14 years on the average) made them semi nomadic. 2) Despite Penn's sincerity in dealing with the Native Americans, Pastorius exaggerated the element of cool calculation in the Delaware negotiations. His motivation here involved one or more of these considerations: this approach would best convince his German readers (especially the potential emigrants hesitant to confront American "barbarism"); Penn's desire to live in Pennsylvania with the "Love and Consent" of the Indians, treating them as "Neighbours and friends," would be misinterpreted as weakness or ridiculed by ethnocentric Europeans; or that even Penn's reasonable dealings benefitted from a history of superior colonial force which made the Delaware compliant, an interpretation that would have weighed upon his conscience.

Pastorius presents the Indians as nomads in preliminary descriptions, adding complexity in the subsequent incremental expansions of *Beschreibung Pennsylvaniae*. The English did not name Pennsylvania before Penn was granted the territory, he reports in Chapter One,

> because the natural inhabitants of the land all roam around naked in the forests and did not have any civil assemblies or established cities after which it could have been named, but instead lived (as they still do) hither and yon in the wilderness in little huts made from the trees.

Chapter Two describes Penn's first treaty negotiations (which in fact yielded the Delaware a generous assortment of fishing, hunting, cooking, sewing and other equipment in addition to blankets, clothing and hats):

It should be noted that William Penn did not use any military force to drive out the inhabitants of the land who go naked in their natural state, but instead, upon his arrival, brought with him special clothing and hats for the Indian leaders, thus *benevolentiam capit* [convincing (or charming) with benevolence], and purchased a twenty-mile stretch of land from them, whereupon they withdrew this distance farther back into the untamed forests. (P. 14.)

Although Penn already had English charter rights to all of Pennsylvania, Pastorius clarifies in Chapter Twelve, "this intelligent and God-fearing sovereign . . . did not want to go ahead and take this inheritance without paying anything for it," so he repeatedly "conferred gifts and placated" the Delaware, and thus "bought up one tract of land after the other, with the result that they retreated farther and farther into the wilderness." Save for fur trading, the colonists in Philadelphia and Germantown no longer had any regular contact with the Delaware tribes, Pastorius writes in 1699, since the Indians had moved "very far away from us into the untamed forests, where they live according to their traditional manner of hunting, shooting game and fowl as well as catching fish" (p. 85). His Poem 353 nevertheless indicates that at least a small group of partially acculturated Delaware still lived near Germantown as late as 1714.

Some of the Indians seem eager to move west, he reported shortly after immigrating (*Sichere Nachricht*, p. 8), "since they are superstitious enough to believe that just as many Indians will have to die each year as there are Europeans arriving here." He later realized the "superstition" was a realistic fear based on the heavy loss of life, predominantly through contagious disease, that was decimating numerous Atlantic coastal tribes. In 1694 he estimated that nearly three-quarters of the Pennsylvania Indians had died during his first decade in the colony (p. 66). Though obviously subjective, the estimate reveals his awareness of catastrophic suffering and loss even during a period of peaceful coexistence.

Despite his defense of encroachments upon Delaware territory, Pastorius repeatedly asserts the priority of Native American culture in *Beschreibung Pennsylvaniae*. He gives the Native Americans first place when he describes Pennsylvania's inhabitants, religions and forms of government, and includes them whenever he describes the economy of the province. He considered European morality inferior to that of the Native American, and European corruption of Indian virtue is a reiterated theme of his reports. His description of the Indians in Chapter Eleven, "Of the Inhabitants of This Province," is twice as long as the combined descriptions of the European immigrants who first explored and settled the region – Dutch, Swedes, and English – and of the English who came after Penn acquired the colony. Even after most of the Delaware had left the Germantown area, Native American culture remains a dominant theme in Pastorius' letters. His most comprehensive reports – the letter to Georg Leonhart Model in 1688 and Chapter Eleven of *Beschreibung Pennsylvaniae* – reveal his concern for anthropological detail just as numerous other references underscore the lessons to be learned from a culture whose complexity amid nature did not defy the sense of divinity that, Pastorius felt, should prevail in all cultures.

4.4.3.2 "Frank in spirit, unassuming": Anthropological Reporting

> Common goods are oftenest lost. Coupled sheep drown (one another) . . . Unless the vessel be preserved, our cabins cannot . . . Among friends all things are common . . . A wise man judges nothing so much his own, as that wherein mankind is allowed a share. Seneca, p. 598 . . . Let us ever forget the words mine and thine. Mamut . . . If all lay in common. Temple . . . The Indians are very charitable to each other; for if any has to spare, he freely imparts it to his friends, and whatever they get by gaming [i.e., hunting game] they share, leaving commonly the least part to themselves. Emp. in Am., p. 80.
>
> -- "Common Goods"

The 1688 text, written for Nürnberg University's Johann Christoph Wagenseil and others intrigued by the varieties of culture, describes the physical appearance, dress and housing of the Delaware as well as their language, economy, government, religion and methods of child-rearing. The Indians "are tall and usually muscular in physique," their unbearded faces painted, and rubbed with bear's grease; they are scantily clad in summer, and in winter wear moccasins of thin deerskin and "rectangular cloths of coarse, thick material that has never seen either shears or the needle of a tailor." They live in simple dwellings made from tree trunks and brushwood, Pastorius reports, "and none of them is so unskilled that he cannot construct a house for himself and his family within three or four hours." The Indians are "frank in spirit, their speech unassuming and brief, simple but at the same time dignified."

Although he does not mention any grammatical principles, Pastorius presents a fictional dialogue in the Delaware language – Pastorius, an Indian brave and Model, "visiting" from Germany, converse in the forest just beyond Germantown – illustrating 42 basic words and phrases, including "apple"/"acothita", "bread"/ "agboon", "fish"/"lamess", "cow"/"muss", "pig"/"kuschkusch", "mother"/"ana", "woman"/"squaa", "Welcome, friend"/"Eitha nithap", "What's your name?"/"Gecho ki hatti?", "I am very hungry"/"Husko lallacuta" and "Look at the tree"/"Hittuck nipa." During the 1690s Pastorius still reported (pp. 29, 39) that he was only gradually learning the language. This beginner's dialogue seems to have been his only lesson in or description of the Delaware language.

Pastorius briefly describes Native American government with comments on criminal punishment, the rules of succession for tribal chiefs, and democratic assemblies. He suggests contrasting concepts of royalty (and government) by juxtaposing "rex" (a king) and "regulus" (a prince, petty king or chieftain) in this comment: "Their kings (or rather chiefs) summon the entire populace to deliberate important matters of government." Although he later noted the benevolent effects of mild punishment, the tone of his remarks here suggests he was only gradually absorbing this lesson:

> No crime, not even murder, is so serious that it cannot be expiated with money. If someone kills a person's wife, however, he has to pay twice as much since she might have still been able to have children, which is not possible for men. A crime committed while drunk is forgiven as the result of intoxication. As long as wine has contributed to the deed, not even the purse has to make amends.

"The female sex," Pastorius reports, is "capricious, talkative, haughty and deceitful" as well as alluring:

> Their [long, black] hair is gathered together in a single knot, their breasts are turgid, their skin swarthy, &c. Yet of her own accord (or: alone, on her own), her dark and inelegant charm is lovely. They burden, and adorn, neck, arms and ears with heavy coins [i.e., wampum].

This description might well reflect at least one romantic encounter frustrated by barriers of language and culture (including differing attitudes on female modesty). He also notes that the women are used to bearing heavy loads and are solely responsible for the difficult tasks of tilling the soil and raising the crops of beans and Indian corn, whereas the males hunt and fish, and are "opposed to all labor."

Although his lively description of child-rearing implies the influence of fathers, it follows his comments on female diligence:

> They [the women] love their children passionately. Following birth they bind the bodies of the babies, still tender and tiny, on smooth wooden slats without first wrapping them in linen cloth. The little creatures are not acquainted with any cradle; when they cry they are calmed down again by being rocked gently back and forth on the backs of their mothers. Later on the tender little ones, who are taught true endurance, are immersed into a flowing river by their stern bathers. Thus initiated through this austere training, the young boys occupy themselves with learning how to fish, and they get little to eat if they neglectfully let their fish-hooks dangle in the water. After having practiced hunting in the forests as they mature, they have to bring home a goodly supply of pelts for several years. If it happens that a youth wants to marry before he has become a good hunter, this is considered a disgrace, and even an offence of the greatest impudence. Marriageable girls indicate their desire to be wed by covering their face with a cloth. Frequently the bride is just thirteen years old and the groom only seventeen when the wedding takes place.

Pastorius is equally detailed – and, for his day, unusually open-minded – in his descriptions of religious belief and custom, which include the practices of burial and mourning, and ceremonial sacrifices and dances that were at once strange and captivating:

> The Indians believe in God and the immortality of the soul. They believe that God dwells in a most glorious land to the south, and that it is the destiny of the soul to enter this land, where it may return to life once more. Their religious observances are celebrated in two ways, through song, as they call it, and through sacrifice. When they kill the first victims of the hunt, which are designated as sacrificial animals, they do so with such agitated bodily motion, burning with passion, that they are fully covered with perspiration. Their singing involves a religious dance in a circle, in the center of which two singers dance animatedly and bellow a doleful song. The chorus sings with loud wailings, a sadness intermixed with tears, murmuring at one time and gnashing their teeth at another, now snapping their fingers, now clapping with their feet, &c., and they all partake in this scene of physical activity and drama with such passion and seriousness that the observer, of one mind with their discord, is moved to sympathy.

4.4.3.3 Bicultural Object Lessons and Cross-Cultural Interaction: Indian Virtue, Universalism, Anti-Chauvinism

> Enough is as good as a feast.
>
> -- "Contentment"
>
> When that old Serpent which lives but on Dust
> Would fill thy Soul with Cares and with Mistrust
> In God's good Providence; Then, then thou must
> Look on these Roses and this Lilly-Bed,
> How finely they're array'd in White and Red;
> And on the Ravens black, yet richly fed:
> Much more on th' Word, which speaks of Daily Bread,
> And bids us not to Sorrow
> For the Day or Morrow.   Phil. 4:6
> Gotts große Gütigkeit,
> Die Gras und Blumen kleidt,   Matt. 6:30
> Und alle Tiere speist,   Ps. 145:15
> Dir solches auch Verheißt.   Ps. 37:23
> [God's great goodness clothes the grass and flowers,
> and feeds every creature; it promises as much to you as well.]
>
> -- Poem 244
>
> Virtue can hardly mount when clogged by
> The pressing weight of servile poverty.
>
> -- Epigram 2334.5

Chapter Eleven of *Beschreibung Pennsylvaniae* presents similar details of life in an exotic culture, and, far more than in the earlier report, interprets Indian life in the context of European culture, foreshadowing the cross-cultural message that predominates in his subsequent letters from Pennsylvania. Describing Delaware dwellings, for example, Pastorius reports the technical details of construction more carefully than in 1688, and at the same time uses physical detail to convey some of the humane values that served as an object lesson for his German readers:

> Their shelters are made from many young trees woven or bent together, which are then expertly covered with tree bark. They use neither table nor chairs nor any other household belongings aside from one single pot, in which they cook their meals. I once watched four of them heartily enjoying a meal with one another, eating squash that had been cooked in plain water without spices or butter. The dear earth was their table and bench, sea-shells were the spoons they used to ladle the warm water as a soup, the leaves from the nearest tree were their plates, and they did not have to go to the trouble of washing them up after the meal or carefully store them away for future use. It occurred to me that these uncivilized people have never in their lives heard the teachings of Jesus about moderation and contentedness, yet they go far beyond the Christians [in following his advice to "take no thought for the morrow" (Matt. 6, 34)] (P. 28.) [61]

In this report Pastorius gives more space to describing Indian virtues, and begins pointing up cultural contrasts from a Native American point of view:

> They take great pains to be honest and sincere, keep their word without fail, and do not cheat or insult anyone; they gladly entertain their guests, and are obliging and devoted to them ... They are usually serious, expressing themselves with few words, and they are amazed to observe such an excess of idle talk and gossip as well as other frivolous conduct among the Christians. (Pp. 28-29.)

In a few instances, he compresses reported details to the bare minimum and supplements these with bicultural interpretation. Thus his brief description of the Indian economy culminates with a didactic message:

> As far as their economy and domestic habits are concerned, the men tend to the hunting and fishing. The women diligently supervise their children, faithfully rearing and admonishing them against bad behavior. They grow Indian corn and beans around their huts but do not concern themselves with extensive farming and cattle-raising, but rather are astonished to note that we Christians are so extremely concerned and preoccupied with our efforts to obtain food and drink as well as satisfying clothing and dwellings, as if we doubted that God could nourish and provide for us. (P. 30.)

Pastorius' description of Pennsylvania "fertility" (Chapter Nine) includes a few details indicating that Indian moderation did not preclude esthetic or economic complexity. The Delaware have "their national currency" consisting of two types of coral beads "cut and polished" from seashells, each type with its own monetary value. "They know how to interweave this coral money very artistically, and wear it like golden necklaces. Their king wears a crown or headdress made from it," Pastorius reports (p. 25). They paint their faces, smoke tobacco, and, for amusement, stroll or march while playing a flute or Jew's harp, he notes in Chapter Eleven.

Chapter Eleven progresses from comparative culture to cultural interaction, commenting on missionary work and colonial trade. Pastorius describes the "previously established Christians" – Swedish, Dutch and English colonists and traders who inhabited the territory before 1681 – from a perspective that includes Native American views:

> They never had the honest intention of instructing these indigenous needy creatures in a living and genuine Christianity but solely pursued their personal worldly interests instead, defrauding the innocent inhabitants in their business transactions and general conduct, with the end result that those Indians who had dealings with them have also turned out to be cunning, deceitful and fraudulent, so that I cannot report anything very praiseworthy about either of these two groups. These corrupted individuals frequently trade the furs and pelts they have attained for hard liquor and get so drunk that they are no longer able to walk or stand up, and they also use almost every available opportunity to commit theft. Thus it is that their kings and superiors have frequently complained about the vices of dishonesty, fraud, theft and drunkenness that were introduced by the Christians, and have stated that these vices were totally unheard of in this land before. (P. 31.)

We Europeans arriving since 1681, he writes here (p. 32), are affiliated with "respectable societies and companies" and have "the intention . . . not only of acquiring temporal gain and sustenance but also of taming the savage people and informing them in the true realization of God." He later admits that the Indians were receiving "gunpowder, lead, woolen blankets and brandy" for their furs, pelts, fish and game even though "selling them brandy as well as all strong drink is forbidden by our laws" (1694, p. 66). "The Indians eat and drink in moderation," he states, and in those instances when an Indian gets drunk "it is usually the nominal Christians who are at fault, since they sell the Indians liquor for the sake of their damnable personal gain" (1693, p. 58). Pastorius here identifies and criticizes colonial practices that had been established before the founding of Pennsylvania, and would continue to complicate American civilization as the frontier advanced.

Complementing his sympathy for Delaware religious ceremonies, Pastorius, in Chapter Eleven, reports on missionary endeavor from a universalist perspective:

> They [the Delaware] gladly listen, and not without visible signs of emotion, to our descriptions of the Creator of heaven and earth and of His divine Light, which illumines all people who have entered this world and will enter it in the future, and of God's wisdom and love, which moved Him to sacrifice for us His only-begotten Son whom He loved above all else... In our religious assemblies they are very peaceful and meditative, so that I fully believe they will appear with those [virtuous heathens] of Tyre and Sidon on that great Day of Judgement to come, and put to shame many thousands of untrue Christians who merely profess or bear the name of Christ. (Pp. 29-30.)

The wording here is unambiguous: "His divine Light ... illumines all people." Pastorius subtly proclaims his universalist beliefs even as he informs his German readers about the Delaware tribes. For Pastorius divine light is anthropological as well as religious, the rationale that explains or demands humane conduct towards all. Although his reports imply that he became less concerned with converting a virtuous people already divinely illumined, Pastorius here argues that he lacked the ability rather than the will to convert:

> It is of course regrettable that we do not yet properly understand their language, and thus cannot convey to them the real thoughts and intentions of our hearts concerning the nature of the strength and salvation that may be found in Christ Jesus. (P. 29.)

Despite his designation of the Native Americans as "needy creatures," a justification of efforts to convert or acculturate them, Pastorius generally recognized a deep-seated "neediness" in Western culture that could be "instructed" by cultures usually considered less advanced. In the 1710s, for example, he read *Propagation of the Gospel in the East* (Parts 1 and 2, 1709-10), epistolary reports primarily by Bartholomaeus Ziegenbalg (1682-1719), a Lutheran Pietist, on efforts to convert the Malabar heathens (actually Tamil Hindus on India's Coromandel Coast). [62] Ziegenbalg studied their religion "to lay open ... [its] folly and falsity" (p. 37) and thus "to rescue ... many souls" (p. 39). Their theology, he states, is "ridiculous," "useless trash," "sottishness" (pp. 24-25, 33), and they are "these poor deluded souls," "such a multitude of wild pagans," "benighted Infidels" (pp. 31, 55; pt. 2, 48). He asserts (p. 58) that God "earnestly ... endeavoureth their conversion, having no pleasure to see them perish in their wild Unbelief and Stupidity." Yet he carefully reported countless theological details.

Pastorius ignored Ziegenbalg's bias as he eagerly absorbed the theological details – the heathens' creation stories, the belief in transmigration of souls, their concept of heaven, their emphasis on moral integrity, etc. – but then he sharply criticized the missionaries' ethnocentrism. In Poem 363, he resorts to the scathing biblical language of Christ in Matthew 23 – "Woe to you, scribes and Pharisees, hypocrites!" – as he denounces the church "hirelings" who "to proselyte poor Souls compass both Sea and land" yet "bring none thereof from Darkness into Light." Because the missionaries were less humane than the local populace, they only managed

> To teach the [Malabar] Youth to talk of Sacramental bread,
> And with European whims to fill their heart and head,
> When they, if left alone, a holier life would lead.

Proper cultural interaction, on the other hand, a true give and take, could help to generate "a holier life" among insensitive Europeans. Adding a biblical notation to Poem 353, Pastorius quietly indicated some of the sensitivity he acquired from the Delaware Indians. The poem reflects upon the death of a man Pastorius had known as a legal client, a poor Germantown neighbor whose struggle for survival had blinded him to Christian love and obedience:

> Long-bearded Thomas Tress
> Himself did dispossess
> Of all his Bills and Bonds,
> And therefore, at his Death,
> Had nothing to bequeath,
> But some ill-gotten lands,
> Besides a silly Soul,
> Most vitious and foule,
> I know not to whose hands:
> The Indians now do talk
> Of hunch-back'd Tress to walk
> On Manatana's strands.
> He was buried the 17th day of the 3d month 1714. Luke 16:22.

Pastorius here presents gently humorous incongruities in lively meter and rhyme, building to a sharp judgement based on traditional views of good and evil. He does not hesitate to describe the viciousness of Thomas Tress' soul, but he is too humane to express explicitly the thoughts of damnation implied in his reference to the hands of God or Satan. This humanity then leads him to reflect upon Delaware attitudes about Tress reported in conversation or heard directly, an antithesis to sharp judgement, and to incorporate Native American theology and Christian charity into his own revised attitudes, reflected in the reference to Luke 16, 22, from Christ's story of Lazarus and Dives: "The poor man died and was carried by the angels to Abraham's bosom." The souls of the dead journey to "the highest heaven," the pantheistic Delaware believed, or to the home of the Great Manito (or Great Spirit), a variation of which is "Manatana's strands" ("Strand" is German for beach). [63] Prompted by his Delaware neighbors, Pastorius senses the futility of speculating on the reward or punishment awaiting his neighbor Thomas Tress, who, maimed and dispossessed in a material world, might well be pardoned for the blemishes of his soul.

Interacting culturally, Pastorius developed a liberality of spirit capable of accepting the humane values of "primitive" cultures, and (as his Epigram 2334.5 on page 236 indicates) the deficiencies of individuals who lacked his cultural advantages. His faith was, of course, quintessentially Christian, but unusually ecumenical and even universalist, including rather than excluding, open to radical mysticism and to the philosophical speculation of pragmatic and scientific ideas. Pastorius may have indicated this liberality most clearly by describing all humanity, regardless of religious persuasion, as illumined by one divine spirit or "light", a point of view he developed through his affinity for theologians and mystics like Johanna Eleonora and Johann Wilhelm Petersen, the Cambridge Platonists, Jane Ward Lead, the Quaker Robert Barclay, and George Keith, who became an Anglican after the Quakers disowned him for leading a Pennsylvania religious schism in 1692. [64]

This liberality even marked his approach to religious strife among the Pennsylvania Quakers. Serving as a Philadelphia judge during the Keithian controversy of 1692, he "admonish[ed] all parties to gentleness and unity" – with a judicial decree in rhymed verse inviting all to "richly dine / With Christ, as at a feast" – rather than consent to a request by one religious faction to impose restraints upon the other (Poem 38, quoted on page 142 of this study). At the same time, though, his intercourse with elite Quakers contains occasional traces of European cultural bias that, presumably, was a part of Pennsylvania society as well. [65]

4.4.3.4   "My unsavage savages": A Common Bond with the Delaware

> Heathen philosophers' divine knowledge. Barclay, p. 361 . . . Of gentiles doing by nature, the things contained in the law [of God]. Pennington, pt. 2, p. 307 . . . If we divide the world into 30 parts, Christianity is but as 5 in 30, Mohammedanism as 6, and ethnicism as 19. Meade, p. 83. To send all the gentiles to hell, who have not heard Christ preached unto them as crucified, &c though they framed their lives according to the Light in them, is a horrible reflection upon both the justice and mercy of God, &c. Keith, Refut., p. 36.
>
> -- "Heathenism"
>
> The Light shineth forth universally, enlightening every man . . . God has allotted unto all mankind an inheritance of eternal life, and written their names in the Book of Life, which appears by the frequent mentioning of blotting them out for sinning against God and man, vid. Exod. 32:33. So they must be first written. Hepburn, p. 21.
>
> -- "Universal Grace"

Pastorius reiterates and supplements his basic views on the Native Americans in the letters and reports appended to *Beschreibung Pennsylvaniae*. The extracts from *Sichere Nachricht* include a narrative of a dying chief's words to his successor indicating the chief's observance of traditional forms of respect and politeness in tribal council, his fairness toward tribesmen as well as Europeans, and his "love for that which is good" (pp. 43-44). Satisfying a request from his young half brother Augustin Adam for information about the court life of the Indians, Pastorius ironically confesses:

> Their royal palaces are so poorly constituted that I can barely describe them. The palace is merely a single room or chamber in a tree hut covered with tree bark, without any chimney, stairs or "Secret" [place of privacy]. These kings go along on the hunt themselves, shoot wild animals, and live from the work of their own hands. They have neither servants nor virgins of state, and what purpose could a stable master serve for someone who does not own a horse but instead walks at all times? There is also no need for a court steward since the king provides for no one other than himself and his wife and children; they live according to nature pure and simple, *quae paucis contenta est* [which is content with little]. (1694, p. 65.)

"I can report but little about the natural inhabitants of this country for the satisfaction of those who give more attention to external professions of faith than to a genuine practice of Christ's commandments," Pastorius notes, since the Indians "live much more contentedly and much less concerned about the needs of the morrow than we Christians do" (1693, pp. 57-58). It was this basic approach to life that enabled them to exist without destructive warfare or violent criminality, he reports here, comparing the pagans of North America with those of ancient Rome and Greece by referring to a Pietist sermon he had read in Pennsylvania:

In the ten years of my existence here I have never yet heard of any case in which they have attempted to use force toward anyone, let alone committed murder, and this in spite of the fact that they would have opportunity enough not only to commit such a crime but also to go into hiding in the dense and vast forests [and thus escape unpunished]; so that when I consider the heinous evil committed among the professing Christians of Europe and, as a direct reproach to this, the guileless simplicity of these, my present West [i.e., American] Indian countrymen, I always think of the sermon on "Christianity Put to Shame with a Reflection on the Heathens" preached among you by Johann Augustin Li[e]tzheimer, which states there on page 45: "Nominal Christians insolently crucify the Son of God and consume their Saviour when, ignoring the Word of God, they esteem the money and possessions of this world or the welfare of this fleeting life above God and His eternal salvation, but in contrast to this the pagan Seneca beneficially advised: 'The more I become devoted and attached to someone like the courtly attendant or hanger-on, the more unwilling I am to do that which God desires. What I long for is what I try to attain. I never reject that in nature which of itself will be comprehended...'..."

In closing let me add on behalf of my unsavage savages that they have completely renounced war and the shedding of human blood, in contrast to which almost all of Christianity have taken up arms and, with the dreadful barbarities of offensive and defensive fighting, are harming each other as much as the most despicable monsters do mangling and tearing each other to pieces. [Here Pastorius quotes six lines of German verse (also used in Poem 38, his 1692 plea for a resolution of religious strife) noting that, unlike the Christians, wolves, tigers, lions and leopards naturally avoid attacking others of their kind.] (Pp. 58-60.)

Intuitively associating Lietzheimer's Windsheim sermon with his deep sympathies for the Delaware Indians, Pastorius indicates a few cross-cultural insights he did not logically define as he addressed his father and other members of the establishment in Germany. Seneca had aligned nature with the divine, and contrasted oneness with God and nature to the attitudes of learned officials (or 'courtly hangers-on') who denied any sense of oneness or community that might impede their selfish pursuit of power and influence. Lietzheimer, preaching his sermon in the Church of Saint Kilian after Pastorius' departure from Windsheim, indicated that the values of a pagan like Seneca put to shame the so-called Christianity of a church and state that elevated the pursuit of power and influence above the humane values of Christ's teachings.

As he contrasts European and Native American cultures, Pastorius notes American virtues capable of correcting European defects. Mild punishment, humane government, religious sincerity, a loving yet disciplined upbringing preparing the young for modest lives of adult productivity – these Native American traits encouraged meaningful values and avoided many of the tensions and compulsions generated by the authoritarianism of Pastorius' youth, culminating with complicity in the "barbarities" of European militarism. His stark image of "despicable monsters" and their self-destructive violence reveals a deep awareness of inborn or acquired depravity reflecting his experience of baroque society, an awareness, transcending any one age, that has moved many intellectuals to contemplate the fragility of civilization, among them Arthur Schopenhauer and Sigmund Freud, both of whom portray human destructiveness and cruelty with images of wild beasts like that of Pastorius. [66] Through his reports on the Delaware (or Native Americans generally), Pastorius suggests that such depravity is acquired rather than inborn, an argument implying the possibility of improvement, and explaining the moral intensity of his transatlantic message.

Commenting on Lietzheimer's theme of pagans and Christians in a German verse meditation (Poem 344), Pastorius rejects these cultural or religious labels and notes that a tree can be recognized by the fruit it bears. Aside from his references to "instructing these ... needy creatures" and "taming the savage people," he avoids ethnocentric attitudes toward Native Americans. "I can best divide the inhabitants [of Pennsylvania] into the natural and the transplanted," he writes in *Sichere Nachricht* (p. 2), "for if I were to call the former savage and the latter Christian, I would be doing great injustice to many in both categories." Although he sometimes uses "Indian" and "uncivilized" or "savage" ("wilde" and the nominalized adjective "die Wilden"), he repeatedly indicates his dissatisfaction with these labels. Underscoring the common bond of humanity he felt for the Delaware, he refers to them as "the *per errorem* so-called savages," "the natural inhabitants of this country," "my West Indian countrymen" and "my unsavage savages."

4.5   The Rights of Blacks Asserted

> A Black-more (Ethiopian) can not change his skin, nor the leopard his spots. Jer. 13:23. Blacks or Negro's to be trained up in the fear of God, G. F. Journal 392/610. Tawnies are mildly & gently to be dealt with & after certain years of servitude to be made free, Id p. 354 ... Scorched & blackened by the sun of Africa, Neg. Xst p. 2. You look on them as part of your possessions Id. Who can tell but that this poor creature may belong to the Election of God &c. Id. p. 3. Treat them not as bruits, but as men, Id. p. 4. Col 4:1 [Masters, give unto your servants that which is just and equitable, knowing that ye also have a Master in Heaven.] They should not be overwrought [over-worked, but be] acquainted with the way to salvation. He is thy neighbor, yea & brother, & to be loved, p. 5. ... It is well known, that the whites are the least part of mankind, & the biggest part copper-coloured & a sort of tawnies, and our English that inhabit some climates (by maternal Imaginations & other accidents) do seem growing apace to be not much unlike to them, Neg. Xst p. 24.
>
> -- "Neger or Negro"
>
> The Negro's trade and usury
> Are sins which loud to Heaven cry.
>
> -- Epigram 623

Living in a multi-ethnic society with extraordinary political and commercial freedoms, Pastorius had occasion to demonstrate that this common bond extended to various races, an awareness some of his fellow Pennsylvanians tried to avoid. Thus in 1688 he and three of his ethnic Germantown neighbors officially protested the practice of black slavery that had been recently introduced into the colony, noting that Christ's Golden Rule ("doe to all men like as we will be done our selves") applied regardless of "generation, descent or colour." To shock insensitive Quakers, they cite the fear of being "taken and sold for slaves into Turkey," a fear white colonists then experienced en route to Pennsylvania, and they warn that the inherent violence of slavery is self-defeating, since the slaves would have "as much right to fight for their freedom, as you [slaveholders] have to keep them slaves."

Pastorius does not mention Pennsylvania's small but increasing black population in his extant transatlantic reports and letters since, as he and his Germantown neighbors state in their protest petition, "you surpass Holland and Germany," where "many [are] oppressed for conscience' sake," by oppressing those "which are of a black colour." Their argument continues: "This makes an ill report in all those countries of Europe, where ... [men and women] are desirous to know in what manner the Quakers do rule in their province; and most of them do look upon us with an envious eye. But if this is done well, what shall we say is done evil?" The petition was presented at local, district and provincial Quaker meetings in 1688, and at each level found to be, according to the Quaker minutes, "a thing of too great a weight" to allow "a positive judgement in the case." The Pennsylvania Quakers advised against slaveholding in 1696, but it was not until 1776 that they excluded from their membership any slaveholders who would not emancipate their slaves. [67]

In Poem 361, among his numerous references to slavery, Pastorius imagines a slaveholder wanting to "swap his great and well-cashed Coffer / With me for mine Estate; But I refuse that Profer" – even if "he would all his Negros give to boot: / No, no! Such high-heel'd Shoes will never fit my foot." In the German Poem 462, describing slavery as "exceedingly indecent" and "unnatural," Pastorius fictively asks a slave owner or trader if he would like to be a slave. The ironically indignant reply: "Oh, God help me! No, no!" "Why then," Pastorius asks, "does a man with his wife and children have to bend their backs under the yoke of slavery, without ever becoming free?" [68]

He evokes esthetic and moral contrasts in Poem 461 (also in German), its earthy imagery enhancing an allusion to Matt. 8, 11 & 12: Just as we fondly gather black whortleberries but let white cherry blossoms fall from the branch, the whitest among us may find themselves denied, and Ethiopians welcomed, into heaven. God "regards no Face," he writes in Poem 204:

> Be't white or black, it matters not,
> God looks unto the Mind,
> The Sin- and not the Sun-burn'd Spot
> Does no Acceptance find.

Linking related sins, Poem 473 describes "biting Usurers" and "Negro-buffeters" as "Satan's Tools, / Abominable Fools," and Poem 470 cites as bound for hell those who

> ... Christ's Precepts transgress,
> Negroes by Slavery oppress,
> And White ones grieve by Usury,
> (Two Evils, which to Heaven cry).

Pastorius also notes in Poem 462 (see page 295, n. 68) that the need for labor (for "Knecht und Magd" or farm hands, servants and maids) encourages insensitivity toward slavery "in American lands" or provinces. He then concludes the poem by implying that so-called Christians who single-mindedly pursue private gain (his paraphrase of slaveholders or traders) might be reformed by the penance of hell:

> Aber, sind sie wahre Christen,   Die da nur zu allen fristen
> Suchen ihren Eigen-Nutz.   Ey das glaub der Höllen büß!

His poetry remains staunchly anti-slavery to the end. Yet the pervasiveness of slavery noted in Poem 462 ("Who can change this?" he asks here) may have caused him to moderate his public stance during the 1710s. [69] This pervasiveness would also account for the presence of an offensive placard or handbill, apparently commissioned by one of his clients, in his "Young Country-Clerk's Collection" of legal and business forms. The advertisement promises "reasonable Satisfaction for his trouble" to anyone who "take[s]... up" and returns a runaway slave identified as "a Negro boy about 18 years of age... named Sam." Not all members of Pennsylvania society, Pastorius eventually had to admit, could enjoy the New World satisfactions proclaimed in *Beschreibung Pennsylvaniae*.

Conclusion

> What plants these Lands afford,
> No Herbalist can Count,
> Nor all their Virtues tell:
> The Mercies of the Lord
> Their number still surmount,
> He does for ever well.
> Truly God is good to such as are Clean of ♥ . Psal. 73:1.
>
> -- Poem 229
>
> This country [i.e. province] exceeds England in affording industrious people means to be wealthy & flourishing, but a licentious idleness & pride obstructs many, by pleasurable horses, fine houses, gay household stuff, shining garments, &c., for tho' they run in debt, yet these must be had. Leeds, 1700. Pennsylvania a country making rich men poor & poor men rich; very well fitting all people, but [except] beggars & gentlemen. Id. 1693. Tho' it be the nature of these woods to make rich men poor & poor men rich, labour being the means to gain wealth; yet such is the influence of this wilderness, that it inclines them to an Indian way of living. Id. 1700... A flourishing countrey, blest with liberty, ease & plenty, beyond what many of ourselves could expect.
>
> -- "Pennsilvania"
>
> As the Outwardness of Friendship [i.e., superficial friendliness] deceives many Simple-hearted, so free, substantial & Christian Friendship seeks at all times & in all places the good of our fellow mortals... True Friends will never flatter nor Dissemble; their Policy consists in being frank & plain, evermore speaking the truth one to another.
>
> -- To Rowland Ellis, 25 Jan. 1717, "Letter Book," p.22

This study has described Franz Daniel Pastorius' early life in the context of his Pennsylvania writings, a context informed by his search for material and ethical satisfactions in a transatlantic community that nowhere attained the societal perfections anticipated by early colonists who "would of Utopia dream," as Pastorius expresses it in Poem 396 (quoted on page 37). Yet despite learned cynicism, ennui or resignation, there was throughout this community a profound hope that mankind might yet achieve a better world, or at least retain control of the varied social and technological forces that, in the analyses and predictions of numerous contemporary intellectuals and religious seers, were heading Western society toward chaos or destruction. Pastorius himself embraced this hope as he coped with complicity and guilt during his final years in Germany, and to some extent it colors all of the personal development that made of him a pious and enlightened moralist, a prolific scholar and poet, a pragmatic farmer, teacher, jurist and politician – in short, one of the most profound and active colonists of early Pennsylvania.

For Pastorius, of course, it was more than just a hope. Particularly in his transatlantic writings, he repeatedly indicates that a better world was in fact attainable, and – despite his criticism of Native American exploitation and his refusal to mention black slavery – that Pennsylvania circumstances were helping to place this world within the grasp of mankind.

What substance is there to Pastorius' claim? A definitive answer is beyond the scope of this biography, which has utilized a large assortment of Pastorius documents to describe, in the framework of his German experience, the hallmarks of his character and ideology. A tentative answer will have to suffice until a full biography of his Pennsylvania years can be produced. This study thus concludes with an analysis of one illustrative passage from the immense store of Pennsylvania documentation awaiting further research, summing up the personality of Pastorius as it has emerged in the preceding chapters, and commenting on the regenerative potential he saw embodied in the circumstances of his life in early Pennsylvania.

In the rough draft of a letter written when he was 67 years old and preserved in a "Letter Book" he was keeping at the time, Pastorius records a Germantown domestic scene that suggests a few basic similarities and differences between his Pennsylvania existence and the life style he had known among European contemporaries who accepted the values of absolutist politics and baroque culture. The letter is addressed to Lloyd Zachary (1701-56), then a 17-year-old student and one of Pastorius' protégés in upper-class Quaker society, a youth who would study medicine with a Philadelphia physician, travel widely in Europe, and cofound Pennsylvania Hospital and the College and Academy of Philadelphia (later University of Pennsylvania). Pastorius had just received a small gift from Zachary, a sketch, painting or collage including some of "the long-nosed Ovid's Latin verse," as Pastorius describes it, and bordered with "counterfeited shadows" and real flowers and leaves betokening Zachary's appreciation for Pastorius' tutelage and friendship:

> Thy last, dated the 25th of this Instant [October, 1718], I received the same day towards Evening, my daughter[-in-law] Hannah bringing it unto me (sitting as one of [the] Muses and Birds before my Beehive [manuscript]) into the Stoveroom, with a Father, here is a letter for thee! ... At first glimpse I had of the Packet, my wild guess made me suppose, that some body did send a Patent or Indenture, to have a deed of sale drawn thereby. But espying thy hand (which I know as well as my right from the left,) I went with it into the kitchen, demanding Scissors to unseal it: they gave me the best they found, (however a very dull tool,) and the Cover being quickly off, I perceived by the Foulding of the Inclosed, (*ex ungue Leonem,*) there would a certain Rarity appear, and so told my Wife, daughters[-in-law and] youngest Son then there present (the Eldest having just brought a bag full of buckwheat to the Mill for his piggs). All the rest of my small family now standing about me, (as people surround Mountebanks,) I unwreathed the Gordian knot, and let them glance upon the green, red, yellowish and purple Sage-Rose and other fine leaves in the Margent. Oh, what a Staring, Gaping and Gazing! One said, O strange and the other, I never saw the like in my life! At last my little grand Child must also take a View of thy Masterpiece of Curiosity, who not yet able to speak seemed to skip for Joy. [70]

This passage, like much of his poetry, shows Pastorius relaxed and at peace with himself and his community, presumably enjoying the spiritual and material satisfactions he had proclaimed in his transatlantic writings. Late of an autumn day in temperate Pennsylvania, Pastorius sits at home near the stove, immersed in the verses and commonplaces he has been writing and compiling during the hours of intellectual recreation that have informed and validated his active pursuits over the past three decades. Like his counterparts in any society, this man of learning and station has known material and cultural advantages not shared by many of his fellow citizens, and these advantages help to explain his critical awareness of societal imperfections and his poetic delight in the simple pleasures of life. His property and his public and private accomplishments have brought him personal security and added to his respect in the community; his spacious garden and his leisure time have enabled him to develop two especially rewarding hobbies – growing flowers, herbs and vegetables, and writing pleasant and instructive verses about them. He shares his intellectual pleasures with his peers, displaying his learnedness in the occasional verse and epistles exchanged with the learned of his generation and with the young who are trained, in varying degrees, to emulate learned attainments. He is, in this respect, a part of genteel culture, remarkable only in that his intellectual productivity far surpasses that of most of his peers. His hobbies have become his passions, he has somehow failed to keep the usual perspective toward art and reality, and thus he can be ranked among the eccentrics, eggheads or geniuses that any genteel culture will occasionally produce.

In these respects Pastorius had much in common with the learned of Europe, men, and occasionally women, who likewise used their intellectual skills and advantages of station to create poetry and prose that delighted and informed their peers, to probe the complexities of the human mind and to criticize social reality. Yet this Pennsylvania scene of scholarly domesticity reveals several elements that could not be found in the lives of many of his upper-class contemporaries in Europe. Instead of stoves or fireplaces in various rooms of a spacious house or mansion, there is just one "stove room" providing warmth for Pastorius' modest two-story house, apparently only slightly better furnished than many of the other houses of Germantown. (The kitchen, of course, would have had its own fireplace or stove, and, in German fashion, was presumably large enough to serve as a dining / living room for other household members as well.) [71]

Instead of a servant or butler it is a daughter-in-law who receives and delivers the letter to the scholar at his desk, and although the individuals in the kitchen might include domestic help as well as family members, there is no clear indication here or in any of the available poetry or prose that the family had any servants after Pastorius ended his bachelor existence in 1688, reflecting either a lack of servants or a reluctance to flaunt one's affluence with any obvious references to the domestic help. Pastorius in fact wrote, in Poem 361, "I have no Master, and no Slave nor Servant neither," and he apparently meant it literally as well as figuratively.

In a similar vein, the report that John Samuel was personally delivering his buckwheat to the mill suggests that members of the family themselves performed some or all of the manual chores of farming, just as numerous passages in his poetry and scholarship give the impression that Pastorius enjoyed physical labor in his garden, orchard, vineyard and fields. [72] Since this level of reality was usually ignored by educated poets celebrating the joys of rustic simplicity amid nature –

and since Pastorius and his European peers were trained to observe distinctions between themselves and the peasants who tilled the fields and tended the animals, and in most cases religiously avoided "demeaning" manual labor – the fact that John Samuel tended his own pigs illustrates the radical break with the past that had transpired within the Pastorius family. Mentioning this fact in discourse with other learned men in the new society of Pennsylvania, furthermore, indicates at least some degree of shared values no longer consistent with the values of the European elite.

In "Genealogia Pastoriana" Pastorius reflects on these changing values with an illustrative anecdote from his European experience and, in contrast, family entries pointing toward a greatly altered future. While journeying toward England and his departure for Pennsylvania in 1683, he reports, "I was kindly received" by the Danish ambassador at Cologne, Germany:

> This [man] had strong inclinations for Pennsylvania, & desired me to prevail with his wife, but her reply was that there they were carried in a coach from one door to the other, but if they should happen to come hither, she was afraid that she must look after the cattle, and milk her cows, &c.

Within a single generation, the Pastorius family overcame whatever reluctance it might have had to performing such menial tasks. Pastorius lists the apprenticeships of his two sons in his family register in "Genealogia Pastoriana," and thus indicates that they lived, like other Germantown residents, as craftsmen and farmers who (beyond the rudiments of French and Latin) did not aspire to the cultural attainments of the learned. In the family register, Pastorius notes that he himself encouraged this unusual mix of old and new values, purchasing a loom and weaving equipment for John Samuel, his elder son, who practiced the weaver's craft in the Pastorius home. Two 1719 letters to Lloyd Zachary reveal that John Samuel became a master weaver who began his day "ere Sun-rise" and could teach an apprentice "besides the Trade, Reading, Writing & Cyphering." Similarly, in a letter of November, 1714, to 22-year-old Henry (then living away from home), Pastorius advises his younger son to "earn good wages" as a laborer "at the mill-race upon Duck Creek," to "perfect thyself in the shoemaker's trade," and to live honestly while "thou art abroad [i.e., away from home], that no just theme may be made against thee." [73]

How this radical change in family values came about has not yet been fully explored. To some extent, Pastorius may have simply capitulated to a variety of factors in frontier Pennsylvania society that, at the beginning of the eighteenth century, were loosening family bonds, and ameliorating oppressive paternal authority. At any rate, his emphasis on common rather than learned values in training his sons is reflected in the family history over generations. Although a number of the descendants of John Samuel lived as middle-class citizens in the Philadelphia area for generations, the descendants of Henry became pioneers who moved westward across the province, eventually settling near Pittsburgh, Pennsylvania, and lived predominantly as farmers and laborers, some of them semi-literate at best, with down-to-earth values far removed from the learned aspirations of their forebears. [74]

Does this family history represent a loss or a gain? Pastorius obviously wrestled with similar questions as he trained his sons and taught the youth of early Pennsylvania, at least occasionally frustrated by youthful resistance to cultural attainment.

The scholarly impulse was deeply imbedded in his character and habits, providing life-long personal satisfactions, but he also enjoyed his many active pursuits in a frontier society, and gained a mature pragmatism from them. He believed that learned attitudes fostered arrogance and social excess, and came to realize the value of practical as well as academic training, especially for children in a colony like Pennsylvania, where learnedness was not the only measure of social standing or success.

Perhaps it was above all his awareness of the innate compulsiveness of scholarship as practiced in his day – the ingrained habits that one generation forced upon the next, frequently with negative consequences – that gradually led Pastorius to adapt a flexible approach toward his sons' careers in Pennsylvania. He remained committed to academic achievement, at least for the youths who were readily motivated, a commitment clearly demonstrated in his correspondence with young Lloyd Zachary of Philadelphia in 1717-19. In French, Latin and English letters on themes ranging from the benefits of printing to the absurdities of metempsychosis, he encouraged Zachary's intellectual growth, praising the young scholar's progress in French and urging him to study Greek, and freely dispensing his own knowledge of ancient and modern literature, science, religion and philosophy. [75] Society needed well-educated leaders with keen insight and broad vision, Pastorius knew, but it also needed citizens and leaders with common decency, with heart and soul – needs that could not be adequately met through compulsive educational methods.

Pastorius' Pennsylvania life thus demonstrates a considerable degree of consistency with the values proclaimed in his transatlantic writings. These were the values he believed would help create a better world – if the human race would only have enough insight and common sense to live by them. Unusual career flexibility within the Pastorius family illustrates one basic reason for his belief that Pennsylvania circumstances provided greater sustenance for these values than could be found in contemporary Europe, although he also identified dangers that emerged as Philadelphia grew increasingly metropolitan and affluent, especially toward the end of his life.

In Pennsylvania, he did not sense deeply-entrenched cultural biases reinforced by the educational establishment, or fear that these biases would be allowed to develop under the colony's liberal system of government. He did worry that new wealth would encourage moral insensitivity, and, anticipating later American critics, that greater freedom might itself lead to complacency among the populace, either politically or religiously. His and other annotations in Germantown court records reveal that average citizens sometimes shirked civic duties (or declined on grounds of conscience), risking a fine rather than serving on a jury, for example, and in the transatlantic correspondence of *Beschreibung Pennsylvaniae* he also notes that in Pennsylvania, where all religions were permitted, the majority of churchgoers attended out of "pure habit" rather than personal conviction (1698, p. 86). Reflecting the increasingly topical issues of fashion and luxury, he epigrammatically notes that "Foolish Dress" will "unbless" the colony ("Symbola Onomastica," no. 724, composed 1717).

Pastorius not infrequently includes well-meant instruction or criticism in his friendship and occasional verse such as that annually addressed, in 1714-19, to the three daughters of Thomas Lloyd, all of them married to affluent and influential Philadelphia merchants and politicians. [76] Commemorating their arrival in the colony with a prose preface to Poem 359 in 1714, he writes that the "Love of Money ... (chopping in between the Lord and our Souls) always and unavoidably darkens and obscures" the "Brother and Sister Love (the Greek name signifying the one as well as the other)" for which Philadelphia was named, and that the former "seems to ... almost totally Eclipse" the latter in many "Microcosms" or residents of the city. Although he feels "Joy and Gladness" because "you and Your Dear Husbands still . . . Love the Brotherhood" as true Christians, he nevertheless advises them "solidly to ponder" biblical citations enjoining brotherly love and affection. He himself might have had "great Riches and Preferments" if he had returned to "my Father's house" in Germany in the early years, he reminds them here, but he chose not to.

Similarly, he addressed his poetic praise of Christ's Golden Rule (1714, in Poem 331, quoted on page 182) to James Logan (1674-1751), Penn's provincial secretary, two years after Logan began exploiting his position to make a quick fortune in land dealings and the fur trade, increasing his net worth fivefold in eight years. [77] These are two of various indications of the moral views he openly expressed among his most affluent and influential friends in the emergent merchant aristocracy of Philadelphia, an expression reflecting the essentially democratic nature of Pennsylvania society as well as the respect and esteem he enjoyed as the colony's leading scholar-poet despite the relative modesty of his Germantown life. "True Friends," he insisted, "will ... evermore speak ... the truth one to another" (page 244).

Although his criticism of usury and luxury, black slavery, and the exploitation of Native Americans illustrates the shortcomings of colonial society, Pastorius only once offers general criticism of Pennsylvania morality in the extant transatlantic writings – a sharp comment that he immediately qualifies cross-culturally: "This province is daily increasing in human population and human evil," he writes (1699, p. 98), "yet I cannot imagine that conditions here will ever be as inhumane as they are at the European universities," where intelligent young men were forced to learn the "useless" scholarly knowledge that kept them living in "abominable ... darkness," their "eyes of understanding" closed to the "light of the Gospels" and the real issues of daily conduct – and it is here that he notes these attitudes were epitomized by the learned of Europe who legally and illegally attained wealth so they and their families could "strut about a la mode".

Even though the accumulation of wealth was finding new adherents in colonial Pennsylvania, Pastorius continued to trust the basic premises of provincial society. All in all, his writings reveal a sustained conviction that Pennsylvania offered the great majority of its people definite advantages over the Old World, and that these advantages could be seen in almost every sphere of existence – in economic opportunity, in liberal politics and religion and a reformed legal system, in the simplicity of life close to nature, in the wholesome pragmatism and energy of intellect and conduct encouraged by frontier living. Particularly for Pastorius, it was a rejuvenating setting in which he could reformulate broadly humanitarian views and propose a new synthesis of the worldly and the spiritual, a life of moderation drawing upon European and Native American cultures, a blend of common and upper-class convictions that could give his contemporaries greater opportunity to live productively and harmoniously within society without surrendering the deepest and most meaningful of personal values. ("The influence of this wilderness," cited on page 244, may have indeed fostered something of "an Indian way of living" among Pastorius and many of his fellow Pennsylvanians.)

Significantly for Pastorius, this colonial setting permitted free expression and bold thought, engendering flexible responses to the restrictive tendencies of any society, and loosening the grip of intellectual hypocrisy and complicity, a climate Pastorius himself helped create with his probing of social and intellectual values – in "Alphabetical Hive" entries on atheism, for example, or in his poetry of flirtation and sensuality – and with his radical opposition to religious conformity and manipulation, to imperial might and destruction, or to the inequities of slavery and ethnic exploitation. (His own theology grew from an early emphasis on sin and the hereafter to a focus on divine love and "light" illuminating all mankind, a redemptive stance far removed from the religious indoctrination of his Windsheim youth.) This mood of free inquiry, coexisting with respect for tradition and authority, thus accounts for a personal maturity distinctly influenced by Enlightenment ideas, and producing (in his light apian verse, for example) some of America's earliest neoclassical poetry as well as social commentary presaging basic themes of later colonial and nineteenth-century American history. Ultimately, Pastorius' life and writings shed light on the Pennsylvania transition from Quaker beginnings to the mid-century era of Enlightenment and pre-Revolutionary thought.

Yet it is more than free inquiry that accounts for the vitality, pertinence and grace of the poetry and prose highlighted throughout this study. Taken together, for example, the epigrams alone constitute a first-rate sampling of colonial American verse. The variety and dexterity of his poetry is exemplary. His blending of erudition and generosity, of irony, skepticism and moral fervor, of learned wit, common sense and down-to-earth humor gave him unusual strengths as one of the outstanding writers of the colonial period.

Pastorius' life and writings, in retrospect, can be seen as forming part of a historical progression involving all of Western culture, and, ultimately, the even larger world culture the West can no longer ignore – a progression that has always been tentative, troubled, precarious, yet one that does indeed imply a purposeful moving forward. It can thus be concluded that Pastorius, through his intellectual breadth and generosity, made a significant contribution to the heritage of the transatlantic community that has been evolving since his lifetime, and that it is such breadth and generosity, shared in varying degrees by so many members of this community past and present, which has enabled it to keep some sense of balance between sustaining cultural values and the forces of disintegration or destruction that threaten its survival. Thus the pragmatic idealism of Franz Daniel Pastorius, responding to needs for self-realization and social responsibility, can be seen to offer guidance for survival even amid the complexities of post-industrial society.

Notes

Introduction

1. Biographical details are from Franz Daniel Pastorius, *Umstandige Geographische Beschreibung Der zu allerletzt erfundenen Provintz Pen[n]sylvaniae, In denen End-Gräntzen Americae In der West-Welt gelegen*, [ed. Melchior Adam Pastorius], (Frankfurt am Main and Leipzig: Andreas Otto, 1700), passim (cited as *Beschreibung Pa.*); and Marion Dexter Learned, *The Life of Francis Daniel Pastorius* (Philadelphia: W. J. Campbell, 1908), passim, esp. pp. 126-34 (founding Germantown), 156-70 (offices held), 221 (the Quaker press plans, proposed in 1697), 170-72 (on immigrant naturalization). Further documentation is provided in subsequent portions of this study.
2. "Artzney und Kunst," p. 2, quoted in Learned, p. 189.
3. Letter of Israel Pemberton to Richard Johns, quoted in Learned, p. 178-79: "The first time I saw him [Pastorius] I told my father that I thought he would prove an angry master he asked me why so I told him I thought so by his nose for which he called me a prating boy." See also pp. 99-100 of this study.
4. Letter of 20 Oct. 1718 to Lloyd Zachary in "Letter Book." The evaluation of Pastorius' library is from Frederick B. Tolles, *Meeting House and Counting House; The Quaker Merchants of Colonial Philadelphia* (Chapel Hill: Univ. of North Carolina Pr., 1948), p. 158, n. 40.
5. The bibliography lists Pastorius' manuscripts and published writings, many of which are described by Learned. The agricultural manuscript, which borrows from and augments many English farming books and German compendia known as "Hausvatterliteratur," is entitled "The Monthly Monitor, briefly shewing When our works ought to be done in Gardens, Orchards, Vineyards, Fields, Meadows & Woods; also in our Houses, Kitchins [sic], Cellars, Garners, Barns, Stables all the year round," 1701-c. 1716 (Historical Society of Pennsylvania, Pastorius Collection, Item 1). The extant medical writings are in "Artzney und Kunst," or "Talia Qualia / Medicinalia, Artificialia & Naturalia" (Historical Society of Pennsylvania, Pastorius Collection, Item 2), compiled between 1695 and about 1710, which includes "Medicus Dilectus," an encyclopedic compendium of 194 pages with 82 chapters arranged by bodily regions and kinds of disease and injury. Another extensive medical ms has been lost. These writings obviously predate Cotton Mather's less comprehensive medical ms of 1724, erroneously designated the first American medical compilation by Otto T. Beall, Jr., and Richard H. Shryock in *Cotton Mather: First Significant Figure in American Medicine* (Baltimore: Johns Hopkins Pr., 1954), p. 53. Pastorius' primer is *A New Primmer, or Methodical Directions to attain the True Spelling, Reading & Writing of English* (New York: Wm. Bradford, [1693]). Bradford had established Pennsylvania's first press in 1685 but, after becoming embroiled in religious and political controversies that briefly landed him in prison, he took a post as royal printer to New York in 1693. Pennsylvania lacked a printer in 1693-98 and 1705-09, a fact which vexed Pastorius and partly explains why so many of his writings were never published. See John Tebbel, *A History of Book Publishing in the United States*, 1 (New York: Bowker, 1972), 38-40, and Carl Bridenbaugh, *Cities in the Wilderness: The First Century of Urban Life in America*, 1625-1742 (1938; rpt. New York: Oxford Univ. Pr., 1971), pp. 132, 293. *Update 2013:* The law treatise quote: Alfred L. Brophy, "'*Ingenium est Fateri per quos profeceris*': Francis Daniel Pastorius' *Young Country Clerk's Collection* and Anglo-American Legal Literature, 1682-1716," 3 *University of Chicago Law School Roundtable* (1996), p. 637.
6. Harrison T. Meserole, ed., *Seventeenth-Century American Poetry* (Garden City, N.Y.: Doubleday, 1968), p. 294.
7. From compilations in the "Beehive" (Univ. of Pennsylvania MS Am 3), pp. 211-14, 633-34, 845-47. Pastorius clearly differentiates the 367 original epigrams collected here – and his other poetry – from the many borrowed rhymes copied elsewhere in his "Alphabetical Hive." Internal evidence including his sequential but incomplete number-

252 | Notes: Introduction

ing suggests he wrote many more epigrams not entered in these pages. Since he used section numbers 2311-2340 of his "Alphabetical Hive" supplement for some of his epigrams, these verses are identified by section and epigram; thus Epigram 2320.1 is the first epigram in section 2320 of the "Hive." The couplets cited here are numbered 648, 652, 2320.1, 2325.3, 2328.1, 2329.1, 2330.5 and 2330.7. The triplet is no. 2324.1. The quatrain, from Poem 419, is also in Meserole, p. 303.

8. The Greek Apelles (fl. 4th cent. B.C.) was the most renowned artist of classical antiquity. Homer describes the original Stentor as a Trojan War herald with the voice of fifty men. Tension between metrical and rhetorical stress in line 2 suggests the clergyman's erratic preaching, catalexis in line 5 emphasizes the swift finality of "death," and the two extra feet of line 6 deliver the ironic coup decisively concluding the poem's thrust and parry. The Germanism "on the pulpit" ("on" for "in" or "behind") derives from "auf der Kanzel."

9. In English, translated as "Circumstantial Geographical Description of Pennsylvania" by Gertrude S. Kimball in *Narratives of Early Pennsylvania, West New Jersey and Delaware*, ed. Albert C. Myers (1912; rpt. New York: Barnes & Noble, 1967), pp. 353- 448. This translation lacks the stylistic verve of the original, and is at times inaccurate, even blatantly so. On p. vi of the foreword, for example, deriding the arrogance of the university educated of his day, Pastorius refers to "der in der Aristotelischen Welt-Weisheit ertrunckener Mann" or, unambiguously, "the man who has drowned in Aristotelian worldly wisdom." Kimball, apparently worried that Pastorius would prove unpalatable or offensive to her readers, translates this as "the man who has drunk deep of the worldly wisdom of the school of Aristotle" (Meyers, ed., p. 363), thus turning sharp criticism into dull praise distorting the original message. See pp. 292-93, n. 60 for simplifications involving the Delaware or Lenape Indians.

10. "Francis Daniel Pastorius, His Hive, Melliotrophium Alvear or, Rusca Apium;" UPenn Ms. Codex 726. This folio volume has various title pages, added as Pastorius repeatedly enlarged and rebound it, one of which reads as follows: "Francis Daniel Pastorius / his / Hive or Bee-stock / Containing above two thousand little Honey-Combs; Begun in the year 1696 / And continued for the use of his children." Pastorius' remarks about the "Alphabetical Hive," taken from the "Beehive" itself, are cited in Learned, pp. 242, 248- 51. The ms includes Pastorius' epigrams and his collected poetry, "Silvula Rhythmorum Germanopolitanorum," or "Poetical Raptures," a numbered sequence of 494 poems on pp. 137- 201; the "Alphabetical Hive" on pp. 415-97 and its supplements on pp. 498- 890; indexes of its poetic themes and prose compilations; and a number of other scholarly works and compilations, including those described on page 92 of this study and one other (not elsewhere described) that deserves mention here.

Upon the birth of John Penn in Pennsylvania in 1699, Pastorius commemorated the event, on behalf of his son Johann Samuel and seven other pupils (all named John) he was then teaching in Philadelphia, by compiling "A Few Onomastical Considerations occasioned by Our Dearly Esteemed Name-Sake John Penn," 66 items of his own composition (from brief sentences to half-page paragraphs) describing "namesakes" of William Penn's son, i.e. men named John throughout history, and reflecting on universal and personal naming and signifying, philosophically and humorously expanding upon Consideration No. 1: "A Name (in the Latin Tongue *Nomen quasi Novimen, a Noscendo*) is the Outside Character, whereby to discern one thing from another." The inspiration for this small commemorative present obviously pleased Pastorius. He first expanded the compilation with versions containing 100 and then 199 items, retitling it "Some Onomastical Considerations . . .," and gradually enlarged his "Beehive" copy to 1829 items. In a letter of 6 Oct. 1710 to eleven-year-old John Penn (from the copy in Pastorius' "Letter Book"), he notes that these "Onomastical Remarks have beyond expectation accrued already to above 1160 Paragraphs. Here thou wilt meet with abundance of Johns, Emperors, Popes, Kings, Pips, Dukes, Generals, Princes, Priests, Doctors, Champions, Lawyers, Lyers, Historiographers, Botanicks, Linguists, Poets, Magicians, Conjurers, &c. &c. [etc.] Johns of all kinds & ranks, good & bad, rich & poor."

Update 2013: This is the one work of Pastorius's most deserving closer examination

11. Gert A. Zischka, *Index Lexicorum* (Wien: Hollinek, 1959), pp. xxx-xxxix.
12. The ms also contains early evidence of German-English linguistic interaction in Pennsylvania, such as Pastorius' 1716 borrowing of the English "fence" (substituted for "Zaun") to explain that he had thrown his Poem 432 over the backyard fence ("über die Fence geworffen") to his learned neighbor Christopher Witt, and that Witt responded in kind, with a poem "die er über die Fence zurück geworffen [hat]." (The poems humorously comment on one of Witt's botanical experiments, growing a fig tree outdoors in temperate Pennsylvania.)
13. Saving applies to time as well as money, Pastorius indicates in Epigram 2329.3: "Spend not your precious Time, but always make / A quick Dispatch of things you undertake;" in two variations on sleep and productivity, he opts for a short night's rest (Epigrams 659, 676):

> To be with Health and Wealth, and Wisdom fed,
> Rise very Early, and go late to Bed.

> Late to Bed, and early up,
> Fills your Platter and your Cup,
> Well to breakfast, dine and sup.

Here he experiments poetically and philosophically, revealing a modern temperament not unlike Franklin's, a lively and flexible pragmatism humorously expressed in Epigram 621:

> In all what thou look'st on,
> There is a Pro and Con.
> But little can be said,
> Of Eggs as yet unlaid.

As with many of his "Alphabetical Hive" notations, Pastorius entered "A penny saved ..." without listing its source. He could have read it in the *Spectator* of 14 Oct. 1712 or possibly in a manuscript of William Penn's *Fruits of a Father's Love: being the Advice of William Penn to his children* (1726) if he did not record it from conversation. An earlier version of "Early to bed ..."is contained in John Clarke, *Paraemiologia Anglo-Latina* (1639). See *Oxford Dictionary of English Proverbs*, 3rd ed., pp. 211, 619, and Tolles, p. 45.

14. Seidensticker, "Franz Daniel Pastorius (1651-1719) und die Gründung von Germantown," *Deutsche Pionier*, 2 (1870), 136-43, 168-78, 206-11, 241-48, 275-79, 300-07, 334-40, 379-83; 3 (1871), 8-12, 56-58, 78-83. For "the father of German-American immigration" see, for example, a *Pastorius-Amerika-Fahrt* leaflet (1933) reproduced in Friedrich Gutmann und Georg Furkel, *Sommerhausen in Wort und Bild* (Würzburg: Selbstverlag der Gemeinde Sommerhausen, 1970), p. 311.

15. For Cotton Mather, see Samuel Eliot Morison, *The Intellectual Life of Colonial New England*, 2nd ed. (Ithaca, N.Y.: Cornell Univ. Pr., 1956), pp. 143, 194-95; Adams, *Provincial Society, 1690-1763* (New York: Macmillan, 1936), p. 7; other instances of the comparison with Mather are in Learned, p. 226, and S. Foster Damon, "Francis Daniel Pastorius," *Poetry*, 14 (1934), 38. Bridenbaugh, *Cities in the Wilderness*, p. 131. Cremin, *American Education: The Colonial Experience 1607-1783* (New York: Harper & Row, 1970), pp. 308-09. Fantel, *William Penn: Apostle of Dissent* (New York: Morrow, 1974), p. 242. Ahlstrom, *A Religious History of the American People* (New Haven: Yale Univ. Pr., 1972), p. 232. *Update 2013:* Anthony Grafton, "The Republic of Letters in the American Colonies: Francis Daniel Pastorius Makes a Notebook," *American Historical Review*, 117 (2012), 2, 18.

16. Seidensticker, "Francis Daniel Pastorius," *The Penn Monthly*, 3 (1872), 66. Learned, ed., "From Pastorius' Bee-Hive or Bee-Stock," *Americana Germanica*, 1 (1897), 67-110; 2 (1898), 33-58 and 65-79. (This project began with Pastorius' early verse, and terminated before it got to his mature poetry.) Learned, *Life*, p. 226. Bridenbaugh, *Cities in the Wilderness*, p. 131.

254 | Notes: Introduction

17. Arthur F. Engelbert, "Francis Daniel Pastorius in his Literary Activities" (Diss. Univ. of Pittsburgh, 1935) examines, in 72 pages, Pastorius' various scientific and philosophical manuscripts and his published religious and educational works in addition to his verse. Along with descriptive summaries and excerpts from the poetry, Engelbert (a theologian) offers some useful evaluation, in particular noting the joy, vitality and humor of many poems, but dismissing the baroque complexity of others as "exaggerated artificiality." Deella Victoria Toms, "Intellectual and Literary Background of Francis Daniel Pastorius" (Diss. Northwestern Univ., 1953) traces many of Pastorius' literary sources and, in a 30-page chapter, discusses the poetry in the context of European and English poetic traditions. [Henry A Pochmann], "The Mingling of Tongues," *Literary History of the United States*, ed. Robert E. Spiller, et. al., 4th ed. (New York: Macmillan, 1974), 1, 678.
18. *Seventeenth-Century American Poetry*, p. 294. A few earlier selections from the poetry are included in G. U. Zimmermann, ed., *Deutsch in Amerika* (Chicago: Eyller, 1894), 1, 3-4; Heinrich A. Rattermann, ed., *Deutsch- Amerikanische Dichter und Dichtungen des 17ten and 18ten Jahrhunderts* (Chicago: German- American Hist. Soc., 1915), pp. 12-20; and John Joseph Stoudt, ed., Pennsylvania German Poetry, 1685-1830 (n.p.: Pennsylvania German Folklore Soc., 1955), pp. 3-7.
19. Columbia, South Carolina: Camden House. As of 1989, most of the poetry in the "Beehive" ms remained unpublished.
20. Just as a gift of paper enabled him to begin the "Beehive" (Learned, *Life*, p. 196), paper scarcity obliged him to write small, Pastorius notes in this excerpt from a discourse on types of quills, one of 36 uncollected "Rimes ... from mine Anvil" listed or referenced in the "Beehive," p. 214:

    The Hen pens, which we Officinas call,
    Are best for me because they Scribble small;
    For should I write so Coarse as some men do,
    Who'ld find me Paper then, pray! tell me who?
21. "Francis Daniel Pastorius, the German-American Poet," *Yearbook of German-American Studies*, 18 (1983), pp.21-28.
22. *The New Oxford Book of Seventeenth Century Verse*, ed. Alastair Fowler (Oxford: Oxford U. Pr., 1992), p. 764; *American Poetry: The Seventeenth and Eighteenth Centuries*, ed. David S. Shields (New York: The Library of America, 2007), pp. 200-15; Marc Shell and Werner Sollors, eds., *The Multilingual Anthology of American Literature: A Reader of Original Texts with English Translations* (New York: New York U. Pr., 2000), pp. 12–41; UPenn Ms. Codex 726, URL= http://dla.library.upenn.edu/dla/medren/pageturn.html?id=MEDREN_2487547&rotation=0&size=0&currentpage=1 ; Hist. Soc. Pa. (hsp.org), Francis Daniel Pastorius papers [0475], URL= http://digitallibrary.hsp.org/index.php/Detail/Collection/Show/collection_id/546. Numerous unpublished colonial poets have been gaining recognition particularly since the 1990s, Shields notes. See "The Library of America Interviews David S. Shields about American Poetry of the 17th and 18th Centuries," 2007, at http://www.loa.org.
23. German population density in the late 17th century was low compared to later eras but high relative to 17th century Pennsylvania.
24. Learned, *Life*, p. 183; Bridenbaugh, pp. 283-84, 446-48; and Louis B. Wright, *The Cultural Life of the American Colonies* (New York: Harper, 1957), pp. 107-08.
25. "Alphabetical Hive," Number 964 ("Doctor"), in "Beehive," p. 619.
26. Larzer Ziff, *The Literature of America: Colonial Period* (New York: McGraw-Hill, 1970), pp. 8-14.
27. Samuel Eliot Morison, *The Oxford History of the American People* (New York: Oxford Univ. Press, 1965), p. 131.
28. The quotation (varying slightly in formulation) is found in English, Scotch and German immigrant letters and travel journals cited by James T. Lemon in *The Best Poor Man's Country: A Geographical Study of Early Southeastern Pennsylvania* (Baltimore: Johns Hopkins Press, 1972), p. xiii. German immigration is described in James S. Olson, *The*

Ethnic Dimension in American History (New York: St. Martin's, 1979), pp. 24-27, 93-110; in Wright, pp. 58-63, and in Christine M. Totten, *Roots in the Rhineland* (New York: German Information Center, 1983), pp. 1-76. Franklin is quoted in Albert B. Faust, *The German Element in the United States* (1909; rpt. New York: Steuben Soc., 1927), 2, 154-55: "Unless the stream of importation [of Germans] could be turned from this to other colonies, ... they will soon so outnumber us that all the advantages we have will, in my opinion, be not able to preserve our language, and even our government will become precarious." Of the 82.7 percent of United States residents identifying their ancestry in the 1980 census, 28.8 percent claimed German descent, followed by 24 percent Irish and 22.3 percent English. See *Newsweek*, 17 January 1983, p. 20, and Andrew Hacker, *U/S: A Statistical Portrait of the American People* (New York: Viking, 1983), p. 46.

29. Seidensticker published Pastorius information in the *Deutsche Pionier* articles cited above; in "Francis Daniel Pastorius," *The Penn Monthly*, 3 (1872), 1-9 and 51-68; and in *Die erste deutsche Einwanderung in Amerika und die Gründung von Germantown* (Philadelphia: n.p., 1883). Pennypacker included supplementary detail in *The Settlement of Germantown Pennsylvania* (1899; rpt. New York: Benj. Blom, 1970). The only earlier publication faintly resembling a scholarly account of Pastorius is *Geographisch-statistische Beschreibung der Provinz Pensylvanien* (Memmingen, Germany: A. Seyler, 1792), anonymously edited, a 44-page summary of Pastorius' *Beschreibung Pennsylvaniae* published under Pastorius' name and updated with commentary for prospective emigrants. Friedrich Kapp summarized Pastorius' life in his introduction (based on Pastorius' reports and Seidensticker's 1883 book) to a reprint of *Beschreibung Pennsylvaniae* entitled *Beschreibung von Pennsylvanien* (Krefeld: Kramer & Baum, 1884), pp. XI-XIX. A few Pastorius studies published in Germany early in this century drew their information from *Beschreibung Pennsylvaniae* and from Seidensticker, Pennypacker and/or Learned.

30. The only detailed account of a Pastorius topic (until the1980s) is Beatrice Pastorius Turner, "William Penn and Pastorius," *Pennsylvania Magazine of History and Biography*, 57 (1933), 66-90. A few articles provide fairly reliable summaries of Pastorius, although some of the reported details have since been corrected: E. Gordon Alderfer, "Pastorius and the Origins of Pennsylvania German Culture," *American-German Review*, 17 (1951), 3, 8-11; George H. Genzmer, "Pastorius, Francis Daniel," *Dictionary of American Biography*, 14 (1934), 290-91; C. F. Jenkins, "Francis Daniel Pastorius," *American-German Review*, 1 (1934), 22-25; Erich Mende, "Franz Daniel Pastorius gründete Germantown," *Damals: Zeitschrift für geschichtliches Wissen*, 10 (1978), 123-36; and "Francis Daniel Pastorius" [headnote] in Meserole, *Poetry*, pp. 293-94. (Mende misleadingly illustrates his article with two representations of Pastorius, by modern artists or sculptors, that have no claim to authenticity.) A bibliography in Toms' diss. includes many other articles that are derivative or non-scholarly in nature. Articles and books commemorating the 1983 tricentennial of the founding of Germantown, then interpreted as the "beginning" of German-American immigration, include numerous additional summaries of the previously available Pastorius studies, among them Dietmar Kügler, *Die Deutschen in Amerika* (Stuttgart: Motorbuch Verlag, 1983), pp.18-23; and Ingrid Schöberl, "Franz Daniel Pastorius and the Foundation of Germantown," in *Germans to America* (Stuttgart: Institut fur Auslandsbeziehungen, 1982), pp. 16-24.

31. Pastorius studies since 1988 include Brophy, op.cit., 3 *University of Chicago Law School Roundtable* 637-742 (1996); Brophy, "The Quaker Bibliographic World of Francis Daniel Pastorius' Bee Hive," *Pennsylvania Magazine of History and Biography* 122 (1998), 241- 291, http://www.law.ua.edu/directory/bio/abrophy/PASTbks.html; Brophy, "The Intellectual World of a Seventeenth-Century Jurist: Francis Daniel Pastorius and the Reconstruction of Pietist Thought," in: *German? American? Literature? New Directions in German-American Studies*, ed. Winfried Fluck und Werner Sollors, New York 2002, pp. 43-63; Patrick M. Erben, "'Honey-combs' and 'paper-hives': positioning Francis Daniel Pastorius's manuscript writings in early Pennsylvania," *Early American Literature* 37 (2002), 2, 157-94; Erben, "Promoting Pennsylvania: Penn, Pastorius, and the

Creation of a Transnational Community," *Resources for American Literary Study* 29 (2003–2004), 25–65; Erben, *A Harmony of the Spirits: Translation and the Language of Community in Early Pennsylvania* (Chapel Hill: Univ. of North Carolina Press, 2012), esp. pp. 159-94 (the latter available too late for use in the updates here); Anthony Grafton, "Jumping Through the Computer Screen," *New York Review of Books*, Dec. 2010; Grafton, "The Republic of Letters," op. cit., 1-39; Margo M. Lambert, "Francis Daniel Pastorius: An American in Early Pennsylvania, 1683-1719/20", Ph.D. diss., Georgetown University, 2007 (Ch. 2 of this broader study is referenced here); Rüdiger Mack, "Franz Daniel Pastorius – sein Einsatz für die Quäker," *Pietismus und Neuzeit* 15 (1989), 132-71; Brooke Palmieri, "'What the Bees Have Taken Pains For': Francis Daniel Pastorius, The Beehive, and Commonplacing in Colonial Pennsylvania" (B.A. thesis, University of Pennsylvania, 2009), URL = http://repository.upenn.edu/uhf_2009/7/; Lyman W. Riley, "Books from the 'Bee Hive' Manuscript of Francis Daniel Pastorius," *Quaker History* 81 (1994), 116-129. Entering "Daniel Pastorius" at amazon.com (or similar sources) yields the new reprints available (some for Francis and others for Franz Daniel Pastorius); online versions include Learned's *Life* at URL = http://archive.org/stream/cu31924028830649#page/n5/mode/2up. Entries in encyclopedias, biographical dictionaries, etc. have not been cited.

Update 2016: Pastorius research continues apace. Andrew L. Thomas, for example, has published "Francis Daniel Pastorius and the Northern Protestant Transatlantic World," *Acta Comeniana: International Review of Comenius Studies and Early Modern Intellectual History* 28 (2014), pp. 95-126. Using a wealth of sources (including the 2013 PDF edition of this book), he traces the influence of Rosicrucianism and Behmenism on Pastorius.

32. Data from church membership archives provided by Lois Fulmer, secretary of the New Holland Evangelical United Methodist Church (email of 17 June 2014).

Prologue

1. *Beschreibung Pa.*, pp. 98, 101-02.
2. *Beschreibung Pa.*, p. 104:
    Ich bin von meiner Kindheit an so vielen seltsamen Fatis und Unglücks-Fällen unterworfen gewesen, daß ich mich offt selbst über die allmächtige Hand Gottes nicht genugsam verwundern kan, wie mich solche so wunderbarlich geführet, ernehret, beschützet und erhalten hat.
3. "Antwort an dieselbige[: Beschreibung meiner Ankunfft und geführten Lebens-Lauff]," *Beschreibung Pa.*, pp. 103-20; rpt. in M. A. Pastorius, *Kurze Beschreibung der Reichsstadt Windsheim 1692*, ed. Alfred Estermann (Bad Windsheim: Delp, 1980), pp. x-xxvi.
4. The following account is based on "Antwort an dieselbige" in *Beschreibung Pa.* and the "Itinerarium" in M. A. Pastorius, *Des Melchior Adam Pastorius . . . Leben und Reisebeschreibungen von ihm selbst erzählt und nebst dessen lyrischen Gedichten . . .* , ed. Albert R. Schmitt. (München: Delp'sche, 1968), pp. 17-82, an English summary of which is in Learned, pp. 12-29. Background information may be found in: Learned, pp. 5-49; Schmitt's introduction to *Des Melchior Adam Pastorius... Leben* , pp. 9-16; Estermann's introduction to *Kurze Beschreibung Windsheim*, pp. i-xxxii; Estermann, *Bad Windsheim. Geschichte einer Stadt in Bildern*, 2nd ed. (Bad Windsheim: Delp, 1975), p. 91; and Alfred Roth, "Der Windsheimer Bürgermeister und Oberrichter Melchior Adam Pastorius als leistungsstarke Persönlichkeit der Barockzeit," (photocopy of ts in Stadtarchiv Bad Windsheim), passim.
5. *Beschreibung Pa.*, pp. 106-07:
    Der König leget ihnen Guarnison ein, schliesset aber die Römisch-Catholischen von der Capitulation aus, in deren Häuser und Klöster die Soldaten anfänglich gantz allein einquartirt worden, welche sie dann gantz ausgeplündert, und die meisten gar niedergerissen und evertirt haben, worunter auch meines Vatters Hause auff dem Roß Marckte gewesen, woraus meine Frau Mutter nichts als ein Erb-Registerlein über etliche Gefäll und Zins-Einnahm darvon gebracht. Wir Kinder aber wurden

von denen Soldaten mit blossen Degen verjagt, und sahen sich allhier die Herren Catholici durch die erstere Persuasion hintergangen...

Mein Herr Vatter, Martinus Pastorius, machte sich schleunig auff, zu seinem Chur-Fursten nacher Mayntz zu verreisen, und das erlittene Excidium zu klagen, er fiel aber unterwegens wieder in derer Schwedischen Soldaten Hände, wurde nackend ausgezogen und mit Schlagen dermassen tractirt, daß er inner wenig Wochen seinen Geist auffgabe.

Nach solchem erlittenen Grundsturtze und eingebüsseten Vatter, wurden wir Kinder durch die betrübte und ruinirte Wittib kümmerlich aufferzogen... Ich Melchior ward bey geringer Kost und Kleidung von der Mutter zu denen Studiis gehalten... Ich bäte meine Frau Mutter sehr, daß sie mich auff eine Universität schicken mögte; sie entschuldigte sich mit dem Unvermögen und obhabenden Last der übrigen Kinder-Verpflegung, doch entlehnete sie auff mein ferners Anhalten bey meinem Tauff-Pathen einen Ducaten, und gab mir solchen mit auff die Reise, mit welchem ich etliche tausend Meilwegs in der Welt herum gereiset, und doch nie keinen Mangel gelitten habe.

6. *Leben*, p. 61:
Drumb, lieber Sohn, Bring Gott fortan sein Preis von Hertzen,
Lieb Ihn, und thu im Geist als Brauth in Liebe schertzen,
Gib rauser von deim Guth dem Armen in der Noth,
So wirst du hier und dort in Gnaden stehn bey Gott.

7. *Leben*, p. 30: "Dise Weise zu leben war gantz wider meine Natur, und hatte ich keine Lust zu dem geistlichen Stande."

8. Quoted, in English translation, in *Learned*, p. 22.

9. *Leben*, p. 43: "... wegen einiger Dispensations Bulla, die ich ihme zu Rom beim Pabste ausgewürcket hatte."

10. *Leben*, p. 24: "Die verwunderten sich sehr, daß in Teutschland die Leute anderst redeten als sie, und daß ich ihre Sprache nicht konte."

11. *Leben*, p. 30: "Auch lernete ich die Romanische Sprache, so in dem verschlossenen Collegio unter denen Teutschen nimmermehr würde geschehen sein."

12. *Leben*, pp. 21-45 passim.

13. *Leben*, p. 23:
... ich [sahe] mit Verwunderung den Schnee uff den Bergen ligend mitten in denen Hundstagen an, und mitt einem Fendrich [Fähnrich] umb einen 1/2 Eymer Wein wettete, innerhalb 4 Stunden dahin zu lauffen und ettliche Schneeballen herab zu holen. Als ich nun 1 1/2 Stunde geloffen war, begegne[te] mir ein Baur, den fragte ich, wie weit es noch zu dem Schnee wäre. Der sagte mir, 3 Stunde hätte ich noch zu lauffen. Da dachte ich, das Spiel wäre verlohren, und fragte den Bauren, ob er keinen Schnee in der Nähe wüste. Da führte er mich bald zu Schnee, davon ich 4 Ballen zusammen druckte, in meinen Huth nam und gen Schwatz sprunge, auch noch eine gute Viertel Stunde vor dem gesetzten Ziel ankame und die Wettung gewanne.

14. *Leben*, p. 53: "Bey.diser Occasion bey Hoffe täglich zu speisen, penetrirte ich den gantzen Statum diser Hoffhaltunge...'

15. *Leben*, pp. 53-55:
Die Castraten und Italienische Hoff Musici... luden mich in ihr Losament uff eine Collation und gut Gespräch... Ich lude sie widerumb in mein Quartier, welches sie mir zwar zugesagten, aber keine gewisse Zeit benennen wolten, damitt ich mich uff sie verkosten [ihretwege Aufwand machen] solte. Ich versprach ihnen, nicht mehr uff zu tragen als zwo Kanten [Kannen] weins... Mein Herr Dresanus aber war darzu abgerichtet, daß wann eine Kanten leer ward, er solche in die Schlaffkammer practicirte und solche gefüllter wider unter die Banck stellete. Wurden also die guten Musicanten gantz truncken, daß sie des andern Tags rauhe Hälse hatten und nicht rein singen konten."

16. Leonard W. Cowie, *Seventeenth-Century Europe* (London: G. Bell, 1960), pp. 302-03.

17. *Leben*, p. 95:

> Zu Rom hat der Leib sein Himmelreich, die Seele ihre Hölle und der Beuttel sein Fegfewer.
>
> *Peregrinationis Dissuasio.*
> Sage mir, was hastu zu Rom gesehen? R.: Bey denen Reichen den Berg des Hochmuths und der Unbarmhertzigkeit, ihre Hertzen voller Sünden von Geitz, Unzucht und Sodomiterey.
> Bey denen Armen den Thal der Trähnen, der Hungers Noth und der Verachtung. Selig ist, der es glaubt und nicht sihet.

18. "Liber Intimissimus" in *Leben*, p.47:
    > Unser Heyland habe ja bey Erlösung und Auffbawung seiner Gemeinde auff kein Pabstumb oder eüserlichen Staat gesehen ... Der Herr Christus [hat] die Intention nicht geführt, eine geistliche Souverainität und päbstlichen Staat wider die vorhin [vorher] aller Orthen wohlbefestigte Landes Regirungen und Obrigkeiten anzurichten, sondern er spricht gantz deutlich: Mein Reich ist nicht von dieser Welt.

19. Ibid., pp. 46-47:
    > In der Statt Rom [hatte ich] alle der Römischen Kirchen Mißbräuche, die Anbetung des Pabsts, der Heiligen, der Reliquien, und der Todten Beine, die Hochhaltung des Weywassers, der Agnus Dei, der Messe, der Wallfahrthen, der Closter Gelibte [Gelübde], des Rosenkrantz Bethens genugsam erfahren und mich zwar überdrüssig daran gesehen.

20. *Leben*, pp. 30, 36, 46-47.

21. *Leben*, p. 31: "... ettliche Kästen, darinnen eitel Schätze ligen, welche ein und anderer Pabst an disen Orth verschaffet hat, die Schatz Cammer zu vermehren."

22. "Itinerarium," Univ. of Pennsylvania MS. Ger 54, f. 22a. (Schmitt included only a paraphrase of this passage in *Leben*, p. 33.)

23. "Liber Intimissimus" in *Leben*, pp. 46-47:
    > Ich konte ... lange Zeit mir nicht in den Kopff bringen, das kein Pabst und kein sichtbares Kirchen Haupt sein solte, und ob es möglich wäre, ohne den Pabst in den Himmel zu kommen. Umb welches Zweiffels willen ich mich einige Jahrlang allen Gebrauchs der Beichte und Communion gar enthalten, und fast so Viel als nichts geglaubet.

24. Franz Petri, "Im Zeitalter der Glaubenskämpfe," *Rheinische Geschichte*, ed. Franz Petri and Georg Droege, 2 (Düsseldorf: Schwann, 1976), 124, 138-43, 146; and Gottfried Kentenich, *Geschichte der Stadt Trier* (Trier: Lintz, 1915), pp. 485-91.

25. "Liber Intimissimus" in *Leben*, p. 47.

26. *Beschreibung Pa.*, pp. 108-09:
    > Man [wiese] mich ... in eine sehr finstere Kammer zu schlaffen, worinnen ein getödteter Menschen-Cörper unter dem Bette lag und einen abscheulichen Gestanck von sich gabe, und ich hatte bey meiner Ankunfft hinter diesem Würthshause ein groß frisch gegrabenes Loch wahrgenommen, darein man den vorigen getödteten und mich hat einscharren wollen, aber Gott halff mir durch Ankunfft etlicher reisenden Pilgramen gnädiglich darvon, daß ich in selbiger Nacht gen Monte Frascon kam ...

27. "Liber Intimissimus" in *Leben*, p. 47:
    > Dann [war] das Lachen sehr theur, und das Nachsinnen scharff und ernstlich, wo ich mit Leib und Seele wurde sein hingefahren, wann ich also in meinen Sünden wäre umbgebracht ... worden.

28. *Leben*, pp. 37-45, and *Beschreibung Pa.*, pp. 109-10.

29. *Beschreibung Pa.*, p. 110: "... unter dem freyen Himmel in nassen Kleidern und grosser Kälte."

30. *Beschreibung Pa.*, p. 110:
    > Da sahen wir gantz von ferne ein Liecht auffgehen, welches sich gemählich immer je höher in die Lufft erhube, biß es gantz nahe zu uns herbey ruckte, und weit grosser als ein grosses Pferd um uns herum funckelte, so daß uns beeden ein Schauer über die Haut lieffe, und wir anfingen nach Gott zu schreyen, und um Rettung zu bitten, da es dann endlichen wieder zurück gienge, und an eben dem Orte, da es zuvor entstanden, wiederum auslöschete und verschwande. Was gewesen, ist Gott bekannt.

Notes: Prologue | 259

31. *Beschreibung Pa.*, p. 110:
    Wir ... fanden auch folgenden Tages in dem Dorffe Beaona gar schlechte Erquickungen, indeme dieser Orten gewöhnlicher Lands-Art nach keine warme Stuben anzutreffen sind.
32. Durant, *Age of Louis XIV*, pp. 3-8; and *Brockhaus Enzyklopädie*, 1, 540; 6, 631-32; 12, 301.
33. *Leben*, p. 44:
    Sie [sprengten]... uns gantz rasender Weise an, und hielten uns für Spionen, namen uns die Degen und wolten uns erstechen. Ich zeigte ihnen meinen Paß vom Churfürsten von Trier, den schmissen sie in den Koth, und muste ich also fast meines Lebens verzeihen [verzichten, aufgeben], bis endlich ein reicher Korn Händler darzue kam, der den Pöfel [Pöbel] stillete und uns den Paß widerumbzustellete, auch mitt sich in sein schon [schönes] Haus nam und von einem gebratenen Geislein zu essen und zu trincken gab.
34. *Leben*, pp. 44-45:
    Ich mietete bey Hn. Dr. Heilmann in der Vorstatt S. Germain ein Zimmer, und kauffte mir einen Vorrath an Victualien, Erbsen, Bonen, Linsen, Kääs, Butter, e[tc], und hielte mich stets zu Hause, weillen täglich ein großes Tumultuiren in der Statt war, und manche über dem Brotkauffen erstochen wurden, und große Theurung dahero entstunde, weillen der Prinz Conde mitt seinen Völckern [Truppen] alle Landstraßen besetzet hatte, das die gewöhnlich wöchentlich hineingehende 2000 Wägen und Kärren mitt Brod nit hinnein kommen mochten. Da lagen alle Hanthierungen darnider und war der gemeine Pöfel schwürig [schwierig] und keinem Frembden wurde kein Wexel ausgezahlet, dorffte doch niemand bey Lebens Straffe sich aus der Statt begeben.
35. *Beschreibung Pa.*, p. 112:
    Dieser tranck mir ein Glas Wein zu, und thate mir alle gute Vertröstungen; aber nach Mittags Zeit simulirte er eine Spatzierfahrt in einen Garten ausser der Stadt zu thun, und kam nimmer wieder gen Paris.
36. *Beschreibung Pa.*, p. 113:
    Als nun obgedachter Hoffmeister etliche Tage sich bey mir verborgen aufgehalten hatte, wollte er endlichen tentiren aus der Stadt zu seinem Herrn Baron zu gehen, welches ich ihm sehr wiederriethe, und bate, nur noch ein paar Tage in Gedult zu stehen, es würde sich die Auffrühr bald legen, und als er auf mein vielfältiges Zusprechen und Bitten nicht verbleiben wollte, gab ich ihm das Geleit biß zum Thor, und ging so fort uff den hohen Wall. Jener war bereits durch die erste und zweyte Schildwacht passirt, von der dritten und letzten aber (so ein Knab von 11. bis 12. Jahren war) angeschrien, wer er wäre, und wo er hin wollte, da er aber seines Gangs immer fortgieng, un[d] auf vielfältige Instantz nicht antworten wollte, wurde er durch und durch so gleich tod geschossen, und bald darauff von etlichen Soldaten in die Stadt geschleppet, auff ein klein Hospital-Kirchhoflein, fine Crux fine Lux, eingescharret, ein Mensch warhafftig von grossen Qualitäten, in Jurisprudentia und diversis linguis wohlerfahren. Dieses Tragödische Spectacul an meinem Schlaff-gesellen, und die Recordatio derer gefährlichen Begebenheiten auff der Reise lehreten mich in meinem Bestand-Zimmerlein stille sitzen, und der Welt Eitelkeiten in etwas zu Gemüte ziehen, darbey meine Conscientz zu erforschen, wie diese gegen dem lieben Gott bestehe, und uff was Weise meine arme Seele von ewiger Verdamnutz [Verdamnis] mochte gerettet werden.
37. *Leben*, pp. 11-12, 42, 62-64, and 74-81.
38. *Leben*, pp. 47, 52; and *Beschreibung Pa.*, pp. 114-15.
39. *Leben*, pp. 46-47.
40. *Leben*, p. 53:
    Ihre Churfürstl. Gen. ließen hierauff einige Ungenade gegen mir nicht verspüren, sondern meldeten mitt einer freundlichen Mine, das der geistliche Stand nicht jedermanns Thun sey. Ich solte mich bey dero Hoffhaltunge gedulden, sie wolten weitters mitt mir reden.

41. *Leben*, p. 55: "Ich war endlich des Hofflebens müde."
42. *Beschreibung Pa.*, pp. 115-16:
    Ich... hielte mich... bey Hofe auff, thate offtmals eine Spazier-Reise nacher Winter- und Sommer-Hausen, ward jedesmahls von daselbstigen Inwohnern sehr höflich tractiret, so daß mir der Ort und die Conversation derer Evangelischen Christen je länger je besser gefiele, dahero ich bey höchstgedacht Ihrer Chur-Fürstlichen Gnaden um Dimission und Recommendation an die Herren Grafen von Limpurg anhielte, auch erlangte, und solchen Orts auf das freundlichste auf- und angenommen ward. Meine erste Arbeit aber war diese, daß ich die Augsburgische Confeßion durchgienge, meinen bißhero geführten Lebens-Lauff von Jahr zu Jahr durchgienge, und mich unterweisen liesse wie man allezeit mehrer den Creatorem als die Creaturen vor Augen haben, und mehrer denen Worten CHristi als denen Menschen-Satzungen und Traditionibus glauben müsse, da ich dann endlich zu derjenigen Erkäntnuß gelanget, daß ich den innern neuen Menschen erkennen lernen, und dargegen den äusserlichen Mund-Christen mit eignem Werck-Verdienst habe fahren lassen, und bin in dem Nahmen deß HErrn den [25. Dez.] 1649. das erste mahl nebst ihrer Hochgräfl. Gn. Schenck, Georg Friederichen von Limpurg zu Sommershausen zum heiligen Abendmahl gegangen, habe auch meine Christliche Glaubens-Bekäntnus aufgesetzt, und hochgedacht seiner Hochgräfl. Gnaden diciciret.
43. *Beschreibung Pa.*, pp. 116-19; *Learned*, pp. 53-57; *Leben*, pp. 111-13.
44. *Beschreibung Pa.*, pp. 117-18
45. *Kurtze Beschreibung des H. R. Reichs Stadt Windsheim / Samt Dero vielfältigen Unglücks-Fällen / und wahrhafftigen Ursachen ihrer so grossen Decadenz und Erbarmungswürdigen Zustandes* (Nürnberg: C. S. Froberg, 1692).
46. The following discussion refers to the poems selected by Schmitt in *Leben*, pp. 56-110, and the poetry in the 257-page "Nucleus Doctrinae Biblicae" (Stadtarchiv Bad Windsheim MS.). The richness of Melchior Adam's worldly and spiritual verse is illustrated in these two excerpts, from "Vom Herbst," in *Leben*, p. 84, and from a poem of penitence in *Geistliche Liebs-Übung* (Nürnberg, 1683), quoted in Roth, p. 127:

    Die Sonn eylt durch die Waag zum Scorpion und Schützen,
    Die Aepffel fallen ab, da hülfft kein Baumes Stützen;
      Die Würmer nähren sich im schönen Apffel Bauch,
      Das außen schöne Bild ist offt ein Sinnen Rauch.

    Den edlen Rebensafft nun aus den fetten Trauben
    Thu in das hohle Vaß durch deine Kelter schrauben.
      Der Most die Zungen löst, macht sie von Sorgen frey,
      Also das Irus offt meint,- das er Croesus sey.

    Kraut, Rüben ligen da, hier, dort, in allen Ecken,
    Darnach die schwartze Kuh ihr weites Maul kann lecken ...

      Suche mich dein Schäflein wieder,
    Du mein Gott und treuer Hirt,
      Welches irrig auf und nieder,
    Wölffen sonst zum Raube wird.
    Schließ in Jesu Wunden ein
    Das verscheuchte Täubelein,
    Daß es Sathan nicht erwische
    In dem wüsten Welt-Gebüsche.

      HErz, ich habe zwar verzogen,
    Bin, nach Noe Raben Art,
      Sicher hin und her geflogen,
    Hab die Busse lang gespart,
    Jetzt thu ich zu dir den Tritt,
    Bringe Reu und Glauben mit,
    Herz, ich komme noch beladen,
    Heile du mein Seelen-Schaden.

Notes: Chapter One | 261

47. *Beschreibung Pa.*, p. 119: "... gleichsam wie in einem geistlichen Erimitorio [bringe ich meine Zeit] mit gottseligen Gedanken und Meditationibus ... zu ..."
48. In 1692 the elder Pastorius had included Franz Daniel's "Kurtze Geographische Beschreibung ... Pensylvania" (a revised version of the 32-page book published without place or date in 1690 or 1691) as an appendix to one of two editions of his Windsheim history, identical except for the inclusion of this appendix.

Chapter One

1. Biographical details are from Pastorius, "Genealogia Pastoriana" (Appendix I) and *Beschreibung Pa.*, passim, and Learned, *Life*, esp. pp. 101-11, and from Pastorius' mss as indicated in subsequent portions of this study.
2. Like all subsequent translations not otherwise attributed, this text was translated anew for this study by the author. The original text, from *Beschreibung Pa.*, p. 15, is in Appendix II. Accounts of initial and subsequent purchases differ in detail. Pastorius apparently confirmed and paid for a purchase of either 15,000 or 25,000 acres earlier arranged by the Frankfurt Pietists.
3. *Beschreibung Pa.*, pp 45-47. Appendix II includes the original text of the letter. Pastorius took his Latin text on being lost forever from St. Augustine, and commented on it lyrically, once in German not long after emigrating and again in English around 1715 (Poems 15 and 415). The reference signifies his concern with the hereafter, which was most pronounced in the early 1680s and regained some of its early prominence in the last few years of his life. The departure from Deal was delayed from 7 June to 10 June 1683.
4. This biography presents a representative selection of themes and opinions from the "Alphabetical Hive," primarily as epigraphs, although scientific and religious topics are under-represented in this general study. The excerpts from the "Hive" are identified by the headings Pastorius gave them. Compiling from his sources, he entered each sentence immediately after the previous entry without indicating the transition from one source to the next except when (relatively infrequently) he identified the name of the quoted author or book, often with an abbreviation. He also included short phrases without context, essentially as thesaurus entries. The typical quotation is a single sentence, offering the reader a moment's pleasure or demanding a moment's contemplation before moving on to the next, which generally has no logical connection aside from its common theme. Thus, in "Cookery," a remark on economical feasting (from an unidentified work of William Penn's) precedes a wry comment on the sin of gluttony and the lusty image of pasta towers and castles (both from unidentified sources), and they in turn are followed by references including Maxim 56 from Penn's *Some Fruits of Solitude* and the note on cooking instructions in John Shirley's *The Accomplished Ladies' Rich Closet of Rarities*, 1687, two works listed in the bibliography of this study along with other identified "Hive" sources, and keyed to the names and/or titles Pastorius used in the "Hive". Unidentified sources have not been traced. Poems and "Hive" entries not identified as entire are excerpted from a longer poem or listing. Where the sense of the passage is not affected, spelling and punctuation have been modernized (although, in the poetry, Pastorius' capitalization is generally observed), and abbreviated words generally spelled out. *Update 2013*: My "Beehive" research (both in Philadelphia and, using a microfilm copy, in Germany) was extensive but selective. I skipped many topics entirely, skimmed those of interest, and carefully studied those I decided to use (textually or as epigraphs).
5. Personal attitudes and habits are frequently revealed in his poetry, most of it in "Sylvula Rhythmorum Germanopolitanorura" in the "Beehive," some of which is also in *Deliciae Hortenses*, occasionally in altered form. Poem 277 describes strawberries in rum, Poems 167 and 491 deal with pipe smoking and tobacco, and Poems 136, 168, 194, 208, 236 and 247 mention turnips, various melons, and forget-me-nots, representative of the dozens of garden herbs, flowers and vegetables scientifically or metaphorically treated in the poetry. Flirtation and sexual allusion are described on pp. 128-37

of this study. A couplet in Poem 167 satirizes non-smoking teetotalers who also avoid snuff tobacco:
> Poor Mad-Caps that refuse to drink, when dry, but rather wheese,
> Will make no Chimneys of their Mouths; Their Noses never sneeze.

6. *Life*, p. 116, n. 1.
7. "Zwei unbekannte Briefe von Pastorius," *German-American Annals*, n.s. 2 (1904), 493: "[Das Bild von Pastorius mutet] uns jetzt leicht als etwas hausbacken und prosaisch an, trotz aller Biederkeit und Ehrlichkeit des Helden."
8. *Vom Rhein zum Delaware: Krefelder gründeten 1683 Germantown* (Krefeld: Formdruck, 1983), p. 5: "Seine Kleidung war aus grobem Tuch und aufs einfachste zugeschnitten. Für jeden des Wegs Kommenden hatte er einen freundlichen Gruß, ohne jedoch ein einziges Mal den Hut zu lüften."
9. Pastorius' inventory of the personal clothing he took with him to Pennsylvania – listed in Learned, p. 115 – includes, along with the usual socks, shoes, trousers and similar items, a generous assortment of linen dress shirts and cravats, white and colored linen handkerchiefs, knitted, leather and white linen dress stockings, crepe caps, and felt hats, as well as a blue overcoat, a full-length brown dress coat, two jackets or suits with a veneer like that of patent leather ("lackene rock mit Hosen"), a leather camisole, two cloth camisoles, one of which was white and thus for formal wear, and the three wigs that seem to have embarrassed him as he copied this inventory into his "Res Propriae" manuscript around 1715, for he obscured their nature by listing them as one of two types of "small caps" ("acht Schlaff- und drei Paruquen mützgen," or "eight small sleeping- and three peruques caps"), thus suggesting that he did not ordinarily wear a wig, at least not after he had adjusted to the village life of Germantown.
10. *Beschreibung Pa.*, pp. 66-67:
    Den 8. Febr. dieses 1694. Jahrs kriegte ich auch einige wenige Zeilen von meinem Baten Frantz Jacob Mercklein, welchen ich im achtzehenden Jahr meines Alters aus dem Wasserbad der heiligen Tauff gehoben habe, selbst noch mit dem heiligen Geist ungetaufft seyende, und Christum noch nicht angezogen habende. Diesen bitte meinetwegen freundlich zu grüßen, und ernstlich zu ermahnen, daß er den Bund, welchen ich zu selbiger Zeit vor ihm mit Gott gemacht, dem Teuffel aber, der Welt, und denen Fleisches-Lüsten in seinem Namen abgesagt habe, treueyfferig halten, und nicht brechen wolle, denn solche erste Zusage gehet allen andern Verpflichtungen weit, weit vor, und ist die wahre Tauffe nicht das Abthun des Unflats vom Fleisch; sondern sie ist der Bund eines guten Gewissens mit Gott, &c.

    The tone of this exhortation reflects Pastorius' Windsheim experience as a young lawyer in 1676-79 as well as Franz Jakob Mercklein's decision to become a lawyer and thus follow the traditions of his upper-class family. Johan Caspar Mercklein (1616-97, named burgomaster in 1692) had chosen Franz Daniel as godfather of his infant son Franz Jakob, baptized on 25 July, 1670. 18-year-old Pastorius was then visiting Windsheim after completing his first two years as a student at Nürnberg University. See pp. 63, 103 and 109 of this study and Alfred Estermann, *Bad Windsheim: Geschichte einer Stadt in Bildern*, 2nd ed. (Bad Windsheim: Delp, 1975), p. 83.
11. Cited in Learned, pp. 52-53.
12. Donald M. Lake, "Baptism," *The New International Dictionary of the Christian Church*, ed. J. D. Douglas (Exeter: Paternoster, 1974), pp. 99-101; and Robert H. Fischer, "Baptism," *The Encyclopedia of the Lutheran Church*, ed. Julius Bodensieck (Minneapolis: Augsburg Publ., 1965), 1, 179-88.
13. "Itinerarium et Vitae Curriculus" (sic), in *Des Melchior Adam Pastorius ... Leben und Reisebeschreibungen*, ed. Albert R. Schmitt (München: Delp'sche, 1968), p. 65. Learned, pp. 52-53, gives an English translation of the Journal notation:
    In the year of Christ 1651, the 26th of Sept., early in the morning between 1 and 2 o'clock in the sign of the crab, Franciscus Daniel Pastorius was born, and the following day baptized under the sponsorship of the High Well-born Franciscus of Limpurg, Hereditary Cupbearer of the Holy Roman Empire and Semper Free, and of the most worthy and erudite Daniel Gering, Doctor of the Laws.

Reflecting upper-class norms, the Latin form "Franciscus" appears in this notation and in the church registry of baptism although Pastorius was called Franz or Franz Daniel (in the 17th century frequently spelled Frantz) as a child and later in Pennsylvania, where he was also known, among his English friends, as Francis Daniel Pastorius. Writing a French dedicatory epistle to William Penn ("A Few Onomastical Considerations"), Pastorius signed his name "François Daniel Pastorius," and he also used Latin and Italian forms of his name in appropriate literary contexts. In his daily life (as reflected in Pennsylvania documents and Poem 220) he was addressed – and referred to himself – as "Daniel Pastorius," an informal compromise that avoided alternating between the English and German forms of his first name. ("Daniel" is both English and German.) As a German male named Franz, Pastorius might not have liked the sound of the English name Francis, a seemingly emasculated form of his robust and hearty German first name. (The German 'z' is an unvoiced 'tz' sound, unlike the soft voiced 'z' of English.) The Pennsylvania record, including legal documents signed "Frantz Daniel Pastorius" (Learned, pp. 161-69, 173-74), does not support Christoph E. Schweitzer's claim that Pastorius "changed his first name" from Franz to Francis in Pennsylvania (*Yearbook of German-American Studies*, 18 (1983), p. 21).

In the poem, Melchior Adam conveys his religious faith through the persona of his son, foreshadowing the paternal influence he would have throughout Franz Daniel's early years. The text in paraphrase: As death is inherent in divine justice, I ask you Jesus, the source of sustaining welfare, to protect me for a long time from approaching death, which all poor mortals must endure. You have suffered for me, you have conquered sin, daemons and death, and in your blood I am redeemed. The original text:

Franciscus Daniel Pastorius
  anagramma:
Fons salutis, parcas diu neci
Si peccatori mortemque necemque minari,
  Numinis est proprium Iustitiaeque Dei,
PARCAS quaeso, DIU IESU FONS alme SALUTIS,
  Venturae, misero quae subeunda NECI.
Passus enim pro me, Peccatum Daemona, Mortem
  Stravisti, inq. tuo Sanguine tutus ovo.

14. *Beschreibung Pa.*, p. 102:
 ... damit wann je einer unter uns nach Gottes Willen einsten hinaus in Teutschland kommen sollte, wir nach der Freundschafft fragen könnten, wollest auch von unsert wegen unsere liebe Vettern und Basen uff das freundlichste grüßen, und dieselbige dahin anweisen, daß sie öffters Brieffe an uns schreiben, welches uns auch nach unsers Vatters tödlichen hingange sehr angenehm seyn solle, und wir nicht ermangeln werden durch anderer frommen Leute Hülffe die Correspondentz zu continuiren.

15. This description is based on *Polyglott-Redaktion, Reiseführer Franken*, 4th ed. (Munich: Polyglott, 1980), pp. 3-7, 14-15, 18-30; and Max Spindler, ed., *Teil Franken* of *Franken, Schwaben, Qberpfalz bis zum Ausgang des 18. Jahrhunderts*, vol. 3 of *Handbuch der Bayerischen Geschichte* (Munchen: Beck, 1971), pp. 196-200, 216-23. Sommerhausen is described in Friedrich Gutmann and Georg Furkel, *Sommerhausen in Wort und Bild*, 2nd ed. (Wiirzburg: Gemeinde Sommerhausen, 1970), pp. 42, 119-30, 158, 187-89. Windsheim is documented in the descriptions of Chapter Two.

16. William Smith, "A Description of the Cittie of Noremberg," ed. Karlheinz Goldmann, *Mitteilungen des Vereins fur Geschichte der Stadt Nürnberg*, 48 (1958), 212-16; Daniel Papebroch, *Eine Gelehrtenreise durch Mainfranken 1660* (Wiirzburg: Freunde Mainfr. Kunst und Geschichte, 1952), pp. 18-25; Balthasar de Monconys, "Eine Reise durch Frankenland im Jahre 1663," ed. A. Bechtold, *Der Fränkische Bund*, II, i, 2-5; Jacques Esprinchard and Sebastian Munster are quoted in Hanns H. Hofmann and Günther Schuhmann, eds., *Franken in alten Ansichten und Schilderungen* (Konstanz: Thorbecke, 1967), pp. 42 and 215.

17. The historical data is from Gerd Zimmermann, "Franken," *Geschichte der deutschen Länder: Territorium Ploetz*, ed. Georg W. Sante (Würzburg: Ploetz, 1964), pp. 211-44;

Karl Brandi, *Deutsche Geschichte itn Zeitalter der Reformation und Gegenreformation* (Munich: Bruckmann, 1960), pp. 428-545 passim; Hajo Holborn, *A History of Modern Germany*, 1 (New York: Knopf, 1959), 284-374 passim; Wilhelm Treue, *Deutsche Geschichte von den Anfängen bis zur Gegenwart*, 3rd ed. (Stuttgart: Kröner, 1965), pp. 276-87; and Walter P. Fuchs, "Das Zeitalter der Reformation," and Ernst W. Zeeden, "Das Zeitalter der Glaubenskämpfe (1555-1648), *Von der Reformation bis zum Ende des Absolutismus*, ed. Max Braubach et al, vol. 2 of *Handbuch der deutschen Geschichte*, 9th ed., ed. Bruno Gebhardt and Herbert Grundmann (Stuttgart: Union, 1970), pp. 27-188 passim.

18. Luther, *Vom unfreien Willen*, quoted in Fuchs, "Zeitalter," 8th ed., p. 69. Luther's text: ". . . auf daß diejenigen, so durchs Wort nicht wollen fromm und gerecht werden, dennoch durch solch weltlich Regiment gedrungen werden, fromm und gerecht zu sein vor der Welt."
19. *Kurze Beschreibung der Reichsstadt Windsheim 1692*, ed. Alfred Estermann (Munich: Delp, 1980), pp. 110-39. The quotation from Pastorius' text: "In der Stadt... war eitel ach und Wehe, weilen das Sterben also überhand nahm, daß die Todten allenthalben auf den Gassen lagen, und täglich mit einem Karren durch die Flurer in eine Gemein-Gruben geführet wurden."
20. The postwar era is described in Holborn, 2, 3-41; Treue, pp. 285-313; Max Braubach, "Vom Westfälischen Frieden bis zur Französischen Revolution," *Handbuch der deutschen Geschichte*, 2, 240-74 passim; and Rudolf Endres, "Staat und Gesellschaft. Zweiter Teil: 1500-1800," *Handbuch der Bayerischen Geschichte*, 3, 349-52.
21. Rudolf Vierhaus, *Deutschland im Zeitalter des Absolutismus (1648-1763)* (Göttingen: Vandenhoeck & Ruprecht, 1978), pp. 50-51:
    Die eifersüchtige Beachtung von sozialen Unterschieden, die Betonung von Vorrechten und Distanzen, das dichte System sozialer Kontrolle, das in Stadt und Dorf bestand, ... erzeugten einen hohen Anpassungsdruck.... Servilität, tatsächliche oder scheinbare Demut des Tieferstehenden gegenüber dem "Höheren" ... haben sich dem allgemeinen Denken und Verhalten der Menschen tief eingeprägt... Standes- und Zunftmentalität herrschte auch bei Juristen, Gelehrten und Pfarrern.
22. "Brim" is defined in OED, 1 (1933), 1105: "Of swine: To be 'in heat,' rut, copulate."
23. This short title, from a list of books Pastorius read (in Learned, p. 257), is used in the poem, and refers to *The Cabinet Open'd, or the secret history of the Amours of Madam de Maintenon, with the French King* (London, 1690). *Update 2013:* The mistress was Françoise d'Aubigné, Marquise de Maintenon (1635-1719), whom Louis XIV secretly married in 1685; see Veronica Buckley, *Madame De Maintenon: The Secret Wife of Louis XIV* (London: Bloomsbury, 2008), reviewed, for example, in *The Economist*, 24 July 2008: URL = http://www.economist.com/node/11785001
24. Will and Ariel Durant, *The Age of Louis XIV*, Part 8 of *The Story of Civilization* (New York: Simon and Schuster, 1963), pp. 415-16.
25. On Pietism generally: "Pietism" in *The Oxford Dictionary of the Christian Church*, 2nd ed., ed. F. L. Cross and E. A. Livingstone (Oxford: Oxford Univ. Pr., 1974), pp. 1089-90; August Langen, "Pietismus," *Reallexikon der deutschen Literaturgeschichte*, 2nd ed., 3 (1977), 103-14; Johannes Wallmann, *Kirchengeschichte Deutschlands* II (Frankfurt: Ullstein, 1973), pp. 133-56; Martin Schmidt, "Einleitung," *Das Zeitalter des Pietismus*, ed. Martin Schmidt and Wilhelm Jannasch (Bremen: Schönemann, 1965), pp. iv-xlviii. On Spener and the Saalhof Pietists: "Pia desideria" and "Spener, Philipp Jakob," in *Oxford Dictionary*, pp. 1088-89, 1298-99; Paul Grünberg, "Spener, Philipp Jakob," *Realenzyklopädie für protestantische Theologie und Kirche*, 3rd ed., 18 (1896, rpt. 1971), 609-22; Friedrich W. Kantzenbach, *Orthodoxie und Pietismus* (Gütersloh: Mohn, 1966), pp. 134-48; Johannes Wallmann, *Philipp Jakob Spener und die Anfänge des Pietismus* (Tubingen: Mohr, 1970), pp. 35-178 passim.
26. Helmut E. Huelsbergen, "The First Thirteen Families: Another Look at the Religious and Ethnic Background of the Emigrants from Crefeld (1683)," *Yearbook of German-American Studies*, 18 (1983), 29-40; and Guido Rotthoff, "Die Auswanderung von Krefeld nach Pennsylvanien im Jahre 1683," *Die Heimat: Krefelder Jahrbuch* (Sonderdruck), 53

(1983), 2-11. Although the simplicity of the Krefelders is still being debated, Pastorius reported, in *Sichere Nachricht auß America* [March, 1684] (N.p., n.d.), p. 3, that "these simple, honest people" ("diese redliche Leutlein") used up their life savings on the journey to Pennsylvania, arriving in a state of destitution that would have required them to enter indentured servitude had it not been for William Penn's generosity in getting them established. The diminutive "Leutlein," meaning simple or common people, indicates the sense of class distinction Pastorius communicated to his Frankfurt associates in 1684.

27. *Sichere Nachricht*, p. 7:
    Dafern ihr nicht... zu Ermanglung der meisten in Teutschland gewohnten Gemächlichkeiten als steinern Häuser, niedlichen Kost und Tranck &c. ein oder zwey Jahr resolviren könnt, so folget meinem Rath und bleibet noch eine Zeitlang wo ihr seyd, fallen euch aber jetztgedachte Puncten nicht zu hart, so gehet je ehender je lieber auß dem Europaeischen Sodom auß...

28. *Theologisches Bedencken Und andere Brieffliche Antworten* (Halle: Buchhandlung des Waisenhauses, 1712), 3, 766:
    Denen die ihre zuflucht dahin nehmen, überlasse ich ihre gedancken: ich könnte niemand rathen, zu fliehen, ehe der Herr austreibt... Meine gedancken sind allezeit, zu bleiben, wo uns der Herr hinsetzt, und wie lang er uns daselbst lässet...
    This letter, dated 1 Aug. 1689, is identified – in Gustav Kramer, *Beiträge zur Geschichte August Hermann Franckes* (Halle: Buchhandlung des Waisenhauses, 1861), p. 329 – as addressed to fellow Pietist August Hermann Francke. Spener here complains that he has not heard from Pastorius for three years (since moving from Frankfurt to Dresden in 1686), and states he would be happy to see a copy of a Pennsylvania tract by Pastorius mentioned in Francke's previous correspondence, since Pastorius "is after all the one who founded Germanstown and has sent the most reports from the colony to Germany." ("Hrn. Lie. Pastorii... ist sonsten derjenige, der Germanstown gebauet, und die meiste nachricht von dem land in Teutschland gebracht hat.")

29. *Beschreibung Pa.*, p. 90:
    Von diesen [die Principal-Participanten] haben noch einige Theils genossen zu mir herüber [zu]kommen, und das Vornehmen zum gewünschten Effect Bringen helffen sollen, so aber biß dato nicht geschehen, weilen sie die Einöde und Langweil scheuen, dessen allen ich Gott Lob nunmehro wohl gewohnet bin, und also gewohnet werde bleiben biß an mein seeliges Ende.

Chapter Two

1. Quoted in Pastorius, *Das Melchior Adam Pastorius... Leben und Reisebeschreibung*, ed. Schmitt, p. 55:
    Aus der Innlage hastu zu ersehen, was der Hochgelehrte, Unser Lieber Besonder Melchior Adam Pastorius, an Uns gelangen lassen. Gleich wie Wir nun dessen Wohlfart gerne befördert sehen mb'chten, also zweiffelt Uns nicht, Du werdest dise Unsere Recommendation so weith gültig sein lassen, damitt selbiger nach seinen Qualitäten bester maßen möge untergebracht und befördert werden.
    The sources here referred to are cited in the notes to the Prologue. Although not mentioned in the sources, Pastorius may have met Georg Friedrich and arranged employment before obtaining Johann Philipp's recommendation in late November.

2. The Latin text (from Pastorius, *Leben*) is quoted in Learned, p. 34.

3. *Franconia Rediviva* (Nürnberg: n.p., 1702), p. 431:
    Sommerhausen / ein schöner Flecken am Mayn gegen Winterhausen übergehört / denen Erbschencken und Semper-Freyen von Limpurg / diese aber tragens von dem Bischoffe zu Wüirtzburg zu Mann-Lehen. Hat ein Freyherrlich Haus und schöne Kirch darinnen / auch ein Kellerey und Schultheissenampt / gesunde Brunnen / und einen herrlichen guten Weinwachs / samt fruchtbaren Obs-Bäumen.

266 | Notes: Chapter Two

4. Pastorius Collection, Item 3, Historical Society of Pennsylvania. The text, quoted passim by Learned, is similar to "Genealogia Pastoriana" but includes supplementary names and dates.
5. Georg S. Ziegler, "Der Limpurgischer Ehrensaal" (MS. Limpurg, 1739) as cited in Learned, pp. 31-32; and Karl O. Müller, "Das Geschlecht der Reichserbschenken zu Limpurg," *Zeitschrift fur württembergische Landesgeschichte*, 5 (1941), 237.
6. Pastorius, *Leben*, p. 65; also in Learned, p. 30:
    Magdalena Pastoriusin Gebohrne Dietzin
        anagramma:
    O IESU, An Dir Hangt Mein Gantze Lieb, O Spare Da.
    Von Kindheit auff im Creutz und Nothstand must ich stecken,
    Mich that der Kriegsschwall und manche Plünderung schrecken.
    Mein's Vatters Haus und Hoff, auch was erwarb mein Mann
    Must mitt dem Rucken ich als Wittib schauen an.
    In solcher Creützes Schuel lernt ich die Welt verachten.
    Und deren Eyttelkeit vonn innern Grund betrachten.
    Ich sprach: O spare da, mein Gott, einst doch die Peyn,
    O IESU an dir hangt mein gantze Lieb allein.
7. Karl-Sigismund Kramer, *Bauern und Bürger im nachmittelalterlichen Unterfranken* (Würzburg; Schöningh, 1957), pp. 15-16, 37-42.
8. Kramer, p. 41: "In gleicher Weise wie eine Hausgemeinschaft muß auch die Dorfgemeinschaft zum Wohle aller Hand in Hand arbeiten, [um] das ... Zusammenprallen verschiedener Temperamente bei den ermüdenden Erfordernissen des arbeitsreichen Alltags [zu vermeiden]."
9. Gutmann and Furkel, *Sommerhausen*, pp. 259-60.
10. Gutmann and Furkel, pp. 165-66:
    Voraus gingen der Flurer mit den Schulbuben, 2 Tambour, 4 Musikanten, die vier Geschwornen mit Gerten, die mit seidenen Bändern geschmückt waren, dann folgte der Gräfl. Amtmann, der Amtsschultheiß, Rathschreiber und andere Herren, 2 Herrn des Rats in Rock und Degen, die Schützenkompagnie mit ihrer Fahne und den Herrn Oberoffiziers, die Bürgerschaft, nämlich voraus: 2 Tambours und 3 Musikanten, der Bürger-Hauptmann, die Bürgerschaft mit der Bürgerfahne, ihren Oberoffizieren und Unteroffizieren, 1 Tambour und 2 Querpfeifer, endlich 1 Corporal mit der jungen Mannschaft ... An dem Festessen, das an zwei Tafeln auf dem Rathaus stattfand, beteiligten sich die Herren des Gräfl. Amtes, der Ortsgeistliche, der Amtsschultheiß, der Amts- und Rathschreiber, die Herren Offiziere der Schützen- und Biirgerkompagnie, die Geschwornen, 7-8 Musikanten und andere Personen.
    For similar observances in other Franconian towns, see Kramer, pp. 60-62, and his *Volksleben im Fiirstentum Ansbach* (Wiirzburg: Schöningh, 1961), pp. 68-69.
11. Kramer, *Volksleben*, pp. 118-19:
    Spieltische und Kramstände waren aufgeschlagen, auf freiem Platz wurde gekocht und Wein ausgeschenkt, von allen Seiten her stromten aus den Nachbarortschaften die Gäste. Tanzmusik tönte vom Plan her und von den Tanzböden, auf denen der "offene Tanz" von den Wirten veranstaltet wurde. Gruppen von Zechenden saßen um die auf der Dorfstraße aufgestellten Tische oder in den Schankstuben... Das Juchzen und Schreien der Tanzenden und Zechenden erfullte die Luft, hie und da flackerten Streitigkeiten auf... Nicht nur die Rauflust, auch die Sinnlichkeit wurde erhitzt. Es ist aktenkundig, daß so mancher Erdenbürger dem Rausch von Tanz und Trunk auf den Kirchweihen sein Dasein verdankt. Der nächtliche Heimweg oder auch das Luftschöpfen im Hofe des Wirtshauses nach erregendem Tanze wurde so manchem Mädchen, war sie auch ehrbar bis zu dieser Stunde, zum Verhängnis.
12. Kramer, *Bauern*, p. 71; *Volksleben*, pp. 121-22.
13. Gutmann and Furkel, pp. 214, 216, 374.
14. Kramer, *Bauern*, p. 177: "Die Freude an kräftigen Genüssen fand nicht nur im gemeinsamen Essen und Trinken bei den verschiedensten Festen des offentlichen und privaten Lebens ihren Ausdruck. Sie gibt auch dem alltäglichen Dasein Würze und Inhalt."
15. Kramer, *Bauern*, pp. 177-89.

Notes: Chapter Two | 267

16. Gutmann and Furkel, pp. 187-88, 203, 209, 214.
17. Kramer, *Bauern*, p. 154:
    [Die] Nachbarn... waren es ..., die im Anschluß an das Leichenbegängnis im Wirtshaus oder im Sterbehause zum Leichentrunk zusammenkamen. Man begnügte sich dabei nicht mit dem von den Angehörigen gespendeten Wein, sondern legte, sicher zu Ehren des Toten, noch weiteres Getränk auf die Anwesenden um ... Daß es dabei dann leicht... zu unwürdigen Szenen kommt, liegt nahe ...
18. Kramer, *Volksleben*, p. 119: "Mitten im Trubel saßen herrschaftliche Beamte, Schultheißen und Bauernmeister und verzehrten auf Gemeindekosten ihr Kirchweihmahl."
19. The following details are from Gutmann and Furkel, pp. 244-45, 256, with supplementary detail on "high court" assemblies in Lower Franconia from Kramer, *Bauern*, p. 83.
20. Kramer, *Bauern*, p. 80:
    [Es] gibt im alltäglichen Leben Anlässe genüg, sich an den altüberkommenen Vorrechten der Herren zu reiben und wundzuscheuern. Das Mißtrauen, übervorteilt zu werden, ist sehr wach und rege. Herrschaftliche Interessen im Dorfe vertreten zu müssen, ist darum keine sehr schätzenswerte Aufgabe; eine Tatsache, die vor allem der Schultheiß immer wieder zu spüren bekam... Durch seine Funktion ist ein sehr deutlicher Abstand zu den übrigen Dorfgenossen geschaffen.
21. Hanns H. Hofmann, *Neustadt-Windsheim. Historischer Atlas von Bayern, Franken* section, ser. 1, no. 2 (München: Komm. fur bay. Landesgeschichte, 1953), 15-33; Herman Delp, *Bad Windsheim*, 3rd ed. (Bad Windsheim: Delp, 1979), passim; Fritz Schnelbögl, "Die fränkischen Reichsstädte," *Zeitschrift fur bay. Landesgeschichte*. 31 (1968), 421- 65 passim.
22. *Leben*, pp. 12, 69; Appendix V ("Lebenslauf," unpaginated) in Roth, "Der Windsheimer Bürgermeister und Oberrichter Melchior Adam Pastorius."
23. Estermann, *Bad Windsheim*, pp. 63, 82-83, 88-90, 92, 95; Kramer, *Volksleben*, pp. 62, 261-65, 290-91, 297-312; and Hermann Kellenbenz, "Wirtschaft zwischen 1555 und 1648," and Ingomar Bog, "Wirtschaft und Gesellschaft im Zeitalter des Merkantilismus," both in *Nürnberg*, ed. Gerhard Pfeiffer (Munich: Beck, 1971), pp. 300-01, 315-22.
24. Estermann, p. 27; Kramer, *Volksleben*, pp. 29-30; M. A. Pastorius, *Windsheim*, pp. 8-9.
25. "Zwei unbekannte Briefe," ed. Goebel, p. 494; and *Sichere Nachricht*, p. 3: "Germantown ist... die helffte umb und umb mit anmuthigen Brunquellen als einem natürlichen Wall bevestigt."
26. Kramer, *Volksleben*, p. 62:
    Im Brauchkalender [Windsheims] sind die alten wichtigen Termine mit Fasnacht, Fasten, Ostern, Pfingsten, Fronleichnam, Martini, Weihnachten und Neujahr reich vertreten. Zumindest werden sie in festlichen Mahlzeiten des Rates auf dem Rathaus sichtbar. Die Fasnacht ist durch Spiele und Tänze der Handwerker hervorgehoben. Auch der Neujahrstag wurde besonders feierlich begangen. Selbstverständlich stehen auch die großen Ereignisse des rechtlichen Gemeindelebens, vor allem die Rats- und Bürgermeisterwahl im Mittelpunkt. Musikanten und Abgesandte fremder Herrschaften kehren das ganze Jahr über in der Stadt ein und werden großzügig bewirtet.
27. Kramer, *Volksleben*, p. 270:
    Die Haufen von Bauernburschen oder Bürgersöhnen, die auf der staubigen Straße mit klingendem Spiel von den verschiedensten Seiten her einem Ziele nahen, einem Dorfe, in dem der Wirt zum Tanz geladen hatte, in dessen Haus nun alles "übereinander wimmelt," wo Bier und Wein in Strömen sich dürstige Kehlen ergießen, Lachen und Fluchen erklingen und viele Musikanten zum Tanze aufspielen . . . Daß die Heimkehr dieser Rotten nicht Lautlos vor sich ging, daß sie im Heimatort, war es mitten in der Nacht, Trommeln und Pfeifen nicht ruhen ließen, daß sich ein "bochisch und unzüchtig schreyen, jauchzen und singen auf den gassen" erhob (Polizeiordnung 1549), läßt sich denken.
28. Friedrich Bock, *Zur Volkskunde der Reichsstadt Nürnberg* (Würzburg: Schöningh, 1959), pp. 31-32; *Bräuche und Feste im fränkischen Jahreslauf*, ed. Joseph Dünninger and Horst Schopf (Kulmbach: Stadtarchiv, 1971), pp. 89-95.

29. Mandate of the Nürnberg senate, 20 June 1653, cited in Dünninger and Schopf, pp. 93-94:
    Und gebieten Ihre Herr.[en] E.[dlen] E.[hrbaren] Rath der Stadt Nürnberg hierauf ernstlich / daß alle Ihre Bürger ... sich ... des anzündens des so genannten Sonnenwendt: oder Simmets Feurs / des dabey vorgangenen Fressen und Sauffens / Tantzens / Springens / und anderer darneben verübten aberglaubischen Werck und unchristlicher Ungebühr / wodurch der Höchste erzörnet / und die Jugend zu sträfflichen Leben und Wandel angewehnet / männiglichs aber geärgert wird / allerdings und gäntzlich enthalten sollen.
30. Windsheim ordinance, 15 Sept. 1650. Reprinted in *Windsheimer Zeitung*, 28 Feb. 1959, and in *Jahresbericht des Historischen Vereins von Mittelfranken*, 24 (1855), 35-38.
31. Windsheim ordinance, 1667. Copied in M. A. Pastorius, "Forma civitatis imperialis liberae" (Stadtarchiv Bad Windsheim, MS. A6), fols. 90-95.
32. M. A. Pastorius, *Windsheim*, pp. 36-39; Estermann, *Bad Windsheim*, pp. 5, 36-37, 72, 109.
33. M. A. Pastorius, *Windsheim*, p. 37:
    Auch stehet in diesem mittlern Theile der Kirchen der Predigstuhl / welchen anno Christi 1600. Georg Brenck Burger und Bildhauer gefertiget / also / daß zu unterst die Statua Mosis mit denen zwo Tafeln stehet / uff dessen Haupte 6. Engel mit ausgebreiteten Flügeln den Predigstuhl / wie die Athlantes tragen / ringsherum sind die Bildnüssen Christi Salvatoris, derer 4. Evangelisten S. Joannis Bapt. und einige Propheten. Oben um den Crantz herum stehen diese Worte: Nach dem Gesetz und nach dem Zeugnüs / werden sie das nicht thun / so werden sie die Morgenröthe nicht sehen. Inwendig an der obern Decke ist die Historia von Ausgiessung des H. Geistes / cum inscriptione: Und er faßte sich auf einen jeglichen unter ihnen / und sie wurden alle voll des H. Geistes. Aussen herum stehen die 12. Aposteln / und 12. Engel uff der Schiltwach fur die Christliche Kirche / und dienen der H. Dreyfaltigkeit / welche zu allerobrist abgebildet ist. An der Thür des Predigstuhls ist der Fall Adam und Evae, Item das Bildnüß Christi / wie er die Böcke von denen Schafen absondert / rings herum sind die 7. Wercke der Barmhertzigkeit. Über dieser Thür sind die damalige Herren Geistliche abgebildet / und zu obrist der von den Todten auferstandne HErr Christus / nebenst welchen zween Engel mit Posaunen das Jüngste Gericht verkündigen.
34. *Beschreibung Pa.*, pp. 34-35:
    Wir haben allhier zu Germantown Ann. 1686. ein Kirchlein fur die Gemeinde gebauet, darbey aber nicht auf äusserliches großes Stein-Gebäude gesehen, sondern daß der Tempel Gottes (welcher wir Glaubige selbst sind) gebauet werde, und wir allesamt heilig und unbefleckt seyn mögen. Die Evangelische Prediger hätten hier eine schöne Gelegenheit dem Befehl Christi nachzukommen: Gehet hin in alle Welt, und prediget das Evangelium. Wann sie lieber Christi Nachfolger, als ihres Leibes Diener seyn wolten, und wann sie mehr der Theologiae interna, als der buchstäblichen Recitirung ergeben wären.
35. For the "stone church" references of Weigel and Boehme see Holborn, *History*. 2, 135-36; and Emanuel Hirsch, *Geschichte der neuern evangelischen Theologie*, 2 (Gütersloh: Bertelsmann, 1951), 234-36.
36. Estermann, "Geistliches Singen und Spielen zu Gott," *Fränkische Landeszeitung*, 25 Aug. 1967: "... ein imponierend vielfältiges Bild sonntäglichen Musizierens und Singens 'ad maiorem gloriam Dei,' zum größeren Ruhm Gottes ..."
37. Estermann, "Geistliches Singen."
38. Windsheim ordinance, 1641, quoted in Estermann, *Bad Windsheim*, p. 114: "... alle Viertelstunden nach allen 4. Seiten ein Zeichen ihrer Wachsamkeit zu geben."
39. M. A. Pastorius, *Windsheim*, p. 39:
    Ausserhalb der Kirchen uff der rechten Seiten des Chors ist im Jahr Christi 1439. ein achteckichter Kirchthurn gebauet worden / so mit Zinn gedecket / auf deme man durch eine steinerne Schneckstiegen gehet / und in dem ersten Zimmer die Glokken / in dem andern darüber derer Wächter oder Musicanten Wohnung / aus dero man

den gantzen Horizonth übersehen kan. Zu allerobrist im Thurn hängt die Schlag-Uhr / welche der Wächter durch einen Zug schlagen machet.
40. Estermann, *Bad Windsheim*, p. 84; Pastorius, *Windsheim*, pp. 84-85.
41. The events summarized here are described in Braubach, "Vom Westfälischen Frieden," *Handbuch der deutschen Geschichte*, 2, 246-48; Holborn, 363-65; Horst Rabe, "Die iberischen Staaten im 16. und 17. Jahrhundert," *Handbuch der europäischen Geschichte*, ed. Theodor Schieder, 3 (Stuttgart: Union, 1971), 634-37; and Juan Reglá, "Spain and her Empire," *The New Cambridge Modern History*, 5, ed. F. L. Carsten (Cambridge: The Univ. Press, 1961), pp. 369, 379-80.
42. For Windsheim's imperial observances in 1659 and 1660 see Estermann, p. 84; Pastorius, *Windsheim*, pp. 84-85; and Christian Schirmer, *Geschichte Windsheims* (Nürnberg: Riegel und Wießner, 1848), p. 191.
43. Pastorius, *Windsheim*, p. 84:
    Der gantze Rath gieng mit entblosten Haupten neben der Gutschen / und ritten 25. Pferde der vornehmsten Burger hinter der Kutschen biß zu Ende der Stadt Marckung gegen Wibelsheim / alldar man in einer Reihen gehalten / und Abschied genommen / mit demüthigster Neigung gegen die beede Potentaten.
    Although Pastorius may have witnessed the royal departure – the only phase of Leopold's visit he described – he did not move his family to Windsheim for another five months.
44. Estermann, p. 84; Pastorius, *Windsheim*, pp. 139-40; Rolf Bauer, *Österreich* (Berlin: Haude & Spenersche, 1970), pp. 169-70; and Herbert Jansky, "Osmanenherrschaft in Südosteuropa von 1648 bis 1789," *Handbuch der europäischen Geschichte*, ed. Schieder, 4, 757.
45. Schirmer, p. 191:
    Auf die Nachricht von der Niederlage bei Neuhäusel (1663) verbot hier der Rath alle Lustbarkeiten, und ließ am 1. Oktober einen Buß- und Bettag halten. Man fürchtete sich so sehr vor den Türken, auch im Frankenlande, daß der Rath die Befestigungen der Stadt herzustellen für nöthig hielt, und 1664 viele Personen aus der Gegend ihre Habe hierher flüchteten.
46. Estermann, p. 84; Schirmer, p. 191.
47. Endres, "Franken in den Auseinandersetzungen," *Handbuch der bayerischen Geschichte*, ed. Spindler, 3, 233.
48. Pastorius, *Windsheim*, p. 105:
    1664. den 22. Julii geschahe die blutige Schlacht bey S. Gotthard in Hungarn an dem Raab Fluß / ward Herr Obrist Bleittner und Hr. Obrist-Lieutenant Buttlar / Obrist-Wachmeister Beck / und die meisten gemeinen vom Regiment durch die Türcken niedergesäbelt. Die Stadt Windsheim hatte den 5. Mann all ihrer Unterthanen etlich und 90. Köpffe gestellt / davon kamen nicht mehr zu rücke als 2. Corporal und 8. Gemeine unter dem Leuten. Lass / die danckete man den 5. Decembris ab / gab jedem nebst seinem Abschiede 3 1/2. Thaler.
49. *Update 2013:* Grafton ("Republic of Letters," p. 27) notes that Pastorius' wheel "reconfigured an image coined more than a century before by the Catholic Kabbalist and historian Michael von Aitzinger."
50. Pastorius, *Windsheim*, pp. 106-07:
    1666. den 3. May Abends kurtz vor dem gar ausschlagen / war zu Windsheim ein grausames Donner- Wetter / und von denen blitzen fast die gantze Stadt mit Feuer angefüllet / endlich schlug ein grosser Schiebel Feuer in den Pfarr-Thurn. Der Fluhrer / Georg Leicht / so zu Wetter leutete / blieb vom Halle todt / bald darauf fieng das allerobriste Thürnlein / darinn die Schlag-Uhr henckt / anzubrennen / und stunde fast zwo Stunden lang in Feuers-Flammen. Auswendig kunte man mit keiner Wasser-Kunst hinauflangen / innwendig war es so eng / daß kaum eine eintzige Person uff der Laiter stehen konnte / man trug alle die Milch aus dem Spital und sonst zusammen / trugens über das lange Haus der Kirchen / und langten einen Feuer-Eimer nach dem andern voll Milch dem Thomas Wagnern / so zu obrist beym Feuer stunde / zu / biß es endlich / mit GOttes Hülffe / geloschet wurde.

Man ließ nachgehends durch die Zimmer-Leute ein neues Thürnlein nach dem alten Model von gutem aichenen Holtze verfertigen / und durch den Schieferdecker von Kitzingen mit zinnernen Blechen bedecken / welcher Meister nach gäntzlich gefertigter Arbeit / Mittwochs den 23. May / auf den Knopff gestiegen / alda ein neues paar Strümpf und Schuh angezogen / eine zinnerne Maaß-Kanten mit Wein auf 3. Trüncke ausgetruncken / und solche herab vor das neue Haus geworffen.

51. Pastorius, *Windsheim*, pp. 61-63. This passage, in a chapter on "other religious institutions" ("Von andern Geistlichen Stiftungen"), follows descriptions of Windsheim's churches and chapels:

    Daß lateinische SchulHaus / ohnweit der Pfarrkirchen und des Rathhauses ist von E. E. Rathe im Jahr Christi 1573. an einem solchen Orte aufgebauet worden / an welchem nicht viel Gethös der Handwercker zu hören ist. . . . In dem untersten Stockwerck werden die kleinsten Knaben in Begreiffung der Buchstaben / des Lesens und Schreibens informiret / auch zum Gebet / und Erlernung des kleinen Catechismi angehalten . . . In dem obristen Stockwerck / dociret der Herr Rector die nunerwachsene Jugend / und spitzet sie zu / daß sie capabel werden auf eine Universität zu reisen / und höhere Studia unter die Hand zu nehmen. Die sämtliche Praeceptores werden von E. E. Rathe angenommen / mit freyen Behausungen versehen und mit nothdürfftigen Salariis versehen. Dagegen müssen sie sich schrifftlich verreversiren / daß sie allen getreuen Fleisses die Jugend in der Gottes-Furcht und freyen Künsten wollen unterweisen / und mit einem guten exemplarischen Leben und Wandel vorgehen / und dem Magistrat pariren.

52. For the inkwell attack and its context see Richard Friedenthal, *Luther* (Munich: Piper, 1967), pp. 357-60. The following description summarizes the educational writings of Luther reproduced with commentary in Theodor Ballauf and Klaus Schaller, *Pädagogik* (Munich: Alber, 1970), 2, 15-31.

53. *An die Bürgermeister und Ratsherrn aller Städte in deutschen Landen*, 1524, in Luther's *Pädagogische Schriften*, 2nd ed., ed. Hermann Lorenzen (Paderborn: Schöningh, 1969), pp. 68, 75:

    Das ist einer Stadt bestes und allerreichstes Gedeihen, Heil und Kraft, daß sie viel feiner, gelehrter, vernünftiger, ehrbarer, wohlerzogener Bürger hat . . . Wenn nun gleich . . . keine Seele wäre, und man der Schulen und Sprachen gar nicht bedürfte um der Schrift und Gottes Willen, so wäre doch allein diese Sache genugsam, die allerbesten Schulen, beide für Knaben und Mädlein, an allen Orten aufzurichten, daß die Welt, auch ihren weltlichen Stand äußerlich zu halten, doch bedarf feiner, geschickter Männer und Frauen, daß die Männer wohl regieren könnten Land und Leute, die Frauen wohl ziehen und halten könnten Haus, Kinder und Gesinde. Nun solche Männer müssen aus Knaben werden, und solche Frauen müssen aus Mädlein werden.

    Lorenzen summarizes Luther's educational values and goals, which also gave importance to mathematics, history and music, in "Martin Luther als Erzieher," appended to *Pädagogische Schriften*, pp. 182-89.

54. Klaus Leder, "Das evangelische Schulwesen," *Handbuch der bayerischen Geschichte*, ed. Spindler, 3, 682.

55. Estermann, pp. 61, 64; Roth, "Pastorius," pp. 88-91.

56. For Luther and Erasmus and Luther's approach to childrearing, see Klaus Petzold, *Die Grundlagen der Erziehungslehre im Spätmittelalter und bei Luther* (Heidelberg: Quelle & Meyer, 1969), pp. 64-67, 84-89; and Ballauf and Schaller, pp. 15-25. Luther's light moods are described, with quotations in English, in a misleadingly one-sided analysis in John C. Sommerville, *The Rise and Fall of Childhood* (Beverly Hills, Calif.: Sage Publ., 1982), pp. 89, 93. The other quotations from Luther, as quoted in Ballauf and Schaller, p. 24: "Wer . . . sein Kind lieb hat, der stäupet es vielmals." "Es ist in eines jeglichen Kindes Herzen törlich Vornehmen; aber die Rute mag das alles austreiben." "Schlägst du dein Kind mit Ruten, so wirst du seine Seele von der Hölle erlösen."

57. "Schulordnung," 1595, in Werner Korndörfer, *Studien zur Geschichte der Reichsstadt Windsheim vornehmlich im 17. Jahrhundert*, Diss. Erlangen-Nürnberg, 1972 (Erlangen: Offsetdruck Hogl, 1972), p. 147:

Alle Schueler... sollen... wie die fromme Schueler für sich selbsten aus Lieb zur Ehr und Tugendt allen schuldigen Gehorsam zu leisten wissen; Also befehlen und gebieten Wir den Praeceptoribus sämbtlich und iedem in sonderheit, hiemit ernstlich, daß dieselbigen die bösen und unartigen Schueler mit gebührender Straff zu schuldigem Gehorsam antreiben und sonderlich die Ruten mit mehrern Ernst, dann bißhero geschehen, nutzen und brauchen sollen. Dargegen erbieten Wir Uns beedes den Praeceptoribus und frommen Schueler allen günstigen Willen und Beförderung zu erweisen.

58. In Korndörfer, p. 160:
 ... damit... der hernachwachsenden lieben Jugendt Nutz und Frommen, ewig und zeitliche Wohlfahrt befördert, hingegen bey derselben alle Mißbreuch und Unordnungen abgestellet, der eingerissenen Faulheit, Muthwillen, und Eigensinnigkeit, bevorab deme in ietziger letzten Weltneige leider! allzusehr überhandt nehmenden, unchristlichen und unerbaren Wandel unsers Orts nach bestem Vermögen zeitlich gesteuert, vorgebogen werden möge.
59. Johann Georg Nehr, *Zur Geschichte der Schulen in Windsheim* (Windsheim: n.p., 1807, 1808), 1, 22 und 2, 8-10.
60. *Windsheim*, pp. 89-94, 99-101.
60a. *Update 2013*: Pastorius does not mention homosexuality directly but instead refers to "that filthy wickedness, whereof the Apostle speaks at the end of his ninth verse" in 1 Corinthians 6. His father's complaint about sodomy in Rome is quoted on p. 18.
61. Teachers and clergy in Windsheim: Nehr, 1, 20-22; 2, 11; Korndörfer, pp. 92-95. In Franconia and Germany: Kramer, *Volksleben*, pp. 75-81; Friedrich Paulsen, *Geschichte des gelehrten Unterrichts*, 3rd ed., 1 (1919; rpt. Berlin: de Gruyter, 1960), 331-37, 484-86, 607-08.
62. In Korndörfer, p. 160.
63. Johann Georg Nehr, *Beitrage zur Kirchengeschichte Windsheims*, 5 (Windsheim: n.p., 1805), 21:
 Ihm dünke, jeder der beyden anwesenden Streiter sage nur mit andern Worten das nämliche. Dieß fiel den beyden Herren wie eine unerhörte Neuigkeit auf. Sie stutzten und nach einigem Nachdenken kam ihnen die Sache gerade so vor, wie Gelchsheimer gesagt hatte.
64. In Korndörfer, pp. 147-71.
65. Motives and personalities here discussed are indicated in the revised code itself and in senate minutes referred to by Nehr, *Zur Geschichte*, 1, 22-23; and Roth, "Pastorius," pp. 92, 96.
66. For background on Pastorius' Latin schooling see Roth, "Pastorius," pp. 88-102; Paulsen, 1, 341-87, 465-92; and Fritz Blättner, "Die Wandlung von der altprotestantischen Gelehrtenschule zum humanistischen Gymnasium," in *Das Gymnasium in Geschichte und Gegenwart*, ed. Hermann Rohrs (Frankfurt: Akademische Verlagsges., 1969), pp. 1-13.
67. The circulated poetry includes "sorry Rimes, scribbled on any vacant page" of books borrowed and then returned to their various owners (Pastorius to Samuel Carpenter, quoted in Toms, p. 152), several commemorative poems to the daughters of Thomas Lloyd (two of which are cited on pp. 36-37, 50, 88 and 248-49 of this study), and *Deliciae Hortenses or Garden-Recreations and Voluptates Apianae*. The emblem collection is cited on pp. 92-98, 117-18 and 139 (and in a few epigraphs), and the Latin letter on pp. 147-48, 229 and 234-35. The allusions and resonances of the letter were noted by Dr. Rolf Lenzen of Cardinal Frings Gymnasium, Bonn, the Latin specialist who helped translate portions of the letter for this study.
68. Learned, *Life*, pp. 99, 127-28; Mack, pp. 139-40; Learned, *Life*, pp.195-212, describes some of Passtorius' Pennsylvania friendships. *Update 2013:* Grafton, "Republic of Letters," p. 4, describes the allusion to the *Aeneid* identified in Learned and provides the English translation of this line. Mack identifies it as pentameter verse.
69. Notation in his book inventory, in Learned, p. 281.
70. For Schumberg's biography and school program see Estermann, p. 98; Roth, "Pastorius," pp. 92-102; and Gerlinde Lamping, *Die Bibliothek der Freien Reichsstadt Winds-*

heim, Diss. Univ. Würzburg, 1966 (Bad Windsheim: Delp, 1966), pp. 49-50. For his friends Dilherr and Seckendorf see Gerhard Schröttel, "Johann Michael Dilherr," *Fränkische Lebensbilder*, ed. Pfeiffer and Wendehorst, 7 (1977), 142-51; Holborn, *Modern Germany*, 2, 51-52; and Michael Stolleis, "Veit Ludwig von Seckendorf," *Staatsdenker*, ed. Stolleis, pp. 148-73. The Comenius titles in Pastorius' book inventory (in Learned, pp. 280, 282) are *Synopsin Physicae ad lumen divinum reformatae, Lexikon atriale & januale,* and two of the *Janua Linguarum* bi- and multilingual handbooks, one for Latin and English, and the other for Latin, German, French and Italian.

71. *Pharus divina philosophiae practicae* (Nürnberg: W. Felsecker, 1663, rev. ed. 1667). The following analysis follows the 1667 ed., which does not vary substantially from the first edition. Johann Michael Dilherr praised Schumberg's clarity and brevity in the textbook's five-line verse foreword:

    Ad Virum Clarissimum. Dn Tobiam Schumbergium.
    Ars est longe; brevis vita. Hinc dignissimus ille
    Laude, brevi methodo qui bene multa docet.
    Hoc Tu, Schumbergi! praestas praesente libello:
    Quem, scio, praeclaris posse placere Viris.

72. "Tolerabilior est reipublicae status, ubi princeps malus, & consiliarii boni sunt, quam ubi princeps bonus, & mali consiliarii."
73. "Basis & fundamentum reipublicae Religio... Cometae, eclipses & terraemotus mutationes in imperiis futuras portendunt."
74. Vier kleine/Doch ungemeine/Und sehr nutzliche Tractätlein (n.p., 1690), described in Learned, pp. 228-29; "De Mundi Vanitate," in *Beschreibung Pa.*, pp. 62-63; also in Learned, pp. 60-61; in a German transl. by Eduard Schauenburg, in Koppen, *Vom Rhein zum Delaware*, pp. 52-53; and in a less satisfactory English transl. by J. Franklin Jameson in Myers, *Narratives*, pp. 423-24.
75. P. 130: "Paterfamilias est princeps persona familae, rem familiarem monarchicè gubernans."
76. *Leben*, p. 67:

    Nach deme es sein Zuestand nicht leyden wolte, mit seinem Söhnlein Francisco Daniele in die Länge in Sommerhausen zu verharren, hat er sich an des wohl-edlen und hochgelehrten Herren Johann Gelchsheimers, der Rechten Doctoris, und des heyl. Röm. Reichs Statt Windsheimb bestellten Consulentens Jungfraw Tochter Evam Margaretham verheüratet, den 9. Febr. 1658.

77. *Leben*, pp. 69-70:

    Nach deme der Wittib Stand bey zu erzihen habendem Söhnlein ettwas beschwerlich fallen wollen, und doch die in letzterer Ehe vorgeloffene, sehr ung[lück]liche Zufalle widerumb zu heyrathen, ihne fast abschrecketen, nam er sich vor, nach einer betagten Matron und fleißigen Haushalterin zu trachten, mitt deren Hülffe er seinen Sohn in studys wohl erzihen möchte. Vermählete sich also den 21. January, Anno 1662, mit der viel ehren- und tugendreichen Frawen Barbara Greülichin, einer gebornen Heiderin, Wittibin zu Hüttenheimb, und lebte mitt ihr in friedlicher Ehe 12 Jahr und 8 Wochen, aber ohne Leibes Erben. Sie starb in Gott seeliglich, den 26. Marty, Anno 1674. War eine gottsförchtige, und in Gottes Wortt wohlbelesene Matron, zu dero Gedächtnuß nachfolgende Reimen gemacht worden...

78. Roth, "Pastorius," p. 66.
79. *Beschreibung Pa.*, pp. 50, 52, 54, 71-72, 75, 93:

    Lasset uns... einander in hertzlicher Affection als Einer in Christo umfassen / woran uns weder die Entlegenheit der Oerter / noch die Gefährlichkeit der See- Rauber / oder einige andere Umbstände verhindern mögen.
    ... daß er mir in dieser Zeitlichkeit gerne mehr gutes erweisen mögte / erkenne ich für einen allzu überflüssigen Affect seiner vätterlichen Zuneigung / von deren ich anitzo / da mir Gott selbsten ein Kind bescheret hat / weit besser denn zuvor urtheilen... kann... Gott der Allerhöchste belohne denselben all an mir erzeigte Liebe / Treue / und Wolthat aufs reicheste...
    Ich.... konte solches nicht sonder fröliche Liebes-Thränen durchlesen.

So kan ich auch kaum aussprechen mit was Freude ich aus des Herrn Vattern letzteren ihren guten Zustand ... verstanden habe / zumahlen ich mich geduldig darein ergeben hatte / weder dessen geehrte Person in dieser Welt / noch einigen Buchstaben von seiner an mich so offtmal gutthätig eröffneten Hand zu erblicken.

[In dieser Kriegszeit] darf [ich] nicht hoffen ... viele weitere Brieff von dessen werthen Hand zu empfangen / um welche ich aber gleichwohl kindlich hiermit anhalte.

... [diesen Brief] schliessende den Herrn Vattern tausend mal grüsse / und durch die Lufft kind-hertzlich Küsse ...

80. *Beschreibung Pa.* pp. 49, 54; and *Copia, eines ... Brieffes* (Appendix Two, no. 3).
81. "Emblematical Recreations" is on pp. 75-107, and "Symbola Onomastica" on pp. 46-48, 105, 129-32 and 215-19 of the "Beehive." A prefatory verse indicates that Pastorius produced at least one copy of "Emblematical Recreations" for friends in Pennsylvania:

    My dear Friends, accept these Emblems & Devices,
    Whereby my Thankfulness your Love forever prizes.
    I never can repay your Favours for me done,
    When once these Papers here are burned, dead & gone.

82. The cultural interpretation of this emblem results in part from discussions with Robert Con Davis of his "Revenge against Time: the Father in Fiction" (Diss. Univ. of California, Davis, 1979).
83. *DNB*, 13 (1888), 286.
84. *A New Primmer*, pp. 32-33.
85. Letters by Pastorius and his pupil Israel Pemberton, cited in Learned, pp. 175-79. "D. P." is short for Daniel Pastorius, the common form of his name, as noted on p. 263 n13.
86. *Beschreibung Pa.*, p. 102:

    Ach daß du hier wärest und in unserm Hause zu Germantown wohnetest, welches einen schönen Obsgarten hat, und der Zeit leer stehet, indeme wir zu Philadelphia wohnen, und täglich 8. Stunden lang in die Schul gehen müssen, ausgenommen den letzten Tag in der Wochen, da wir Nachmittag daheim bleiben dörffen.

    School was not held on Sunday, a fact so obvious Pastorius did not bother to mention it. Following Quaker custom, Pastorius commonly used numbers instead of names for days and months.

87. *Beschreibung Pa.*, p. 75:

    Mir war sehr lieb zu vernehmen / daß mein vielgeliebter Bruder Augustin Adam Pastorius zu mir zu kommen geneigt seye / nicht zweifflende wir wolten in brüderliche Liebe einträchtig beyeinander wohnen / und in ohnverbrochener beständiger und ungefärbter hertzlichen Affection stehen. Wie gern ich aber auch denselben bey mir haben mögte / so ersuche und bitte ich ihn doch hiermit gantz freundlich er wolle ja ohne seiner in Ehren zu haltenden Eltern Wissen und Willen night weggehen / gestallten derselbe solchen falls mir überaus unwillkommen seyn würde.

88. Nürnberg University matriculation records, cited by Learned, p. 63; "Genealogia Pastoriana" and "Res Propriae."
89. "Reichsstadt Windsheim," ed. Wilhelm Dannheimer, in *Pfarrerbuch der Reichsstädte Dinkelsbühl, Schweinfurt, Weißenburg i. Bay, und Windsheim*, ed. Matthias Simon (Nürnberg: Selbstverlag des Vereins fur Bayerische Kirchengeschichte, 1962), p. 97; Estermann, *Bad Windsheim*, pp. 87, 114; Johann Jacob Geiß (Geysen), *Ansehnlicher und volckreicher Leich-Begangnis Des Hoch-Wohl-Ehrwürdigen Hoch-Achtbar- und Hoch-Wohlgelehrten Herrn M. Georg Leonhart Models* (Windsheim: Eitel H. Schmiden, 1714), pp. 19-29 (biography published with the funeral sermon).
90. Geiß, p. 24:

    Er hatte mitten in der Eitelkeit wenig eitles an sich ... Sahe Er irrige in der Religion / so kunte Er nicht ruhen / biß Er sie auff den rechten Weeg gebracht ... Sahe Er gottlose Welt-Kinder / die in allerhand Sünden und Lastern ersoffen waren / so gieng Er ihnen nach / biß Er sie auß des Teuffels Rachen wiederum herauß gerissen.

91. Biographical detail on Stellwag: Estermann, p. 90; Pastorius, *Windsheim*, pp. 21-26 passim; "Taufbuch 1648-77" (Archiv des Evang.-Luth. Pfarramts Bad Windsheim, MS.

274 | Notes: Chapter Three

K9), p. 67. Stellwag cannot be traced beyond his university years; like Pastorius, he probably pursued a career elsewhere as a result of the Windsheim dissension of 1676-79. On Mercklein: Estermann, pp. 83, 90, 92; Pastorius, *Windsheim*, pp. 24-27 passim; "Bestattungen 1653-1717" (Archiv des Evang.-Luth. Pfarramts Bad Windsheim, MS.), p. 428.

Chapter Three

1. Pp. iii-vii; see Appendix II for the German text.
2. *New Cambridge Modern History*, 2, 316-17.
3. Biographical detail not otherwise attributed is taken from "Genealogia Pastoriana" (Appendix I) and "Res Propriae," Pastorius' German autobiographical sketch (also cited by Learned, pp. 63-78 passim).
4. Franklin L. Ford, *Strasbourg in Transition* (Cambridge, Mass.: Harvard Univ. Press, 1958), pp. 35-37; Ernst Jirgal, "Johann Heinrich Bökler (1611-72)," *Mitteilungen des Instituts für österreichische Geschichtsforschung*, 45 (1931), 322-84 passim.
5. On Altdorf: Georg Andreas Will, *Geschichte und Beschreibung der nürnbergischen Universität Altdorf*, 2nd ed. (1801; rpt. Aalen: Scientia, 1975), p. 154. This description of the university is based on: Will, pp. 125-27, 140-41, 154-57, 212-19, 267-70; Horst C. Recktenwald, *Die fränkische Universität Altdorf* (Nürnberg: Spindler, 1966), pp. 12-18, 30, 42-45; Konrad Lengenfelder, *Johann Georg Puschners Ansichten von der Nürnbergischen Universitat Altdorf* (Nürnberg: Spindler, 1958), pp. 34, 52; Artur Kreiner, "Die jährlichen Neueinschreibungen an Gymnasium, Academie und Universität Altdorf von 1579-1809," *Mitteilungen des Vereins für Geschichte der Stadt Nürnberg*, 37 (1940), 341-42; and *Catalogus Lectionem... Altdorffina*, 1665-75 (annual academic catalogs).
6. "Tantum Quantum," no. 22, in "Beehive," p. 58, cited in Toms, "Background of Pastorius," pp. 220-21.
7. For Nürnberg's professors see: Andreas Kraus, "Der Beitrag Frankens zur Entwicklung der Wissenschaften," *Handbuch der bayerischen Geschichte*, ed. Spindler, 3, 603-15; Andreas Kraus, "Bürgerlicher Geist und Wissenschaft," *Archiv für Kulturgeschichte*, 49 (1967), 345-52; Peter Petersen, *Geschichte der aristotelischen Philosophie im protestantischen Deutschland* (1921; rpt. Stuttgart: Frommann, 1964), pp. 151, 353; biographies of Dürr and Wagenseil in Georg Andreas Will, *Nürnbergisches Gelehrten-Lexikon* (Nürnberg, 1755- 58).
8. Will, *Altdorf*, pp. 248-50; Dürr biography in Will, *Lexikon*; Friedrich Schulze and Paul Ssymanck, *Das Deutsche Studententum*, 2nd ed. (Leipzig: Voigtländers, 1910), pp. 85-87.
9. Will, *Altdorf*, pp. 196-98; Ernst Mummenhoff, "Die Juristenfakultät Altdorf" (Diss. Erlangen-Nürnberg, 1959), p. 51; Toms, p. 36.
10. Will, *Altdorf*, pp. 190-91; Mummenhoff, pp. 51-52.
11. Inventory in "Res Propriae," cited in Learned, p. 276.
12. John Bowie, *A History of Europe* (London: Secker & Warburg, 1979), p. 452.
13. Paulsen, *Geschichte*, 1, 260-61, 492-94; Paul Wentzcke, "Die alte Universität Straßburg," *Elsaß-Lothringisches Jahrbuch*, 17 (1938), 88-89 (illus. 5 and 6); Will, *Altdorf*, pp. 268-75. Reporting that Pastorius' generation wore red gowns, Learned (p. 69) misinterpreted Will, who states (p. 270) that the red gowns were worn during the first half of the eighteenth century, and Toms (p. 40) repeats Learned's error.
14. Max Steinmetz, ed., *Geschichte der Universitat Jena* (Jena: G. Fisher, 1958, 1962), 1, 107, and 2, 647-48.
15. *Ein Send-Brieff Offenhertziger Liebesbezeugung an die sogenannte Pietisten in Hoch-Teutschland* (Amsterdam, 1697), p. 14. This "confession" is a short embedded clause in a long paragraph on true faith in which Pastorius expresses his gratitude for regaining his belief: "bis [ich] endlich von meinen Unglauben und denen auff Universitäten tieff bey mir eingewurtzelten Gottlosigkeit mehr und mehr erlöst wurde." *Beschreibung Pa.*, pp. 99-100: The son Pastorius explicitly referred to was his 16-year-old half-brother in Windsheim, but internal evidence suggests his emotions and thoughts were not with his brother at all. Pastorius wrote: "I only regret that... my dear brother Johann Samuel

... may lose his piety while at the university... at extreme danger to his mortal soul." Pastorius had momentarily forgotten that his Windsheim brother was Augustin Adam, and that his "dear brother Johann Samuel" had died eleven years earlier in 1687. The full text is quoted on p. 173 of this study.

16. Pastorius' "Itinerarium," more than 600 pages in length, is not extant, but portions of it are preserved in a section of the "Beehive" ms entitled "Tantum Quantum, or A Few Inscriptions, gathered out of my own Itinerary." This collection includes hundreds of inscriptions and begins with the following indication of its contents:
    The Heads of the following Inscriptions: 1. Sun-dials. 2. Clock-dials & Bells. 3. Steeple-houses, Altars, Organs, Images, &c. 4. Cloisters & Cells. 5. Hospitals, Infirmaries, &c. 6. Schools. 7. Libraries. 8. Senate houses & Guild halls. 9. Bridewells. 10. Prisons. 11. Armouries or Magazines for Weapons. 12. Utensils of war, Standards & the like. 13. Mints, & Treasure-houses. 14. Burses or Royal Exchanges for merchants to meet in. 15. Palaces. 16. Tennis-Courts, Bowling-greens, &c. 17. Market places, Shambles, &c. 18. Apothecary-Shops. 19. Inns and Ordinaries. 20. Private Dwelling-houses. 21. Doors, Chimneys, Tables, &c. 22. Gardens. 23. Fountains. 24. Ships. 26. Bridges. 27. Monuments. 28. Statues. 29. Cities & Fortresses. 30. Fenster-Schrifften [window inscriptions]. 31. Stambuch-Andenck-Sprüch [dedicatory verses and proverbs from genealogical and commemorative books]. 32. A Miscellaneous Appendix. 33. Privy Houses. Post num. 6. Arms or Coat of Arms.
    This and other extracts are reproduced in Learned, pp. 94-100.

17. *A New Primmer*, p. 48. Pastorius used this European ms as a literary thesaurus in Pennsylvania, he indicates here, which made it a convenient source for many of the Latin and German quotations listed with the predominantly English gleanings of the "Alphabetical Hive."

18. Robert M. Browning, *German Baroque Poetry* (University Park: Pennsylvania State Univ. Press, 1971), pp. 3-30, 269-70; Karl F. Otto, *Die Sprachgesellschaften des 17. Jahrhunderts* (Stuttgart: Metzler, 1972), pp. 7-13.

19. Toms, pp. 160-83. Especially on the issue of comedies and operas, or theater in general, Pastorius displays both moral censure and cultural liberality in his Pennsylvania writings. In three consecutive "Beehive" entries ("Some Onomastical Considerations," nos. 874-76), for example, he blames Socrates' death on a "ridiculous" play by "the vain theatrical wit" Aristophanes, and states that "wicked Play-wrights... stir up unwary minds to prophanness [sic], Immorality & ungodly Projects," but also shows his delight in a large variety of "fine & magnificent" titles given "infectious" (i.e. potentially immoral) plays by men like Thomas Nash, John Ford, John Dryden and James Shirley. He used a play title for a 1713 report circulated in Pennsylvania – "Exemplum sine Exemplo, or (to borrow the Inscription of one of John Wilson's Plays) The Cheats and the Projectors" – and quoted classical playwrights in his scholarly writing, for instance with a witty reference to Publius Syrus cited on p. 148.

20. Paulsen, pp. 503-04.

21. The "&c" concluding his enumeration of countries visited (a variant of "et cetera") refers to the unspecified portions of Germany Pastorius also toured on this journey, as he specifies in "Res Propriae": "Ich... that... eine Reis durch Holland, Engelland, Franckreich, Schweitz, und einen Strich Hochteutschlands." Toms hypothesizes that Pastorius toured Italy, and refers to Italian entries in "Tantum Quantum" (the collection of inscriptions predominantly from Pastorius' travel journals). Pastorius notes, however, that the Italian inscriptions are from the journals of "my relatives and me" ("ich die Meinige und mich"), presumably referring to Melchior Adam's "Itinerario" of his Italian travels, a copy of which Melchior Adam had apparently given to his son, and which has been preserved in Pennsylvania to the present (Univ. of Penna. MS Ger 54). He would surely have mentioned Italy in his enumeration of countries toured if he had actually been there.

22. *Beschreibung Pa.*, p. 52, and "Res Propriae," cited in Learned, p. 113. *Update 2013:* Karsten Dietsch, "Über das Geldverhältnis alter deutscher Münzwährung (theoretische Kaufkraft zur heutigen Zeit)," Teichwolframsdorf, 2005 (PDF), p. 11. URL=

www.mohlsdorf.de/01-ges/mo-1-5-geldwertvergleich-w.pdf

23. Cited in Learned, p. 96: "Dergleichen sind in meinem Itinerario mehr, die anher zu überschreiben der Zeit u. Papiers nicht wehrt."

24. Embellishing the paradox of Sir John Denham's concluding couplet in "Directions to a Painter" – "Poems and Paints can speak some times bold Truths, / Poets and Painters are licentious Youths" – Pastorius, in Poem 376 (composed 1714), constructed an elaborate joke involving verbal ambiguity as well as biblical allusion:

> Our Painters and Poets are re-so-lute men,
> Presumptiously working with Pencil and Pen;
> And tho' they but seldom in Riches do thrive,
> Their Emblems and Poems poor Dives survive,
> Who fared deliciously every day, and in
> Purple, not Eclogues, his Money would spend.

By syllabifying "resolute," Pastorius indicates it may also be read as the Latin "resolutum," meaning undone, physically relaxed, or set free, just as "presumptiously" can be read literally or as "presumptively" (now an obsolete meaning); i.e., artists either arrogantly pursue vain pleasures or valiantly follow a high calling. Freely interpreting Christ's parable, Pastorius here presents Dives as an affluent cultural philistine.

25. Art, music and theater in Nürnberg: Blake Lee Spahr, "Nürnbergs Stellung im Literarischen Leben des 17. Jahrhunderts," *Stadt - Schule - Universitat - Buchwesen*, ed. Albrecht Schöne (Munich: Beck, 1976), pp. 72-83. Articles by H. Brunner and E. Strasser, F. Krautwurst, K. Oettinger, K. A. Knappe, W. Schwemmer, and P. Kertz in *Nürnberg*, ed. Pfeiffer, 1, 207-18, 250-62, 283-95, 344-57; Ewald V. Nolte, "Pachelbel, Johann," *New Grove Dictionary of Music*, ed. Sadie, 14 (1980), 46-54.

26. The son of a Nürnberg tinsmith, Pachelbel had to leave Nürnberg for financial reasons less than a year after enrolling even though he worked as church organist while attending the university; he then received a scholarship at Regensburg, and thus qualified for high cultural achievement despite his modest origins.

27. The Nürnberg poets: K. Wölfel, "Barockdichtung in Nürnberg," *Nürnberg*, ed. Pfeiffer, 1, 338-44; Richard Newald, *Deutsche Literatur*, 6th ed. (Munich: Beck, 1967), pp. 210-22; Joachim Kröll, "Sigmund Birken," *Fränkische Lebensbilder*, ed. Pfeiffer and Wendehorst, 9 (1980), 187-203; Conrad Wiedemann, "Sigmund von Birken," *Fränkische Klassiker*, ed. Wolfgang Buhl (Nürnberg: Nürnberger Presse, 1971), pp. 325-36; Marian Szyrocki, *Deutsche Literatur des Barock* (Reinbek: Rowohlt, 1968), pp. 99-105; Robert Haas, *Die Musik des Barocks* (Potsdam: Akademische Verlags-ges., 1929), pp. 11, 168-73. Toms, pp. 32-35, 57-59, describes influences on Pastorius.

28. The Austrian exiles: Browning, pp. 68-77; Newald, pp. 248-50, 356-60; Wölfel, pp. 342-43.

29. Browning, p. 68.

30. Bartholomäus Dietwar, quoted in Albrecht Schübel, *Das Evangelium in Mainfranken* (Munich: Evang. Presseverband, 1958), pp. 132-33: "... ein stolzer prächtiger Mann, dem es nur um große Besoldung zu tun war ..."

31. Kröll, ibid.; Wiedemann, ibid.

32. Rudolf Endres, "Markgraf Christian Ernst von Bayreuth," *Fränkische Lebensbilder*, ed. Pfeiffer and Wendehorst, 2 (1968), 260-89; Melchior Adam's commentary, from *Franconia Rediviva*, pp. 66-68, concludes as follows:

> His honor the Margrave Christian Ernst, whose praiseworthy government continues to this day, has shown very great concern for the entire Fatherland of Germany from the beginning of his administration to the present, and committed large sums of money from his patrimony as well as his own worthy personage to the cause, refusing to let up until the entire war [actually numerous wars] has been allayed and composed, which great loyalty the Roman [i.e., Hapsburg] Imperial Majesty has recognized with gratitude, appointing His Princely Highness [Christian Ernst] Imperial Field Marshall [of the Hapsburg armies].
>
> Dieser noch heut zu Tag Löblichst-regierende Herr Markgraf Christian Ernst, hat von Antritt seiner Regierung bis hiehero für das allgemeine Vaterland Teutscher Nation

sehr grosse Sorge getragen und nicht allein grosse Geld-Summen *de substantia Patrimoniali*, sondern auch dero hohe Person selbsten aufgesetzet, und nicht ehender nachgelassen, bis der gantze Krieg gestillet, und componirt worden ist, welche grosse Treue die Rom. Kayserl. Majestät zu Danck erkennet, und Se[in] Hoch-fürstl. Durchl. zu Dero Kayserl. Feld-Marschallen verordnet haben.

33. Poem 14 (entire):
Dieweil die Welt aus Nichts gemacht,
So nennt man sie auch nichtig;
Der Mann aus Erden fortgebracht
Heißt irdisch. Sofern richtig.
Das Weib formiert aus einem Bein
Muß darumb auch ja beinern (peinend) sein.

33a. *Update 2013:* Marguerite Deslauriers, "Lucrezia Marinella", The Stanford Encyclopedia of Philosophy (Winter 2012 Edition), Edward N. Zalta (ed.), URL = <http://plato.stanford.edu/archives/win2012/entries/lucrezia-marinella/>.
Marinella was also a poet, but this is a philosophical treatise in vernacular Italian prose (English transl. by A. Dunhill, Chicago: Univ. of Chicago Press, 1999).

34. On 26 Nov. 1688, Pastorius married Ennecke Klostermanns (b. 1658), the daughter of a physician from Müllheim on the Ruhr, Germany, known in Pennsylvania (at least among English-speaking friends) as Anne. She bore their two sons on 30 Mar. 1690 and 1 Apr. 1692, sustaining a "maternal" (presumably vaginal or uterine) illness or injury during her second childbirth that remained with her "all her life," Pastorius reports in "Res Propriae": "In diesem ihre Zweyten Kindbett kriegte sie einen solchen Anstoß, oder Mutterkrankheit, die ihr all ihr Leben lang Anhieng." Thus some degree of sexual abstinence may have compounded tensions between a husband and wife who had relinquished the privileges of European affluence for an essentially frontier existence in a modest household that apparently did not employ servants.

35. Poem 190 (entire):
Amara-Dulcis heißt mein Weib,
Ein bitter-süßer Zeit Vertreib;
Doch die sie nicht kennen,
Die lachen hierüber
Und wollen sie nennen,
Je länger, je lieber.

36. "FDP" ms ("Common Place Book"), p. 589. Learned implies original composition, stating this song or poem is "in his writings" (p. 189). Unlike other early poetry contained in this ms, however, Pastorius did not transfer the "Corinna" lyric to his collected poetry in the "Beehive," and Toms (pp. 101-06) has identified it as a lyric by Johann Georg Schoch (1627-90).

37. Anne Bradstreet is spelled "Broadstreet" in Edward Phillips' *Theatrum Poetarium*, apparently Pastorius' source. In his admirably concise lesson in scansion, Pastorius comments on Fenn's meter, or lack of it, and offers encouragement in a few lines of iambic pentameter and hexameter, and then adds a prose explanation:

One [verse] wants some Feet, the other does abound,
Which matters not, the Matter being Sound.
Go thou but on! Thou willst <u>Most of</u> thy Sex surpass,
And be a Poetess, as <u>famous</u> Sappho was.
Mind, that each of these my two last Verses having two feet more than the former, are of a different race or species; But leave out the underlined words and they'll be of due length.

37a. *Update 2013:* Poem 163 continues:

Go now, and on thy Tulips feed,
To such like Flow'rs I give no heed,
My heart nothing in them espy's
Than Stirring up the Lust of th' Eyes.
. . .
I newly saw Two Lips together,

278 | Notes: Chapter Three

>And could not think much good of them;
>But said Two Lips & Tulips rather
>Should hang & wither,
>Than thus hem.
>Beauté sans Bonté ne vaut rien.
>[Beauty without goodness is not worth anything.]
>Nuptas [et] Innuptas generis damnosa Voluptas.
>[Wives and unmarried young women beget injurious sensual pleasure.]

"Hang & wither" refers to the flowers' fading, wilting and dying; Pastorius seems to wish that youthful beauty would fade as quickly, thus sparing him the prolonged frustration of repeatedly observing the enticing girl and her two lips. "Hem" can mean either "equivocate" (as in "hem and haw") or confine ("hem in"), or, of course, a combination of the two – female equivocation, and potential confinement perceived by the male. It is almost as if he were describing a pouting, sexy young woman or teenager.

38. Despite its obviously sexual allusion (and apparent reference to the "maternal" illness or injury of his wife Anne), the poem reflects real experience with trumpet roses (also called tuberoses and Indian hyacinths). Pastorius here notes:

    >Anno 1712. One of the Tuberoses in Germantown flourished 15 weeks, was 4½ foot high, and brought forth 143 flowers, besides 7 that were withered with the Cold, out of one single root.

39. Letters of 24 and 30 Jan. 1718/19 to Lloyd Zachary of Philadelphia, in "Letter Book," pp. 73, 75-80. Pastorius had challenged 17-year-old Zachary to write on "the Preeminence or Preferableness of the Female Sex above ours," a topic he had encountered years earlier (he noted) in *de Vanitate Omnium Scientiarium* by Heinrich Cornelius Agrippa (1486-1535). [*Update 2013:* The actual title is *De nobilitate et praecellentia foeminei sexus* (On the Nobility and Excellence of the Feminine Sex), 1529; see Charles Nauert, "Heinrich Cornelius Agrippa von Nettesheim", The Stanford Encyclopedia of Philosophy (Summer 2011 Edition), Edward N. Zalta (ed.), URL = <http://plato.stanford.edu/archives/sum2011/entries/agrippa-nettesheim/>.] With his cousin Elizabeth Hill (like himself a grandchild of Deputy Governor Thomas Lloyd), Zachary composed a response so good "that thereby thou Deservest the Love and Favour of the Best of 'em." (Zachary and Hill's essay was not available for this study.) Pastorius "enlarges" upon the topic (in what he calls "this my Additional Rhapsody") "not by way of amending, but of augmenting" their essay, in the process reminding them of methods of argumentation ("Artificial or Inartificial, Synthetick or Analytick"); he begins with the "sure Foundation" of a syllogism advancing formally from first to second premise and conclusion, yet combines this logic with a lively and informal style, and ends by spoofing his own scholarly seriousness:

    >... Item, ... Item, ... Thus I might heap on mine Items till next Lammas Day [i.e., infinitely; cf. "latter Lammas," *OED* 6, 40] ... There would be Items above Items; But having already said too much in what the Females overtop us, and not being able to say enough of it, I heartily bid thee Farewell ...

    His willingness to address the young on gender issues exemplifies his encouragement of liberal thought in early Pennsylvania. The verve and humor of this letter also shows how relaxed and open he had become in his full maturity in Pennsylvania.

40. One of many poems freely mixing philosophy and gardening observations, Poem 278 moves from physical to scriptural purity, but returns to the initial theme of virginal lilies with its joke about transforming lilies to roses. The full text:

    >White Lilies yield the sweetest Smell
    >When Virgin like they stand;
    >I mean, when (understand me well)
    >Untouch'd by human hand:
    >So is the Sacred Writ of Old
    >Without the Newish Gloss,
    >Of Glossers, and of Glossers bold.
    >Away with all their Dross!
    >Q. Wie willstu weise Lilien

Zu rothen Rosen machen?
A. Küss unversehens dein Polyxen,
Sie wird erröthet lachen.
White Lilies presently
One may Metamorphose
By kissing Margery (Dorothy, etc.)
Into a Damask-Rose.

41. Will, *Lexikon*, 4 (1758), 274-76.
42. D. F. Fritz, "Johann Georg Rosenbach," *Zeitschrift für bayerische Kirchengeschichte*, 18 (1949), 21-59 passim. Passing reference to *Wunder- und Gnaden-volle Führung Gottes* (n.p.: n.p., [1704]).
43. Cited in Fritz, p. 42:
    ... einem denen fanatischen Meinungen und eitlen *Visionibus* ergebenen Idioten, der leicht die studierende Jugend irremachen und der Universität bei den *exteris* eine üble blame erwecken könnte.
44. Ibid. Long: "anstatt des Geistes und der Kraft [ist] schulfüchsisches Kunst- und Hirnwissen eingerissen." Rotenbeck:
    ... von den fleischlich gesinnten teils Pharisäern und pedantischen *Theoligis*, welche den geistlichen Weinberg als listige, bissige Schulfüchse verderben, teils gottlosen Baalspfaffen und wollüstigen Bauchdienern, welche ihn als wilde Säue zerwühlen.
45. The poetic texts:
    419. Lach, liebe Einfalt, lach!
          Dein lieber Rosenbach
          Bekehret viele Seelen
          Vors Fluchen, Sauffen, Stehlen
          Was bessers zuerwehlen.
          Ach! Mit Teuffelischer Rach,
          Mordmesser an der kehlen,
          Und list, nicht zu erzehlen
          Sein Hertz in Liebe quälen.
          Willkom all Ungemach!
          Verbied't ihm Dach und Fach;
          Ja, unter scharffer wach,
          Die Wahrheit zu verhehlen,
          So wird doch Rosenbach,
          Der Lehre Christi nach,
          Sein gantz gerechte Sach
          dem Höchsten Gott empfehlen.
          Die Pfarrer schreyen ach!
          Veritatis Indici, Mendaciofum Vindici.

    428. Wann Einjeder Christi Sach
          Förderte wie Rosenbach,
          Hätten wir in kurtzer Zeit
          Eine bess're Christenheit.
          Item, Wer gottselig sucht zu leben,
          Muss dem Creutze sich ergeben,
          Und durch viel Verfolgung schweben.
                    2. Corinthians 3:12
46. Etienne Gilson and Thomas Langan, *Modern Philosophy* (New York: Random House, 1963), pp. 1-6, 16-24; Petersen, pp. 118-27, 258-277, 412; Rolf Schäfer, "Abendländischer Aristotelismus," *Theologische Realenzyklopadie*, ed. Krause and Müller, 3 (1978), 789-96. Galileo is quoted in Gilson and Langan, p. 19. Gerhard and Andreae are paraphrased from Schäfer, p. 794, and Petersen, pp. 268-73.
47. Paulsen, 1, 263-75; Wentzke, p. 59.
48. *Beschreibung Pa.*, pp. 98-99. See Appendix II for the German text.
49. *Beschreibung Pa.*, pp. 72-73. See Appendix II for the German text.

50. Petersen, pp. 149-53; Christian C. Jöcher, *Allgemeines Gelehrten-Lexicon* (1750-1897; rpt. Hildesheim: Olms, 1960-61), 4, 730; passing reference to the *Physical Treatises* in *The Works of Aristotle* (Chicago: Encyclopaedia Britannica, 1952), 1, 255-494.
51. Sturm biography in Will, *Lexikon*; Petersen, pp. 156-61; Kraus, "Beitrag Frankens," p. 611.
52. Petersen, pp. 277-338 passim; Paul Harvey, *Oxford Companion to Classical Literature* (Oxford: Oxford Univ. Press, 1937), pp. 45-46; Egidius Schmalzriedt, "Ta Meta Ta Physika," *Hauptwerke der antiken Literatur*, ed. Schmalzriedt (München: Kindler, 1976), pp. 181-82; passing reference to the *Metaphysics* in *Works*, 1, 495- 626.
53. Felwinger biography in Will, *Lexikon*; Petersen, p. 285; Max Wundt, *Die deutsche Schulmetaphysik des 17. Jahrhunderts* (Tubingen: Mohr, 1939), pp. xiv, 55-56, 149.
54. Dürr biography in Will, *Lexikon*; Petersen, pp. 168-69.
55. Wagenseil biography in Will, *Lexikon*; Julius Pirson, "J. Chr. Wagenseil und Jean Chapelain," *Gedächtnisschrift für Adalbert Hämel*, ed. Heinrich Kuen (Würzburg: Triltsch, 1953), pp. 197-222; Artur Kreiner, "Professorenschicksale und Charakterköpfe aus der Universitätsgeschichte Altdorfs," *Mitteilungen ... Nürnberg*, 37 (1940), 334; Helmut Coing, "Die juristische Fakultät und ihr Lehrprogramm," *Handbuch der Quellen und Literatur der neueren europäischen Privatrechtsgeschichte*, ed. Coing, 2 (Munich: Beck'sche, 1977), 27. The Wagenseil quotation, from Pirson, p. 199: "Wir wollen uns, so oft es sein kann, in Italien und Franckreich fleißig dabei einfinden, weilen man hierdurch mit den allerwackersten Leuten bekannt wird und auch geschickter nachhause gehet."
56. This background is interpolated from Pastorius' Latin letter of 1 Dec. 1688 to Model, published by Wilhelm Ernst Tentzel of Leipzig in the April, 1691, issue of his monthly journal *Monatlichen Unterredungen*. How Pastorius came to Wagenseil's attention is not known, although his emigration was surely noted by various friends and relatives in Nürnberg. Significantly, this 1688 letter is his only extant Windsheim correspondence from 1684 to 1691, years during which he and Melchior Adam were not communicating (see p. 189). It is conceivable that Model himself was at least indirectly involved in awakening Wagenseil's interest in Pastorius (which provided the *modus vivendi* for reestablishing contact), possibly as a favor to Melchior Adam, who must have been anxious for word of his son even though affronted pride seems to have kept him from corresponding for another three years. Reflecting a typical mix of learned pride and qualms of conscience, Wagenseil (then 70 years old) had become a supporter of Pietism by the time the dispute over Johann Georg Rosenbach erupted in 1703.
57. Pastorius' commentary on education was omitted from the 1691 publication. In a letter to his father of 1 Mar. 1697 (*Beschreibung Pa.*, p. 72), Pastorius indicates that his proposals to Model had included giving all Gymnasium pupils practical training as craftsmen that would enable them to earn a decent living anywhere in the world. The text from *Monatlichen Unterredungen*, in Latin, was reproduced with a German transl. in Goebel, "Zwei unbekannte Briefe," pp. 492-503.
58. Pastorius' reference to forms of water transport apparently spoofs Wagenseil's new "hydraspis," or "water shield" invention, a mode of sea transport the scholar was allowed to demonstrate to Emperor Leopold I in 1691. The text from Goebel, p. 494:
    Cujus nos supplicio cauti porro pedem efferentes exspatiemur tantisper ad Indos, & in momentariae hujus excursionis solatium hanc exsorbeamus phialam. Tu vero, mea Coquula, leporem interim istum succensis ignibus assa, quern a reditu nostro Attico condiemus lepore. Salva jam res est, Modeli, pergamus, & ne silentio viam transigamus veluti pecora, sermocinemur aliquid de Nili, vel quae aeque obscura est, Indorum nostrorum origine. Nam licet non desint, qui eos Ebraeorum arbitrentur prosapiam, non sine signis verosimillimis: quosdam tamen longius nine habitantium ex Cambria emersisse, nativa illorum loquutio innuit. Quibus antem temporibus atque navigiis Atlanticum hoc mare exantlaverint, Polyhistor tuus Altdorfinus distinctius explicet: ego nee ullo pene libro instructus tarn dubiam litem meam non facio. Ingenuae potius interrogationi ex Virgilio Tuae: Quod genus hoc hominum? uberiorem responsionem parturiens in novo prooemio aurium tuarum patientiam obtestor.

Notes: Chapter Three | 281

59. Schwäger biography in Will, *Lexikon*; Nürnberg Univ. annual catalogs, 1659-75.
60. Will, *Lexikon*:
    Er lies lange allerhand Unanständiges, Aergerliches und Lächerliches selbst auf der Kanzel in Worten, Gebehrden und Handlungen blicken. Einst predigte er über die Worte des Titels eines Katechismus-Büchleins: Gedruckt bey Balthasar Scherf, Universitäts-Buchdrucker. Die Predigt handelte vom Nutzen der Buchdruckerey und war zwar nicht ungelehrt, auch einigermassen zur Erbauung eingerichtet: alleine gleichwol konnte sie nicht ohne Gespotte der Zuhörer abgeleget werden. . . . Er gieng hierauf noch viele Jahre, und zwar in einem langen griechischen Talar mit einem fortwachsenden scheuslichen Barte und einem Stecken einher, suchte auf der Strasse alle Papiere zusammen und trug sie heim, und machte überhaupt viele Possen und Kindereyen.
61. Zischka, *Index Lexicorum*, pp. xxx-xxxi. Pastorius humorously reflects the intellectual intensity of his era in an epigram on sleeping habits (Poem 54):
    Five hours a Scholar sleeps by right,
    A Merchant six, an upstart Knight
    Full seven & a Lollard eight;
    But cup-shot People, Babes and Sucklings all the Night.
62. Konig biography in Will, *Lexikon*: "So viel unser König geschrieben, so wenig hat er herausgegeben, und insbesondere, welches zu bewundern ist, keine einzige academische Disputation."
63. Molitor biography in Will, *Lexikon*:
    Fleiß, Ehrlichkeit und Bescheidenheit wurden ihm vornehmlich nachgerühmet; die letzte Tugend war in der That mit einiger Furcht verknüpft, daß er wenigstens kaum dahin gebracht werden konnte, etwas im öffentlichen Druck auszugeben.
64. Reinhart biography in Will, *Lexikon*:
    . . . in seinen Schrifften herrschte . . . so wie in allen seinen Handlungen Vorsicht, Demuth und Liebe. Auch zog er die Einsamkeit allem Umgange vor, und war mit einem Worte in dem wahresten und besten Verstande ein *Theologus Irenicus* . . . Reinhart war . . . von ganzem Hertzen ein Calixtiner: doch hatte er so viel Klugheit und Bescheidenheit, daß er auf beyden Kathedern nichts davon einmischte . . . ja es war mehr als eine Bescheidenheit, und eine allzugrosse Schüchternheit und Furcht, daß er sich auch nicht *privatim* getrauete, seine Meynung von irgend einer theologischen Uneinigkeit und Streitsache zu eröffnen. Er schrieb auch deswegen, ohngeachtet er 39 Jahre Professor war, kaum eine oder die andere Disputation, damit er ja nicht in Streitigkeiten verwickelt würde.
65. Ibid.; Johannes Wallmann, "Calixt, Georg," *Theologische Realenzyklopädie*, ed. Krause and Müller, 7 (1981), 552-59; Gerhard Pfeiffer, "Altdorf, Universität," *Theologische Realenzyklopädie*, 2 (1977), 328; "Colloquy of Thorn," *Oxford Dictionary*. ed. Cross and Livingstone, p. 1374.
66. Will, ibid.; Weinmann biography in Will, *Lexikon*.
67. The funeral sermon is among Reinhart's publications listed in the Reinhart biography in Will, *Lexikon*.
68. Hermann Schüssler, "Dannhauer, Johann Konrad," *Neue Deutsche Biographie*, 3 (1957), 512.
69. Wallmann, *Philipp Jakob Spener*, pp. 62-124, 159-78 passim; Paul Schaudig, *Der Pietismus und Separatismus im Aischgrund* (Schwäbisch-Gmünd: Aupperle, 1925), p. 4; Max Göbel, *Geschichte des christlichen Lebens*, 2 (Koblenz: Bädeker, 1852), 591-95; Werner Korndörfer, "Ein sehr umstrittener Mann seiner Kirche," *Windsheimer Zeitung*, 21 Aug. 1964; Gustav C. Knod, ed., *Die alten Matrikeln der Universität Strassburg* (Strasbourg: Trübner, 1897, 1902), 1, 364, 367 and 2, 291; "Reichsstadt Windsheim," ed. Dannheimer, p. 96.
70. "Reichsstadt Windsheim," ed. Dannheimer, p. 96; Johann Heinrich Horb, *Der Christen Seligkeit in dieser Gnaden-Zeit* (n.p.: n.p., [1684]), pp. 460, 493-510 (biography with funeral sermon); Johann Augustin Lietzheimer, *Evangelische Sabbaths-Bedancken* (Sulzbach: A. Lichtenthaler, 1676), pp. i-ix.

Quote from Lietzheimer (p. v): "Soll der Bücher schreiben, welcher . . . auf der Universitäten . . . ja kaum das Maul hat fortbringen können . . . ?" Quotes from Horb (pp. 496-97):

> Gott gab ihm aber in sein hertz, daß er für sich die heilige Schrifft und unsers theuren Luthers bücher fleissig lase, und darauß eine ob wohl einfältige doch feine erkäntnüß Gottes und seines heiligen willens gefasset . . . Doch wunschte er sich zuweilen nur die tröpfflein weins oder gutes bröcklein, so von des Reichen tische gefallen, oder offt so gar unnützlich verschwendet werden.

Learned, p. 283, item 64, cites the "Res Propriae" entry for Lietzheimer's *Schriften* in Pastorius' Pennsylvania library.

71. *Update 2013: Ein Send-Brieff Offenhertziger Liebsbezeugung*, 1697, pp. 11-13. Pastorius reports the prior argued that the Bible alone could not be the basis of Christianity because that would lead to an endless proliferation of interpretations with every clever preacher establishing yet another sect; the Catholic church, on the other hand, was sustained by enshrined traditions passed down through generations and providing authenticity and stability. These arguments, Pastorius reports, were too weak to convince him, but they added to his growing doubts about the Lutheran establishment.

71a. *Update 2013:* See "Biography: Cotton Mather (1662/3-1727/8)" at The Mather Project, URL = http://matherproject.org/node/22 and Cotton Mather, *Memorable Providences, Relating to Witchcrafts and Possessions* (1689), passim, at URL = http://law2.umkc.edu/faculty/projects/ftrials/salem/ASA_MATH.HTM

72. Letter of 24 Aug. 1718, in "Letter Book," also cited in part in Toms, pp. 204-05.

73. *Beschreibung Pa.*, pp. 86-89.

74. John Passmore, "Cambridge Platonists," *Encyclopedia of Philosophy*, ed. Edwards, 2 (1967), 9-11.

75. *Update 2013: Ein Send-Brieff*, pp. 5-6, 9 and 11-12. The German report was "Eine Missiv ex Antipodibus, oder America Pennsylvaniae . . . von einem Studioso Theologiae [Johann Georg Seelig] : . . ." (Appendix 5) in *Grundforschendes Gespräch zweyer Personen / gehalten über die Formulam Concordiae, Pietismus, Chiliasmus . . ."* (Frankfurt: Heinrich Wilhelmi, 1695), cited in Mack, p. 160. Pastorius' quotes:

> so ungütlich diffamirter getreuen Zeugen und Dienstknecht Jesu Christi / deren Bücher ich großen theils gelesen / auch vieler mündliche Erklärungen und Predigten mehr dann 13. Jahr lang zum öfftern angehört habe. (P. 6) . . . dieselbe festiglich und einhelliglich bekennen / dass Christus Jesus der Ewige Eingebohrne Sohn Gottes uns von seinem Himlischen Vatter gemacht sey beedes zur Erlösung und Gerechtigkeit . . . dass wir . . . in seinem Liecht / Krafft und Stärcke seinen Fußstapffen nachfolgen / I Petr. 2:21. das ist / wandeln / gleichwie Er gewandelt hat / I Joh. 2:6. . . . und dero . . . Lehrer bezeugen und predigen einmüthiglich / dass das Blut des unbefleckten Lambs Gottes / welches erwürgt ist von Anfang der Welt / von allen Sünden reinige / heilige und vor Gott ewiglich gerecht mache / alle die ans Liecht glauben / und in Kindschuldigem Gehorsam darin wandeln. (P. 9) . . . Die so genannte Quaker sind diese fast halb hundert jährige Zeit über / da sie der Herr auffgeweckt hat / so wol in Engelland / als hier in Amerika durch ihre schier unzehlbare Schrifften / Christtugendsames Leben / und gedultiges Leiden dermassen bekannt . . . (p. 11) Ich entsinne mich sehr wol / dass in meiner Jugend tausend und tausend mahl den Nahmen Quäker und Enthusiasten (von denen hachtrabenden und aufgebrüsteten Hahnen / welche auff ihrem eigenen Mist (der Kantzel) am lautesten krähen dürffen) habe ausruffen hören; demnach aber versichert bin / dass viele derselben weder des einen noch andern Worts eigentliche bedeutung nicht verstehen . . . Anderseits bejammere ich noch vielmehr diejene / welche . . . nicht nur den euffern Worten nach verstehen / was sie widerrsprechen / sondern auch inwendig in ihrem Gewissen eines bessern überzeugt sind / und alles dessen ungeachtet / den schmahlen Kreutzweg Christi nicht bewandeln wollen. (P. 12)

76. *Update 2013:* Lambert, "Francis Daniel Pastorius," pp. 87-147 passim, uses "Alphabetical Hive" entries and some of the books therein cited to trace Pastorius' relationship to Quaker ideas. She relates this to his Pietist background, but does not examine the secu-

Notes: Chapter Three | 283

lar and (pre-)Enlightenment influences. (The following description of Pastorius' early poems is also a *2013 update*.)

77. Coing, 2, 29-47; Egidius Schmalzriedt, "Corpus juris civilis," *Hauptwerke*, ed. Schmalzriedt, pp. 483-84; Heinrich Mitteis, *Deutsche Rechtsgeschichte*, 15th ed. (Munich: Beck'sche, 1978), pp. 254-62, 281-83. Textbooks and authors are listed in "Res Propriae"; supplementary detail from: Alfred Söllner, "Literatur in Deutschland ... und der Schweiz," *Handbuch der Quellen*, ed. Coing, 2, 536, 549, 607; Roderich Stintzing and Ernst Landsberg, *Geschichte der deutschen Rechtswissenschaft* (1880-1910; rpt. Aalen: Scientia, 1957), 3, 1, 13.
78. Coing, 2, 42-43; Mitteis, pp. 265-83, Wolfgang Huschke, "Politische Geschichte von 1572 bis 1775," *Geschichte Thüringens*, 5, ed. Hans Patze and Walter Schlesinger (Köln: Böhlau, 1982), 221-23, supplements "Res Propriae" on Gotha.
79. Wallmann, *Spener*, pp. 80-81; Paul Wentzcke, "Boeckler, Johann Heinrich," *Neue Deutsche Biographie*. 2 (1955), 372-73; Dietmar Willoweit, "Hermann Conring," and Hasso Hofmann, "Hugo Grotius," in *Staatsdenker*, ed. Stolleis, pp. 51-77, 129-47.
80. Erich Maschke, *Universität Jena* (Köln: Böhlau, 1969), pp. 28-38; Steinmetz, ed., *Geschichte der Universität Jena*, 1, 111-65 passim; Notker Hammerstein, "Samuel Pufendorf," *Staatsdenker*, ed. Stolleis, pp. 177-80. Pastorius' sources for information about Halle were the *Works* and the *Pietas Hallensis* of August Hermann Francke, both of which were in his Pennsylvania library (Learned, p. 281, item 60, and p. 283, item 64).
81. Linck biography in Will, *Lexikon*; Stintzing and Landsberg, 3, 1, 51-52; Johann F. von Schulte, *Geschichte ... des canonischen Rechts*, 3 (Stuttgart: Enke, 1880), 1, 62-63. The quotations, from Will:
    ... durch Rechtssprüche, Urtheile und Bedenken einen Einfluß in die grössere Staats-Welt haben konnte ... Und in der That, er war zum academischen Lehramte gebohren, indem er bey seiner grossen Gelehrsamkeit ein mit Freundlichkeit temperirtes ernsthafftes Ansehen hatte, wodurch er die Gemüther aller Lernenden an sich zog.
82. Holborn, *Modern Germany*, 2, 68-79; Braubach, "Vom Westfälischen Frieden," *Handbuch der deutschen Geschichte*, ed. Grundmann, 2, 263-67; Guido Hable, *Geschichte Regensburgs* (Regensburg: Mittelbayerische Druckerei, 1970), pp. 170-75; Walter Fürnrohr, *Der immerwährende Reichstag zu Regensburg* (Regensburg: Lassleben, 1963), pp. 14-20, plates 2, 3, 12; Frederick Bracher, ed., *Letters of Sir George Etherege* (Berkeley: Univ. of California Press, 1974), pp. xi-xxiii.
83. *Etherege*, ed. Bracher, p. 68. Etherege, in Regensburg from 1685 to 1689, observed essentially the same Regensburg society as Pastorius had a decade earlier. Pastorius lists Etherege's *Works* among the books cited in the "Beehive."
84. In *Leben*, pp. 70-71:
    Vocatio Melchioris Adami Pastori ad
    Quartas Nuptias, Educato iam Filio Francisco

    Wie wunderlich Gott sey in allen seinen Thaten,
    Bezeuget dise Eh', die Er selbst eingerathen;
       Und das sie für sich gieng, must helffen insgemein
       Freund, Feind, Holland, Franzos, viel Herren gros und klein.

    Hätt Holland nicht so hoch in stoltzem Glück floriret,
    So hätte Franckreich nicht aus Mißgunst aemuliret,
       Der Kayser hätte nicht den Erstern Hülff geleist,
       Die Frantzen wären nicht dem Reich so nah gereist.

    Viel Leute wären nicht in feste Stätt geflogen.
    Mein' Esther wäre wohl gebliben zu Beyreuth,
       Ich hätt in Nürenberg nicht funden sie zur Beuth.

    Mann hätte nicht gewust von manches Craises Tagen,
    Herr Würffel hätte nichts von Frembden können sagen,
       Pastorius wär nicht gekommen zu der Ehr,
       Zu sehen dises Kind, so er ietzt liebet sehr.

> Pastorius wär nicht in Pirckens Freundschafft kommen,
> Dem Neuhoff wäre nicht sein Pflegkind abgenommen.
>> Mein hochgeschätzte Gäst, diß Tisches Ehr und Zier,
>> Ia selbst mein liebe Brauth wär ietzund nicht bey mir.
>
> Danck hab, du großer Gott, Danck habet, all ihr Freunde,
> Danck habt (: uff sondre Weis :) ihr des Teutschlandes Feinde,
>> Das ihr die Forcht und Flucht in Esther Hertz gebracht.
>> Ietzt wünscht ich, das ihr wart durchs teutsche Schwerd geschlacht.
>
> Ich habe das, so Gott durch Euch mir zu geschicket,
> Mir ist nach allem Wunsch mein Vorsatz wohl geglücket.
>> Euch aber wird der Herr Noth, Tod, Spott, Angst und Hohn
>> Bald geben nach Verdienst der Tyranney zu Lohn.
>
> Uns aber segne Gott mitt seinem Fried in Gnaden,
> Sein Güthe wende ab von uns, was uns mag schaden,
>> Er einig und verknüpff die beede Hertzen so,
>> Das wir so hier als dortt verbleiben stethig froh.

85. The detailed notes and the wedding list of "Res Propriae" do not mention his father's wedding, a clear indication he did not attend. See also Appendix I.
86. *Windsheim*, p. 148:
    > ... die ... in Noth, Gefahr, Kummer, Sorg und Elend schwebende, ja agonizirende löbl. Burgerschafft, die ... Trost und Hülffe ... aber uff andere Weise nicht gegeben werden kan, als durch ... Wieder-Einführung des lieben Friedens, oder seelige Aufflös- und Entbindung von diesen sterblichen Leibern.
87. From "Breutigams Gedancken," in *Leben*, p. 71: "... / Du bist meines Hertzens Zier / . . . / Als auff Regen Sonnenschein. / ... / O Du meines Lebens Leben. / ..."
88. Will, *Altdorf*, pp. 120-22. For disputing at German universities generally, see Paulsen, 1, 371-74. Will's text:
    > Von den nützlichen Disputirübungen kann man wol behaupten, daß sie, wenn irgendwo, vorzüglich zu Altdorf, von ieher zu Hause gewesen seyen. Wir haben hier öffentliche und Privat-Disputationen. Bei den öffentlichen erscheinet der Rektor und der Dekan der Fakultät im Habit, die sämtlichen Professoren aber sind ihnen beizuwohnen verpflichtet. Sie werden entweder zur Uebung unter dem Vorsitz eines Professors ... oder von Privatlehrern, die sich habilitiren, oder auch üben wollen, oder endlich zur Erlangung der höchsten Würde, gehalten ... Mit den Privat- Disputationen hat es hier eine ganz eigne Bewandniß. Ob sie gleich von den öffentlichen unterschieden werden, gehen sie doch in einem Auditorium vor, und werden wie andere besuchet, nur sind die Professoren nicht besonders verpflichtet, dabei zu erscheinen ... Diese gute, von ieher angeordnete und 1627. wieder erneuerte Anstalt war mit Ursache, daß in Altdorf eine so gar große Anzahl von Disputationen zum Vorschein kam ... Ehehin nemlich sind alle Wochen in den 4. sämtlichen Fakultaten [Privat]- Disputationen gehalten worden.
89. Will, *Altdorf*, pp. 26-27, 61-63, and Coing, 1, 50-52, supplement "Res Propriae" and *Learned*, pp. 78-81.
90. Will, *Altdorf*, p. 61: "... damit nemlich nichts nachtheiliges fur die Staatsverfassung und Rechte des deutschen Reichs und der Stadt Nürnberg eingemischet werde."
91. *Disputatio Inauguralis de Rasura Documentorum* (Altdorf: H. Maier, 1676), 25 pp. *Update 2013*: Pastorius had intended to deal with the reasons why "the credibility of documents was often called into question in court" but then limited his topic to the meanings of "rasura" (scraping, erasing, etc.) in the context of legal documentation (Grafton, "Republic of Letters," pp. 23-24).
92. *Disputatio Inauguralis*, pp. 22-24. The corollaries, in English paraphrase:
    > I. A husband is not legally bound to mourn his wife, but he creates a scandal by becoming engaged to another upon her death; II. A young man does not violate the law by kissing a maiden against her will; III. Allowing a wife to rule the household is contrary to nature and morality; IV. Committing a crime in secret complicates

matters once the secret is out, but a Roman proverb says, "What no one knows has hardly even taken place;" V. The death penalty may be imposed following a conviction based on testimony of witnesses in cases where the accused does not confess his guilt; VI. An agreement among drinking companions to transfer the ownership of wine is binding, but only until revoked; VII. A brother may marry his brother's sister if she is not his own sister; VIII. Children who do not have a father can easily be given away; IX. Professors, lawyers, doctors and other learned men may legally prohibit craftsmen from moving in next door to them; X. Emperor Justinian unsuitably revised the punishment of female adultery; XI. Aristotle's claim that slavery naturally exists does not contradict the Christian view that slavery is unnatural; XII. If a vassal kisses the wife of his overlord, he may legally be robbed of his fief.

93. Graduation is described in Will, *Altdorf*, pp. 16-17, 33-36, 41, 109-10 and 366; and in Mummenhoff, pp. 192- 94. Pastorius omits the June graduation from his detailed lists of university events and dates in "Res Propriae," an obviously deliberate omission that, like his father's 1674 wedding, he does not comment upon in the autobiographical jottings. He merely states ("Genealogia Pastoriana") that he disputed and received his doctorate on November 23 "and then turned back to my old Home, to wit Win[d]sheim."
94. Will, *Altdorf.* p. 110.
95. *Beschreibung Pa.*, pp. 99-100. See Appendix II for the German text.

Chapter Four

1. Hildegard Weiss, "Das Agrarwesen vom Spätmittelalter bis zum Ende des 18. Jahrhunderts," *Handbuch der bayerischen Geschichte*, ed. Spindler, 3, 456-72; Ingomar Bog, *Dorfgemeinde, Freiheit und Unfreiheit in Franken* (Stuttgart; Fischer, 1956), pp. 58-77.
2. "Prognosticon" ms, f. 343 a, cited in Learned, p. 84. The German epigram:

    Uff alle Sättel gerecht
    Häng den Mantel nach dem Wind
    Gibts kein Ochsen, gibts ein Rind.
3. Korndörfer, *Studien*, pp. 55, 58, 71-80; Estermann, *Bad Windsheim*, pp. 20-21, 51-52, 82, 84-87, 106, 113, 116; Schirmer, *Geschichte Windsheims*, pp. 58-65; Werner Schultheiß, "Bad Windsheim," *Bayerisches Städtebuch*, ed. Erich Keyser and Heinz Stoob (Stuttgart: Kohlhammer, 1971), l, 89-91.
4. Windsheim, p. 16: "Diese Stadt wird fast Aristocratisch von einem Ober-Richter und 24. Raths-Herren ... administriret."
5. Korndörfer, pp. 106-35; Schirmer, pp. 191-92.
6. Cited in Korndörfer, pp. 191-92:

    Nach deren Anheimbskunft Ihnen sobaldten der Raths-standt und andere Ehrenämbter offenstehen, da Sie dann balden zum Wohlgefallen der Alten ihr dominium über die arme nothleidende Burgerschafft sehen lassen, sich in verbottenen fleischlichen Wollüsten einlaßen, ehrlicher Burger Weiber verführen, und deren Töchter nothzüchtigen, jedennoch in den Rathsstandt erduldet werden ...
6a. *Update 2013*: Not all saltpetermen were itinerants, but their working conditions, involving the "stinking fundament of the human environment," were similar (Kelly, p. 33). Jack Kelly, *Gunpowder: A History of the Explosive That Changed the World* (London: Atlantic Books, 2004), pp. 33-36, 164; "Salpetersieder" in Wikipedia (DE), URL = http://de.wikipedia.org/wiki/Salpetersieder; "Saltpeter," URL = http://www. musketeer.ch/blackpowder/saltpeter.html
7. Estermann, *Bad Windsheim*, pp. 90, 94-113 passim.
8. Cited in Korndörfer, pp. 189-90:

    Gleicher Gestalt befindet sich auch eine Erbare Burgerschafft contra Herrn Burgermeister Pastorium in specie eußersten graviret, weilen Er bey diesen erlittenen schwehren Einquartierungen baldt diesen Burger mit schwehrer Gefängnuß und

Thurm thrauet, den andern vor einen Rebellen gescholten, den dritten den Weg zum Thor hinauß zu verweisen höchst schimpflicherweiß sich vernehmen läßet, wie Er denn dergleichen zu Georg Lentzen, Hannß Nicolaus Gilligen und Melchior Zehen geredet und sich öffentlich hören laßen, wie man noch ein- und den anderen Burger ehistens zum Thor hinaus fitzen und die Stadt verweisen müßte . . .

9. Cited in Korndörfer, p. 189:

Es kommt auch einer Erbaren Burgerschafft sehr Schmertz-lichen vor, daß Herr Burgermeister und Oberrichter Stellwag, und Herr Burgermeister Pastorius sich keineswegs miteinander vertragen können, wie dann der Letztere ohne Scheu vorgibet, daß Er neben Herrn Stellwagen nicht mehr regieren und subsistiren könnte, sondern deßwegen aus der Stadt annoch ziehen müßte, worüber dann nicht nur die heilsame Justiz mercklichen gehemmet, und die betrangten Burger an ihrem Recht verkürtzet werden, sondern auch hierdurch das gemeine Stadtwesen Selbsten euserst periclitiret.

10. Korndörfer, pp. 124-25.

11. *Großes vollständiges Universal-Lexicon aller Wissenschafften und Künste*, 57 (1748), cols. 792-93:

Die Streitigkeiten [in und um Windsheim sind] . . . Sachen, die nichts hauptsächliches ausmachen . . . Ihr Interesse ist, als wie der ändern Reichs-Städte ihres, sich nehmlich unverbrüchlich an Kayserliche Majestät und das Reich zu halten, und zugleich in sich selbsten auf Friede, Ruhe und Einigkeit, bedacht zu seyn . . . [um] sich eines stets florirenden Standes versichern [zu] können.

12. Schirmer, p. 192. In two additional sentences Schirmer briefly reported that an imperial commission decided against the citizens, and that some of them were punished:

Da die Bürger diese Lasten [die Einquartierungen] nicht mehr glaubten ertragen zu können, erlaubten sie sich Widersetzlichkeiten, und klagten sogar in Wien. Eine Kaiserliche SubdelegationsKommission entschied jedoch zu ihrem Nachteile. Drei Bürger wurden aus der Stadt verwiesen, andre kamen mit Verweisen und Strafandrohungen davon.

13. Two examples: Even though Paul Schaudig had carefully examined the archival records, his detailed account of Johann Heinrich Horb and early Pietism in Windsheim, published in 1925 (*Der Pietismus*, pp. 3-23), does not even mention the insurrection, a simplification now addressed on pages 192-200 of this study. As recently as 1982, in his ts. biography of Melchior Adam Pastorius ("Der Windsheimer Bürgermeister," pp. 49-56), Alfred Roth ignores or misinterprets significant details of the uprising and its causes, and takes an unjustifiably cavalier attitude toward the citizenry, admitting only that "not all of the complaints were completely unfounded": "It was predominantly insignificant trifles that the well-intentioned citizens expressed against the so-called oppression by Senate rule . . . It refreshes one's spirits to read" the 62 gravamina. His text:

Es waren meist unbedeutende Kleinigkeiten, die von den wohlmeinenden Bürgern gegen die sogenannte Unterdrückung durch die Ratsherrschaft vorgebracht wurden . . . Es ist herzerfrischend sie zu lesen . . . Die Beschwerden waren nicht alle aus der Luft gegriffen. (Pp. 50, 56.)

14. *Copia, eines . . . Brieffes* (Appendix II).

15. *Beschreibung Pa.*, pp. 61-62:

Darzu gratulire ich darum, dieweilen derselbe nun mehrern Anlaß und Vermögen empfangen hat, den armen Windsheimb ersprießliche Dienste zu leisten, *juxta monitum Divi Bernhardi: Vae tibi si prae es, & non podes.* Derohalben lasset uns unaufhörlich betrachten, wie daß der Aller-Obriste Richter der Lebendigen und der Todten uns sothane Obrigkeitliche Macht nicht anvertrauet habe umb unsers privat Nutzens, sondern umb des gemeinen bestens willen, und daß er an dem großen Tage des letzten Urtheils von denen, welchen viel geben war, auch viel fordern werde. *Juxta illud: Potentes potenter tormenta patientur.*

16. *Beschreibung Pa.*, p. 91. The letter itself (pp. 81-93) answers five questions about Pennsylvania enumerated by Melchior Adam as he planned his emigration. Pastorius delays

this personal attestation until near the end of the letter, perhaps indicating ambiguous emotions at the thought of living with his father again after a separation that had seemed so complete. The quoted text:
> Inmassen mich dann des Herrn Vattern gefassete Resolution hier selbst zu leben, und Gott zu dienen sehr vergnüget und erfreuet hat. O ein gesegneter Vorschmack dessen, worvon wir nach abgelegter Hütten dieses Fleisches die Fülle in der Ewigkeit zu erwarten haben.
> O seelige Führung des heiligen Geistes! denn was anders solten es doch seyn oder genannt werden können, als die heilige Gnade Gottes, die den Herrn Vattern (nachdeme er zu Windsheimb in vieler Aempter Bedienung grau worden ist) daß ihme GOtt der HErr auch endlichen an der Seelen und Gemüte so weiß gemacht hat, daß er die überschwengliche Boßheit der Menschen erkennet, und deßhalb von Babel ausgegangen ist. Diese Eingabe des Heil. Geistes, wolle der himmlische Vatter aller Lichter in des Herrn Vattern Hertzen bewahren biß an seinen letzten Abdruck und Ubersprung in die Ewigkeit.

17. Upon receiving this twelve-page letter, Melchior Adam, relying on his European experience rather than his son's advice, wrote to Penn in England (20 June 1698) on the pretext that he had not "had any definite information [from Franz Daniel] for a long time now" ("nun eine geraume Zeit keine gewisse Nachricht gehabt"). Melchior Adam sought Penn's sympathy by stating he had lost all hope that Franz Daniel would be his supporting "staff and consolation in my old age" ("in meinem Alter einen Stab und Trost"), asked Penn to have one of his officials describe Franz Daniel's "circumstances and biography" ("Zustande und Lebenslauf"), and excused "my audacity in writing" ("meine Kühnheit im Schreiben") by explaining it arose out of fatherly concern. In his response (20 Feb. 1699), Penn, with his preference for "sound and true words," encouraged Melchior Adam to write directly to Franz Daniel "as a pledge of your love for him" ("*Amoris tui pignus*"); Penn nevertheless described, briefly, Franz Daniel's Pennsylvania existence, and summarized his character: Your son is "regarded as a man of reason, decency, prudence and piety, esteemed among all men, most blameless in reputation:" ("filius tuus... est... Vir sobrius, probus, prudens & pius audit, spectatae inter oranes, inculpatae que famae..."). Melchior Adam included his letter and Penn's response, in both Latin and German, in *Beschreibung Pa.*, pp. 93-98, prefacing them with the explanation that he had wanted a report from "a third party" ("einem *Tertio*").

18. *Beschreibung Pa.*, p. 91:
> Daß aber der barmhertzige GOtt dem Herrn Vattern samt lieben Seinigen in diesem letztmaligen Frantzösischen Kriegs-Feuer so gnädiglich erhalten hat, gibt mir solches Anlaß dessen ewigwährende Gütigkeit zu preisen, und dieselbe inniglich anzuflehen, daß sie euch noch ferner vor allen Unglücks-Fällen mild-vätterlich bewahren, absonderlich aber je mehr und mehr in seine heilsame Forcht und Gehorsam bringen wolle, damit wir einen Abscheu ihme zu beleidigen, und dargegen mit freudigen Hertzen seinen heiligen Willen zu vollbringen trachten mögen.

19. *Beschreibung Pa.*. pp. 92-93:
> So ist es zwar nicht ohne, daß ich, mein Weib und kleinster Sohn harte Krankheiten ausgestanden, aber Gott Lob, völlig wieder restituirt sind. Es sind aber solches Erinnerungen unserer Sterblichkeit. Alles muß ein Ende haben, und also auch dieser Brieff, welchen schliessende den Herrn Vattern tausend mal grüsse, und durch die Lufft kind-hertzlich küsse vielleicht zum letzten mahl, und euch mit uns, und uns mit euch Göttlicher heylsamen Schutz- und Leitungs-Hand getreulichst empfehle und verbleibe
> Des Herrn Vatters
Treu-gehorsamster Sohn
F. D. P.

20. Carl Bertheau, "Johann Heinrich Horb," *Allgemeine Deutsche Biographie*, 13 (1881), 120-24; Göbel, *Geschichte des christlichen Lebens*, 2, 591-606; Korndörfer, "Ein sehr umstrittener Mann," *Windsheimer Zeitung*, 21 and 28 Aug. 1964; Otto T. Müller. "Heinrich Horbius (1645-1695)," *Monatshefte für Evangelische Kirchengeschichte des Rhein-*

landes, 15 (1966), 127-33; Alfred Roth, "Leben und Wirken des Superintendenten Horb," *Zeitschrift für bayerische Kirchengeschichte*, 51 (1982), 111-15; Schaudig, *Der Pietismus*, pp. 3-23; Estermann, *Bad Windsheim*, pp. 87, 92.

21. *Gottes gnädige Heimsuchung der Reichsstadt Windsheim, nach Exod. 20, vers 20 bei vorscheinendem ungemeinen Cometen*... (Frankfurt: D: Zeumer, 1681).
22. "Erstes Christliches Bedencken" in Spener, *Pia desideria* (Frankfurt am Main: J. Zunners, 1680), pp. 163-314; Göbel, 2, 596-99, supplements "Bedencken," pp. 245- 46.
23. Quoted in Göbel, 2, 601:
    Im Uebrigen werden Eure hochfürstliche Durchlaut ohne Zweifel erfreulichst vernommen haben, wie herrliche *progressus* unsere *pia desideria* durch ganz Deutschland schon haben ... Alle Welt erkennet, daß, was wir geschrieben, die pure Wahrheit sei.
24. *Theosophia Horbio Speneriana* (Würzburg: n.p., 1679), pp. 10-12:
    ... ein fleißiger Studiosus Theologiae [kann sein Wissen] ohne sonderbahre Gnade des heiligen Geistes erlangen und erhalten, ja so er auch schon, wie woll offte geschehen möchte, solte Gottlos seyn, und in herrschenden Sünden wider das Gewissen leben ... Und bezeiget die tägliche Erfahrung, daß offte die allerbösesten *Studiosi Theologiae*, so etwa ihre gute *Ingenia* und Fleiß dran gestrecket, für andern dißfals excelliret haben.
    In this passage Dilfeld was ridiculing Horb for trying to become a clergyman whose theology was enriched with the spirit of the prophets ("Bedencken," p. 171: "ein *Specimen*, Gottsgelahrter *Theologorum* Prophetischem Geist") and for encouraging others to do the same. The theological dispute is described in Johannes Wallmann, "Spener und Dilfeld," *Theologie in Geschichte und Kunst*, ed. Siegfried Herrmann and Oskar Söhngen (Witten: Luther-Verlag, 1968), pp. 214-35.
25. *Beschreibung Pa.*, p. 65:
    Ein vertraulicher Freund aus Frankfurt berichtete mich neulich, was massen die kaltgesinnete Lutherische Prediger durch die Pietisten, die Päpstische werck-heiligen aber durch die Quietisten etwas angefochten und erschüttert würden ... Ich habe aber anbey mit Verwunderung vernommen, daß beederseits [die Quietisten], so dann auch die uff den thätigen Glauben tringende Pietisten, als göttlichen Wahrheits Zeugen, fast hefftig verfolget werden, als wolte man den Rathe Gottes widerstehen, und über der Menschen Gewissen herrschen ... Sie werden einstens sehen in weme sie gestochen haben. *Verbum Domini manet in aeternum*. Gottes Wort und die Wahrheit lassen sich nicht unterdrucken.
26. *Beschreibung Pa.*, p. 84:
    Ich [habe] dieselbige für raisonable und zu Begreiffung guter Lehr und Sitten capable Leute gefunden, ... und sich in der That viel begieriger zur Göttlichen Erkäntnuß sich erwiesen als viele bey euch sind die uff der Cantzel mit Worten Christum lehren, durch ihr ungöttliches Leben aber denselben verläugnen ...
27. *Beschreibung Pa.*, p. 65: "die uff den thätigen Glauben tringende Pietisten"
28. Roth, "Pastorius," pp. 56-57, 59, 78.
29. "Bedencken," pp. 181-86.
30. Letters quoted in Johannes Geffcken, *Johann Winckler* (Hamburg: G. Nolte, 1861), pp. 402-05. The quoted excerpts:
    ... von solcher schweren Consequenz, daß ich nicht ohne Seufzen daran gedenken kann.
    Wenn ich bedenke, ... was mir noch bevorsteht, wie ruhig ich dagegen hier sterben könnte, so ist leicht zu erachten, welche Gedanken mir da einfallen.
    Ach Herr Jesu, wie schwer ist es mir worden, mich zur mutation nach Hamburg zu resolviren, ich habe solchen Kampf Tag und Nacht auszustehen gehabt, daß ich nicht mehr gewußt, ob ich Glauben und menschlichen Verstand bei mir habe; daher wollte es für höchst gefährlich halten, mit baufälligem Leib, schwachen Gemüthskräften, geringen Studien aus einem ruhigen Ort und da ich die meisten Schwierigkeiten überwunden, an einen Ort zu kommen, da so viel Sorge, Gefahr, menschliche erudition, mühsame Arbeit sich findet.

31. Letter of 3 Mär. 1685 to Winckler, quoted in Geffcken, p. 404: "... wobei viel Weinen, Geschrei, Wehklagen und Nachlaufen Jung und Alt, großer und geringer Leut [gewesen]."
32. The extent to which Spener was aware of the rift between Pastorius and his father is not known. *Theologisches Bedencken*, 3, 763:
    Daß im übrigen auch dessen leiblicher Vater sich nicht nur unter den widersprechern dieser göttl. warheit finden lasse, sondern von demselben dieser ursach wegen alle väterl. liebe abziehe, bekenne ich daß es wol eines der schweresten leiden, so einer seelen widerfahren könne, seyn müsse ... Also ob alle welt sich widersetzte, und auch unsre Eltern, so wollen wir dennoch an dem treu bleiben, welcher der rechte Vater ist ...
    The reference to Pastorius is quoted on p. 265 n28 of this study.
33. *Deutsche Städtebuch*, ed. Keyser and Stoob, 4,1 (1957), 122-54 passim; *Handbuch der Historischen Stätten Deutschlands*, ed. Georg W. Sante, 4 (1967), 130-36. Wealthy members of the Bodeck, Günderode and Lersner families are listed on pp. 738-44 of an appendix ("Größe Vermögen," or "Large Fortunes") in Alexander Dietz, *Frankfurter Handelsgeschichte*, vol. 4 (1923; rpt. Glashütten im Taunus: Auvermann, 1970). Young Bodeck is probably the Johann Bonaventura von Bodeck who left a fortune of 258,324 gulden when he died in 1700, presumably around the age of forty, but the identity is not certain since Dietz does not give years of birth. "Juncker" (the variant spelling of "Junker") identifies an aristocrat with an estate. Pastorius was probably referring to Philipp Wilhelm von Günderode (d. 1689) and Heinrich Ludwig von Lersner (d. 1696), both city stewards (Stadtschultheißen), or Maximillian von Lersner, a Pietist friend described on pp. 208 of this study.
34. Update 2013: For the Latin pun, see Grafton, "The Republic of Letters," p. 9
35. *Handbuch der Historischen Stätten*, 5 (1965), 356-57, 414-15; 6 (1965), 420-21; *Deutsche Städtebuch*. 4,2 (1959), 110-23 passim; articles on Friedrich IV and Karl Ludwig in *Neue Deutsche Biographie*, 5 (1961), 532-35, and 11 (1977), 246-49; Friedrich Walter, *Aufgabe und Vermächtnis einer Deutschen Stadt; Drei Jahrhunderte Alt-Mannheim* (Frankfurt/M.: F. Knapp, 1952), pp. 9-28.
36. *Handbuch der Deutschen Geschichte*, ed. Braubach, 2, 270-77; *Rheinische Geschichte*, ed. Petri and Droege, 2, 246-55; *New Cambridge History of Modern Europe*, ed. Clark et al., 5, 219-21, 494-98, 512-17.
37. Hartmut Lehmann, *Das Zeitalter des Absolutismus* (Stuttgart: Kohlhammer, 1980), pp. 105-35 passim; Wilhelm Heß, *Himmels- und Naturerscheinungen in Einblattdrucken des XV. bis XVIII. Jahrhunderts* (Leipzig: Drugulin, 1911), pp. 51-75 passim, 104-05, 112-13.
38. *Handbuch der Deutschen Geschichte*, 2, 278-82; *Rheinische Geschichte*, 2, 255-57; Walter, *Aufgabe*, pp. 32-37.
39. Letter of 20 March 1689 quoted in Walter, *Aufgabe*, pp. 37-38:
    Was mich am meisten daran schmerzt, ist, daß man sich meines Namens gebraucht, um die armen Leute ins äußerste Unglück zu stürzen, und wenn ich darüber schreie, weiß man mirs gar großen Undank und man protzt mit mir drüber. Sollte man mir aber das Leben darüber nehmen wollen, so kann ich doch nicht lassen zu bedauern und zu beweinen ... Ja, ich habe einen solchen Abscheu vor alles, wo man abgesprengt hat, daß alle Nacht, sobald ich ein wenig einschlafe, deucht mir, ich sei zu Heidelberg oder zu Mannheim und sehe alle die Verwüstung, und dann fahr ich im Schlaf auf und kann in zwei ganzen Stunden nicht wieder einschlafen; dann kommt mir in Sinn, wie alles zu meiner Zeit war, in welchem Stand es nun ist, ja in welchem Stand ich selber bin, und dann kann ich mich des Flennens nicht enthalten.
40. *Beschreibung Pa.*, p. 49:
    Dann deren Frantzosen barbarische Proceduren mit Verwüstung so schöner Städte, Kirchen, und Kayserlicher Begräbnussen, auch Mord-brennerey haben wir hier zu Lande mitleydentlich angehört, und sind dardurch in unsern Glauben gestärcket worden, daß man nicht auff fleischliche Macht und veste Castellen, sondern eintzig und allein auff die göttliche Schutzhand vertrauen solle, deren es so leichte ist uns

gegen alle feindliche Anfälle zu beschirmen, als unmöglich es sothane steinerne Schantzen thun können.

41. Pastorius reported (*Beschreibung Pa.*, p. 53) that his Pennsylvania friend Mordacai Lloyd, then on the Caribbean island, was saved from death "through the marvelous dispensation of God" ("durch Göttliche wunderbahre Schickung") because Lloyd was able to crawl out of a cavernous tunnel after having been swallowed up ("verschlungen") by the quake, which destroyed the capital of Port Royal and 2500 of its inhabitants, including "some females dressed a la mode, who were strolling along in high headdresses and Fontanges [ornamental headwear] as if they had two heads, and then sank into the earth up to their waists, and could not be freed by any means or removed from the spot, until they died and their bodies stiffened [while still vertical], and they were forced, as it were, to represent the Devil's pillory-columns [in Hell]" ("einige a la mode gekleidete Weibspersonen, die mit hohen Auffsätzen und Fontangen als mit doppelten Köpffen daher zogen, biß halben Leibs in die Erde versuncken, die man auf keine weise ausgraben oder von dem Orte removiren konnte, biß sie deß Todes erstarret, und gleichsam des Teuffels Prang-Säulen agiren müssen").

42. *The Select Works of William Penn*, 4th ed. (1825; rpt. New York: Kraus Reprint, 1971), 2, 420-32. Penn visited Holland and Germany on behalf of the Quakers in 1670 or 1671 and in 1677. In England, he became involved in organizing the Quaker colony of West New Jersey in 1675, applied for the land grant of Pennsylvania in 1680, sent the first colonizing party to Pennsylvania the following year, and sailed to the colony himself in 1682, where he lived in 1682-84 and 1699-1701. *Update 2013*: In the "Alphabetical Hive" (no. 1095), Pastorius includes this citation from Penn's epistle: "This I have to tell you in the Vision of the Almighty, that the day of the breaking up of the Nations about you and of the Sounding of the Gospel-Trumpet unto the Inhabitants of the Earth is just at the door."

43. Learned, pp. 106-09, 120-21, 139, 256, 280; Pennypacker, *Settlement*, pp. 21-22, 28-31; Wallmann, *Spener*, pp. 253-335 passim; *Lebens lauff... der... Maria Juliana Baurin von Eyseneck* (Frankfurt, 1684), rpt. in *Das Leben der Glaubigen*, ed. Gottfried Arnold (Halle: Waisenhaus, 1701), pp. 1121-43; Hermann Dechent, *Kirchengeschichte von Frankfurt am Main*, 2 (Frankfurt: Kesselring, 1921), 79-83, 94-97; Dechent, "Johann Jakob Schütz," *Christliche Welt*, 3 (1889), 849-54, 864-68, 935-37, 952-56; Dietz, *Handelsgeschichte*. 4, 300-05; Eise Oswalt, "Christian Fende" (Diss. Univ. Frankfurt, 1921), pp. 3-17; "Schuurmann, Anna Maria van," *Religion in Geschichte und Gegenwart*. 3rd ed., ed. Galling, 5 (1961), 1585.

44. "Some Onomastical Considerations," no. 435, mentions Jean de Labadie as one of various authors who published pseudonymously (a naming theme), and no. 436 describes Labadie and his book *Justum Judicium*, 1673, referring to Bohemia Manor in Maryland, a Dutch Labadist commune, founded in 1683, that permitted private ownership in 1698, and had disappeared by 1727:

> This our French namesake, not fully satisfied with John Calvin's Reformation in point of Doctrine [following conversion from Catholicism], made it his sincere Endeavours, to reform likewise the Immoralities of the formerly Reformed ... [in part by establishing in Germany a group of Christian communists] without meum & teum [mine and thine], and living by one common Purse & Patrimony. But as touching our Neighbouring Labadists on Bohemia River in Marieland, us thinks we hear their sd Patriarch take up this Lamentation: O foolish Bohemians, who has bewitched you to part your Joint Stock & to return to the worldly Principle of mine & thine again? Had your hearts been one, your Estate would not have been divided...

Bohemia Manor is described in Delburn Carpenter, *The Radical Pietists* (New York: AMS Press, 1975), pp. 19-36.

"Some Onomastical Considerations," No. 814 mentions Schuurmann and other female poets, also describing Anne Bradstreet's *A New-England Poetess, or the Tenth Muse Sprung up in America*, 1650.

45. Letter of 18 Apr. 1719 to Lloyd Zachary, in "Letter Book," quoted in Toms, p. 123; Johanna Eleonora Petersen, *Eine Kurze Erzehlung* (1688, rev. 1718, 1719), rpt. as

"Selbstbiographie" in *Der deutsche Pietismus*, ed. Werner Mahrholz (Berlin: Furche, 1921), pp. 201-45; Wallmann, ibid.; Dechent, "Schütz," pp. 853, 866, 867; Albrecht Ritschl, *Geschichte des Pietismus*, 2 (1884; rpt. Berlin: de Gruyter, 1966), 225-49; Carl Bertheau, "Petersen, Johann Wilhelm," *Realencyklopädie für protestantische Theologie und Kirche*, 3d ed., ed. Albert Hauck, 15 (1904), 169-75; Daniel Jacoby, "Petersen, Johann Wilhelm," *Allgemeine Deutsche Biographie*, 25 (1887), 508-15; Emanuel Hirsch, *Geschichte der neuern evangelischen Theologie*, 2 (Gütersloh: Bertelsmann, 1951), 232-33; "Merlau," *Neues allgemeines Deutsches Adels-Lexicon*, ed. Ernst H. Kneschke, 6 (1865), 246; Gotthold Ephraim Lessing, *Briefe, die neueste Litteratur betreffend* (1759), in *Sämtliche Schriften*, ed. Karl Lachmann, 3d ed. (1892; rpt. Berlin: de Gruyter, 1968), 8, 14-18; Johann Gottfried Herder, *Adrastea* (1801-03), in *Sämtliche Werke*, ed. Bernard Suphan (1885, rpt. Hildesheim: G: Olms, 1967), 23, 491-92. Herder's words to Goethe are quoted in "Herder, Johann Gottfried," *Brockhaus Enzyklopädie*, 8 (1969), 392; Merlau's criticism of Petersen's anti-Calvinist disputation is from Petersen's autobiography as quoted by Jacoby; all other direct quotations are translated from Merlau's autobiography in Mahrholz.

46. *Beschreibung Pa.*, p. 90. See Appendix II for the original German texts of this and other passages from the transatlantic writings quoted in translation in the following pages.
47. Pastorius' reports are here presented in the context of his transatlantic experience and thought, with background information from Gary B. Nash, *Quakers and Politics: Pennsylvania, 1681-1726* (Princeton, N.J.: Princeton Univ. Pr., 1968), passim; Joseph E. Illick, *Colonial Pennsylvania; A History* (New York: Scribner's, 1976), pp. 1-169 passim; and Stephanie Grauman Wolf, *Urban Village* (Princeton: Princeton Univ. Pr., 1976), passim. This analysis notes obvious simplifications in the reports, but does not consider technical issues more appropriate to a sequel biography describing Pastorius' Pennsylvania years in detail. Such issues would include his failure to mention either the Provincial Council, which limited the power of the popularly-elected Assembly, or the merchant elite, whose economics differed from his own and in part account for the criticism of usury in his poetry. [*Update 2013*: In 1990 I planned to publish this study and continue my research on a sequel biography, but things turned out otherwise.]
48. Published without place, date or publisher, the original text of 32 pages was reviewed in *Monatlichen Unterredungen*, ed. Tentzel, in Dec. 1691 (pp. 1037-41), and this review – presented in the form of a learned conversation between Herr Constantin and Herr Antoni – illustrates the sort of feedback that led to later revisions. Pastorius begins his report, Herr Constantin explains, by describing his worldly education and European grand tour, his conversion to Pietism in Frankfurt, and his admiration for those of "'the sect in England . . . who try to attain salvation through fear and trembling and live without guile . . .' Oh, those are the Quakers, interrupted Herr Antoni, who tremble when they are overcome by the Spirit. It's just too bad that . . . Pastorius allowed himself to be led astray by these people." Since the review was generally favorable, noting that Pastorius' historical and geographical reporting would permit "the still relatively unknown province of Pennsylvania [to] be better known among the people of learning and curiosity," it was undoubtedly one of the factors that convinced Pastorius to avoid specifying his religious preferences in at least two revisions, the first of which was appended to one of two 1692 editions of M. A. Pastorius' *Kurtze Beschreibung . . . Windsheim*.

Other early mention of Pastorius includes Gottfried Zenner's description of Pastorius' 32-page text in his four-part review of "forty gallant works of learned curiosity" entitled *Frühlings-Parnaß oder Abhandlung von viertzig galant-gelehrten Curiositäten* (Frankfurt: A. Boetius, 1694), 4, 27-31; a balanced and detailed digest or review of *Bechreibung Pa.* in an anonymously-edited review journal of newly-published books, *Monatlicher Auszug aus allerhand neu-herausgegebenen nützlichen und artigen Büchern* (Hannover: Nic. Förstern, 1700), pp. 895-902; and the listing of *Beschreibung Pa.* in Christian Gryphius' bibliography of world and regional histories, *Apparatus sive Dissertatio Isagogica de Scriptoribus Historiam* (Leipzig: Fritsch, 1710), p. 599, which summarily comments:

"germanice sed ineptissime scripta," or "sincerely but very unsuitably [or: foolishly] written."
49. Charles Francis Atkinson, "Gibralter," *Encyclopaedia Britannica*, 11th ed., 11 (1910), 941; and "Heracles" in *The Oxford Classical Dictionary*, 2nd ed., ed. N. G. L. Hammond and H. H. Sculland (Oxford: Oxford Univ. Press, 1970), pp. 498-99.
50. J. K. Laughton, "Penn, Sir William (1621-1670)," *Dictionary of National Biography*, ed. Sidney Lee, 44 (1895), 308-11.
51. Maurice Ashley, *England in the Seventeenth Century*, 3rd ed. rev. (Harmondsworth: Penquin, 1967), pp. 26-41, 108-20; John Bowle, *A History of Europe* (London: Secker & Warburg, 1979), pp. 418-24, 450-51, 458-64; and John Morrill, "The Stuarts," and Paul Langford, "The Eighteenth Century," both in *The Oxford Illustrated History of Britain*, ed. Kenneth O. Morgan (Oxford: Oxford Univ. Pr., 1984), pp. 285-359 passim. Melchior Adam Pastorius was so impressed with the fealty payment of two beaver pelts – which symbolized both the traditional continuities and, because of its token nature, the innovations of Pennsylvania – that he called attention to it in his two-page preface introducing German readers to his son's Pennsylvania reports (*Beschreibung Pa.*, p. ii).
52. Louis B. Wright, *The Cultural Life of the American Colonies* (New York: Harper, 1957), pp. 58-62.
53. See pp. 231-42 of this study and Elémire Zolla, *The Writer and the Shaman*, trans. Raymond Rosenthal (New York: Harcourt, 1973), p. 110.
54. "General Court Book of the Corporation of Germantown" (Hist. Soc. of Pennsylvania MS Am .3713), passim; and Pennypacker, *Settlement*. pp. 157-60, 256-57.
55. W. H. Barber, "Montesquieu, Charles-Louis de Secondat," *Penquin Guide to European Literature*, ed. Anthony Thorlby (New York: McGraw-Hill, 1969), pp. 545-46; Maurice Cranston, "Montesquieu, Baron de," *Encyclopedia of Philosophy*, ed. Paul Edwards (New York: Macmillan and the Free Press, 1967), 5, 368-71.
56. Dechent, *Kirchengeschichte*, 2, 79-83; Dechent, "Schütz," pp. 867-68, 935, 952-53; Oswalt, "Christian Fende," pp. 7-12.
57. Learned, pp. 138-39, 145-49; and Pennypacker, pp. 30-31, 38.
58. Reflecting the insecurities of the novice entrepreneur, Pastorius may have exaggerated his business, legal and farming activities as a"junior executive" reporting to Frankfurt "headquarters" in 1684. The extent of land he actually cleared and farmed is not known, but it seems to have involved only a small portion of the 1000 acres (600 in his German conversion) he bought through the German Company in 1683, holdings he lost in fraudulent land transactions in 1708, with compensation (a land grant of 893 acres) delayed until 1713. See Learned, pp. 149-55 and Pennypacker, pp. 38-50, 74-79.
59. He describes his painstaking efforts to develop a Germantown vineyard during 1706-16 (apparently not his first such attempt) in a section of "Monthly Monitor" entitled "*Observationes propriae Vineales*." A 1710 entry celebrates eating the first grapes with his family – on "the anniversary day of mine arrival in Philad[a]." – with a paean of praise "to God for all his Mercies & Blessings," but his observations conclude with this note: "Anno 1715. My Grapes were worth but little, anno 1716. good for nothing. *Spes alit agricolas, me mea ferme necat*. Oh! who would toil in such a Soil?" Thus his description of "sorry sow'r Clusters" of grapes in Poem 220 depicting Noah's viticulture (quoted on p. 96) probably reflects personal experience.
60. Poem 476 is theologically ambiguous, and does not directly refer to Pennsylvania. The most pertinent biblical reference: "Heaven is my throne, and the earth is my footstool" (Acts 7, 49 and Isaiah 66, 1). "Proprietary" suggests the Pennsylvania context. "Friends of His" is, arguably, ambiguous. "Free legacy" and "merit," of course, refer to grace versus good works.
Background on the Delaware Indians and Pennsylvania Indian policy: Gary B. Nash, *Red, White and Black; The Peoples of Early America*, 2nd ed. (Englewood Cliffs, N.J.: Prentice-Hall, 1982), pp. 95-98; William W. Newcomb, Jr., *The Culture and Acculturation of the Delaware Indians* (Ann Arbor, Mich.: Univ. of Michigan, 1956), pp. 1-78 passim; C. A. Weslager, *The Delaware Indians: A History* (New Brunswick, N.J.: Rutgers Univ. Pr., 1972), pp. 50-76, 155-72; and articles on the Delaware in *Encyclopaedia Britannica*,

15th ed. (1974), *Micropaedia*, 3, 444, and *Encyclopedia Americana International*, 7th ed. (1976), 8, 662-63. Penn's words on love and friendship are quoted from a letter he wrote to the Delaware chiefs in 1681 or 1682, cited in Weslager, p. 156.

Present-day knowledge of the Delaware Indians (who migrated westward from Pennsylvania, eventually to Oklahoma) utilizes seventeenth-century reports by Pastorius, William Penn and others, and generally confirms Pastorius' views. Weslager (p. 73) lists Pastorius as one of several authors of "valuable contemporary descriptions;" Newcomb (p. 130) states that Pastorius provides "limited" knowledge of the Delaware "but what he did say about them I have found to be of value." Pastorius' contribution is more valuable than Weslager and Newcomb realized, since they both relied on the English translations in Myers, *Narratives*, incomplete and sometimes misleading texts here corrected for the first time in English. Pastorius scholarship in English, including the *Narratives* translations, has ignored his most detailed and scholarly description of the Delaware, the 1688 Latin letter to Georg Leonhart Model, which was included in *Beschreibung Pa.* (and, retranslated, in *Narratives*) in a condensed translation that omits much useful detail and, in one important instance, misinterprets a passage including the Latin word "ludicri" (meaning drama or sport, but from the same root as ludicrous). Thus the English text in *Narratives*, based on the German condensation of the Latin original, has Pastorius describing a religious ceremony as "this laughable spectacle [executed] quite ardently and seriously" – a far remove from Pastorius' words (Appendix II) translated here (p. 235) as "and they all partake in this scene of physical activity and drama with such passion and seriousness that the observer, of one mind with their discord, is moved to sympathy." Weslager could not realize that Pastorius was an exception to the seventeenth-century Europeans he summarizes on p. 65: "White observers saw the Indian ceremonies either as childish antics, or pagan rites, instead of a sincere expression of a religious fervor based on deep-seated spiritual convictions."

61. Watching this Indian meal, Pastorius reports in *Sichere Nachricht* (1684, p. 4), "moved me to the depths of my soul, and made me ponder our Saviour's well-meant exhortation to take no thought for the morrow if we are his disciples," and he notes "everything is so totally reversed! If we Christians do not have our provisions for a month or several months in advance, don't we become so very fainthearted? But these heathens, so marvelously calm and patient, let God take care of them."

62. *Update 2013: Propagation of the Gospel in the East: Being an Account of the Success of two Danish Missionaries, Lately sent to the East-Indies, for the Conversion of the Heathens in Malabar... Rendered into English from the High-Dutch* [Ed. Anton Wilhelm Böhme], (London: J. Downing, 1709) and *Propagation of the Gospel in the East. Pt. 2, Being a further account of the Progress Made by some Missionaries to Tranquebar, Upon the Coast of Coromandel, For the Conversion of the Malabarians... The Second Edition.* (London: Downing, 1711). URL = http://www.francke-halle.de/main/index2.php?cf=3_1_3_3_2. The citations here are from Part 1 (with one exception, indicated as "pt. 2"). Pastorius quoted or paraphrased from these books in the "Alphabetical Hive," Nos. 1465 and 1680-85, and in "Some Onomastical Considerations," Nos. 1097, 1503, 1533 and 1736. This excerpt displays his lively interest in world cultures ("Beehive," p. 726):

> The Malabarians in the East Indies have many hundreds of gods, & own nevertheless but one Divine Being, which they call Isparetta, whom they say, before any thing was created, to have transformed himself into an egg, out of which the whole system of heaven & earth, & all that is contained therein, was afterwards produced, Ibid. p. 19. Their divinity is interlaced with a world of fables, and idolatrous fictions, the which they set out in such fine flourishes of wit, & adorn'd with such a poetical air, that it may be pleasant enough to read 'em, Id. That at last the great serpent, which bears the earth, would let it fall; and this should be the period of this world, & the beginning of another, Id. p. 24.... They desired of the two Danish missionaries to thrust a book containing the Christian principles into the fire, & they would do the same with another of their own worship; if either of them should be burn'd, the owners thereof should turn to the religion of those whose book should remain unhurt; but

in case the fire should destroy both, then none of the contending parties to be in the right, Id. p. 34.

Ziegenbalg and fellow theologian Heinrich Plütschau (1677-1747) were Germans (erroneously described as Danes) educated at Halle under August Hermann Francke. They were sent to the Danish East India Company's colony of Tranquebar by King Friedrich IV of Denmark in 1706. See Kurt Liebau, "Einleitung," *Die Malabarische Korrespondenz: Tamilische Briefe an deutsche Missionare*, (Sigmaringen: Jan Thorbecke Verlag, 1998), pp. 7-36 (esp. 7-14). Examples of Ziegenbalg's chauvinism: He once was so angered by the sight of countless "foppish" porcelain idols at a pagoda, he reports, that he "threw some of them down to the ground, and [struck] off the heads of others" (p. 57). When he realized that the adults resist Christianity but the young children are pliable, he had the mission build a charity school and developed a plan to increase enrollment by "buy[ing] up...some Malabar children" from their destitute parents. While arguing for increased mission funding, he even complained about the "high rate" demanded for such children in, essentially, a fluctuating market. He clarified, though, that the Danish East India Company now bought children (presumably as company slaves) only from their parents and had meanwhile stopped the practice of buying them from known kidnappers (pp. 58, 60-61). These details help to explain the tone of Pastorius' criticism. In the poem, "hirelings" implies criticism of their being salaried by the Danish king and also contrasts the Good Shepherd (Christ) with the hirelings of John 10, 13: "The hireling fleeth because he is a hireling, and careth not for the sheep." Despite his long history of Pietist sympathy, Pastorius was not swayed by the missionaries' proclaimed allegiance to Lutheran Pietism. (Later on, Pastorius apparently also read *Propagation of the Gospel in the East*, Part 3 (1714), not referenced here.)

63. Weslager, pp. 55, 66.
64. *Update 2013:* He seems ambiguous in his attitudes toward George Keith, collecting Keith's ideas in the "Alphabetical Hive" yet complaining about him in letters and occasional verse to William Penn and Philadelphia Quakers. (The complaints may have reflected Quaker dissatisfaction over Pastorius' neutrality during the 1692 controversy.) Jane Ward Lead (also spelled Leade) was a mystic whose beliefs appealed to Pastorius, particularly her theology of universal salvation and her emphasis on "the feminine aspect of the divine, embodied in Sophia, the Christian figure of Wisdom." ("Jane Ward Lead Essay - Critical Essays" in Enotes: URL=http://www.enotes.com/topics/jane-ward-lead). Pastorius cites from at least three of her books in the "Alphabetical Hive:" *The Heavenly Cloud now Breaking, Or the Lord Christ's Ascension Ladder Sent Down*, 1682; *The Laws of Paradise given forth by Wisdom to a translated Spirit*, 1695; and *Message to the Philadelphian Society*, 1696. And in "Books published by those of the Philadelphian Society" ("Beehive," p. 632) he lists six more books written by her along with numerous publications by other Philadelphians.
65. *Update 2013*: In a 1714 letter or prose preface to Poem 359, for example (to the daughters of Thomas Lloyd), he states his gratitude toward Thomas Lloyd (then deceased) while hypothetically considering "the blackest ingratitude (worse than that of the most unthankful Negro's);" recalls a presumed maritime escape from "the cruel enslaving Turks" (a reference cited in Chapter 2); and compares potentially mutinous passengers aboard ship with "the malcontent Jews" rebelling against Moses (Exodus 32). (The "unthankful Negro" comment might have been made to offset his anti-slavery reputation among elite Quakers directly or indirectly involved in the slave trade.)
66. Schopenhauer and Freud are cited in a discussion of decadence and brutality in Michael Grant, *Die Gladiatoren*, trans. Brigitte Mannsperger (Frankfurt/Main: Ullstein,1982), pp. 91-96 (originally entitled *Gladiators*, 1967). Grant's treatment of sexual perversion and imperial conquest (in a Roman context) might also suggest a link between the animalistic images here and in Pastorius' description of Louis XIV quoted on p. 42. Given his generally healthy and robust attitudes toward sexuality, Pastorius seems to have viewed the sexual excesses of the court as symptomatic of a "deep structure" of decadence in his day.

67. "Germantown Friends' Protest Against Slavery" and Quaker minutes in Learned, pp. 260-63; C. Duncan Rice, *The Rise and Fall of Black Slavery* (London: Macmillan, 1975), p. 188; and John Keils Ingram, "Slavery," *Encyclopaedia Britannica* (1961), 20, 779-83.
68. Poem 462 (with "double" lines, presumably to save ms space):
    Allermassen ungebührlich   ist der Handel dieser Zeit,
    Daß ein Mensch so unnatürlich   and're druckt mit Dienstbarkeit:
    Ich möcht einen solchen fragen,   Ob er wohl ein Sclav wolt seyn?
    Sonder Zweiffel wird er sagen,   Ach bewahr mich Gott! Nein, Nein.
    Warum müssen dann den rücken   Mann mit weib und kindern bücken
    Unter's Joch der Sclaverey,   ohne einst zu werden frey?
    Antwort: Wer kan Dieses ändern?   In Americanschen Ländern
    Nimmet man es nicht so scharff,   weil man Knecht und Magd bedarff.
    Aber, sind sie wahre Christen,   Die da nur zu allen fristen
    Suchen ihren Eigen-Nutz.   Ey das glaub der Höllen büß!
69. *Update 2013*: See his comment on "unthankful" Negroes in his 1714 letter to the daughters of Thomas Lloyd (note 65 above).
70. Letter of 29 Oct. 1718, in "Letter Book;" Lloyd Zachary is described in Toms, pp. 155-56; and Tolles, p. 122. *Update 2013:* URL=http://www.archives.upenn.edu/people/1700s/zachary_lloyd.html
71. According to information filed at the Historical Society of Pennsylvania (Autograph Collection, Case 21, Box 32), Pastorius, in 1685, built a modest two-story house that remained the family home for several generations. The house was depicted (before being torn down in 1860) in a painting or print that appears on a 1908 commemorative postcard reproduced in Learned, facing p. iii. Misleadingly entitled "Homestead of Francis Daniel Pastorius," the picture actually shows three buildings: the eighteenth century Green Tree Tavern to the left; a large house, on the right, built by descendants of Pastorius in 1796; and, in the middle, the low two-story dwelling built by Pastorius. The modest furnishing of the house is reflected in a 1720 property inventory, in Learned, following p. 286.
72. Various quotations from his poetry and correspondence in this study show his endorsement of labor and opposition to idleness. Numerous poems testify to the joys of gardening, or present him at work in his garden, as in Poem 141 (quoted on pp. 128-29), where neighbors stop to chat with the gardener, whose labor is thus enhanced by its natural and social setting. He indicates he worked at weaving and masonry in several references (including a quote on p. 3), revealing his enjoyment of the regularity these crafts share with poetry, as in this excerpt from Poem 125 (where "measure" playfully refers to arithmetic or mathematics and to poetry):
    Mason-work affords me Treasure,
    Trow'l and Plumb-Rule yield much Pleasure,
    And the Winter Ev'nings Leisure
    To sit down, and learn to Measure.
Various entries in the "Monthly Monitor" reflect personal work experience: His vineyard entries (cited in n. 59) describe the work of creating a small vineyard and his bitter disappointment when his "toil" was not rewarded. Similarly, he describes a method of growing superb asparagus that requires a multilayered bed dug six feet deep; for the less energetic gardener he then describes a bed two feet deep that suffices for asparagus of good quality. His Poem 220, an agricultural history of the world, concludes with examples of kings and a poet who became gardeners, and a self-congratulatory paean on the liberating rewards of agrarian endeavor, the ultimate response to the debilitations of courtly dependence:
    King Cyrus of Persia (oh glorious pelf!)
    Was hoeing and sowing in Gardens himself.
    Angeas, a Grecian Prince, dunged his own,
    Diocletian abandon'd th' Imperial Crown,
    Exchanging the Sceptre for a Weeding-hook, and
    Preferring the harrow to Clubs of Command.
    Brave [Abraham] Cowley but lately has plaid for the nonce

296 | Notes: Chapter Four

> The Poet and Gardner near Barnelius at once.
> So, since the Almighty, and remarkable men
> Were Terricultores, what wonder you then
> That Daniel Pastorius here many hours spends,
> And having no Money, on Usury lends
> To's Garden, Orchard and Vineyard such Times,
> Wherein he helps Nature, and Nature his Rimes,
> Because they produce him both Victuals and Drink,
> Both Medicine and Nose-gays, both Paper and Ink. vide 183.
> Moreover beholding his Mother, the Dust,
> He after his heavenly Father does lust.
> Matt. 13:8. Ager nunquam sine Usura reddit, quod accepit, says Cicero. And the same Pastorius in his Treatise against Usury, page 213, excepts Erd-Wucher, or lending to the Earth, as lawful, the 30, 60, yea and 100 bushels for one. [Pastorius' note.]

"Vide 183" is a reference to Poem 183, describing turmeric, which indicates Pastorius made his own ink from this herb: "And those who have no Ink supply / The Want thereof (look here) thereby."

73. From a photographically-reproduced copy of the letter in Learned, following p. 246; see also Learned, pp. 193-94.
74. Learned, pp. 304-12, and S. Foster Damon, "One Line of the Pastorius Family" (Library of Congress copy of TS Cambridge, Mass., 1926; 22pp.); copy of the Damon article provided by Gary Pastorius of Pittsburgh, Pa. Although Learned and Damon did not trace the descendants of Henry, research by Thomas V. and Mary Beth Pastorius of Sewickley, Pa., has now established the lineage of Franz Daniel's youngest son as well. The early descendants of John Samuel include a saddler and innkeeper, a carpenter, a Loyalist who was dispossessed and went to Canada in 1779, and three sea-captain brothers (one captured by pirates and involved in a plot to rescue Napoleon, and the other two lost or drowned at sea); more recently, they have included distant cousins of Presidents Abraham Lincoln and Theodore Roosevelt. Typifying much of immigrant American experience, both branches of the Pastorius family now include a broad range of professions, among them businessman, librarian, technical writer, chemical engineer, lobbyist and lawyer. The brilliant electric bassist John Francis ("Jaco") Pastorius, of Fort Lauderdale, Fla., is the most famous Pastorius since Franz Daniel; he recorded and toured with Joni Mitchell, Weather Report, and Blood, Sweat and Tears, and influenced jazz musicians worldwide until his death at 35 in 1987. Numbering around 200 families, Pastorius descendants are now dispersed throughout the United States, predominantly in California, Florida, Indiana, Minnesota, Ohio and Wisconsin, with more than one-third of the known families still located in Pennsylvania. Interviews of 30 Aug. 1983 with Thomas V. Pastorius and of 27 Aug. 1987 with Gary Pastorius, both in Bonn, Germany, and various letters from Gary, Mary Beth and Thomas V. Pastorius; obituaries of Jaco Pastorius: *Philadelphia Inquirer*, 22 Sept. 1987; Scott Benarde and Tom Moon, "Bassist Jaco Pastorius dead at thirty-five," *Rolling Stone*, 19 Nov. 1987, pp. 29-30. Research to date has failed to find any trace of the Pastorius family in Europe since a late journal entry by Melchior Adam Pastorius reporting that his youngest son Augustin Adam was learning engineering instead of studying law, a response to Franz Daniel's plea on behalf of the trades (Melchior Adam indicates) and to Augustin Adam's frustrations with his learned upbringing.
75. Toms, pp. 155-61.
76. Richard Hill, Samuel Preston and Isaac Norris, described in Tolles, pp. 43-44, 117-19.
77. Illick, pp. 109-11.

Appendix One
From "Genealogia Pastoriana"

The most basic text for Pastorius' years in Germany, this brief autobiography contains precise details (names, dates, etc.) taken from earlier notations and journals, but largely avoids the human aspects of his early life while focusing on the events leading to his emigration, a narrative pattern reflecting the distance in time, place and attitude that separated him from childhood as well as the sense of release and renewal that accompanied his departure from Germany. The text contains a few typical Germanisms as well as some grammatical errors that are not typical of most of the writing Pastorius did after mastering English around 1690, which suggests it was written during one of several periods of sickness late in his life. (Written "above 30 years" after his emigration, its earliest date of composition is 1713 or 1714.) The text is from the "Beehive," pp. 221-26, a photographic reproduction of which is in Learned, following p. 312.

Altho I heartily abhor that Sottish Kind of Pride & Arrogance, whereby some fetching their Pedigree from one or other renowned person in old times, think themselves the better for having the like worthies of the world among their Forefathers, & mind not at all, whether their own Names be written in the Book of Live [sic], or no, & Yet to acquaint my two sons, (who were born in Pensilvania [sic], where I now lived [sic] above 30. years) what Ancestors they had, and what Relations they still may have alive in High Germany, or elsewhere, I shall set down on this Leaf a Summary Account of my Parents, &c. and of my own self, humbly praying the Lord, to keep the sd my two Sons & all the Offspring, which He shall be pleased to give unto them, in His Fear & Favour, & thus to guide them by his Holy Spirit through this troublesome Vale of Tears, that at last they may happily arrive in the eternal Mansions of Bliss, Rest & Glory, there to praise Him for ever and ever, Amen.

[The three following sections, describing the lives of Pastorius' father, mother and other relatives (grandfather, uncles and aunts), are here omitted.]

I, Francis Daniel Pastorius, was born at Sommerhausen in Franckenland the 26th of September between 1. & 2. a Clock in the morning, Anno 1651. & had (after the Lutheran fashion,) for my God-fathers Franciscus, Semperfrey of Limburg, and Daniel Gering J.U.D. living at Segnitz. At the removal of my Father from Sommerhausen to Win[d]sheim [sic] the sd Semperfrey clothed me in red Scarlet, giving me also a little Sword, a hat with three plumes of Feathers & a pair of white boots, &c. making a fool of me, even in my tenderest years. In Winsheim I had a good Schooling, & mostly twenty or more young Earls, Baronets & Noble mens Children for School-fellows, there being then an excellent Rector of the Gymnasium, by name Tobias Schumberg, a Hungarian by birth, who could speak almost no Dutch [i.e., German], so that it was not allow'd to use any other Language but the Latin, &c. Anno 1668. the 31st of July I went with some others to the University of Altdorf, there to be Innitiated among Students, (which they call Deponiren,) giving to those Novices with abundance of impertinent Ceremonies the Salt of Wisdom, Sal sapientiae, &c. and Anno 1670. the 11th of August to the University of Strassburg, where I studied the Laws & likewise made a beginning to learn French. Anno 1672. mense July I visited also the University of Basel, & was by the way (at Schletstadt) strangely attacked by the Prior of a Monastery, to stay & read over the Books of St. Augustin & these Patres that might convince me, &c. The 25th of November, eodem Anno [1672], I returned to Winsheim, where I stayed all that Winter, and the next 13th of April 1673. I went again to Altdorf, but not liking the Place for some reasons, left it the 2d of July, going to Nürnberg, thence to Erford [Erfurt], and so on to Jena, where I arrived the 13th of the aforesd month of July & continued the Study of the Laws, learning moreover of Dr. Carolo Caffa the Italian Tongue, in which I publickly Disputed the 18th of April, 1674. upon some printed Theses inscrib'd dalle Leggi, as I had done before mense January sub praesidio Doctoris Linckii ad lib. 3. Pandectarum. Having from hence viewed Naumburg, Gotha and other Towns of that Countrey, I travelled unto Regenspurg, where the Diet of the Empire then was kept, in order to be the fuller instructed in Jure publico, whereof I formerly was taught some certain principles by the renowned Dr. Böckler at Strassburg. So therefore I lodged the greatest part with Dr. Völcker, Embassadour of Niirnberg and the rest of the Imperial Cities of

Franckenland. Anno 1675. the 16th of April I rode the post to Bayreut[h], where Anna Maria Völckmann (the eldest Sister of my present Stepmother,) was celebrating her Marriage with [Georg] Roth, Lehen Secretary of that Marquisata of Brandenburg, and thence in a Coach with my parents down to Winsheim, and afterwards, the 27th of September the third time to Altdorf, where I at last made an End of my Academical Learning, exantiabis [?] examinibus did Dispute Inauguraliter & pro Gradii Docterati the 23rd of November 1676. and then turn'd back to my old Home, to wit Winsheim. Here I practised above two years & an half, keeping mine own horse, marching from one Nobleman's house in the Province unto the other, (auff der Wurst herumb, as they use to speak,) and in short making nothing but work for Repentence. Anno 1679. the 24th of April I went (by persuasion of Dr. Horb, a godly Man & good Friend of Mine,) to Franckfort upon the Meyn, where I still plaid the Lawyer & kept Collegia privata Juris to some young Patriciis of the sd City, having my lodging for a while with Dr. Schutz, and then with an old & merry-hearted Gentleman call'd Juncker Fichard, as likewise good Opportunity to see Worms, Man[n]heim, Speyer & other places of the Neighbourhood. Anno 1680. the 26th of June, I upon the recommendation of Dr. Spener (that brave Patriarch of the Pietists,) undertook to be (Hoffmeister or) Conducteur & Guide to a Noble young Spark called Johanes Bonaventura von Bodeck in his Travels through Holland, England, France, Switzerland, &c. & so went to Mentz, where we did meet, and happily perform our sd Voyage, as does appear by a peculiar Manuscript Journal of mine in 8° arriving again at Francfort in perfect health & Safety, the 18th of November 1682. And forasmuch as I after this my Return was glad to enjoy the ancient familiarity of my former Acquaintances (rather than to be with the afores[ai]d von Bodeck feasting, dancing, &c.) especially of those Christian Friends who frequently assembled together in a house, called the Saalhof, viz. Dr. Spener, Dr. Schutz, Notarius Fenda, Jacobus van de Walle, Maximillian (bynamed the pious) Lersner, Eleonora von Merlau, Maria Juliana Baurin, &c. who sometimes made mention of William Penn & of Pennsilvania, and moreover communicated unto me as well some private letters from Benjamin Furly of Rotterdam, as also a printed Relation concerning the sd province, and finally the whole Secret could not be withholden from me, viz. that they purchased 15000. acres of land in this remote part of the world, some of 'em entirely resolv'd to transport themselves, families & all; this begat such a desire in my Soul to continue in their Society, and with them to lead a quiet, godly & honest life in a howling wilderness, (which I observed to be a heavy Task for any to perform among the bad examples & numberless Vanitates Vanitatum in Europe,) that by several letters I requested of my sd Father his Consent and approbation, and at length Obtained the same, with a Bill of Exchange of 250. rixdollars; Thereupon I sent a large Chest full of Books & other Rarities by me heretofore gathered as a free Gift to my brother Johanes Samuel Pastorius, and after One weeks Visit, wch I gave to Friends at Krisheim, to wit, Peter Shoemaker, Gerhard Henrix, Arnold Cassel, &c., I prepared myself for this the farthermost Journey, that I as yet ever had done or dreamed of. Anno 1683. the 2nd of April I set out from Francfort, came the 5th of ditto to Collein, where I was kindly received of David van Enden, Danniel Mitz and ..... Dozen, the then Resident of the King of Denmark in the sd City, (This Dozen had strong Inclinations for Pennsilvania, & desired me to prevail with his wife, but her Reply was that there they were carried in a Coach from one door to the other, but if they should happen to come hither, she was afraid that she must look after the Cattle, and milk her cows, &c.) and the 11th ditto all along upon the R[h]ein to Oerdingen, from whence I went a foot to Crefelt and there did speak to Denis Kunders & his Wife, Dirk, Herman & Abraham op den Graeff, &c. who with many others came about Six weeks after me into the aforesd Province. The 16th ditto I arrived at Rotterdam, Lodged with our Friend Marieke Vettekueke; saw here Benjamin Furly, Peter Hendrics, Jacob Tellner, &c. The 4th of May I sailed from Rotterdam accompanied by Tob. Lud. Kohlhans, and the servant, then with me, and came the 8th of ditto to London, taking our Lodging at John Hodgkins in Lombard street. After I had done my business with Hellmont & those I had letters for, I with Jacob Shoemaker (who came with me from Mentz,) Georg Wertmuller, Isaac Dilbeek, his wife Marieke & his two boys Abraham & Jacob, Thomas Gasper, Cunrad Backer, (alias Rutter,) and an English Maid, called Frances Simson, went a board of a Ship, which had the name of America, (the Captain whereof was Joseph Wasey,) and being gone the 6th of June from Gravesend, we arrived the 7th ditto at

Deal, and left England the 10th of the sd month of June, and saw the 16th of August this new World, arriving the 18th ditto in the Bay of Delawarre, and the 20th ditto at Philadelphia. Post Francofortum Fessus Desidero Portum. This our sd Passage described more at large, my sons may find in the abovesd Journal or Itinerary in 8° as likewise many of my Transactions for & in behalf of Others in a Manuscript in 4° so that it is altogether needless to repeat it here, &c.

Appendix Two
Selections from Pastorius' German Texts

1. Letter of 7 June 1683 from Deal, England (*Beschreibung Pa.*, pp. 45-47):
Nachdeme ich die Europäische Provinzien und Landschafften zur genüge besichtiget / und die bevorstehende *motus belli*, und dahero besorgliche Veränderungen und Zerrüttungen des Vatterlandes zu Hertzen genommen / habe ich mich durch den sonderbaren Zug des Allerhöchsten bewegen lassen in Pensylvanien überzufahren / der Hoffnung gelebende / daß dieses mein Vorhaben zu mein / und meiner lieben Geschwistrigten Besten / zuforderist aber zur Beförderung Göttlicher Ehre / (so mein allervornehmster Zweck ist) hinaus schlagen werde / wann zumahlen der Europäischen Welt-Frechheit und Sünden sich von Tag zu Tage / je mehr und mehr häuffen / und dahero die gerechte Straff- Gerichte Gottes in die Länge nicht aussen bleiben können. Ich hatte in allen meinem thun diese Eitelkeit und Frechheit wohl zu Hertzen genommen / und deren endlichen Ausgang mit tieffen Nachsinnen betrachtet / wie daß nemlichen Leib und Leben / Haab und Gut / Ehr und Wollust allzumal dem Tode und der Zergänglichkeit unterworffen. Die Seele aber einmahl verlohren / ist vor ewig verlohren.
Semel periisse aeternum est.
Derowegen ich zeitlichen und ewigen Unheil zu entfliehen / diese Reise und Uberfarth über den grossen Oceanum unter Gottes heiligen Geleite um so lieber angetretten / und samt 9. mir angehörigen Personen in Begleitung verschiedener ansehnlichen Familien den 7. Jun. 1683. von Deal abgesegelt / in Hoffnung / der HErr / welcher mich biß auff diese Stunde so reichlich gesegnet / und seinen Engeln über mir befohlen Wache zu halten / werde meinen Aus-und Eingang dergestalt regiren / daß dardurch sein allerheiligster Name auch jenseits des Meers an unbekannten Orten gepriesen werde.
Ich befehle darauff den Herrn Vatern und alle liebe Angehörige in dessen Allwaltende Schutzhand / und so bald mir der HErr in Pensylvanien überhilfft / werde ich von allen weitläufftigere Relation abstatten. Ist es aber sein heiliger Wille mich auff dem Wege abzufordern / bin ich von Hertzen bereit / und nehme deßwegen von dem Herrn Vatter kindgebührlichen Abschied / mit nochmahlig gehorsamer Dancksagung für alle so überflüssig erwiesene Lieb und Treue; GOtt vergelte es in Zeit und Ewigkeit.
Ich erinnere mich auch in meinem Reise-Tour eine Grabschrifft gelesen zu haben / welche also lautete:
Der ich bey frembder Grufft so manche Schrifft gelesen / Und deren gute Zahl in dieses Buch gebracht / Weiß nicht wo? wann? und wie? ich selbsten werd verwesen / Drum gib ich Welt-Lust dir nun tausend gute Nacht.
Sehen wir einander derowegen nicht mehr unter dem Himmel / so wird es seyn in dem Himmel / wo wir anderst den Willen GOttes allhier auff Erden vollbringen / welches ich von Grund der Seelen wünsche und biß in Tod verbleibe
      Des Herrn Vatters
       Treugehorsamster Sohn
        F. D. P.
2. From the Foreword to *Beschreibung Pennsylvaniae* (pp. iii-viii):
Es ist denen Meinigen insgesamt zur Genüge bekannt auf was Weise ich von meinen Kindes-Beinen an / nach abgelegten Kinder-Schuhen auf dem Wege dieser Zeitlichkeit meinen Lebens-Lauff gegen die frohe Ewigkeit zu / eingerichtet / und in allem meinem Thun dahin getrachtet habe / wie ich den allein guten Willen GOttes erkennen / seine hohe Allmacht fürchten / und seine unergründliche Güte und Barmhertzigkeit hertzlich lieben / loben und ehren lernen möchte. Und obwohlen ich nebst andern gemeinen

Wissenschafften der freyen Künste / das Studium juris feliciter begriffen und absolviret. Danebens die Italiänische und Frantzösische Sprachen zur Genüge mir bekannt gemacht / darauff den sogenannten grossen Tour mit guter Gesellschafft durch die Landschafften gethan. So habe ich jedoch an allen Orten und Enden meinen grösten Fleiß und Bemühung an anderst nichts gewendet / als eigentlich zu erfahren / wo und bey welchen Menschen und Nationen doch eine wahre Devotion, Liebe / Erkänntnuß und Forcht GOttes anzutreffen und zu erlernen seyn möchte. Ich fande auff Universitäten und Academien der gelehrten Leuthe Anzahl fast ohne Zahl / aber so mancherley Köpff / so mancherley Religionen und Secten / hochgeführte Sinnen und spitzige Quaestiones, in Summa / es war von der eitelen Welt-Weisheit ein so grosses Gespräch und Gepränge von welchen der Apostel spricht: *Scientia inflat.*

Aber daß ich an einigem Ort in Niderland und Franckreich einen Professorem solte gesehen haben / der von gantzem Hertzen eines Knabens und Discipuls Seele solte zu der reinen Liebe JEsu und zur Erkantnus der heiligen Dreyfaltigkeit mit Ernst angewiesen haben / daß kan ich mit gutem Gewissen nicht von mir schreiben.

An Maul- und Namen-Christen / die mit Welt-Witz aufgeblasen umher gehen / und Fleisches-Lust / Augen-Lust / und hoffärtiges Wesen (des Teuffeis Trifolium) liebhaben / ist zwar kein Mangel. Aber die da mit Forcht und Zittern ihre Seeligkeit zu würcken gedächten / ohne Betrug lebeten / und mit allen Seelen-Kräfften in ihr Centrum, in GOtt das allerhöchste Gut eindringeten / da war *rara avis in terris*.

Ich fande doch endlich in der Universität Cambridge und in der Stadt Gend einige heimlich latitirende / dem lieben Gott von gantzem Gemüt resignirte und ergebene Männer / welche auf verspürte meine ernstliche Nachforschung / mir viel gute Lehren beybrachten / und mich in meinem Vorsatze sehr besteiffeten / auch sonsten mir an Hand giengen / daß mir in dem printzlichen Hofe zu Gend des glorwürdigsten Kaysers Caroli V. Geburts-Stuben (so nur 4. Elen lang 4. Elen weit ist) gezeiget wurde / mit der Erinnerung / wie diesem neu- gebornen Printzen von einem seiner Tauff-Pathen eine kostbar gebundene Bibel mit der güldenen Uberschrifft: *Scrutamini scripturas*, seye eingebunden worden / die er auch fleissig gelesen / und daraus erlernet / daß er auf das allein gültige Verdienst JESU Christi sterben müsse.

Ich sahe ferner in diesem meinem Tour zu Orleans / Paris / Avignion, Marseille, Lyon und Geneve viel tausend junge Personen aus Teutschland / meistens vom Adel / die da im Gebrauch haben nur denen Eitelkeiten der Kleidungen / Sprachen / frembden Sitten und Ceremonien nachzuziehen / und in Erlernung des Pferd-Hupffens / Reutens / Dantzens / Fechtens / Piquen- und Fahnen-Schwingens unglaubliche Depensen machen. Also daß ein groß Stuck ihres Teutschen Patrimonii an die unnütze Welt-Eitelkeit verwendet / darbey aber an die Liebe Gottes / und an die Gott- wohlgefällige Klugheit der Nachfolgung Christi nicht ein einiges mahl gedacht wird; Ja wer von des heiligen Augustini, Tauleri, Arndii, und anderer Gottesgelehrten Männer Schrifften und *Soliloquiis cum Deo* etwas reden will / der muß für einen Pietisten / Sectirer und Ketzer ausgeschryen werden; und will sich kein in der Aristotelischen Welt-Weisheit ertrunckener Mann mehr einreden / noch von dem Geiste GOttes straffen lassen.

Derowegen setzte ich mich nach Endigung meines Tours in mein Cabinet in eine kurtze Retirade, und revocirte mir in mein Gedächtnuß alles das / was bißhero dieses Welt-Theatrum mir vor die Augen gestellet hatte / und konte in keinem Dinge eine beständige Vergnüglichkeit finden / desperirte auch / daß in meinem Vatterlande / und gantz Teutschland einiger Ort für künfftige würde erfunden werden / in welchem man von der alten Gewonheit des blossen *Operis operati* abtretten / und die reine Liebe zu GOTT aus gantzem Hertzen / aus gantzen Gemüte und aus allen Kräfften antretten / auch den Nächsten lieben würde wie sich selbsten.

Gedachte also bey mir / ob es nicht besser wäre / daß ich die von dem höchsten Geber / und Vatter des Liechtes mir aus Gnaden geschenckte Wissenschafft zum guten denen neu-gefundenen Amerikanischen Völckern in Pensylvanien vortragen / und dieselbe hierdurch die wahre Erkäntnuß der heiligen Dreyfaltigkeit / und des wahren Christenthums theilhafftig machen thäte.

Weilen aber die Provintz und Landschafft Pensylvania an denen End gräntzen Americae sich situiret befindet / so muß nothwendig zuvor etwas weniges von der Repartition der Welt-Kugel und in specie von gantz America (als den vierten Theil der Welt) praemittirt und gemeldet werden ...

3. *Copia, eines von einem Sohn an seine Eltern auss America abgelassenen Brieffes sub dato Philadelphia, den 7. Martii 1684*:
Liebwerthester Herr Vatter und Frau Mutter!
Gleichwie ich allschon vor mehr als einem viertel Jahr meine Gott lob! gesegnete Anherokunfft in schuldiger Obliegenheit berichtet / und anbey bekandt gemacht / daß von allhiesigem Landsherrn William Penn mir sehr affectionirter Freundlichkeit empfangen worden; So sol anitzo kürtzlich zu notificiren nicht umb / daß iztgedachter rühmliche Regent seine zu mir tragende Gewogenheit täglich mehr und mehr im Werck verspüren lasset / mir auch dißseitige Landschafft von Zeit zu Zeit besser gefällt / daß ich dahero dickmals wünsche / euch nebenst meinen lieben Geschwistern bey mir zu haben / wol wissend / daß weder euch noch sie sothaner Wexel gereuen würde. Dann ob ich zwar dem Liebe nach eurer Anwesenheit beraubt seyn muß / bin ich jedennoch in kindlicher Liebe Euch allzeit gegenwärtig / und sehe die trübselige Zorn- und schwere Straff-Gerichte / welche nach dem unhintertreiblichen Lauff göttlicher Gerechtigkeit über Europa biß zur gäntzlichen Verderbung dieses abscheulichen Babylons / außgegossen werden. Wolt ihr nun / liebwerthiste Eltern / diesen über Teutchland bestimmten Plagen entfliehen / so macht euch nicht theilhafftig ihrer Sünden / sondern N B. gehet davon aus!
Ich sage nicht von einem leiblichen Außgang / welcher alleinlich wenig nutzen würde / sondern von dem geistlichen / so darinn bestehet / daß ihr euch solchen jenseits die Oberhand habenden Babilonischen Eitelkeiten und verwirrten Menschen-Satzungen nicht unterwerffen / auch keinen andern Lehrmeister erkennen wollet / als JEsum Christum den Sohn deß allmächtigen Gottes / welcher denselben zu uns gesandt / daß Er uns sey der Weg / die Wahrheit / und das ewige Leben.
Geht ihr nun solcher Gestalt auß / so mögt ihr wol in eurem Vatterland (wofern ihr keinen innerlichen von Gott herrührenden Antrieb / dasselbe zu verlassen / bey Euch empfindet) verbleiben / eben als Loth zu Sodoma wohnete / und sich von der alldar im Schwang gehenden Hoffart / Füllerey und Geilheit unbefleckt erhielte.
Weil ich aber auß trifftigen Ursachen befahre / daß der Feuer-und Schwefel-Regen göttlichen Zorns in kürtzem über das teutsche Gomorra abfallen werde / ist mein hertzlicher Wunsch / daß ihr solchem auch dem äussern Menschen nach entgehen möget. Prüffet so wol hierinn / als in allen andern Stücken den guten Willen Gottes / umb denselben zu vollbringen / dann / wer solchen thut / wird nicht umbkommen / mit der Rotte der Gottlosen / sondern hat die Verheissung / daß er bleiben werde in Ewigkeit / &c.
Hiesige Provintz betreffend / haben wir gesunde reine Lufft / anmuthige Brunnquellen / Fisch- und Schiffreiche Ström / fruchtbaren Grund / nachdem er erstlich von starcken unverdrossenen Armen handthieret wird / allerhand zahme und wilde Thiere. Die Hauptstadt Philadelphia / worinnen ich mich noch zur Zeit mit meinen Knechten und Mägden bey erwünschtem Wolstand aufhalte / nimt täglich an Gebäuen und Einwohnern starck zu / wie auch hier und da im Land andere Stadt fundirt werden. Den 24. Octobr. legte ich eine an / und / dieweil sie von Teutschen bewohnt / Germantown genennet wird; liegt nur 2. Stund von hier / und begreifft 6000 Morgen Felds / leben allbereits 12. Familien (von 42. Personen) sehr vergnüglich daselbst / wiewol diß Jahr die Lebensmittel wegen der grossen Menge des von vielen Orten anher gekommenen Volcks ziemlich kostbar / und wir durch göttlichen Segen das nechste einen mehrern Überfluß verhoffen.
Neben nunerwehnten Germantown hat W. Penn uns noch einen Strich Landes von 12000 Ackers assigniret / welches Er Neu-Franckenland benahmset / worinnen / so der Herr will / in kurtzem noch etliche Städte anzuordnen verhoffe.
Über diß / so eine grössere Anzahl Teutschen (woran ich nicht zweiffele) anhero kommen / können wir noch wohl 20000 Ackers dabey / und also ein klein Teutschland! / auch eigene Freyheiten kriegen / und unter unserm Recht- und Gerechtigkeits- liebenden Gouverneur ein friedsam und stilles Leben führen / in aller gottseligen Erbarkeit / Amen!
Betrachtet nun / liebwertheste Eltern / ob ich auff diese Weiß Gott und meinem Neben-Menschen nicht weiterspießlichere Dienste leisten möge / als da ich bey euch / wie andere *rabulae forenses* und Gewissenlose Beutelfegende Schand Vocaten Hader zwischen Brüdern via Juris anrichten hülffte?

Minstens finde ich bey meinem nunmahligen Beruff einen gnädigerem Gott / und unverletzte Conscientz, welche 2. Stück ich allen Schätzen Aegypti unvergleichlich weit vorziehe. Der N. und seine Frau wären diesem Land / und diß Land ihnen hinwieder sehr nützlich / könnten in wenig Jahren durch redliche Arbeit ihrer Hände einen so reichen Seegen von Gott gewarten / woran sie in eurem Ort nicht gedencken dörffen: Allein niemand muß ehender lauffen / er werde dann vom HErrn gezogen / im Gegensatz aber auch diesem Göttlichen Zug nicht ungehorsam seyn / worvon viel zu sagen wäre / wann unsere Hertzen nicht noch allzufleischlich &c. Ich schliesse derowegen / und nechst warhafftiger Contestation, daß Meine Seele voll Lieb / Ehrerbietung und Dienstwilligkeit gegen euch und meine liebe Geschwistere / die ich hiermit grundhertzlich grüsse und küsse / und Sie versichere / daß ich ihrenthalben die gefährliche und beschwerliche Reiß gern noch einmal thun wolte / umb / so es Gottes heiliger Wolgefallen wäre / selbige anhero zu holen &c. Verbleibe ich unter der allwaltenden Schutzhand unsers ImmanuELs
   Des Herrn Vatters und Frau Mutter
    auch in America treugehorsamer
      Sohn N. N.
P. S. Ich habe vergessen ein paar Wort von den so genannten Indianern oder Wilden zu gedencken: Es sind guthertzige redliche Leut / die dermaleinst an dem grossen Gerichts-Tag mit denen von Tyro und Sidon auftretten werden / die falsche Maul-Christen zu beschämen. Zwey von ihren Königen und Königinnen haben mich etliche mal besucht / auch kommen ihrer zum öfftern sehr viel in mein Hauß / denen ich nach Möglichkeit alle Lieb erweisse. Der Herr erleuchte Sie / und uns alle / Amen.

4. From Letter of 1 March 1697:
Ich habe ehedessen den 1. Dec. 1688. an meinen guten Freund / Herrn Georg Leonhard Modeln / Rectorem der Schulen in Windsheimb fast ausführlichen geschrieben / worauff mich Kürtze halber beziehe. Auch hatte ich ihme qua Educationem juventutis eingerathen / daß ein jeder Knab pro capacitate auch ein leichtes Handwerk nebens der notitiam literarum, erlernen sollte / um im Nothfall solches in fremden Provinzien zutreiben / und sich darmit aus dem Lande zu helffen und in aller Welt / ohne Verschwendung ihres Patrimonii, mit der Eltern Betrübnuß / fortzukommen... Ich selbsten gebe so fort etliche 100. Reichsthaler darum / daß ich die köstliche Zeit / welche ich zu Erlernung der Sperlingischen Physic, Metaphysic und andern unnöthigen sophistischen Argumentationibus und arguitionibus angewendet / uff Ingenier-Sachen oder Buchdruckerey-Kunst gekehret hätte / welches mir nun mehr zu statten kommen / ja mir und meinem Neben-Christen nützlicher und ergetzlicher fallen sollte / als sothane Physic, Metaphysic, und alle Aristotelische Elenchi und Sylochismi, durch welche kein wilder Mensch oder Unchrist zu GOtt gebracht / vielweniger ein Stuck Brods erworben werden kan.

5. From Letter of 4 March 1699:
Sonsten nimt hiesige Landschafft noch täglich zu an Menschen und menschlicher Boßheit / jedoch verhoffe ich es werde nimmermehr so unmenschlich darinnen zugehen / als in denen Europäischen hohen Schulen / auff denen man meistentheils lauter dediscenda erlernen muß. Multi enim Professores inutilibus quaestionibus & acutis tricis nugalibus tempus terunt, & dum discentium mentes in super-vacaneis quaestionibua detinent, impediunt eas ne ad solidiora aspirent. Nituatur explorare quid sit Jupiter & Vulcanus, sed non quid sit Christus? Conantur quoque sanctissimum Verbum Dei Aristotelicis Syllogismis illuminare & defendere, quasi vero Spiritus ille Sanctus (qui solus verus Author & Dictator scripturae est) per damnatum Ethnicura & in Inferno ejulans Ingenium Aristotelis posset reformati aut illustrari.
Andere vertreiben die edle Zeit mit lauter unnützen Fragen und indagationibus, an vera sit illa Inscriptio sepulchralis in Monte Fiascone: Propter Verbum est est Dominus meus mortuus est. Andere suchen bey denen Griechischen Declinationibus den Ablativi casum, worzu sie solchen aber verlangen / wissen sie selbst nicht.
Ja so gar fangen heut zu Tage die Studenten an einander / und zwar unter ihnen den zehenden zu tode zu sauffen / und den leidigen Satan in sein Hollen-Reich zuzuschicken / welches in Warheits-Grund höchstens zu betauren ist / und von GOtt zu wünschen

wäre / daß so wohlen denen Herren Professoribus als Studiosis die Augen ihres Verstandes geöffnet würden / daß sie erkennen möchten / wie vergebens es seye sich deß Lichts des Evangelii zu berühmen / und doch unter so abscheulichen Wercken der Finsternuß zu stecken.
Betaure ich solchem nach meinen lieben Brudern Joannen Samuelem / wann er zu Hause von seinen lieben Eltern und Praeceptore domestico die Pietät und Gottesfurcht erlernet hat / solche hernach uff Universitäten wieder verlieren / und mit äusserister Seelen-Gefahr so viel dediscinda erfahren solte / und wolte ich ihme viel lieber hertzbrüderlich einrathen / daß er ein ihme anständiges leichtbegreiffliches Handwerck erlernete / bey deme er GOtt und dem Neben-Christen dienen möchte; welches / wiewol es bey euch verächtlich und gering geachtet wird / so ist es doch göttlicher Verordnung / und Apostolischer Lehre viel gemässer / als alles scholastische Grillisiren; denn meistentheils sind die Hochgelehrte Hochverkehrte / und scientia mundana inflat, dergleichen hohe hoffärtige Geister wollen hernachmahls einen grossen Staat führen / hierzu bedörffen sie grosse Geld Summen / diese suchen sie per fas & nefas mit ihres Nechsten Schaden zu erlangen / damit nur ihre Weiber und Kinder stets a la mode einher schwäntzen können.
Herentgegen sagen die demüthige gottsgelehrte Leute mit dem Antonio: Non data non cupio, und halten mit Palingenio für gut / contentum vivere parvo, cum quibus concordat S. Paulus Hebr. 13 v. 5.

6. The following selection includes the texts quoted on pp. 215-42 of this study:

a. From *Sichere Nachricht*:
Meine Gesellschafft bestund auß vielerley Sort Leuten / da war ein D. Medicinae mit seinem Weib und 8. Kindern / ein Frantzos. Capitain / ein Niederteutscher Kuchenbecker / ein Apothecker / Glaßblaser / Maurer / Schmidt / Wagner / Schreiner / Küfer / Hutmacher / Schuster / Schneider / Gärtner / Bauern / Näderinnen / &c. in allem etlich und 80. Personen / ausser dem Schiffvolck. Solche nun sind nicht nur ihrem Alter (massen unsere älteste Frau 60. Jahr / das jüngste Kind aber nur 12. Wochen alt waren) und nunerwehnten Handthierung nach unterschieden / sondern auch so differenten Religionen und Wandels / daß ich die Schiff / welche sie anhero tragen / nicht unfüglich mit der Archen Noä vergleichen könte / wofern nicht mehr unreine / als reine (vernünfftige) Thier darinnen befindlich. Unter meinem Gesinde habe ich / die es mit der Römischen / mit der Lutherischen / mit der Calvinischen / mit der Widertäufferischen / und mit der Englischen Kirche halten / und nur einen Quäcker. (P. 2.)
[Die alte Einwohner] sind schlechte Oeconomi / haben theils weder Scheunen noch Ställe / lassen ihr Geträyd etliche Jahr lang unaußgedroschen / unter freyem Himmel ligen / und ihr Vieh / Pferd / Küh / Schwein / &c. Sommer und Winter im Busch lauffen / daher sie auch geringen Nutzen darvon schöpffen. (Pp. 2-3.)
Philadelphia nimt täglich an Häusern und Einwohnern mehr und mehr zu / und wird nun auch ein Zuchthäuß gebaut / damit die jenige / so nicht Philadelphisch leben wollen / disciplinirt werden mögen... Die Einwohner belangend / kan ich solche nicht besser abtheilen / als in die Natürliche und Eingepfropffte; Dann so ich jene wild / und diese Christen nennte / thät ich vielen von beeden groß unrecht ... an frommen Gottsfürchtigen Leuten ist ... auch kein Mangel / und kan ich mit Grund der Warheit versichern / daß ich in Europa nirgendswo gleich als in unserm Philadelphia / angeschlagen gesehen: Diß und das hat der gefunden / der Verlierer mag sich bey ihm anmelden. (Pp. 3-4.)
[Ich will] von denen per errorem so genannten Wilden meine Nachricht kürtzlich ertheilen. Die ersten / die mir vor Augen kommen / waren die jenigen zwey / so bey Upland auf einem Canu an unser Schiff anfuhren / ich präsentirte ihnen ein Sopje Brandewein / welches sie mir mit einem halben Kopffstück bezahlen wolten / und da ich solch Geld refusirte / gaben sie mir die Hand und sprachen: Danck Bruder!, .. Einer von ihren Königen ... kam also den 3. Octobr. wie auch den 12. Decembr. ein anderer König und Königin in mein Hauß. Item überlauffen mich viel Gemeine sehr offt / denen ich doch fast allzeit meine Lieb mit einem Stück Brod und Trunck Bier erweise / wodurch dann eine Gegen-Lieb in ihnen erweckt wird. (P. 4.)

Nachdem ich [W. Penn] aber repraesentirt / daß ihr die Vorgänger von allen Teutschen / und dahero in mehrere Consideration zu ziehen / &c. Hat Er mir zu Anfang der Stadt drey Loß hintereinander von seines Jüngern Sohns Antheil abmessen lassen. (P. 5.) Sie [wollen] meistentheils hiesige Land quittiren / und etlich hundert Meil weiter Buschwarts einziehen: Dann sie stehen in einem solchen Aberglauben / daß eben so viel Indianer jährlich sterben mussen / als viel / nemlich Europaeer anhero kommen / &c. (P. 8.)

b. From the letters in *Monatlichen Unterredungen* (In "Zwei unbekannte Briefe," ed. Goebel, pp. 493-95, 502-03.):
Quanquam enim anno 1683. tredecim tantum inchoaverimus, unius tamen lustri intervallo numerum excreverunt quinquagenarium. Et quod turn rudis erat quercuum densitas, nunc domus sunt, caulae, horrea. Quod tunc spinae ac vepres, nunc agri, pometa, hortuli. Moenia vero nondum alia nostrum pagum tutantur, quam quae Romulus urbi suae neotericae circumliravit aratro.
Infantes suos effusissime diligunt. A partu tamen adhuc molles scindulis (vix recens corpusculum aequantibus) duriter superilligant, sine linteo. Cunarum etiam agitationi inassuetos, cum vagiunt, in dorsum leviter impactos repentino motu compescunt. Mox tenellos, quo solidius obdurescant, aestuantibus fluviis immergunt baptizadores rigidi. Sic austerae educationi initiatos, piscium tendiculis occupant parvulos pupos, malo ac frugaliter pransuros, si perfunctorie pendeat hamus. Post nemoribus maturatos venatico exercent pulvere, & ni numerosam aliquot annis praedam exuviarum reportaverint, turpe est hisce Actaeonibus. & pudendae audaciae scelus, maritari. Puellae viri potentes faciem velo obnubilantes propensionem suam ad jugum publicant, & procos vino, etiam sine hac hedera vendibili, alliciunt. Sponsa 13. plerumque anno nata, Sponsus non plus 17. foedus connubiale sanciunt. Nullum tam enorme facinus, quod poena pecuniaria non eluat, ipsum etiam homicidium. Interemtio tamen mulieris duplione vindicatur, cum, quod viri nequeunt, ipsa pariat. Delicta ebriorum crapula excusat: neque enim marsupium vapulat, si merum peccavit... Deum credunt & immortalitatem animarum. Illum terram australem habitare gloriosissimam, has vero post fatum illuc proficisci & reviviscere. Religio illorum duplici absolvitur cultu. Cantico nimirum, ut sua lingua nuncupant, & sacrificiis. Primitias equidem venaturae tam ferventi corporis motione flammis concremandas caedunt, ut sudore toti perfluant. Cantico a. illorum orbis est saltatorius, in cujus centro bini chorastates praesultant, & lugubre carmen demugiunt. His chorus ejulabili vociferatu, tristibus intermixto lacrymis, ad murmurans, nunc dentibus frendet, nunc concrepat digitis, nunc pedibus plaudit &c. & ludicri spectaculi scenam tam ardenter & serio omnes peragunt, ut concors eorum discordia miserationem intuenti moveat.
Wir haben diese geraume Zeit her in Fried und Sicherheit gewohnet, wie ich denn meine Hauss-Thüren des Nachts noch nie geschlossen habe ... Das von mir angelegte Germantown hat Zeit dieses letzten Kriegs-Wesens nicht stark zugenommen, doch ... können wir in kurtzen Jahren aus unser Zucht ein oder ander Dorff besetzen. Denn wie fast niemand gestorben, so wachsen unsere Kinder an wie Oel-Pflanzen an Wasser-Bächen.

c. From *Beschreibung Pennsylvaniae*:
Die Welt-Kugel zertheile ich in 4. Theile: der 1. ist Europa ... Dieser Theil ist unter denen andern der kleinste aber wegen der Kunst u. Christi. Religion der berühmste ... Der dritte Theil ist Africa ... Es ist ein sehr heisses unfruchtbares / und theils unbewohntes Land / voller vergiffteten Thiere ... America ... ist der grössete Theil der Welt-Kugel / ja fast so groß als die gantze alte Welt / Europa / Asia und Africa zusammen. Und dieses ist das Land darinnen Gold / Silber / Edelgesteine / Zucker / Gewürtz und mancherley Raritäten überflüssig zu befinden sind / wie die jährlich daraus kommende Silber-Flotten uns dessen klare Zeugnus geben -... Das grosse unbekannte Sud-Land ... ist ferne nach dem Mittage hinweg nach dem Sud-Pol gelegen / darein sich biß dato noch niemand hat begeben dörffen / des Nachts scheinet es / als wann die gantze Gegend in vollem Feur stünde. (Pp. viii-x.)
Wiewohlen von denen Zeiten Christophori Columbi und Vesputii Americi an / viel Colonien und Plantagien successive auferbauet worden ... So hat sich jedoch noch ferner

zugetragen / daß in Anno 1665.... noch ein grosses neues Land weit hinter diesen jetzt erzählten Ländern gelegen / ist erfunden worden. Deme aber gedachter König bey seinen Lebzeiten keinen gewissen Nahmen zu geben gewußt / weilen die natürliche Inwohner des Landes alle nackend in denen Wäldern herumb vagirten / und keine civile Versammlungen noch einige erbauete Städte hatten davon man sie hätte benamsen können / sondern sie wohneten (wie noch) hier und dar in Tuguriis und Baum-Hüttlein in denen Wildnussen. (P. 5.)

... die allergrausamste und zuvor niemals erhörte Tragoedia mit obgedachten Könige Carolo I. hat sich zugetragen / daß er von seinen eigenen Unterthanen verfolget / gefangen / und gar mit dem Beyl enthauptet worden. Dessen Sohn Carolus II. dessen Herrn Vatters Tod zu rächen / und sein Königreich zu behaupten / eylig eine Armee colligirte / und sich in Battaille einliesse / aber auf dem Felde geschlagen und zum Tode aufgesuchet wurde / welcher ihme dann auch ohnfehlbar wurde angethan worden seyn / woferne nicht sein General / der Lord Penn / ihme verkleidet in einem Schiffe nacher Franckreich übergebracht hätte; um welcher That willen diesem Lord Penn alle seine Landgüter / Schlösser und Dörffer in die Aschen gelegt / und er selbst ins Exilium verjagt worden ist / darinnen er auch gestorben / ehender als Carolus Stuardus II. wieder auff den Königlichen Thron gesetzet wurde.

Nach wieder erlangten Scepter und Krone / fände sich William Penn (deß Lord Penns einiger Sohn) bey ihme ein / wurde sehr freundlich empfangen / und ihme zur Vergeltung seines Vaters geleisteter treuen Dienste diese neu- gefundene Landschafft / samt dem Schloß Neu-Castle auff ewig eigenthumlich übergeben ...

Dieser William Penn ließ in der Stadt London kunt und public machen / wie daß er gesonnen wäre einige Colonien und Städte in dieser Landschafft anzulegen / welche Leute nun Lust und Lieb mit hinein zu schiffen hätten / denen wolte er jeden Morgen Landes nicht theurer als um 1. Kopffstucke verkauffen. Da liessen sich viel Leute auf ein gewisses Stück Landes in ein Buch einschreiben / und reiseten mit ihme sehr viel Familien hinein / da er denn für sich und die Seinige die Stadt Philadelphiam anlegte. In Specie aber verbandte sich eine Teutsche Compagnia zusammen / welche etliche tausend Morgen Landes einhandelten / um eine Teutsche Coloniam darinnen anzurichten. Die gantze Provintz aber wurde Pensylvania (deß Pens Wildnus) genannt / dieweilen es mit lauter Waldung und Wildnus überwachsen war. (Pp. 6-7.)

Ist zu wissen / daß William Penn / die natürliche nackend gehende Inwohner des Landes gar nicht mit militärischer Macht ausgetrieben / sondern bey seiner Dahinkunfft / denen vornehmen Indianern sonderbare Kleider und Hüte mitgebracht / dadurch benevolentiam capirt / und auf 20. Meilwegs lang ihnen Grund und Boden abgekaufft / und sie darauf um so weit weiters zurück in die wilden Wälder hineingewichen sind. (P. 14.)

Mann sihet in dieser Landschafft einige neue schöne Sterne ... die ... denen Europaeischen Astrologis zuvor nicht bekannt gewesen sind. Der delaWare-Strom ist so herrlich / daß er seines gleichens in gantz Europa nicht hat ... Bey Philadelphia ist er 2. ... Englische Meilwegs breit ... Die frische Quellen und Bronnen sind fast nicht zu zehlen. Das schattichte Gesträuch und Buschwerck ist aller Orten mit Vögeln angefüllet / deren rare Farben und mancherley Stimmen ihres Schöpffers Lob herrlich ausbreiten. Und gibt sonsten einen Überfluß an wilden Gänsen / Enden / Calicunen / Rebhünern / wilden Tauben / Wasser-Schnepffen und dergleichen. (Pp. 19-20.)

Als sie noch zimlich weit vom Lande waren / kam ihnen ein so lieblicher Geruch in der Lufft entgegen als aus einem neublühenden Garten. (P. 20.)

Daß Wasser bey der Stadt ist tieff genug / daß die grosse Schiffe biß an die Banck ohngefehr einen Steinwurff von der Stadt anfahren können ...

Den 24. Octobr. 168[3]. habe ich Franciscus Daniel Pastorius auf Gutbefinden unsers Gouverneurs noch eine neue Stadt Namens Germanton oder Germanopolim zwo Stund Wegs von Philadelphia angelegt / allwo ein gut schwartz tragbares Erdreich / und viel frische gesunde Brunnenquellen / viel Eichen / Nuß- und Castanien-Bäume / auch eine gute Weyde für das Vieh hat. Der Anfang bestünde nur in 12. Familien von 41. Köpffen / meistens Hochteutschen Handwercks-Leuten und Webern / weilen ich wahrgenommen / daß man des leinen Tuches nicht würde entbehren können.

Die Haupt-Gasse dieser Stadt machte ich 60. Schuh breit und die Zwerch-strassen 40. das Spatium oder Grundplatz zu einem jeglichen Hause und Garten ist so viel als 3. Morgen Ackers / für meine Wohnung aber doppelt so viel. (Pp. 22-23.)
Ich habe auch für meine Hoch-Teutsche Societät 15000. Morgen Ackers an einem Stucke zuwegen gebracht ... Also / daß wir Hoch-Teutsche eine seperate kleine Provintz erhalten / und uns von aller Unterdruckung desto mehr versichert halten können... . der Gouverneur [sagte] erst vorgestern zu mir: daß ihm der Eyffer der Hoch-Teutschen im Bauen sehr wohl gefalle / und daß er sie vor denen Englischen liebe / auch ihnen gewisse Privilegia ertheilen wolte. (P. 24.)
Gleichwie dieser Landschafft Polus- Höhe sich wie Mompellier und Neapolis befindet / aber mit weit mehrern Flüssen und Brunnenquellen als eine begabet ist / also ist ohnschwer zu erachten / daß solch Land zu vielen Edlen Früchten sehr bequem sey. Die Lufft ist hell und lieblich / der Sommer länger / und wärmer als in Teutschland / und hat man nunmehro dieser Orten an allerhand Früchten ein genügliches Auskommen / und wird uns unsere Arbeit im bauen redlich belohnen. (P. 24.)
... bißweilen verkaufen [die Indianer ihre Kaufmannschaften] umb ihr Landgeld / welches nur langlechte an Faden angeschnürte Corallen sind / aus Meer-Muscheln geschliffen ... Solch Corallen-Geld wissen sie gantz künstlich ineinander zu flechten / und tragens für güldene Ketten. Ihr König trägt eine Krone oder Haube davon ... Edelgesteine haben wir diß Orts nicht / verlangen sie auch nicht / und können dem jenigen kein grosses Nachlob zuschreiben / der zu erst das Gold und die Edelgesteine aus denen duncklen und verborgenen Orten der Erden hervor gegrübelt hat / dann diese edle Geschöpffe Gottes / ob sie wol an sich selbsten gut sind / so werden sie doch durch den Mißbrauch schröcklich geschändet / und müssen wider ihren Willen dem Dienste der Eytelkeit unterworffen seyn. (Pp. 25-26.)
Wiewohlen dieser weitentlegene Welt-Ort in lauter Wildnussen bestanden / und erst von kurtzer Zeit her zum Gebrauch der Christen-Menschen angerichtet zu werden beginnet / so ist sich doch höchlich zu verwundern / wie schnell es unter Gottes Seegen empor steiget und von Tag zu Tage augenscheinlich zunimmt; Dann ob wir im ersten Anfange unsere Victualien etwas theuer aus Jersey umb unser Geld haben herbey bringen müssen / so können wir doch / Gott lob / nunmehro andern Benachbarten dienen.
Mit denen meisten und nötigsten Handwerckern sind wir versehen / die Taglöhne uff ein Leydentliches eingerichtet und haben an Mühlen und Ziegelöffen die Nothdurfft. Unsern Überfluß an Geträid und Viehe verhandlen wir gen Barbados umb Brandwein / Syrupp / Zucker / und Saltz / das rare Beltzwerck aber übersenden wir in Engeland. Sonsten sind wir beflissen den Wein-Bau / und die Tuchweberey dieser Orten in Schwang zu bringen / umb das Geld im Lande zu behalten / deßwegen wir auch bereits Jahrs-Märckte angerichtet / nicht umb leidigen Wuchers und Gewinns willen / sondern umb einander das jenige kaufflich zukommen zu lassen / was einer oder der andere zuviel und übrig hat / damit man deswegen nicht in die benachbarte Insuln überfahren / und das Geld dorthin tragen dörffte. (Pp. 26-27.)
Sie befleissigen sich einer auffrichtigen Redligkeit / halten genau über ihren Versprechen / betriegen und beleidigen niemanden; sie beherbergen die Leute gerne / und sind ihren Gästen dienstfertig und treue.
Ihre Hütten sind aus etlichen zusammen geflochtenen oder gebogenen jungen Bäumen gemacht / die sie mit Baumrinden zu bedecken wissen. Sie gebrauchen weder Tisch noch Bänck / noch andern Hausrath / als etwa einen eintzigen Topff / darinnen sie ihre Speise sieden.
Ich sahe ihrer einsten viere in hertzlicher Vergnügung miteinander speisen / und einen im blossen Wasser / ohne Butter und Gewürtz gekochten Kürbis essen. Ihre Tafel und Banck war die liebe Erde / ihre Löfel waren Muscheln / damit sie das warme Wasser aussuppeten / ihre Teller waren des nechsten Baumes Blätter die sie nach der Mahlzeit weder mühsam abspühlen / noch zu künfftigem Gebrauch sorgsam bewahren dörffen. Ich dachte bey mir / diese wilde Leute haben die Lehre JEsu von der Mässigkeit und Vergnügsamkeit ihr lebtag nicht gehöret / und thun es doch denen Christen weit bevor. [From *Sichere Nachricht*, p. 4: (Dies) stieg mir ... tieff zu Hertzen / da ich die treugemeinte Vermahnung unsers Seligmachers erwegte / daß wir seine Jünger nicht vor den morgenden Tag sorgen selten / weil solches die Heyden thun. Ach gedachte ich bey

mir selbsten / wie ist nun alles so gar verkehrt! Wann wir Christen nicht proviantirt sind auff ein und mehr Monat / wie kleinmütig werden wir? Diese Heyden (aber stellen) ihre Versorgung in einer so wundersamen Gelassenheit GOTT heim ...]
Sie sind sonsten ernsthafft und von wenigen Worten / verwundern sich wann sie bey den Christen ein so überflüssig Geschwätz nebst andern leichtfertigen Geberden wahrnehmen ...
Sie hören sehr gerne / und nicht ohne merckliche Gemüts-Bewegung reden von dem Schöpfer Himmels und der Erden / und von seinem Göttlichen Liechte / welches alle Menschen erleuchtet die in diese Welt kommen sind / und noch kommen werden / und von GOttes Weisheit und Liebe / aus welcher er seinen eingebohrnen allerliebsten Sohn für uns in den Tod gegeben hat. Nur ist zu betauren / daß wir ihre Sprache noch nicht recht können / and dahero ihnen unsere eigentliche Hertzens Gedancken und Intention nicht beybringen können / was nehmlich in Christo JEsu für eine Krafft und grosses Heyl verborgen lige. Sie sind in unsern Versammlungen sehr stille und andächtig / daß ich gäntzlich glaube sie werden dermaleins an jenem grossen Gerichts-Tage mit denen von Tyro und Sydon aufftretten / und viel tausend falsche Nahmen- und Maul-Christen beschämen.
Ihre Oeconomiam und Hauswesen betreffend / so warten die Männer ihres Jagens und Fischens. Die Weiber thun ihre Kinder in fleissiger Aufsicht treulich erziehen und von Lastern abmahnen. Sie bauen umb ihre Hütten herum Indianish Korn und Bonen / aber umb weitläufftigen Feld-Bau und Vieh-Zucht sind sie unbekümmert / verwundern sich vielmehr / daß wir Christen umb Essens und Trinckens auch bequemlicher Kleidung und Wohnunge willen so vielfältig bemühet und bekümmert sind / als zweiffelten wir / daß uns Gott nicht versorgen und ernähren könnte. (Pp. 28-30.)
Diese [aus Europa angekommene alte Christen] haben niemahls die aufrichtige intention gehabt diesen eingebohrnen Hülff bedürfftigen Creaturen eine Unterweisung in dem lebendigen wahren Christenthum zu thun / sondern haben nur ihr propre Welt-Interesse gesuchet / und die einfältige Innwohner im Handel und Wandel betrogen / dahero endlichen die jenige Wilden so mit diesen Christen umgiengen / sich mehrentheils auch arglistig / lugenhafft / und betrüglich erwiesen / also daß ich von beeden nicht viel ruhmwürdigs melden kan. Diese verführte Leute pflegen ihre erlangte Fell und Beltzwerck gegen starckes Geträncke zu vertauschen / und sich so voll zu trincken / daß sie weder gehen noch stehen können / auch pflegen sie bey ereignender Gelegenheit allerhand Diebstähle zu begehen.
Also daß sich ihre Könige und Vorgesetzte zum öfftern über die durch die Christen eingeführte Laster der Falschheit / des Betrugs / der Dieberey und des Vollsauffens beschweret haben / als welche zuvor in diesen Landen gantz unbekannt gewesen sind ...
Wir Letzt-Angekommene in ehrlichen Gesellschafften und Compagnien begriffene Christen / haben ... der Intention neue Städte und Colonien auffzurichten / und darinn nicht allein unsern zeitlichen Nutzen und Nahrung zu erwerben / sondern auch die wilden Leute mansuet und zahm zu machen / und sie in der wahren Erkäntnuß GOttes zu informiren ... (Pp. 31-32.)
Dieser kluge und gottsförchtige Regent [William Penn] aber hat bey seiner Ankunfft dieses Erbteil der Heyden nicht so bloß umsonst annehmen wollen / sondern hat die natürliche Inwohner und ihre vorgesetzte Könige beschencket und begütiget / so dann ein Stück Landes nach dem andern abgekauffet / so daß sie immer je weiter in die Wildnuß hinein gewichen ... Und obwohlen dickerwehnter William Penn der Sect der Tremulanten oder bebenden zugethan ist / so zwinget er doch niemand zu einiger Religion / sondern überläst einer jeden Nation deß Glaubens Freyheit. (P. 33.)
... in meiner neu-angelegten Stadt Germanton [stehen] bereits 64. Haushaltungen im Flor. Solche Inwohner nun / wie auch andere ankommende zu ernähren / da müssen die Feldungen angebaut / und Aecker zugerichtet werden. Man wende sich aber hin wo man wolle / da heisset es: Itur in antiquam sylvam, und ist alles mit Holtz überwachsen / also daß ich mir offt ein paar dutzet starcke Tyroler gewünschet / welche die dicke Aychen-Bäume darnider geworffen hätten / so wir aber nach und nach selbst haben verrichten müssen / worbey ich mir eingebildet / daß die jenige Pönitentz / mit welcher GOtt den Ungehorsam des Adams gestraffet hat / nemlich daß er im Schweis seines Angesichtes sein Brod essen solle / auch uns Nachkömmlingen in diesem Lande

dictiret und gegeben seye / dann es heisset hier: Hie opus, hie labor est, und ist nicht genug Geld / sondern auch Geneigtheit zur Arbeit mit anhero zu bringen... (Pp. 38-39.) Wer nun die ernstliche Resolution hat über zu fahren... soll mit sich nehme[n] Butter / Käß / Zucker / Wein / Brandwein / Gewürtz / Baumöl / Cerbalar-Würst / Hirs / Reiß / gerennelte Gersten / allerhand Feld- und Garten-Saamen / eiserne Häfen / Kesselein / Flinden-Röhr zum Wild schiessen / &c. (P. 42.)

Es scheinet fast / daß die meisten ihre gute Intention (allhier in Pensylvania GOTT und dem Rechsten in Stilligkeit ihres Gemüts zu dienen) nicht so vollkommlich erreichen können... Ich meines Orts kan nunmehro selbsten nicht anderst / als daß meine Gedancken bald zu Philadelphia / bald zu Germanopel habe / welche ich doch allerliebsts allezeit in dem Himmlischen Jerusalem haben möchte / in der zukünfftigen Stadt des HErrn / welche da ewig währet und mit allem Ernst von mir und allen Gottlieben den zu suchen ist. Alleine das Amt eines getreuen Auffsehers / welches mir anvertrauet ist / muß auch mit möglichem Fleiß und Treu verwaltet seyn. (Pp. 47-48.)

Inmassen wir friedsam und vergnügt leben / ohne Appetit deß vergänglichen Reichthums / so wir nur Kleider und Nahrung in dieser unserer Pilgerschafft haben / so wenden wir übrigens unsere Augen allezeit vorwärts zu dem himmlischen Jerusalem unserm rechten Vatterlande. (P. 52.)

So hat der grundgütige GOTT diese provintz die zehen Jahr über meines Hierseyns dergestalt unter denen Flügeln seiner Barmhertzigkeit genädig beschirmet / daß kein feindliches Geschrey / weder Trummel noch Musqueten-Schall unsere tägliche Arbeit / und nächtliche Ruhe gebrochen. Ja wir haben so lange Jahr über keinen Heller weder Kriegs- noch andere Contributionen zu entrichten gehabt / biß etwa vor 5. Wochen im Namen des Königs Wilhelmi III. der neue Gouverneur Benjamin Fletscher / zu Philadelphia ankam... Deme wir zu Ersetzung der Reise-Kosten den 240sten Pfennig / semel pro semper consentiret. (Pp. 54-55.)

Von diesen natürlichen Inwohnern dieser Landen kan ich wenig melden zu Satisfaction derer / so ihr Augenmerck mehr auff eine eusserliche Mund-Bekäntnuß / als auf eine würckliche Ausübung der Gebotten und Verbotten Christi gerichtet ist... Sie leben viel vergnügter und sorgloser für den künfftigen Morgen / als wir Christen... Sie... sind mässig in Speiß und Tranck / und wann sich einer bißweilen vollsaufft / so sind gemeiniglich die Maul-Christen daran schuldig / die umb ihres vermaledeyten Eigen-Nutzes willen denenselben starckes Getränck verkauffen.

Ich habe in meiner zehenjährigen allhiesigen Anwesenheit noch nie gehört / daß sie einigem Menschen Gewalt anzuthun versuchet / viel minder jemanden ermordet hätten / da sie doch nicht nur dergleichen zu vollbringen / sondern auch in dem dicken und grossen Walde zu verbergen offtmahlige Gelegenheit hätten; So daß ich in Betrachtung der greulichen Bosheit die in Europa unter denen Schein-Christen getrieben wird / und in reiffer Dargegenhaltung dieser meiner jetztmahligen West-Indischen Landsleute auffrichtiger Einfalt jederzeit an Herrn Johann Augustin Litzheimers bey euch gehaltenen Predigt / von dem beschämten Christenthum durch betrachtetes Heydenthum / gedencke / der da pag. 45. meldet: Die Maul-Christen creutzigen den Sohn GOttes / und verspeysen ihren Seeligmacher mit allem Trotz / wann sie wider GOttes Wort dieses zeitliche Geld und Gut / oder dieses vergänglichen Lebens Wohlfarth höher achten als GOtt und die ewige Seeligkeit / dahingegen der Heyd Seneca profitiret: Semper magis nolo, quod Deus vult, quam quod ego, adjungar & adhaerebo illi velut Minister & assecla. Cum illo appeto, cum illo desidero. Nihil recuso omnium quae ipsi vidibuntur...

Ich muß zum Beschluß zu Recommendation meiner unwilden Wilden noch dieses beyfügen / daß sie gantz abkehrig vom Krieg und Vergiessung menschlichen Bludes sind / vielmehro Friede halten mit jederman / da hingegen fast die gantze Christenheit im Harnisch ist / und mit barbarischer Grausamkeit offensive & defensive einander viel ärger als die abscheuligste Unthiere auffreiben und zerreissen. (Pp. 57-60.)

Ich und die liebe Meinige befinden uns annoch bey dergleichen wohlergehen / als in meinem vorigen gemeldet / in einer stillen und friedlichen privat Lebens-Art / und ob ich wohl noch mit der Inspection über das Justitz-Wesen so wohl zu Germanton als zu Philadelphia beladen bin / so hindern doch solche äusserliche Ampts-Geschäffte das inwendige Gefühl des sanfft- und demüthigen privat-Lebens JEsu Christi so gar nit / daß ich auch mitten in jener Verrichtunge wohl sagen kan: revertere anima mea in requiem tuam...

Nun auff meines lieben Bruders Augustini Adami Fragen zu antworten / wie es umb der hiesigen Wilden Könige Hofhaltungen beschaffen seye? So ist zu wissen / daß ihre königliche Palläste dermassen schlecht beschaffen sind / daß ich sie nicht wohl beschreiben kan. Es ist nur ein einziges Gemach oder Zimmer in einer Baum-Hütten mit BaumRinden gedeckt / ohne Schorstein / Stiegen und Secret. Diese Könige gehen selbst mit auff die Jagt / schiessen wilde Thiere / und nahren sich ihrer Hand Arbeit. Sie haben weder Knechte / noch Laqueyen / weder Mägde noch Staats-Jungfrauen / und was soll ein Stallmeister deme der kein Pferd hält / sondern allezeit zu Fusse gehet. So ist auch kein Hofmeister vonnothen / wo man ausser seinem Leib / Weib und Kindern niemand anders zu versorgen hat / sie leben schlecht und recht der Natur gemäß / quae paucis contenta est. ... sie [handeln] Pulver / Bley / wolline Decken / und Brandwein ein / welches letztere doch / wie auch sonst alles starcke Getränck an sie zu verkauffen in unsern Gesetzen verbotten und straffbar ist ... (Pp. 64-66.)

Diß Landischen Zustand betreffend / kan und muß ich Göttliche Gütigkeit und Providentz höchlich rühmen / wir leben in Ruh und Frieden / mit aller Nothdurfft reichlich versehen und versorget. (P. 69.)

... jedes Jahrs [werden] von dem gantzen Volck gewisse Personen erwehlet / welche der Zeit und des Volcks Beschaffenheit nach für solches Jahr nothdürfftige Gesetze und Ordnungen stellen / und dardurch denen einreissenden Lastern vorbiegen / und übrigens das gantze Jahr hindurch in allen Occurrentien das gemeine Beste mit und neben dem Landes-Gouverneur versorgen helffen. Inmassen dann mehrgedachter Landes-Herr / William Penn / aus solchen erwehlten 12. Personen etliche Justitiarios ordnet / welche nach also gemachten Gesetzen alle vorfällige Streitigkeiten entscheiden / nachdeme zuvor die Species Facti von 12. Nachbaren untersuchet worden ist. Und all dieses wird gethan in publica Curia, da jedermänniglich Groß und Klein eingehen und zuhören mag ... So viel die Besteurung und Tribut der Unterthanen in hiesiger Landschafft anbetrifft / so wird es gehalten wie mit der Engelländischen Nation / da weder der König selbst / noch seine Gesandten / Landpfleger oder Gouverneurs einigerley Schantzunge oder Steuer uff die Unterthanen nicht legen dörffen / es haben dann solche Unterthanen zuvorhero selbst freywillig ein gewisses zu geben beschlossen und eingewilliget / und mag nach denen Fundamental-Gesetzen keine Steuer länger währen als ein eintziges Jahr. (Pp. 82-84.)

... diese Stadt [hat] ihr eigenes Gericht / eigenen Burgermeister und Rath / samt benöthigten Bedienten / und wohleingerichteten Stadt-Gesetzen / Raths- Regeln / und Stadt-Sigill. Die Inwohner dieser Stadt sind meistentheils Handwercks-Leute / als Zeug- Barchet- und Leinenweber / Schneider / Schuster / Schlosser / Zimmerleuthe / die aber allezumahl auch mit Ackerbau und Viehzucht versehen sind. Der Orth wäre sufficient noch zweymal so viel Inwohner zu unterhalten als für jetzo würcklich darinnen sind. (P. 83.)

[Die Indianer haben sich] sehr weit von uns hinweg in den wilden Wald hinein begeben / allwo sie ihrer angebohrnen Art nach sich mit jagen / Wild- und Vogelschiessen / auch Fischfangen ernehren / und nur in Hütten / von Büsch und Bäumen zusammen gezogen / wohnen. (P. 85.)

... unsere Teutsche Compagni und Brüderschafft [ist] von einigen frommen und gottsförchtigen Personen begonnen worden / nicht so sehr um zeitlichen Gewinns willen / als vielmehr vor sie und andere redliche Landsleute eine Pella oder Zufluchts-Platz zu haben / wann der gerechte GOtt seine Zorn-Schaalen über das sündliche Europa ausschütten würde. (P. 90.)

Bibliography

1. Manuscripts and Publications of Franz Daniel Pastorius

This list includes the items cited in this study as well as representative titles from the "Beehive" and from the nonextant mss. For reasonably complete listings, see Learned, Life, pp. 245-48 and 275-76. Items from the Historical Society of Pennsylvania Pastorius Collection are identified "Past. Coll."

"Alphabetical Hive" with Supplements. In "Beehive," pp. 415-97, 498-890. Microfilm selections provided by Univ. of Pennsylvania Library, which also permitted extensive recorded dictations from the ms.

"Alvearialia, or such Phrases and Sentences, which in haste were Booked down here, before I had Time to Carry them to their respective proper Places in my English-Folio-Bee- hive." Past. Coll., no. 4.

"Angling & other Tracts of Husbandry." Nonextant ms.

"Ansprach an die Nachkömmlingschaft, und Alle, die dieses Lager-Buch continuiren oder fortsetzen." / "Address to posterity and all who shall continue or keep up this Land Record." (German and English texts by Pastorius.) In "The General Court Book of the Corporation of Germantown. oder Raths-Buch der Germantownischen Gemeinde, angefangen den 2 ten tag des 4 ten Monats Anno 1691." Hist. Soc. of Pa. MS. Am .3713. In Learned, with introductory poem "Salve Posteritas" trans. John Greenleaf Whittier, pp. 267-74.

"Apiarium: oder Bienenbüchlein." Nonextant ms on beekeeping.

"Artzney und Kunst," or "Talia Qualia / Medicinalia, Artificialia & Naturalia" with "Medicus Dilectus." Past. Coll., no. 2. Microfilm copy provided by Hist. Soc. of Pa. (Order no. 5022, 22 Dec. 1976).

"Beehive." Univ. of Pennsylvania Van Pelt Library ms Amer. MS 3 and Mic 238 pos (the latter via Brown Univ. John Hay Library).

"Circumstantial Geographical Description of Pennsylvania," trans. Gertrude S. Kimball. With "Positive Information from America, concerning the Country of Pennsylvania, from a German who has migrated thither; dated Philadelphia, March 7, 1684," trans. J. Franklin Jameson. In *Narratives of Early Pennsylvania, West New Jersey and Delaware 1630-1707.* Ed. Albert Cook Myers. *Original Narratives of Early American History.* Ed. J. Franklin Jameson. 1912; rpt. New York: Barnes & Noble, 1967, pp. 392-411.

"Confusanea Geometriae" Nonextant ms.

Copia, eines von einem Sohn an seine Eltern auss America abgelassenen Brieffes sub dato Philadelphia, den 7. Martii 1684. N.p., n.d. Microfilm copy provided by Zentralbibliothek Zürich. In Appendix II of this study.

Deliciae Hortenses or Garden-Recreations and Voluptates Apianae. Ed. Christoph E. Schweitzer. Columbia, South Carolina: Camden House, 1982.

Disputatio Inauguralis De Rasura Documentorum, Qvam, Divina suffragante Gratia, Auctoritate Magnifici JCtorum Ordinis in Incluto Noribergensium Athenaeo, pro Licentia Summos in Utroqve Jure Honores ac Privilegia Doctoralia, more Majorum, ritè capessendi, Publico Eruditorum Examini sistit Franciscus Daniel Pastorius, Windtsheimensis. Diss. Univ. Nürnberg, 1676. Altdorf: H. Maier, 1676.

"Emblematical Recreations." In "Beehive," pp. 75-103, 127-29.

"Exemplum sine Exemplo. Or (to borrow the Inscription of One of John Wilson's Plays) The Cheats and the Projectors." In Pennypacker, *Settlement*, pp. 74-79, and Learned, pp. 294-97.

"F. D. P. Franciscus Daniel Pastorius. Fortunante Deo Pietas Fert Deniq. Palmam. Fideliter Deus Providebit. &c." Past. Coll., no. 5. Commonplace book, the original title page of which is missing.

"A few Onomastical Considerations, enlarged From the Number of Sixty Six To that of One Hundred, and Presented or rather Re-presented To William Penn, Proprietary and Governour of Pennsilvania, & Territories thereunto belonging. Patri Patria, The Father of this Province, and lately also the Father of John Penn, an innocent & hopeful Babe, by whose Nativity & Names sake they were first contrived." Later version entitled "A Few Onomastical Considerations." With *A New Primmer* in Photostat Americana. 2nd ser. (1936), no. 80.

"Francis Daniel Pastorius." Selected poetry. In *Seventeenth-Century American Poetry.* Ed. Harrison T. Meserole. Anchor Seventeenth-Century Series. Garden City, New York: Doubleday, 1968, pp. 293-304.

"Francis Daniel Pastorius." Selected poetry. In *Pennsylvania German Poetry, 1685-1830.* Ed. John Joseph Stoudt. *Pennsylvania German Folklore Society Proceedings*, 20. N.p.: Pennsylvania German Folklore Soc., 1955.

"Franz Daniel Pastorius." Selected poetry. In *Deutsch-Amerikanische Dichter und Dichtungen des 17ten und 18ten Jahrhunderts*. Ed. H[einrich] A. Rattermann. [Chicago]: German-American Hist. Soc., 1915, pp. 12-20.

"Franz Daniel Pastorius." Selected Poetry. In *Deutsch in Amerika. Beiträge zur Geschichte der Deutsch-amerikanischen Literatur*. 2nd ed. Vol. 1. Chicago: Eyller, 1894, pp. 3-4.

"From Pastorius' Bee-Hive or Bee-Stock." Ed. Marion Dexter Learned. In *Americana-Germanica*, 1 (1897), 67-110; 2 (1898), 33-58 and 65-79.

"Genealogia Pastoriana." In "Beehive," pp. 221-26. Three pages photographically reproduced in Learned, following p. 312. Appendix I of this study includes the autobiographical portions of the text.

Geographisch-statistische Beschreibung der Provinz Pensylvanien. Memmingen, Germany: A. Seyler, 1792. Based on Pastorius, *Beschreibung Pennsylvaniae*, 1700.

"Germantown Friends' Protest Against Slavery." 1688. In Learned, pp. 261-62. Pastorius is one of four signatories.

"Good Counsel for bad Lawyers & Attornies." Nonextant ms.

"Grammatical Rudiments of the Latin Tongue." Nonextant ms.

Henry Bernhard Koster, William Davis, Thomas Rutter & Thomas Bowyer, four Boasting Disputers Of this World briefly Rebuked, And Answered according to their Folly, which they themselves have manifested in a late Pamphlet, entituled, Advice for all Professors and writers. New York: Wm. Bradford, 1697.

"J. Saml. Pastorius his Cherry harvest of Arithmetick." Nonextant ms.

Kurtze Beschreibung von der allerneulichst erfundenen Americanischen Landschafft Pensylvanien. N.p., [1690 or 1691].

"Kurtze Geographische Beschreibung der letzmahls erfundenen Amerikanischen Landschafft Pensylvania, Mit angehenckten einigen notablen Begebenheiten und Bericht-Schreiben an dessen Hrn. Vattern / Patrioten und gute Freunde." In Melchior Adam Pastorius, *Kurtze Beschreibung . . . Windsheim*. Nürnberg, 1692, supplemental pp. 1-32 following p. 148. Microfilm copy provided by Hist. Soc. of Pennsylvania.

"Law-Terms added to the Compleat Justice." Nonextant ms.

"Letter Book." Past. Coll., no. 6. Microfilm copy provided by Hist. Soc. of Pennsylvania.

"Letter from Francis Daniel Pastorius, March 7, 1684." In Pennypacker, *Settlement*, pp. 81-99.

"Lex Pennsylvaniensis in Compendium redacta.: h. e. The Great Law of Pennsylvania – abridged, for the particular use of Francis Daniel Pastorius. Salus Populi Suprema Lex esto!" 1693. Bound with "Leges Pennsilvanianae h. e. The great Law of the Province of Penn Silvania," 1690, and "1. Copia des Germantownischen Charters. 2. Gesetz, Ordnungen und Statuten der Gemeinden zu Germantown, in denen daselbstigen generalen Raths Versamblungen von Zeit zu Zeit gemacht und publicirt. 3. The Laws of the Province of Pennsylvania antecedent to the sd Charter & By-Laws," 1693. Past. Coll., no. 8.

"The Matter of Taxes & Contributions briefly Examined by plain Scripture Testimonies & Sound Reason." Printed as "Pastorius' Essay on Taxes." Ed. and introd. Henry J. Cadbury. In *Pennsylvania Magazine of History and Biography*, 58 (1934), 255-59.

"Meine Reisebeschreibung oder Itlnerarium." Nonextant ms.

"The Monthly Monitor, briefly shewing When our works ought to be done in Gardens, Orchards, Vineyards, Fields, Meadows & Woods; also in our Houses, Kitchins, Cellars,
Garners, Barns, Stables all the year round." 1701-c. 1716. Past. Coll., no. 1.

"Moral Sayings meeterly Versified." Nonextant ms.

A New Primmer or Methodical Directions To attain the True Spelling, Reading & Writing of English. Whereunto are added, some things Necessary & Useful both for the Youth of this Province, and likewise for those, who from forreign Countries and Nations come to settle amongst us. New York: Wm. Bradford, [1698]. In Photostat Americana. 2nd. ser. (1936), no. 80.

"Phraseologia Teutonica." Nonextant ms.

"Poetica Pastoriana." Nonextant ms.

"Res Propriae." 1715. Past. Coll., no. 3. Microfilm copy provided by Hist. Soc. of Pennsylvania.

Ein Send-Brieff Offenhertziger Liebsbezeugung an die so genannte Pietisten in Hoch-Teutschland. Amsterdam: J. Claus, 1697. PDF copy provided by State Library of Pennsylvania, Harrisburg, Pa.

"Ship-Mate-Ship (An Omer full of Manna)." 1714. Past. Coll., no. 7. Poetry presented to daughters of Thomas Lloyd.

312 | Bibliography

Sichere Nachricht auß America, wegen der Landschafft Pennsylvania / von einem dorthin gereißten Teutschen / de dato Philadelphia, den 7. Martii 1684. N.p., n.d. Microfilm copy provided by Zentralbibliothek Zürich. Rpt. in Gutmann and Furkel, *Sommerhausen,* pp. 336-47.

"Silvula Rhythmorum Germanopolitanorum," or "Poetical Raptures." In "Beehive," pp. 137-201. Microfilm copy provided by Univ. of Pennsylvania Library. Draft ts provided by Prof. Harrison T. Meserole, Pennsylvania State University.

"Some Onomastical Considerations" see "A few Onomastical Considerations"

Umständige Geographische Beschreibung Der zu allerletzt erfundenen Provintz Pensylvaniae, In denen End-Gräntzen Americae In der West-Welt gelegen Durch Franciscum Danielem Pastorium, J. V. Lic. und Friedens-Richtern daselbsten. Worbey angehencket sind einige notable Begebenheiten / und Bericht-Schreiben an dessen Herrn Vattern Melchiorem Adamum Pastorium, und andere gute Freunde. [Ed. Melchior Adam Pastorius.] Frankfurt am Main and Leipzig: Andreas Otto, 1700. 2nd ed. 1702. Copy of 1st ed. provided by Haverford College. Also rpt. as *Franz Daniel Pastorius' Beschreibung von Pennsylvanien.* Introd. Friedrich Kapp. Crefeld, Germany: Kramer & Baum, 1884; and with the original title (a facsimile of the 1st ed.) Introd. Ulrich Bister. Kommern, Germany: Eigenverlag Förderverein Rheinisches Freilichtmuseum, 2000.

Vier kleine Doch ungemeine Und sehr nutzliche Tractätlein I. De omnium Sanctorum Vitis II. De omnium Pontificum Statutis III. De Conciliorum Decisionibus IV. De Episcopis & Patriarchis Constantinopolitanis. Das ist: l. Von Aller Heiligen Lebens-Ubung 2. Von Aller Päpste Gesetz- Einführung 3. Von der Concilien Stritt-Sopirung. 4. Von denen Bischöffen und Patriarchen zu Constantinopel. Zum Grunde Der künfftighin noch ferner darauf zu bauen Vorhabender Warheit praemittiret. N.p., n.d. [Title page: "Durch Franciscum Danielem Pastoriu[m] J. U. L. Aus der ... Stadt Germanopoli Anno Christi M.DC.XC.," ("By Franz Daniel Pastorius from ... Germantown, 1690.")]

"Wm Penns Früchte der Einsamk[eit], von mir verteutscht." Nonextant ms. Pastorius' German trans. of Penn's *Some Fruits of Solitude,* 1693.

"The young Country-Clerk's Collection of the best Presidents of Bills, Bonds, Conditions, Acquittances, Releases, Indentures, Deeds of Sale, Letters of Attorney, Last Wills & Testaments, &c. With many other necessary and useful Forms of such like Writings as are vulgarly in use between Man and Man. An Alphabetical Table whereof is thereunto prefixed." Univ. of Pennsylvania MS. 49M-54.

"Zwei unbekannte Briefe von Pastorius." Ed. Julius Goebel. In *German-American Annals,* n.s. 2 (1904), 492-503.

2. Selected "Alphabetical Hive" Sources

The following sources, cited in "Alphabetical Hive" entries in this study, are from "The Several Authors out of which this present Hive is collected" and "The Writings of Some called Quakers, as also some other honest Men," two alphabetical listings with Supplements in the "Beehive," pp. 106, 627-32. A few of the cited sources could not be located in these lists, apparently omitted inadvertently by Pastorius.

Ac. Compl.	*A New Academy of Complements, or [the Lover's Secretary: Being] Wit and Mirth Improved [by the most elegant expressions used in the art of courtship],* London, 1717.
Agrippa	Henricius Cornelius Agrippa. *Libellus De [incertitudine et] Vanitate omnium Scientiarum [et artium liber],* 1643.
Ainsworth	Henry Ainsworth. *Annotations upon the Five Books of Moses, Psalms and Canticles,* 1627.
Andreae	Johann Valentin Andreae. *Menippus, sive Dialogi, Satyrici* [*sive Dialogorum satyricorum encturia inanitatum nostratium speculum*],1673.
Ath. Oracle	[John Dunton, ed.] *The Athenian Oracle: Being an Entire Collection in Three Volumes of all the Valuable Questions and Answers in the Old Athenian Mercuries &c. By a Member of the Athenian Society.* Vol. I, the 2d. Edition, 1704.
Bacon	Francis Bacon. *Essays and Religious Meditations,* 1688.
Barclay	Robert Barclay. *Christian Labours & Writings Collected,* 1692. [Also references to other publications by Barclay.]
Beaumont	John Beaumont. *Treatise of Spirits, Apparitions, Witchcrafts and other Magical Practices,* 1705.
Beller	John Beller. *Essays about the Poor, Manufactures, Trade, Plantations and Immorality,* 1699.
Boehm, Epiph.	Anthony William Boehm [Anton Wilhelm Boehme]. *His Sermon upon the Epiphany of Christ.* 1710.

Bibliography | 313

Boehm, Lud.	---------. *The Faithful Steward* (at Henry William Ludolf's Funeral), 1712.
Boehm. Orig.	---------. *The Doctrine of Original Sin*, 1711.
Boehm, Piet.	---------. *A Short Account of Pietism*, n.d.
Chr. Mon.	[John Rawlet.] *The Christian Monitor, Containing an Earnest Exhortation to an Holy Life*, 1687.
Chr. Rights	[Matthew Tindal.] *The Rights of the Christian Church Asserted against the Romish & all other Priests [who claim an Independent Power over it]*, 3d ed., pt I, 1707.
Closet	See Shirley.
Creech	Thomas Creech. *The Life & Unpararalleled Actions of Alexander the Great, King of Macedonia*, 1715.
Culpeper	Nicholas Culpeper. *Last Legacy left & bequeathed to his wife for the public good*, n.d. (Also references to other publications by Culpeper.)
Dan. Miss.	*An Account of the Success of Two Danish Missionaries, viz. Barthol. Ziegenbalgh & Henry Flutsche lately sent to the East Indies*, Parts 1-3, 1709-14.
Defoe	See Trueborn.
Dell	William Dell. *The Tryall of Spirits both in Teachers & Spirits*, n.d.
Denham	Sir John Denham. *Directions to a Painter for Describing Our Naval Business*, 1667.
Dewsb.	William D. Dewsberry. *To All Faithful Brethren born of the Immortal Seed*, 1661.
Emp. in Am.	R. B. [Nathaniel Crouch]. *The English Empire in America: Or a Prospect of his Majesties Dominions*, n.d. [1685].
E. M. Mod.	[E. M.] *A Brief Answer unto the Cambridge Modell: [which is to go to the two universities to be read by all the doctors . . . and this is to go amongst all the country-men, that they may see the fruits of the learning from the doctors, which fruits is persecution . . .*, London,] 1658.
Fox	George Fox. *Journal*, vol. I, 1694.
Fox, Sal.	--------. *Noble Salutation*, n.d.
Franck, Orph.	August Herman Franck[e]. *Pietas Hallensis, or Historical Narration of the Orphan-House and other Charitable Institutions at Glaucha near Hall in Saxony*, 1705.
Freeholder	[Joseph Addison.] *The Freeholder* [London journal], nos. 1 (23 Dec. 1715), 4, 6, 10, 21, 26-28, 31-34.
Genes.	[Anon.] *The History of Genesis: [being an account of the holy lives and actions of the patriarchs, explained with pious and edifying explications, and illustrated with near forty figures]*, [London,] 1708.
Hepburn	John Hepburn. *Essay to Prove the Unlawfullness of making slaves of men*, 1715.
Heywood	Oliver Heywood. *Heavenly Converse [: or, A discourse concerning the communion between the saints on Earth, and the spirits of just men made perfect in heaven: Grounded Upon Heb. XII. XXIII]*, 1697.
Hill	J[ohn] Hill [Jr.]. *The Young Secretary's Guide, or a Speedy Help to Learning*, 1687.
Julian	[Anon.] *Julian the Apostate: Being a Short Account of his Life &c; [together with a Comparison of Popery & Paganism]*, 1682.
Keith	George Keith. *[The] True Christ Owned [as he is, true God and perfect man]*, 1679.
Keith, Reexam.	--------. *The Pretended Examination of John Alexander of Leith reexamined*, 1682.
Keith, Ref.	--------. *Refutation of three Opposers of Truth*, 1690.
Keith, Ser. Appeal	--------. *Serious Appeal to all the more sober . . . People in New England*, 1692.
Leeds	Daniel Leeds [ed.]. *Almanacks*. (Published annually.)
Locke	John Locke. *An essay concerning humane understanding*, 2 vols., 1710.
Ludolf	Henry William Ludolf. *Reliquiae Ludolfiana: The Pious Remains of Mr. Henry William Ludolf*, 1712.
Maint.	*The Cabinet Open'd, or the secret history of the Amours of Madam de Maintenon, with the French King*, 1690.
Mamut	[? Giovanni Paolo Marana.] *Letters writ by a Turkish Spy (Mamut the Arabian, who took upon him the name of Moldavian) who lived five & forty years undiscovered at Paris*, vols. 7 & 8, 1687.

Max[im(s)]	William Penn. *Some Fruits of Solitude*, 1693.
Medley	*The Medley [, publish'd every Thursday & Saturday* (journal, circa 1710)], nos. 3, 14, 17.
Meade	Joseph Meade. *Diatriba Pars IV. Item his Letters, Life & Death*, 1652.
Miscellanea	See Tryon.
Neg. X[st.]	[Cotton Mather.] *The Negro Christianized [. An Essay to Excite and Assist that Good Work, the Instruction of Negro-Servants in Christianity]*, Boston, 1706.
Newb.	T[homas] D[eloney]'s *Pleasant History of John Winchcomb, or Jack of Newberie the [famous and worthy] Clothier [of England ... and how he set continually five hundred poore people at work, to the great benefit of the Common-wealth]*, 1597.
Peace Eur.	[William Penn.] *An Essay towards the present and future Peace of Europe [by the Establishment of an European Dyet, Parliament or Estates]*, 1696.
Peacham	Henry Peacham. *Minerva Britanna or a Garden of heroical Devices [, furnished, and adorned with Emblemes and Impresa's of sundry natures]. 1612.*
Penn	William Penn. (Any of numerous texts not identified by title. See also Max[-im(s)], Peace Eur., Ser. Apology, Truth.)
Penn, Address	———. *Address to Protestants of all Persuasions*, 1692.
Pennington	Isaac Pennington. *Works, in Two Parts*, 1681.
Petry	W. Petry. [Title(s) not identified.]
Phillips	Edward Phillips. *Theatrum Poetarium [, or a Compleat Collection of the most eminent Poets of all Ages, antient & modern]*, 1675.
Piggott	John Piggott. *Sermon Preached the 7th of Sept. 1704 [Being the Solemn Thanksgiving-Day for the Late Glorious Victory obtain'd over the French and Bavarians at Bleinheim]*, 1704.
Quarles	Francis Quarles. *Emblems* (5 Books) and *Hieroglyphicks* (1 Book), n.d.
Quevedo	Francisco de Quevedo (Specific source not located).
Reynell	Carew Reynell. *The True English Interest or an Account of the Chief Natural Improvements [and some Political Observations demonstrating an Infallible Advance of this Nation to infinite Wealth and Greatness, Trade and Populacy, with Employment and Preferment for all Persons]*, 1674.
Saavedre	Don Diego Saavedra. *The Royal Politician Represented in One Hundred Emblems*, tr. Sir James Astry, Vols. l & 2, 1700.
Salmon	William Salmon. *Polygraphices, or the Arts of Drawing, Engraving, Etching, ... Painting, ... &c.*, 1685.
Seneca	Sir Roger L'Estrange [ed./tr.]. *Seneca's Morals by way of abstract*, 6th ed., 1696.
Ser. Apology	George Whitehead and William Penn. *A Serious Apology [for the Principles & Practices of the People call'd Quakers]*, Pts. 1 & 2, 1671.
Shewen	William Shewen. *True Christian's Faith and Experience*, 1676.
Shirley	John Shirley. *The Accomplished Ladies Rich Closet of Rarities [: or, The ingenious gentlewoman and servant-maids delightfull companion]*, 1687.
Spectator	[Joseph Addison and Richard Steele.] *The Spectator*, vols. 1-4, 1712-13.
Temple	Sir William Temple. *Letters*, 1700.
Trueborn	[Daniel Defoe.] *A Collection of the Writings of the Author of the Trueborn Englishman*, 1703.
Truth	[William Penn.] *Truth Exalted [: In A Short, But Sure Testimony, Against All Those Religions, Faiths, And Worships, That Have Been Formed And Followed In The Darkness Of Apostacy: And For That Glorious Light Which Is Now Risen, And Shines Forth, In The Life And Doctrine Of The Despised Quakers, As The Alone Good Old Way Of Life And Salvation]*, n.d. [1668].
Tryon	Thomas Tryon. *Miscellanea [; or, a Collection of Tracts on Variety of Subjects]*, 1696.
Tryon, Mem.	———. *Some Memoirs of the Life of Thomas Tryon written by himself*, 1705.
Tusser	Thomas Tusser. *Book of Husbandry*, n.d. [? *Five Hundred Points of Good Husbandrie to as many of Good Huswifery*, 1573].
Tusser, Belief	———. *Belief*, n.d.

3. Historical Documents and Other Primary Texts

Aristotle. *The Works of Aristotle.* Chicago: Encyclopaedia Britannica, 1952. Vol. 1.

Dilfeld, Georg C. *Theosophia Horbio Speneriana oder Sonderbare Gottesgelährtheit Herrn Horbii und seines Schwagers Speneri . . . zu fernerem Nachsinnen vorgestellt.* Würzburg: n.p., 1679. Copy provided by Stadtarchiv Soest.

Dünninger, Joseph, and Horst Schöpf, eds. *Bräuche und Feste im fränkischen Jahreslauf. Texte vom 16. bis zum 18. Jahrhundert.* Die Plassenburg, 30. Kulmbach: Stadtarchiv, 1971.

Etherege, George. *Letters of Sir George Etherege.* Ed. Frederick Bracher. Berkeley: Univ. of California Press, 1974.

Geiß (Geysen), Johann Jacob. *Ansehnlicher und volckreicher Leich-Begängnis / Des Hoch-Wohl-Ehrwürdigen / Hoch- Achtbar- und Hoch-Wohlgelehrten Herrn M[agister] Georg Leonhart Models.* With "Lebenslauf." Windsheim: E. H. Schmiden, 1714. Photocopy provided by Stadtarchiv Rothenburg ob der Tauber.

Gryphius, Christian, ed. *Apparatus sive Dissertatio Isagogica de Scriptoribus Historiam.* Leipzig: Fritsch, 1710.

Herder, Johann Gottfried. *Adrastea.* 1801-03. In *Sämtliche Werke.* Ed. Bernard Suphan. 1885; rpt. Hildesheim: G. Olms, 1967. Vol. 23, Pp. 19-506.

The Holy Bible. Authorized or King James Version. 1611; rpt. New York: Books, Inc., n.d.

Horb, Johann Heinrich. *Der Christen Seligkeit in dieser Gnaden-Zeit . . . Bey Volckreicher und recht traurigen Leich-begängnuß Des weyland Wohl-Ehrwürdigen und von Gott gelahrten Herrn Joh. Augustin Liezheimers Gewesen treu-fleissigen Evangel. Predigers der Hauptkirchen zu S. Kilian in des H. Reichs Statt Windsheim.* N.p., [1684], Microfilm copy provided by Herzog-August Bibliothek Wolfenbüttel.

-------. "Erstes Christliche Theologische Bedencken." Appended to Philipp Jakob Spener, *Pia Desideria.* Frankfurt am Main: J. Zunners, 1680, pp. 163-314. This ed. provided by Stadtbibliothek Wuppertal.

Lebens-Lauff und Abschieds-Reden einer recht Christlichen Wittwe, der Wohl-Edelgebohrnen, Viel Ehr- und Tugendreichen Frau Maria Juliana Baurin von Eyseneck. Frankfurt am Main, 1684. Rpt. in *Das Leben der Gläubigen.* Ed. Gottfried Arnold. Halle: Waisenhaus, 1701, pp. 1121-43. Copy provided by Universitätsbibliothek Bonn.

Lessing, Gotthold Ephraim. *Briefe, die neueste Litteratur betreffend.* 1759. In *Sämtliche Schriften.* Ed. Karl Lachmann. 3d ed. 1892; rpt. Berlin: de Gruyter, 1968. Vol. 8, pp. 3-285.

Lietzheimer, Johann Augustin. *Evangelische Sabbaths-Bedancken. In welchen der heutigen verkehrten, Grund-bösen und zum Ruin geneigten Laster-Welt meiste Sünden vor Augen gestellet werden, selbige aber hingegen . . . zu einem neuen, heiligen, reinen, untadlichen, unsträfflichen Gottseeligen Leben aufgewecket wird.* Sulzbach: A. Lichtenthaler, 1676. Copy provided by Stadtsbibliothek Solingen.

Luther, Martin. *An die Bürgermeister und Ratsherrn aller Städte in deutschen Landen, daß sie christliche Schulen aufrichten und halten sollen.* 1524. In *Pädagogische Schriften.* Ed. Hermann Lorenzen. 2nd ed. Paderborn: Schöningh, 1969, pp. 62-81.

Monatlicher Auszug aus allerhand neu-herausgegebenen nützlichen und artigen Büchern. Dec. 1700. Photocopy provided by Stadtarchiv Hildesheim.

Monconys, Balthasar de. "Eine Reise durchs Frankenland im Jahre 1663." Ed. A. Bechtold. In *Der Fränkische Bund,* 2,1 (1925), 1-11.

Nürnbergische Universität Altdorf. *Catalogus Lectionem atque Exercitationum in Universitate Norimbergensium Altdorffina.* Altdorf, 1659-75. Provided by Universitätsbibliothek Erlangen-Nürnberg.

Papebroch, Daniel. *Eine Gelehrtenreise durch Mainfranken 1660.* Würzburg: Freunde Mainfr. Kunst und Geschichte, 1952.

Pastorius, Melchior Adam. "Antwort an dieselbige [: Beschreibung meiner Ankunfft und geführten Lebens-Lauff]." Appended to F. D. Pastorius' *Beschreibung Pennsylvaniae,* pp. 103-20. Rpt. in Estermann ed. of M. A. Pastorius' *Kurze Beschreibung Windsheim,* pp. x-xxvi.

-------. "Forma civitatis imperialis liberae d. i. grundliche Beschreibung des Heiligen römischen Reiches Stadt Windsheimensis." 1670. Stadtarchiv Bad Windsheim MS. A6.

-------. *Franconia Rediviva. Das ist: Des Hochlöblichen Fränckischen Craises So wohl Genealogische als Historische Beschreibung.* Nürnberg: privately printed, 1702. Provided by Herzog-August Bibliothek Wolfenbüttel.

-------. "Itinerarium et Vitae Curriculus. Das ist: Seine völlige Reis-Beschreibunge und gantzer LebensLauff." Univ. of Pennsylvania MS. Ger 54.

-------. *Kurtze Beschreibung des H. R. Reichs Stadt Windsheim / Samt Dero vielfältigen Unglücks-Fällen / und wahrhafftigen Ursachen ihrer so grossen Decadenz und Erbarmungs-würdigen*

Zustandes. Nürnberg: C. S. Froberg, 1692. Provided by Herzog-August Bibliothek Wolfenbüttel. Rpt. as *Kurze Beschreibung der Reichsstadt Windsheim 1692.* Ed. Alfred Estermann. München: Delp, 1980.

------. *Des Melchior Adam Pastorius... Leben und Reisebeschreibungen von ihm selbst erzählt und nebst dessen lyrischen Gedichten*... Ed. Albert R. Schmitt. München: Delp, 1968.

------. "Nucleus Doctrinae Biblicae Intima Christianismi fundamenta omni remoto tegmine ad oculum exhibens." Stadtarchiv Bad Windsheim MS. A9.

Penn, William. *Travels in Holland and Germany.* In *The Select Works of William Penn in Three Volumes.* 4th ed. Vol. 2. 1825; rpt. New York: Kraus Reprints, 1971, pp. 398-503.

Petersen, Johanna Eleonora. *Eine Kurze Erzehlung, wie mich die leitende Hand Gottes bisher gefuhret.* 1688, rev. 1718, 1719. Rpt. as "Selbstbiographie" in *Der deutsche Pietismus. Eine Auswahl.* Ed. Werner Mahrholz. Berlin: Furche-Verlag, 1921, pp. 201-45.

Propagation of the Gospel in the East: Being an Account of the Success of two Danish Missionaries, Lately sent to the East-Indies, for the Conversion of the Heathens in Malabar... Rendered into English from the High-Dutch. [Ed. Anton Wilhelm Böhme]. London: J. Downing, 1709.

Propagation of the Gospel in the East. Pt. 2, Being a further account of the Progress Made by some Missionaries to Tranquebar, Upon the Coast of Coromandel, For the Conversion of the Malabarians... The Second Edition. London: Downing, 1711. URL (both volumes) = http://www.francke-halle.de/main/index2.php?cf=3_1_3_3_2

Reichsstadt Windsheim. "Bestattungen 1653-1717." Archiv des Evang.-Luth. Pfarramts Bad Windsheim MS.

------. "Eines Erbarn Raths dieser des Heiligen Reichs Statt Windsheim Schuelordnung anno 1595." In Korndörfer, *Studien*, pp. 147-59.

------. "Erneuerte Schuel-Ordnung 1667." In Korndörfer, *Studien*, pp. 159-71.

------. "Gravamina Einer Löbl. Bürgerschafft des H. Reichs Stadt Windsheimb. Contra Die Woledle, Vest- und Hochgelahrte, dann Wolehrenveste, Fürsichtig- Hoch- und Wolweise Herren Burgermeister und auch daselbst." In Korndörfer, *Studien*, pp. 172-200.

------. "Policey Ordtnung des Heyl. Rom. Reichs Statt Windtsheimb. Verneuert den 18., und von dem Predigtstuhl abgelesen den 20. 8bris. 1667." In M. A. Pastorius, "Forma Civitatis," fols. 90-95.

------. "Taufbuch 1648-77." Archiv des Evang.-Luth. Pfarramts Bad Windsheim MS. K9.

------. "Verordnung des Magistrats der Reichsstadt Windsheim vom 15. September 1650." Ed. Johann Georg Nehr. In *Jahresbericht des Historischen Vereins von Mittelfranken*, 24 (1855), Beilage 3, pp. 35-38. Rpt. in *Windsheimer Zeitung*, 28 Feb. 1959.

Rosenbach, Johann Georg. *Wunder- und Gnaden-volle Führung Gottes Eines auff dem Wege der Bekehrung Christo nachfolgenden Schaffs.* Wetzlar: n.p., 1704. Provided by Bibliothek P. R. Stuttgart.

Schumberg, Tobias. *Pharus divina philosophiae practicae, Illustrissima facilitatis suae face errabundas mentes ad prudentiae portum dirigens. h. e. Idea Ethicae, Oeconomicae, Politicae.* Nürnberg: W. Felsecker, 1663, rev. 1667. Both eds. provided by Bayerische Staatsbibliothek.

Smith, William. "A Description of the Cittie of Noremberg, 1594." Ed. Karlheinz Goldmann. In *Mitteilungen des Vereins für Geschichte der Stadt Nürnberg*, 48 (1958), 194-216.

Spener, Philipp Jakob. *Pia desideria, oder hertzliches Verlangen, nach Gottgefälliger Besserung der wahren Evangelischen Kirchen.* 1675. Ed. Kurt Aland. Berlin: de Gruyter, 1955.

------. *Theologisches Bedencken Und andere Brieffliche Antworten.* Halle: Waisenhaus, 1712. Vol. 3.

Tentzel, Wilhelm Ernst, ed. *Monatlichen Unterredungen einiger guten Freunde von allerhand Buechern und anderen annehmlichen Geschichten.* Issues of Apr. 1691, Dec. 1691 and Feb. 1693.

4. Essential Reference Works

Bodensieck, Julius, ed. *The Encyclopedia of the Lutheran Church.* 3 vols. Minneapolis: Augsburg Publ., 1965.

Bodnar, John E. *Ethnic History in Pennsylvania: A Selected Bibliography.* Harrisburg: Pa. Hist. and Museum Comm., 1974.

Brockhaus Enzyklopädie in zwanzig Bänden with *Ergänzungen.* 17th ed. 22 vols. Wiesbaden: Brockhaus, 1966-76.

Clark, Sir George, et al., eds. *The New Cambridge Modern History.* Vols. 4 and 5. Cambridge: Univ. Press, 1961, 1970.

Coing, Helmut, ed. *Handbuch der Quellen und Literatur der neueren europäischen Privatrechtsgeschichte*. Vol. 2, Teilband 1. München: Beck'sche, 1977.

Cross, F. L. and E. A. Livingstone, eds. *The Oxford Dictionary of the Christian Church*. 2nd ed. Oxford: Oxford Univ. Press, 1974.

Deppermann, Klaus, and Dietrich Blaufuß, eds. "Pietismus-Bibliographie." In *Pietismus und Neuzeit: Ein Jahrbuch zur Geschichte des neueren Protestantismus*. Ed. Alfred Schindler, et al. Vols. 1-11. Bielefeld: Luther Verlag, 1974-85.

Douglas, J. D., ed. *The New International Dictionary of the Christian Church*. Exeter, England: Paternoster, 1974.

Edwards, Paul, ed. *The Encyclopedia of Philosophy*. 8 vols. New York: Macmillan and the Free Press, 1967.

The Encyclopedia Americana. 7th (International) ed. 30 vols. New York: Americana Corp., 1976.

The Encyclopaedia Britannica. 11th ed. 29 vols. Cambridge: Cambridge Univ. Pr., 1910-11. Also 1961 and 15th (1974) eds.

Erman, Wilhelm, and Ewald Horn, eds. *Bibliographie der deutschen Universitäten*. 2 vols. Leipzig: Teubner, 1904-05.

Faber du Faur, Curt von, ed. *German Baroque Literature: A Catalogue of the Collection in the Yale University Library*. 2 vols. New Haven: Yale Univ. Press, 1958, 1969.

Galling, Kurt, ed. *Die Religion in Geschichte und Gegenwart*. 3rd. ed. 6 vols. Tübingen: Mohr, 1957-65.

Gebhardt, Bruno, and Herbert Grundmann, eds. *Handbuch der deutschen Geschichte*. 9th ed. Vol. 2. Stuttgart: Union Verlag, 1970.

German Baroque Literature: A. Descriptive Catalogue of the Collection of Harold Jantz and a Guide to the Collection on Microfilm. 2 vols. New Haven: Research Publs., 1974.

Greschat, Martin. "Zur neueren Pietismusforschung. Ein Literaturbericht." *Jahrband des Vereins für Westfälische Kirchengeschichte*, 65 (1972), 220-68.

Hammond, N. G. L., and H. H. Sculland, eds. *The Oxford Classical Dictionary*. 2nd ed. Oxford: Oxford Univ. Press, 1970.

Harvey, Paul. *The Oxford Companion to Classical Literature*. Oxford: Oxford Univ. Press, 1937.

Hassinger, Erich, ed. *Bibliographie zur Universitätsgeschichte. Verzeichnis der im Gebiet der Bundesrepublik Deutschland 1945-1971 veröffentlichten Literatur*. Freiburg: Alber, 1974.

Hauck, Albert, ed. *Realencyklopädie für protestantische Theologie und Kirche*. 3rd ed. 24 vols. Leipzig: Hinrichs, 1896-1913.

Hirsching, Friedrich Carl Gottlob, ed. *Historisch-literarisches Handbuch berühmter und denkwürdiger Personen, welche in dem 18. Jahrhunderte gestorben sind*. 17 vols. 1794-1815; rpt. Graz: Akademische Druck, 1972-76.

Historische Commission bei der Bayerischen Akademie der Wissenschaften, eds. *Neue Deutsche Biographie*. Berlin: Duncker & Humblot, 1953-. (1985: Vol. 14, Lav-Loc.)

Historische Commission bei der Königl. Akademie der Wissenschaften, ed. *Allgemeine Deutsche Biographie*. 56 vols. Leipzig: Duncker & Humblot, 1875-1912.

Hofer, Joseph, and Karl Rahner, eds. *Lexikon für Theologie und Kirche*. 2nd ed. 10 Vols. Freiburg im Br.: Herder, 1957-67.

Illick, Joseph E. "Bibliography." In *Colonial Pennsylvania: A History*. New York: Scribner's, 1976, pp. 322-38.

Jöcher, Christian G. *Allgemeines Gelehrten-Lexicon*. 4 vols. 7 supplementary vols. ed. J. C. Adelung and H. W. Rotermund. 1750-51, 1784-1897; rpt. Hildesheim: Olms, 1960-61.

Keyser, Erich, and Heinz Stoob, eds. *Bayerisches Städtebuch*. Vol. 5 of *Deutsches Städtebuch*. Stuttgart: Kohlhammer, 1971.

Kneschke, Ernst H., ed. *Neues allgemeines Deutsches Adels-Lexicon*. 8 vols. Leipzig: Voigt, 1859-68.

Knod, Gustav C., ed. *Die Alten Matrikeln der Universität Strassburg*. 3 vols. Strasbourg: Trübner, 1897-1902.

Kommission für bayerische Landesgeschichte and Generaldirektion der Bayerischen Staatlichen Bibliotheken. *Bayerische Bibliographie*. München: Beck'sche, 1966-. (1981: Vol. 8.)

Krause, Gerhard, and Gerhard Müller, eds. *Theologische Realenzyklopädie*. Berlin: de Gruyter, 1977-. (1984: Vol. 13, Ges-Got.)

Meynen, Emil, ed. *Bibliography on German Settlements in Colonial North America*. Leipzig: Harrassowitz, 1937.

Pfeiffer, Gerhard, ed. *Fränkische Bibliographie. Schriftennachweis zur historischen Landeskunde Frankens bis zum Jahre 1945*. 4 vols. Würzburg: Schöningh, 1965-78.

——————. "Sammelbericht Franken." *Blätter für deutsche Landesgeschichte*, 98 (1962), 353- 406; 102 (1966), 313-46.

——————and Alfred Wendehorst, eds. *Fränkische Lebensbilder*. Würzburg: Schöningh, 1967-. (1984: Vol. 11.)

Pochmann, Henry A., and Arthur R. Schultz, eds. *Bibliography of German Culture in America to 1940*. Madison: Univ. of Wisconsin Press, 1953.

Schieder, Theodor, ed. *Handbuch der Europäischen Geschichte*. Vols. 3 and 4. Stuttgart: Union Verlag, 1968, 1971.

Schmalzriedt, Egidius, ed. *Hauptwerke der antiken Literatur*. München: Kindler, 1976.

Scupin, Hans Ulrich and Ulrich Scheuner, eds. *Althusius-Bibliographie. Bibliographie zur politischen Ideengeschichte und Staatslehre, zum Staatsrecht und zur Verfassungsgeschichte des 16. bis 18. Jahrhunderts*. 2 vols. Berlin: Duncker & Humblot, 1973.

Simon, Matthias. "Bibliography." In *Evangelische Kirchengeschichte Bayerns*. Vol. 2. München: P. Müller, 1942.

Spindler, Max, ed. *Handbuch der bayerischen Geschichte*. Vol. 3. München: Beck'sche, 1971.

Steiger, Günter, ed. *Die Matrikel der Universität Jena*. Vol. 2, parts 1 and 2. Weimar: Böhlaus, 1961, 1964.

Steinmeyer, Elias von, ed. *Die Matrikel der Universität Altdorf*. Würzburg: H. Stürtz, 1912.

Thorlby, Anthony, ed. *The Penquin Guide to European Literature*. New York: McGraw-Hill, 1969.

Tolzmann, Don Heinrich, ed. *German-Americana: A Bibliography*. Metuchen, N. J.: Scarecrow Press, 1975.

Ziegler, Konrat, and Walther Sontheimer, eds. *Der kleine Pauly. Lexikon der Antike*. 5 vols. Stuttgart: Druckenmüller, 1964-75.

5. Other Sources

Adams, James Truslow. *Provincial Society, 1690-1763*. Vol. 3 of *A History of American Life*. Ed. Arthur M. Schlesinger and Dixon Ryan Fox. New York: Macmillan, 1936.

Ahlstrom, Sydney E. *A Religious History of the American People*. New Haven: Yale Univ. Press, 1972.

Alderfer, E. Gordon. "Pastorius and the Origins of Pennsylvania-German Culture." In *American-German Review*, 17, no. 3 (1951), 8-11.

Ashley, Maurice. *England in the Seventeenth Century*. 3rd ed. rev. Pelican History of England, 6. Harmondsworth: Penquin, 1967.

Ballauff, Theodor, and Klaus Schaller. *Pädagogik. Eine Geschichte der Bildung und Erziehung*. Vol 2. Freiburg: Aalber, 1970.

Bauer, Rolf. *Österreich*. Berlin: Haude & Spenersche, 1970.

Beall, Otto T., Jr., and Richard H. Shryock. *Cotton Mather: First Significant Figure in American Medicine*. Baltimore: Johns Hopkins Press, 1954.

Blättner, Fritz. "Die Wandlung von der altprotestantischen Gelehrtenschule zum humanistischen Gymnasium." In *Das Gymnasium in Geschichte und Gegenwart*. Ed. Hermann Rohrs. Frankfurt: Akademische Verlagsges., 1969, pp. 1-13.

Bock, Friedrich. *Zur Volkskunde der Reichsstadt Nürnberg*. Veröffentlichungen der Gesellschaft für Fränkische Geschichte, 14. Würzburg: Schöningh, 1959.

Bog, Ingomar. *Dorfgemeinde, Freiheit und Unfreiheit in Franken*. Quellen und Forschungen zur Agrargeschichte, 3. Stuttgart: Fischer, 1956.

Brandi, Karl. *Deutsche Geschichte im Zeitalter der Reformation und Gegenreformation*. München: Bruckmann, 1960.

Bridenbaugh, Carl. *Cities in the Wilderness: The First Century of Urban Life in America, 1625-1742*. 1938; rpt. New York: Oxford Univ. Press, 1971.

Brophy, Alfred L. "'*Ingenium est Fateri per quos profeceris*': Francis Daniel Pastorius' Young Country Clerk's Collection and Anglo-American Legal Literature, 1682-1716," 3 *University of Chicago Law School Roundtable* (1996), pp. 637-742.

——————. "The Quaker Bibliographic World of Francis Daniel Pastorius' Bee Hive," *Pennsylvania Magazine of History and Biography* 122 (1998), 241-291, URL= http://www.law.ua.edu/directory/bio/abrophy/PASTbks.html.

——————. "The Intellectual World of a Seventeenth-Century Jurist: Francis Daniel Pastorius and the Reconstruction of Pietist Thought," in: *German? American? Literature? New Directions in German-American Studies*, ed. Winfried Fluck und Werner Sollors, New York, 2002, pp. 43-63.

Browning, Robert M. *German Baroque Poetry, 1618-1723*. University Park, Pa.: Pennsylvania State Univ. Press, 1971.

Carpenter, Delburn. *The Radical Pietists*. New York: AMS Press, 1975
Cowie, Leonard W. *Seventeenth-Century Europe*. London: G. Bell, 1960.
Dannheimer, Wilhelm, ed. "Reichsstadt Windsheim." In *Pfarrerbuch der Reichsstädte Dinkelsbühl, Schweinfurt, Weißenburg i. Bay. und Windsheim*. Ed. Matthias Simon. Nürnberg: Verein für Bay. Kirchengesch., 1962, pp. 83-114.
Dechent, Hermann. "Johann Jakob Schütz. Der Dichter des Liedes 'Sei Lob und Ehr dem höchsten Gut.'" In *Christliche Welt*, 3 (1899), 849-54, 864-68, 935-37, 952-56.
---------. *Kirchengeschichte von Frankfurt am Main seit der Reformation*. Vol. 2. Frankfurt/M.: Kesselring, 1921.
Delp, Hermann. *Bad Windsheim. Kurze Beschreibung der ehemaligen Reichs- und heutigen Bäderstadt*. 3rd ed. Bad Windsheim: Delp, 1979.
Dietz, Alexander. *Frankfurter Handelsgeschichte*. Vol. 4. 1923; rpt. Glashütten im Taunus: Auvermann, 1970.
Durant, Will and Ariel. *The Age of Louis XIV*. Vol. 8 of *The Story of Civilization*. New York: Simon & Schuster, 1963.
Englebert, Arthur F. "Francis Daniel Pastorius in his Literary Activities." Diss. Univ. of Pittsburgh, 1935.
Erben, Patrick M. *A Harmony of the Spirits: Translation and the Language of Community in Early Pennsylvania*. Chapel Hill: Univ. of North Carolina Press, 2012.
---------. " 'Honey-combs' and 'paper-hives': positioning Francis Daniel Pastorius's manuscript writings in early Pennsylvania," *Early American Literature* 37 (2002), 2, 157-94.
---------. "Promoting Pennsylvania: Penn, Pastorius, and the Creation of a Transnational Community," *Resources for American Literary Study* 29 (2003–2004), pp. 25–65.
Estermann, Alfred. *Bad Windsheim. Geschichte einer Stadt in Bildern*. 2nd ed. Bad Windsheim: Delp, 1975.
--------. "Geistliches Singen und Spielen zu Gott." *Fränkische Landeszeitung*, 25 Aug. 1967.
Fantel, Hans. *William Penn: Apostle of Dissent*. New York: Morrow, 1974.
Faust, Albert B. *The German Element in the United States, with Special Reference to its Political, Moral, Social, and Educational Influence*. 2 vols. 1909; rpt. New York: Steuben Soc., 1927.
Ford, Franklin L. *Strasbourg in Transition 1648-1789*. Cambridge, Mass.: Harvard Univ. Press, 1958.
Fowler, Alastair, ed., *The New Oxford Book of Seventeenth Century Verse*. Oxford: Oxford Univ. Press, 1992.
Friedenthal, Richard. *Luther. Sein Leben und seine Zeit*. München: Piper, 1967.
Fritz, D. F. "Johann Georg Rosenbach." *Zeitschrift für Bayerische Kirchengeschichte*, 18 (1949), 21-59.
Fürnrohr, Walter. *Der immerwährende Reichstag zu Regensburg. Das Parlament des alten Reiches*. Regensburg: Lassleben, 1963.
Geffcken, Johannes. *Johann Winckler und die Hamburgische Kirche in seiner Zeit (1684-1705)*. Hamburg: G. Nolte, 1861.
Genzmer, George H. "Pastorius, Francis Daniel." *DAB*, 14 (1934), 290-91.
Gilson, Etienne, and Thomas Langan. *Modern Philosophy: Descarte to Kant*. Vol. 3 of *A History of Modern Philosophy*. Ed. Etienne Gilson. New York: Random House, 1963.
Göbel, Max. *Geschichte des Christlichen Lebens in der rheinisch-westphälischen evangelischen Kirche*. Vol 2. Koblenz: Bädeker, 1852.
Grafton, Anthony. "Jumping Through the Computer Screen," *New York Review of Books*, Dec. 2010.
---------. "The Republic of Letters in the American Colonies: Francis Daniel Pastorius Makes a Notebook," *American Historical Review*, 117 (2012), 2, 1-39
Gutmann, Friedrich, and Georg Furkel. *Sommerhausen in Wort und Bild; Geschichtliche und kulturgeschichtliche Darlegungen nach Quellen*. 2nd ed. Würzburg: Gemeinde Sommerhausen, 1970.
Haas, Robert. *Die Musik des Barocks*. Potsdam: Akademische Verlagsges., 1929.
Hable, Guido. *Geschichte Regensburgs. Eine Übersicht nach Sachgebieten*. Regensburg: Mittelbay. Druckerei, 1970.
Hirsch, Emanuel. *Geschichte der neuern evangelischen Theologie*. Vol. 2. Gütersloh: Bertelsmann, 1951.
Hofmann, Hanns H. *Neustadt-Windsheim. Historischer Atlas von Bayern*. Franken section, ser. l, no. 2. München: Komm. für bay. Landesgeschichte, 1953.
--------, and Günther Schuhmann, eds. *Franken in alten Ansichten und Schilderungen*. Konstanz: Thorbecke, 1967.
Holborn, Hajo. *A History of Modern Germany*. Vols. l and 2. New York: Knopf, 1959, 1964.

Huelsbergen, Helmut E. "The First Thirteen Families: Another Look at the Religious and Ethnic Background of the Emigrants from Crefeld (1683)." In *Yearbook of German-American Studies*, 18 (1983), 29-40.
Huschke, Wolfgang. "Politische Geschichte von 1572 bis 1775." In *Geschichte Thüringens*. Ed. Hans Patze and Walter Schlesinger. Vol. 5. Köln: Böhlau, 1982.
Jenkins, C. F. "Francis Daniel Pastorius." In *American-German Review*, 1 (1934), 22-25.
Jirgal, Ernst. "Johann Heinrich Böckler (1611-72)." *Mitteilungen des Instituts für österreichische Geschichtsforschung*, 45 (1931), 322-384.
Kantzenbach, Friedrich W. *Orthodoxie und Pietismus*. Vol. 11/12 of *Evangelische Enzyklopädie*. Ed. Helmut Thielicke and Hans Thimme. Gütersloh: Mohn, 1966.
Kelly, Jack. *Gunpowder: A History of the Explosive That Changed the World*. London: Atlantic Books, 2004.
Kentenich, Gottfried. *Geschichte der Stadt Trier von ihrer Gründung bis zur Gegenwart*. Trier: Lintz, 1915.
Koppen, Ernst. *Vom Rhein zum Delaware: Krefelder gründeten 1683 Germantown*. Issued by Oberstadtdirektor and Verkehrsverein Krefeld. Krefeld: Formdruck, 1983.
Korndörfer, Werner. "Ein sehr umstrittener Mann seiner Kirche: Johann Heinrich Horb." *Windsheimer Zeitung*, 22 Aug., 28 Aug. and 12 Sept. 1964.
---------. *Studien zur Geschichte der Reichsstadt Windsheim vornehmlich im 17. Jahrhundert*. Diss. Univ. Erlangen-Nürnberg, 1972. Erlangen: Offsetdruck Hogl, 1972.
Kramer, Gustav. *Beiträge zur Geschichte August Hermann Franckes, enthaltend den Briefwechsel Franckes und Speners*. Halle: Waisenhaus, 1861.
Kramer, Karl-Sigismund. *Bauern und Bürger im nachmittelalterlichen Unterfranken*. Veröffentlichungen der Gesellschaft für fränkische Geschichte, ser. 9, vol. 12. Würzburg: Schöningh, 1957.
---------. *Volksleben im Fürstentum Ansbach und seinen Nachbargebieten 1500-1800*. Veröffentlichungen der Gesellschaft für Fränkische Geschichte, ser. 9, vol. 15. Würzburg: Schöningh, 1961.
Kraus, Andreas. "Bürgerlicher Geist und Wissenschaft." In *Archiv für Kulturgeschichte*, 49 (1967), 340-75.
Kreiner, Artur. "Die jährlichen Neueinschreibungen an Gymnasium, Academie und Universität Altdorf von 1575-1809." In *Mitteilungen des Vereins für Geschichte der Stadt Nürnberg*, 37 (1940), 340-45.
------. "Professorenschicksale und Charakterköpfe aus der Universitätsgeschichte Altdorfs." In *Mitteilungen des Vereins für Geschichte der Stadt Nürnberg*, 37 (1940), 322-40.
Lambert, Margo M. "Francis Daniel Pastorius: An American in Early Pennsylvania, 1683-1719/20", Ph.D. diss., Georgetown University, 2007.
Lamping, Gerlinde. *Die Bibliothek der freien Reichsstadt Windsheim*. Diss. Univ. Würzburg, 1966. Bad Windsheim: Delp, 1966.
Laughton, J. K. "Penn, Sir William (1621-1670)." *DNB*, 44 (1895), 308-11.
Learned, Marion Dexter. *The Life of Francis Daniel Pastorius, the Founder of Germantown*. Philadelphia: W. J. Campbell, 1908.
Lehmann, Hartmut. *Das Zeitalter des Absolutismus. Gottesgnadentum und Kriegsnot*. Stuttgart: Kohlhammer, 1980.
Lengenfelder, Konrad. *Johann Georg Puschners Ansichten von der Nürnbergischen Universität Altdorf*. Nürnberg: Spindler, 1958.
Liebau, Kurt. "Einleitung." *Die Malabarische Korrespondenz: Tamilische Briefe an deutsche Missionare*, pp. 7-36. Sigmaringen: Jan Thorbecke Verlag, 1998.
Lorenzen, Hermann. "Martin Luther als Erzieher." In Martin Luther, *Pädagogische Schriften*. 2nd ed. Paderborn: Schöningh, 1969, pp. 182-89.
Mack, Rüdiger. "Franz Daniel Pastorius – Sein Einsatz für die Quäker." *Pietismus und Neuzeit*, 15 (1989), pp. 132-171.
Maschke, Erich. *Universität Jena*. Mitteldeutsche Hochschulen, 6. Köln: Böhlau, 1969.
Mende, Erich. "Franz Daniel Pastorius gründete Germantown." *Damals. Zeitschrift für geschichtliches Wissen*, 10 (1978), 123-36.
Mitteis, Heinrich. *Deutsche Rechtsgeschichte. Ein Studienbuch*. Neubearbeitet von Heinz Lieberich. 15th ed. München: Beck'sche, 1978.
Morison, Samuel Eliot. *The Intellectual Life of Colonial New England*. 2nd ed. Ithaca, N. Y.: Cornell Univ. Press, 1956.
---------. *The Oxford History of the American People*. New York: Oxford Univ. Press, 1965.

Müller, Karl O. "Das Geschlecht der Reichserbschenken zu Limpurg bis zum Aussterben des Mannesstammes." In *Zeitschrift für württembergische Landesgeschichte*, 5 (1941), 215- 43.
Müller, Otto T. "Heinrich Horbius (1645-1695), ein tragisches Pfarrerschicksal." In *Monatshefte für evangelische Kirchengeschichte des Rheinlandes*, 15, Heft 4 (1966), 127-33.
Mummenhoff, Ernst. "Die Juristenfakultät Altdorf in den ersten fünf Jahrzehnten ihres Bestehens 1576-1626." Diss. Univ. Erlangen-Nürnberg, 1959.
Nauert, Charles. "Heinrich Cornelius Agrippa von Nettesheim." In The Stanford Encyclopedia of Philosophy (Summer 2011 Edition), ed Edward N. Zalta. URL = <http://plato.stanford.edu/archives/sum2011/entries/agrippa-nettesheim/>.
Nehr, Johann Georg. *Beiträge zur Kirchengeschichte Windsheims*. 5 pamphlets. Windsheim, 1800-05.
--------. *Zur Geschichte der Schulen in Windsheim*, 2 vols. Windsheim, 1807, 1808.
Newald, Richard. *Die Deutsche Literatur vom Späthumanismus zur Empfindsamkeit*. 6th ed. München: Beck'sche, 1967.
Nolte, Ewald V. "Pachelbel, Johann." In *New Grove Dictionary of Music and Musicians*. Ed. Stanley Sadie. Vol. 14. Washington, D. C.: Grove's Dictionaries, 1980, pp. 46-54.
Olson, James S. *The Ethnic Dimension in American History*. New York: St. Martin's, 1979.
Oswalt, Else. "Christian Fende. Ein Beitrag zur Geschichte des Pietismus in Frankfurt/Main," Diss. Univ. Frankfurt, 1921.
Otto, Karl F. *Die Sprachgesellschaften des 17. Jahrhunderts*. Stuttgart: Metzler, 1972.
Palmieri, Brooke. "'What the Bees Have Taken Pains For': Francis Daniel Pastorius, *The Beehive*, and Commonplacing in Colonial Pennsylvania" (B.A. thesis, University of Pennsylvania, 2009). URL = http://repository.upenn.edu/uhf_2009/7/.
Pastorius, Thomas V. Personal interview on the Pastorius family history. 30 Aug. 1983 in Bonn-Bad Godesberg, Germany. Also letter of 11 Jan. 1985.
Paulsen, Friedrich. *Geschichte des gelehrten Unterrichts auf den deutschen Schulen und Universitäten vom Ausgang des Mittelalters bis zur Gegenwart*. 3rd ed. 2 vols. 1919-21.; rpt. Berlin: de Gruyter, 1960.
Pennypacker, Samuel W. *The Settlement of Germantown, Pennsylvania, and the Beginning of German Immigration to North America*. 1899; rpt. New York: Benj. Blom, 1970.
Petersen, Peter. *Geschichte der aristotelischen Philosophie im protestantischen Deutschland*. 1921; rpt. Stuttgart: Frommann, 1964.
Petri, Franz, and Georg Droege, eds. *Rheinische Geschichte in drei Bänden*. Vol. 2. Düsseldorf: Schwann, 1976.
Petzold, Klaus. *Die Grundlagen der Erziehungslehre im Spätmittelalter und bei Luther*. Heidelberg: Quelle & Meyer, 1969.
Pfeiffer, Gerhard, ed. *Nürnberg. Geschichte einer europäischen Stadt*. Vol. 1. München: Beck'sche, 1971.
Pirson, Julius. "J. Chr. Wagenseil und Jean Chapelain: die Universität Altforf im Dienste Colberts." *Gedächtnisschrift für Adalbert Hamel*. Ed. Heinrich Kuen. Würzburg: Triltsch, 1953, pp. 197-222.
Pochmann, Henry A. "The Mingling of Tongues." In *Literary History of the United States*. Ed. Robert E. Spiller, et al. 4th ed. rev. Vol. 1. New York: Macmillan, 1977, pp. 676-93.
Polyglott-Redaktion. *Reiseführer Franken*. 4th ed. München: Polyglott, 1980.
Recktenwald, Horst C. *Die fränkische Universität Altdorf*. Nürnberg: Spindler, 1966.
"Reichsstadt Windsheim." In *Großes vollständiges Universal-Lexicon aller Wissenschafften und Künste*. Ed. Johann H. Zedler. Vol. 57. Leipzig: Zedler, 1748, cols. 757-97.
Rice, C. Duncan. *The Rise and Fall of Black Slavery*. London: Macmillan, 1975.
Riley, Lyman W. "Books from the 'Bee Hive' Manuscript of Francis Daniel Pastorius," *Quaker History* 81 (1994), 116-129.
Ritschl, Albrecht. *Geschichte des Pietismus in der lutherischen Kirche des 17. und 18. Jahrhunderts*. 3 vols. 1880-86; rpt. Berlin: de Gruyter, 1966.
Roth, Alfred. "Das Leben und Wirken des Superintendenten Johann Heinrich Horb in der Reichsstadt Windsheim." *Zeitschrift für bayerische Kirchengeschichte*, 51 (1982), 111- 15.
--------. "Der Windsheimer Bürgermeister und Oberrichter Melchior Adam Pastorius als leistungsstarke Persönlichkeit der Barockzeit. Ein Beitrag zur süddeutschen Reichsstadtgeschichte." 1981. Copy of 212-p. ts in Stadtarchiv Bad Windsheim and in Universitätsbibliothek Erlangen-Nürnberg.
Rotthoff, Guido. "Die Auswanderung von Krefeld nach Pennsylvanien im Jahre 1683." In *Die Heimat. Krefelder Jahrbuch* (Sonderdruck), 53 (1983), 2-11.

Schaudig, Paul. *Der Pietismus und Separatismus im Aischgrund.* Schwabisch-Gmünd: Aupperle, 1925.
Schirmer, Christian Wilhelm. *Geschichte Windsheims und seiner Nachbarorte.* Nürnberg: Riegel und Wießner, 1848.
Schmidt, Martin, and Wilhelm Jannasch, eds. *Das Zeitalter des Pietismus.* Klassiker des Protestantismus, 6. Bremen: Schünemann, 1965.
Schnelbögl, Fritz. "Die fränkischen Reichsstädte." *Zeitschrift für bayerische Landesgeschichte,* 31 (1968), 421-74.
Schübel, Albrecht. *Das Evangelium in Mainfranken.* München: Evangel. Presseverband, 1958.
Schulte, Johann F. von. *Die Geschichte der Quellen und Literatur des canonischen Rechts von Gratian bis auf die Gegenwart.* Vol. 3. Stuttgart: Enke, 1880.
Schulze, Friedrich, and Paul Ssymanck. *Das Deutsche Studententum.* 2nd ed. Leipzig: Voigtländers, 1910.
Seidensticker, Oswald. *Die erste Deutsche Einwanderung in Amerika und die Gründung von Germantown, im Jahre 1683.* Philadelphia: n.p., 1883.
--------. "Francis Daniel Pastorius." In *The Penn Monthly,* 3 (1872), 1-9, 51-68.
--------. "Franz Daniel Pastorius (1651-1719) und die Gründung von Germantown in 1683." In *Der Deutsche Pionier,* 2 (1870), 136-43, 168-78, 206-11, 241-48, 275-79, 300-07, 334-40, 379-83; 3 (1871), 8-12, 56-58, 78-83. Film 3434 E, Reel 1, L. C. Photoduplication Service.
Shell, Marc and Werner Sollors, eds. *The Multilingual Anthology of American Literature: A Reader of Original Texts with English Translations.* New York: New York Univ. Press, 2000.
Shields, David S., ed. *American Poetry: The Seventeenth and Eighteenth Centuries.* New York: The Library of America, 2007.
Sommerville, John C. *The Rise and Fall of Childhood.* Beverly Hills, Calif: Sage Publ., 1982.
Spahr, Blake Lee. "Nürnberg's Stellung im Literarischen Leben des 17. Jahrhunderts." In *Stadt - Schule - Universität - Buchwesen und die deutsche literatur im 17. Jahrhundert.* Ed. Albrecht Schöne. München: Beck, 1976, pp. 72-83.
Steinmetz, Max, ed. *Geschichte der Universität Jena.* 2 vols. Jena: G. Fischer, 1958, 1962.
Stintzing, Roderich, and Ernst Landesberg. *Geschichte der deutschen Rechtswissenschaft.* Vol. 3. 1910; rpt. Aalen: Scientia, 1957.
Stoeffler, F. Ernest. "Introduction" and "The Influence of Pietism in Colonial American Lutheranism." In *Continental Pietism and Early American Christianity.* Ed. F. Ernest Stoeffler. Grand Rapids: Eerdmans Publ., 1976, pp. 8-33.
Stolleis, Michael, ed. *Staatsdenker im 17. und 18. Jahrhundert: Reichspublizistik, Politik, Naturrecht.* Frankfurt/ Main, 1977.
Szyrocki, Marian. *Die deutsche Literatur des Barock. Eine Einführung.* Reinbek: Rowohlt, 1968.
Tebbel, John. *A History of Book Publishing in the United States.* Vol. 1. New York: Bowker, 1972.
Tolles, Frederick B. *Meeting House and Counting House: The Quaker Merchants of Colonial Philadelphia 1682-1763.* Chapel Hill: Univ. of N. Carolina Press, 1948.
Toms, Deella V. "The Intellectual and Literary Background of Francis Daniel Pastorius." Diss. Northwestern Univ., 1953.
Treue, Wilhelm. *Deutsche Geschichte von den Anfängen bis zur Gegenwart.* 3rd ed. Stuttgart: Kröner, 1965.
Turner, Beatrice Pastorius. "William Penn and Pastorius." In *Pennsylvania Magazine of History and Biography,* 57 (1933), 66-90.
Vierhaus, Rudolf. *Deutschland im Zeitalter des Absolutismus (1648-1763).* Vol. 6 of *Deutsche Geschichte.* Ed. Joachim Leuschner. Göttingen: Vandenhoeck & Ruprecht, 1978.
Wallmann, Johannes. *Kirchengeschichte Deutschlands II. Deutsche Geschichte,* 12. Frankfurt am Main: Ullstein, 1973.
--------. *Philipp Jakob Spener und die Anfänge des Pietismus.* Beiträge zur historischen Theologie, 42. Tübingen: Mohr, 1970.
--------. "Spener und Dilfeld: Der Hintergrund des ersten pietistischen Streites." In *Theologie in Geschichte und Kunst.* Ed. Siegfried Herrmann and Oskar Söhngen. Witten: Luther-Verlag, 1968.
Weaver, John. "Franz Daniel Pastorius (1651-c. 1720): Early Life in Germany with Glimpses of his Removal to Pennsylvania." Diss. Univ. of California, Davis, 1985.
Wentzcke, Paul. "Die alte Universität Straßburg, 1621-1793." In *Elsaß-lothringisches Jahrbuch,* 17 (1938), 37-112.

Wiedemann, Conrad. "Sigmund von Birken." In *Fränkische Klassiker: Eine Literaturgeschichte in Einzeldarstellungen.* Ed. Wolfgang Buhl. Nürnberg: Verlag Nürnberger Presse, 1971, pp. 325-36.

Will, Georg Andreas. *Geschichte und Beschreibung der nürnbergischen Universität Altdorf.* 2nd ed. 1801; rpt. Aalen: Scientia, 1975.

----------. *Nürnbergisches Gelehrten-Lexikon.* 4 vols. + 4 supplementary vols. Nürnberg, 1755-58, 1802-08. Photocopies of biographies provided by Bayerische Staatsbibliothek and Staats- und Stadtbibliothek Augsburg.

Wolf, Stephanie Grauman. *Urban Village: Population, Community and Family Structure in Germantown, Pennsylvania 1683-1800.* Princeton: Princeton Univ. Press, 1976.

Wright, Louis B. *The Cultural Life of the American Colonies, 1607-1763.* New York: Harper, 1957.

Wundt, Max. *Die deutsche Schulmetaphysik des 17. Jahrhunderts.* Tübingen: Mohr, 1939.

Zimmermann, Gerd. "Franken." In *Geschichte der deutschen Länder. Territorium-Ploetz.* Ed. Georg Wilhelm Sante. Würzburg: Ploetz, 1964, pp. 211-44.

Zolla, Elemire. *The Writer and the Shaman: A Morphology of the American Indian.* Trans. Raymond Rosenthal. New York: Harcourt, 1973.

Index: "Alphabetical Hive" topics cited

"Absurdity" 1
"Admonishing" 99
"Adversity" 178, 192
"Anger" 185, 196
"Articles of Faith" 61, 194
"Atheism" 157
"Banishment" 35
"Baptism" 32
"Bee" 134
"Bell" 67
"Boasting" 180
"Body" 81
"Book" 1
"Brave Woman" 123, 134-35
"Calling" 57, 140
"Certainty" 150
"Child" 49, 89
"Childhood" 47, 74
"Chiliasm" 206-07
"Christianity" 156
"Christ" 30
"Church" 61
"Comets" 202
"Common Goods" 234
"Communion" 207
"Company" 112, 207
"Complaint of Times" 42
"Conscience" 175
"Contentment" 236
"Cookery" 30
"Courting" 167
"Court" 121
"Custom" 1, 42
"Disobedience" 99
"Doctor" 9 (254n25), 73
"Doctrine" 68, 153
"Dog" 27
"Drinking of Healths" 51-52
"Eloquence" 140, 145, 170
"Fortune" 13
"Friendship" 102
"Germany" 37, 40, 166
"Government" 218
"Grammar" 78
"Grandeur" 54, 57, 67
"Gun" 166
"Heathenism" 240
"Home" 56, 227
"Hospitality" 64
"Hunger" 64
"Husbandry" 57, 220, 227
"Idleness" 220
"Inn & Innkeeper" 60, 112
"Instrument" 57
"Joy" 51, 211
"Kiss" 123
"Language" 35
"Latin" 77-78
"Laughter" 112, 128, 147

"Lawyer" 48, 161
"Law" 180, 211, 218
"Lay People" 140
"Learning" 70, 73, 114-15, 148
"Liberality" 64
"Liberty of Conscience" 156, 224
"Logic" 139
"Love of the World" 103
"Love of Woman" 128
"Magistrate" 179
"Memory" 78
"Modesty" 126
"Music" 119
"Native Country" 27, 34-35
"Neger or Negro" 242
"Obedience" 178
"OEconomy" 85
"Original Sin" 32, 71
"Original Tongues" 70
"Pardon" 71, 151
"Parents" 86, 185
"Parsimony" 7
"Patience" 99
"Peace" 64, 165
"Pedantry" 115, 148, 149, 151, 153
"Pennsilvania" 244
"Persecution" 40
"Persuasion" 140
"Piety" 153, 222
"Pilgrimage" 27
"The Privy Parts" 125
"Punishment" 71
"Rules" 165, 182
"Schoole" 69
"Self" 145
"Self-confident" 150
"Self-Knowledge" 196
"Self-Love" 145
"Self-Praise" 145
"Simulation" 73
"Singing" 61, 120
"Spider" 161
"Student" 109
"Theologia scholastica" 142, 170
"To Court or to Woo" 48
"Try all things" 163
"Universal Grace" 240
"Universalists" 151-52
"University" 109, 141, 163
"Variety" 128
"Victory" 67
"War" 202
"Wife" 125
"Woman" 124, 126, 134
"Womanish" 125
"Woman's Beating" 125
"Woman's Imperiousness" 125
"Woman's Wit" 125
"Youth" 68

Index

[Abbreviations: MAP: Melchior Adam Pastorius
FDP: Franz Daniel Pastorius]

Absolutism, Age of 41, 119, 145, 151, 196, 211
acculturation: of FDP 2, 36, 99, 231
Adam: and original sin 34, "Alphabetical Hive" entries on 32, 135; in FDP poetry and commentary 96, 135, 221;
Adam and Eve (fall of): depicted on Windsheim pulpit 62; in MAP poetry 24; in FDP poetry 125. *See also* Eve
Adams, James Truslow 7
Addison, Joseph 6. *See also Freeholder, The*
Aeneas *see* Virgil
African Americans *see* blacks
Angst, Age of 205
agriculture: in Thirty Years War 41, in Windsheim 57-58; in Pennsylvania 221, 228; FDP on 3, 58, 122, 222, 251n5, 295n71. *See also* husbandry
Agrippa, Heinrich Cornelius 6, 158, 279n39; cited by FDP 142
Ahlstrom, Sydney E. 7
Ainsworth, Henry: cited by FDP 153, 228
Alsace: FDP in 109, 115, 156; French annexation of 204
Altdorf *see* Nürnberg Univ.
Ambrose, Saint 144
Ames, William 122
Andreae, Johann Valentin 22, 81, 142, 158; cited by FDP 35, 142
Anne, Queen of Austria 20
Anne, Lady, of Britain 123
Anne, Queen of England 33
Anne Sophia of Denmark, Princess 43
Apelles: in FDP poem 5; in "Alphabetical Hive" entries 134
Apocalypse 204; apocalyptic views 5, 189, 204, 216. *See also* Armageddon; millennialism; retribution, divine
Aquinas, Thomas 6
aristocracy *see* nobility
Aristotelians, scholastic 141-144; FDP on 106-07; 143, 173; FDP's criticism of A.s mistranslated 31, 252n9
Aristotle 81, 82, 172; golden mean of 61, 81, 82-83
Armageddon 11, 205. *See also* Apocalypse, millennialism
Arndt, Johann 43, 106, 144, 158
artist(s) 43, 52, 252n8; of Jena 114; of Nürnberg 111, 120, 140; of Regensburg 167; of Strasbourg 113, 114; patronage of Louis XIV for 146; FDP poem on 118, 276n24. *See also* painters
artist, striptease: in FDP poem 129
Asseburg, Rosamunde Juliane von 214
assimilation *see* acculturation
Athenian Oracle: cited by FDP 110, 128, 145, 147; on Germans 37; on courting 48, 167; on music 119, 120; on kissing 123; on women 124, 134; on teachers 148

atheism: "Alphabetical Hive" entries on 157
Augsburg: view of A. with comets 204
Augustine, Saint 6, 144, 156, 261n3; cited by FDP 42, 106
authority, governmental: Windsheim citizens' resentment of 73; ambiguous attitudes toward 139; Windsheim rebellion against 179-81; excesses of MAP criticized by citizens 186; FDP opposing 84, 173, 181, 191-92
authority, paternal or parental 69, 85, 90, 93, 96, 97-98; FDP opposing 168-69, 172; ameliorated in Pennsylvania 247. *See also* fathers and sons
authoritarianism: of Prince Philipp Christoph 19; condoned by M. Luther 40, 71; in Windsheim schooling 75-77, 82-84; in university education 142-43, 154; of Lutheran clergy 103, 154, 195; Pietist resistance to 140-41, 155, 208-10, 211-12; FDP and 84, 98-100, 140-41, 172. *See also* childrearing, obedience
Avignon, FDP in 106
Babel 70, 154, 187, 190
Babylon (metaphorical) 188, 206, 207, 215; whores of (scholastics as) 142
Bacon, Francis 6, 143, 157-58, 219; cited by FDP 13, 68, 102, 114, 145
Baier, Johann Wilhelm 164
baptism, infant: and FDP 32-34. *See also* godfather
Barbados 227; B. journal criticized by FDP 158
Barclay, Robert 33, 43, 239; cited by FDP 32, 119, 165, 240; on illiterate Christians 139; on ecumenicalism 151; on conscience 175, on separatism 207
Basel, Switzerland: FDP in 109, 154, 156
Bayreuth: FDP in 169
Beaumont, John cited by FDP 67
"Beehive" *see under* Pastorius, Franz Daniel
bees: on FDP's farm 127, 130; "Alphabetical Hive" entries on 134; FDP poem on 136-137; FDP ms. on beekeeping 310
Beller, John cited by FDP 227
Bernegger, Mattheus 142
Birken, Sigmund von 120-122
blacks 2, 36, 242-44. *See also* Negro(s), slavery
Bodeck, Johann Bonaventura von 116, 201
Boeckler, Johann Heinrich 109, 147, 162-63
Boehme, Jakob 62; FDP and 6, 62, 158, 214
Boehm(e), Anton Wilhelm 33; cited by FDP 32, 61, 71, 202
Bohemia: 1680 peasant revolt 203
Bohemia Manor, Md.: FDP on 290n44
Boyle, Robert: FDP compiling from 158
Bradstreet, Anne 131, 290n44
Bridenbaugh, Carl 7-8
Brophy, Alfred L. 10, 255n31
Calixt, Georg 152
Calixtinianism 152, 164; *see also* ecumenicalism
Calvinism 109, 152, 156; in the Palatinate 200, 202; C. predestination 214; in Pennsylvania 222-23

326 | Index

Cambridge University: FDP on 106, 114
Cambridge Platonists 159, 219, 239
Catholicism, Roman: in Franconia 38; FDP and 85-86, 107-08, 156-57, 159; MAP and 13-16, 18-19, 85
Chapelain, Jean 145-46
Charles I, King 218
Charles II, King 218-19
Charles V, Emperor 106, 107-08
chauvinism, cultural (of Pietist missionaries) 238; FDP criticizing 238
chauvinism, male: in FDP writings 2, 126-27, 245. See also misogyny
childhood: of FDP 49-51, 54-55, 56-57, 58-59, 62-63, 68-69, 85-88; "Alphabetical Hive" entries on 47, 49, 74; FDP poetry on 50, 74, 88, 100
child-rearing: in Windsheim 72, 74-77; FDP emblems on 92-98; FDP school primer on 99; M. Luther on 71; among Delaware Indians (FDP reports) 235, 237; See also education, upbringing
chiliasm 31; "Alphabetical Hive" entries on 206-07. See also millennialism
Christian Ernst, Margrave 64, 181; MAP and 24, 122-23, 168-69
clergy, Lutheran: in Windsheim 73-74, 181, 183, 184, 198; opposing Pietists 140, 195, 199; arrogance and hypocrisy of 122, 195; MAP and 22, 25, 62; FDP and 33-34, 177; FDP criticism of 5, 59, 62, 141, 159, 195-96, 223. See also disputatiousness, Lutheranism
Columbus, Christopher 217, 218
comedies: at Windsheim Gymnasium 82; in Nürnberg 120-21. See also theater
Comenius, Johannes Amos 82; books of C. owned by FDP 272n70
comets: portentousness of 84, 194, 202, 204, 206
communion: "Alphabetical Hive" entries on 207
Communion, Holy: MAP abstaining from 19; MAP participating in 23; as Franconian ritual 35; in Windsheim schooling 75; Pietist refusing C. as heresy 209; "Alphabetical Hive" entries on 207
Conring, Hermann 163, 165
conscience: atheists on 157; Lutheran clergy ignoring 159, 195; J. A. Lietzheimer and 155; MAP and 19, 21, 24; FDP on 33, 84, 159, 175, 224; "Alphabetical Hive" entries on 71, 125, 148, 175, 224
conscience, freedom of: "Alphabetical Hive" entries on 156, 224; FDP on 225
Copernicus, Nicolaus 112
Corpus juris civilis see Justinian legal code
court(s) (of monarch or nobleman): FDP on 106, 122-23; MAP and 15-16, 17, 23, 89, 169; of Leopold I in Windsheim 65; "Alphabetical Hive" entries on 121; of Native Americans (FDP report) 240
court patronage: of Louis XIV 146
courtly delights: of FDP 107, 119, 120
courtly satire: in FDP prose and poetry 121, 123
Court, Imperial High (in Speyer) 201; FDP commentary on 201-02

court(s), legal: in Sommerhausen 55; in Windsheim 72, 74; criticism of (by Pietist J. H. Horb) 198-99; in Pennsylvania 225
courtship: "Alphabetical Hive" citations on 48, 167; of MAP 89, 168, 169
Cowley, Abraham 116, 295n71
crafts, the: FDP practicing 2, FDP commentary on 173
craftsmen: in Windsheim 57, 58, 60, 65, 67, 69; in Pennsylvania 222, 225, 226, 227; in Germantown 228, 229; "Alphabetical Hive" entries on 57, 140; FDP poetry on 59, 70; FDP's sons as 9, 80, 100, 246-47
Creech, Thomas: cited by FDP 37
Cremin, Lawrence A. 7
crime and punishment: in Windsheim (MAP on) 73; among Delaware Indians (FDP on) 234, 240-41
cuckoldry: FDP on 127, 129
Culpeper, Nicholas 99; cited by FDP 1, 81, 99, 163; on love of country 27, 35, 56; on friendship 102, on learning 114; on orators 170; on the law 180; on idleness 220
cultural contrasts: in life of FDP 8-9, 245-47
cultural attainment: of FDP 7, 108, 115-18
cultural imperialism see chauvinism, cultural
culture, costs of 117, 118-19; in Windsheim 62, 64-65, 185
damnation: FDP and 107, 124, 176; J. A. Lietzheimer and 154; MAP on 21; Merlau and Petersen on 214; FDP on 237, 239
dancing: in Sommerhausen 53; in Windsheim 60, 61, 181; at universities 109, 111; Nürnberg performances 120; on FDP's grand tour 116, 207; of Delaware Indians (FDP report) 235; FDP on 106, 121
Dannhauer, Johann Conrad 153, 154
de Montesquieu, Charles-Louis 226
de Walle, Jakob van 208
Deal, England: FDP in 29, 188
death(s): in Thirty Years' War 41; in Sommerhausen 54; of Windsheim soldiers 66; of J. A. Lietzheimer 155; MAP and 19, 21-22, 24; FDP and 50, 51, 87, 168; FDP on 5, 29, 30, 84, 87, 160, 166, 192, 216, 239
Defoe, Daniel 4, 116; cited by FDP 198
de Labadie, Jean, see Labadie, Jean de
Delaware tribe(s) 148, 162, 231, 232-38, 240-42, 293n60. See also Native Americans
Dell, William: cited by FDP 141
Deloney, Thomas (Jack of Newberie): cited by FDP 128
Denham, Sir John 4, 116, 276n24; cited by FDP 151, 166, 218
Descartes, Rene 143
Devastation, Palatine see Palatine Devastation
devil, the see Satan
Dienst, Burgomaster Georg Andreas 181, 192
Diet, Imperial see Reichstag
Dilfeld, Georg Konrad 195
Dilherr, Johann Michael 82, 121, 152, 153, 272n71

Diogenes: cited in "Beehive" 1, 56, 119
disobedience: of Pastorius family servant (betrayal) 15; inherent d. of children (M. Luther) 71; of J. G. Rosenbach 140; in Windsheim insurrection 179-84, 186; of FDP 168-69; to God (FDP's psychology) 176; "Alphabetical Hive" entries on 99, 185; FDP on 85, 98,
disputation(s): of scholastic professors 142, 143, 144; at Nürnberg Univ. 111, 149-50, 151-153, 165, 170-71; by FDP 116, 170, 171-72
disputatiousness: among Windsheim clergy 74, 192-93; of Lutheran clergy 152-53, 209, 213; of MAP 25, 101, 186; of Nürnberg professors 140, 151-53, 170-71; of lawyers 224; FDP on 151, 171, 224; FDP satirizing 148
Dives and Lazarus 118, 155, 181; cited by FDP 115, 117, 118, 239, 276n24
divorce: marriage and (in FDP's poetry) 127
doctorate, the: its rank equaling that of the nobility 173; FDP completing 171-72; FDP refusing to attend graduation ceremonies 173
drinking, festive: in Sommerhausen 52, 53-54; in Windsheim 60; at Nürnberg Univ. graduation 173; MAP and 17, 49; FDP and 30; FDP on 44, 172, 262n5; "Alphabetical Hive" entries on 51-52
drinking, excessive: in Sommerhausen 54; Windsheim senate opposing 61, 194; Nürnberg senate opposing 61; among university students 114; among German statesmen 167; among aristocrats 212; and Native Americans 237; FDP on 114, 143, 237;
Dryden, John 275n19
Dürer, Albrecht 120
Dürr, Johann Conrad 112, 113, 144, 171
Dutch, the *see* Netherlands, the
Dutch War (of Louis XIV) 111, 203
"E. M.": cited by FDP 70
Eckard, Michael 193
ecumenicalism 152; of FDP 157, 159, 239. *See also* Calixtinianism, universalism
education: Luther's approach to 70-71; in Windsheim (of FDP) 69-70, 71-72, 75-77, 78-79, 81-82, 84; in Pennsylvania 9, 99-101; "Alphabetical Hive" entries on 69, 78; FDP on 84, 147-48, 278n39, 280n57; FDP's poetry on 69, 78. *See also* child-rearing, emblems, upbringing
education, university *see* Aristotelians, scholastic; learned, the; Nürnberg University
Ellis, Rowland: FDP letter to 244
emblems 47, 79, 83, 176, 187, 229; defined by FDP 118; depicting childhood and upbringing 92-98
emblematic verse: of Nürnberg poets 121
"Emblematical Merriments" (in FDP's garden) 79
empire *see* imperialism, Hapsburg Empire
engineering: FDP on 143; half-brother Augustin Adam learning 296n74
England: political influences of 219, 225-26; FDP in 28-29, 106, 116
English (language): FDP and 3-4, 6, 35, 80-81
Enlightenment, the 9, 185; Pietism and 43, 214; FDP and 2, 6, 8, 201, 215, 250, 282-83n76

Epicurus 110; atomism of 157
Erasmus, Desiderius (of Rotterdam) 71, 158
Erben, Patrick M. 10
Erfurt: MAP and 14-16, FDP in 86, 109
Ernst the Pious, Duke 162
eschatology *see* millennialism
esthetic awareness: sacrificed by Reichstag artists 167; of Deleware tribes (FDP report) 237; of MAP 17, 62; of FDP 63, 118, 119, 123, 243
eternity: FDP references to 29, 106, 160, 187, 189, 190, 209
Etherege, Sir George 167
ethnocentrism *see* chauvinism, cultural
Eucharist, the *see* Communion, Holy
Eve: in FDP commentary and poetry 125, 135. *See also* Adam and Eve
exile(s): in FDP's writing 34-35
expatriate: FDP as 36-37
Eyseneck, Maria Juliana Baur von 208, 209, 212
family, nuclear: of FDP 85
family, extended: of FDP 85-86
Fantel, Hans 7
fashion (changes in): at universities 113; in "Alphabetical Hive" entries 42, 61; FDP on 116, 129, 248
father and son relationship: of FDP and MAP 13-14, 28, 31, 85-86, 101-02, 168-69, 172, 188-91; FDP on 89-92
Felwinger, Johann Paul 144, 146, 171
females: preeminence over males 126, 278n39; FDP on youthful encounters with 116; in FDP poems 128-33; FDP on Native American f. 235; FDP treatise on f. preeminence over males 135. *See also* gender, misogyny
fencing: at universities 109, 111; FDP and 116; FDP criticizes 106
Fenda, Christian 209-10
Ferdinand III, Emperor 65, 163; MAP and 16
Ferdinand IV, Emperor 49
Fetzer, Magnus 138, 171
Fleming, Paul 116
flirtation: in FDP's poetry 123, 128-33. *See also* sensuality
flower(s): FDP poetry on 98, 128-34, 136-37, 222, 236. *See also* garden(s)
Ford, John 275n19
Fox, George 43; cited by FDP 61, 139, 179, 180
France: weakening German nation 41; as 'protector' of the Rhineland 65; tensions with F. at Strasbourg 109; Hapsburg Empire (1674) declares war on 166-67: aggressive expansionism of (1679-84) 200, 203; FDP in 106, 109, 115, 156; MAP in 20-22. *See also* Louis XIV
Francis, Saint MAP and 18
Francke, August Hermann 155, 194, 265n28, 283 n80, 294n62; cited by FDP 151-52
Franconia 37-39, 47; in Thirty Years' War 41. *See also* Sommerhausen, Windsheim
Frankfurt am Main 201; Pietists of 34, 43-44, 207-09, 228; FDP in 27-28, 200-01, 207-10

Frankfurt Land Company *see* German Company
Franklin, Benjamin 7, 9
Franz, Graf von Limpurg 48, 49-50, 55
Freeholder, The (journal) 116; cited by FDP 218; *see also* Addison, Joseph
Freiburg (ceded to France) 203
Friedrich IV, Elector 202
Friedrich IV, King of Denmark 294n62
Friedrich Wilhelm, Elector 65, 166
Friedrichsburg citadel 202, 203
Friends, Society of *see* Quakers
friendship: FDP and 63, 102-03, 108, 199-200, 227; T. Schumberg on 83; "Alphabetical Hive" entries on 27, 60, 102, 234; FDP on 4, 168, 187, 244; MAP on 25
French: FDP and106, 109, 115, 116
Galileo (Galilei, Galileo) 112, 142
garden(s): Nürnberg Univ. botanical 111; in Germantown 228; FDP planting tree in MAP's g. 190; FDP's emblematical mottoes in his 79; FDP poetry on 4, 8, 98, 100, 128-29, 131-32, 164, 216-17, 222, 229-30. *See also* flowers
Geiger, Johann Anton 171, 173
Gelchsheimer, Johann (step-grandfather) 51, 56, 74, 86, 87
gender: in mystic theology (feminist perspective) 211-12; 294n64
gender bias: in "Alphabetical Hive" entries 125-26; in FDP treatise on female superiority 135. *See also* misogyny
gender identity *see* homosexuality
Genesis, The History of cited by FDP 27, 35, 185
Geneva: MAP in 22; FDP in 106
Georg Friedrich, Graf 23, 48, 55, 265n1
Gerhard, Johann 141-42
German Company, the 2, 29, 208, 209, 210, 215, 219, 226, 227, 228
Germans: as immigrants to Pa. 9, 227; at European courts (FDP on) 106; lacking knowledge of Quakerism (FDP on) 159; apocalyptic mood of many in 1680s 204; reacting to Palatine Devastation 205-06; as hardy farmers in Pennsylvania 222;
Germantown 1-2; lack of protective walls 59; similarities with Windsheim 59; church built in 62; FDP's fictive tour of G. with boyhood friend 147-48; FDP reports on 221, 228-30; citizens protesting black slavery 242-43
Germany: in Reformation era 40-42; Pietists in 42-44; Luther seeking cultural rebirth of 70-71; baroque culture in 116; FDP leaving 27-29, 44-45; FDP considers returning to 35-36, 249; FDP unable to live morally in 107; FDP predicting divine punishment and calamity in 188; tension and warfare in G. as FDP emigrates 203; described by W. Penn as 'desolate' 208; improved by Pietists (J. G. Herder) 214; "Alphabetical Hive" entries on 37, 40, 166; *See also* Franconia, Hapsburg Empire
Ghent: FDP in 106, 107, 159
Glanvill, Joseph: FDP on G.'s witchcraft reports 158
Glorious Revolution (of 1688) 201, 219, 225

godfather: FDP as 33, 109, 181, 184, 262n10
God's punishment *see* retribution, divine
Goethe, Johann Wolfgang von 43, 214
golden mean *see* Aristotle
Golden Rule 43; FDP and 182, 187, 189, 242, 249 *see also* love, neighborly
Gomorrah: Germany as (FDP commentary) 189
Gotha: FDP in 109, 162
Grafton, Anthony 7, 10
grammar 79; importance of 78; FDP on 70; his grammar books 116
grand tour: German custom of 115; of FDP 27, 80, 107, 116, 201, 207; FDP's journal of his 115; FDP on 29, 106
Greiffenberg, Catharina von 122
Groß, Johann Philipp 184, 192, 193
Grotius, Hugo 43, 163, 164
guilds *see* crafts, the
guilt *see* conscience
Günderode, Juncker 201
Gymnasium *see* education
Hall, Joseph 122
Hamburg: orthodox v. Pietist Lutherans in 193, 199
Hapsburg Empire 38-39, 65; following the Reformation 40-42; in 1660s in Windsheim 64-67; conflict with France 65, 109, 166-67, 200, 205; conflict with Turkey 200, 203, 205; legal system 161; MAP in 14-17, 20-23. *See also* court(s), Charles V, Christian Ernst, Johann Philipp von Schönborn, Philipp Christoph von Sötern, Reichstag
Harsdörffer, Georg Philipp 111, 121, 122
Hartmann, Johann Ludwig 192, 193, 196
Haßler, Hans Leo 120
Heidelberg 202, 203, 206
hell: Merlau and Petersen diminishing Lutheran emphasis on 214; "Alphabetical Hive" entries on 124, 126, 157, 166, 194, 202, 240; FDP references to 137, 160, 206, 216, 243
Hepburn, John: cited by FDP 240
Hercules 95, 217
Herder, Johann Gottfried 43, 214
Heywood, Oliver: cited by FDP 220
Hill, Elizabeth 278n39
Hill, John Jr. cited by FDP 67, 68
Hill, Richard 80, 296n75
Hindus, Tamil *see* Malabar "heathens"
Hirten- und Blumen-Orden an der Pegnitz, Löblicher *see* Pegnitz Shepherds
Hobbes, Thomas 157, 164, 219
Hohberg, Wolfgang Helmhard von 122
Holland *see* Netherlands, the
Holy Roman Empire *see* Hapsburg Empire
homosexuality: in Windsheim 72, 73, 193, 197; FDP on 73. *See also* sodomy
Horb, Johann Heinrich: at Strasbourg 153; and J. A. Lietzheimer 154-55; in Windsheim 192-99, 286n13; and FDP 192, 199-200, 206
Hungary: war with Turkey in 64, 66; and Hapsburg Empire 200, 203, 205
husband and wife *see* marital relationship

husbandry: "Alphabetical Hive" entries on 57, 114, 220, 227
husbands: "Alphabetical Hive" entries on 125; FDP on 59, 126, 127, 129, 133-34, 135, 172
imperialism: FDP on187, 188, 200, 206, 207
India: Pietist missionaries in (FDP on) 238
Innocent X, Pope 18
Innocent XI, Pope 203
Inquisition 18-19, 142
intellectuals *see* learned, the
Italy: MAP in 17, 19
Italian (language): MAP and 17, 90; FDP and 106, 109, 115-16
Jakobi, Daniel Caspar 193, 197
Jena University 164; depiction of student dissipation at 114; FDP at 109, 115-16, 154, 161
Jews: in Windsheim 185; in Frankfurt 201; FDP on 148, 156, 294n64
Johns, Johann Ludwig (half-brother) 49, 51, 54
Johns, Margareta (half-sister) 49, 51, 54
Johann Philipp von Schönborn, Prince-Bishop: Rhineland Alliance of 65; and MAP 16, 22-23, 48; and J. H. Boeckler 163; Regensburg procession depicted 167
Julian the Apostate (Anon.), cited by FDP 77-78
Justinian I, Emperor 161, 285n92
Justinian legal code 161, 171
Karl Ludwig, Elector 201, 202-03
Keget, Burgomaster Augustin 193, 194, 197
Keith, George 33, 239; FDP and 294n64; cited by FDP 32, 81, 240
Khotyn, Battle of iv, 167
Kimball, Gertrude S. 31, 252n9
Klaj, Johann 121, 122
Köppen, Ernst 31
Krefeld: FDP in 31
Krefeld immigrants 1, 28, 31, 44, 201, 227, 228-29
Kriegsheim, FDP in 201
Labadie, Jean de 43, 108, 209, 210, 290n44
labor, manual: of Sommerhausen villagers 52; FDP engaging in 246; the need for l. in Pennsylvania (FDP on) 221-22, 226, 243; FDP poetry on 51, 78, 136, 219; "Alphabetical Hive" entries on 57, 220, 227, 244
Lambert, Margo M. 10, 282n76
languages: FDP and 115-16;
Latin (as element of classical learnedness): FDP and 79-81
law, the: "Alphabetical Hive" entries on 180, 211, 218; FDP on 202; FDP poem on perversion of 162; J. H. Horb on 'sins' against 198-99; J. J. Schütz criticism of 209; Pa. Quaker reform of 10, 225; FDP in Pa. and 10, 177, 182, 225-26
law career: of MAP 23, 24, 48; of FDP 176-77, 200-02
law study: of FDP 161-63, 171
lawyer(s) "Alphabetical Hive" entries on 48, 161, 177, 199; FDP on 194, 224; FDP poem criticizing 177; FDP response to letter from l. godson 33
Lazarus and Dives *see* Dives and Lazarus

Lead, Jane Ward 6, 214, 239, 294n64
learned, the: arrogance of 78, 107, 122, 173, 195; camaraderie of 36, 79-80, 111; compulsions of 42, 73, 99, 101, 118, 151; idealism of 92, 111, 119; insecurities of 101, 151; misogyny of 125; perceived superiority of 9, 41, 57-58, 76; pursuing courtly favor 122, 146, 163, 169; taboo on insurrection 186-87, 191; FDP as prime example of 108, 115-17, 245-46; "Alphabetical Hive" entries on 9, 114-15; FDP on 106-107, 173; FDP poetry on 58, 84, 115, 149; FDP satirizing 148. *See also* disputatiousness; doctorate, the
Learned, Marion Dexter 7, 10, 31
Lechner, Leonhard 120
Leeds, Daniel 6, 126; cited by FDP: on lawyers 48, 161; on women 124, 126; on chiliasm 207; on Pennsylvania 244
legal system *see* law, the
Leibniz, Gottfried Wilhelm von 43, 111, 112, 163
Lenni Lenapi *see* Delaware tribe(s)
Leopold I, Emperor 65, 66, 68, 166; and J. C. Wagenseil, 146, 280n58; and Windsheim insurrection 179, 180, 181, 184; and the Palatinate 203, 205
Lersner, Junker 201
Lersner, Maximillian von 208
Lessing, Gotthold Ephraim 214
Levellers 219
Lietzheimer, Johann Augustin 153-155, 198; FDP and 154, 155, 156, 241-42
light (Christ's, divine, God's, inner): FDP and 1, 108, 160, 207, 215, 239; "Alphabetical Hive" commentary on 156, 207, 240; FDP on 88, 107, 159, 187, 190, 238, 249; W. Penn on 208; J. W. Petersen on 215
Linck, Heinrich 165; FDP and 109, 110, 116, 161-62, 170, 171
Lipsius, Justice 43
Liselotte, Palatine Princess 203, 205-06
literacy: FDP on 80-81
literature: FDP and 116, 121-22
Locke, John 6; FDP on 158; cited by FDP 115, 142, 163
Logan, James 80, 133, 249; FDP's poems to 182, 187, 249
Logau, Friedrich von 111, 113
logic: taught in Windsheim 74, 82; at Nürnberg Univ. 111; of misogynists 125; in FDP's teaching 278n39; cited by FDP 139; in FDP poem 182; "Alphabetical Hive" entries on 139. *See also* Aristotelians, scholastic
London: FDP in 28-29
Long, Johann Michael 140
Louis XIV 41, 116, 263; and Franconia 65; Dutch War of 109; and C. K. Wölcker 138; and J.C. Wagenseil 146; "donee's list" of 146, 163; "subsidies" paid by 41, 203; sexual exploits criticized by FDP 42, 124, 294n65; "reunions" of 1679-84 203; and Palatine Devastation 205-06
Lloyd, Thomas 50, 80, 294n64; FDP's poems to daughters of 36-37, 50, 88, 248-49, 294n64

love, neighborly 209; FDP and 107, 118, 181, 187. See also Golden Rule

Ludolf, Henry William: cited by FDP 165

Luther, Martin 40; "two kingdoms" of 40; on education and child-rearing 70-71; cited by FDP 141

Lutheranism: baptism in 33-34; MAP and 14, 22, 23, 24; Reformation 40; Windsheim altar depicting L. tenets 62; in Windsheim schooling 69, 72, 75-76, 79; and scholastic Aristotelianism 141-42; FDP and 63, 86, 88, 158, 160; FDP criticism of 62. See also clergy, Lutheran; Pietism, Lutheran

Lyon: FDP in 108; MAP in 22

L'Estrange, Sir Roger: FDP and 80, 116; cited by FDP 35, 202; see also Seneca

Maintenon, Marquise de (Françoise d'Aubigné,) 42, 127, 264n23

Malabar "heathens" 159, 238, 293n62

Mamut the Arabian 125; cited by FDP 134, 202, 234; on Germany 40, 166; on husbandry 227; on music 119; on women 124, 126, 128, 134, 167; see also Marana, G. P.

Mannheim 202-03; and FDP 201, 206; and the Palatine Devastation 205-06

Marana, Giovanni Paolo 80, 125 see also *Mamut the Arabian*

Marienberg Castle see Würzberg

Marinella, Lucrezia 126

marital relationship: in FDP's poetry 126-28, 133-34. See also newlyweds

marriage: FDP postponing 175; of FDP 189, 277 n34; in Deleware tribes 235. See also divorce, marital relationship

Marseille: FDP in 106

Mather, Cotton 7, 158, 251n5; *The Negro Christianized* cited by FDP 242

Meade, Joseph: cited by FDP 240

medical writings: of FDP 3, 111, 158, 251n5

Medley, The (journal) 116; cited by FDP 163

Melanchthon, Philipp 71, 78, 110, 141, 144

Mennonites 1, 28, 223

Mercklein, Franz Jacob (godson) 33, 63, 103, 109

Mercklein, Johann Caspar 262n10

Mercklein, Johannes Joachim 103, 196; and FDP 153, 154, 184

Merlau, Johanna Eleonora von 208, 209, 211-215; and FDP 208, 211, 215

Meserole, Harrison T. 8

metaphysics, Aristotelian 144; FDP on 143. See also Aristotelians, scholastic

millennialism 188, 204; of Pietists 43, 209, 213-14; of FDP 5, 31, 204, 206-07, 215. See also Apocalypse, chiliasm,

misogyny 125-126. See also gender bias; chauvinism, male

missionaries, Pietist see chauvinism, cultural

Model, Georg Leonhart 103; FDP letter to 147-48, 216, 229, 234-35, 280n56

Model, Johannes 74

Molière, Jean Baptiste: performed in Nürnberg 120; in Mannheim 203

Molinos, Miguel de: FDP on 158

music: in Nürnberg 120; at Nürnberg Univ. 111; in Sommerhausen 52, 53, 54; in Windsheim 60, 61, 62; in Windsheim schooling 63, 75, 76, 79; in Würzburg 39; "Alphabetical Hive" entries on 57, 61, 119, 120

music, religious: in Windsheim 62, 63; influencing FDP's prose and poetry 63;

musicians: MAP entertaining 17-18; of Windsheim (doubling as sentinels) 63

Muslims see Turks [i.e. Muslims]

Nagel, Bartholomeus: MAP and 20-21, 22

Nash, Thomas 275n19

Native American(s) 107, 108, 148, 155, 196, 222-23, 231-37, 240-42. See also Delaware tribe(s)

Negro(s) 242-244, 294n64. See also blacks, slavery

neoclassicism: in Philadelphia culture 123; of FDP 11, 137, 250

nepotism: among Frankfurt patricians 201; in Windsheim senate 178, 180, 185

Netherlands, the 166, 167; and FDP 106, 108, 201; in MAP poem 168

Netherlands, the Spanish 107-08, 146, 167

Neubert, Georg Erhard 192, 193

New Academy of Complements: cited by FDP 109, 120

newlyweds: in FDP poem 129

Newton, Isaac 143

nobility, the 38, 110, 113, 173; and FDP 8, 49-50, 81, 106, 113, 177, 201; and MAP 14, 16, 19, 23; and S. von Birken 122; in FDP's poems 162, 166; in MAP's poetry 24; J. E. von Merlau on 212

nonconformity: in Germany 40; FDP and 32, 141, 157; "Alphabetical Hive" entry on 40

Norton, Lydia 158

Nuremberg see Nürnberg

Nürnberg 38, 39; summer solstice celebration 61; Lutheran education in 71; Pietist reform in 82; influence on Windsheim 56, 58, 61; MAP in 89; as cultural center influencing FDP 108, 120-22; FDP in 138; FDP's ambiguous attitudes toward 139, 141

Nürnberg poets see Pegnitz Shepherds

Nürnberg University 110-12; professors at 142-44, 146, 149-53; FDP at 109, 142-44, 170-72;

obedience: of Sommerhausen citizens to lord 55; of Windsheim citizens to emperor 65-66; demanded of children (M. Luther) 71; demanded of pupils (Windsheim) 72, 83-84; "Alphabetical Hive" entries on 86, 89, 178, 185; FDP on 99, 100, 159, 190, 210. See also disobedience

obedience, filial: symbols of 92-93, 95-98; FDP and 99; FDP on 98; FDP expressing 89, 90-91, 191

Obrecht, Georg 109

opera: in Nürnberg 120, 121; FDP on 275n19; in "Alphabetical Hive" citation 120

Opitz, Martin 116; FDP on 116

original sin 34; "Alphabetical Hive" entries on

Index | 331

32-33, 71; Luther and 71. *See also* baptism, Adam
Orleans: FDP in 106; J. C. Wagenseil at 146
Ovid 6; *Metamorphoses* 79; cited by FDP 216
Owen, Griffith 80
Pachelbel, Johann 120, 276n26
painter(s): of Nürnberg 120; FDP on 135; FDP poetry on 5, 118, 276n24
painting(s): of student dissipation 114; of Regensburg procession 167; FDP observations of 115, 117
Palatinate 40, 201, 202-03; FDP in 1, 11, 201-202
Palatine Devastation 5, 11, 205; FDP on 206
Palmieri, Brooke 10
panderer, courtly: FDP poem satirizing 123
Paracelcus, Theophrastus 6
Paris 146; FDP in 80, 106; MAP in 21, 22
Pastorius, Anna Katharina (half-sister) 190
Pastorius, Anne (Ennecke neé Klostermanns) (wife) 33, 127, 133, 134, 189, 191, 245, 277 n34
Pastorius, Augustin Adam (half-brother) 102, 173, 176, 190, 240, 275n15, 296n73
Pastorius, Barbara Greulich (step-mother) 87-88, 109
Pastorius, Brigitta (grandmother) 14, 15, 16
Pastorius, Caspar (uncle) 86
Pastorius, Dorothea Esther neé Volckmann (stepmother) 25, 89, 91, 168, 169, 170, 190
Pastorius, Eva Margareta neé Gelchsheimer (step-mother) 51, 56, 86-87, 89
Pastorius, Franz Daniel: general description 1-7, 8-10, 244-48. *See also* "FDP" entries throughout this index
"Alphabetical Hive": described 5-6, 33, 35, 261n4. *See also* topics index on page 324
"Beehive" ms. 5-6, 8; research on 10; FDP translations in 81; FDP at his ms. 245
Beschreibung Pennsylvaniae 5, 14, 33-34, 63, 80, 91, 106-07, 159, 189-91, 215-33, 236-38, 240-42, 248
"Emblematical Recreations" 92-98, 115, 117-18, 138, 139, 218, 231, 273n81
"Genealogia Pastoriana" (autobiographical citations) 14, 15, 49, 50, 81, 85-87, 90, 112, 116, 138, 156-57, 170, 177, 192, 201, 207, 208, 228, 247, 297-98
"Some Onomastical Considerations" 73, 79, 80, 210, 252n10, 263n13, 275n19
"Symbola Onomastica": described 92; cited 37, 40, 98, 116, 118, 121, 124, 126, 145, 166, 171, 194, 211, 225, 248
Umständige Geographische Beschreibung . . . Pen[n]sylvaniae see *Beschreibung Pennsylvaniae*
Pastorius, Heinrich (Henry) (son) 14, 33, 36, 80, 91, 245, 247
Pastorius, Johann Augustin (uncle) 16, 85-86
Pastorius, Johann(es) Samuel (half-brother) 24, 92, 172, 173, 190, 256, 275n15
Pastorius, Johann (John) Samuel (son) 14, 33, 36, 80, 82, 91, 127, 130, 245, 246, 247, 252n10,

Pastorius, Magdalena neé Frischmann (mother) 48, 49, 50, 51
Pastorius, Margareta Barbara (half-sister) 190
Pastorius, Martin (grandfather) 14-15
Pastorius, Melchior Adam (father): early life and travels 13-18, 19-21; on Catholicism 18-19; in Paris 21-22; Protestant conversion 22-23; legal and political career 23-24; scholarship and poetry of 23, 24-25; political setback and desire to emigrate 25; his four marriages 48, 51, 87-89, 168-69; early career in Sommerhausen 48-49, 55-56; move to Windsheim 51, 56; his history of Windsheim cited 41, 62-67 *passim*, 69, 73, 169, 178; and Windsheim education 69, 76, 82; described by FDP 90; traits as a father 101-02; financing FDP at university 117, 169; and Margrave Christian Ernst 122, 168-69; conduct during Windsheim insurrection (1677-79) 185-86; tensions in relationship with FDP 168-69, 189-90
Pastorius, Rebecca (aunt) 86
patricians, Frankfurt 201
Peacham, Henry 116; cited by FDP 134
peasants: Bohemian uprising of 203; in Windsheim 57-58; "Alphabetical Hive" entries on 57; FDP poetry on 58
Peasants' Revolt of 1525 40, 176, 187
Pegnitz Shepherds 121, 122
Pella (Palestine) 215, 228
Pemberton, Israel 100
Penn, William: and FDP 1, 2, 32, 79, 80, 190, 227, 231-32, 252n10, 263n13; and MAP 190, 287 n17; founding Pennsylvania 27, 218-19, 220, 221, 225, 229, 265 n26, 290n42; on education 9; on German colonists 227; touring Germany 43, 208; Native American policies of 232-33; cited by FDP 30, 40, 51, 71, 109, 224; *Address to Protestants* cited by FDP 156, 163; *Some Fruits of Solitude* cited by FDP 1, 30, 64, 81, 85, 86, 89, 102, 163, 164, 165, 185
Penn, Sir William (father of W.P.) 218-19
Pennington, Isaac: cited by FDP 240
Pennsylvania: FDP reports on 216. *See also Beschreibung Pennsylvaniae* under Pastorius, F. D.
Pennypacker, Samuel 10, 255n29
persecution, religious 44; "Alphabetical Hive" entries on 40, 143, 211; FDP on 140-41, 195; J. E. v. Merlau on 208
Petersen, Johann Wilhelm 211, 213-15, 239
Petry, W.: cited by FDP 114
Philadelphia: FDP and 1-3, 80, 100, 123, 137, 228; in FDP poetry 129, 232; in FDP reports 219, 226, 230
Philadelphia Friends' School: FDP at 99, 100
Philip IV, King of Spain 65
Philipp Christoph von Sötern, Prince-Bishop 16, 19, 24
Phillips, Edward: cited by FDP 42, 123, 126, 277 n37
Pietism, Lutheran 43-44; in Frankfurt 27-28, 44, 207-09; at Strasbourg University 153-54; J. V.

Andreae and 22; J. W. Baier and 164; J. M. Dilherr and 82; A. H. Francke and 155; J. H. Horb and 192-95, 198-99; J. A. Lietzheimer and 154-55; J. E. v. Merlau and 211, 213-14; J. W. Petersen and 213-14; P. J. Spener and 43-44; J. G. Rosenbach and 140-41. *See also* millennialism, Saalhof Pietists
Piggott, John: cited by FDP 61
pipe, smoking *see* tobacco, smoking
Plato 158; cited by FDP 227
Platonists *see* Cambridge Platonists
Poland 203
Polish-Ottoman War *see* Khotyn, Battle of
poverty: in Windsheim 64-65, 177, 178; M. Luther on 70; contrasted with university cost 117; warfare increasing 67, 169; peasants living in 176; FDP on 67, 236
predestination, Calvinist 214
Preston, Samuel 80, 296n75
Pride: "Alphabetical Hive" entries on 112, 142, 166, 244; FDP poetry on 4, 67, 130, 145, 149, 211, 225
printing: at Nürnberg Univ. 111; in Pennsylvania 251n5; FDP and 2, 3; FDP on 143
Protestantism *see* Lutheranism
Prussia 167
Pufendorf, Samuel 164; cited by FDP 142
punishment: of children 71-72, 94; of Windsheim pupils 72, 76, 77; of Altdorf students 113; "Alphabetical Hive" entries on 71; FDP on 99. *See also* crime and punishment
punishment, divine *see* retribution, divine
Quakerism: perceived as radical in Germany 158-59, 215, 291n48; preaching tours in Germany 43, 208; German Pietist interest in 208, 215; FDP and 84, 100, 108, 135, 158-59, 159-160, 239-40, 242-43; FDP on 159; in FDP's poetry 231; in FDP's Pennsylvania reports 218, 220, 223
Quarles, Francis 4, 116, 229; cited by FDP 112, 125, 198
Quevedo, Francisco de: cited by FDP 161, 198
Quietism 43, 195, 208, 209. *See also* Labadie, Jean
Ratke, Wolfgang 82
Rawlet, John (*Christian Monitor*): cited by FDP 222
Reformation *see* Luther, Lutheranism
Regensburg: FDP in 138-39, 165, 166-67, 169
Reichstag (Imperial Diet) 66, 110, 166-67, 203
Reinhart, Lucas Friedrich 111-12, 151-53
retribution, divine 176, 204; FDP on 36, 187-89, 204, 206, 207. *See also* comets
Reynell, Carew: cited by FDP 70
Rhein, Johann Adolf 193, 197
Rhineland Alliance (1654) 65
Riley, Lyman W. 10
Roman Catholicism *see* Catholicism, Roman
Rome: MAP in 16-17, 18-19
Rosenbach, Johann Georg 140-41; FDP on 140-41
Rotterdam: FDP in 28
Rötenbeck, Georg Paul 140
Saalhof Pietists 44, 200, 204, 207-212, 228

Saavedra, Don Diego: cited by FDP 47, 163, 218; FDP poem inspired by 187
Sachs, Hans 116
Salmon, William: cited by FDP 13
saltpeter gatherers 181, 285n6a
Sandrat, Joachim von 120
Sappho of Lesbos: cited by FDP 131
Satan (also: the devil): M. Luther and 70; Windsheim pupil and 72; G. L. Model and 103; M. Luther on 70; Merlau and Petersen on 214; "Alphabetical Hive" entries on 211, 220; FDP on 33, 106, 160, 171, 175, 239, 243, 290n41; scholastic critics on 142
Schirmer, Christian Wilhelm 187, 286n12
Schmidt, Michael 181
scholastics *see* Aristotelians, scholastic
Schönborn, Johann Philipp von *see* Johann Philipp von Schönborn
Schumberg, Tobias 76-77, 81-84, 85, 192, 193, 272n71; FDP on 81, 84
Schütz, Johann Jakob 209, 210, 211, 212, 213, 224; FDP and 209-10, 224
Schwäger, Johann Leonhard 149-50
Schweitzer, Christoph E. 8, 263n13
Scotus, Duns ("Doctor Subtlety") 142, 144
Seckendorf, Veit Ludwig von 43, 82, 162
Seidensticker, Oswald 7, 10
Seneca, Lucius 15, 80, 241; cited by FDP 34, 42, 57, 74: on fortune 13, on banishment 35, on pardoning 71, on philosophy 110, on pedantry 115, 153, on royal courts 121, on bees 134, on the Germans 166, on anger 196, on war 202, on sharing 234
sensuality: FDP poetry on 129-33; 136-37; FDP criticism of 125-26. *See also* flirtation
Shewen, William: cited by FDP 32, 211, 224
Shirley, James 275n19
Shirley, John 261n4; cited by FDP 30, 89, 126, 128
sin, original *see* original sin
slavery: FDP on 2, 36, 242-244, 298n64
smoking *see* tobacco, smoking
snuff: in FDP poem 262 n5
Socrates: cited by FDP 110, 125, 127, 151, 163, 275n19
sodomy: in Rome (MAP on) 18; Windsheim trials of 1656 72-73. *See also* homosexuality
Sommerhausen: described by MAP 49; communal village life in 52-54; tension between citizens and leaders 55-56
Sonntag, Christoph 140
Sötern, Philipp Christoph von, *see* Philipp Christoph von Sötern
Spain 65, 146, 166
Spanish Netherlands 107, 146, 167
Spectator, The 116, 253n13; cited by FDP on German honesty 37, on Latin 78, on music 120, on courtly obeisance 121, on women 126, 128, 134
Spener, Philipp Jakob: and Pietism 43-44, 199; and FDP 44, 200-01, 208, 265n28; at Strasbourg 153-54; and J. H. Boeckler 163; and J. H. Horb 192, 199; on fathers and sons 200;

and Saalhof Pietists 208-09; and J. E. v. Merlau 213; and J. W. Petersen 213
Sperling, Johannes 143
Speyer 202, 205; FDP in 201. *See also* Court, Imperial High
Spinoza, Benedictus 157
Steele, Richard 6; see also *Spectator, The*
Stellwag, Johann Georg 103; and MAP 76, 183, 186; and the Windsheim insurrection 178, 181-84, 186; and J. H. Horb 192-93, 196-97
Stellwag, Johannes Mathias 103, 154, 274n91
Strasbourg 109
Strasbourg University 109, 203; elegant dress of students 113; and Pietism 153-154; FDP at 109, 116, 147, 153, 154
striptease *see* artist, striptease
student career: of FDP 109-10, 115-16
student conduct (at universities) 112-114; FDP on 114
Sturm, Johann Christoph 112, 143
Sweden: in Thirty Years' War 14-15; fighting Hapsburg Germany (1674) 110, 167; FDP on 36
Swedes: in Pennsylvania (FDP reports) 221-22, 223, 226, 233, 237
Switzerland: MAP in 16-17, 22; FDP in 109, 116, 156;
syncretism *see* Calixtinianism
Tacitus: on German drinking 167
Tauler, Johann 158, 209; mentioned by FDP 106
Temple, Sir William 116; FDP on 80; cited by FDP 40, 234
theater: in Nürnberg 120-21; FDP on 275n19
Thirty Years' War 41
Thoreau, Henry David 84
Thorn (Poland), Colloquy of 152
Thuringia 109, 115
Tindal, Matthew (*Christian Rights*): cited by FDP 140, 142, 218
tobacco, smoking 30; Native Americans and (FDP report) 237; FDP poetry on 3, 129, 261n5
trades, the *see* crafts, the
Trew, Abdias 112
Trier 19, 167, 203; MAP in 16
Tryon, Thomas (*Memoirs*): cited by FDP 109, 151; *Miscellanea* cited by FDP 64
Turkey: threatens Hapsburg Europe 64, 66; battles in Europe 203, 205; seen by FDP as instrument of divine punishment 36, 189; and slavery 242. *See also* Vienna
Turkish Spy, The see *Mamut the Arabian*; Marana, G. P.
Turks (i.e. Muslims): in FDP poem 156; in universalist treatise 215
Tusser, Thomas: cited by FDP 57, 194, 220
universal salvation, theology of 214, 215
universalism: of FDP 157, 159-60, 214-15, 238; cited by FDP 151-52, 240; and Native Americans 231, 238. *See also* Calixtinianism, ecumenicalism
universities *see* Aristotelians, scholastic; learned, the; Nürnberg University
upbringing: of FDP 33-34, 49-51, 54-55, 57, 58, 68-69, 85-88; *See also* child-rearing, emblems, father and son
usury: FDP on 36, 156, 227, 242, 243, 291n47, 295-96n71
utopia: FDP on 36, 37, 244
Vatican, the: MAP at 16-18
Vespucci, Amerigo: referenced by FDP 217, 218
Vienna: MAP in 17; Turkish siege of 66, 167, 200; and the Windsheim insurrection 179, 180, 182, 183
Virgil 6, 80; cited by FDP 34-35; *Aeneid* cited by FDP 80; FDP emblem based on *Aeneid* 92-93
Virgin Mary, the: in FDP letter 136
virgins: in "Alphabetical Hive" entries 124; in FDP poetry and prose 130, 132, 135
Volckmann, Dorothea Esther *see* Pastorius, Dorothea Esther
von Limpurg, Graf Georg Friedrich *see* Georg Friedrich, Graf
Wagenseil, Johann Christoph 112, 145-146; FDP and 145, 147-48, 171, 280n56
Wallenstein, Albrecht von 111, 113
Waller, Edmund 116
Weigel, Erhart 164
Weigel, Valentin 62
Weinmann, Johann 152-53
Westphalia, Peace (Treaty) of 20, 41
Whitehead, George and William Penn: cited by FDP 77, 141
widows / widowers: in FDP poetry 127, 130
wig(s): at Nürnberg Univ. 113; of J. C. Wagenseil 146; of FDP 117, 262n9; FDP on 166
Will, Georg Andreas 170
William of Orange, King 201
Wilson, John 116, 275n19
Winckler, Johann 199, 210
Windsheim 57-59; Pastorius family moving to 56-57; boisterous celebration in 60-61; religious observances in 61-64; political developments of 1660s in 64-66; Gymnasium education in 68-69, 72, 74-77; sodomy trials of 1656 72-73; poverty of its citizens 169, 178; insurrection of 1677-79 177-181, 183-84; in early 18th century 185; Pietist interregnum of 1679-85 192-99
Witt, Christopher 36, 80, 253n12
wives: "Alphabetical Hive" entries on 60, 124, 125, 126, 135; in FDP poetry and prose 59, 126, 127, 129, 133-34, 135, 278n37
Wölcker, Christoph Karl 138, 169
women *see* females
work, physical *see* labor, manual
Worms 202, 205; FDP in 201
Worthy Order of Shepherds and Blossoms *see* Pegnitz Shepherds
writing (good or bad): FDP on 158
Würzburg 38-40; MAP in 16, 17, 22
Ziegenbalg, Bartholomaeus 238, 293-94n62; FDP on 238

About the Author

John Weaver (b. 1942) grew up in rural Pennsylvania (Lebanon and Lancaster counties) and studied at Lafayette College (B.A.), California State University, San Jose (M.A.), and the University of California, Davis (Ph.D.). A Davis teaching exchange provided a year in Mainz, Germany (1977-78), and that led to a career as an English and American Studies lecturer at Bonn University. Weaver chaired the foreign-language lecturers' association (*Lektorenverband*) at Bonn, coordinated language courses in the English Department, and was elected to the Bonn University *Personalrat* (staff council), serving as academic staff representative over two decades. He acted modern and Shakespearean roles with the British Embassy Players (later the Bonn Players) and played a Village Elder in Peter Greenaway's "The Baby of Mâcon." Childhood experience shaped later sensibilities: Roaming a hillside farm with a valley creek running through woods and meadows (ages 5-9); attending one-room schools (ages 6-12); traveling to Georgia and Alabama (ages 10 and 12); above all, knowing the humor, warmth, generosity and wisdom of Miss Steiner in grades 1-3 at Nacetown School, a liberal and liberated woman who integrated the children of Lutherans, Mennonites, Evangelicals and Roman Catholics, and challenged the boy to read way beyond the prescribed levels. Early jobs grounded him in the real world: farm hand, supermarket checker, auto parts clerk, forklift operator, taxi driver. More recently, Weaver has traveled widely in Europe and the United States, experiencing on-the-road epiphanies, yet he was most alive in the classroom, engaging in discussion or, in lectures, with eager and inquiring young faces fixed upon him. He now walks the dog (Sally, a Welsh terrier) and dabbles in amateur photography, often simultaneously (photos at google plus and flickr).  Before starting graduate school in 1970, Weaver served as a U. S. Army officer (1964-66, mostly in Germany) and worked as an insurance claims adjuster and print journalist. He also taught at a Gymnasium in Norderstedt, Germany (1973-74). He retired in 2008 and has been living with his German-born wife in Bamberg and Potsdam, Germany. They have two children and five grandchildren, also living in Germany.

A page of poetry from Pastorius' "Beehive" manuscript

Poem 167, adorned with two clay pipes, humorously debates the merits of smoking tobacco. It is cited on pages 3 and 129 of this study. Poems 163, 164 and 165 involve tulips, cowslips and "two lips" as well as asparagus shoots and literal and metaphorical virgins – illustrating the liveliness of Pastorius' verse. They are discussed on pages 130 and 132-33. From Univ. Of Penna. Ms. Codex 726, p 160 (used with permission); online image at: http://dla.library.upenn.edu/dla/medren/pageturn.html?id=MEDREN_2487547& currentpage=170&rotation=0&size=1

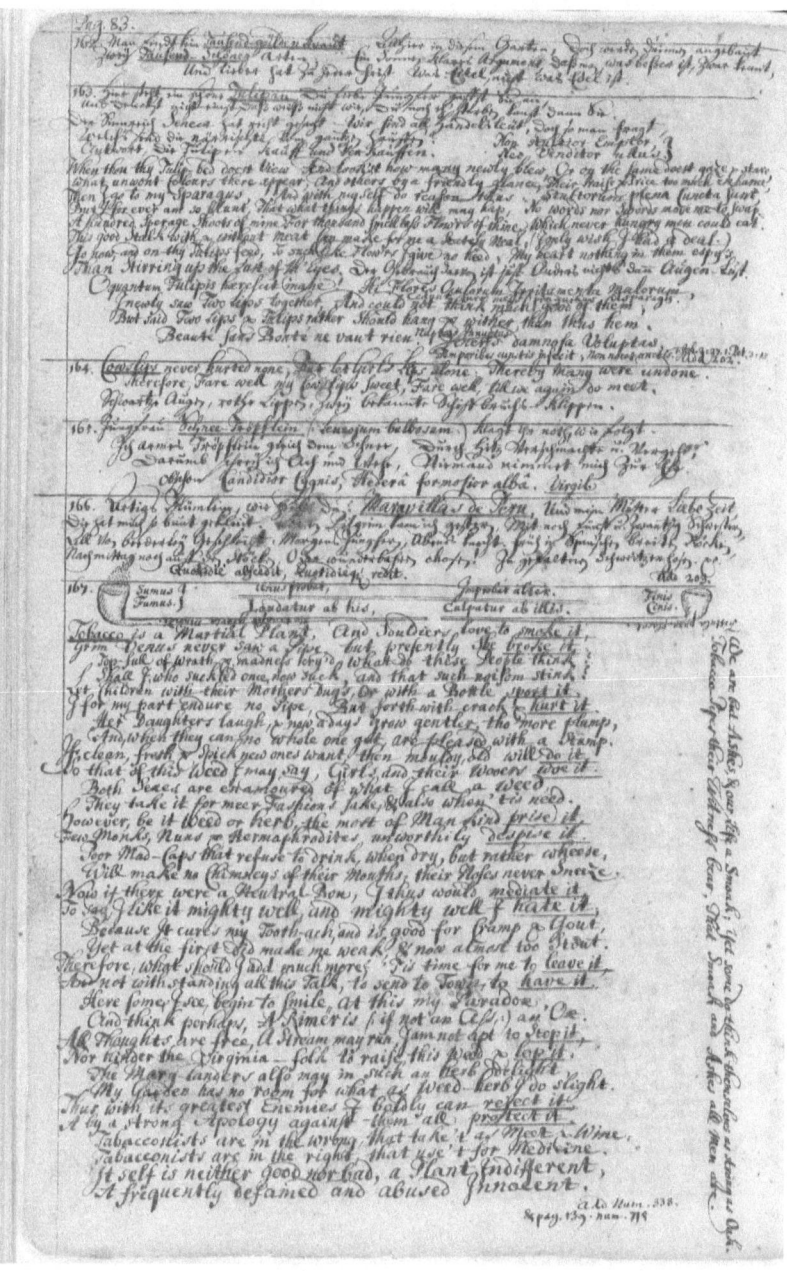

www.ingramcontent.com/pod-product-compliance
Lightning Source LLC
Chambersburg PA
CBHW021336230426
43666CB00006B/307